Introduction to Paralegal Studies

Introduction to Paralegal Studies

A Critical Thinking Approach

Seventh Edition

KATHERINE A. CURRIER
Professor Emeritus
Elms College

THOMAS E. EIMERMANN
Emeritus Professor
Illinois State University

MARISA S. CAMPBELL
Director, Paralegal Program
Meredith College

© 2021 Katherine A. Currier, Thomas E. Eimermann, and Marisa S. Campbell

Published by Wolters Kluwer in New York.

Wolters Kluwer Legal & Regulatory U.S. serves customers worldwide with CCH, Aspen Publishers, and Kluwer Law International products. (www.WKLegaledu.com)

Cover image: Wisconsinart/Dreamstime.com

To contact Customer Service, e-mail customer.service@wolterskluwer.com, call 1-800-234-1660, fax 1-800-901-9075, or mail correspondence to:

Wolters Kluwer
Attn: Order Department
PO Box 990
Frederick, MD 21705

1 2 3 4 5 6 7 8 9 0

ISBN 978-1-5438-0890-2

Library of Congress Cataloging-in-Publication Data

Names: Currier, Katherine A., 1949- author. | Eimermann, Thomas E., author. | Campbell, Marisa Szabo, author.
Title: Introduction to paralegal studies : a critical thinking approach / Katherine A. Currier (Professor Emeritus, Elms College), Thomas E. Eimermann (Professor Emeritus, Illinois State University), Marisa S. Campbell (Director, Paralegal Program, Meredith College).
Description: Seventh edition. | New York : Wolters Kluwer, [2021] | Series: Paralegal series | Includes bibliographical references and index. | Summary: "This is an introduction to paralegal studies text for undergraduate students"—Provided by publisher.
Identifiers: LCCN 2020053838 (print) | LCCN 2020053839 (ebook) | ISBN 9781543808902 (paperback) | ISBN 9781543831108 (ebook)
Subjects: LCSH: Legal assistants—United States. | Practice of law—United States.
Classification: LCC KF320.L4 C87 2021 (print) | LCC KF320.L4 (ebook) | DDC 340.023/73—dc23
LC record available at https://lccn.loc.gov/2020053838
LC ebook record available at https://lccn.loc.gov/2020053839

About Wolters Kluwer Legal & Regulatory U.S.

Wolters Kluwer Legal & Regulatory U.S. delivers expert content and solutions in the areas of law, corporate compliance, health compliance, reimbursement, and legal education. Its practical solutions help customers successfully navigate the demands of a changing environment to drive their daily activities, enhance decision quality and inspire confident outcomes.

Serving customers worldwide, its legal and regulatory portfolio includes products under the Aspen Publishers, CCH Incorporated, Kluwer Law International, ftwilliam.com and MediRegs names. They are regarded as exceptional and trusted resources for general legal and practice-specific knowledge, compliance and risk management, dynamic workflow solutions, and expert commentary.

To our spouses and children
for their understanding and support

About the Authors

Katherine A. Currier, J.D., served as the Elms College Paralegal and Legal Studies program director for many years. She developed and taught many law-related courses, including Legal Reasoning, Research, and Writing; Introduction to Legal Studies I and II; Law Office Computer Literacy; Law Office Applications; Interviewing, Counseling, and Negotiating; and Law and Literature. In addition to the three texts she has coauthored with Professor Eimermann, Professor Currier has publications in the areas of legal ethics as applied to paralegals and law office computing.

Professor Currier has been actively involved in the development of undergraduate legal education at both the regional and the national levels, particularly through her work with the American Association for Paralegal Education (AAfPE) and the American Bar Association (ABA) Approval Commission on Paralegals. Professor Currier served on the national board of AAfPE, first as its parliamentarian and then later as the elected representative of four-year paralegal programs. She served many years as the AAfPE publications chair, charged with the final responsibility for overseeing the *Journal of Paralegal Education and Practice* and *The Educator*. Professor Currier frequently speaks at both the AAfPE Northeast regional meetings and the annual AAfPE conferences on topics as diverse as the use of computer shareware, paralegals and the unauthorized practice of law, creative teaching techniques, and conducting legal research on the Internet. Professor Currier also chaired the American Bar Association Approval Commission on Paralegals, the body charged with conducting site visits of paralegal programs that are seeking their initial ABA approval or reapproval. She also served on the Board of Directors of the International Assembly for Collegiate Business Education (IACBE), an organization dedicated to promoting excellence in business education.

Prior to teaching at Elms College, Professor Currier taught at Suffolk Law School and Western New England College School of Law. She graduated magna cum laude with her B.A. in Political Science from Carleton College, with her M.A. in Political Philosophy from the University of California, Berkeley, and with her J.D. from Northeastern University Law School.

Thomas E. Eimermann is Emeritus Professor of Political Science and a former Director of the Legal Studies Program at Illinois State University. Dr. Eimermann helped establish the paralegal program there in 1976 and served as director until 2005. He has taught the Introduction to Paralegal Studies, Legal Research and Writing, and Constitutional Law courses.

Professor Eimermann was a member of the American Association for Paralegal Education's Board of Directors from 1986 to 1993 and served as president of that organization from 1991 to 1992. He has also served in the Certification Board and Specialty Task Force of the National Association of Legal

Assistants; as a member of the Illinois State Bar Association Committee on the Delivery of Legal Services; and as a member of the Hearing Board, the Inquiry Board, and the Oversight Committee of the Illinois Attorney Registration and Disciplinary Commission. He was also a consultant for the Illinois Department of Corrections, where he designed its Uniform Law Clerk Training Program.

In addition to the three paralegal texts he has coauthored with Professor Currier, Professor Eimermann's publications include *Fundamentals of Criminal Law and Procedure for Paralegals* (co-authored with Thomas McClure), and journal articles on paralegals, jury behavior, and free speech issues. He earned his B.A. in Political Science at North Central College. He went on to receive an M.A. and a Ph.D. in Political Science from the University of Illinois-Urbana/Champaign campus.

Marisa S. Campbell, J.D., has served as the program director for the Meredith College Paralegal Program since 2000 and has taught the Legal Survey and Legal Research and Writing courses. In addition, she has taught Constitutional Law in the Political Science department and business law classes in both the undergraduate and MBA programs. She taught international law students introduction to American law and culture in the Summer Institute at the Fuqua School of Business at Duke University. She has spoken on a number of topics, nationally and regionally, including paralegal regulation, ethics, professionalism, and assessment.

Ms. Campbell served as President of the American Association for Paralegal Education (AAfPE) from 2007 to 2008 after serving as South East Regional Representative. She served on the American Bar Association Approval Commission on Paralegals from 2009 to 2010. She has served on the North Carolina State Board of Continuing Legal Education. From 2001 to 2004, she served on the Board of the Alliance for Paralegal Professional Standards and on a joint committee with the North Carolina State Bar to develop the North Carolina paralegal certification standards. She served on the inaugural North Carolina State Bar Board of Paralegal Certification from 2004 to 2010. She served as a member of the North Carolina Bar Association CLE Committee, as Chair of that Committee from 2014 to 2016; as a member of the Publication Committee; as a member of the Law Office Management and Technology Section Council; and as a member of the Membership Committee. In 2013, she was awarded the Women of Justice Award for North Carolina Lawyers Weekly in the Legal Scholars Award category.

In addition to this text, she coauthored the *North Carolina State Bar Paralegal Certification Exam Guide* in 2013 as well as numerous articles and manuscripts. She graduated with Honors in Political Science and Honors in Studies in Religion from the University of Michigan, Ann Arbor. She earned her Master in International Affairs from Columbia University and her J.D. from the University of Michigan Law School.

Currier, Eimermann, and Campbell have also authored *Introduction to Law for Paralegals: A Critical Thinking Approach* and *The Study of Law: A Critical Thinking Approach*.

Summary of Contents

Contents

List of Illustrations

Preface

NEW TO THIS EDITION

This seventh edition keeps pace with many new developments in the law and the paralegal profession. We have added new topics, expanded others, and incorporated discussions of recent court decisions. We have also included new Legal Reasoning exercises, Discussion Questions, Review Questions, and updated the Web Exercises.

This edition was completed during the Covid pandemic; changes that were happening in the law and how the legal system works were accelerated during this time. We were able to capture those changes in this edition. We also made major organizational changes. Criminal Law and Procedure, Chapter 9 in the sixth edition, was split into two chapters, Chapter 8, Criminal Law and Chapter 9, Criminal Procedures. This change made the chapters more manageable for students to read and understand. We also made it easier to compare and contrast Criminal Law and Criminal Procedure with Civil Litigation and Torts by moving the chapter on Contracts, Chapter 8 in the sixth edition, to Chapter 10 in this edition. This also helped with the flow of the topics that followed in the chapter on Specialized Practice Areas.

APPROACH

As the subtitle of this book indicates, it uses a critical thinking approach to paralegal studies. Paralegal studies focus on the functions and duties of paralegals in the American legal system. The critical thinking approach to paralegal studies places great emphasis on the development of analytical thinking skills.

We use this critical thinking approach because we believe it is the best way for students to learn the fundamental principles of law. By learning how to read and interpret statutes, cases, regulations, and court documents, students will be better able to learn how to perform paralegal duties in a variety of specialty areas. Therefore, this book emphasizes careful reading for detail, analytical thinking, and the written presentation of arguments.

Another key element of this critical thinking approach is the interactive nature of the book. We have included Hypothetical Cases, Discussion Questions, Legal Reasoning Exercises, Practice Tips, and Ethics Alerts to stimulate students to think about and discuss the underlying assumptions behind various aspects of the law and the ramifications of different approaches to legal problems.

We purposely dispersed these items throughout the chapters so that the students would be encouraged to think about them while the material is fresh from recent reading and to be readily available for instructors to use as springboards for classroom discussion. While we did relegate the Review Questions to the end of each chapter, we have labeled them with the pages they cover so that you can easily assign just part of a chapter with its accompanying review questions.

ORGANIZATION OF THE BOOK

Part 1, Paralegals and the American Legal System, introduces students to the study of law, the organization of the legal system, and the role of paralegals in that system. It includes the classification of different types of paralegals and what they do, as well as coverage of the issues of paralegal education, registration, certification, licensure, and ethics. Chapters in this section also cover such topics as sources of the law, the different ways in which law is classified, the structure of the courts, and the various stages involved in litigation and alternative dispute resolution.

Part 2, Substance of the Law, introduces readers to the basic concepts involved in the areas of torts, criminal law, criminal procedure, and contracts and the Uniform Commercial Code. It also provides an overview of specialized practice areas, such as business law, employment and labor law, debt collection and bankruptcy, administrative law, immigration, real estate, intellectual property, estate planning and probate, and family law. Part 3, Legal Analysis and Research, contains chapters that build the critical thinking skills students need for reading and analyzing the law. Chapters 12 and 13 cover finding and interpreting statutory law and court opinions. Chapter 14 discusses basic legal research tools, and Chapter 15 shows students how to apply what they have found to specific legal problems. Chapter 15 also discusses how to use the IRAC approach to legal analysis and how to report research findings in a legal memorandum.

Whereas Part 3 builds skills for finding and analyzing the law, Part 4, Paralegals and the Work World, builds skills related to gathering and managing relevant factual information. Chapter 16 focuses on interviewing while Chapter 17 covers the gathering, preservation, and use of different types of evidence. Chapter 18 introduces readers to case management and the various types of computer programs that attorneys and paralegals can use to manage case information.

KEY FEATURES

The many features that set this book apart are

- Chapter Objectives
- Discussion Questions integrated into each chapter
- Legal Reasoning Exercises
- Marginal definitions of key terms
- Practice Tips

- Ethics Alerts
- NetNotes
- Web Exercises
- Review Questions
- An appendix on the fundamentals of good writing
- A glossary that includes definitions for all bold-faced words and phrases found in the text

Because this book stresses the critical thinking approach, we illustrate our points with hypothetical situations and with real case decisions that students will understand and to which they can relate. Discussion Questions and Legal Reasoning Exercises force the students to synthesize and analyze the material rather than simply regurgitating an answer. The Practice Tips help connect the theoretical textbook learning to the reality of the work world. They provide checklists and other "words of wisdom' " regarding practical paralegal tasks. By bringing the text to life, the Discussion Questions, Legal Reasoning Exercises, and Practice Tips all help maintain student attention and aid in the students' retention of the material.

Ethics Alert boxes are placed throughout the text to draw attention to the ethical issues involved in various aspects of the law. These boxes warn students of actions that would be considered unethical; they also give advice on how to act appropriately. NetNotes provide students with handy links to key Internet resources, and Web Exercises require students to utilize the Internet to find specific types of practical information.

Because so much of learning the law involves mastering legal vocabulary, we have included marginal notes containing key definitions. The end-of-the chapter Review Questions also help students reinforce basic concepts.

Of special note are the appendices. Appendix A contains the U.S. Constitution. Appendix B provides students with a convenient and easy-to-understand primer on the basics of grammar, including verb tense, pronoun agreement, placement of modifiers, punctuation, and style. Appendix C provides a useful summary of all of the NetNotes found in the text.

An instructor's manual that includes suggested answers for all the Discussion Questions, Review Questions, Legal Reasoning Exercises, and Web Exercises, as well as teaching tips, is available to help teachers make the most effective use of this book. Also available is a PowerPoint presentation to assist with classroom lectures and an electronic test bank. Instructors can download these materials at the product page that accompanies the text, at www.wklegaledu.com.

RELATIONSHIP TO THE AUTHORS' OTHER TEXTS

Those familiar with *Introduction to Law for Paralegals: A Critical Thinking Approach* and *The Study of Law: A Critical Thinking Approach* will recognize many similarities to this text. All three books emphasize the critical thinking approach to understanding the law. All three include Discussion Questions,

NetNotes, references to ethical questions, and either Legal Reasoning or Critical Thinking exercises. Topics such as sources of law, classification of the law, structure of the court system, overviews of civil and criminal litigation, overviews of torts, contracts, property, and criminal law, and analysis of statutes and cases are covered in all three books.

These books differ in terms of their intended audiences. *The Study of Law* is directed at a more general-education/pre-law audience, whereas both the *Introduction to Law for Paralegals* and this text are specifically directed at paralegals. Whereas *Introduction to Law for Paralegals* goes into more detail in its coverage of substantive areas of the law and includes excerpts from actual court opinions, this text provides greater coverage of the role of the paralegal and the types of skills involved in interviewing, investigations, and computerized case management.

SPECIAL THANKS

Naturally, we owe a great deal of thanks to the many students, educators, paralegals, and attorneys who contributed ideas for this book. Special recognition should go to Victoria Joseph for her contribution to the criminal law chapter.

We would also like to thank the staff at Aspen Publishers for the excellent support we have received on the books we have done with them. We especially want to thank Betsy Kenny for the key role that she continues to play in the development of each new edition of our books.

Finally, we also want to thank our spouses and children for their continued support and understanding of our professional activities.

Katherine A. Currier
Thomas E. Eimermann
Marisa S. Campbell

November 2020

Acknowledgments

We are grateful to copyright holders for permission to reprint excerpts from the following items:

Shepard's, Massachusetts Citations, Case Edition, Part 4, 1993, page 318. Reprinted with permission of LexisNexis.

Thomson Reuters,

___, *Callow v. Thomas*, 78 N.E.2d 637, 637-641. Reprinted with permission of Thomas Reuters.

___, *Lewis v. Lewis*, 351 N.E.2d 526, 526-533. Reprinted with permission of Thomas Reuters.

___, Massachusetts Digest, 12 Mass. Digest 2d 623; Table of Cases, page 233. Reprinted with permission of Thomas Reuters.

___, Massachusetts General Laws Annotated, Ch. 209 §6, pages 351-352, 354, Pocket Part. Reprinted with permission of Thomas Reuters.

___, Massachusetts Digest Case Summaries, 13 Mass. Digest 2d, 623. Reprinted with permission of Thomson Reuters.

Introduction to
Paralegal Studies

PART

1

Paralegals and the American Legal System

Chapter 1

Introduction to the Study of Law and the Paralegal Profession

[P]aralegals are capable of carrying out many tasks, under the supervision of an attorney, that might otherwise be performed by a lawyer.
Justice William Brennan

Chapter Objectives

After reading this chapter, you should be able to:

- Give a commonly accepted definition of paralegal.
- Describe the various settings in which paralegals and lawyers work.
- Compare the educational requirements for becoming a lawyer with those of becoming a paralegal.
- List the major professional organizations that have an impact on paralegal education and practice.
- Describe the various types of paralegal credentials.
- Describe the various tasks that paralegals typically perform.

INTRODUCTION

The purpose of this text is to help you understand the American legal system and how paralegals and lawyers work within it. People often turn to the legal system for help in planning their affairs. For example, a group of entrepreneurs may seek legal advice regarding the best way to organize a new business, or a young, married couple may come to a lawyer for help with the purchase of their first home. Sometimes, however, people become involved with the legal system because they are in trouble. Perhaps they are facing criminal charges or have been injured in an automobile accident. Their stories illustrate how society has developed a set of rules to help people resolve conflicts they cannot resolve on their own.

Take a few minutes to read the following fact situations involving a distressed grandfather and a harassed student. We will be using their stories, and those of others, throughout this text to help you understand how the legal system works.

Case 1: The Distressed Grandfather

Approximately one year ago, Donald Drake and his six-year-old grandson, Philip, were walking down a residential road on their way home from visiting one of Philip's friends. Philip was walking on the sidewalk approximately thirty feet in front of Drake. Suddenly, a car sped past Drake, seemingly went out of control, jumped the curb, and hit Philip. Drake ran to Philip's side, but it was too late. Philip had been killed instantly. The driver of the car, Wilma Small, was unhurt. Based on skid marks and testimony from both Small and Drake, the police investigation following the accident determined that excessive speed was the cause of the accident.

Drake said that at the time of the accident, his only concern was for the welfare of his grandson because he himself was clear of the danger. Naturally, Drake suffered a great deal of mental pain and shock because of seeing his grandson killed. While being driven home from the accident, he suffered a heart attack that necessitated a lengthy hospital stay.

One year later, he still does not feel completely recovered and often suffers from nightmares reliving the accident and his grandson's death. Following the advice of trusted friends, he decided to make an appointment at the law office of Darrow and Bryan to see if he could sue Small to recover for his hospital bills, for his pain and suffering, and for the emotional distress he felt in seeing his grandson killed.

Case 2: The Harassed Student

Wanda Smith, a 20-year-old college student, was walking past a construction site on campus when several of the construction workers began to whistle and make catcalls. Smith did not appreciate being treated as a sex object and greatly resented the way in which these construction workers were behaving. She avoided the construction site, regularly making her late for her contracts class.

After talking it over with a few of her friends, Smith decided to talk to one of the lawyers at Darrow and Bryan to see if she could take legal action. She does not want other women to have to undergo similar treatment and wondered if she could collect damages for mental suffering.

Keep these two stories in mind as you read this chapter and our explanation of how one goes about becoming a paralegal, how paralegals differ from lawyers, and the types of work paralegals typically do.

A. PARALEGALS AND LAWYERS

While this book focuses on paralegals, you cannot understand or fully appreciate the role of paralegals without also knowing some basic things about lawyers. Remember that only lawyers can provide legal advice, appear in court, or set legal fees. The terms **lawyer** and **attorney** are generally used interchangeably to refer to a person who has been officially licensed to practice law. However, in some contexts, people use "lawyer" to refer to a person who is authorized to practice law and "attorney" to refer to a job title. Thus, an organizational chart may carry titles such as attorney, associate attorney, enforcement attorney, District Attorney, United States Attorney, or Attorney General.

In the late 1960s, the terms "paralegal" and "legal assistant" began to be used to refer to persons who assist lawyers in ways that go beyond the duties of traditional legal secretaries and file clerks. Because the term **paralegal** is the most common and the most generic, it will be the term most often employed in this book.

In the early 1970s, the legitimacy of this new occupational classification was established when it was officially endorsed by the **American Bar Association (ABA),** the largest and most prominent national organization of lawyers. The ABA has periodically changed its definition of "paralegal." Most recently, in 2020, the ABA amended its officially adopted definition to read:

> A paralegal is a person, qualified by education, training or work experience who is employed or retained by a lawyer, law office, corporation, governmental agency or other entity and who performs specifically delegated substantive legal work for which a lawyer is responsible.[1]

Because this is a rather long definition, we can better understand it by dividing it into its separate components. A paralegal is:

- ∎ "a person, *qualified* by education, training or work experience"
- ∎ "who is *employed or retained by* a lawyer, law office, corporation, governmental agency or other entity" and
- ∎ "who performs specifically delegated *substantive legal work*"
- ∎ "for which a *lawyer is responsible.*"

More than half the states have developed some form of definition for the term "paralegal" as well. None of the states require adherence to its definition for employment. Other definitions of paralegal have also been developed by NALA: The Paralegal Association and the National Federation of Paralegal Associations (NFPA). Each association is discussed later in this chapter.

While there are differences among these definitions, all of them suggest that paralegals perform many of the same tasks normally performed by lawyers. They gather and analyze facts relevant to legal disputes, perform legal research, draft legal documents, prepare witnesses and evidence for presentation at legal proceedings, and even represent clients in some types of administrative hearings.

Lawyer
A person who has been officially licensed to practice law in a state or federal jurisdiction. Also referred to as an attorney.

Attorney
A lawyer; a person licensed by a court to practice law. This term is often used to refer to a job title.

Paralegal
A person who assists a lawyer and, working under a lawyer's supervision, does tasks that, absent the paralegal, the lawyer would do. A paralegal cannot give legal advice or appear in court, nor can they set legal fees.

American Bar Association (ABA)
americanbar.org
A national voluntary organization of lawyers.

---

[1] Adopted by the ABA House of Delegates, February 2020.

However, even though paralegals carry out many of the same tasks performed by lawyers, paralegals are not licensed to practice law. Therefore, they can perform many of these tasks only when working under the supervision of a lawyer. In addition, even then, they are not allowed to give direct legal advice to clients or to represent clients in most types of judicial proceedings.

DISCUSSION QUESTION

1. Until August 1997, the ABA definition of legal assistant read:

A legal assistant is a person, qualified through education, training, or work experience, who is employed or retained by a lawyer, law office, governmental agency, or other entity in a capacity or function which involves the performance, under the ultimate direction and supervision of an attorney, of specifically-delegated substantive legal work, which work, for the most part, requires a sufficient knowledge of legal concepts that, absent such assistant, the attorney would perform the task.

You will see this definition quoted in most of the court opinions decided prior to 1997 that deal with the role of paralegals. In what ways do you think this definition differs from the one that the ABA adopted in 2020? Which ABA definition do you prefer? Why?

B. PARALEGALS AND OTHER LAW-RELATED PARAPROFESSIONALS

Traditional paralegals are paralegals who work as employees or independent contractors and are supervised directly by attorneys. Paralegal employees can be found within law firms, corporate in-house law departments, governmental agencies, and non-profits. Paralegal contractors can be self-employed or work for an agency. According to the U.S. Bureau of Labor Statistics, by 2018 there were about 325,700 paralegal jobs. The Bureau projects that the number of paralegal jobs will grow 12 percent between 2018 and 2029, "much faster than average for all occupations."[2]

An alternative and expanding group of law-related paraprofessionals go by a number of titles, including "legal document preparers (LDPs)," "limited licensed legal technicians (LLLTs)," and "lay advocates." They are distinguished from traditional paralegals in that they deal directly with the public, without attorney supervision.

Finally, another exciting area of job growth is developing within nontraditional work settings. Here, we see paralegals taking the skills they have honed and applying them to a variety of nonparalegal but still law-related occupations.

As Karen Decrescenzo explains in her Paralegal Profile, paralegals who are employed by the government, such as in municipal law offices, work in a wide variety of legal areas.

---

[2] Bureau of Labor Statistics, U.S. Department of Labor, *Occupational Outlook Handbook*, "Paralegals and Legal Assistants," www.bls.gov/ooh/legal/paralegals-and-legal-assistants.htm (visited April 6, 2020).

PARALEGAL PROFILE

Karen Decrescenzo
Principal Paralegal/Legal Intern Coordinator
Office of the City Attorney, Civil Division

I work in the office that services all of the legal needs for the city of San Diego. We have approximately 80 attorneys and 20 paralegals, with every four to five paralegals being supervised by one of four senior paralegals. It is my job to supervise those supervisors.

In addition, I am responsible for the process that leads to new hires. I chair the interview panels and make recommendations about whom to hire. I also hire and supervise temporary paralegals whom we hire to cover short-term spikes in the workload. Finally, I supervise the librarian and recruit, hire, and supervise legal interns (law students). In a nutshell, my job is managing everything that relates to the paralegal staff, librarian, and law clerks, including recruitment, interviewing, hiring, training and development, utilization, workload, workflow, performance management, rewards, and recognition.

The attorneys and paralegals in our office work on a wide variety of legal issues, as we handle civil litigation and advisory matters for all of the city's departments, such as police, fire, park and recreation, and water. Cases can range from allegations of civil rights violations, to trip and fall, to First Amendment issues regarding sign ordinances, to collections, condemnations, contract disputes—really, anything about which a city can sue or be sued. Working in so many different areas means that the paralegals are called upon to engage in a lot of legal research and writing. Our paralegals particularly enjoy working on temporary restraining orders to protect city employees who receive threats from the public, as the paralegals are able to appear in court for the preliminary injunctions, being careful, of course, to announce who they are and why they are there. As anyone who works for a governmental office can tell you, it's not about the money; it's about doing interesting, challenging, and rewarding work.

As with most governmental offices, ours suffers from a lack of resources. This lack of resources is both my biggest challenge and the greatest source of job satisfaction, as it forces me to be creative and innovative and to use my imagination to solve problems.

I think the best preparation I had for this job was being a parent. Being a parent taught me how to juggle multiple responsibilities and how to deal with sometimes difficult personnel issues. Those skills have come in particularly handy lately, as I have been working full-time while finishing my master's degree in public administration.

My parting advice to students is to say that I cannot stress strongly enough the huge benefits to be gained from joining paralegal associations. It is never too early to join. Students should become active in any clubs on their campus and investigate student membership in their local paralegal association. Through that networking, they will form relationships that will support and enrich them throughout their careers. Both the Association of Legal Administrators (ALA) and the International Paralegal Management Association (IPMA) have given me tremendous networking opportunities. I was the first and only person to work in my position. When I found IPMA, I practically cried as I walked into the meeting room and found it full of people, all of whom do what I do and understand what it takes to do my job well. The connection I formed with them has helped me throughout the years. Because of my colleagues in IPMA, I never feel isolated.

1. Traditional Paralegals Working as Employees

Approximately 70 percent of all paralegals work in private law firms. There are five main types of private practice: sole proprietorships, partnerships, limited liability partnerships, professional corporations, and office-sharing arrangements. We discuss each of these business types in Chapter 10. Other common places of employment include the legal department of a business and a governmental agency.

Paralegals may also be employed in the legal departments of private non-business organizations, such as labor unions, trade associations, consumer groups, and charities. The operation of such legal departments parallels that of a business corporation or a governmental agency.

Finally, you may find paralegals working for legal clinics or legal service offices. These terms are frequently used incorrectly and interchangeably. **Legal clinics** provide low-cost legal services on routine matters by stressing low overhead and high volume. They frequently operate out of storefront offices and make extensive use of paralegals. The lawyers who operate the clinic are usually organized as either a partnership or a professional corporation. **Legal services offices** are affiliated with the federal government's **Legal Services Corporation.** The lawyers who work in such offices are salaried employees of a not-for-profit corporation that receives both public funds and private donations to provide free legal services to the poor. They hold positions similar to lawyers working for a public defender's office, except that they handle civil rather than criminal cases. Such offices frequently rely heavily on the assistance of paralegals, as much of the work of a legal services office involves representation before administrative agencies, an area where paralegals are usually allowed to practice without running afoul of the unauthorized practice of law statutes.

2. Freelance/Independent Paralegals

Paralegals who work as **independent contractors,** rather than as employees of law firms or corporations, may also be referred to as **freelance paralegals.** Because freelance paralegals usually contract to do specific jobs for several lawyers at the same time, the lawyer supervising the paralegal will differ from one case to the next. The advantages of being a freelance paralegal include having the capacity to choose what kinds of projects you will work on and setting your own hours. Lawyers find that in this type of contractual relationship, they can use paralegals on an "as needed" basis without having to pay fringe benefits and unemployment compensation insurance and without worrying about what to do with the paralegals during a slack time in the business cycle.

Legal clinic
Usually organized as either a partnership or a professional corporation, law clinics provide low-cost legal services on routine matters by stressing low overhead and high volume.

Legal services offices
Affiliated with the federal government's Legal Services Corporation, these offices serve those who would otherwise be unable to afford legal assistance.

Freelance paralegal
A paralegal who works as an independent contractor rather than as an employee of a law firm or corporation.

Some freelance paralegals are self-employed. Others work for specialized staffing agencies that provide law firms with qualified paralegals to work on a temporary basis, often on unusually large or complex cases.

PARALEGAL PROFILE

Jennifer Lerner
Freelance Paralegal

Although I worked in a personal injury firm while attending school for my paralegal degree, when I graduated I found I could make more money if I contracted my services than if I remained an employee. Freelance work also enables me to decide what types of duties I want to accept and allows me to work from my home. I do personal injury work for area attorneys, with a specialty in writing demands for completed cases to be sent to insurance claims representatives. The demands are based on the medical expenses incurred and the expectation as to future medical and hospital expenses, pain and suffering, and lost wages. I take the file, investigate it, make sure all of the information is there, and then come up with the price. I present the information as persuasively as possible, using spreadsheets and including particulars, such as how many hours the client had to wait in the doctor's office each week. I do all of my work on a disk that I give to the attorney. The attorney then makes any desired changes and sends the demand to the insurance company.

I like the variety that can come at you at any time and the unpredictability. I love working with the law because the whole concept of how conflicts arise and then how people go about getting rid of conflict is fascinating. For some, arbitration or mediation is the best choice. Working as a paralegal teaches you a lot about people. For example, people have very different ways of dealing with their injuries. We are in a people business, and what we do changes the lives of people.

Recently, I was also hired on a part-time basis to use my paralegal skills in an unusual way. A maritime company was interested in hiring someone to research regulations, to prepare documents for ships coming into port, to ensure that crew members have all required paperwork, and to communicate with ships at sea. Even though the company did not start out looking for someone with paralegal skills, during the interview process it became evident that those skills were exactly what they needed, and I got the job. Those skills include the abilities to sustain independent thought, understand the need to maintain confidentiality in negotiations, project a professional image, understand the intricacies of dealing with contracts and government regulations, and not make a judgment before having all of the necessary information.

Even if I didn't use any of my paralegal skills as a paralegal, the education and experience I have received have armed me for what the world may throw my way. It has helped me to deal with a lack of predictability and enabled me to reason and see both sides of issues. Rather than jumping to conclusions, I now tend to back up and think of all the reasons before choosing a course of action.

3. Legal Document Preparers, Limited Licensed Legal Technicians, and Lay Advocates

Legal document preparer (LDP)
A nonlawyer, not working under the supervision of a lawyer, who assists with the preparation of legal documents for individuals or companies representing themselves.

Limited licensed legal technician (LLLT)
A nonlawyer in Washington who meets certain educational requirements and is permitted to advise and assist clients in approved practice areas.

Pro se
Representing oneself in a legal matter.

Traditional paralegals, whether working as employees or on a freelance basis, work under the supervision of a licensed lawyer. In contrast, those who fall under the terms described in this section are nonlawyers who provide legal services directly to the public without being under the supervision of a lawyer. They fall into three broad categories: **legal document preparers (LDPs), limited licensed legal technicians (LLLTs),** and lay advocates.

Individuals who prepare standardized legal documents for people who are attempting to handle their own legal matters **pro se** (that is, to handle the case on their own without using a lawyer) go by various titles, but are generally referred to as LDPs. So long as they do not give legal advice, they are generally allowed to communicate about general, published, and factual information relating to the format and content of certain types of legal documents. They can also assist with the entering of information into those documents, so long as that information is supplied by their clients and the document preparer does not alter it in any way.[3]

Two states, California and Arizona, have carved out specialized areas for document preparers. In California, they have unlawful detainer assistants (UDAs) who are authorized to assist landlord and tenants in eviction proceedings, and legal document assistants (LDAs). Both must satisfy very basic educational requirements and be registered with the state. They cannot offer legal advice, but they can assist consumers in filling out complex forms. In Arizona, LDPs can prepare documents and give general legal information, but not legal advice. They must meet certain education or work experience requirements and pass an examination that includes "legal terminology, client communication, data gathering, document preparation, ethical issues, and professional and administrative responsibilities pertaining to legal document preparation."[4] A third state, Louisiana, gives notary publics some authority to draft legal documents for the public.

The role of nonlawyers dealing directly with the public is controversial, but many states have created commissions to study enlarging the role of nonlawyers in the legal system. Advocates for expanding the role of nonlawyers argue that legal aid lawyers and lawyers providing *pro bono* legal services have not been able to fully serve the needs of indigent clients who cannot pay the going price for regular legal services. On the other hand, many opponents are concerned about the quality of the services that nonlawyers could provide and the enforcement of the ethical duties that go with such representation.

Two states, Washington and Utah, were among the first to apply a more expansive approach to allowing nonlawyers to deal directly with the public. In 2012, the Washington Supreme Court adopted a rule that authorized LLLTs who

---

[3] See Chapter 2 for a discussion on the unauthorized practice of law.
[4] Arizona Code of Judicial Administration, Part 7: Administrative Office of the Courts, Chapter 2: Certification and Licensing Programs, Section 7-208: Legal Document Preparer, www.azcourts.gov/Portals/26/ACJA%20Code/7-208_Amend_2013.pdf (visited April 6, 2020).

meet certain educational requirements to advise and assist clients in approved practice areas. Family law was chosen as the first practice area for these new licenses. In June 2020, the Washington Supreme Court sunsetted the LLLT program, citing administrative costs and the low number of LLLTs. The current LLLTs and those in the process of applying for LLLT status may continue to practice, but no new LLLTs will be allowed to apply.

The Utah Supreme Court approved a new class of legal professional, called the **licensed paralegal practitioner (LPP).** Similar to the Washington approach, LPPs can assist clients with family law, eviction, and debt collection issues. The first 4 LPPs were licensed at the end of 2019, and it is anticipated that there will be 20 LPPs by 2021 and 200 by 2029.[5]

Finally, a **lay advocate** is generally a nonlawyer who is authorized to represent clients in administrative hearings. Statutes that establish administrative agencies sometimes allow for representation by nonlawyers or give the agency the power to decide who may represent clients in agency matters.

> **Licensed paralegal practitioner (LPP)**
> A paralegal in Utah meeting certain educational requirements, who is permitted to advise and assist clients in approved practice areas.
>
> **Lay advocate**
> Generally a nonlawyer who represents persons before administrative agencies that permit this practice.

DISCUSSION QUESTIONS

2. The state of Washington's LLLT system initially applied only to certain types of family law tasks. In what other areas of the law do you think there would be a role for LLLTs?

3. Do you think there are any situations in which nonlawyers, working either independently or under supervision, should be allowed to give legal advice?

4. Other Law-Related Positions

In her Paralegal Profile on page 9, Jennifer Lerner talked about how she was able to take the skills she had developed as a paralegal and use them to attain a position with a maritime company. Curtis Linder's Paralegal Profile on page 12 provides another example of using the knowledge and skills acquired as a paralegal to open up other occupational opportunities. This ability to take a specific skill set and refashion it into a variety of nontraditional jobs is something that is becoming more and more common. Paralegals are moving into a wide variety of new positions. These include work as investigators, law librarians, claims representatives, risk management professionals, compliance officers, legal technology specialists, sales representatives for legal software vendors, contract negotiators, and office managers. While these positions do not carry the title of paralegal, they require similar skills and aptitudes: namely, an ability to communicate effectively, both orally and in writing; analytical reasoning skills; top-notch research capabilities; and a sense of professionalism.

---

[5] Lyle Moran, *Utah's Licensed Paralegal Practitioner Program Starts Small*, Above the Law, Dec. 12, 2019, abovethelaw.com/2019/12/utahs-licensed-paralegal-practitioner-program-starts-small/ (visited April 6, 2020).

PARALEGAL PROFILE

Curtis A. Linder
Founder and President
Linder Legal Staffing Inc.

As part of my political science major, I took several paralegal courses and had two outstanding internship experiences: one with a general practice law firm and the other with a circuit court judge.

I started my paralegal career working as a temporary/contract paralegal in a Chicago law firm, where I reviewed and indexed discovery documents in a federal antitrust suit. The documents I was indexing were located in off-site storage, and I was told to dress appropriately for warehouse work and was given a handheld tape recorder. I created audio cassette tape recordings that were later transcribed into documents—indexes—of what were in those hundreds of bankers boxes. I really enjoyed the energy, pace, and excitement of working on such a large and important case.

And that is how I found my passion: in temporary staffing. I was then hired by the staffing company to work at their offices to interview and place paralegals, lawyers, and other support professionals on assignments with law firms and corporate legal departments throughout Chicagoland. I also later managed the legal divisions of two staffing companies before founding my own firm.

For the better part of the past three decades, I have been in the paralegal placement and staffing field. Since the late 1980s I have interviewed, hired, and placed hundreds of legal professionals—mostly paralegals but also lawyers. And as the legal profession (business!) has grown, this has come to include other key support staff such as law firm marketers, conflicts managers, and other types of critical project support staff.

On a day-to-day basis I meet with and personally interview two to four candidates each day. I try to meet with as many different types of law-related candidates as possible because I never know what my clients (Chicago-area law firms and companies large enough to have an in-house legal department) will ask for.

I strongly advise recent graduates of paralegal programs to consider the benefits of working with a firm like mine. Landing a temporary assignment is usually a faster way to get hired than searching and applying for direct-hire positions. In fact, you might get interviewed by the staffing firm on a Wednesday and start an assignment the following Monday. These temporary assignments provide on-the-job experience, and many contract assignments result in the paralegal getting an offer for a permanent position. If you do receive an offer to stay on as one of their regular employees, you will be better able to evaluate the offer in light of what you already know about the quality of the firm and the people that work there.

Qualifications	Paralegal	Lawyer
Undergraduate education	None required in general (However, an associate's degree is rapidly becoming the minimum acceptable degree for employment; many employers require a bachelor 's degree.)	Bachelor's degree
Specialized education	None required (Some employers give preference to graduates of ABA-approved paralegal programs.)	Usually a degree from an ABA-accredited law school
Testing	None required (Some employers give preference to those who pass a voluntary exam administered by one of the national paralegal associations.)	Passage of a state bar exam (Most exams have multi-state and state-specific questions.)
License and morals check	None required	Must be licensed

Figure 1-1   Paralegal versus Lawyer Qualifications

C. PARALEGAL EDUCATION

There are significant differences in the qualifications for becoming a paralegal or a lawyer. Figure 1-1 summarizes those differences. Becoming a licensed lawyer generally involves attaining a bachelor's degree, a graduate legal education (normally three years if attending full time, or four years part time), passing a state bar exam, and passing a morals or character check.[6] In some states, to be authorized to practice law, lawyers must also join their state bar association and fulfill annual continuing education requirements.

In contrast, nothing prevents a person with no college credits and no paralegal training from being hired to work as a paralegal. This is true because currently there are no minimum legal requirements that must be satisfied to be able to work as a paralegal. Nor are there any informal standards universally accepted by all lawyers who hire paralegals.

---

[6]While it may not be formally required by the state, most law schools today will not admit new students who have not completed a bachelor's degree. California, Maine, New York, Vermont, Virginia, Washington, and West Virginia have provisions that potentially allow someone without a law school degree to take their bar exam after having studied in a law office for an extended period of time. Comprehensive Guide to Bar Admission Requirements 2020, *Chart 3: Domestic Legal Education*, www.ncbex.org/pdfviewer/?file=%2Fassets%2FBarAdmissionGuide%2FCompGuide2020_021820_Online_Final.pdf#page=13 (visited April 6, 2020).

Both lawyer and paralegal organizations, however, have worked to develop a set of educational and credentialing standards. According to the U.S. Bureau of Labor Statistics, while many paralegals have an associate's degree or a certificate in paralegal studies, "many employers prefer, or even require, applicants to have a bachelor's degree" in paralegal studies, or in any field along with a certificate in paralegal studies.[7]

1. Basic Qualifications

To be an effective paralegal, one must have a great deal of specific knowledge, whether gained through formal education or on-the-job training. But in addition to a sound grasp of both substantive and procedural law, an effective paralegal should possess certain intellectual and personality traits.

Because the law is complex and often ambiguous, paralegals must be able to think analytically and logically so that they can recognize and evaluate relevant facts and legal concepts. Paralegals must then be able to effectively communicate their conclusions both verbally and, what is particularly important, in clear, concise prose.

Certain personality traits are also important for success in this field. At times paralegals work closely with lawyers, clients, and members of the public. Therefore, paralegals should be congenial and diplomatic and present a good professional image. At other times, however, they must work long, solitary hours drafting, organizing, or digesting legal documents. These activities require patience, persistence, and the ability to work with a minimum of supervision. Paralegals should function well in stressful conditions because they live in a world of deadlines and often have conflicting demands placed on their time by lawyers.

Perhaps the most important characteristics for success in the paralegal field are ingenuity and good judgment. The best paralegals are innovative and resourceful. Once they understand the nature of the problem, they develop their own solutions. Because they exercise good judgment, they know when to proceed independently and when to bring matters to the attention of their supervising lawyers.

2. Formal Paralegal Education

Before 1970 there were no formal educational programs for paralegals; the necessary skills were learned exclusively through on-the-job training. Many lawyers simply gave their secretaries a variety of paralegal tasks, along with their own instructions as to how they were to be done. Occasionally a law firm brought in someone with a special skill, such as accounting, to help with a specific area of the law, such as assisting with the processing of tax returns.

The late 1960s and early 1970s saw the development of paralegal programs at both community colleges and proprietary schools. Today many four-year colleges and universities also have formal paralegal programs. Many employers prefer to hire graduates of a formal paralegal educational program rather than relying completely on their own in-house training.

---

[7] Bureau of Labor Statistics, U.S. Department of Labor, *Occupational Outlook Handbook*, www.bls.gov/ooh/legal/paralegals-and-legal-assistants.htm#tab-4 (visited April 6, 2020).

> ### PRACTICE TIP
>
> Sometimes supervising lawyers do not fully understand the type of education you have received. Therefore, you may need to let your supervisor know the full range of responsibilities you are capable of handling.

3. The ABA Approval Process

In 1974, to help establish appropriate standards for paralegal educators and to assist potential students and employers in judging the quality of different paralegal programs, the ABA formally adopted a set of standards for granting its approval to educational programs. To date, the ABA remains the only official body to have a formal process for approving paralegal programs. In larger urban areas, some employers prefer paralegals who have graduated from an ABA-approved paralegal program, although this is rarely a requirement.

As of 2020, the ABA had approved approximately 270 paralegal programs. This does not mean that the remaining programs could not meet the ABA requirements, although some may not be able to do so. It may simply mean that those programs have chosen not to seek ABA approval for either philosophical or economic reasons. Those programs that do meet ABA requirements but have not applied for ABA approval are often spoken of as being in "substantial compliance."

PARALEGAL PROFILE

Susan Wozniak
Paralegal
City of Champaign Legal Department

I have been employed as the sole paralegal for the city of Champaign, Illinois, for the past 14 years. My primary focus is the administration of the city of Champaign municipal court system. The purpose of this system is to prosecute individuals accused of violating the city of Champaign municipal code. I am responsible for these cases from start to finish. I receive and review the reports from the police department and prepare the charging instrument for review by an assistant city attorney. I assist in settlement negotiations and trial preparation, including obtaining victim and witness statements, and prepare the necessary documents for jury trials or appeals as necessary.

On regular municipal court days, approximately 200 cases are heard per morning, at least twice a month. The sheer volume of these cases makes this a very challenging task. Additionally, bench trials are usually held once a month, and it is not unusual for the court to hear several trials in a morning.

After trial, it is my job to monitor compliance with the sentence imposed by the Court. I have also assisted with the development of a web-based database program to track city ordinance violation cases; and most recently with an online payment component that will aid in the collection of fines and save valuable personnel time — all while making the process easier for the offender.

In addition to prosecuting ordinance violations, I have also been responsible for acting as the liaison between the legal department and outside counsel that has been retained to defend the city in federal civil rights actions and other similar civil cases against the city. It is my job to monitor and assist outside counsel with the defense and to keep the city attorney informed as to the progress of the case. This starts from the time the initial complaint is received through trial and sometimes appeal. These civil cases are quite complex and often take a year or more to resolve so they are quite the contrast to what I do in city court. They require in-depth research and regular contact with the city employees involved in the case. Because of their complexity, I spend a lot of time at the federal courthouse and meeting with outside counsel to make sure they have what they need to defend the case. In between these assignments I have also taken on the responsibility for orientation for our law clerks and work with any of the 711 law students in our department who are able to practice in court under attorney supervision.

Finally, one of my favorite responsibilities is to provide information to the citizens of the city of Champaign. As municipal employees, we take pride in serving the public. We feel it is our responsibility to share information about the city — and help citizens understand the Champaign Municipal Code.

All of this variety is what makes my position so enjoyable and challenging at the same time. The skill to navigate these varied environments has taken years to acquire. In order to be a successful paralegal, a person must be organized, a self-starter, and be able to prioritize all the different tasks assigned. It is also very important to stay current with technology as well as the areas of law that affect your practice. Joining professional associations is a good way to meet other paralegals and people who work in the legal field — while obtaining the latest information on continuing education options and changes in the law.

When I was hired, the position required one of the following: (1) a certificate from an ABA-approved paralegal/legal assistant program; (2) bachelor's or associate's degree in legal studies; or (3) a bachelor's degree plus one year's experience as a paralegal. The City is currently adding a second paralegal to the legal department and the paralegal experience qualification has increased to three years.

In addition to my employment with the city of Champaign, I have been a member of the Illinois State University Paralegal Advisory Board since 2008 and during my tenure the board assisted the university in obtaining ABA certification for their paralegal degree. I am also involved in the Central Illinois Paralegal Association and enjoy attending the annual education seminar to catch up with my fellow central Illinois paralegals while learning about new areas of law and growing my present skill set.

4. American Association for Paralegal Education

In 1981 educators from a variety of paralegal programs formed the **American Association for Paralegal Education (AAfPE)**. This national organization was chartered to promote high standards for paralegal education, provide a forum for professional improvement for paralegal educators, and promote research and dissemination of information regarding the paralegal profession and paralegal education. Its membership includes approximately 400 educational institutions offering programs at the community college, baccalaureate, and postgraduate levels.

American Association for Paralegal Education (AAfPE) *www.aafpe.org* A national organization of paralegal programs that promotes high standards for paralegal education.

D. PARALEGAL PROFESSIONAL ASSOCIATIONS

There are two major, national, not-for-profit professional associations dedicated to meeting the needs of working paralegals. They are the National Federation of Paralegal Associations and NALA: The Paralegal Organization.

The **National Federation of Paralegal Associations (NFPA)** was formed in 1974 as a federation of local paralegal groups. Its mission is to promote a global presence for the paralegal profession and leadership in the legal community. **NALA: The Paralegal Association** was formed in 1975 as a direct membership organization for paralegals and its mission is to advance paralegals through certification and professional development. Its organizational structure includes local chapter affiliates.

National Federation of Paralegal Associations (NFPA) *www.paralegals.org* A national association of paralegal associations advancing the paralegal profession.

Both organizations seek to promote the paralegal profession and monitor activities of courts, bar associations, and legislatures that might affect their members' interests. Each association has developed its own formal set of ethical guidelines, which their members are pledged to follow. Some of their differences lie in the policy positions taken by each organization on such issues as certification, licensure, the nature of the relationship between paralegals and bar associations, and the extent to which paralegals should be permitted to operate without being under the direct supervision of a lawyer.

NALA: The Paralegal Association *www.nala.org* A national association of paralegals advancing paralegals through certification and professional development.

While the existence of competing organizations demonstrates the diversity of the profession, some observers fear that paralegals may be losing political influence because they lack a single organization to speak with one voice for the entire paralegal profession. Because each organization has its own traditions and "personality," it is highly unlikely that they will merge any time in the near future.

While NFPA and NALA are the two most prominent national paralegal organizations, there are a variety of other paralegal associations at the national, state, and local levels. Membership in these other associations may be general or may be limited to a particular type of paralegal, such as paralegal managers, corporate paralegals, plaintiff paralegals, defense paralegals, or freelance paralegals. One notable example is the **International Paralegal Management Association (IPMA)**, an influential organization representing paralegal managers in large law firms and corporate law departments.

Now would be a good time to find out which paralegal associations are strong in your community and whether they have a special membership rate for

PRACTICE TIP

Join your local paralegal association.

International Paralegal Management Association (IPMA) *www.theipma.org* A national association of paralegal managers.

students. Joining a paralegal association will give you the opportunity to meet working paralegals and to participate in the association's benefits by, for example, attending seminars and being listed in their job bank.

PARALEGAL PROFILE ||||

Laurie Roselle
Director of Legal Services
Clifford Chance US LLP

I work at Clifford Chance US LLP, one of the largest law firms in the world. We have offices in thirty-seven countries. I work in the New York office. My official title is Director of Legal Services.

As Director of Legal Services, I supervise the managers who coordinate the full-time paralegals, the temporary paralegals and attorneys, the clerks (court filers), technology support, conflicts clearance, and records groups. I often handle facilities and space-related issues and generally troubleshoot for the practice groups.

I don't think I have ever had a typical day. I generally get to the office by 7 A.M. with a "To Do" list of about five items. By 9 P.M. when I've only finished one, I declare it a victory and head home, usually by hired car so I can work and bill for another hour before arriving home.

What I really like about my work is that the people are fabulous. They are passionate, resilient, fun, and, most of all, they take very seriously what the client needs, not what suits them. We work as hard as we play. I also like that no two days are ever alike. It's like a new three-ring circus every day.

Thinking back on my education and what best prepared me for my work, I would have to say that business, math, and statistics were the courses that have helped me the most. When those math teachers tell you that you will use basic algebra all your life, believe them. Business is all a numbers game, and the more you know how to slice and dice them, the better off you'll be.

The International Paralegal Management Association (IPMA) is a great source of information and networking for the paralegal management piece of my job. Their annual conference is always well done and timely on issues directly impacting the paralegals I supervise. The Association of Legal Administrators (ALA) is an excellent group for networking and information on a wide variety of topics that cover the myriad of other items for which I am responsible. The ALA annual conference makes me giddy like a kid in a candy shop, as there are so many sessions to attend. For real estate it is all about "location, location, location," and for networking, it is all about IPMA/ALA for me.

My advice to students thinking about a career as a paralegal is to act like a sponge: soak up information on both "soft" and "legal" topics. You never know where this field will lead you, so the more information you gather, the better equipped you will be to take the next step up the ladder. Embrace technology (even though we may never really see a paperless courtroom!) and never say "never." The attitude you bring to the table is what an employer is looking for . . . they can teach you the legal skills, but they cannot teach you attitude. If you don't have a "can-do" attitude, legal is not the field for you. Lawyers do not want to hear the reasons why you cannot do something. They want to hear that it has been done.

In my free time I do stand-up comedy, spoil my nieces and nephews, and do volunteer work with Delta Gamma Sorority, the Smile Train (a non-profit organization committed to eradicating the problem of cleft lips and palates), and the Princess Project (a non-profit organization that distributes donated new and "gently worn" formal dresses to students who might otherwise not be able to attend their proms).

E. REGISTRATION, CERTIFICATION, AND LICENSURE

Although many employers hire only paralegals who have completed an ABA-approved or other well-established paralegal education program, the lack of formal licensing requirements allows for situations in which people with no formal training or experience can be hired and given the job title of paralegal. This situation often leads to a great deal of variation among paralegals in terms of background and quality, and that in turn is seen by many as harming the image of the profession. "Real" paralegals are justifiably upset when they find some law firms giving the "paralegal" or "legal assistant" job title to administrative assistants as a reward for loyal service to the firm, even though they will continue to do the same clerical work they have always done. Many paralegals are looking for ways to set themselves apart. The possibilities include registration, certification, and licensing.

1. Registration

Registration is a process by which individuals or organizations have their names placed on an official list kept by some private organization or governmental agency. Depending on the purpose of the registration process, placing one's name on this list is either voluntary or mandatory. Both Florida and Indiana have adopted voluntary paralegal registration programs, whereby any person who is qualified by education, training, or work experience and who works under the supervision of a lawyer performing delegated, substantive work for which that lawyer is responsible may register as a paralegal.

2. Certification

When special qualifications are established as a requirement for registration, the system moves from registration to certification (see Figure 1-2). **Certification** refers to the formal recognition by an organization that an individual has met

Registration
The process by which individuals or organizations have their names placed on an official list kept by some private organization or governmental agency.

Certified
The status of being formally recognized by a governmental or nongovernmental organization for having met special criteria, such as fulfilling educational requirements and passing an exam, established by that organization.

some predetermined set of qualifications, which typically includes meeting educational requirements and passing an exam. Only those who meet these criteria are allowed to claim the title that goes with the designated status, but a person without such certification is not legally restricted from working in that occupational area. The advantage of certification is that potential employers and clients know that the individual has met certain standards. Therefore, presumably they are more likely to employ this individual than someone who is not certified. Three states have created a certified paralegal designation: North Carolina, Ohio, and Wisconsin.

A few states, along with the two major paralegal organizations discussed above, provide a method by which paralegals can become certified. For example, the only paralegals who can call themselves a "Certified Legal Assistant" or a "Certified Paralegal" and use the letters "CLA" or "CP" after their names are those who have completed the requirements of NALA's voluntary certification program. The terms "Certified Legal Assistant (CLA)" and "Certified Paralegal (CP)" are registered trademarks of NALA.

NALA's certification requirements include passing an exam and completing five units of continuing legal assistant education every five years. NALA also offers an advanced certification program.

Similarly, NFPA administers two certification exams. The first is the Paralegal CORE Competency Exam (PCCE), with a target audience of entry-level and early-career paralegals. The second exam is a proficiency exam for experienced paralegals, known as the Paralegal Advanced Competency Exam (PACE). Paralegals who successfully complete NFPA's certification program are authorized to use a "Registered Paralegal (RP)" designation.

These exams are national in scope and test for general legal knowledge that is not state specific. Some states have developed their own state-specific exams. These certification programs are all voluntary in that certification is not a legal requirement for working in the paralegal field. However, in some regions of the country, employers are more likely to employ someone who is certified than someone who is not.

It is important to distinguish between being certified by a state agency, such as the North Carolina State Bar, or a voluntary organization, such as NALA or NFPA, and being certificated. A person is **certificated** when that person has successfully completed a formal paralegal program that offers a certificate of completion, whether instead of or in addition to awarding a degree. Such people can appropriately be called "certificated legal assistants" or "certificated paralegals" but should not be called "certified paralegals" unless they have followed the certification requirements of a state or NALA.

Certificated
The status of having received a certificate documenting that the person has successfully completed an educational paralegal program.

Figure 1-2 Increasing Levels of Regulation

Registration ⟶ Certification ⟶ Licensure

Even though no state has as yet licensed paralegals, paralegals must always remember that as part of the legal profession, they are required to maintain demanding ethical standards. The following three points are of special importance to paralegals:

Ethics Alert

1. Paralegals are not lawyers and therefore cannot give legal advice, sign court documents, or appear in court on behalf of a client. To do so is the unauthorized practice of law, which is a crime in most states.
2. Lawyers and their staff must respect the confidentiality of the client-attorney relationship. You must treat anything you learn in the law firm as confidential and not discuss it with anyone outside the firm—even your spouse or other family member.
3. Clients expect their lawyers and staff to be loyal to them. Therefore, if you change employers, you must alert your new employer to any cases with which you were involved while working for your former firm. Not to do so means running the risk of creating a conflict of interest for the firm.

As you read through the materials in this book, watch for potential ethical issues posed in the readings or chapter questions.

3. Licensing

Licensing refers to the process by which governmental agencies establish standards and then prohibit those who have not met those standards from working in that occupational field. Thus a person who has not been admitted to the bar is prohibited from practicing law because he or she is not a licensed lawyer. Based on the prevailing definitions of what constitutes the unauthorized practice of law, paralegals can perform a variety of legal tasks without a license to practice law, so long as they work under the supervision of a licensed lawyer. Some have argued, however, that a separate system of licensing should be established for paralegals in the same way that nurses are licensed separately from doctors.

Over the past twenty-five years, a few states have considered proposals for licensing paralegals. Certification of paralegals has spread to several states, but licensing has not. Part of the reason for this is that opponents of licensure argue that licensing is not needed, as the state can hold the supervising lawyers responsible for ensuring the quality of the work done by their paralegals, as well as their ethical behavior.

While the licensing of paralegals has not been widely accepted, many states have expressed concerns that access to lawyers is a significant problem, so they have been looking for ways to remove barriers to civil justice for low-income and disadvantaged people. Washington and Utah have formally adopted a type

Licensing
Governmental permission to engage in a profession.

of licensing for non-lawyers who can provide limited legal services without the supervision of a lawyer. A number of other states have either adopted similar legislation or have formed task forces to examine this type of licensing.

DISCUSSION QUESTIONS

4. What is the difference between registration and certification? Compare Florida's registration to North Carolina's certification.

5. What reasons were given for discontinuing Washington State's LLLT system? What were the arguments in favor of continuing the system? What argument did you find more compelling, and why?

6. Compare the Washington LLLT system with Utah's LPP system. What areas of the law were covered? What were the criteria for becoming an LLLT or an LPP?

F. WHAT PARALEGALS DO

Earlier in this chapter, we said that when working under the supervision of a lawyer, paralegals can do just about anything related to the practice of law except give legal advice to clients and represent clients in most types of judicial proceedings. In a landmark U.S. Supreme Court case dealing with the awarding of fees for paralegal work, Justice William Brennan noted that

> paralegals are capable of carrying out many tasks, under the supervision of an attorney, that might otherwise be performed by a lawyer and billed at a higher rate. Such work might include, for example, factual investigation, including locating and interviewing witnesses; assistance with depositions, interrogatories, and document production; compilation of statistical and financial data; checking legal citations and drafting correspondence. Much of this work lies in a gray area of tasks that might appropriately be performed either by an attorney or a paralegal.[8]

The tasks listed by Justice Brennan involve communication with clients, research, drafting, and case management. In order to perform these duties effectively, paralegals need not only a thorough understanding of the legal system, but also sound critical thinking skills. These skills include:

- gathering and analyzing facts;
- conducting legal research to identify the appropriate legal rules;
- applying the rules to the facts; and
- acting on the results.

Take a moment to reread the two hypothetical cases we introduced at the beginning of this chapter, as we will be using them to illustrate these four basic steps.

---

[8] Missouri v. Jenkins, 491 U.S. 274, 288, n.10 (1989).

PRACTICE TIP

Everything you read in this book is wrong! Or at least it might be. Remember that law keeps changing, and it also varies from state to state. Further, there are exceptions to many rules.

1. Gathering and Analyzing Facts

The answer to any legal question depends on the specific facts of the individual case. Even a minor change in the facts may alter the outcome of the case. Lawyers say that a case is **fact bound**.

    Just as a medical doctor cannot give a competent medical diagnosis without a thorough examination of the patient, a lawyer cannot render legal advice without a complete understanding of all of the relevant facts. In some areas of the law, such as those dealing with negligence of landlords and tenants, the legal outcome is particularly tied to the specific facts. For example, assume a stranger approaches a lawyer at a party with questions such as, "My landlord is trying to evict me. Can he do that?" or "My husband is trying to get custody of my kids. Will he succeed?" It would be impossible for the lawyer to answer without gathering a lot more information and personally reviewing key documents.

    Paralegals often assist in the fact-gathering process by participating in or conducting interviews, summarizing those interviews, and reading and summarizing relevant documents. For example, when Donald Drake and Wanda Smith came to the law office of Darrow and Bryan to seek advice, they were each interviewed by Pat Harper, a lawyer with the firm. Chris Kendall, one of the firm's senior paralegals, also sat in on the interviews to help take notes and to become familiar with the facts of the cases.

    While the client will supply many of the important facts in the case, a lawyer can never rely solely on the client's perception of those facts. Invariably clients will overlook some facts, while allowing their personal prejudices and self-interest to color their perception of other facts. The paralegal can play an important role in interviewing both the client and other witnesses and then accurately recording the results of those interviews. A paralegal may also draft documents to gather information from the opposing party or witnesses.

Fact bound
The principle that even a minor change in facts can change the outcome of a case.

2. Conducting Legal Research to Identify the Appropriate Legal Rules

After meeting with the clients, the first thing that Harper, the lawyer, needed to determine was whether either client had a basis for proceeding with a lawsuit. If a client does not have a valid **cause of action** (i.e., a claim that, based on the law and facts, would be sufficient to support a lawsuit), then the client's case will be dismissed before it even goes to trial. For example, in Wanda Smith's case, she was clearly upset and disturbed by what had happened to her. However, that does not mean she has a legal remedy. Her lawyers will have to prove not only

Cause of action
A claim that based on the law and the facts is sufficient to support a lawsuit.

that the construction workers harassed and upset her, but also that these actions violated some law. It is important to understand that not every problem is a problem for which the courts will supply a remedy.

NETNOTE

One way to stay current with the changes in the law is through the Internet. You can find the latest legal news by going to *lp.findlaw.com*.

Thus, the second stage of legal analysis involves the identification of the specific provisions of the law that are applicable to the client's situation. Because there are so many laws at the federal, state, and local levels, and because the law covers such a wide variety of topics, it is impossible for any lawyer to know everything there is to know about the law. Furthermore, because the law is constantly changing, one's legal knowledge must be continually updated. Therefore, even lawyers who specialize and strive to keep current by reading legal newspapers, journals, and bar publications on a daily basis may still need to do legal research.

Legal research
The process of finding the law.

Legal research is a very time-consuming process, and lawyers often rely on paralegals to assist them in locating and summarizing the relevant statutes and cases they need to properly interpret the current status of the law. Because Harper has not recently handled a similar case, Kendall was assigned in Smith's case to research the law on sexual harassment and, in Drake's case, to see what law existed regarding the right to sue for emotional distress. We will discuss legal research in greater detail in Part III of this text.

3. Applying the Rules to the Facts

Even after a lawyer or paralegal has found the applicable legal rule through legal research, the job is far from completed. Because each client's problem is unique, simply knowing a general rule will not answer the problem in question. These general rules must be applied to the client's specific facts. We call this process **legal reasoning.**

Legal reasoning
The application of legal rules to a client's specific factual situation; also known as *legal analysis.*

Often this is a very straightforward process. For example, assume that your firm is representing a husband seeking a divorce. He wants to know if the court will take into consideration the years his wife worked as a stay-at-home mother when it decides on the appropriate division of the marital assets. Through legal research, you find a state statute that requires the court to take into account homemaker services when dividing marital property. In this case, assuming that your client's wife did indeed perform homemaking services, applying the law to your client's facts is very straightforward, and your supervising lawyer would report to the husband that, unfortunately for him, the court will take into account her years as a homemaker when dividing the marital assets. At other times, this process is much less clear-cut, and the result in a client's case may depend on how the courts have handled similar situations in the past.

To find out how similar situations have been handled in the past, a lawyer or paralegal will examine prior court decisions, **precedent**, and then apply them to the client's situation. This is because our legal system is based on a doctrine known as **stare decisis** (literally, "the decision stands"). If the facts of the client's situation and a prior court decision are similar (i.e., they are **analogous**), it is likely that the result in the client's case will be similar to the result reached in the prior case. If the facts are significantly different (i.e., **distinguishable**), it is likely that the result in the client's case will not be the same as the result reached in the prior case.

Unfortunately for Wanda Smith, Kendall's research indicated that she did not appear to have a legal basis for suing the construction workers. If Smith had been employed as one of the construction workers and her boss had been harassing her, she would have had the basis for suing the company. However, as a mere passerby, she lacked such protection. Her facts combined with the law do not give her a right to sue.

As recently as 30 years ago, Smith would not have been able to sue even if her employer had been the one to harass her. But as societal values change, the law usually changes as well. In recent years, our society has become more sensitive to issues of gender equality, and new laws have developed to provide new protections. Societal values change, and the law evolves in order to respond to those changes.

DISCUSSION QUESTION

7. Why do you suppose there are certain types of harm, such as the humiliation Wanda Smith felt when the construction workers whistled at her, that courts will not help individuals resolve?

With regard to Donald Drake's case, Kendall's research proved more promising. He found one case in which a mother who saw her young child killed by a negligent driver was allowed to recover for the emotional distress the accident caused her. However, five years later, in another decision involving a similar situation, a female bystander who happened to witness the death of a young boy was not allowed to recover for her emotional distress.

In assessing the strength of Drake's case, Harper must decide whether the courts would treat a grandfather as they did the mother or as they did the bystander. Take a few minutes to list as many arguments as you can muster for each side of the debate. The most important part of legal reasoning is seeking factual similarities and differences between prior decisions and your client's case, and then explaining why you think those similarities or differences matter. In that process, you will find that you and your classmates often differ as to the "right" answer.

In actuality, there is no "right" answer, only better or worse arguments for your client. A judge may be the final arbiter as to what the answer is in a particular case, but even then it is not the "right" answer in any cosmic sense. Any decision about what the law should be is a choice between competing values. This is why some cases go to trial instead of settling — that is, because the two litigants have differing viewpoints as to which of two competing values is the most important. The important point to remember is that your goal is to learn

Precedent
One or more prior court decisions.

Stare decisis
The doctrine stating that, normally, once a court has decided one way on a particular issue in the past, it and other courts in the same jurisdiction will decide the same way on that issue in future cases, given a similar set of facts, unless they can be convinced of the need for change.

Analogous cases
Cases that involve similar facts and rules of law.

Distinguishable cases
Cases that involve dissimilar facts or rules of law.

how to develop arguments that will help persuade the other side that your answer is more correct than theirs.

4. Acting on the Results

Throughout this process, lawyers and paralegals must commit their thoughts to writing. At some point they will take informal, working notes for their own use. At other times they will make more formal reports that are designed to be read by colleagues, clients, opposing lawyers, or judges. You will be introduced to various examples of these more specialized forms of **legal writing** throughout the text.

After a lawyer has thoroughly analyzed the application of the law to the client's situation and has advised the client as to the options available under the law, the lawyer and client may agree to take some action on the client's behalf. These actions might include trying to settle the case without having to resort to **litigation** (i.e., without having to rely on the courts to resolve the dispute). For example, the lawyers for the two sides might be able to negotiate a compromise either with or without the help of a neutral third party, such as a mediator.

If litigation cannot be avoided, the lawyer may represent the client in a civil lawsuit. In these situations the lawyer is responsible for submitting court documents called **pleadings** in order to initiate the lawsuit. Prior to trial, the lawyer will also conduct **discovery** in order to find out as much about the case as possible from witnesses and the parties on the opposite side. If the case does proceed to trial, the lawyer will also be responsible for conducting direct and cross-examinations of witnesses and making appropriate arguments to the judge and the jury. Paralegals often assist in all these stages, from drafting pleadings to preparing witnesses and evidence for trial.

In Donald Drake's case, Harper concluded that, although victory was not assured, there were good grounds for a lawsuit. Because Drake was anxious to proceed, she directed Kendall to begin preparing the documents needed to officially begin the lawsuit. After carefully reviewing these documents, Harper signed them and directed Kendall to file them at the local courthouse.

Legal writing
Examples of legal writing include case briefs, law office memoranda, and documents filed with the court.

Litigation
A lawsuit; a controversy to be settled in a court.

Pleadings
The papers that begin a lawsuit; generally, the complaint and the answer.

Discovery
The modern pretrial procedure by which one party gains information from the adverse party.

Ethics Alert

Although paralegals can draft legal documents, the documents cannot be filed with the court until a lawyer has reviewed, approved, and signed them.

As the case progresses, the paralegal can serve as a link between lawyer and client. Once the lawyer has established the client-lawyer relationship, paralegals can and do play a very important role in maintaining effective communications between lawyer and client. For example, whereas many lawyers are notorious for being too busy to return phone calls to their clients, paralegals are usually far more accessible. If they are properly prepared, paralegals can relay important information about the case from client to attorney, and vice versa. Due to their specialized training, paralegals can help explain legal procedures to clients, and they can communicate effectively with other lawyers and court officials.

When talking with clients, keep in mind that everything that is said must be kept confidential. Also, there may be times when you are alone with a client and the client will ask you for legal advice. Remember that only the lawyer can give that advice. For you to do so would be the unauthorized practice of law.

Legal Reasoning Exercise

1. Imagine that you are interning in Harper's law firm. She has asked you to give her your thoughts on Drake's case. Specifically, Harper wants you to list all the ways in which you think Donald Drake's case is similar to that of the mother who saw her child injured. Then list all the ways in which you think Drake's case could be likened to that of the bystander. Finally, give Harper your evaluation as to why you think that a court would see Drake's case as more similar to that of the mother or to that of the bystander. Also, let her know if you think there are additional facts that you would want to gather before making a final recommendation.

PARALEGAL PROFILE

Amy J. Inlander
Director of Paralegals and Chicago Office
Taft Stettinius & Hollister LLP

Taft Stettinius & Hollister LLP (Taft) is a prominent Midwest law firm with multiple offices located in Illinois, Indiana, Michigan, northern Kentucky, and Ohio. The firm practices across a wide range of industries, in virtually every area of law. Taft has approximately 400 lawyers and 50 paralegals firm-wide. The Chicago office is one of our larger locations with 150 employees. I serve as a general manager of the Chicago office and director of all paralegals.

My paralegal-related responsibility is to manage and distribute work assignments to all of the paralegals. My position requires occasional travel to all of the Taft offices. It is important for me to know the paralegals that I am managing in addition to the attorneys that work closely with them. All firm partners and employees must feel comfortable communicating with me. I am a problem solver and project facilitator. My communication and analytical and people skills were established and sharpened early in my career through exposure to the frenzied environment of a law firm.

I began my career as a full-time practicing paralegal, focusing in the transactional area. My paralegal classes and internship provided a wonderful foundation for my first paralegal position. However, it was a paralegal that I met at my first job that served as my mentor and assisted me with polishing my general office skills. Mentoring or teaching is the greatest gift one paralegal can give another. Mentoring is often manifested through one-on-one training, teaching a paralegal class, or participating in professional seminars. I am fortunate enough to have participated in all of the above. The reaction that I receive from other people confirms that my work experiences can be valuable in enhancing the professional lives of many as they contemplate or enter into a paralegal career.

Being a member of the paralegal community also leads to more global responsibilities. Participation in professional law firm associations promotes networking with colleagues and provides useful information to share with others. This type of communal activity can reinforce necessary skills that lead to a higher level of performance.

Ultimately, the choice to become a paralegal has given me an opportunity to expand my professional career. My paralegal foundation gave me valuable skills and many business successes, which I could never have imagined when first reading *Fundamentals of Paralegalism*.

NETNOTE

As you may have noticed by reading the marginal definitions, all of the major associations mentioned in Chapter 1 have websites. Take a few minutes to visit each.

American Association for Paralegal Education (AAfPE):

www.aafpe.org

American Bar Association (ABA):

www.abanet.org

National Federation of Paralegal Associations (NFPA):

www.paralegals.org

NALA: The Paralegal Association:

www.nala.org

International Paralegal Management Association (IPMA):

www.theipma.org

SUMMARY

Over the past 50 years, the paralegal profession has grown rapidly, and paralegals are now found in a variety of legal settings. In this chapter, we have discussed what paralegals do and how their work relates to other legal professionals.

We have also examined how paralegals are educated and credentialed. Lawyer and paralegal associations are working to further develop educational and testing standards. These efforts include the ABA paralegal program approval process, the NALA certification program, the NFPA Advanced Proficiency and CORE Competency exams, and AAfPE's core competencies, as well as state certification, registration, and licensure.

The most common legal work environments are private practice arrangements, but paralegals can also be found in the legal departments of businesses, non-profits, and governmental agencies. Take a few minutes to compare the paralegal profiles of Karen Decrescenzo and Susan Wozniak. Note how much variation there is in what they do, even though they both work in municipal legal departments.

Then, read Amy Inlander's paralegal profile, and compare it with the one of Laurie Roselle. Both provide examples of how paralegals can work their way up into managerial positions in large law firms. Also, note what all of them have to say about the importance of networking and becoming active in local professional associations.

In order to achieve the kinds of success these paralegals have achieved, you will need to develop strong critical thinking skills that include the ability to analyze the facts, identify the appropriate legal rules, apply the legal rules to the facts, report the results, and take actions on behalf of the client. Although we have presented each stage in a linear fashion, the reality is that these various stages are intertwined. Legal reasoning often reveals the need to do more research. In the process of reporting your findings, you may discover flaws in your analysis. Thinking, researching, and writing are inseparable.

Do not be dismayed if you are sometimes overwhelmed by the complexity and sheer volume of legal concepts and materials. Learning law is a lot like learning a foreign language. Although many of these terms may be new to you now, they will become increasingly familiar to you as you progress through the text. In the end, you will be amazed at how these diverse pieces end up fitting into a logical and effective system.

REVIEW QUESTIONS

Pages 3 through 11
1. What is the definition of a paralegal?
2. What is a freelance paralegal?
3. How do document preparers, LLLTs, and lay advocates differ from traditional paralegals?

Pages 13 through 19
4. What are the requirements for becoming a lawyer?
5. What are the requirements for becoming a paralegal?
6. When did formal paralegal education begin?
7. What role does the ABA play in paralegal education?
8. What are the names of the two major paralegal associations?

Pages 19 through 22
9. What is involved in the process of registration?
10. What are the major differences between certification and licensure?
11. Who has the right to use the title CLA?
12. What are the three ethical issues of which paralegals must be particularly aware?
13. What is an LPP?

Pages 22 through 30
14. Why does the study of law involve more than simply memorizing rules?
15. What is legal reasoning?
16. Why is it important to know whether your client's facts are analogous to or distinguishable from those in prior court decisions?
17. Why does law change? Should it?
18. Why is there no one "right" answer to a legal problem?
19. What are some of the basic tasks that most traditional paralegals perform?
20. Should it be the lawyer or the paralegal who signs a client letter that analyzes the law? Why?

WEB EXERCISES

1. In this chapter, we gave you an overview of what paralegals do. To read more about the paralegal profession, including typical job duties, go to the U.S. Bureau of Labor Statistics' website (*www.bls.gov*). Do a search on the word "paralegal."
   a. What skills and personality traits appear to be particularly important for someone to be successful as a paralegal?
   b. What pay range should you expect if you work as a paralegal?

2. Visit the websites of the two major paralegal associations, NFPA (*www .paralegals.org*) and NALA (*www.nala.org*).
   a. Does either organization sponsor a local branch near you?
   b. Read about the test given by each organization. Which seems better suited to recent graduates of a paralegal program?
   c. Take a few minutes to simply browse within each website. You will find many things of interest.
      i. Take a look at NFPA's "Position Statement on Non-Lawyer Practice." Do you agree with its support of legislation and court rules that would allow non-lawyers to deliver limited legal services directly to members of the public?
      ii. On the NALA site, you can find their Model Standards and Guidelines for Utilization of Paralegals. How do the NALA Guidelines contrast with the NFPA Position Statement?
3. Visit the AAfPE website (*www.aafpe.org*). On the site, you can find a page to assist students in evaluating paralegal educational programs. What special considerations should you take into account if you would like to enroll in a distance education program?

Chapter 2

Legal Ethics

A lawyer should avoid even the appearance of professional impropriety.
ABA Model Code of Professional Responsibility
Canon 9

Chapter Objectives

After reading this chapter, you should be able to:

- List the five principal ways of regulating paralegal ethical behavior.
- Describe the types of client confidentiality situations that can arise in a law practice.
- Distinguish between client confidentiality and attorney-client privilege.
- Describe the types of conflict of interest situations that can arise in a law practice and when it is necessary to erect an ethical screen.
- Define the practice of law and explain what can make it the unauthorized practice of law.
- Describe the various billing methods that lawyers use and possible ethical issues that can arise when dealing with client funds.
- Describe the various ways that ethical rules are enforced.

INTRODUCTION

Knowledge of the ethical responsibilities that govern what paralegals do is one of the most critical aspects of being a member of the paralegal profession. As professionals who hold positions of responsibility and trust, paralegals have ethical responsibilities that extend to the lawyers who employ them, the clients they serve, and the administration of justice.

Lawyers are bound by the ethical rules that have been officially adopted in the states in which they practice. While the specific wording of these ethical guidelines varies from state to state, every state except for California has chosen to adopt rules based on the American Bar Association (ABA)'s **Model Rules of Professional Conduct**. Because these ethical codes are tied to state licensing provisions, if an attorney lawyer, or someone working for a lawyer, commits a serious ethical violation, that violation can result in sanctions, including the loss of the attorney's lawyer's license to practice law.

As employees of lawyers, paralegals are also expected to abide by these lawyer guidelines as well. To date, however, no state has adopted a code of ethics for paralegals. The states treat the paralegals as an extensions of the lawyer, and lawyers are held liable for the ethical breaches of those who work for them. In addition, as we saw in Chapter 1, no state has taken the step of requiring that paralegals be licensed. If such legislation licensing paralegals is passed, those licensing statutes will undoubtedly place specific obligations or restrictions on those who receive such a license. In the meantime, the two major paralegal associations, the NALA: The Paralegal Association and the National Federation of Paralegal Associations (NFPA), have each adopted a model code of ethics for its members to follow.

Paralegals are also affected by the laws regarding liability for negligent acts and the unauthorized practice of law (UPL). Paralegals who are notary publics are obliged to follow the laws regarding notary publics in the states in which they are commissioned. Finally, the two major paralegal associations, NALA and NFPA, have each adopted a model code of ethics for its members.

Therefore, paralegals currently are regulated in five ways:

1. indirectly, by the bar's regulation of lawyers through ethical codes;
2. directly, by NALA's or NFPA's ethical codes (for members of those organizations);
3. directly, by laws on the unauthorized practice of law (UPL);
4. directly, by the tort law of negligence; and
5. directly, by notary public law (for members who are notary publics).

As we will discuss in this chapter, there are three main ethical areas about which paralegals must be particularly knowledgeable: client confidentiality and attorney-client privilege, conflict of interest, and UPL. In addition, we will be discussing the proper procedures for handling client funds, the limits to zealous representation, and liability for legal malpractice.

As you read the chapter, see if you can pinpoint all the possible ethical violations raised in the following fact scenario.

Model Rules of Professional Conduct
A set of ethical rules developed by the American Bar Association (ABA). The Model Rules have been adopted in whole or in part by every state and the District of Columbia.

Case 3: The Ethically Challenged Paralegal

One day, John Bloom, a lawyer, asked Sally Green, a paralegal with his firm, to sit in on an initial client interview. Bloom introduced Green to the client, Sara Smith, and to Smith's friend, Bertha. Smith was very nervous about going to a lawyer and so had brought her friend Bertha for support. Bloom explained to them that Green is a paralegal. Smith told them the following story:

She recently served a pot roast to her family. That night, her entire family developed severe stomach cramps and diarrhea. The doctors in the hospital emergency room told them that they were suffering from food poisoning. Smith wanted to know if she could sue the grocery store that sold her the meat.

Bloom told Smith they would be happy to accept her as a client and that they handled cases such as hers on a contingency basis. He explained that that meant she would owe them one-third of whatever they recovered for her. He then told her they would get back to her as soon as they completed some preliminary research. After the interview, Bloom asked Green to conduct a factual investigation, research the issue, and draft the complaint.

As part of her research, Green called the grocery store. Saying she was from the Department of Health, she asked the store manager how many customer complaints they had in the past month regarding spoiled meat purchased from the store.

Later that afternoon, Bloom asked Green to write the paychecks for herself and the firm receptionist. Because the firm was temporarily a little short of cash, Bloom told her to take the money from the client escrow account. He assured her that he would replace the money before the end of the week and that no clients would be harmed. Bloom also asked Green to notarize a stack of documents on his desk. Green did as Bloom requested.

The next day, Smith called the office. As Bloom was in court, Green took the call. Smith said that she was confused about some of the terminology that Bloom had used the day before. First, she asked Green to explain to her what a complaint is. Green did so. Then Smith asked her what sorts of information would be put in the complaint. Green pulled out the complaint that she had just drafted (but had not yet shown to Bloom) and read it to Smith. Finally, Smith asked whether Green thought she would win her negligence claim. Green told Smith that she was not a lawyer and could not give legal advice. However, her personal opinion was that Smith had a very good chance of winning her case.

Right after Green got off the phone with Smith, Joan Doe, the firm's receptionist, brought a letter into her office. The letter had just been faxed to them from another lawyer's office. The letterhead indicated that the letter was from the firm Smith and Smith, was signed by Sam Smith, and was addressed to Mr. Defendant. The letter stated that Smith was representing Mr. Defendant in a lawsuit that Bloom had initiated on behalf of Ms. Plaintiff, one of Bloom's clients. Green assumed that someone in Smith's office had mistakenly sent the letter to her firm, as it was obvious Mr. Defendant was the intended recipient. Quickly reading through the letter, she saw it contained information that could be very helpful to Bloom. The fax cover sheet stated that the enclosed material contained information protected by the attorney-client privilege.

Later that evening, while unwinding over a leisurely dinner with her husband, Green told him of the day's events. She discussed various client cases but was always very careful never to reveal any names. She also told her husband that another law firm had offered her a job. It would entail a significant increase in pay. However, she said that it made her feel a bit sad to know that the new firm might ask her to work on the opposite side of some cases that she was currently working on with Bloom.

A. THE MODEL RULES OF PROFESSIONAL CONDUCT

Historically, state supreme courts have claimed the power to regulate lawyers and to determine who can or cannot "practice law." Typically, they establish specialized boards or agencies to administer bar exams, investigate the character and fitness of applicants, review complaints against lawyers, and discipline those who violate their rules of professional conduct. While each state is responsible for establishing its own rules of professional conduct, the content of these rules generally follows the Model Rules promulgated by the ABA. The ABA adopted the Model Rules of Professional Conduct in 1983, but it has amended them many times since then. In 2016, the ABA amended Model Rule 8.4 to prohibit "engag[ing] in conduct that the lawyer knows or reasonably should know is harassment or discrimination on the basis of race, sex, religion, national origin, ethnicity, disability, age, sexual orientation, gender identity, marital status or socioeconomic status in conduct related to the practice of law."

Technological advances and the advent of social media have created special challenges in updating the rules. This continuous amendment process has resulted in a great deal of variation among the states. While all states base their codes of ethics on the Model Rules, they do not necessarily keep pace with the changes suggested by the ABA amendments. In addition, individual states often adopt their own unique variations of some of the more controversial provisions, such as those affecting client confidentiality and how to incorporate new technology, such as videoconferencing and the limitations on a judge's use of social media.

With so many different approaches, you may ask how any of these sets of rules can claim to guide lawyers as to ethical behavior. One answer is that none of these are actually ethical codes based on moral values; rather, they are simply rules to govern lawyer behavior. This explanation is supported by the name: the Rules of Professional *Conduct*, not the Rules of Professional *Ethics*. That is, arguably these rules are not meant to offer lawyers moral guidance, but rather to set forth a strict set of rules that lawyers must follow at the peril of losing their license to practice law. Therefore, when they study these rules in law school, law students are not really studying a code of ethics but rather a series of rules governing behavior, the violation of which could result in disbarment. Hence, when confronted with what might be seen as an ethical dilemma, lawyers may not immediately ask, "What is the right thing to do?" but rather, "What does the rule say I *have* to do?"[1]

In recognition of the distinction between rules of conduct and ethics, a number of state bar associations have started to focus on the concept that there are standards to which the legal professional should strive that are higher than those required by the Rules of Professional Conduct. Many state courts and bar associations have created professionalism commissions, and some have promulgated codes of professionalism and civility.

In addition to the Model Rules, the ABA has adopted a set of Formal Ethics Opinions, which address questions that lawyers have asked regarding particular Model Rules. Each state has adopted a similar system to help lawyers meet their

---

[1] For further discussion of this concept, see *Ethics + a changed world = Neoethics*, available at bucklin.org/articles/legal-ethics/ethics-a-changed-world-neoethics/ (last visited October 1, 2020).

obligations under the rules. These opinions are advisory, but they can be helpful in understanding how each state bar, or the ABA, interprets specific provisions of the Model Rules or Model Code. For example, if you had a question about the use of social media in advertising for your law firm, you would first read the rules regarding lawyers advertising in your state's Model Code. If your question is not directly answered (perhaps social media is not addressed in the rules), read the ethics opinions written for the rules. They very well may provide the answer you are seeking. If not, you can call or send a question to your state bar's ethics counsel, and your lawyer may get an advisory opinion over the phone; if it is seen as a particularly important question, the answer may be published as a formal ethics opinion to provide non-binding guidance to other lawyers. Note that the ABA adopted new guidelines for advertising in their most recent amendments to Rules 7.1-7.5 in August 2018.

Lawyers are required to follow the Rules of Professional Conduct of each state in which they are licensed. Each state's rules are influenced greatly by the Model Rules of the ABA. In summary, although the ABA was responsible for drafting the Model Rules of Professional Conduct, it is a voluntary association. Lawyers are not required to become ABA members, and the ABA has no authority to require lawyers to abide by the Model Rules of Professional Conduct. States, however, through their licensing power, do have the power to require lawyers to abide by a Code of Professional Responsibilities. It is the version of the code that a particular state has adopted that is binding on the lawyers in that state. As previously noted, if a lawyer, or a nonlawyer whom they supervise, is found to have violated an ethical rule, the lawyer can be subjected to sanctions, including suspension and disbarment.

By April 2020, most state bars provided their members with ethical guidelines during the COVID-19 pandemic. Social distancing orders and the closure of numerous legal entities, including courts and register of deeds offices, created questions of how lawyers could best fulfill their ethical duties. Common topics in those ethical guidelines included communication, diligence, competence, confidentiality, conflicts of interest, incapacity, supervision, disaster preparedness plans, technology, and social media. In addition to broad ethical guidelines, many lawyers contacted their state bars for guidance on how to ethically serve clients in specific circumstances. That caused the state bars to issue a number of opinions to help lawyers meet their ethical responsibilities when confronting these unforeseen new circumstances.

NETNOTE

You can locate the most current ABA Model Rules of Professional Conduct on the organization's website. When reviewing the rules, be sure to also locate the updates under "Other Model Rules Resources" at the bottom of the text of the Model Rules of Professional Conduct.

DISCUSSION QUESTIONS

1. In the popular media, lawyers are often referred to as "hired guns." We have also all heard the lawyer jokes: "How do you know when a lawyer is lying? His lips are moving." Why do you think there is this negative perception of lawyers and what they do? Do you think it is a fair characterization?

2. Locate the website for the Florida Bar's *Professionalism Handbook*. Review the "Professional Expectations" section (pages 6-14 in the 2017-2019 handbook). How does the content of "Professional Expectations" differ from the ABA Model Rules of Professional Conduct? Why are states creating these types of expectations in addition to their Model Rules?

B. ETHICAL CODES GOVERNING PARALEGAL CONDUCT

No state has yet adopted a code of ethics that directly governs the ethical behavior of paralegals. However, both major national paralegal organizations, NALA and NFPA, have adopted model codes. The ABA has also developed standards to guide lawyers in their ethical employment of paralegals.

The NALA Code of Ethics and Professional Responsibility consists of nine canons. The first five of these focus on a legal assistant's avoiding UPL. Canon 6 stresses the importance of maintaining competency through continuing education, and Canon 7 deals with protecting client confidences. Canons 8 and 9 both emphasize the need to follow rules of ethics as defined by statute, court rule, or bar association.

NETNOTE

Both NALA and NFPA have placed their codes of ethics on their websites. The ABA website also has the Model Guidelines for the Utilization of Paralegal Services, a set of guidelines that they developed to provide lawyers with guidance when working with paralegals. The ABA website also includes their 2013 ethical comments on Guidelines 2 and 3.

NFPA's Model Code of Ethics and Responsibility contains eight canons, as well as ethical considerations. While this code also has provisions regarding UPL (Canons 5 and 6) and client confidences (Canon 7), it goes beyond NALA's code in that it specifically deals with conflicts of interest (Canon 8). In its first four canons, NFPA's code emphasizes that paralegals should maintain a high level of competence, integrity, and professional conduct. An expansionist document, NFPA's code encourages paralegals to dedicate themselves "to the improvement of the legal system and [to expanding] the paralegal role in the delivery of legal services."

Because paralegals work under the supervision of a lawyer and must follow the Rules for Professional Responsibility for lawyers in the state where they practice, most states have not adopted special guidelines for paralegals. Increasingly, however, states have created official ethics guidelines specifically for paralegals, typically through the paralegal division of the regulatory agency for lawyers in states such as Florida, Utah, and Texas. Further, North Carolina is an example of a state that has promulgated its own guidelines for the use of paralegals.[2]

As the name implies, the ABA Model Guidelines for the Utilization of Paralegal Services are directed to lawyers employing paralegals rather than to paralegals themselves. For example, guideline 6 states: "A lawyer is responsible for taking reasonable measures to ensure that all client confidences are preserved by a paralegal." The ABA Standing Committee on Paralegals developed these guidelines in the hope that they would encourage lawyers to make better use of paralegal skills. The Committee also hoped that these model guidelines would encourage states to develop their own rules regarding paralegal employment. Rule 5.3 of the Model Rules of Professional Conduct outlines a lawyer's responsibilities when supervising or employing paralegals. A partner or supervising lawyers must ensure that a nonlawyer's conduct "is compatible with the professional obligations of the lawyer." In addition, a lawyer will be held accountable for a nonlawyer's unprofessional acts if the lawyer ordered or ratified those acts. However, even if the lawyer does not know of or ratify the conduct, a partner or supervising lawyer will be held accountable if the lawyer knows of the conduct in time to avoid or mitigate any harm but fails to take "reasonable remedial action."

DISCUSSION QUESTION

3. Locate the Ethics Opinions page of the ABA website. Read the ethical opinions from 2020 regarding ethical considerations related to the COVID-19 pandemic. Do you think these considerations are relevant outside of a pandemic situation?

C. THE BIG THREE: CONFIDENTIALITY, CONFLICT OF INTEREST, AND THE UNAUTHORIZED PRACTICE OF LAW

Three critical areas covered by most of the ethical codes mentioned above are of particular concern to paralegals. They are the rules regarding client confidentiality and lawyer-client privilege, conflict of interest, and UPL. In addition, paralegals should be aware of the proper procedures for managing client funds, the limits on zealous representation, the law regarding legal malpractice, and notary public law.

---

[2] Guidelines for the Use of Paralegals in Rendering Legal Services, the North Carolina State Bar (2010), *www.nccertifiedparalegal.gov/guidelines/guidelines-on-the-use-of-paralegals/* (visited April 15, 2020).

1. Client Confidentiality and Attorney-Client Privilege

Confidentiality
The ethical rule prohibiting lawyers and paralegals from disclosing information regarding a client or a client's case.

A lawyer cannot effectively serve a client without knowing all the facts of a particular case. Without the assurance of **confidentiality** many clients would be reluctant to reveal potentially embarrassing or incriminating information that their lawyers need to effectively represent them. When dealing with information they have learned while representing a client, lawyers and paralegals have to be aware of:

- their ethical obligations to maintain client confidences and
- the court-imposed protections provided by what is known as the lawyer-client privilege.

a. Ethical Rules on Confidentiality

The rules against revealing client confidences apply not only to current clients, but to potential clients and former clients as well. It is crucial that paralegals realize that they can never mention any aspect of a client's case to those outside the law firm. In fact, the very presence of the client in the firm should be kept confidential.

Ethics Alert

DON'T	DO
Speak to the lawyer about your client while in an elevator in the courthouse.	Go to an isolated place in the courthouse where you cannot be overheard before you call the lawyer.
Talk about cases over lunch in a restaurant, where other patrons can overhear you.	Have regular case meetings in your office, where you cannot be overheard.
Leave paperwork with the names of clients on your desk when you meet with other clients.	Make certain that paperwork for clients is put away or covered before meeting with other clients.
Blog, tweet, or share information about your job that can potentially identify any of your clients.	Be certain to use social media in a responsible manner.
Tell one of your friends that you saw her son at your law office the other day.	Keep what happens at your law office completely separate from your social life.

The ethical codes of the paralegal associations and the ABA Guidelines on the Utilization of Paralegals all emphasize the importance of maintaining confidentiality. The ABA Model Rules of Professional Conduct Rule 1.6 state the following:

(a) A lawyer shall not reveal information relating to representation of a client unless the client gives informed consent, the disclosure is impliedly authorized in order to carry out the representation or the disclosure is permitted by paragraph (b). [Paragraph (b) provides a list of specific exceptions.]

Exceptions to the Model Rules can be found in Model Rule 1.6, including "to prevent reasonably certain death or substantial bodily harm." (Rule 1.6(b)(1))

Several states, though not the ABA, have mandatory disclosure rules. In Wisconsin, for instance, Rule 20:1.6(b) states that disclosure is mandatory in instances in which it is likely that disclosure will "prevent the client from committing a criminal or fraudulent act that the lawyer reasonably believes is likely to result in death or substantial bodily harm or in substantial injury to the financial interests or property of another."[3] In Texas, Rule 1.05(e) requires mandatory disclosure "when a lawyer has confidential information clearly establishing that a client is likely to commit a criminal or fraudulent act that is likely to result in death or substantial bodily harm to a person."[4]

With so many variations to this rule, if a paralegal becomes aware of situations involving any exceptions, the safest course would be to notify the supervising lawyer so that the lawyer can determine the proper course of action.

DISCUSSION QUESTIONS

4. The common justification for having such strict limits on when a lawyer may reveal client confidences is that without such restrictions, clients would be afraid to give their lawyers the complete story. Do you think this is really true? Given the complexities of the legal system, and hence the need for a lawyer to help people through it, do you think that a client would risk not getting adequate representation by not being forthcoming with the lawyer?

5. What do you make of the fact that in every jurisdiction, the confidentiality rules do not apply when the litigation is between a lawyer and the client and the issue is the lawyer's fees?

6. Do you think there are ANY circumstances in which a lawyer should be required to reveal a client's planned future activities? Classify each of the following according to whether you think a lawyer should be required to report the future activity, allowed to do so at his or her discretion, or prohibited from disclosing it at all. You should also consider whether the test should be a subjective one, based on what the lawyer actually thought was likely to happen, or an objective test, based on what a reasonable person would think would happen.

    a. A deliberately wrongful act
    b. Harm to a financial or property interest
    c. Substantial harm to a financial or property interest
    d. Any crime
    e. A serious violent crime
    f. Bodily harm
    g. Substantial bodily harm
    h. Death
    i. Imminent death

7. A lawyer is representing a man charged with several murders. In the course of one of their conversations, the client admits that in addition to the murders with which he is currently charged, he killed an elderly lady. Currently, an innocent person is serving a life sentence for that murder. What do you think the lawyer should do? What if the murder of the elderly lady were unsolved, and

---

[3] *See* SCR (2020).
[4] *See* Tex. Disciplinary R. Prof. Conduct, (2020).

no one had been charged with that crime? What if the elderly lady were considered a missing person rather than a murder victim?

b. Attorney-Client Privilege

Attorney-client privilege
A rule of evidence that prevents a lawyer or a paralegal from being compelled to testify about confidential client information.

In addition to the exceptions to client confidentiality contained in the ethical codes, under certain circumstances a court may order a lawyer or a paralegal to testify, thereby forcing the revelation of confidential information. Rather than testifying, the lawyer or paralegal may object on the grounds of **attorney-client privilege**. The attorney-client privilege is not part of the ethical codes. Rather, it is contained within the rules of evidence.

In state and federal courts, rules of evidence govern what testimony and documentary evidence can be used at trial. Some evidence is not allowed because it is considered privileged. That is, in some instances it is more important to protect the communication than it is to allow the evidence to be heard. An example is the privilege that prohibits the use of a spouse's statement against the other spouse. Similarly, the attorney-client privilege generally protects a lawyer or a paralegal from being compelled to supply information when called as a witness.

For the attorney-client privilege to apply, the client, while seeking legal advice, must speak directly to a lawyer or his or her employee, with no unnecessary third parties present. This is more restrictive than the ethical rule protecting client confidences. The ethical rule applies no matter how the lawyer or paralegal acquired the confidential information.

Problems often arise in a corporate business setting, when an employee or officer of the corporation makes incriminating admissions to a lawyer who has been hired to represent the corporation. Because the lawyer represents the corporate entity rather than the employee or the officer making the statements, those statements made to the lawyer are not covered by the attorney-client privilege. Therefore, lawyers doing these types of investigations must inform the persons they interview that they are not representing them and that they need to retain their own lawyer if they wish legal representation.

Figure 2-1 summarizes the differences between the attorney-client privilege and the ethical rules regarding confidentiality. As you can see, the attorney-client privilege does not cover as many situations as do the ethical rules regarding confidentiality. The ethical rules generally cover any confidence regarding the client, no matter the source. Therefore, a paralegal cannot voluntarily repeat that information without the client's consent. However, a court could require the paralegal to testify regarding that information unless it also meets the four-part test for satisfying the attorney-client privilege:

1. The *client* made a statement
2. to the paralegal or lawyer
3. while seeking legal advice, and
4. no unnecessary persons were present.

Therefore, you can think of information covered by the attorney-client privilege as a subset of all confidential information. See Figure 2-2.

When talking outside of the law firm, paralegals must be constantly vigilant so as not to reveal confidential information. But even within the law firm,

Ethical Rule Regarding Confidentiality	Attorney-Client Privilege
Under the Model Code, applies to: ■ confidences and secrets ■ learned from any source ■ regarding anything and ■ made anywhere *Under the Model Rules, applies to* ■ information ■ relating to representation of the client	*Applies to:* ■ a client statement ■ to a lawyer or paralegal ■ made while seeking legal advice and ■ given in confidence (i.e., no unnecessary persons present)
Result: If all of the conditions are present, the lawyer or paralegal may not voluntarily reveal the information (but may be compelled to testify unless statements also satisfy the criteria for the attorney-client privilege.)	*Result:* If any of these four conditions is missing, the lawyer can be compelled to testify.

Figure 2-1 A Comparison of the Ethical Rule Regarding Confidentiality and the Attorney-Client Privilege

paralegals need to remain conscious of the need for confidentiality so as to maintain the attorney-client privilege. Consider, for example, the case of *People v. Mitchell.*[5] The defendant, John Mitchell, had been indicted for the stabbing death of his girlfriend. Lapin was the lawyer representing him in that case. On January 5, a prostitute died of 11 stab wounds. The next morning, the defendant went to Lapin's office. Lapin was not in, and the defendant spoke to a legal secretary who was stationed in the reception area. He told her that "he had been out drinking and met a girl and then he woke up in the morning and she was dead." While he was talking to the first secretary, a second secretary entered the reception area. He then muttered something about a knife. Finally, a paralegal entered the room. She asked Mr. Mitchell what was wrong. He told her "that there was a dead body and he felt that he had done it and that the person was dead, that she was dead because of being stabbed."

Figure 2-2 Attorney-Client Privilege: A Subset of Confidentiality

The prosecution found out about these conversations and subpoenaed the two secretaries and the paralegal to testify at Mitchell's trial. Naturally, Mitchell's lawyer tried to have this testimony kept out of the trial for violating the lawyer-client privilege. Review the criteria for establishing an attorney-client privilege. Do you think the secretaries and paralegal were required to testify? What additional facts do you think you would want to know before making that decision?

The trial court ordered the secretaries and paralegal to testify, stating that their testimony was not protected by the attorney-client privilege. The appellate court agreed. The conversation had happened in a reception area, where "unnecessary

[5] 448 N.Y.S.2d 332 (1982).

persons" might have been present. Also, while the lawyer, Lapin, was representing the defendant regarding a prior murder, because Lapin was away from the office, he had had no opportunity to accept the defendant as his client with regard to this second murder. Therefore, the court ruled that the communication could not have been "for the purposes of securing legal advice or assistance."[6]

Closely related to the concept of attorney-client privilege is the doctrine of **lawyer work product.** If materials can be categorized as lawyer work product, then they are protected from discovery requests and need not be disclosed even during trial. Generally, to be protected, the materials must be prepared by a lawyer or an agent of the lawyer, such as a paralegal, contain thoughts, strategies, or opinions of the lawyer or paralegal, and be prepared in anticipation of litigation or for trial. Examples include notes outlining trial strategy or evaluation of the effectiveness of a witness's testimony. Items that would not be included are those that are prepared routinely, not in anticipation of litigation.

While the attorney-client privilege in effect belongs to the client and can be waived only by the client, the doctrine of lawyer-work product is meant to protect the mental impressions and creativity of the lawyer. It is particularly important to note that this privilege also covers paralegal employees, and so the paralegal's notes are also part of the protected work product.

Issues regarding the privileged status of documents generally arise during the discovery phase of the litigation. When one of the parties subpoenas documents that the other side considers to be privileged, the responding party has the burden of establishing their privileged status. They usually do so by submitting a **privilege log,** which sets forth

- the general nature of each document,
- the identity and position of the document's creator,
- the date it was prepared,
- the identity and position of the recipient and all other parties who received copies,
- the document's current location, and
- a declaration that it contains privileged materials.

Paralegals are frequently involved in preparing these logs.

Lawyer work product
Materials prepared by a lawyer or paralegal in anticipation of litigation.

Privilege log
A list of factors relevant to determining if evidence in documents and other materials is covered by attorney-client privilege.

NETNOTE

The ABA website offers, "Is It Privileged? A Young Lawyer's Guide to Preparing a Privilege Log in Commercial Litigation," an article with tips for creating a privilege log.

---

[6] Id. at 333.

An interesting issue arises when a lawyer or paralegal accidentally sends privileged information to an opposing law firm. It is all too easy to enter the wrong e-mail address or use reply all. Model Rule 4.4 requires that the lawyer who receives the materials notify the lawyer who inadvertently sent them. There is no obligation to comply with the other lawyer's request as to how to dispose of the materials; however, the lawyer is required to follow any applicable laws, such as the waiver provisions of Rule 26(b)(5)(B) of the Federal Rules of Evidence.[7]

The issue of inadvertent disclosure of protected information becomes even more complicated in situations involving electronically stored information (ESI), such as Microsoft Word and Excel files, client databases, and e-mails. During the discovery process, a client may be required to turn over ESI files numbering in the thousands. Trying to weed out protected from non-protected material can be quite a daunting task, and mistakes are often made. When that happens, a reviewing court is likely to take one of three different approaches.

The first and most lenient is to find no waiver. The strictest is to find a waiver under the theory that once privileged information is disclosed, there can no longer be any expectation of confidentiality. Some courts have adopted a third middle approach and balance a number of factors, such as whether the lawyer took reasonable precautions to prevent the inadvertent disclosure.[8]

Of course, when a lawyer or paralegal receives privileged material not through the mistake of the opponent but through some other means, such as disclosure by a third party, the appropriate response is to notify the opponent and dispose of or return the material. Consider the situation where a paralegal was asked to review a disk from one of the firm's clients. The client was suing his former employer, and the disk contained approximately 100,000 e-mails from and to the client and various other company personnel, including the defendant company's lawyers. Many of the e-mails were clearly marked "Lawyer-Client Privileged." The paralegal stated that he had seen the notation but had chosen to ignore it. The defendant moved to have the plaintiff's firm disqualified.

The court found that a portion of the e-mails that the paralegal had read were relevant to the case and were protected by lawyer-client privilege. The plaintiff's firm tried to argue that no *lawyer* knew of the privileged information. However, the court held that the rules regarding confidential information apply equally to paralegals as to lawyers, and that the conduct and knowledge of the paralegal must be imputed to the law firm. The paralegal's "review of privileged material was an ethical violation regardless of his status as a paralegal."[9] Finally, the court found that the paralegal's review of the documents had tainted the proceedings so severely that the only remedy was to disqualify the firm from its continuing representation of the plaintiff.

DISCUSSION QUESTIONS

8. When a lawyer receives information that the opposing side has sent accidentally, that lawyer has four options:

---

[7] Fed. R. Evid. 25(b)(5)(B) (2019).
[8] Victor Stanley, Inc. v. Creative Pipe, Inc., 250 F.R.D. 251 (D. Md. 2008).
[9] Richards v. Jain, 168 F. Supp.2d 1195, 1200 (W.D. Wash. 2001).

   a. to refrain from reading the information, and then to contact the opposing lawyer and return the document unread;
   b. to read the information, contact the opposing lawyer, and return the document;
   c. to read the information, contact the opposing lawyer, and refuse to return the document; or
   d. to read the information and use it.

Given our adversarial system and your own sense of justice, which approach do you think is best?

9. White, a lawyer, represents a plaintiff who was injured in an automobile accident. She and her client have decided to settle the case if they can obtain at least $200,000. The settlement talks are set to begin tomorrow, and her strategy is to start by asking for $300,000, hoping to end up at $200,000. As White is reviewing the files in preparation for the settlement talks, she discovers a one-page memo that she had not noticed before. It is from the defendant's insurer and addressed to Attorney Sherwood, the defendant's lawyer. It contains just one line: "Offer $100,000, but you have authority to settle for up to $500,000."

   a. What should White do?
   b. Do you think that it should matter that the one-page memo was intermixed with other documents?
   c. What if White received this by email? The email was addressed to her, but from the content, it was obvious to her that it was meant for the defendant's attorney. The bottom of the email contained the following language:

Privileged and Confidential—All information transmitted hereby is intended only for the use of the addressee(s) named above. If the reader of this message is not the intended recipient or the employee or agent responsible for delivering the message to the intended recipient(s), please note that any use, distribution, or copying of this communication is strictly prohibited. Anyone who receives this communication in error should notify us immediately by telephone.

What should she do?

10. How do you think the situation should be handled when the inadvertently sent communication is from the client and not the lawyer? Recently, a defendant's lawyer sent an e-mail to the opposing lawyer. He blind-copied his own client. The client responded to the e-mail by hitting the Reply All button, thinking he was replying only to his lawyer. Of course, instead the e-mail was sent to the opposing lawyer as well. Do you think the opposing lawyer should be able to use the contents of the e-mail at trial, or should it be excluded as being protected by the lawyer-client privilege? Why? What should lawyers do to prevent this type of situation from arising in the future?

2. Conflict of Interest

Our legal system is classified as adversarial because it requires that lawyers zealously represent their clients. The best interest of a client is most likely in opposition with the opposing client. The legal system relies on attorneys to present all the relevant facts and arguments on behalf of their clients so that a neutral judge or jury may reach a proper decision. In this type of adversarial system, lawyers may not represent parties with conflicting interests. For example, by representing both the plaintiff and the defendant in a negligence action, a lawyer creates a **conflict of interest**. A lawyer's duty to the client is impaired when the lawyer cannot consider and recommend a particular action because it may adversely affect the interests of another client.

Conflict of interest
The ethical rule prohibiting lawyers and paralegals from working for opposing sides in a case.

Paralegals must be careful how they respond to situations that present possible conflicts of interest. A serious problem could develop if the law firm for which a paralegal works takes a case that involves a friend, relative, former employer, former client, or business interest of the paralegal. Problems can also arise when a paralegal changes jobs if the new employer represents clients on the opposite side of cases handled by the paralegal's previous employer. It is therefore very important that paralegals understand the prevailing interpretations as to what constitutes a conflict and that they inform their supervising lawyer of any interest that could result in such a conflict—or even the appearance of such a conflict.

There are two basic types of conflicts of interest. The first occurs when lawyers or paralegals have a personal or business interest that suggests they cannot give their undivided loyalty to a client. The second involves either present or past client representation that presents a conflict with the representation of a new client.

Conflicts of the first type can occur when a lawyer is related to another lawyer or paralegal who represents the opposite side of a case. This can also occur if the lawyer is related to the opposing party or to any of the ancillary individuals related to the opposing party's case such as witnesses or experts. Other examples include entering into certain types of business relationships with clients, preparing instruments for a client that give some benefit to the lawyer or a family member of the lawyer (such as a bequest in a will), providing financial assistance to a client in connection with pending litigation, and accepting compensation from third parties. Each of these situations poses either a real or a potential conflict of interest.

As an example of this first type of conflict, assume that Mrs. Abbot is a lawyer working for a defendant's firm. Her husband is a lawyer who works for a plaintiff's firm. One of Mr. Abbot's clients is suing the local grocery store for allegedly selling tainted meat. Mrs. Abbot represents the grocery store. (See Figure 2-3.) Mr. and Mrs. Abbot had been hoping for some time to get away

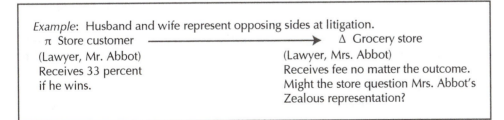

Example: Husband and wife represent opposing sides at litigation.
π Store customer ⟶ Δ Grocery store
(Lawyer, Mr. Abbot)   (Lawyer, Mrs. Abbot)
Receives 33 percent   Receives fee no matter the outcome.
if he wins.   Might the store question Mrs. Abbot's
                                       Zealous representation?

Figure 2-3   Personal Conflict

from the pressures of work for a week or so, but their lack of finances was standing in their way. If Mr. Abbot wins his case against the grocery store (through either a settlement or a court judgment), he will earn 33 percent of the amount awarded to his client. This is quite ethical and a common practice for plaintiffs' lawyers. Defendants' lawyers, however, usually receive a fee that does not vary based on whether their clients win. Can you see any potential conflict of interest? Would anyone knowing all the facts think that perhaps Mrs. Abbot might not be quite as diligent in her representation of the grocery store as she would be if another lawyer were representing the plaintiff? In addition, do you think anyone might be concerned that in a careless moment, either Mr. or Mrs. Abbot might let some confidential information slip?

The second type of conflict of interest occurs when the lawyer or paralegal has information about the client on the opposite side of the case, and therefore may know something that will be detrimental to that person. For example, assume that Smith, a lawyer, and Jones, a paralegal, worked for Pat Brown when he was getting a divorce. During the divorce proceedings, Smith and Jones naturally became quite informed regarding Brown's financial state, including his partnership interest in a local gymnasium. It is now two years later, and one of Brown's partners has approached the firm seeking representation in a case he wants to bring against Brown. If Smith is allowed to take the case, his knowledge of Brown's finances that he gained while he represented him in his divorce might put Brown at an unfair disadvantage.

As you can see, client confidentiality and conflicts of interest are very closely related. In the case of Mr. and Mrs. Abbot, there is the fear that confidentiality might be breached because of the close relationship between the lawyers representing the two sides. In the second case, the fear is more real, as Smith actually knows confidential information, and the only issue is whether he might use it against his former client. Because of this possibility, the ethics codes require that Smith either obtain Pat Brown's consent to proceed as the lawyer representing the partner or resign from the case. In addition, all other lawyers at Smith's firm would be barred from representing Brown's partner.

Conflicts of interest that involve representing two potentially adverse clients can be classified as **concurrent** (representing both clients simultaneously) or **successive** (representing one client and then later representing the second client). The conflicts can also be classified as actual or potential.

a. Concurrent Representation/Actual Conflict

Rule 1.7 of the Model Rules of Professional Conduct prohibits a lawyer from representing a client "if the representation involves a concurrent conflict of interest" unless "the lawyer reasonably believes that the lawyer will be able to provide competent and diligent representation to each affected client," the representation is not "prohibited by law," the lawyer is not representing one client against another client in the same proceeding, and each client "gives informed consent, confirmed in writing."

Notice that there are four parts to this test. First, the lawyer must reasonably believe that he or she can zealously and equally represent both clients. Second, the representation must not run afoul of some other prohibition. Third,

Concurrent conflict of interest
Simultaneously representing adverse clients.

Successive conflict of interest
Representing someone who is in a position adverse to a prior client.

Figure 2-4   Concurrent Representation/Actual Conflict

the lawyer cannot represent both sides of a matter in litigation. Finally, each client must be informed of the conflict, consent, and verify that consent in writing. Note that all four requirements must be met. If any are missing, then the concurrent representation is prohibited. Therefore, consent alone will not suffice. The other three conditions must also be true.

Assume that Baker, a lawyer, is representing Deb Driver against Tracy Trucker. If Trucker asks Baker to also represent her, this is an obvious conflict of interest. If Baker is to fully represent Driver, she must try to get the maximum settlement from Trucker. However, to fully represent Trucker, she would have to try to minimize any settlement that Trucker would have to pay. Baker may not represent both Driver and Trucker. See Figure 2-4.

b. Concurrent Representation/Potential Conflict

Now assume that Patti Passenger, who was in Deb Driver's car, also wants to sue Tracy Trucker. Can Baker represent Passenger? It appears that there is no conflict, as both Passenger and Driver want to sue Trucker. But let's stop for a moment and think about what could happen. Assume that Trucker decides to countersue Driver, claiming the accident was really Driver's fault. If the jury awards Passenger damages by finding Driver 50 percent at fault and Trucker 50 percent at fault, Baker is put in an untenable position. Baker will have to decide whether to appeal the decision (to the detriment of Passenger, who would have to wait for her damages award or might lose it entirely) or not appeal the decision (to the detriment of Driver). Figure 2-5 illustrates the problems inherent in this type of situation. In such cases of a **potential conflict**, Baker probably should decline to represent both the driver and the passenger.

Similar situations arise when two potential partners ask a lawyer to draft a partnership agreement for them, when spouses assume that a lawyer can represent both of them in a no-fault divorce, and when two criminal defendants want the same lawyer to represent them. If the clients are insistent about wanting joint representation, the lawyer must completely explain the situation to the potential clients and obtain their consent. In addition, it must be obvious to the lawyer that he or she can adequately represent the interests of each client.

Potential conflict
A situation in which a conflict of interest may arise in the future—for example, representing business partners.

c. Successive Representation

Even after an lawyer-client relationship has ended, according to Rule 1.9 of the Model Rules, lawyers have an ongoing obligation not to represent anyone in a "substantially related matter" if the new client's interests are materially adverse to those of a former client.

As you can imagine, there are frequent disagreements as to whether two matters are "substantially related." Consider the example we cited earlier, where Smith represented Pat Brown when he was getting his divorce. Two years later, one of Brown's partners approached Smith, seeking representation in a case he wants to bring against Brown. These two matters are certainly different. However, as already stated, there is the possibility that Smith's knowledge of Brown's business dealings that he acquired during the divorce proceedings may give her an unfair advantage in representing the business partner. Therefore, Smith should decline the representation of the business partner. See Figure 2-6.

To summarize, in cases of actual conflict, a lawyer can never represent both sides. In those situations involving potential conflict or successive representation, a court might allow the representation, so long as the client consented after being fully informed of the potential problems. However, the court could still disallow the representation if it thought that there was in fact an actual conflict or that the client had not been fully informed.

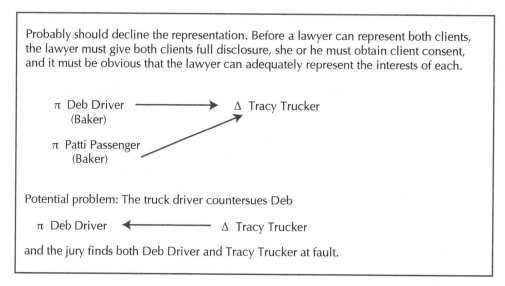

Figure 2-5   Concurrent Representation/Potential Conflict

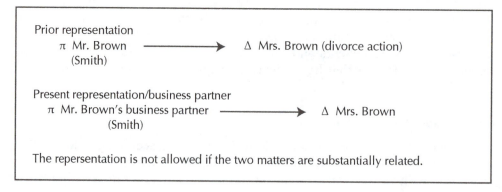

Figure 2-6   Successive Representation

d. Vicarious Representation

Under the Model Rules of Professional Conduct, if one lawyer in a firm is disqualified from representing a client, then all of the lawyers are disqualified. This is known as **vicarious representation**, whereby all members of a law firm are treated as though they had represented the client.

This rule creates problems when a lawyer leaves one firm to join another. Assume that a lawyer is representing Mary Dula in the case of Mary Dula versus Tom Chen. Clearly, he cannot also represent Chen. Then assume that the lawyer switches firms and now works for the firm representing Chen. May that firm continue in its representation of Chen? Traditionally, the rules indicated that it may not. This is because this scenario is really no different from the prior example. A lawyer in the firm has confidential information about the opposing party. On the other hand, if every time a lawyer switches firms, it means that no one in the new firm can ever take a case against one of that lawyer's former clients, then it is very difficult for lawyers to make necessary career moves.

Because of the perceived hardships created by this rule, Model Rule 1.10 allows a law firm to hire a lawyer with a conflict of interest without a waiver from the former client, so long as the hiring firm gives written notice with an explanation of how the firm will ensure that it will not receive any confidential information from the lawyer with the conflict. It is said that the lawyer will be "screened" from the case. Screened lawyers are also barred from directly sharing in compensation earned from matters where a potential conflict exists.

It is important to note, however, that not all states have adopted this more permissive standard. For example, in a recent case, the New Mexico Supreme Court held that a defendant's law firm should be disqualified even though the firm had erected a screen around one of its newly hired associates. Before being hired by the defendant's firm, the associate had worked on the same case for the plaintiff's firm:

> When an attorney has played a substantial role on one side of a lawsuit and subsequently joins a law firm on the opposing side of that lawsuit, both the lawyer *and* the new firm are disqualified from any further representation. [S]creening the new lawyer from any involvement in the lawsuit is *not* an adequate response to the conflict.[10]

> **Vicarious representation**
> The rule whereby all members of a law firm are treated as though they had represented the former client, even if only one lawyer did so.

PRACTICE TIP

Use a computerized conflict-checking program. Years after the fact, you do not want to have to rely on your memory as to the names of all the clients with whom you have had significant contact. See ABA Ethics Rule 1.18 regarding prospective clients.

---

[10] Roy D. Mercer, LLC v. Reynolds, 292 P.3d 466, 467 (N. Mex. 2012).

Because paralegals have access to confidential information about a firm's clients, the movement of a paralegal from one law firm to another presents similar issues of conflict of interest. Most courts that have addressed this issue have concluded that a law firm should not automatically be disqualified from a case simply because a paralegal employee's former employer represents someone who is suing one of the paralegal's current firm's clients. The paralegal must be cautioned

1. not to disclose any information relating to the representation of a client of the former employer *and*
2. not to work on any matter on which the paralegal worked for the prior employer, or about which the paralegal has information relating to the representation of the client of the former employer.

The key requirement in these types of situations is that the new law firm must strictly adhere to a formal written screening process (variously referred to as an **ethical wall** or **cone of silence**) that effectively isolates the new employee from any participation in the case. To create an effective wall, the firm must undertake the following steps:

Ethical screen, ethical wall, or cone of silence
A system developed to shield a lawyer or a paralegal from a case that otherwise would create a conflict of interest.

1. Develop an educational program for employees that includes warning all employees of the firm about the importance of not sharing information. Have firm-wide meetings to discuss the importance of confidentiality and why ethical walls must be built.
2. Specifically prohibit those with confidential information from discussing the case or client in question with others in the firm.
3. Restrict access to files. This can be done by "flagging" the files so they are easily identifiable at a distance and by physically removing them from areas where the person with the conflict can have access to them.
4. Write a memorandum to all personnel instructing them not to discuss the conflict matter with the conflict person.
5. Separate those working on the file from those with the information.
6. Circulate a policy statement concerning the specific wall, and announce the methods for enforcement, including sanctions.
7. Notify the client. The client's consent may be necessary to avoid disqualification.

DISCUSSION QUESTION

11. Which of the following situations would involve an unethical conflict of interest?
    a. A lawyer agrees to represent a friend in a real estate matter. The lawyer has done some unrelated legal work for the corporation that employs the friend.
    b. A lawyer who drafted a will later represents one of the client's children in a dispute over the terms of the will.

    c. After defending a client against manslaughter charges related to an automobile accident, the lawyer represented the victim's estate in a civil suit against the former client's insurance company.

3. Unauthorized Practice of Law

As you know, lawyers are licensed to practice law; paralegals are not. This difference has important consequences for paralegals. Many of the issues regarding UPL by nonlawyers are bound to change if the licensing of paralegals becomes a reality. Meanwhile, however, you need to be aware that most states have statutes that prohibit nonlawyers from practicing law, and UPL is subject to several sanctions, including injunction, contempt, and criminal. Typically, nonlawyers found to be practicing UPL will be sent a cease-and-desist letter prior to criminal proceedings being initiated. These orders usually result in compliance with the UPL statutes, and so criminal sanctions are rarely used.

> **Unauthorized practice of law (UPL)**
> When nonlawyers do things that only lawyers are allowed to do. In most states, this is a crime.

While statutes prohibit nonlawyers from practicing law, the amount of guidance as to what is prohibited varies from state to state. Where the guidance is less specific, courts have generally held that what constitutes UPL must be determined on a case-by-case basis.

One approach that some courts have followed is to start by citing the older ABA Model Code's definition of the **practice of law**—an activity that calls for the exercise of professional judgment. **Professional judgment** is further defined as the "educated ability to relate the general body and philosophy of law to a specific legal problem of a client." Contrast this definition of professional judgment with the definition of what a paralegal or legal assistant does, developed by NALA in its Code of Ethics and Professional Responsibility:

> **Practice of law**
> An activity that requires professional judgment, or the educated ability to relate law to a specific legal problem.
>
> **Professional judgment**
> The educated ability to apply law to specific facts.

> Legal assistants, also known as paralegals, are a distinguishable group of persons who assist attorneys in the delivery of legal services. Through formal education, training and experience, legal assistants have *knowledge and expertise regarding the legal system and substantive and procedural law* which qualify them to do work of a legal nature under the supervision of an attorney. (*Emphasis added.*)

In this course, you have been acquiring knowledge "regarding the legal system and substantive and procedural law." But you have also been gaining an "educated ability to relate the general body and philosophy of law to a specific legal problem of a client." Does this mean that once you are working as a paralegal, you can rely on your knowledge of the law, but you cannot use your ability to apply that knowledge to a specific situation? The short answer is no, if you work under the supervision of a lawyer and you avoid doing any of the following:

1. establishing a lawyer-client relationship or setting the legal fee
2. giving legal advice to clients to inform them of their rights and obligations
3. preparing directly for clients (as opposed to your supervising lawyer) documents that require knowledge of legal principles not possessed by ordinary lay people
4. appearing for clients in court

This does not mean that paralegals cannot meet with clients. They can, if they refrain from establishing the lawyer-client relationship, setting the fee, and giving legal advice. They can also draft documents if a supervising lawyer reviews those documents and takes full responsibility for their content. Finally, paralegals can be present in court to assist a lawyer.

Some argue that UPL statutes have historically been used to protect lawyers from competition with lay persons seeking to perform similar services for less money. Others defend UPL statutes based on the "public interest." Restatement of the Law 3d states:

> The primary justification given for unauthorized practice limitations was that of consumer protection—to protect consumers of unauthorized practitioner services against the significant risk of harm believed to be threatened by the nonlawyer practitioner's incompetence or lack of ethical constraints.[11]

Over the past few decades, UPL restrictions have lessened for a number of reasons. A large number of federal and state administrative agencies, such as the Bureau of Indian Affairs, the Departments of Agriculture, Justice, Labor, and Veterans Affairs, the Environmental Protection Agency, the Food and Drug Administration, the Immigration and Naturalization Service, the Internal Revenue Service, the Patent and Trademark Office, and the Social Security Administration, have been allowing nonlawyers to advise and represent individuals in legal proceedings for decades. In the early 2000s, the U.S. Department of Justice and the Federal Trade Commission sent letters to states and the ABA concerning antitrust issues with UPL rules, particularly those related to real estate closings and other similar matters. The Access to Justice movement has called for states to loosen their UPL regulations so that nonlawyers can fill this gap by providing legal services less expensively and increasing access for low-income people.

In addition, courts have begun to adopt standardized forms and frequently asked questions documents to assist members of the general public with instructions for how to complete legal forms. Do-it-yourself legal form books, companies like LegalZoom, and software like TurboTax have further eroded what UPL means in the twenty-first century. The culmination of these factors can be seen in the growth of the legal technician movement we discussed in Chapter 1, which allows nonlawyers to be licensed to practice in limited designated areas of the law without endangering the public interest. The statutes governing UPL are still important. However, state bars are allowing more and more exceptions so that nonlawyers can provide services that previously had been restricted to lawyers.

a. Prohibited Tasks

Certain tasks traditionally have been considered tasks that only lawyers could perform. They include making courtroom appearances, preparing legal documents, and giving legal advice. As you will see, while it is still true that nonlawyers are limited in what they can do in each of these areas, there is room for paralegal involvement.

---

[11] Rest 3d L GOVL §4 (2019).

(1) Courtroom and administrative agency representation

The application of UPL statutes is least ambiguous in the area of courtroom representation. With very few exceptions, only licensed lawyers are allowed to present motions and argue cases in court. Although the courts have recognized a constitutional right to self-representation, they have rejected interpreting the Sixth Amendment right to counsel as requiring the courts to allow a defendant who so wishes to be represented by a nonlawyer.

However, nonlawyers are sometimes allowed to act in a representative capacity at administrative hearings. At the federal level, the Administrative Procedure Act states:

> A person compelled to appear in person before an agency or representative thereof is entitled to be accompanied, represented, and advised by counsel or, if permitted by the agency, *by other qualified representatives.*[12]

At the state level, some statutes and administrative regulations also permit lay representation at agency proceedings. Workers' compensation boards, unemployment compensation boards, and public utility commissions are most apt to have made such allowances.

(2) Preparation of legal documents

In *Davies v. Unauthorized Practice Committee,* the Texas Supreme Court noted that

> the practice of law is not confined to cases conducted in court. In fact, the major portion of the practice of any capable lawyer consists of work done outside of the courts . . . and includes the giving of advice or the rendering of any service requiring the use of legal skill or knowledge, such as preparing a will, contract or other instrument. . . .[13]

Court cases regarding the preparation of legal documents have generally arisen in the areas of real estate, divorce, workers' compensation, and estate planning. As we saw in Chapter 1, such document preparation by nonlawyers is generally allowed, so long as the nonlawyer is supervised by a lawyer or meets the requirements laid out in those states that have carved out exceptions for nonlawyer document preparers, such as California's legal document assistants (LDAs) or Washington's limited licensed legal technicians (LLLTs). Note that in addition, Louisiana gives notary publics the authority to draft some legal instruments.

In the real estate area, some courts have adopted an additional exemption for lay persons to prepare standard business forms when such preparation is incidental to their business. Thus, for example, in several states, real estate agents and brokers have been allowed to draft sales contracts and leases. This is especially true when they are merely filling in the blanks on standardized forms drafted by lawyers.

---

[12] 5 U.S.C.S. §555(b) (2014) (emphasis added).
[13] 431 S.W.2d 590, 593 (Tex. 1968).

A number of companies now offer document automation software that allows an online user to select and complete a variety of legal forms, such as corporate bylaws, uncontested divorces, wills, and livings trusts. LegalZoom is one such company. The bar associations in a number of states challenged LegalZoom's activities as constituting UPL. A South Carolina court approved a settlement agreement, finding that the business practices of LegalZoom did "not constitute the unauthorized practice of law. . . . [T]he customer's selection identifies the form, and the customer completes the form. . . . The software . . . operates automatically in the same fashion as a 'mail merge' program."[14]

(3) Giving legal advice

As the LegalZoom situation illustrates, a lay person or computer program can act as a scrivener, entering a client's answers onto a standardized legal form, but a lay person or a computer program cannot advise the client as to which form to use or how to word the answers. Paralegals can meet with clients and gather information necessary to draft legal documents, so long as a lawyer supervises their work. The need for adequate supervision was illustrated by the case of *In re Hessinger & Associates*.[15] Hessinger & Associates was a bankruptcy firm that hired paralegals to meet with new clients, to get the clients to sign a contract agreeing to retain the firm, and then to prepare the bankruptcy papers. The paralegals worked in an office where no lawyer was present. Once a number of bankruptcy petitions had been completed, a courier picked them up and took them to another office, where a lawyer signed and filed them. Typically, a lawyer saw the client debtor for the first time at the bankruptcy hearing. The court noted that merely reviewing the paperwork was insufficient supervision, as the lawyer could not possibly know what advice the paralegal had given or whether that advice was correct. "The incidental availability of a lawyer does not make the practice legal where the attorney exercised no actual and significant supervision of the nonlawyers."[16] The court concluded that the firm had violated the Rules of Professional Conduct by assisting the paralegals in engaging in UPL.

DISCUSSION QUESTION

12. An insurance marketing agency sold estate planning services, including wills and trusts. It did a targeted mailing to prospective clients, with information on how to avoid probate. An agent then met with the client, and if the efforts were successful, got the client to select and pay for an estate plan. The agency employed a panel of lawyers, one of whom would then call the client to provide legal advice. The panel lawyer was paid a flat fee of $225. After discussing various options with the lawyer of the 1,306 clients to whom estate plans were sold, only 9 chose a less expensive plan. Do you think the panel lawyers provided the clients with independent professional judgment, or did the agency commit UPL?

---

[14] See *Report on Findings of Fact and Recommendations to Approve the Settlement Agreement*, www.abajournal.com/files/SC_Supreme_Court_report_findings_fact_and_settlement_agreement.pdf (last accessed April 3, 2020).
[15] 171 B.R. 366 (Bankr. N.D. Cal. 1994), aff'd in part & rev'd in part by In re Hessinger & Assocs, 192 B.R. 211 (N.D. Cal 1996).
[16] Id. at 372.

b. Appropriate Paralegal Tasks

The cases discussed in the previous section all involved the activities of nonlawyers who were working independently or without adequate lawyer supervision. The situation changes when a paralegal is working under the proper supervision of a licensed lawyer. So long as the lawyer maintains a direct relationship with the client, supervises the delegated work, and has complete professional responsibility for the work product, a paralegal can perform various legal tasks that otherwise would be considered UPL. While these tasks may still be considered part of the practice of law, they are no longer unauthorized.

(1) Contact with clients and people outside the office

So long as paralegals clearly identify their lay status, they can deal directly with clients, lawyers, witnesses, and other relevant people. The major limitations are that they cannot commit a lawyer to represent a client or negotiate fee arrangements for the lawyer's services and that they cannot give legal advice.

Paralegals can gather and summarize information from clients and can keep clients informed as to developments in their cases. However, they are limited to being information conduits; that is, they can relay instructions from lawyers to clients but cannot provide their own opinions.

Paralegals can make telephone calls, send out correspondence, and in other ways interact with third parties on behalf of the client, so long as they identify their status with the law firm and act only within the bounds of their delegated authority. In most states, paralegals may be listed on a firm's letterhead and may have their own business cards, so long as the listing makes it clear that they are not lawyers. For example, they can list themselves as "paralegal" or "legal assistant," but should avoid ambiguous terms such as "law clerk," which is usually used to designate a law school student.

The UPL statutes of a number of states also prohibit the use of the title "notario public." The title "notario," or the equivalent, in many other countries means that an individual is an attorney. That is not the case in the United States. The concern is a direct consequence of nonlawyers holding themselves as "notarios," and overcharging clients for legal services that were never performed.

(2) Participation in legal proceedings

A lay person working under the supervision of a lawyer can, of course, directly represent clients in those situations discussed above in which lay representation is authorized (as it is in some administrative agencies and inferior courts). Thus legal aid agencies frequently assign paralegals to handle government benefits cases involving administrative hearings.

States differ on such things as whether a paralegal can supervise will executions and represent clients at real estate closings. Although paralegals can apparently attend and observe depositions, they are not allowed to question the deponent on the record.

A few states allow paralegals to answer calendar calls and make purely ministerial motions for such things as uncontested continuances. When working under the supervision of a lawyer, a lay person can, of course, perform various "second-chair" duties by assisting a lawyer during a trial.

(3) Drafting legal documents

Lay personnel who are working under the supervision of a lawyer can draft a wide range of legal documents from contracts to pleadings and briefs. However, the supervising lawyer is responsible for approving the final draft. A lawyer must sign all court documents, and they can be filed only with the lawyer's approval.

c. *Nature of the Supervision*

The ABA Model Guidelines for the Utilization of Paralegals clearly hold lawyers responsible for reviewing and supervising the work done by paralegals who are either employed or retained by them. Guideline 1 instructs the lawyer to "take reasonable measures to ensure that the paralegal's conduct is consistent with the lawyer's obligations under the rules of professional conduct of the jurisdiction in which the lawyer practices." The other guidelines contain phrases such as "provided the lawyer maintains responsibility" and "it is the responsibility of a lawyer to. . . ."

However, this does not mean that all of the responsibility rests with the lawyer. In a case involving the question of whether freelance paralegals working for a law firm were committing UPL, the New Jersey Supreme Court first cited with approval the 1989 United States Supreme Court opinion *Missouri v. Jenkins*, 491 U.S. 274 (1989), agreeing that the use of paralegals represents a means for achieving the goal of providing legal services to the public at an affordable cost while maintaining the quality of legal services.[17]

Next, the court noted that "[t]here is no question that paralegals' work constitutes the practice of law. . . . However, paralegals who are supervised by attorneys do not engage in the unauthorized practice of law."[18] Therefore, *any* lack of supervision is a problem. However, the court held that there is no logical reason to distinguish between the degree of supervision required with regard to freelance as opposed to employed paralegals. "The key is supervision, and that supervision must occur regardless of whether the paralegal is employed by the attorney or retained by the attorney."[19] Of special note to all paralegals was the court's admonition that

NETNOTE

You can read about developments in legal ethics at the blog created by Professor Alberto Bernabe at the University of Illinois at Chicago John Marshall Law School at *bernabepr.blogspot.com/*.

---

[17] In re Opinion No. 24 of the Committee on the Unauthorized Practice of Law, 128 N.J. 114, 123, 607 A.2d 962, 966 (1992).

[18] Id. at 122-123, 607 A.2d at 966.

[19] Id. at 127, 607 A.2d at 969.

[a]lthough fulfilling the ethical requirements of RPC 5.3 is primarily the attorney's obligation and responsibility, a paralegal is not relieved from an independent obligation to refrain from illegal conduct and to work directly under the supervision of the attorney. A paralegal who recognizes that the attorney is not directly supervising his or her work or that such supervision is illusory because the attorney knows nothing about the field in which the paralegal is working must understand that he or she is engaged in the unauthorized practice of law. In such a situation an independent paralegal must withdraw from representation of the client.[20]

Legal Reasoning Exercise

1. John Patel has worked as a paralegal for 10 years. Over the years, he has gained a great deal of expertise, especially in the area of personal injury work. Recently, his boss, Amanda Butler, asked him to draft a complaint alleging fraud and negligence as alternate claims. He drafted the complaint, and Butler read it and then signed it. As was customary practice in the firm, Patel then sent a copy of the complaint to the client with the following cover letter. Discuss each of Patel's activities, beginning with his drafting of the complaint, and decide whether he has or has not committed UPL.

LAW OFFICES OF
PROCTOR & WHITNEY

Jonathan Proctor, Esq.	Cynthia Shore, Esq.
William Whitney, Esq.	John Jake, Paralegal
Maria Garcia, Esq.	Janet Smith, Esq.
Amanda Butler, Esq.	

May 7, 2020

Dear Ms. Brown:

Enclosed please find a copy of the complaint that this law firm has filed on your behalf. Do not be confused by the seemingly inconsistent claims of fraud and negligence. Although fraud requires an intent to deceive, while negligence only requires unreasonable conduct, we do not yet have enough facts to know which is the most appropriate theory. However, based on the facts as you presented them, we will probably end up proceeding under the fraud theory.

Sincerely,
John Patel
John Patel, Legal Aide

---

[20] Id. at 127, 607 A.2d at 969.

D. MONEY MATTERS

Lawyers use various methods to charge for their services. The three most common methods are flat fee, hourly rate, and contingency fee. Typically, lawyers charge a flat fee for simple matters where the total time that will need to be spent can be estimated fairly accurately before the services are rendered. Examples include drafting a simple will, preparing the documents for an uncontested divorce when children and substantial assets are not involved, and representing a criminal client on a misdemeanor charge. When it is more difficult to estimate the total amount of time that will be required to complete a project, lawyers frequently charge by the hour. The third method is the **contingency fee**. Clients can hire a lawyer and only owe a fee "contingent upon" the lawyer's winning the case. If the plaintiff loses, the plaintiff is responsible for the costs of litigation but owes the lawyer nothing. If the plaintiff wins, however, then the lawyer's fee is a percentage of what the plaintiff has won. Typically, that amount is 33 percent of the plaintiff's recovery. Contingency fee agreements must be in writing.

Contingency fee
Lawyer compensation that is calculated as a percentage of the amount recovered rather than a flat or an hourly fee.

There are five ethical issues related to money that are particularly important for you to know. First, because a contingency fee arrangement creates the possibility that a lawyer could recover a very large fee for very little time spent, the use of such arrangements can raise ethical issues. Second, the firm's money and the client's money must be kept in separate accounts with no possible commingling. Third, lawyers may charge clients for the time that paralegals spend working on a case, but it is unethical to charge paralegal fees for clerical work or to charge lawyer fees for work that a paralegal actually accomplished. Fourth, usually lawyers are forbidden from forming partnerships and sharing profits with nonlawyers. Fifth, lawyers may not pay paralegals for bringing new clients into the firm.

1. The Contingency Fee System

Charging a contingency fee is often seen as one way to provide representation to those who have been injured and who could not otherwise afford a lawyer. Because typically lower-income clients do not have enough money to pay a lawyer on an hourly basis, many argue that contingency fees make it possible for those clients to pursue claims that they would otherwise have to abandon.

However, some have questioned if it is ethical for a lawyer to take one-third of the money that would otherwise be going to compensate the client for his or her injuries. If the goal in awarding a plaintiff money, either through a jury award or settlement, is to compensate the plaintiff 100 percent for the plaintiff's loss, that will not happen if the lawyer takes one-third of the payment.

As mentioned above, contingency fees also create the possibility that a lawyer could recover a very large fee for very little time spent. This issue was raised in a case involving a Massachusetts lawyer, Goodman, who represented Donald Gagnon, who was severely injured in a highway accident when he tried to assist another driver who was parked in the breakdown lane. Donald Shoblom, driving a loaded garbage truck, veered off the highway into the breakdown lane and crashed into the tractor-trailer, killing the driver and severely injuring Gagnon, leaving him a paraplegic. As liability was clear and the only question was the amount of damages, the case quickly settled for approximately $3 million. Goodman and Gagnon had signed a standard contingency fee agreement providing for a contingency fee of 33 percent in the case of a settlement. The trial judge, without a request from either party, found that the fee was unreasonable even though Mr. Gagnon testified that he had voluntarily signed the agreement and was satisfied that Goodman had earned his fee. On appeal, the court determined that the trial judge should not have reduced the fee. The court stated: "[T]he one-third percentage has become institutionalized in the practice of the litigation bar as the minimum rate to be charged in the typical tort case. Change, if it is to come, should not come suddenly and to the disappointment of long-standing expectations."[21]

2. Client Funds

Generally, lawyers maintain two types of accounts: a general office account out of which they pay their daily operating expenses and **client trust accounts** into which they deposit client funds. For example, when the firm receives a retainer fee from a client, the fee is deposited in the client trust account, and sums are withdrawn from that account only as the firm earns them. All moneys in client trust accounts belong to the clients, and the lawyer managing the accounts must be scrupulous in making sure that there is no commingling of funds; that is, money the lawyer has earned must always be kept entirely separate from the client funds.

Client trust account
A bank account used to hold money belonging to the client or to a third party.

A particularly sad case of a lawyer being caught borrowing client funds is *In re Warhtig*.[22] Warhtig, a real estate lawyer, found himself in dire financial straits created by his wife's having to undergo cancer treatment and his son's need for extensive psychiatric counseling. Mr. Warhtig routinely deposited large sums of money into a trust account in anticipation of a real estate closing. Periodically, prior to the closing, he would advance himself his fee that would be due at the closing. He always made the proper disbursements at the closing, and no clients ever lost any money. The New Jersey Disciplinary Review Board recommended a public reprimand. The NJ Supreme Court refused to accept that recommendation, however, and instead ordered Mr. Warhtig disbarred.

PRACTICE TIP

Color-code your checks so that there can be no danger of your accidentally using a client account check when you mean to use a general office account check.

3. Charging Clients for Paralegal Time

Some federal and state statutes allow courts to award lawyer's fees to the prevailing party. This presents the interesting question of whether paralegal work can be included as part of lawyer's fees. If so, a firm could bill for the paralegal's time at an hourly rate that would be greater than the cost to the firm of employing the

---

[21] Gagnon v. Shoblom, 409 Mass 63, 565 N.E.2d 775 (1991).
[22] 524 A.2d 398 (N.J. 1987).

paralegal. It appeared that this question had been answered in 1990 in the case of *Missouri v. Jenkins*,[23] in which the Supreme Court determined that lawyer's fees included the work done by paralegals. This was in contrast to the work done by secretaries and other clerical personnel. Such work cannot be included as part of lawyer's fees, as that type of expense is simply considered part of the firm's overhead costs.

In 2008, a unanimous Supreme Court held that a firm could recover paralegal fees at the prevailing market rates typically charged for the paralegal's services, as opposed to the actual cost to the firm.[24] As it had done in *Jenkins,* the Court found that it was "self-evident" that an "attorney's fee" embraced the fees of paralegals as well as lawyers.[25]

However, the amount billed for work done by a paralegal must be reasonable. If the amount billed is disputed, a court may be asked to determine whether the amount was reasonable. In making that determination, a judge will look at the rate charged, as well as whether the work done was of a substantive legal nature (as opposed to clerical work). The court may also inquire as to the paralegal's education and experience to ensure that the paralegal was qualified to handle such work.

Because many firms have a target number of hours that they expect their lawyers and paralegals to bill, there is often a temptation to pad the hours actually spent or to double-bill. Double-billing occurs when, for example, a lawyer waiting in court for a case to begin works on another client's file. Occasionally, paralegals may even see lawyers billing out time at the lawyer rate for work done by the paralegal. Obviously, these practices are unethical and illegal, as they result in the lawyer's unlawfully taking money from the client.

4. Fee-Splitting

When lawyers use lay assistants, traditionally they have not been allowed to share fees with them or to form a partnership, an association, or a professional corporation with a nonlawyer if any of the activities of the partnership, association, or corporation involve the practice of law. The rule prohibiting lawyers from forming partnerships with nonlawyers has periodically come under attack, and the practice is now allowed, at least on a limited basis, in some states. ABA Formal Ethics Opinion 464 does allow lawyers in one jurisdiction that follow the Model Rules to share fees with lawyers in another jurisdiction that allows fee-splitting, knowing that a portion of the fees may go to nonlawyers.

Model Utilization Guideline 8 authorizes lawyers to charge separately for work performed by a paralegal. However, Guideline 9 prohibits the lawyer from splitting legal fees with a paralegal or paying a paralegal for the referral of legal business. A lawyer may compensate a paralegal based on the quantity and quality of his or her work and the value of that work to the law practice. The compensation cannot, by advance agreement, be contingent on the profitability of the lawyer's practice. The commentary accompanying Guideline 9 states:

---

[23] 491 U.S. 274 (1990).
[24] Richlin Security Service Co. v. Chertoff, 553 U.S. 571 (2008).
[25] Id. at 581.

The linchpin of the prohibition seems to be the advance agreement of the lawyer to "split" a fee based on a preexisting contingent arrangement. . . . There is no general prohibition against a lawyer who enjoys a particularly profitable period recognizing the contribution of the paralegal to that profitability with a discretionary bonus so long as the bonus is based on the overall success of the firm and not the fees generated from any particular case.

5. Avoiding Solicitation

In August 2018, the ABA amended Rules 7.1 through 7.5, its rules on advertising and solicitation.[26] These rules were amended in acknowledgment that they were no longer responsive to technology. When the rules were promulgated, the Internet did not exist. The new version of Model Rule 7.3 specifically addresses the solicitation of clients. Posting online is no longer considered solicitation, nor is e-mailing a prospective client about a particular matter.

Rule 7.2(a) allows lawyers "to communicate information regarding the lawyer's services through any media." However, although lawyers may pay for such communications, they cannot pay another person for sending them clients. Thus paralegals cannot go out and solicit clients on behalf of their employers, although the new Rule 7.2(b)(5) does allow a very small exception: nominal gifts as an expression of appreciation that is "neither intended nor reasonably expected to be a form of compensation recommending a lawyer's services." Make certain that you check the rules of your own state on issues regarding solicitation. It will take years for the new ABA Model Rules to be adopted by other states, though some, such as Virginia, had issued new rules in anticipation of these revisions.

E. OVERZEALOUS REPRESENTATION

Lawyers are expected to be zealous advocates for their clients. As a lawyer's assistant, a paralegal is also expected to actively support the client's cause. However, there are limits to how far either a lawyer or a paralegal can go in that zealous representation. Specifically, paralegals must be aware that they usually may not talk to an adverse party who is represented by a lawyer and that they must always avoid any form of deception when dealing with persons outside the law firm.

1. Talking to the Opposing Party or Jurors

A lawyer may not communicate directly with the opposing party if the lawyer knows that the party is represented by a lawyer. Therefore, a paralegal cannot interview the opposing party in a civil case or a co-defendant in a criminal case without first receiving the permission of that party's lawyer. In addition, in a few states, there are very specific prohibitions, such as one limiting the right of a lawyer or a paralegal to talk to jurors during or after a case is concluded.

---

[26] A red-lined and annotated copy of the revisions can be found at www.americanbar.org/content/dam/aba/images/abanews/2018-AM-Resolutions/101.pdf.

To be on the safe side, be sure to check your local rules and consult with your supervising lawyer.

2. Avoiding Deception

Model Rule 8.4 provides that it is "professional misconduct for a lawyer to . . . engage in conduct involving dishonesty, fraud, deceit or misrepresentation." Lawyers must be candid when dealing with the court, opposing counsel, and third parties. Usually, there is no affirmative duty to inform an opposing party of relevant facts. But misrepresentation can occur if you affirm a statement made by someone else when you know it is false.

Also, lawyers must not make statements or present evidence that they know is false. Model Rule 4.1(a) states that when a lawyer is dealing with others on the client's behalf, the lawyer may not make a false statement of material fact. Because paralegals act as agents for their supervising lawyers, they must live by the same restrictions.

Model Rule 4.4 is of special importance to paralegals who do investigative or collections work. It states:

> In representing a client, a lawyer shall not use means that have no substantial purpose other than to embarrass, delay, or burden a third person, or use methods of obtaining evidence that violate the legal rights of such a person.

These restrictions mean that paralegals cannot misrepresent their identity or make other false statements in order to gain the confidence of a reluctant witness. Nor can any compensation beyond ordinary witness fees be offered to a lay witness as an inducement to testify.

Laws regarding secretly taping conversations are divided between one-party states and two-party states. Most jurisdictions legally allow recording conversations, so long as one party knows of the recording, and that person can be the person making the recording. In a two-party state, though, every person being recorded must know that the conversation is being recorded.

According to Formal Ethics Opinion 01-422,

> A lawyer who electronically records a conversation without the knowledge of the other party or parties to the conversation does not necessarily violate the Model Rules . . . A lawyer may not, however record conversations in violation of the law in a jurisdiction that forbids such conduct without the consent of all parties. . . . The Committee is divided as to whether a lawyer may record a client-lawyer conversation without the knowledge of the client, but agrees it is inadvisable to do so.

Finally, the duty of candor also arises in the context of drafting legal memoranda and appellate court briefs. Model Rule 3.3 (Comment 3) notes that a "lawyer is not required to make a disinterested exposition of the law, but must recognize the existence of pertinent legal authority." This means there is an ethical duty not to mislead judges about the existence (or lack thereof) of relevant statutes and cases. In addition to facing the consequences for violating the ethical rules, lawyers who fail to disclose directly adverse legal authority may find themselves facing court sanctions.

F. ENFORCEMENT

The legal and ethical restrictions mentioned above are enforced through a variety of sanctions. Many states have a special administrative agency, usually staffed by full-time professional employees, that reports directly to the state's supreme court. It administers the state's bar exams, registers lawyers practicing in the state, and disciplines lawyers who violate their ethical standards. In other states, the investigation and sanctioning of lawyers are left to special committees of state bar associations.

Lawyers who are found to have breached ethical standards can be reprimanded, suspended, or disbarred. A **reprimand or censure** is an announcement that the lawyer's conduct violated the code of ethics. **Suspension** means that the lawyer may not practice law for a specified time, and **disbarment** means that the lawyer's license to practice is revoked. The specific mechanisms for imposing these sanctions vary from one state to another, but it is ultimately up to the state's judiciary to impose a suspension or a disbarment.

Because paralegals are not licensed, they cannot be suspended or sanctioned as lawyers can. Lawyers can, however, be sanctioned for the misdeeds of their employees because the codes of ethics hold them responsible for adequately supervising their lay employees. This gives lawyers a vested interest in sanctioning their own employees. Any breach of their ethical duties means that the employees will probably lose their jobs and have difficulty finding new ones. Finally, if lawyers or paralegals commit acts of fraud, bribery, obstruction of justice, or engage in other criminal behavior, those actions can result in felony convictions and imprisonment. In most states, violation of UPL statutes may result in a misdemeanor conviction; however, the courts usually respond to UPL charges with injunctions and the threat of contempt charges.

Reprimand or censure
A public or private statement that a lawyer's conduct violated the code of ethics.

Suspension
A determination that a lawyer may not practice law for a set period of time.

Disbarment
The revocation of a lawyer's license.

G. TORT LAW OF NEGLIGENCE

In general, the law of **negligence** requires that all of us act reasonably given the circumstances. For paralegals, this means that they must perform their job duties in a reasonable manner or they may find themselves being sued for negligence. In addition, a supervising lawyer might be liable in a negligence suit if the plaintiff shows that the lawyer was negligent. Negligence can occur in the supervision of the paralegal, in the improper delegation of duties to the paralegal, or in the hiring of the paralegal.

Generally, to prove a **legal malpractice** case, it must be shown that

1. a lawyer-client relationship existed (the duty element),
2. the duty was breached by the lawyer's negligence,
3. the negligence caused
4. harm, and
5. the client's original claim would have succeeded but for the negligence.

This last element is known as having to **prove a case within a case**.

Negligence
The failure of a person to act reasonably under the circumstances.

Legal malpractice
The failure of a lawyer to act reasonably.

Proving a case within a case
The requirement in a legal malpractice case that the plaintiff-client prove that but for the lawyer's negligence, the client would have won.

In determining whether a professional is liable for negligence, the courts look to see whether the defendant exercised the skill and knowledge normally possessed by members of that profession. Furthermore, some courts have held that any violation of prescribed standards (such as codes of ethics or licensing statutes) constitutes negligence per se. Finally, breach of a confidential or fiduciary relationship could also constitute an intentional tort.

Discussion Questions

13. Janice Brown is a lawyer with an extremely busy practice. A few months ago, she began complaining of stress headaches and chest pain. Her paralegal, Susan Smith, became concerned that if Brown did not slow down her practice, she would become ill. Trying to help, Smith started screening all of Brown's telephone calls, only telling her about the ones that Smith felt it was essential for Brown to deal with herself. In her efforts to be helpful, what problems may Smith be creating for her boss?

14. Lale Graham, a paralegal, misplaces a client's file. By the time it is found, the statute of limitations has run out on the case. The client wants to sue the firm for malpractice. An objective evaluator would say that the client had very little chance of winning his original claim. What problems will the client have in succeeding in a malpractice claim?

H. NOTARY PUBLIC LAW

Many paralegals also become notary publics, who witness and authenticate the signing of documents. They provide a safeguard against fraud and forgery. The two most common notarial acts are the acknowledgment, where a signer appears in person in front of a notary and **acknowledges** that the signature on the document is his or her own, and that it was willingly made; and the **jurat**, also known in some states as a "verification upon oath or affirmation," where a signer appears in front of a notary and speaks aloud an oath or affirmation that the statements in the document are true.

The critical role that notaries play is in authenticating signatures. In any notarial act, the notary must ask the signer for identification, and the signer must appear before the notary personally. This is true whether it is a signing on paper or an e-notarization, which simply means that the document being signed is electronic and being signed on an electronic device such as a computer or tablet. Some states list the types of ID that a notary may accept. If your state does not list the types of ID that signers may use, a photo ID issued by a state or other government entity is generally accepted. Always remember to ask for an ID and keep a record of it.

By 2020, 23 states had enacted legislation to allow remote online notarization (RON) using audiovisual technology rather than requiring that the signer be physically present before a notary public. As a result of social distancing orders during the COVID-19 pandemic, by April 2020, most states enabled

Acknowledgment
A formal declaration of a signature before a public official.

Jurat
A document whose contents are sworn to or affirmed to be true by the signer, verbally, before a public official.

RON through temporary executive orders. RON does not negate the need for the signer to "appear" before the notary, even if it is via a video feed, nor does it alter the need for the signer to show a valid ID.

It is equally important that when signing the jurat, when the words "sworn to and subscribed before me" are written, the notary must require that the signer swear an oath or affirm verbally that the document being signed is true. While it may be tempting to skip this step, and swearing or affirming someone may seem awkward the first few times you do it, it is imperative that signers understand the importance of what they are signing. If the signer fails to be truthful on a jurat, that can lead to the person being prosecuted for perjury.

In many states, a paralegal's failure to require identification or to administer an oath is grounds for losing her or his commission as a notary and, in some instances, can result in civil or criminal liability as well. In some states, a notary's employer can also be held liable. Keeping a log of the documents being notarized, with a description of the ID provided by the signer, is either required or recommended in all jurisdictions.

Legal Reasoning Exercise

2. Reread the situation presented at the beginning of the chapter. Write a legal analysis discussing any ethical issues raised by each of Green's activities. As part of your answer, be sure to include the generally accepted definition for UPL and to explain why Green, a nonlawyer, must nonetheless worry about abiding by the lawyer's code of ethics.

SUMMARY

As members of the legal team, paralegals must abide by the lawyers' code of ethics adopted in their state. While both paralegal associations, NALA and NFPA, have developed ethical codes specifically designed to cover paralegal behavior, to date no state has adopted such a code.

The three main ethical areas of concern for paralegals are UPL, client confidentiality, and conflicts of interest. In addition, paralegals must be aware of the need to keep client and office funds separate and of the limits to zealous representation. Finally, the tort law of negligence can come into play if a paralegal does not perform his or her job duties in a reasonable manner. Following notary public law is critical for paralegals who are also notaries.

||| REVIEW QUESTIONS

Pages 33 through 38

1. What ethical rules govern lawyers?
2. Explain the following statement: Although paralegals are not yet licensed, they are still bound by ethical standards.
3. What steps have NFPA, NALA, the ABA, and various states taken toward the development of a set of ethical standards for paralegals?

Pages 38 through 46

4. For each of the following, discuss whether you think the lawyer can reveal the information.
   a. A client tells her lawyer that she murdered her husband.
   b. A client tells her lawyer that she is planning to murder her husband.
   c. A client tells her lawyer that at the end of the week, she is planning to steal all her employer's cash receipts, as she has access to his safe.
   d. A client tells her lawyer that her husband is so upset with how the litigation is going that he is planning to kill the opposing lawyer.
   e. A client tells her lawyer that it was she, and not the woman who is on trial for murder, who killed the victim.
5. How does the lawyer-client privilege differ from the ethical rules regarding confidentiality?
6. Mrs. Smith, who is seeking a divorce, entered Black's law office for her first interview. Because she was very disturbed over the prospect of a divorce, Mrs. Smith brought her best friend along with her to the interview. Should Black let Mrs. Smith's best friend sit in on the interview? Why?
7. At a cocktail party, Sims, a paralegal, sees one of his firm's clients kissing someone who is not the client's wife. At the client's divorce hearing, could Sims be required to testify about what he saw at the party? Could Sims ethically tell his wife about what he saw at the party? Why?
8. What does the lawyer-client work product doctrine protect?
9. What should lawyers or paralegals do if they receive confidential information from the other side? Should it matter how they receive the information—that is, whether the opposing side accidentally sent it to them or whether they acquired it by some other means?

Pages 46 through 53

10. What are the two major causes of conflict of interest?
11. In each of the following situations, determine whether you see any potential conflict of interest problems.
    a. Stewart was injured in an automobile accident when the car he was riding in was struck in an intersection by a pickup truck. Both Stewart and the driver of the car want Black, a lawyer, to represent them against the driver of the pickup truck.
    b. Smith and Davis were arrested for the attempted robbery of United Bank. They would like Jones, a lawyer, to represent both of them.
    c. Taylor Lacy is the prosecuting lawyer for the murder trial of Tom Black. Jim White represents the defendant. Halfway through the murder trial, Lacy and White start dating.

12. What should a paralegal do if she suspects that she has confidential information pertaining to the opposite side of a case?

13. What is the function of an ethical wall (or cone of silence), and how do you erect one?

Pages 53 through 59

14. Give the generally accepted definition of the practice of law. What are the problems with applying it to paralegals working under the supervision of a lawyer?

15. What tasks can a lawyer perform that a paralegal cannot?

16. What is the major justification for enforcing UPL statutes?

17. What should paralegals do to avoid UPL?

Pages 60 through 64

18. Why do lawyers keep two separate types of bank accounts?

19. What are the limitations on a lawyer's billing for paralegal time?

20. Each year at Christmas, if the Goodman firm has had a particularly profitable year, it rewards its employees by giving them bonuses based on the quality of their work throughout the year. Is this an ethical practice? Why?

21. Mary Bisset, a paralegal with the Goodman firm, is taking classes at a local paralegal school. In her family law class, classmates who are going through a divorce frequently complain about how uncaring their lawyers are. Bisset thinks the Goodman lawyers would be much more supportive. Would there be anything wrong in Bisset's handing out her firm's card to her fellow students?

22. What limitations on zealous representation are of particular importance to paralegals?

Pages 65 through 67

23. Describe the various sanctions that can be applied to a lawyer who violates the ethical codes.

24. What elements must a plaintiff prove to win a legal malpractice case?

25. In a legal malpractice case what does it mean to say that the plaintiff must prove a case within a case?

26. What is the difference between an acknowledgment and a jurat?

27. What is the purpose of a notary public?

WEB EXERCISES

1. The ABA website has a Directory of Lawyer Disciplinary Agencies. Find your state's agency and look up your state's Rules of Professional Responsibility. How do your state's confidentiality rules compare to the ABA's Model Rules?

2. Go to Professor Alberto Bernabe's blog on Professional Responsibility and select a current ethical issue that interests you. For example, if you choose confidentiality, you will find that many problems are being created by the ever-increasing use of devices such as smartphones and the staggering amount of communication carried on through videoconferencing, e-mails, blogs, text messaging, and Twittering. What area did you research? Be prepared to discuss what you found with your classmates.

Chapter 3

Sources of Law

We hold these truths to be self-evident . . .
Declaration of Independence

Chapter Objectives

After reading this chapter, you should be able to:

- Define "law" and explain its role in our modern society.
- Describe the two main functions of the U.S. Constitution.
- Explain what federalism is and how it affects our legal system.
- Explain the rationale behind our system of checks and balances.
- Contrast statutory with administrative law.
- Compare enacted law to the common law.

INTRODUCTION

No modern society can exist without a strong legal system, and when a person has a problem or is trying to avoid a problem, that person frequently turns to lawyers and the legal system for help. While there may be a great deal of debate over the wisdom and appropriateness of a particular law (as there is, for example, over laws relating to the ownership and licensing of handguns or legalizing the recreational use of marijuana), there is general agreement that laws themselves are necessary. In this chapter, we examine who actually makes our **laws** and the format that these laws take.

Most people recall something from high school civics class about the three branches of government and that the legislature makes the law, the executive

Laws
Rules of conduct promulgated and enforced by a government.

branch enforces the law, and the courts interpret the law. The truth is that the legislative, executive, and judicial branches are all involved in making the law. The legislature creates statutes, executive agencies promulgate regulations, and the judicial branch issues court decisions.

To help illustrate the application of constitutional, statutory, and administrative laws, we will be referring to the following case involving a pregnant waitress, Diane Dobbs, who has brought a problem to lawyer Harper, a lawyer with the law firm of Darrow and Bryan. As you read the chapter, think about the nature of Diane's problem, and the extent to which the law may, or may not, provide a remedy for her.

Case 4: The Pregnant Waitress

Diane Dobbs had been employed by the Western Rib Eye Restaurant for the past three years. Throughout that time, her work record had been exemplary. Customers often spoke to the manager to tell him how Dobbs' service and personality contributed to their especially enjoyable dining experience at the restaurant.

Six months ago, Dobbs, who is not married, found out that she was pregnant. When she approached her manager, Ben Fischer, to discuss arrangements for a maternity leave, instead of the favorable reception she had expected, Fischer reached over, patted her stomach, and said, "Well, I guess we can't have you working for us any longer." Fischer then grabbed her by the arm and escorted her out of the restaurant. Dobbs protested and asked to be allowed to collect her personal belongings from her locker, but the manager just laughed and said she was "history." When Dobbs began to cry, he softened his demeanor a little and said, "Look, we simply can't have a pregnant lady working here. It just wouldn't be good for business."

Although she has been actively looking, Dobbs has not yet been able to find suitable employment.

When a client presents a problem to a lawyer, the lawyer will seek to identify which laws are relevant to solving the problem and what steps need to be taken to utilize those laws on the client's behalf. However, as we indicated in Chapter 1, not every problem can be resolved by the legal system. In order to better appreciate why this is so, we need to study the function of law, the history of the American legal system, and the sources of U.S. laws. You also need to understand the sources of law in order to do legal research and analysis.

As you read about the different sources of law, answer the following questions related to this case:

- Does Diane Dobbs have a constitutional claim against her employer?
- Does she have a statutory claim against her employer?
- Does she have an administrative claim against her employer?
- Is there a provision in the common law that gives the waitress a claim against her employer?

DISCUSSION QUESTION

1. Do you agree with the statement "Laws are necessary"?

A. CONSTITUTIONAL LAW

The term **constitutional law** refers to the principles and rules that are either explicitly stated in, or inferred from, government constitutions. At the federal level, it is the U.S. Constitution, and at the state level, it is the constitution of each of the 50 states. The United States was the first nation to adopt a written constitution. It provides the framework within which all our laws are made. Take a few minutes now to turn to Appendix A at the back of this book to see how the U.S. Constitution is organized and the type of language used.

Constitutions are usually written by specially selected delegates to a "constitutional convention." The text that is agreed upon by these delegates then has to be "ratified" (approved) by either a direct vote of the people or by some representative body.[1] A constitution also includes the steps required to amend it.[2]

The first major function of the U.S. Constitution is to establish the organizational structure of the government and the allocation of those governmental powers. Its second major function is to protect individual rights from governmental overreaching. These two functions are summarized in Figure 3-1.

The first major function, establishing an organizational structure for the government, and on the national level, the Constitution divides governmental powers among the legislative (Article I), executive (Article II), and judicial branches (Article III). This is commonly referred to as the **separation of powers**, but it is more accurate to describe this as a system of shared powers exercised by separate branches of government. Because they share power, each branch of government has the ability to limit the actions of the other branches. In the Federalist Papers, James Madison explained that this system of **checks and balances** is designed to guard against "a gradual concentration of the several powers in the same department." For example, under the Constitution, Congress has the

Constitutional law
A body of principles and rules that are either explicitly stated in, or inferred from, the constitutions of the United States and those of the individual states.

Separation of powers
The division of governmental power among the legislative, executive, and judicial branches.

Checks and balances
Division among the three branches of the federal government so that each one acts as a check on the power of the other two, thereby maintaining a balance of power among the branches.

> 1) Establish the Organization of Government
>   a. Federal Government: Three Branches (Separation of Powers; Checks and Balances)
>   i.   Legislative (Article I)
>   ii. Executive (Article II)
>   iii. Judicial (Article III)
>   b. Division of Power between the Federal and State Governments: Federalism (Tenth Amendment)
> 2) Protect Individual Rights from Governmental Overreaching (Bill of Rights)

Figure 3-1   Functions of the U.S. Constitution

---

[1] The U.S. Constitution had to be ratified by conventions of at least nine states. Most state constitutions require ratification by a majority vote of the general electorate.

[2] Article V of the U.S. Constitution requires that amendments be proposed by two-thirds of both houses (the House of Representatives and the Senate), or by a special convention called at the request of the legislatures of two-thirds of the states. Three-fourths of the state legislatures or conventions must then ratify the proposed amendment.

Power of judicial review
A court's power to review statutes to decide if they conform to the federal or a state constitution.

power to make laws, but the president has the power to veto them. The executive branch is responsible for administering the law, but it cannot spend money to do so unless Congress provides for the appropriate funding in the budget.

The check and balance most relevant to the legal system is the **power of judicial review**. The U.S. Constitution and its amendments constitute the "supreme law of the land," and based on the concept of judicial review, it is left up to the courts to determine what the Constitution means and whether laws passed by the legislative branch are constitutional or whether the law is valid.

It could be argued that because the U.S. Constitution established three coequal branches, each branch should be free to interpret the Constitution as it sees fit. However, there are times in which there is disagreement among the three branches about the interpretation of the Constitution, and in those situations, someone has to have the final say.

In *Marbury v. Madison*,[3] the U.S. Supreme Court claimed this power for the courts. The Court held that it was inherent in the nature of a court's work to resolve conflicting interpretations of the law before it can carry out its assigned task of applying the law. If a court determines that a statute does not conform to the Constitution, then the statute is invalid and the court cannot enforce it. The Court stated:

> It is emphatically the province and duty of the judicial department to say what the law is. Those who apply the rule to particular cases, must of necessity expound and interpret that rule. If two laws conflict with each other, the courts must decide on the operation of each.[4]

Over the years, the U.S. Supreme Court has used this power of judicial review to invalidate a number of federal and state laws that it found to be in conflict with the U.S. Constitution. Some of the most controversial applications of judicial review include decisions invalidating laws involving racial segregation, abortion, limitations on campaign spending, and same-sex marriage.

Whenever the courts use their power of judicial review and find a governmental action unconstitutional, the legislative and executive branches are powerless to reverse that particular decision. Legislatures do have some other options, however. First, they can sometimes enact new laws to accomplish their intended goal if they can do so without violating the constitutional provisions in questions. Alternatively, they can start the difficult process of amending the Constitution to more explicitly allow them to do what they want to accomplish their goal with a differently worded statute or propose a constitutional amendment. And at the federal level, as vacancies occur, the President can appoint new justices who may interpret the constitution differently.

The U.S. Constitution also divides governmental power between the national government and the states. This division of power between the national government and the states is referred to as **federalism**. Certain powers are explicitly granted to the federal government, while all others are reserved to the states

Federalism
A system of government in which the authority to govern is split between a single, nationwide central government and several regional governments that control specific geographical areas.

---

[3] 5 U.S. (1 Cranch) 137 (1803).
[4] Id. at 177-78.

and the people. We will discuss this federal/state division of power more fully in the next chapter.

The second major function of the Constitution is to protect individual rights from governmental overreaching. Because the first Congress perceived a lack of such protection in the Constitution, as soon as it was ratified, the members began work on the first ten amendments, commonly known as the **Bill of Rights.** These amendments include protections for freedom of speech and press, freedom of religion, a privilege against self-incrimination, the right to a lawyer and a trial by jury, and protections against unreasonable searches and seizures, among others.

At the time the Bill of Rights was written, the major concern of the drafters was overreaching by the federal government, not the state governments. Therefore, they wrote the amendments specifically to limit only the federal government's power. For example, the First Amendment states "Congress shall make no law . . . abridging the freedom of speech." During the Civil War, however, it became clear that the states could also be guilty of infringing on the rights of their citizens and the Thirteenth (banning slavery), Fourteenth (guaranteeing due process and equal protection), and Fifteenth Amendments (giving the right to vote to all males), were added with language that made it clear that they applied to the states.

Gradually, in a series of cases, the U.S. Supreme Court interpreted the Fourteenth Amendment's prohibition against states depriving any person of "life, liberty, or property, without due process of law" as meaning that many of the rights contained within the Bill of Rights also apply to the states. This is known as the **doctrine of incorporation,** and it means that the first ten amendments, along with the Fourteenth Amendment, serve to prevent state or federal government officials from interfering with civil rights and liberties.

Notice that the Constitution's Bill of Rights limits the actions of the federal and state governments, but not those of ordinary individuals. So while the First Amendment protects your freedom of religion from governmental interference and the Fourth Amendment protects against unreasonable searches by agents of the government, neither provides protection from the actions of a private employer or a nosy neighbor. This is known as the **state action requirement.**

Therefore, in our opening scenario involving the pregnant waitress, as we will discuss in the next section, the restaurant manager may have violated a federal statute prohibiting sex discrimination. However, as a private citizen, the manager personally cannot be charged with violating any of Dobbs' constitutional rights.

DISCUSSION QUESTION

2. Arguably, if Congress passes a statute, it means that the majority of both the House of Representatives and the Senate believed that it was not in conflict with the Constitution. Why should the decision of the people's elected representatives be overridden by unelected, appointed judges?

Each of the 50 states also has a written constitution that defines the organization and powers of its government. Most also include an equivalent of the

Bill of Rights
The first ten amendments to the U.S. Constitution.

Doctrine of incorporation
In constitutional law, the application of the Fourteenth Amendment's due process protections to incorporate the provisions of the Bill of Rights and make them applicable to the states.

State action requirement
A requirement that a defendant cannot be charged with a violation of constitutional rights unless the defendant was acting as an agent of a governmental entity.

P R A C T I C E   T I P
In areas having to do with individual rights, sometimes a state constitution will give more protection than the U.S. Constitution.

federal Bill of Rights. The supreme court, or highest court, of a state is the final arbiter of what its state constitution means, so long as the state constitution does not conflict with the federal constitution.

In the past, many lawyers tended to ignore their own state's constitutional provisions. Recently, however, there has been an increase in litigation based on state constitutional law. This is partly because many state constitutions provide more protection of individual rights than does the federal constitution. For example, in the state of Washington, parents of student athletes sued their children's school district, which had adopted a policy of random and suspicionless drug testing of all student athletes. The parents argued that this violated the students' rights under the Washington Constitution. Thirteen years earlier, the U.S. Supreme Court had ruled that a similar policy in Oregon violated neither the Oregon nor the U.S. Constitution.[5] In the Washington case, however, the Washington Supreme Court held in 2008 that the policy violated the student athletes' rights under the Washington Constitution.[6] Hence, student athletes in Oregon are subject to random drug tests because their privacy rights are not protected by either their state or the federal constitution; but in the neighboring state of Washington, student athletes *cannot* be forced to undergo similar drug testing because their privacy rights are protected under their state's constitution.

NETNOTE

You can read the full texts of the Declaration of Independence, the Constitution, and the Bill of Rights at the National Archives website: *www.archives.gov*.

B. STATUTORY LAW

As explained above, federal and state constitutions delineate the general framework within which the government must operate. Although these documents do list some major substantive and procedural rights, they were not designed to contain the types of detailed laws and regulations we need to operate in today's complex society. Rather, the federal and state constitutions specifically delegate the power to make these laws to the legislative branches of government.

At the federal level, the U.S. Congress is the source of statutory law. The process of creating a **statute** starts with the introduction of a bill in either the House of Representatives or the Senate.[7] Bills are assigned to an appropriate committee. The committee often conducts hearings on the bill's merit and then

Statute
A law enacted by a state legislature or by Congress.

---

[5] Vernonia School Dist. 47J v. Acton, 515 U.S. 646 (1995).
[6] York v. Wahkiakum School District No. 200, 178 P.3d 995 (Wash. 2008).
[7] The exception to this is for bills raising revenues, which must originate in the House.

votes on whether it should be brought to the full House for consideration. For the bill to become law, the Constitution requires a majority vote of both the House and the Senate,[8] and the language of the Senate and House bills must be identical. If it is not, then a conference committee made up of members of both houses is formed to try to work out language agreeable to a majority of both chambers. If the conference committee is able to find language that is agreeable to a majority of both the House and Senate, then the bill is sent to the president. If the president signs the bill, a new statute will have been created. If the president does not want to see the bill become law, the president can veto the proposed law.[9] Congress can override a presidential veto with a vote of at least two-thirds of both chambers.

At the state level, legislatures also create statutory law. In addition, a variety of local bodies, such as city councils and village boards, enact **ordinances**, a subcategory of statutory law.

These statutes and ordinances lay down general rules that govern future conduct. They are general in the sense that they apply to broad categories of people rather than to specific individuals. Furthermore, the requirements they impose generally cannot be applied to actions taken *before* the law went into effect. Because a law typically cannot be passed retroactively, it is often passed stating the date on which the law will be enforceable.

The formulation of such future-oriented rules is a difficult task because legislatures cannot foresee all the possible circumstances that might arise. Statutes therefore often contain general prohibitions that are somewhat ambiguous and open to differing interpretations. Ambiguity in statutes can also result from sloppy draftsmanship or be intentionally inserted to avoid creating conflicts among the legislation's supporters.

An example of the ambiguity contained in statutes can be found in the following excerpt from Title VII of the 1964 Civil Rights Act. It states:

> It shall be an unlawful employment practice for an employer (1) to . . . discriminate against any individual . . . because of such individual's race, color, religion, sex, or national origin.[10]

Recall the situation of Diane Dobbs, mentioned at the beginning of the chapter. Was the restaurant manager discriminating against Dobbs because of

Ordinance
A law enacted by a local government; a subcategory of statutory law.

---

[8] However, both chambers of Congress have adopted internal rules that have created various roadblocks, which can slow or even kill a bill. For example, in Senate Rule XXII, through the use of a filibuster, one or more senators can carry on debate, thereby preventing a vote, until three-fifths of the senators vote to end debate. Senate Rule XX can be used to overturn Rule XXII and allow the Senate to decide any issue by a simple majority and ending the filibuster. In November 2013 the democrats ended the filibuster for executive branch nominations and federal judicial appointments except for the Supreme Court. In 2017, the republicans extended the simple majority vote for Supreme Court nominations as well.

[9] In rare instances, the president can exercise a pocket veto. The Constitution grants the president ten days to review a measure passed by the Congress. If Congress has not adjourned within that ten-day period, the measure becomes law without his signature. However, if Congress adjourns during the ten-day period, and the president has not signed it, the bill does *not* become law. This latter situation is referred to as a "pocket veto" because the president can veto it by leaving the bill "in his pocket" rather than signing it

[10] 42 U.S.C. §2000e-2(a) (2020).

her sex when he fired her for being pregnant? While the statute clearly states that employers cannot discriminate on the basis of sex, it is not clear what types of actions should be considered sex discrimination. After the enactment of Title VII, some people argued that pregnancy discrimination should be considered a form of sex discrimination because only women can become pregnant. Others argued that it should not be considered sex discrimination because the differential treatment is based on the condition of being pregnant rather than on the employee's sex. Although only women can become pregnant, the employer was legitimately differentiating between two different types of women—those who were pregnant and those who were not—rather than discriminating between women and men.

As with ambiguities in constitutional provisions, when disagreements such as this arise over the meaning of a statute, a court must resolve the ambiguity. Thus, in *General Elec. Co. v. Gilbert,*[11] the U.S. Supreme Court was called upon to determine if discrimination based on pregnancy was a form of sex discrimination under Title VII. The Supreme Court ruled in *Gilbert* that Title VII allowed employers to discriminate based on pregnancy.

The Supreme Court's interpretation would have left Dobbs without a remedy under the statute. However, luckily for her, if the legislative branch disagrees with the interpretation a court gives to one of its statutes, Congress can always introduce new legislation that amends the original statute to make clear that a different result or interpretation was intended. If this new legislation passes, the court's interpretation is superseded by the new statute. In this instance, Congress reacted by amending the statute to include pregnancy discrimination in the definition of sex discrimination.[12] Thus, under the amended statute, it was unlawful for Dobbs' employer to fire her based upon her pregnancy.

Note, however, the difference between interpreting a statute and determining that it is unconstitutional. Whereas the legislative branch can amend one of its statutes to override a judicial interpretation, the courts retain the final authority with respect to deciding whether it is constitutional.

C. ADMINISTRATIVE LAW

Administrative law
Rules and regulations created by administrative agencies.

Administrative law can be found at both the state and the federal levels. At the federal level, it is created most often by agencies, through rules and regulations, and at times by presidential executive orders or memoranda. A similar structure exists at the state level, with governors.

Enabling act
A statute establishing and setting out the powers of an administrative agency.

Administrative agencies can be created by Congress or by state legislatures. On the federal level, Congress creates administrative agencies through an **enabling act** that sets out the parameters of the powers of the agency being created. Once an administrative agency is created, it will run independently or fall under the authority of the executive branch. Administrative law is similar to statutory law, in that it lays down rules designed to regulate future conduct.

---

[11] 429 U.S. 125 (1976).
[12] Bennett Amendment, 42 U.S.C. §2000e(k) (2020).

However, these rules are usually drawn more narrowly and directed to a more specialized group. Often the legislative branch intentionally leaves it to the executive branch and to independent regulatory agencies to "fill in the details" of a law within a general structure set down by the legislature. Through the process of filling in these details, the executive branch is actually making the law.

NETNOTE

You can find a listing of the U.S. departments and agencies at *www.usa.gov/ federal-agencies*.

For example, assume that a taxpayer wins $50 in the lottery. Must she pay taxes on it? The Internal Revenue Code, a federal statute, provides that she must pay tax on income, but it only includes general categories of income. The Internal Revenue Service (IRS), a federal agency, has developed **regulations** that define in much more detail what the word *income* means. Without the IRS, Congress would be forced to make constant revisions in the federal tax laws and would be hard-pressed to see that they were enforced.

Regulation
A law promulgated by an administrative agency.

At both the federal and state levels, administrative agencies begin the process of creating or amending regulations through what is known as a "notice and comment" period. First, the administrative agency gives notice of its intent by publishing the proposed changes in the *Federal Register* (or its state equivalent). Second, interested parties have a set time in which to inform the agency of their support, opposition, or suggestions for change. At the close of this "comment" period, the agency formally promulgates the regulation through its publication in the *Federal Register* (or its state equivalent).

Just as the courts are drawn into the lawmaking process when they must interpret constitutions and statutes, so, too, are they called on to be the final arbiters of the meaning of administrative regulations. If someone disagrees with the administrative interpretation of a statute, the dissatisfied party can go to court to challenge the agency's interpretation. The court must support

PRACTICE TIP

Your understanding of a statute may be incomplete without also checking for related regulations. For example, policies such as the right of the police to conduct breathalyzer tests may be set by state statutes. However, how those policies are to be implemented (e.g., how a breathalyzer test is to be conducted) may be set by administrative regulations.

the agency's interpretation unless the court determines that the regulation is outside the authorization Congress gave to the administrative agency or that the regulation is unconstitutional. To determine whether the agency has stepped out of the bounds created for it by Congress, the court will examine the enabling act for the agency. The court will also seek to determine the underlying legislative intent of the statute that the agency is attempting to interpret through its regulations.

Returning once again to the case of the pregnant waitress, Harper may decide to sue Dobbs's employer for sexual harassment. A sexual harassment case would be based on the same federal statute, Title VII, discussed above. The statute makes no specific reference to sexual harassment. The Equal Employment Opportunity Commission (EEOC), however, acting under authority given it in the statute, has declared that acts of sexual harassment are a form of sex discrimination. One of its administrative regulations states:

> Unwelcome sexual advances, requests for sexual favors, and other verbal or physical conduct of a sexual nature constitute sexual harassment when (1) submission to such conduct is made either explicitly or implicitly a term or condition of an individual's employment, (2) submission to or rejection of such conduct by an individual is used as the basis for employment decisions affecting such individual, or (3) such conduct has the purpose or effect of unreasonably interfering with an individual's work performance or creating an intimidating, hostile, or offensive working environment.[13]

Fourth branch of government
Administrative agencies.

Executive order
An official policy directive issued by the president for the federal government, or by the governor of a state, which directs government employees as to how they should implement a law. At the federal level, executive orders are published in the *Federal Register.*

Executive memorandum
An official policy directive issued by the president for the federal government, or by the governor of a state, which directs government employees as to how they should implement a law.

Note how much more specific the wording of the regulation is compared to the wording of the statute.

Recall that Dobbs alleged that the manager patted her on the stomach as he was firing her for being pregnant. Do you think that is sufficient to support a claim of sexual harassment? Is there any language in the regulation that could support such a claim?

In addition to their power to promulgate regulations, and as part of their enforcement powers, most agencies have investigatory and adjudicative powers. For example, if Dobbs wants to pursue her claim of sexual harassment, Title VII mandates that she first take her complaint to the EEOC or a comparable state agency. The agency will investigate her case and, if it deems it appropriate, will hold a hearing to determine the truth of her claims. If she or her employer is not satisfied with the results they obtain at the agency, they can then take the case to court. Ultimately, the court would be the final arbiter of whether Dobbs's situation fits the agency definition of sexual harassment.

Because administrative agencies combine the legislative, executive, and judicial functions, they are sometimes referred to as the **fourth branch of government.**

Executive orders and **executive memoranda** are also forms of administrative law. They are policy directives issued by the president (or, at the state level, by governors) that direct government employees as to how they should implement either statutes passed by the legislature, rules and regulations enacted by administrative agencies, or executive powers listed in the federal or state constitution.[14]

---

[13] 29 C.F.R. §1604.11 (2020).

[14] For instance, the U.S. Constitution, Article II, Section 1, states, "The executive Power shall be vested in a President of the United States of America."

The terms "executive order" and "executive memorandum" are often used interchangeably, the primary difference being that executive orders are published in the *Federal Register* and executive memoranda are not. Perhaps the most famous example of such an executive action was President Abraham Lincoln's Emancipation Proclamation. Other notable historical examples include President Franklin Delano Roosevelt's detention of Japanese citizens in internment camps during World War II; President John Kennedy's prohibition of discrimination in federally funded housing; President Richard Nixon's freezing of all prices, rents, wages, and salaries to stop inflation; President George W. Bush's creation of the U.S. Department of Homeland Security after the September 11 terrorist attacks; President Barack Obama's deferral of deportation proceedings for a set number of years for illegal immigrants who met specified criteria; and President Donald Trump's phasing out of this deferral of deportation policy. As with the rules and regulations issued by administrative agencies, executive orders and memoranda clarifying how executive agencies enforce their regulations can be found by courts to be unconstitutional or to be outside the authorization given by Congress.

DISCUSSION QUESTION

3. If Congress and state legislatures have given administrative agencies the ability to create rules and regulations, why do presidents create executive orders and memoranda? Some executive orders and memoranda can be controversial. Should the president, or a governor, have the power to issue unpopular executive orders and memoranda?

D. COMMON LAW

Constitutions, statutes, and administrative regulations are classified as enacted law because they are written documents that have been formally authorized by governmental entities. As we have noted above, courts play a vital role in interpreting constitutions and the laws created by legislatures and agencies. At times, however, no constitutional, statutory, or administrative regulations govern a situation. When that happens, courts must look to their own earlier opinions, known as the **common law.** Therefore, courts have three roles to play:

Common law
Law created by the courts. The body of law that has evolved from judicial decisions in cases that do not involve constitutional, statutory, or administrative regulation interpretation.

- ∎ to determine the constitutionality of a statute or executive action;
- ∎ to interpret ambiguous statutes and regulations; and
- ∎ when no written law exists, to create the common law.

The common law consists of legal principles that have evolved through the years from the analysis of prior court decisions. Ultimately, these principles can be traced to medieval England, although they have been modified through the years by various state courts up through modern times. When a legal dispute involves a subject that is not adequately covered by the other types of law, the judge applies the principles of the common law. In other words, in the absence of pronouncements from the Constitution or a legislative or administrative body, the judge looks to earlier decisions by other judges in similar circumstances.

When the United States was established, the English common law formed the foundation of our legal system. Unless there is a good reason for doing otherwise, judges are expected to follow the legal rules laid down in prior decisions. This was how the doctrine of **stare decisis** developed. Once courts had determined the law in an area, other courts followed that rule unless a court thought that there was a good reason to change it.

Today, there are areas of state law that are still totally governed by the common law, such as most matters dealing with torts. However, over the years, many areas of the common law have been enacted into statutes. This process of converting the common law into statutory form is known as the **codification of the common law**. Sometimes, however, instead of following the common law, a statute will differ from that approach. When the common law is changed through legislation, the statute is said to be in **derogation of the common law**.

In addition to the common law created by law courts discussed above, another part of our common law heritage involves the use of **equity** courts. Law courts had the power to settle disputes by requiring one party to compensate the other with money damages. But there are times when money is not what the litigants want. Rather, they would like the court to order the other party to do something, such as living up to contractual obligations, or to cease doing something, such as having loud parties in the wee hours of the morning. In response to this need, the English created equity courts.

Equity powers include a judge's ability to issue an **injunction** or to order **specific performance**. An injunction is a court order requiring someone to act or to refrain from acting. Specific performance requires that a party fulfill his or her contractual obligations. In the 1800s most states merged their law and equity courts. Therefore, today judges have the power to give either monetary awards or equitable relief or both, as they deem appropriate.

DISCUSSION QUESTION

4. For each of the following, which source of law—a constitution, a statute, an administrative regulation, or a court opinion—would be best able to handle the problem, and why? Before answering, keep in mind that constitutional provisions generally cover the most general, basic rights, such as freedom of speech. Statutes are more detailed and administrative regulations are even more specific, often going into great detail as to what is to be regulated. Statutes and regulations are forward looking; that is, legislatures enact statutes and administrative agencies issue regulations with an eye to what they expect to happen in the future. On the other hand, court decisions are designed to address something that has already happened; by their nature, they are very fact specific.

a. A requirement that all motorcycle riders wear helmets.
b. A rule making a bar owner liable for any injuries caused by a patron to whom the bar sold drinks.

Stare decisis
The doctrine stating that normally once a court has decided one way on a particular issue, it and other courts in the same jurisdiction will decide the same way on that issue in future cases given similar facts unless they can be convinced of the need for change.

Codification of the common law
The process of legislative enactment of areas of the law previously governed solely by the common law.

Derogation of the common law
A term referring to legislation that changes the common law.

Equity
A principle that allows judges to take actions such as issuing injunctions and ordering specific performance when the law would otherwise limit their decisions to monetary awards.

Injunction
A court order requiring a party to perform a specific act or to cease doing a specific act.

Specific performance
A requirement that a party fulfill his or her contractual obligations.

   c. A rule that all semi-trailers traveling on interstate highways use con-cave mud flaps.
   d. A requirement that employers not discriminate on the basis of reli-gion or sexual orientation.
   e. A requirement that no more than a certain percentage of a known pollutant be released by factory smokestacks.
   f. A question as to whether a person not wearing a seat belt should be able to recover for injuries that person sustained in an automobile accident that was not her or his fault.
   g. A law prohibiting government from interfering with an individual's right to own an assault weapon.

E. THE HIERARCHY OF LAWS

In this chapter, you have seen that our laws come in different formats: consti-tutions, statutes, administrative regulations, executive orders and memoranda, and court decisions. In analyzing Dobbs' situation, we found that statutory and administrative laws, as well as court decisions, would affect her legal situation.

Constitutional law is at the top of the established "hierarchy of law." In fact, the U.S. Constitution provides that it and the laws made pursuant to it are the "Supreme Law of the Land." With their power of judicial review, the courts are the final arbiters of what the Constitution means.

Most legal problems, however, do not involve constitutional issues unless an argument arises over the underlying constitutional validity of a statute or administrative regulation. Instead, most legal situations involve the application and interpretation of state and federal statutes, along with any relevant admin-istrative regulations.

If a statute contains any ambiguities, lawyers look to relevant court deci-sions for assistance in interpreting the statutory language. Therefore, the courts have a great deal of power in their role as interpreters of enacted law.

As noted earlier, always keep in mind the crucial difference between court decisions that interpret the meaning of statutory language and those that strike down a statute because it conflicts with provisions of the federal or state con-stitution. Whereas the legislative branch can amend one of its statutes to clarify its intent and thus override a judicial interpretation, the courts retain the final authority with respect to deciding whether a statute is constitutional. When the courts declare a statute unconstitutional, the legislature's only recourse is to seek to amend the constitution or to wait for a change in court membership. This important difference is outlined in Figure 3-2.

It is only when no applicable constitutional or statutory provision governs the situation that the courts will apply court-made common law. While today most areas of the law are governed by statutes, the common law still has a role to play, most notably in the areas of property, tort, and contract law.

Judicial Statutory Interpretation	Versus	Judicial Constitutional Determination
Congress enacts a statute; the terms are unclear.		Congress enacts a statute; the terms are clear, but its constitutionality is questionable.
Example: Statute: It shall be an unlawful employment practice for an employer to discriminate because of such individual's sex. Court interpretation: Pregnancy discrimination is not a form of sex discrimination.		**Example:** Statute: It shall be a criminal offense to desecrate the U.S. flag. Court determination: The statute is not constitutional, as it violates the First Amendment's right to free speech.
If the legislature disagrees with the court's interpretation, it can amend the statute.		Even if the legislature disagrees with the court's decision regarding the constitutionality of the statute, it is bound by that decision.
Example: Congress amends the statute to add a definition of sex discrimination that includes pregnancy discrimination.		**Example:** Congress can do nothing short of working toward a constitutional amendment.

Figure 3-2 Judicial Statutory Interpretation versus Determination of Constitutionality

Legal Reasoning Exercises

1. Assume that Congress enacted a statute making it a federal crime for "anyone" to kidnap children and take them across state lines. Assume further that the U.S. Supreme Court decided that the word "anyone" did not include a parent. If it wanted to do so, could Congress amend the statute to say that the word "anyone" does include parents? Why?

2. Assume that Congress enacted a statute making rape a federal crime. Assume further that the U.S. Supreme Court declared the statute to be unconstitutional because it exceeded congressional power under the Commerce and Equal Protection clauses. If it wanted to do so, could the executive branch prosecute individuals for violating the statute? In other words, does Congress or the Supreme Court have the final word on what is constitutional? Why?

SUMMARY

While our laws come from different sources, they all establish rules of conduct that can be enforced by the governments that enacted them. They play an important role in managing conflict and insuring the rule of law in modern democratic societies. In this chapter, we have looked at four sources of law: constitutions, statutes, administrative regulations, and the common law.

Our country was the first to adopt a written constitution, and it is our federal constitution that provides the framework within which all our laws are made. Similarly, states' constitutions provide the legal basis for their governments to act.

Even though traditionally we say that the legislature makes the law, the executive branch enforces the law, and the courts interpret the law, the truth is that the legislative, executive, and judicial branches, as well as administrative agencies, are all involved in making law. Legislatures create law by enacting statutes; agencies create law by promulgating regulations; the executive branch creates laws through executive orders and memoranda, which clarify how administrative agencies should enforce statutes and regulations; and appellate courts create law through their written opinions, known as "court decisions."

The example with which we began this chapter provides a good illustration of how statutory, regulatory, and court-made law work together. Congress enacted a statute that prohibited "sex discrimination." Because this phrase is so broad, the EEOC, an administrative agency, has issued regulations that more clearly define some types of sex discrimination, such as sexual harassment. Even the most detailed regulation cannot cover every individual case, however. Therefore, the courts are constantly called on to interpret the meanings of both statutes and regulations. In the case of women such as Diane Dobbs, the U.S. Supreme Court determined that the federal statute prohibiting sex discrimination did not cover pregnancy. Because the Court based its ruling on its interpretation of the statute, not on any constitutional authority, Congress was able to reverse this result by enacting a statute that more explicitly prohibits discrimination based on pregnancy.

Where no constitution, statute, or administrative regulation applies, the courts rely on the common law to resolve the problem. But it is in their role as interpreters of constitutional, statutory, and administrative provisions that courts have the greatest power: By interpreting the law, the courts end up creating the law. Figure 3-3 summarizes the major sources of law.

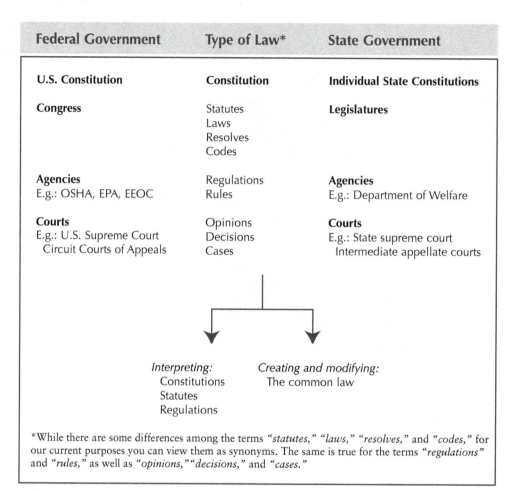

Federal Government	Type of Law*	State Government
U.S. Constitution	**Constitution**	**Individual State Constitutions**
Congress	Statutes Laws Resolves Codes	**Legislatures**
Agencies E.g.: OSHA, EPA, EEOC	Regulations Rules	**Agencies** E.g.: Department of Welfare

Courts
E.g.: U.S. Supreme Court
    Circuit Courts of Appeals
	Opinions
	Decisions
	Cases
		Courts
		E.g.: State supreme court
		    Intermediate appellate courts

Interpreting:
   Constitutions
   Statutes
   Regulations

Creating and modifying:
   The common law

*While there are some differences among the terms *"statutes," "laws," "resolves,"* and *"codes,"* for our current purposes you can view them as synonyms. The same is true for the terms *"regulations"* and *"rules,"* as well as *"opinions," "decisions,"* and *"cases."*

Figure 3-3   Sources of Law

REVIEW QUESTIONS

Pages 71 through 76

1. What are the two primary functions of the U.S. Constitution?
2. Read the excerpts from the U.S. Constitution and the Bill of Rights located in Appendix A. Then answer the following questions:
   a. Which article deals specifically with the legislature? With the executive? With the judiciary? (This may seem like trivia necessary only for *Jeopardy* contestants, but lawyers often refer to Article I, Article II, or Article III powers.)
   b. Which amendment states that the powers not specifically delegated to the federal government are reserved to the states?
   c. Make a list of the rights protected by the first ten amendments (Bill of Rights).
3. What is the doctrine of separation of powers, and how does it relate to our system of checks and balances?

4. What is the power of judicial review, and why is it so important to our legal system?

5. What is the doctrine of incorporation, and why is it important for understanding our rights under the U.S. Constitution?

6. John is upset with his neighbor because on weekends the neighbor plays loud music, disturbing John's sleep. John is so angry that he wants to sue his neighbor for violating his federal constitutional right to privacy. Why will John not be able to win his lawsuit?

7. Are the protections provided by state constitutions the same as those given by the U.S. Constitution? Why might that matter?

Pages 76 through 81

8. Why do constitutions and statutes frequently include ambiguous language?

9. How do courts become involved in the legislative process?

10. How are statutes and administrative regulations similar? How do they differ?

11. What is an enabling act?

12. Why are administrative agencies referred to as the fourth branch of government?

13. How are administrative regulations and executive orders and executive memoranda similar? How do they differ?

14. Can executive orders and executive memoranda be reviewed by the courts?

Pages 81 through 83

15. What is the common law?

16. What does it mean to say the common law has been codified? That a statute is in derogation of the common law?

17. Why were equity courts created, and what special powers were they given?

Pages 83 through 86

18. Who has the final say as to what a statute means: the legislature or the courts?

19. Who has the final say as to the constitutionality of a statute, the legislature or the courts?

WEB EXERCISES

1. In these exercises, you will have the opportunity to delve further into each of the four main sources of law.

   a. **The Constitution:** Use Google or another search engine to find your state's constitution. The Fourteenth Amendment to the U.S. Constitution states that no state can "deny to any person within its jurisdiction the equal protection of the laws." Does your state constitution have a similar provision? Do you think it provides less or more protections than that given by the U.S. Constitution?

   b. **Statutory Law and the Legislative Branch:** Go to *www.votesmart.org*. Enter your ZIP code near the top of the page and then click on the "Current Officials" link to obtain a list of your state's two U.S. senators and your local U.S. congressional representative, as well as the elected representatives to your state legislature. Click on any of their names to read more information about them, as well as to view their record on key votes.

   c. **Administrative Law:** Go to the website for the EEOC *www.eeoc.gov*. On the home page under "Employees & Applicants," take some time to browse through the information on the different types of discrimination, such as age, race, religion, and sex. Then return to the home page, and under "Contact Us," click on "Frequently Asked Questions." Select one of the questions that interests you and read the answer. Summarize the question and answer. Were you satisfied with the answer provided? Why or why not?

d. **Courts and the Common Law:** First, read about the common law at *definitions.uslegal.com/c/common-law*, and then specifically about statutes enacted in derogation of the common law at *definitions.uslegal .com/d/ derogation*. Then read a provision from the Montana statutes at *leg.mt.gov/bills/mca/title_0010/chapter_0020/part_0010/section_0030/ 0010-0020-0010-0030.html*. Why do you think the Montana legislature thought it necessary to enact the provision here?

2. Read a short article on the purpose of our system of checks and balances at *www.auburn.edu/~johnspm/gloss/checks_and_balances*.

a. According to the author of this article, what are the advantages and disadvantages of this system?

b. How would the system of checks and balances handle a situation in which Congress passed a law stating that college students who say anything negative about a professor will be incarcerated in federal prison for a minimum of one year?

Chapter 4

Classification of the Law

Logically, everything ought to come first.
Jean-Jacques Rousseau

Chapter Objectives

After reading this chapter, you should be able to:

- Explain what it means to say that Congress has limited powers.
- Identify areas of the law that could be federal only, state only, or both.
- Describe the basic differences between civil and criminal law.
- Distinguish substantive from procedural law.

INTRODUCTION

In this chapter, we will discuss the most common ways in which lawyers have traditionally categorized law. However, keep in mind that although it is necessary to categorize a client's legal problem in order to help the client, you should not fall into the trap of seeing a client as only a set of legal problems that can be neatly sorted into predefined categories. There is a person behind every legal problem.

In Chapter 3, we explained how law is made not only by legislatures, but also by administrative agencies, executive orders and memoranda, and the courts. Based on its source, we classified law in terms of constitutional, statutory, administrative, or common law, or law made by executive orders or memoranda. You can also classify law based on whether it involves

1. state or federal law (every state, as well as the federal government, has its own laws);
2. civil or criminal law (**civil law** deals with harm against an individual—for example, a broken contract—whereas **criminal law** deals with harm against society as a whole—as when violence leads to someone's death); and
3. substantive or procedural law (**substantive law** defines our legal rights and duties—for example, the duty to obey speed limits and the right of freedom of speech—whereas **procedural law** is comprised of the rules that govern how the legal system operates).

Civil law
Law that deals with harm to an individual.

Criminal law
Law that deals with harm to society as a whole.

These categories are not mutually exclusive. A client's situation may involve both federal and state laws, both civil and criminal issues, and procedural and substantive questions. Figure 4-1 illustrates how these categories relate to each other. At this point, do not be concerned about understanding all of the terms listed in the chart. As the chapter proceeds, we will discuss each term in more detail.

To illustrate key points in this chapter, we will be making frequent references to events surrounding the aftermath of the Boston Marathon bombing.

Figure 4-1   How Lawyers Classify the Law

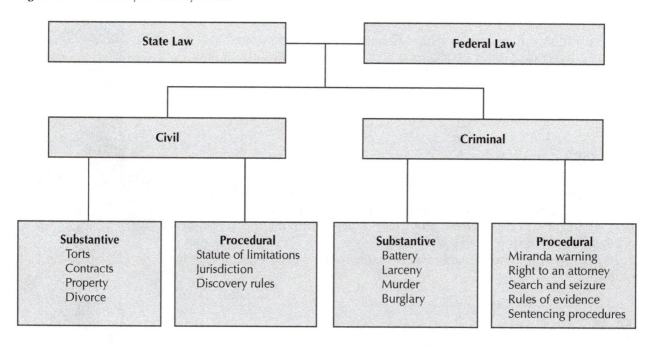

Case 5: The Boston Marathon Bombings

On April 15, 2013, two bombs were detonated near the finish line of the annual Boston Marathon, killing three and injuring more than two hundred runners and spectators. The government alleged that the attack was carried out by 26-year-old Tamerlan Tsarnaev and his 19-year-old brother, Dzhokhar Tsarnaev. In the ensuing manhunt, Tamerlan was killed, but Dzhokhar was captured and charged with committing a host of crimes.

As you read about the different ways that the law can be classified, think about how you might answer the following questions:

- Should Dzhokhar be charged with state or federal crimes, or both? What are the implications of bringing federal versus state charges?
- How would the victims go about trying to receive compensation for the injuries they suffered?
- What procedural issues might arise as the government proceeds with its case?

A. FEDERAL VERSUS STATE LAW

In the previous chapter, we noted how the U.S. Constitution created a system of government, known as **federalism,** in which the power to make various types of laws is divided between the federal government in Washington, D.C., and the 50 state governments. Each of the 50 states, along with the federal government, has its own legal system. Each determines how its court system will be organized and what laws it will enforce. Although the laws of one state are often similar to the laws of another, each state ultimately decides for itself what those laws will be. A client's problem may involve state law, federal law, or both state and federal law.

Federalism
A system of government in which the authority to govern is split between a single, nationwide central government and several regional governments that control specific geographical areas.

1. Federal Law

Federal law is involved if the situation concerns any of the following:

1. an issue involving the U.S. Constitution (such as whether a branch of the federal government has exceeded its delegated powers, or whether an individual's freedoms guaranteed by the Bill of Rights have been violated);
2. a federal statute, such as the Internal Revenue Code or the PATRIOT Act; or
3. a regulation of a federal agency, such as the Internal Revenue Service (IRS) or the Environmental Protection Agency (EPA).

When a client's problem is covered by one of these three areas, you will hear lawyers referring to this as raising a federal issue or a **federal question.** As we will see later in Chapter 6, on civil litigation, the raising of a federal question is one basis for establishing jurisdiction in the federal courts.

Federal question
A legal question involving the application of federal law.

While states have "inherent power" to take actions designed to advance the health, welfare, safety, and morals of the people, the federal government is limited to those powers that are delegated to it in the U.S. Constitution. Therefore, for example, Congress has the power to enact legislation regarding taxation, but not a national divorce law.

However, even though the federal government is limited to the powers that are delegated to it in the Constitution, these powers are quite sweeping. Take a moment to look at Article I, Section 8 of the U.S. Constitution (in Appendix A). The government can lay and collect taxes, regulate currency, fix weights and measures, establish post offices, raise armies, and declare war, just to name a few. In addition, several constitutional amendments such as the Fourteenth Amendment, have provisions enabling Congress to pass legislation necessary to enforce those specific amendments.

Congress also has the ability to enact laws that are "necessary and proper" to carry out its delegated powers. The last clause in Article I, Section 8, states: "[And] to make all Laws, which shall be necessary and proper for carrying into Execution the foregoing Powers vested by this Constitution in the Government of the United States, or in any Department or Officer thereof."

Doctrine of implied powers
Powers not stated in the Constitution but that are necessary for Congress to carry out other, expressly granted powers.

This is commonly called the **doctrine of implied powers.** For example, even though the Constitution did not explicitly delegate to Congress the power to create a national bank, in the 1819 case of *McCulloch v. Maryland*,[1] the U.S. Supreme Court determined that its ability to do so was implied because the Constitution had expressly delegated to Congress the power to collect taxes and borrow money.

Finally, one of the most expansive powers involves the application of the commerce clause. Article I, Section 8, also provides that "Congress shall have power to regulate commerce . . . among the several states." On its face, this seems quite straightforward, that is, whenever something crosses state lines, the federal government, rather than the individual states, should be the appropriate source of authority so as to create a uniform system. For example, if a river flows through several states, the federal government should be able to impose uniform limits as to what can be dumped into the river, as what is dumped in one state will inevitably flow into and affect the next. However, it is not always clear when something will have an impact on interstate commerce, especially when an activity is carried out entirely within just one state.

In the landmark case of *Wickard v. Filburn*, the U.S. Supreme Court interpreted the commerce clause as giving the federal government the power to regulate not only the movement of things that cross state lines but also any activity that has an "effect upon" interstate commerce.[2] In that case, a farmer had harvested more wheat than allowed under a federal statute. He argued that the wheat was to be used solely on his farm and so its production would have no impact on interstate commerce. The Court disagreed. "[E]ven if appellee's activity be local and though it may not be regarded as commerce, it may still,

---

[1] 17 U.S. (4 Wheat.) 316 (1819).
[2] 317 U.S. 111 (1942).

whatever its nature, be reached by Congress if it exerts a substantial economic effect on interstate commerce."[3] Since setting this standard, the Supreme Court has grappled many times with whether a particular action has a great enough effect upon interstate commerce to justify federal regulation.

For example, in the 1960s, Congress relied upon those powers when it enacted the 1964 Civil Rights Act, making it unlawful to discriminate on the basis of race, color, religion, sex, or national origin. As the provisions were challenged, the Supreme Court continued to uphold the right of Congress to legislate through a broad reading of the commerce clause. In *Heart of Atlanta Motel, Inc. v. United States,* a motel in Georgia refused to rent rooms to black patrons, in direct violation of the Civil Rights of Act of 1964, which banned racial discrimination in public accommodations. The motel argued that by depriving places of public accommodation of the right to choose with whom they wished to do business, Congress had exceeded its Commerce Clause powers. The U.S. Supreme Court held that the statute was within the scope of the commerce clause because the existence of racially discriminatory practices made it more difficult for minorities to travel from one state to another, and this had a negative impact on the free flow of interstate commerce.[4]

Beginning in the 1990s, the Supreme Court began to interpret the commerce clause less expansively. In *United States v. Lopez,*[5] the Court ruled that the Gun-Free School Zones Act of 1990 was unconstitutional because it "exceeded Congress' power to legislate under the Commerce Clause." The Court rejected the argument that guns in school had an economic impact on interstate commerce and reasoned that the creation of a gun-free school zone was the sort of intrastate activity that can be regulated by the state, but not by the federal government. Most recently, in *Nat'l Fed'n of Indep. Bus. v. Sebelius,*[6] opponents of the Patient Protection and Affordable Care Act (PPACA) (commonly referred to as Obamacare),[7] argued that Congress, by requiring most Americans to maintain "minimum essential" health insurance coverage or pay a "penalty" for not doing so, had exceeded its constitutional authority. The federal government countered that the individual mandate was constitutional, as it came within Congress's commerce clause powers. It argued the provision for mandatory coverage was a reasonable part of a comprehensive program to address the delivery of health services, an industry that has a major effect on interstate commerce. The Supreme Court ruled that the PPACA could not be justified under the commerce clause. A majority of the justices, however, did uphold most parts of the act on the basis of the federal government's taxing power.[8]

---

[3] Id. at 125.
[4] Heart of Atlanta Motel, Inc. v. U.S., 379 U.S. 241 (1964).
[5] United States v. Lopez, 514 U.S. 549 (1995).
[6] Nat'l Fed'n of Indep. Bus. v. Sebelius, 567 U.S. 519 (2012).
[7] Patient Protection and Affordable Care Act of 2010, Pub. L. No. 111-148, 124 Stat. 119 (codified in scattered sections of the U.S.C.). The reduction of the penalty for not carrying insurance to $0 as part of the 2017 tax overhaul led to a second challenge of the PPACA as unconstitutional. The Supreme Court scheduled that case to be heard in the 2020 term.
[8] Article I, Section 8, gives Congress the power to "lay and collect Taxes, Duties, Imposts and Excises, to pay the Debts and provide for the common Defense and general Welfare of the United States."

2. State Law

Whereas the federal government must trace all of its powers back to a specific constitutional authorization, the states are allowed to make any laws they deem appropriate for the health, welfare, safety, and morals of their citizens, so long as those laws are not prohibited by the U.S. Constitution.[9] Typical examples of areas covered by state law are criminal behavior (from murder and rape to burglary and fraud), contracts, torts, property, and family matters. Figure 4-2 compares federal and state law.

While much of the law from one state to the next is quite similar, the states are free to create their own unique laws. Where one state may choose to create a state lottery, another may not; where one state may choose to allow no-fault divorces, another may not.

Some see this diversity as one of the great strengths of our political system. They argue that it encourages experimentation and innovation by allowing the residents of Georgia, for example, to establish rules of conduct that differ from those established by the residents of Nevada. Critics, on the other hand, point to the problems it creates for interstate business and travel—for example, forcing large corporations and other out-of-state parties to hire local lawyers and making it difficult for a lawyer to move a practice from one state to another. They also point out that states are sometimes reluctant to impose needed regulations

	Federal	**State**
Who enacts	Congress	State legislature
Limitations on legislative powers	Must be found in the Constitution: Article I, Section 8 delegated power Implied power Effect on interstate commerce Amendment enabling provision	Essentially none, so long as not prohibited by the U.S. Constitution and related to the welfare of its citizens
Examples	Income taxes Creation of a national bank Regulation of interstate train travel The Americans with Disabilities Act	Divorce laws Laws governing gambling Landlord/tenant law

Figure 4-2   A Comparison of Federal and State Law

[9]The Tenth Amendment to the U.S. Constitution declares that "powers not delegated to the United States by the Constitution, nor prohibited by it to the States, are reserved to the States respectively, or to the people."

(in areas such as environmental protection and worker safety) for fear that the affected businesses will move to another state with fewer restrictions.

As we become an ever more interdependent nation, however, state laws are tending to become more and more uniform, especially in the area of commercial law. Businesses with dealings in more than one state would rather not have to worry about adhering to a multiplicity of state laws. Therefore, most states have voluntarily moved to adopt uniform laws in areas such as commercial sales.

While state legislatures enact statutes that can affect everyone in the state, local governmental units can enact laws (usually referred to as "ordinances") that have a more localized effect. Local governments are considered to be part of the state government, and can only make laws when they have been specifically authorized to do so by the state legislature.

3. The Supremacy Clause and Preemption

The federal and state governments often pass laws that overlap. So long as state laws do not interfere with the enforcement of federal laws, states are usually free to pass additional regulations or protections for their citizens.

For example, the Civil Rights Act of 1964 is a federal statute prohibiting employers from discriminating on the basis of race, sex, color, religion, or national origin. State or local governments may pass laws prohibiting such discrimination as well. Michigan, for example, has a statute that also prohibits discrimination based on height or weight; this is acceptable because the state statute does not interfere with the enforcement of federal law. Michigan could not pass a statute allowing discrimination based on religion, however, because that would be in direct conflict with federal law.

The **Supremacy Clause** gives the federal government the power to prohibit states from passing any law on a particular subject. This is known as **preemption.** For example, the Federal Railroad Safety Act[10] created uniform standards related to railroad safety, such as maximum train speed and train length, preempting any type of state or local government regulation of trains. A more recent example of supremacy and preemption is the Supreme Court's decision in *Obergefell v. Hodges.*[11] In that case, the U.S. Supreme Court found that same-sex marriage is a fundamental right under the Fourteenth Amendment and the Equal Protection Clause. Prior to *Obergefell*, some states passed laws allowing same-sex marriage and others passed laws prohibiting it. Once the U.S. Supreme Court determined that same-sex marriage is a fundamental right under the U.S. Constitution, the state laws prohibiting same-sex marriage became invalid because they conflicted with the U.S. Constitution. States may, however, still legislate regarding marriage where their laws do not conflict with federal law, such as the requirement to obtain a marriage license.

The Supremacy Clause and preemption do have limits, however. In *Murphy v. National College Athletic Assn.,*[12] the Supreme Court found the Professional and Amateur Sports Protection Act of 1992 (PASPA)[13] to be unconstitutional.

Supremacy Clause
A clause in the U.S. Constitution that dictates if there is a conflict between federal law and state law, federal law takes precedence.

Preemption
The power of the federal government to prevent the states from passing conflicting laws, and sometimes even to prohibit states from passing any laws on a particular subject.

---

[10] 49 U.S.C.A. §20106 (2020).
[11] Obergefell v. Hodges, 135 S. Ct. 2584 (2015).
[12] Murphy v. National Collegiate Athletic Assn., 138 S. Ct. 1461 (2018).
[13] 28 U.S. Code §3702 (2020).

That statute prohibited states from allowing individuals to operate, sponsor, or promote sports gambling schemes. The state of New Jersey challenged that statute's constitutionality because New Jersey wanted to legalize sports gambling. In finding that PASPA was an unconstitutional assertion of congressional authority, the Court held that preemption can occur only if (1) there is a valid federal law, and (2) that valid federal law conflicts with state law, expressly preempts state law, or so dominates the field covered by the federal law as to leave no room for state action. Here, the Court ruled that there was no valid federal law because under the Tenth Amendment, all legislative power not conferred on Congress by the Constitution is reserved for the states. Absent from the list of conferred powers is the power to issue direct orders to state legislatures.

4. Application of Federal versus State Law

The Boston bombing case described at the beginning of this chapter illustrates a situation in which an action can violate both federal and state laws. In thinking about that case, criminal charges for murder are the first thing that comes to most people's minds, and murder is traditionally an area covered by state criminal law. Indeed, Massachusetts authorities charged Dzhokhar Tsarnaev with violating a number of Massachusetts state laws, including murder. However, federal authorities also charged him with a number of federal offenses, including the use of a weapon of mass destruction.[14] One consequence of Tsarnaev being charged with federal crimes is that the federal charges also carried the possibility of the death penalty, something not available to Massachusetts state prosecutors, as Massachusetts does not have the death penalty.

Double jeopardy
A constitutional prohibition against being tried twice for the same crime.

Note that being charged with both state and federal criminal violations does not raise double jeopardy concerns. **Double jeopardy** is a constitutional prohibition against being tried twice for the same crime. However, the courts have interpreted the "same crime" to refer to a violation of the same section of the same criminal code.

5. Summary

As we have seen, a legal problem could be governed by federal law, state law, or both. Keep the following three possibilities in mind:

> First, there are some areas in which only the states can legislate—areas reserved to the states—such as divorce.
> Second, there are some areas in which both the states and Congress can legislate—such as criminal behavior that crosses state lines.
> Third, there are a few areas in which only Congress can legislate—areas of total preemption—such as certain safety issues involving trains traveling across state lines.

---

[14] 18 USCA §2332a (West 2020). Under federal law, the type of bomb that Tsarnaev used would qualify as a "weapon of mass destruction," so long as its use also affected interstate commerce. This latter requirement was easily satisfied, as the annual Boston Marathon attracts runners and fans from all over the United States, and even the world. Their travel across state lines, as well as their spending millions of dollars at local hotels, restaurants, and stores, has a direct impact on interstate commerce.

DISCUSSION QUESTIONS

1. Can you think of any areas of the law that are not now regulated on a federal level but should be? Conversely, can you think of any areas of the law that should be left solely to state and local governments? If so, what are they, and why do you think the federal government should not be involved?

2. In 1970, the U.S. Congress passed the Controlled Substance Act (CSA), making it unlawful to manufacture, distribute, dispense, or possess any Schedule I substance. From then on, marijuana, or cannabis, has been a Schedule I substance, considered to have no acceptable medical use and a high potential for abuse. By 2020, 30 states had legalized marijuana for medical use, and 9 states had legalized marijuana for recreational purposes. How should our federal legal system resolve this conflict between federal and state laws? In 2018, the Food and Drug Administration (FDA) approved the first cannabis-based medication. How might this change the federal laws regarding marijuana in the future?

Legal Reasoning Exercise

1. For each situation, determine whether you think the law involved is federal, state, or both.

   a. A person is liable for slander if that person intentionally says that someone is a thief when she knows it is not true.
   b. To be valid, a contract for the sale of real estate must be in writing.
   c. Trucks traveling on interstate highways must be equipped with concave mud flaps.
   d. No employer with ten or more employees may discriminate on the basis of race, color, religion, sex, or national origin.
   e. A manufacturer of inherently dangerous products will be liable for any defective product that causes injury.

B. CRIMINAL VERSUS CIVIL LAW

Another major classification within the law is the division between criminal law and civil law. Both provide mechanisms for addressing violations of the law, but they differ regarding the procedures you must use and the types of sanctions or remedies that are available. In this section, we will first compare criminal and civil law. Next, we will take a quick look at the major substantive areas of criminal and civil law. We cover substantive civil law in more depth in Chapters 7, 10, and 11 and criminal law in Chapter 8.

1. A Comparison of Criminal and Civil Law

Some of the major differences between criminal and civil law are listed in Figure 4-3, on page 99. When you are analyzing a fact pattern, it is important to be able to differentiate between criminal and civil law and to understand the different procedures entailed in each.

While the Boston bombing case that started this chapter dealt mostly with criminal activities, civil lawsuits by the victims and their families were also a possibility. However, very few civil lawsuits were actually filed, partly because there was no reasonable expectation that Tsarnaev had the funds to pay for the harm he caused, and also, there was no evidence to suggest that anyone else was to blame based on theories such as failure to maintain adequate security.

a. Double Jeopardy and Res Judicata

Keep in mind that a single event can become the basis for actions in both the criminal and the civil courts. For example, the victim of a battery could sue the attacker for civil damages at the same time the state is prosecuting the attacker on a criminal charge. The driver of an automobile involved in a traffic accident may receive a traffic ticket from the police and at the same time be sued by someone else involved in the accident. In certain types of antitrust cases, the government can choose between seeking criminal charges and seeking civil damages.

In the prior section, we mentioned that being charged with a state crime and a federal crime does not constitute double jeopardy. Charging a person with a criminal violation and suing that person civilly also does not constitute double jeopardy.

Res judicata
Occurs when a civil case has a final judgment and is no longer subject to appeal; at that point, the case cannot be relitigated between the original parties.

Civil law has a principle similar to double jeopardy, **res judicata**, which precludes trying a civil case more than once.

b. Type of Harm

Civil law is invoked when one individual harms another. When an individual violates a part of the **criminal law,** society considers itself the offended party and takes an active role in the sanctioning process. Thus, if Peter Jones burglarizes Sam Smith's home, criminal law views that act as an offense against society itself, rather than simply as a matter between Smith and Jones.

But what determines when an act such as burglarizing someone's home is a wrong against society as a whole? It is up to the legislative branch of government to decide when the consequences of certain acts are viewed as grave enough to classify the act as a crime against the state. Thus, when the legislature perceives that a particular act, such as drunk driving, has that broader impact, it can criminalize such behavior.

Plaintiff
A person who initiates a lawsuit.

Prosecutor
A person representing the government who brings criminal charges and presents cases for criminal trial.

Defendant
In a lawsuit, the person who is sued; in a criminal case, the person who is being charged with a crime.

c. Names of the Parties and the "Prosecutor" of the Claim

The person who brings a civil suit (also known as a "civil action" or a "civil lawsuit") is known as the **plaintiff,** and the person sued is called the **defendant.** For example, recall the situation involving the pregnant waitress presented at the beginning of Chapter 3. If Diane Dobbs were to sue the restaurant, she would be the plaintiff. Both the corporation that owns the Western Rib Eye Restaurant and the restaurant manager would probably be named as defendants. Although civil suits are usually between individuals, a governmental unit (federal, state, or local) can become a plaintiff in a civil suit. In a criminal case, the governmental unit that brings the charge is the prosecutor, and the accused is the defendant. For example, in the Boston bombing case, the federal case would be cited as *United States v. Tsarnaev* and the Massachusetts state case as *Commonwealth v. Tsarnaev*. Governmental lawyers prosecute the accused party (the defendant), and the victim is a witness, not a party to the action.

d. Standard of Proof

Because of the serious consequences of violating criminal laws, the standard of proof is different from that used in civil cases. On the criminal side, the prosecution is required to prove its case **beyond a reasonable doubt**. Judges usually explain the "beyond a reasonable doubt" standard to jurors as the degree of doubt that causes a reasonable person to refrain from acting. The proof must be so conclusive and complete that all reasonable doubts regarding the facts are removed from the jurors' minds.

In most civil actions, the plaintiff need only meet the **preponderance of the evidence** standard. A preponderance of the evidence is usually understood to mean that the facts asserted are more likely to be true than not true. One study showed that judges equate "beyond a reasonable doubt" with a median probability of approximately 8.8 out of 10. Jurors averaged approximately 8.6 out of 10.

Beyond a reasonable doubt
The standard of proof used in criminal trials. The evidence presented must be so conclusive and complete that no reasonable doubts regarding the facts remain.

Preponderance of the evidence
The standard of proof most commonly used in civil trials. The evidence presented must prove that it is more likely than not the defendant committed the wrong.

	Civil	Criminal
Principle governing relitigation	Res judicata	Double jeopardy
Type of harm	Private injury	Harm to society
Names of the parties	Plaintiff/defendant	State*/defendant
"Prosecutor" of the claim	Usually an individual; sometimes the government	Government
Standard of proof	Preponderance of the evidence	Beyond a reasonable doubt
Judgment	Liable/not liable	Guilty/not guilty
Sanctions/remedies	Damages/injunction	Imprisonment/fines/death
Source of law	Common law/statutes	Statutes

*The state may also be referred to as "the Commonwealth" or "the People." Although the state is the named party, it is actually a government employee, the prosecutor (also known as the "district attorney," "state's attorney," or "attorney general"), who brings the lawsuit as the state's representative.

Figure 4-3   A Comparison of Civil and Criminal Law

The judges interpreted preponderance of the evidence as a median probability of 5.4 out of 10. For jurors, the median was 7.1 out of 10.[15] These results indicate that although judges and jurors may disagree as to the precise meaning of the standards, they agree that the criminal law requires a greater degree of proof before its sanctions can be applied.

Clear and convincing
The standard of proof used in some civil trials. The evidence presented must be greater than a preponderance of the evidence, but less than beyond a reasonable doubt.

There are a few occasions in which a higher, **"clear and convincing** evidence" standard, is used in civil actions. Examples include situations in which someone is being denied an important government benefit or is facing involuntary commitment to a mental institution. This standard is also used when a court has to determine whether to terminate a parent's rights. Generally, the state must prove the parent is "unfit" by clear and convincing evidence.

DISCUSSION QUESTIONS

3. What do you think of the differences between judges' and jurors' definitions of "beyond a reasonable doubt" and a "preponderance of the evidence"? Do you think this causes any problems for our legal system?

4. Think about the different standards of proof: beyond a reasonable doubt, preponderance of the evidence, and clear and convincing evidence.
   a. What factors do you think should be considered in determining which standard should be applied?
   b. Specifically, do you think that preponderance of the evidence is the appropriate standard when determining whether to terminate the parental rights of an "unfit" parent? Why?

5. On June 12, 1994, Nicole Brown Simpson and Ron Goldman were murdered in Los Angeles. The State of California charged Nicole Brown Simpson's ex-husband, O. J. Simpson, with the murders. After a lengthy trial, the jury found him not guilty. After the trial, the families of Nicole Brown Simpson and Ron Goldman sued O. J. Simpson for damages in civil court. O. J. Simpson was found responsible. Why did the two cases, on the same facts, have different results? Does this undermine our justice system? Why or why not?

e. Judgment

The result of the court's actions in a civil suit is a finding of liability or no liability. Do not use the term *guilty* when referring to a civil defendant. Only in a criminal case do we say that the defendant was found guilty or not guilty.

f. Sanctions/Remedies

Damages
Monetary compensation, including compensatory, punitive, and nominal damages.

Injunction
A court order requiring a party to perform a specific act or to cease doing a specific act.

The typical remedy in a civil case is either **damages,** where the defendant pays the plaintiff for the harm that he or she has done, or an **injunction,** where the court orders the defendant to take some specific action or to cease acting in a specific way. For example, a restaurant libeled by a newspaper might ask for damages to pay for lost business and an injunction ordering the paper to print a

---

[15] Simon & Mahan, *Quantifying Burdens of Proofs*, 5 L. & Soc'y. Rev. 319 (1971).

retraction. In the case of the waitress, Diane Dobbs, she might ask to be paid for the time she has been out of work (damages) and request a court order requiring the restaurant to rehire her (an injunction).

While the focus of civil law is on redressing the losses of the plaintiff, in criminal law the sanctions are designed to punish the offender and deter not only the offender but future offenders as well. If a court of law determines that a provision of criminal law has been violated, it may impose two broad types of sanctions—loss of liberty and financial penalty. The loss of liberty can range from receiving unsupervised probation to spending a few days in the county jail to serving several years in a state penitentiary to receiving the death penalty. The fines assessed as part of the criminal process become the property of the state rather than the victim. Only occasionally will a negotiated settlement with a criminal defendant contain some provisions for restitution for the victim. Usually, if the victim wishes to receive money from the criminal defendant to compensate her for the harm done to her, she must hire a lawyer and initiate a civil suit.

PRACTICE TIP

Even though we sometimes talk about civil versus criminal law, keep in mind that the same facts may give rise to both civil and criminal lawsuits. If a potential defendant in a civil case has been convicted at a criminal trial, it will be easier for the plaintiff to win a civil case. However, even if the defendant was acquitted at the criminal trial, because of the different standards of proof and evidentiary requirements the plaintiff may still win in a civil case.

g. Sources of Law

A final difference relates to the sources of criminal and civil law. Criminal law is almost entirely statutory, while civil law is rooted in the common law (court-made law). Gradually, however, this distinction is being eroded as more and more areas of the civil law are becoming controlled by statutory law.

h. Summary

Common ways of differentiating criminal from civil law include the following: In a civil case, the harm is to an individual, while in a criminal case, the action is said to harm society itself; in a civil case, the parties are labeled the plaintiff and the defendant, whereas in a criminal case, they are the state and the defendant; the government prosecutes criminal cases, while individual plaintiffs initiate civil cases; in a criminal case, the government must prove its case beyond a reasonable doubt, whereas in a civil case, the plaintiff must prove his or her case by a preponderance of the evidence; a finding of guilt in a criminal case results in a fine or imprisonment, while a finding of liability in a civil case results in a monetary award or an injunction; and the source of law for civil cases is both court-made law and statutes, whereas almost all criminal law is based in statutes.

2. Criminal Law

Murder, robbery, and arson are examples of criminal behavior. However, it is much easier to list types of criminal behavior than it is to define the difference between criminal and civil law. As mentioned earlier, usually it is said that a criminal act harms not just the victim, but also society as a whole. That definition does not get us very far. What is a wrong against society as a whole? One way of viewing that is to say that the act hurts not only the individual victim, but also society as a whole because the act's consequences are so grave as to cause concern to the rest of the population. When the legislature perceives that a particular act such as arson has that broader impact, it enacts a statute outlining the elements of the crime and its punishment.

a. Types of Crimes

Serious crimes, such as murder, rape, armed robbery, and aggravated assault, are classified as **felonies**, and they generally involve a punishment that can include a year or more in a state prison. **Misdemeanors** include such lesser charges as disorderly conduct and criminal damage to property. When incarceration is called for in these cases, it usually is for less than one year and is served in a county jail.

b. Establishing a Prima Facie Case

In order for a person to be convicted in a criminal trial, the prosecution must establish that the defendant committed an act defined as being illegal in the criminal code. This involves proving that the accused both had the requisite bad intent (called **mens rea**) and the requisite bad behavior (called **actus reus**). Different acts—killing someone, burning down a building, robbing a store—can give rise to different crimes. It is also true that the same act accompanied by different types of intent can give rise to different crimes. For example, the act of killing could be categorized as murder or manslaughter, depending on the defendant's state of mind when he or she committed the act.

At the trial, the prosecution must first present a **prima facie case**, one that establishes the elements of the crime, the requisite bad intent and bad behavior. A prima facie case contains enough evidence to support a finding of guilty if the defense presents no contrary evidence. If the prosecution fails to present a prima facie case, the judge must issue a not guilty verdict without the defense even presenting its case.

Mens rea
Bad intent.

Actus reus
Bad act.

Prima facie case
What the prosecutor or plaintiff must be able to prove in order for the case to go to the jury—that is, the elements of the prosecution's case or the plaintiff's cause of action.

Legal Reasoning Exercise

2. Take a moment to read the following Massachusetts statute regarding larceny.

Whoever steals . . . and with intent to steal . . . the property of another . . . shall be guilty of larceny. . . .[16]

    a. Assume that Alan got into a car, knowing that it was not his, "hot-wired" it, and then drove off in it. Is he guilty of violating the statute? Why?

    b. Assume that Bill approached a car that he intended to steal but was scared away by a passerby. Is he guilty of violating the statute? Why?

    c. Assume that Charles got into a car, thinking he was getting into his friend's car, and "hot-wired" it, but he only meant to borrow it. Is he guilty of violating the statute? Why?

c. Defenses

If the prosecution does present a prima facie case, the defense then has the opportunity to present evidence that either contradicts that presented by the prosecutor or establishes a legally recognized justification. This evidence could involve witnesses who contradict the testimony of prosecution witnesses or evidence that establishes an alibi, self-defense, or an insanity defense.

There are essentially two types of criminal **defenses**. The first type justifies the act. The second type negates the requisite mens rea. An example of the first type of defense, which justifies the act, is self-defense. The defendant admits killing the victim but argues that he or she had no choice. Examples of the second type of defense, which negates the requisite intent, are insanity, infancy, and intoxication. Each of these defenses has as its premise the fact that the defendant was incapable of forming the requisite intent to commit the crime.

Defense
In a criminal case, a fact or legal argument that would relieve the defendant of guilt.

After the defense has presented its evidence, the prosecution has a chance to respond with rebuttal witnesses to attack these defenses and reestablish the credibility of its own witnesses.

3. Civil Law

Civil law involves private actions brought by individuals to address perceived wrongs. In this section, we will discuss what is necessary to prove a civil prima facie case, the defenses to a civil suit, the damages that a plaintiff can recover, and the main areas of civil law.

[16] Mass. Gen. Laws ch. 266, §30(1) (2020).

a. Establishing a Prima Facie Case

Just as the prosecution has the burden of establishing a prima facie case in a criminal case, so too does the plaintiff share a similar burden in a civil case. The plaintiff has the burden of proving that the various elements listed in his or her complaint show the plaintiff has a valid **cause of action**. A cause of action is a claim that based on the law and the facts is sufficient to demand judicial action. The plaintiff must prove these elements by a preponderance of the evidence, which means it is more likely than not that the defendant committed the wrong.

Cause of action
A claim that based on the law and the facts is sufficient to support a lawsuit. If the plaintiff does not state a valid cause of action in the complaint, the court will dismiss it.

For example, assume that a car and a truck collide at an intersection. The driver of the car is injured and wants to sue the truck driver, alleging that the truck driver ran a red light. The car driver will be the plaintiff, and his cause of action will be based on the law of **negligence** (acting unreasonably under the circumstances) and the facts of what happened at the intersection. To succeed in a lawsuit, the plaintiff will have to present evidence that it is more likely than not that the truck driver was negligent. If the plaintiff/driver is able to do so, then he has satisfied his prima facie case. Every area of civil law has its own required elements that constitute the plaintiff's prima facie case. Later in this chapter, as you read about torts, contracts, and property law, note the requirements of each for the plaintiff to prove a prima facie case.

b. Defenses

The defendant/truck driver can respond first by trying to negate the plaintiff's case. Perhaps he has a witness who will testify that the light was green for the truck driver and red for the plaintiff. In addition to attempting to negate the plaintiff's case, the defendant can raise defenses of his own, known as **affirmative defenses**. In effect, the defendant is saying this: Even if you are right and I did something wrong, I have a good excuse or a reason why my liability should be reduced.

Affirmative defense
A defense whereby the defendant offers new evidence to avoid judgment.

For example, in the accident mentioned above, the truck driver might ask the car driver's passenger to testify that the car driver was not being as attentive to his driving as he should have been. This behavior could have contributed to the accident, thereby decreasing the defendant's share of the liability.

It is very important to keep these two approaches separate: First, the defendant tries to negate the plaintiff's case. Second, the defendant raises defenses that could limit his liability even if the plaintiff's version of the law and facts is true.

Depending on the area of law, different defenses will be available. For example, it might be a valid defense to a contract claim that the defendant was only 15 years old when he signed the contract. However, being 15 years old may not be a defense to an intentional tort, such as battery.

Sovereign immunity
The prohibition against suing the government without the government's consent.

In some cases, statutes or constitutions protect certain classes of people or institutions from being sued by granting them either full or partial immunity. One of the oldest and most important forms of immunity is **sovereign immunity**. Historically, the doctrine of sovereign immunity prohibited injured parties from suing the government unless the government gave its consent. This protection can be traced back to the concept of the divine right of kings and the idea that "the king can do no wrong." Later in this book, we also discuss the related concepts of spousal and parental immunity.

c. Damages

If a court determines that the plaintiff should recover, the issue of damages (monetary compensation) arises. There are three types of damages: compensatory, punitive, and nominal. **Compensatory damages** are intended to compensate the plaintiff for the harm done to her or him. In a tort action involving harm to a person, that might mean the cost of medical bills, lost time from work, and pain and suffering. **Punitive damages** are designed to punish the defendant and typically are awarded only for intentional torts when the court deems that the **tortfeasor** (the person who committed the tort) deserves additional punishment beyond just compensating the plaintiff for the harm done to him or her. Finally, **nominal damages** are awarded when the law has been violated, but the plaintiff cannot prove any monetary harm. As mentioned earlier, in addition to or instead of damages, the court might issue an injunctionan order to the defendant telling the defendant to do a specific act or to cease doing a specific act.

d. Areas of Civil Law

Civil law covers a very broad range of subjects, including adoption, admiralty, collections, corporate, divorce, employment, environmental, intellectual property, personal injury, probate, and real estate law. We believe it is helpful to think of civil law as falling into three main categories: making deals, owning property, and protecting people and property from harm. The most basic principles of each are covered in the standard law school courses of contracts, property, and torts, respectively. The various specialty fields listed above all involve applications of the principles taught in these three courses.

(1) Contract law

Contract law involves identifying the elements of a valid contract and the procedures used to enforce those agreements. A **contract** is a written or verbal agreement that is legally enforceable, supported by consideration. Therefore, contract law deals with two-sided agreements or bargains. I agree to sell you my diamond ring, and you agree to give me $500 in return. We have struck a bargain, entered into a contract. If something should go wrong—if I refuse to hand over the ring or you refuse to give me the money—we would find our actions governed by contract law.

For a contract to be valid, there must be an offer, an acceptance of the offer, and **consideration**; that is, something of value must be exchanged. It is the consideration that differentiates a contract from a gift. Common defenses to a contract action include breach by the other side and incapacity to contract, as when one party is underage. Questions raised in contract law include the following:

- ∎ When does a contract become enforceable?
- ∎ What is the difference between an offer and an invitation to negotiate?
- ∎ Under what circumstances can a mistake justify ending a contract?

We will cover the answers to these and other contract questions in Chapter 8.

Compensatory damages
Money awarded to a plaintiff in payment for his or her actual losses.

Punitive damages
Money awarded to a plaintiff in cases of intentional torts in order to punish the defendant and serve as a warning to others.

Tortfeasor
A person who commits a tort.

Nominal damages
A token sum awarded when liability has been found, but monetary damages cannot be shown.

Contract
A legally enforceable written or verbal agreement, supported by consideration.

Consideration
Something of value exchanged to form the basis of a contract.

(2) Property law

Property law is an area of the law that deals with the ownership and use of property. It covers topics such as the difference between **real property,** land and objects permanently attached to land, and **personal property,** all other property; the acquisition and disposition of property; and the use of property. Questions raised in property law involve issues such as:

- whether a room air conditioner should be treated as real or personal property;
- what types of materials can be copyrighted and what types of inventions can be patented; and
- under what circumstances the government can take private property for government use.

We will discuss these and additional property law topics in Chapter 10.

(3) Tort law

Issues of **tort law** arise when one person harms another person or that person's property. A tort is defined as a private wrong (other than a breach of contract) in which a person is harmed because of another's failure to carry out a legal duty. Through the common law the courts have defined legal duties as occasionally including the affirmative obligation to take action to protect others. More commonly, courts require that everyone refrain from taking actions that inflict harm on others. Torts are traditionally categorized as intentional, negligent, or the result of strict liability. Questions raised in tort law include the following:

- How do negligence laws vary from state to state?
- What is the difference between intentional torts and negligence?
- What remedies are available?

As the name indicates, an **intentional tort** occurs when someone deliberately harms a person or that person's property. If one of your classmates deliberately hits you, your classmate has committed the intentional tort known as battery. **Battery** is the intentional, harmful, or offensive physical contact by one person with another person. Libel, slander, invasion of privacy, and false imprisonment are other examples of intentional torts.

The most common category of tort law is that of **negligence,** the failure to act as a reasonably prudent and careful person is expected to act under the circumstances. This is known as the "reasonable person standard."

You are walking along the beach and see a young child drowning. No one else is in sight. Should the law require you to try to save the child? Should it matter if you are an off-duty lifeguard?

Property law
Law dealing with ownership of things, tangible and intangible, and land

Real property
Land and items growing on or permanently attached to that land.

Personal property
All property that is not real property.

Tort law
Law that involves harm to a person or a person's property.

Intentional tort
A tort committed by one who intends to do the act that creates the harm.

Negligence
The failure to act reasonably under the circumstances.

Case 6: Mr. Whipple

Mr. Whipple owns a grocery store. A customer breaks a bottle of apple juice and promptly reports it to Mr. Whipple. Nonetheless, Mr. Whipple fails to have the broken jar and spilled juice cleaned up. Another 20 minutes later, another customer slips on the wet floor, breaking her leg.

Mr. Whipple may be found liable for negligence. Clearly, he did not intend for the customer to slip and break her leg. Therefore, there was no intentional tort. But a jury might find that a reasonable store owner would have ordered the spill cleaned up within the 20 minutes after learning of it.

For a plaintiff to prove negligence, he or she must show that

1. the defendant owed the plaintiff a duty of care;
2. the defendant breached that duty; and
3. the breach caused
4. the plaintiff harm.

These four basic prerequisites (elements) in a negligence case are known as duty, breach, causation, and harm. In the case just mentioned Mr. Whipple had a duty to act as a reasonable store owner would under the circumstances. The circumstances were a broken jar of apple juice about which Mr. Whipple was informed and a 20-minute time period in which he did nothing. If the jurors believe Mr. Whipple breached his duty to act as a reasonable store owner, then they will find liability if they also think that breach caused the customer harm.

As the store owner, Mr. Whipple would, of course, try to defend himself through rebutting the plaintiff's evidence. Perhaps it had been only 2 and not 20 minutes since he learned of the spill. In addition, he might try to raise an affirmative defense. As mentioned previously, an affirmative defense is a defense whereby the defendant offers new evidence to avoid or limit the judgment. The two main affirmative defenses to negligence are **contributory negligence** and **assumption of the risk.** Contributory negligence means that the plaintiff was also negligent, and through that negligence contributed to his or her own injury. In Mr. Whipple's case, perhaps the customer was in a hurry and was not looking where she was going. Assumption of the risk means that the plaintiff voluntarily and knowingly subjected himself or herself to a known danger. Perhaps the customer saw the spilled juice but chose to walk through it anyway. In many states, assumption of the risk is no longer a separate defense to negligence, as it has been subsumed under the more general category of contributory negligence.

Historically, any showing of contributory negligence or assumption of the risk meant that the plaintiff could recover nothing from the defendant even if the

Contributory negligence
Negligence by the plaintiff that contributed to his or her injury. Normally, any finding of contributory negligence acts as a complete bar to a plaintiff's recovery.

Assumption of the risk
Voluntarily and knowingly subjecting oneself to danger.

Comparative negligence
A method for measuring the relative negligence of the plaintiff and the defendant, with a commensurate decrease in the compensation for the injuries.

Strict liability
Liability without a showing of fault.

defendant's actions were much more culpable than those of the plaintiff. Only five states currently continue to allow this pure contributory negligence defense. Most states now allow some variation of the **comparative negligence** defense. Under comparative negligence, instead of the plaintiff's own negligence relieving the defendant of liability, the jury compares the negligence of the plaintiff to that of the defendant and apportions the responsibility. The plaintiff's recovery is reduced by his or her degree of negligence.

The third category of tort law is called **strict liability.** In some cases, persons or corporations can be held liable for injuries that resulted from their actions, even when their actions were reasonable under the circumstances and they did not intend to harm anyone. The doctrine of strict liability holds that persons who engage in activities that are inherently dangerous are responsible for any injury that results, even though they carried out the activities in the safest and most prudent way possible. For example, someone who uses explosives or who keeps wild animals is liable for all resulting injuries, even if that person used the utmost care. In recent years, many courts have held manufacturers and sellers to be strictly liable when a defective product the defendant manufactured or sold caused harm to the user or consumer, even when the user or consumer could not show that the manufacturer's negligence caused the defect.

We will discuss tort law in greater detail in Chapter 7.

Legal Reasoning Exercises

3. For each question, decide whether the facts raise an issue of tort, contract, or property law, or more than one area of law.

   a. You buy a new car. Two days later, as you are driving, the brakes fail and you go off the road, hitting a telephone pole. Luckily you are unhurt, but the car is badly damaged.

   b. You rent an apartment. One night, as you are leaving the building through the central stairway, the railing gives way and you fall, breaking your leg.

   c. You agree to purchase a bicycle from your neighbor for $50. The next day, your neighbor decides not to sell you the bike.

   d. You put in an offer for a house. A week later, you have a pest inspection and discover that the house is infested with active termites.

   e. You are riding your bicycle in the middle of the afternoon on a dedicated bike path. While you are riding, someone runs over to you and pushes you and your bike, causing you to crash.

4. For each of the following situations, decide if you think liability should be found based on an intentional tort, negligence, or strict liability, or whether no liability should be found.

   a. Sally was angry with Martha. One night after leaving class, she deliberately drove her car into the side of Martha's car.

   b. One night after leaving class, Sally was in a hurry. When she arrived at the stop sign at the student parking lot entrance to

> Main Street, she did a "rolling stop." Martha was driving by on Main Street. Sally's car hit the side of Martha's car.
>
> c. One night after leaving class, Sally got into her brand-new Dodge van. When she arrived at the stop sign at the student parking lot entrance to Main Street, she pressed on the brakes, but nothing happened. Martha was driving by on Main Street. Sally's van hit the side of Martha's car.
>
> d. One night after leaving class, Sally got into her car. When she arrived at the stop sign at the student parking entrance to Main Street, she suddenly got a tremendous cramp in her side and momentarily lost control of her car. Martha was driving by on Main Street. Sally's car hit the side of Martha's car.

C. SUBSTANTIVE VERSUS PROCEDURAL LAW

Finally, law can also be classified as either substantive or procedural. **Substantive law** refers to the laws that define our rights and duties. It defines what actions will violate criminal law and what our obligations are in civil law. For example, substantive law includes the statutes that govern the legal speed limits, the circumstances under which someone can be convicted of robbery, and when a contract is enforceable. **Procedural law,** on the other hand, deals with how the legal system operates. For example, it specifies such things as which types of cases have to be filed in which courts and what has to be included in those court documents. It defines the procedures the police must follow in conducting a search or interrogating a suspect. Further examples are included in Figure 4-4.

Substantive law
Law that creates rights and duties.

Procedural law
Law that regulates how the legal system operates.

Every case is founded in substantive law, and lawyers must determine what their client's obligations and liabilities are. However, they must be equally aware of the procedural aspects of the case. For example, even if the substantive law is on the client's side, the case may be lost if a claim is not filed within the time prescribed in the **statute of limitations,** a limitation imposed by the legal system on how much time a plaintiff has before he or she can no longer bring suit. Those limitations vary given the type of case involved. A plaintiff could also lose if the complaint, the initial document that starts a lawsuit, fails to include all the required information.

Statute of limitations
The law that sets the length of time from when something happens to when a lawsuit must be filed before the right to bring it is lost.

We have all heard of the criminal who was set free due to a "technicality." These rules of criminal procedure have their roots in the Constitution and are intended to protect the innocent from the overreaching of possibly overzealous law enforcement officials. These rules govern everything from the way in which the arresting police officer must inform a suspect of his or her rights to how evidence is introduced at trial. For example, in the Boston bombing case, one of the first procedural issues that arose was the question of whether it was proper for federal agents to question Dzhokhar Tsarnaev for 16 hours before reading him his Miranda rights.[17]

We will discuss civil procedure in more detail in Chapter 6, and criminal procedure in more depth in Chapter 9.

---

[17]The government argued that it was appropriate and not a violation of Tsarnaev's rights under a "public safety" exception.

	Substantive	Procedural
Definition	Creates rights and duties	Regulates how the legal system operates
Civil Law Examples	*Requirements of an enforceable contract. *Negligence is acting unreasonably. *A gift requires offer, acceptance, and delivery.	*The statute of limitations for tort actions is usually two years. *A complaint must state the grounds for the lawsuit. *Only claims worth up to a certain dollar amount can be filed in small claims court.
Criminal Law Examples	*Murder is the unlawful killing of a human being. *Burglary is the breaking and entering of a dwelling at nighttime. *Self-defense is the justified use of force to protect oneself or others.	*A person cannot be tried twice for the same crime. *The necessity for a search warrant. *Requirement to read a suspect Miranda rights.

Figure 4-4   A Comparison of Substantive and Procedural Law

Legal Reasoning Exercise

5. Review the hypothetical case of the pregnant waitress that began Chapter 3. How would you categorize Diane's legal problems?

SUMMARY

In this chapter, we have seen how lawyers categorize law as either state or federal, civil or criminal, and substantive or procedural. The first category, state or federal, arises because the United States operates under a system of federalism. Under our federal system, governmental authority is split between the national government and the 50 state governments. Some areas of the law, such as divorce, are reserved exclusively to the states; some are reserved to the federal government; and some are shared by the states and the federal government. If you are in doubt as to which law applies, check state law first. Federal law will be involved only if the U.S. Constitution, a federal statute, or a federal regulation is involved.

Civil law involves harm to an individual, while criminal law deals with harms to society as a whole. In both criminal and civil cases, the party with the burden of proof must first establish a prima facie case. Once that is established, the other side is given the opportunity to negate the prima facie case or to raise affirmative defenses. While the law has become increasingly specialized, the main areas of civil law are contracts, property, and torts. Tort law can be further subdivided into those involving intentional acts, those based on negligent behavior, and those that result from an imposition of strict liability.

Finally, substantive law defines our rights and duties. Procedural law deals with how the legal system operates.

REVIEW QUESTIONS

Pages 89 through 97
1. What are the three major ways in which lawyers categorize the law?
2. What is federalism?
3. True or false: Every state must have the same laws regarding divorce. Why?
4. What does it mean to say that the federal government is a government of limited powers?
5. Do you think Congress could (not should) enact a national divorce statute? Why?
6. Why are some areas of the law preempted by the federal government?

Pages 97 through 102
6. Name at least four ways in which civil law differs from criminal law.
7. When is the burden of proof "beyond a reasonable doubt" and when is it a "preponderance of the evidence"? What is the difference between them?
8. In a civil case, if a jury is evenly split, leaning equally toward the plaintiff's and the defendant's views of the facts, who will win, the plaintiff or the defendant? Why?

Pages 102 through 105
9. What two basic elements must be established for the government to prove the prima facie case in a criminal case?
10. Why can the same act constitute several different crimes?
11. What are the two basic defenses to a criminal action?
12. In a criminal case, does the government or the defendant present its case first? Why?
13. What is the general definition of a civil cause of action?
14. In a civil case, does the plaintiff or the defendant present its case first? Why?
15. What are the three types of damages available in a civil case?
16. In addition to damages, what might a plaintiff seek in a civil case?

Pages 105 through 109
17. What must be present for a contract to be valid?
18. What is the basic difference between a contract and a gift?
19. What is the difference between real property and personal property?
20. What are the three main areas of tort law?
21. Give the general definition of negligence, and list the elements necessary to prove a prima facie case.
22. What are the main defenses to negligence?

Pages 109 through 111

23. What is the difference between substantive and procedural law?

24. What is the function of a statute of limitations?

ⅢⅢ WEB EXERCISES

1. In May 2009, soon after Barack Obama took office, several newspapers, including the *Washington Post*, reported that he had issued a memorandum to federal agency heads regarding the prior administration's approach to federal regulations preempting state laws. Use Google, or another search engine of your choice, to read the memorandum, and then locate one of those news articles. According to the article you found, what were President Obama's views regarding federal preemption versus state's rights? Do you agree with that policy, or do you think that the U.S. Chamber of Commerce's position that this policy could "wreak havoc on businesses" is more accurate?

2. View a video showing examples of violence in professional hockey at *www.youtube .com/watch?v=VjSEflGUKNk&feature=related*. Based on what you have read in this chapter about the differences between civil and criminal law, if one of the hockey players was seriously hurt, do you think you would be viewing an example of a violation of civil or criminal law, or neither? Why? Would your answer be different if instead of a player, one of the referees or a fan had been hurt? Assuming there is the basis for a civil lawsuit, what area of civil law would be involved? What types of damages do you think would be appropriate?

Chapter 5

Courts

Trial courts search for truth and appellate courts search for error.
Unknown

Chapter Objectives

After reading this chapter, you should be able to:

- Categorize courts as either trial or appellate.
- Distinguish between questions of law and questions of fact.
- List the major courts in the federal system.
- Describe a typical state court system.
- Explain the concept of jurisdiction.

Court
A unit of the judicial branch of government that has authority to decide legal disputes.

Jurisdiction
The power of a court to hear particular types of cases or to hear cases within a specific geographic area.

INTRODUCTION

Now that we have identified the functions, sources, and classifications of law, we turn our attention to the manner in which the judicial system enforces the law. Although the law provides rules about how people should behave in different types of situations, these rules are not self-enforcing. It is to the courts and the judicial system that we must turn for interpretation and enforcement of the law.

A **court** is a unit of the judicial branch of government that has authority to decide legal disputes. However, depending on the nature of the dispute, only certain courts will have jurisdiction to hear the case. **Jurisdiction** refers to the power of a court to hear a particular type of case or to hear cases within a specific geographic area.

113

We will begin by describing how courts are classified as either trial or appellate and either federal or state, but before we do so, please read over Case 7.

Case 7: Alibi to a Murder

Frederick Jones could not believe it when he was arrested for murder, because he thought he had an ironclad alibi.

At his trial, an elderly gentleman testified that he saw Jones near the scene of the murder shortly after it took place. At one point in the trial, over the objection of the defendant's lawyer, the prosecutor showed the jury bloody and gruesome pictures of the deceased victim.

Jones testified that not only did he *not* commit the murder, but that he was attending an out-of-town wedding at the time the murder was supposed to have taken place. Ten witnesses then took the stand in succession and testified that they had been at the wedding and seen the defendant there

At the end of the trial, the jury convicted Jones. As he had so many witnesses testifying as to his whereabouts on the night of the murder, Jones could not understand how the jury could possibly have found him guilty, so he wants his lawyer to appeal his case.

As you read this chapter, think about:

■ the differing roles of the trial and appellate courts, and
■ if you were Jones's lawyer, on what grounds do you think you would base an appeal of his conviction?

A. TRIAL VERSUS APPELLATE COURTS

One major way of classifying courts is in terms of whether they are trial or appellate courts. Most court cases begin in a **trial court**.[1] Sometimes the losing party is able to appeal what it sees as an error of law (but not of fact) to the appropriate **appellate court**. In this section, we will discuss the differences between trial and appellate courts and between questions of fact and questions of law.

1. Trial Courts

Trial courts
Courts that determine the facts and apply the law to the facts.

Trial courts are said to be courts of **original jurisdiction** because trial courts are where actions are initiated and heard for the first time. In addition to conducting trials, much of a trial court's time is spent in far less dramatic proceedings, such as receiving plea agreements and ratifying out-of-court settlements. When a trial is held, the lawyers present witness testimony and other evidence. After considering the evidence and the lawyers' arguments, trial courts have two functions. First, they must determine whose version of the facts is most credible. Second,

Original jurisdiction
The authority of a court to hear a case when it is initiated, as opposed to appellate jurisdiction.

---

[1] The primary exception to this pattern occurs when a dispute is adjudicated in an administrative agency and then appealed to the courts. In very rare circumstances, a case can be filed directly with the U.S. Supreme Court under its original jurisdiction.

they must apply the law to those facts to reach a decision. Therefore, trial courts must determine both questions of fact and questions of law.

Questions of fact relate to the determination of what took place: who, what, when, where, and how. **Questions of law** relate to how the law is interpreted and applied and include such issues as how a statute is to be interpreted and whether a specific piece of evidence is admissible.

In most cases that go to trial, the meaning of the law is clear but the facts themselves are very much in dispute. For example, under the criminal codes of most states, it is a violation of the law for a person to forcibly take someone else's property without the owner's permission—a crime called robbery. When someone is tried for robbery, the trial usually focuses on such factual questions as the identification of the alleged robber and the ownership of the property taken.

Although the primary focus of most trials is on factual issues, legal issues are involved as well. In the example cited above, the judge may have to interpret what the word "forcibly" means. The judge will also have to decide if certain testimony or evidence is admissible. These are questions of law. If the judge decides that the testimony or evidence is not admissible, then the trial proceeds without it. Also, if the judge rules that a search was illegal or that disputed pictures are too prejudicial, then the objects discovered in that search or the pictures are not admitted as evidence. Based on the evidence that has been allowed, the jury then resolves the questions of fact.

Consider the following example. In most states, it is a crime for someone other than a physician, pharmacist, or other authorized medical person to sell or distribute narcotic drugs. When someone is on trial for selling narcotics, the prosecution must present evidence that shows the accused did in fact sell a substance that fits the legal definition of a prohibited narcotic drug. These are issues of fact. The evidence often consists of an undercover police agent testifying that the accused sold the agent a substance that laboratory reports identify as a narcotic.

It is possible, however, that the defendant might admit to selling the drug, but then claim **entrapment.** The entrapment doctrine prohibits law enforcement officers from instigating criminal acts to lure otherwise innocent persons into committing a crime. One question of fact relating to the entrapment defense is whether the defendant ever committed such a criminal act or thought of committing such an act before. However, in addition to the factual questions, and depending on the circumstances of a given case, a legal issue of what constitutes entrapment could arise. For example, assume that government agents supplied the defendant with a drug and then later arrested him for selling the very same drug to another government agent. Here, no one would be disputing what happened (the facts). But an appellate court could be asked to decide whether such actions legally qualify as entrapment. In *Hampton v. United States,*[2] the U.S. Supreme Court held that so long as the defendant is predisposed to commit the crime, it is not entrapment when government agents supply the defendant with a drug and then later arrest him for selling the very same drug to another government agent.

It is not always easy to determine if something is a question of fact or a question of law. Because appellate courts will rule only on issues involving

Questions of fact
Questions relating to what happened: who, what, when, where, and how.

Questions of law
Questions relating to the interpretation or application of the law.

Entrapment
A defense requiring proof that the defendant would not have committed the crime but for police trickery.

---

[2] 425 U.S. 484 (1976).

questions of law, appellate judges determine what they will treat as a question of law. To illustrate the nature of the problem, let us consider the situation presented in Case 7, set out at the beginning of the chapter. Do you think there is any basis for launching an appeal in Jones's case? Remember that a losing party can only appeal questions of law.

It is a question of fact whether on the night of the murder, Jones was present at the scene of the murder (as testified to by one elderly witness) or out of town attending a wedding (as testified to by ten other witnesses). Therefore, his whereabouts on the night of the murder cannot form the basis for an appeal.

On the other hand, it is a question of law as to whether the judge should have allowed the jury to see pictures of the victim's bloody corpse. It can be argued that the viewing of those pictures was so inflammatory as to prejudice the jury. Therefore, the showing of the pictures could form the basis of an appeal. Keep in mind that this does not mean that Jones would win at the appellate level. It simply means that he will be given the opportunity to argue his case to the appellate court.

Legal Reasoning Exercises

1. It is not always easy to know whether something is a question of fact or a question of law. In fact, there have been cases when the issue on appeal was whether something was a question of fact or a question of law. That question is itself a question of law. To see how that can happen, assume that there was a negligence trial in which a grocer was sued when a customer slipped and fell. The customer testified that she slipped on a banana peel in the produce section. The grocery store owner testified that when he came to the assistance of the customer, there was no peel on the floor. One of the store employees also testified that he had mopped the floor in that area just five minutes before the accident, and that there were no banana peels on the floor. Nonetheless, the jury found the store liable. Can the store appeal on the grounds that it was telling the truth and the customer was lying? No. Why? Because that is a question of fact, and factual determinations generally cannot be appealed. But can the store appeal on the grounds that the jury should not have found that it acted negligently because even if there were a banana peel, such hazards are to be expected in the produce section, and the store had done all it could to make the area safe? Is that issue—that is, whether the store acted as a reasonable store should—a question of fact or a question of law?

2. In the following cases, do you think the losing party has a valid basis for appeal? Why?

　　a. A prosecutor commented on a defendant's failure to take the stand in his own defense. His lawyer argued that this violated his client's constitutional right to remain silent. The defendant was convicted.

b. The prosecutor introduced evidence showing that the defendant purposely set fire to his neighbor's garage. This included testimony by the fire chief and a forensic scientist who examined the remains of the burned building. The defendant took the stand and claimed that the fire was an accident. The jury convicted the defendant of intentionally starting the fire.

c. John signed a will in front of two witnesses. The will made no provision for his son, Jimmy. When John died, Jimmy contested the will, arguing that his father was not of sound mind. At the trial, the two witnesses present at the signing testified that John had been legally competent when he signed the will. The court found that the will was valid.

d. June was walking her miniature poodle, Suzy, in her front yard. Suddenly a German Shepherd leaped over the fence and bit Suzy several times, killing her. June was distraught and sued the owner of the German Shepherd for $30,000 for her pain and suffering. The trial judge dismissed the case, stating that as Suzy was property, the most June could recover was the cost of a new dog.

In a **jury trial,** questions of fact are determined by the jury, while questions of law are determined by the judge. If it is a **bench trial** rather than a jury trial, the judge will decide the factual questions as well as the legal ones.

Bench trial
A trial conducted without a jury.

2. Appellate Courts

Appellate courts, usually working in a panel of three or more judges, review alleged trial court errors (and, in some cases, the actions of administrative agencies) to determine whether the law was correctly interpreted and applied. When the person who loses in a trial court is able to appeal the decision to an appellate court, that party (the one filing the appeal) is called the **appellant** or the **petitioner.** The party who won in the trial court is called the **appellee** or the **respondent.** It is important to note that most states and the federal government provide for only one appeal as a matter of right. Additional appeals are usually at the discretion of the higher court.

Appellate courts
Courts that determine whether lower courts have made errors of law.

Appellant or petitioner
The party in a case who has initiated an appeal.

a. Questions of Law

Unlike trial courts, appellate courts do not hear testimony. They rely on the written record of what occurred in the trial to determine whether the trial court made an error regarding the law. They do so because when conducting a review, appellate courts limit themselves to "legal" as opposed to "factual" issues that are specifically raised by the party who is bringing the appeal. Therefore, you can appeal a lower court decision only when you raise a valid legal issue. Appellate courts will not reconsider the facts; they will consider only whether the trial court made an error of law.

Appellee or respondent
The party in a case against whom an appeal has been filed.

Legal issues can arise in three ways:

- They can involve interpretation of the meaning of the laws that underlie the cause of action (e.g., whether entrapment had occurred).
- They can involve the manner in which the trial was conducted. Examples include whether a particular piece of evidence should be excluded because it is the product of an illegal search and seizure, whether the plaintiff's lawyer should be allowed to pursue a certain line of questioning, whether the judge should present a particular set of instructions to the jury, or whether prejudicial publicity has tainted the defendant's trial.
- They can involve challenges to the constitutionality of the law that is being applied. For example, a doctor charged with performing an illegal abortion could argue that the law he is charged with violating is itself unconstitutional.

b. Reversible Errors

There is one limited exception to the rule that appellate courts review only questions of law. Occasionally, the courts will review a case when it is alleged that no "reasonable" jury could have reached the verdict they did. This is extremely rare, however, as normally appellate courts will accept a jury's determination as to which witnesses and evidence were most credible.

In Case 7 at the beginning of the chapter, Jones' lawyer may try to appeal on the facts of the case rather than the law. Jones had ten witnesses testify that Jones was at a wedding and the prosecutor had only one witness testify that Jones was at the scene of the crime. In this instance, the appeals court is likely to find that since the prosecutor had a witness testify as to Jones' whereabouts, that the jury was within its purview to find that the prosecutor's one witness was simply more credible than the defendant's ten witnesses.

If the appellate court determines that no legal error occurred, the court will **affirm** the lower court's decision. In addition, if a legal error occurred but the court determines that it was minor and did not affect the result, the court labels it a **harmless error** and allows the decision to stand. However, if the court finds that a significant legal error was made in the way that the trial was conducted, it will usually cancel the original outcome by **reversing** the trial court's decision. It may also **remand** the case, returning it to the trial court for further consideration.

In criminal cases, when a court reverses a conviction and remands the case, it does not necessarily mean that the defendant will go free, as the government then has the option of retrying the case. However, if the basis for the reversal was the appellate court ruling that a key piece of evidence was inadmissible, the government may choose not to retry the defendant because it may feel that its case is too weak without the excluded evidence.

If the government chooses to proceed with a new trial, this does not violate the constitutional provision regarding **double jeopardy**. Double jeopardy occurs when a person is tried more than once for the same criminal offense. The Fifth and Fourteenth Amendments to the U.S. Constitution prohibit various forms of double jeopardy. However, when a defendant voluntarily appeals a conviction, he or she waives the right not to be retried for the same crime.

Affirm
When the higher court agrees with what the lower court has done.

Harmless error
A trial court error that is not sufficient to warrant reversing the decision.

Reverse
A decision is reversed when the litigants appeal the lower court decision and the higher court disagrees with the decision of a lower court.

Remand
When an appellate court sends a case back to the trial court for a new trial or another action.

c. The Structure of Appellate Decisions

Appellate court judges reach their decisions by majority vote. Someone from the majority writes the **majority opinion** explaining the court's decision and how that decision was reached. In cases where the decision is not unanimous, judges may also write concurring or dissenting opinions to explain the nature of their disagreements. In a **concurring opinion,** the judge agrees with the result reached by the majority, but not with its reasoning. In a **dissenting opinion,** the judge disagrees with the result and with the reasoning.

Majority opinion
An opinion in which a majority of the court joins.

Concurring opinion
An opinion that agrees with the majority's result but disagrees with its reasoning.

Dissenting opinion
An opinion that disagrees with the majority's decision and its reasoning.

3. Conclusion

In summary, there are several major differences between trial and appellate courts. As we noted in Chapter 4, at the trial-court level, the parties are called the plaintiff and the defendant in a civil case and the state and the defendant in a criminal case. At the appellate-court level, the party who lost in the trial court is called either the appellant or the petitioner, while the party who won is called either the appellee or the respondent. In the trial court, the jury decides the facts and the judge determines the law. In a bench trial, the judge serves as both the finder of fact and determiner of the law. In the appellate court, a panel of three or more judges decides questions of law based on the lawyers' briefs (written arguments) and oral arguments. No witnesses give testimony in appellate court, and there are no juries. The judges merely review the trial transcript and the written briefs from the lawyers. Sometimes oral arguments from the opposing lawyers are heard, during which the judges have an opportunity to pose questions. Lower-level appellate judges usually work in rotating panels of three, while in the upper-level appellate courts, all the judges jointly decide each case.

Most of these differences are directly related to the most important distinction between trial and appellate courts: Trial courts determine the facts and apply the law to those facts; appellate courts deal only with questions of law. Three basic types of legal questions can arise at the appellate level. First are those that relate to the meaning of the underlying legal cause of action or defense, such as what qualifies as entrapment. Second, legal issues can arise that have nothing to do with the underlying legal claim, but rather relate to how the trial was conducted. Finally, one of the parties can argue that the law being applied is unconstitutional, as when a doctor challenges an abortion law. Figure 5-1 summarizes the differences between trial and appellate courts.

DISCUSSION QUESTIONS

1. Do you think it is a good or a bad idea that only questions of law can be appealed?

2. Can you think of a situation when an appellate judge might reverse and remand a case? How about when a judge might reverse but not remand a case?

B. FEDERAL AND STATE COURT SYSTEMS

Trial and appellate courts exist in both the federal and the state court systems. At first glance, the federal and state judicial systems of this country present a confusing mixture of titles and functions. In large part, this is because there are actually 51 different court systems (the federal system, plus one for each state). To complicate matters, the same types of courts often have different names. For example, the basic trial court is called the court of common pleas in Pennsylvania, the district court in Minnesota, the circuit court in Illinois, the superior court in California, and the supreme court in New York. Although New York uses the "supreme court" designation for its trial courts, most states reserve that title for their highest appellate court.

It is in the state courts where most legal business is conducted. However, we begin our discussion with an examination of the federal court system because it is uniform throughout the country. Although the diversity among state court systems prevents us from covering them in any detail, we will point out some of the common patterns. For example, most state courts follow the federal pattern of being organized on three levels: the trial courts, the intermediate appellate courts, and one appellate court of last resort.

1. The Federal System

Inferior courts
In the federal system, all courts other than the U.S. Supreme Court.

The structure for the federal court system is set forth in the U.S. Constitution. Article III, Section 1, provides that "[t]he judicial Power of the United States, shall be vested in one supreme Court, and in such inferior Courts as the Congress may from time to time ordain and establish." Those **inferior courts** are the district courts and courts of appeals. Congress established the first inferior courts through the Judiciary Act of 1789. That act provided for 13 districts and

Figure 5-1   A Comparison of Trial and Appellate Courts

	Trial Court	Appellate Court
Parties' names	Plaintiff/defendant State/defendant	Appellant/appellee or petitioner/respondent
Decision maker	Judge and sometimes a jury	Majority vote of three or more judges
Attorney arguments	Yes	Yes
Witness testimony	Yes	No
Evidence introduced	Yes	No
Questions of fact decided	Yes	No
Questions of law decided	Yes	Yes

3 circuits. Over the years, Congress has increased the number of both district and federal circuits. Figure 5-2 shows how cases flow through these three types of federal **constitutional courts:**

- **U.S. District Courts:** These trial courts are organized into 94 different districts located throughout the 50 states, the District of Columbia, and U.S. territories. (See Figure 5-3, which shows district court boundaries.)
- **U.S. Courts of Appeals:** These first-level appellate courts are organized into 12 regional circuits and hear appeals from the district courts located within the circuit. They also hear appeals from decisions of federal administrative agencies. (Figure 5-3 also shows circuit court boundaries.)
- **U.S. Supreme Court:** This is the highest court in the federal system. At its discretion, and within certain guidelines established by Congress, it hears a limited number of the cases involving the most important constitutional issues and conflicts among the circuits. In addition to reviewing decisions of the U.S. Courts of Appeals, it can review decisions of state courts if they involve important questions about the Constitution or federal law.

Article II of the Constitution gives the president the power to appoint the judges who serve on these federal courts. But before an appointment can become final, the Senate must confirm it. Article III, Section 1, provides that "[t]he Judges,

Constitutional courts
A court established by Article III of the U.S. Constitution.

U.S. district courts
The general jurisdiction trial courts in the federal system.

U.S. courts of appeals
The intermediate appellate courts in the federal system.

U.S. Supreme Court
The highest federal appellate court, consisting of nine appointed members.

Figure 5-2 The Federal Court System

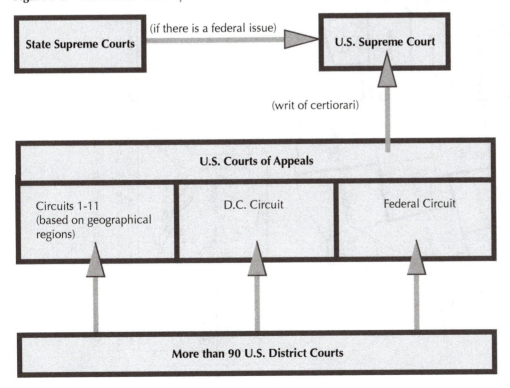

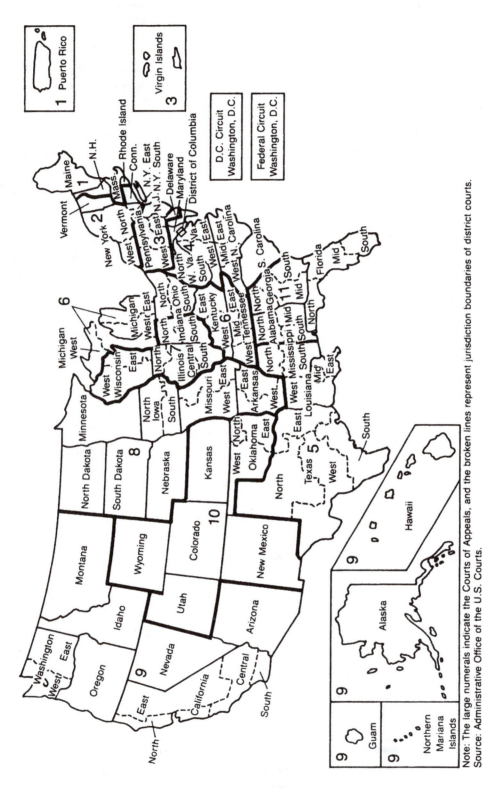

Figure 5-3   District and Circuit Court Boundaries

Note: The large numerals indicate the Courts of Appeals, and the broken lines represent jurisdiction boundaries of district courts.
Source: Administrative Office of the U.S. Courts.

both of the supreme and inferior Courts, shall hold their Offices during good Behaviour, and shall, at stated Times, receive for their Services, a Compensation, which shall not be diminished during their Continuance in Office." This means that "constitutional" judges are guaranteed lifetime tenure unless they resign or are impeached and are protected from any salary reductions.

a. U.S. District Courts

The U.S. District Courts are the trial courts in the federal system. Within limits set by Congress and the Constitution, the district courts have jurisdiction to hear nearly all categories of federal cases, including both civil and criminal matters.

The number of judges assigned to each district varies from 2 to 28 depending on the caseload of the district. Usually, cases are heard by a single judge or a judge and a jury. In criminal cases, the default is a jury trial unless the defendant requests a bench trial. In civil cases, a bench trial is the default. One of the parties must request a jury in the pleadings or else the right to a jury is waived.

The district court judges are assisted by **magistrate judges**. The magistrate judges supervise court calendars, hear procedural motions, issue **subpoenas**, hear minor criminal offenses, and conduct civil pretrial hearings. In some district courts, the magistrate judges, with the consent of the parties involved, conduct trials and enter judgments in civil cases. They are selected by a majority of the active judges in each district for full-time terms of eight years or part-time terms of four years. They can be removed for cause.

Magistrate judge
A court official who exercises limited judicial powers such as issuing subpoenas, conducting preliminary hearings, and ruling on procedural motions.

Subpoena
A court order requiring a person to appear to testify at a trial or deposition.

b. U.S. Courts of Appeals (Circuit Courts)

If a litigant wants to appeal a district court decision, the appeal must be filed with the U.S. Court of Appeals for the circuit within which the district court operates. For example, cases from California district courts are appealed to the Court of Appeals for the Ninth Circuit.

Each of the 12 regular circuits has from 6 to 29 judges. In the federal courts of appeals, cases are usually heard by a panel of 3 judges randomly selected from that Court of Appeals. Decisions in the cases are based on a majority vote of the judges on the panel. Occasionally, all the judges sit together and decide a case **en banc.** This happens most frequently when the losing party in a case already decided by a panel of the court requests a rehearing before the full membership of the court.

En banc
When an appellate court that normally sits in panels sits as a whole.

c. U.S. Supreme Court

Sitting at the top of the federal judicial system is the U.S. Supreme Court. The Court is composed of nine justices, who hear all appeals as a group. It is interesting to note that the Judiciary Act of 1789, mentioned above, provided for a Supreme Court with one chief justice and five associate justices. As with the number of courts, the number of Supreme Court justices has also changed over the years as the volume of the Court's work has increased.

A case seldom goes any further than a court of appeals, as the U.S. Supreme Court has the power to choose which cases it wants to hear from among the

Writ of certiorari
A means of gaining appellate review; in the U.S. Supreme Court, the writ is discretionary and will be issued to another court to review a federal question if four of the nine justices vote to hear the case.

thousands of cases brought to it every year. Most of the cases come to the Court as a petition for a **writ of certiorari.**[3] In this petition, the losing party does not argue the merits of the case but rather asks the Supreme Court to review the case. At least four of the nine justices must agree to grant *cert* before the case will be placed on the Court's docket. If there are not at least four votes to review, it is simply announced that *cert* was denied, without any further explanation. The denial of *cert* does not mean that the Court agrees with the lower court's decision. It simply means that the Court does not want to hear that case. The Supreme Court usually hears no more than 80 of the approximately 7,000 to 8,000 requests that it receives each year. An additional 100 or more cases are decided without oral arguments.

Unlike the U.S. Courts of Appeals, where cases are typically heard by a panel of three judges, the U.S. Supreme Court always considers cases en banc. Unless there is a vacancy on the Court or a justice has chosen not to participate in the decision in a case,[4] all nine justices vote on every case the Court hears. With the exception of the decision to review or not review a case, the outcome is decided by a majority of the justices participating. In situations where there is a tie vote, the lower court's decision is left unchanged.

NETNOTE

The official website of the federal judiciary is *www.uscourts.gov*. It contains links to the U.S. Supreme Court, the U.S. courts of appeals, the U.S. district courts, and the U.S. bankruptcy courts. The U.S. Supreme Court's site, at *www.supremecourt.gov,* contains helpful information on the Court's procedures and its caseload. Biographies of the current Justices can be found at *supremecourt.gov/about/biographies.aspx*.

DISCUSSION QUESTIONS

3. Do you think it is appropriate that the Supreme Court hears no more than 80 of the thousands of requests it receives each year? What criteria should the Court use in deciding which cases it will hear?

4. The Supreme Court has sometimes been criticized for being too political. When then-president Barack Obama, a Democrat, nominated Merrick Garland to join the Supreme Court in March 2016, the Republican controlled Senate

---

[3] In this process, the party seeking review of a lower court decision petitions (asks) the court to issue a writ of certiorari. This writ is an order to the lower court to send a certified record of the case to the Supreme Court so that the Court can be "be informed about" the previous proceedings.

[4] A justice might be disqualified because of a potential conflict of interest or for medical or personal reasons.

refused to hold a hearing or vote on his nomination. That allowed the newly elected Republican president, Donald Trump, to nominate a new candidate, who was then confirmed by the Senate. In September 2020 President Donald Trump, a Republican, nominated Amy Coney Barrett to join the Supreme Court. A Republican controlled Senate scheduled the hearing and voted within one month of her nomination, so that she was able to join the Supreme Court prior to the presidential election in November 2020.

a. Do these actions have an effect on how people view the legitimacy of the decisions of the Justices?

b. To what extent do you think decisions made by judges appointed by Democratic presidents differ from those appointed by Republican presidents? What difference, if any, do you think it makes?

c. How are state and local judges selected where you live? In what way do you think the selection process is better or worse than the federal system of judicial selection?

d. Other Federal Courts

In addition to the Article III **constitutional courts**, there are also several highly specialized **legislative courts** that Congress has created using its Article I powers. These legislative courts include, among others, the Bankruptcy Courts, U.S. Court of Military Appeals, the U.S. Tax Court, and the U.S. Court of Federal Claims.

Legislative courts Courts created under Congress's Article I powers.

For example, Congress was able to establish the bankruptcy courts because Article I, Section 8 grants Congress the power to "establish . . . uniform Laws on the subject of Bankruptcies throughout the United States," and to do what is "necessary and proper" to accomplish that goal. Because the Bankruptcy Court is an Article I and not an Article III court, its judges do not enjoy life-time tenure and instead are appointed for 14-year terms. Also, Article I court jurisdiction is more limited than that of Article III courts. In the case of the Bankruptcy Court, that limitation is to hearing all "core" proceedings arising under the federal Bankruptcy Code. However, what is "core" is not always clear. For example, if litigants in a bankruptcy case raise related state law claims, such as fraud, questions as to the scope of the court's jurisdiction occur. The U.S. Supreme Court has determined that with regard to state law claims, such as common law fraud, a bankruptcy court can make recommendations but not enter a final judgment.[5]

> **PRACTICE TIP**
>
> Find the time to take a walking tour of your local courts. Note the location of the clerk's offices, the courtrooms, and the nearest law library.

2. State Court Systems

While many important cases and significant constitutional issues are decided in the federal courts, it is in state courts where over 90 percent of all legal business occurs. While paralegals may have some opportunities to work with federal courts, most will spend their time operating within state court systems.

---

[5] See Stern v. Marshall, 564 U.S. 462 (2011).

NETNOTE

You can find great visual representations of all of the state court systems at *courtstatistics.org/other-pages/state_court_structure_charts.aspx.*

Rather than attempting to describe each of these 51 court systems, we will review some general patterns and leave it to you to search out the details for your specific state. Organizational charts of state court systems can generally be found on each state's official government website. (See Web Exercise 2.)

Most states have court systems that are very similar to the federal system, with three basic types of courts: trial, first level appellate, and one appellate court of last resort. Figure 5-4 shows the organization of a typical state court system. Note how closely it parallels Figure 5-2, showing the core of the federal court system. The path for appeals in most state court systems is from the trial court to an intermediate appellate court (if one exists), and then, usually only at the court's discretion, to the state's highest appellate court (usually called the supreme court).

General jurisdiction
A court's power to hear any type of case arising within its geographical area.

Limited jurisdiction
A court's power to hear only specialized cases.

Starting at the bottom of Figure 5-4, you can see that states can have either **general jurisdiction** or **limited jurisdiction** trial courts.[6] The former can hear any type of case, not specifically reserved for the federal courts. General jurisdiction courts typically carry a name such as circuit court, district court, county court, or superior court. Many states also have a confusing variety of specialized courts with limited jurisdiction. These courts hear a narrow range of cases on a specific subject (such as probate, domestic relations, or traffic) and sometimes even overlap regarding the types of cases they can hear. For example, in Massachusetts, both the probate court and the superior court can hear divorce cases.

States maintain either one or two levels of appellate courts. The larger states have generally gone to a two-tiered system like that in operation at the federal level. The intermediate-level appellate courts usually sit in panels, while the court of last resort sits en banc. On some matters appeals to the highest court are discretionary, while on others they are a matter of right. A few states have established separate courts to handle criminal versus civil appeals at the intermediate or highest level. Finally, as noted earlier in this chapter, even the name of the highest-level appellate court varies from state to state. While most states identify their highest court as the state supreme court, in New York and Maryland it is called the court of appeals.

---

[6] In some states, below the trial courts shown in Figure 5-4 is a system of inferior courts with names such as justice of the peace, city, and magistrate courts. Those courts are not **courts of record**. This means that no permanent record is kept of the testimony, lawyers' remarks, or judges' rulings. The absence of a record eliminates the possibility of an appeal and requires the losing party to initiate a completely new trial in a higher-level trial court if that party wishes to have the matter reconsidered.

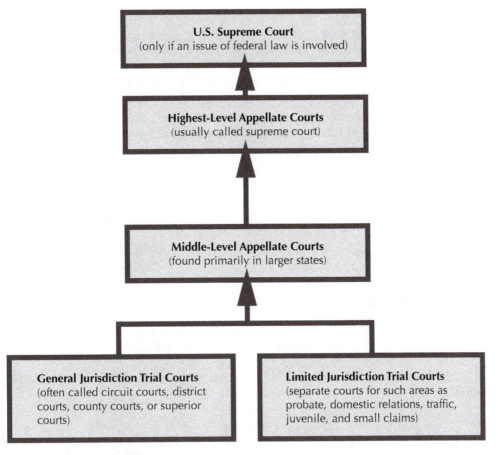

Figure 5-4   Organization of a Typical State Court System

In most cases, a state's top appellate court issues the final judgment because cases can be appealed to the U.S. Supreme Court only if they raise a federal issue. For example, in criminal cases, state courts must accord the due process rights guaranteed by the U.S. Constitution. This can involve resolving issues regarding the right to counsel, the admissibility of evidence resulting from an allegedly illegal search, jury selection procedures, and so on. If the defendant thinks these constitutional rights have been violated, she or he may be able to appeal the case to the federal courts on the basis that a federal issue is involved. Whenever a federal law or a provision of the U.S. Constitution is involved, the federal courts have the right to make the final determination as to what that law or constitutional provision means. But remember that a criminal defendant has no right to appeal his or her conviction in a state court to a federal court unless such federal issues are raised. Under the principles of federalism the state courts are the final arbiters as to the meaning of state statutes and state constitutional provisions.

Unlike federal judges, state court judges are selected in a variety of ways. They are appointed by the state's chief executive or the state legislature in only a few states. In others, they are selected in either partisan or nonpartisan elections. While some see the appointment of judges as undermining the democratic process, others fear that elected judges may be influenced by those who make large contributions to their election campaigns.

Partially in response to this disagreement about whether it is best to appoint or elect judges, some states have developed a modified system that has become known as merit selection, or the Missouri plan. Under that type of plan, a special panel of lawyers and lay persons is convened, and they nominate a few candidates for a vacancy. The governor then appoints from among this select group. A year or two later, the person who was appointed goes before the general electorate in a special retention election. In such an election, the candidate runs unopposed and the voters are asked simply whether that judge should be retained.

Some states also use **justices of the peace, court commissioners,** or **magistrates** in their court systems. Although they are not judges, state laws authorize these individuals to exercise limited judicial powers in specified types of cases. For example, they may handle criminal arraignments or hear small claims or probate cases. In a few states, they do not need to be licensed lawyers. They may be either elected or appointed.

DISCUSSION QUESTIONS

5. Why do you think the framers of the Constitution chose to give federal judges lifetime tenure and protect them from salary reductions? Explain whether you think that was a wise decision.

6. Do you think judges should be elected or appointed? Why? If appointed, what do you think the criteria should be?

3. Choice of State or Federal Court

As you have seen, there are 50 state court systems in operation in the United States, in addition to the federal court system. Choosing the right court requires knowing which court has jurisdiction over the case. That is, a lawyer must select a court that has the power to hear the case. The first decision is whether to select a state or federal court.

State courts generally have the power to hear any type of case, state or federal. The only time state courts are prohibited from hearing cases involving federal law is when Congress has expressly included that limitation in a federal statute.

As to whether the federal courts have jurisdiction, you will recall from Chapter 4 that the federal government is a government of limited powers. Just as Congress can legislate only if the Constitution has given it the power to do so, federal courts can hear cases only if the Constitution has given them the power to do so. Article III, Section 2 of the Constitution describes the jurisdiction of the federal courts in terms of (1) the nature of the subject matter of the case, and (2) the parties involved. Figure 5-5 lists the requirements for federal court jurisdiction.

Two of the grounds for federal court jurisdiction require particular emphasis, as they account for the bulk of federal cases. The federal courts have jurisdiction when the case involves

- a federal question, or
- diversity of citizenship.

Figure 5-5   Jurisdiction of Federal Courts

Based on the subject matter (federal question):
Any case involving the interpretation or application of
1. the U.S. Constitution,
2. a federal law or regulation,
3. a treaty, or
4. admiralty and maritime laws.

Based on the parties involved:
Any case or controversy in law and equity in which
1. the case affects ambassadors or other public ministers and counsels,
2. the United States is a party to the suit,
3. the controversy is between two or more states,
4. the controversy is between a state and citizens of another state,*
5. the parties are citizens of different states (known as diversity jurisdiction),
6. the controversy is between citizens of the same state claiming lands under grants of different states, or
7. the controversy is between (a) a state or the citizens thereof and (b) foreign states, citizens, or subjects.*

Based on the amount of money involved:
In addition to the constitutional requirements stated above, Congress has the power to add a minimum dollar value to suits between citizens of different states. The current federal statute states that the amount in controversy in diversity actions must exceed $75,000 to qualify for original federal jurisdiction.

*The Eleventh Amendment modified this to exclude situations where the suit was commenced or prosecuted against a state by an individual.

A **federal question** is involved when there is an issue dealing with a federal statute, a federal regulation, or the U.S. Constitution. **Diversity of citizenship** occurs when the plaintiff and the defendant are residents of different states. Congress has limited jurisdiction in diversity cases to those where the amount of money involved in the case exceeds $75,000.

That federal courts have jurisdiction over cases involving federal law seems obvious. But why should federal courts have jurisdiction over matters relating to state law simply because the litigants are from differing states and the amount in controversy exceeds $75,000? Traditionally, it has been argued that diversity jurisdiction is necessary to protect out-of-state litigants from the biases they would suffer in state court. Today, however, many disagree as to whether there is a continuing need for diversity jurisdiction.

While it might seem as though it should be relatively easy to decide whether there are valid grounds for finding federal jurisdiction based on the case involving either a federal question or citizens of differing states, this is not always so. In fact, before the parties can resolve the underlying legal issues, they often have to litigate whether a state or federal court is the proper forum.

Questions of diversity jurisdiction can be particularly troubling. For the litigants to be able to proceed in federal court, there must be complete diversity

Federal question
A legal issue involving the application of a federal law.

Diversity of citizenship
A situation where the opposing parties are from different states and the amount in controversy exceeds $75,000.

of citizenship. This means that no plaintiff can be from the same state as any of the defendants. If they are, then they must proceed in state court.

For example, in a widely publicized breach of contract dispute involving Facebook, the plaintiffs, New York residents, filed suit against Mark Zuckerberg, the founder of Facebook, in New York state court. New York was Zuckerberg's legal residence while in college. However, since then he had moved to California where he owned property, registered his automobile, and paid taxes. Zuckerberg was able to remove the case to federal court on the grounds of diversity by showing he was no longer a New York resident.[7]

Exclusive jurisdiction
When only one court has the power to hear a case.

Sometimes only one court is authorized to hear the type of case in question. That is known as **exclusive jurisdiction.** When more than one court is authorized to hear the same type of case, they each have **concurrent jurisdiction.** For example, if a case involves state law and is between citizens of different states, then the state and federal courts would have concurrent jurisdiction. In those situations where both the state and the federal courts have jurisdiction, the plaintiff makes the initial decision as to which court to use. However, as illustrated by the Zuckerberg case, when the plaintiff selects a state court and the federal courts also have jurisdiction, the defendant may be able to **remove** the case to federal court.

Concurrent jurisdiction
When more than one court has jurisdiction to hear a case.

Removal
The transfer of a case from one state court to another, or from a state court to a federal court.

It is very important to understand that deciding whether to go to state or federal court is not the same as deciding whether the court will apply state or federal law to the case. See Figure 5-6. For example, in a negligence case, a federal court might have jurisdiction based on the diversity of citizenship of the parties. However, the federal court must follow state negligence law in deciding the case. If the case involves an area of unsettled state law, the federal court must base its decision on its best guess as to what the state's highest court would do if faced with the same situation. Because the federal court is only guessing at what the state court would do, the federal court's decision is binding on the current litigants but is not binding on the state courts. Therefore, no matter how the federal court decides the case, it will still be open to the state courts to change the law in that area the next time a litigant brings a case on the same issue to the state courts. Likewise, when a state court hears a case involving a federal matter, it must follow the guidance of the federal courts.

DISCUSSION QUESTION

7. As the federal courts face an increasingly heavy workload, many have argued that it is time to either raise the required amount in controversy or eliminate diversity jurisdiction entirely. The requirement that the amount in controversy exceed $75,000 is to help ensure that federal courts are not inundated with cases of minimal importance. In 1789, Congress set the amount at $500, but over the years, it has increased it to the present-day $75,000. Would you be in favor of such changes?

---

[7] Ceglia v. Zuckerberg, 772 F. Supp. 2d 453 (W.D. N.Y. 2011).

Legal Reasoning Exercise

3. For each of these situations determine whether you think the matter should be heard in state or federal *court*. Also decide whether you think a court would apply state or federal *law*.

    a. A wife wants to divorce her husband.

    b. Martha, a Massachusetts resident, wants to sue Susan, a Massachusetts resident, for $80,000 based on breach of contract.

    c. Sam, a Massachusetts resident, wants to sue Jill, a Vermont resident, for $80,000 based on breach of contract.

    d. A teacher in a public school wants to challenge a state law requiring all teachers to start each day of class with a minute of silent prayer.

C. COURT PERSONNEL

It takes many different participants to make the judicial system work effectively. Court personnel include not only the judges who preside over the court proceedings and lawyers appearing before them, but also court clerks, court reporters, and bailiffs.

The trial court judge is, of course, one of the most powerful members of the judicial system. Within the limits of the law, the judge decides whether to dismiss a case before it reaches trial, the extent of pretrial discovery, and the amount of time the lawyers will have to prepare their cases. Once the trial is underway, the judge acts as the presiding officer, rules on objections, and determines when recesses will occur. If a jury is involved, the judge supervises its selection, removes jury members from the courtroom at key times to protect them from improper influences, and instructs them on the meaning of the law they are to apply. When a jury is not involved, the judge also acts as the fact finder and decides whether the defendant is guilty (in criminal cases) or liable (in civil cases). In criminal cases the judge is also responsible for sentencing the convicted defendant. If the

Figure 5-6 Two Separate Questions: State or Federal Court *and* State or Federal Law?

Does a State or Federal **Court** Have **Jurisdiction**?	Does State or Federal **Law Apply**?
Federal court—federal question jurisdiction **Federal court**—diversity jurisdiction	**Federal law**—(1) issues arising from the U.S. Constitution, (2) federal statutes, or (3) federal agency regulations. **State law**
State courts—generally have jurisdiction over **any type of case** unless Congress has provided for exclusive federal jurisdiction.	**State law or federal law**

PRACTICE TIP

When dealing with court personnel, remember that sometimes a few kind words and a professional attitude will get you the assistance you need.

litigants want to contest a trial judge's findings, they must present their arguments to appellate judges.

Lawyers play the most visible role in court proceedings. In addition to being advocates for their clients, lawyers are officers of the court. As such, they are responsible for maintaining proper decorum in the courtroom and acting within the ethical restraints imposed on them by the courts and their profession.

Court clerks are responsible for keeping the court files in proper condition and ensuring that the various motions filed by lawyers and the actions taken by judges are properly recorded. A head clerk of the courts is usually responsible for running the central records section of the courthouse; his or her assistants are assigned to sit in on the actual courtroom proceedings.

The **court reporter** prepares verbatim transcripts of courtroom proceedings. Most reporters use a stenotype machine rather than shorthand. Because it is expensive, they prepare a written transcript only if the case is being appealed.

Bailiffs are responsible for maintaining order in the courtrooms. They are also responsible for watching over the juries when they are in recess or when they have been sequestered. When a jury is sequestered, the members sleep at a hotel and are kept isolated from the public and their families to prevent them from being exposed to prejudicial publicity, threats, bribes, or any other improper influences.

Finally, sheriffs and marshals also serve as officers of the court. They serve summonses and other court documents, collect money as required by court judgments, and otherwise help in carrying out the court's orders.

SUMMARY

In this chapter, we have seen that although the U.S. legal system may seem to involve a confusing mix of names and functions, all courts can be classified in two ways:

1. They are either trial or appellate courts. Some trial courts have only limited jurisdiction; for example, they only hear cases in which less than a certain amount of money is in dispute.
2. They are part of either the federal or a state system.

The federal court system and most state court systems are based on a three-tier model. At the bottom are the trial courts, which decide both factual and legal issues. Above the trial courts, you will generally find an intermediate appellate court. At the top of every system is the highest appellate court. Appellate courts decide questions of law only. In the federal system, the trial courts are called district courts, the intermediate appellate courts are called courts of appeals, and the highest court is the U.S. Supreme Court.

The power of a particular court to hear certain types of cases is known as its jurisdiction. The U.S. Constitution limits all federal courts' jurisdiction by allowing them to hear only the types of cases listed under Article III, Section 2.

The two most common grounds for federal court jurisdiction are federal question and diversity of citizenship.

The judges that sit on these various courts are selected through a variety of different methods. While federal constitutional judges are appointed by the president with the advice and consent of the Senate, some state court judges are appointed, some are chosen by the electorate in elections, and others are chosen through a modified appointment process followed by an election.

Lawyers are considered to be "officers of the court" and are critical to the effective operation of the adversary system of justice. Other key court personnel include court clerks, court reporters, bailiffs, sheriffs, and marshals.

Due to the degree of ambiguity contained in constitutions, statutes, administrative regulations, and the common law, judges have a great deal of discretion when it comes to interpreting and applying the law in the cases that come before them. In exercising this discretion, it can be fairly said that they are "making law."

REVIEW QUESTIONS

Pages 113 through 119

1. What are the two basic functions of trial courts?
2. What is the difference between questions of law and questions of fact? Why is it important to know the difference?
3. Give an example of a question of fact that might arise during a murder trial. Give an example of a question of law that might arise in that same trial.
4. What is the difference between a bench and a jury trial?
5. What will an appellate court usually do if it finds that the trial court made a harmless error?
6. What is the difference between reversing and remanding a case?
7. How do majority, dissenting, and concurring opinions differ from each other?
8. List the major differences between trial and appellate courts.

Pages 120 through 125

9. In the federal court system what are the names given to
   a. the highest appellate court,
   b. the intermediate appellate courts, and
   c. the trial courts?
10. Look at the map in Figure 5-3. How many district courts are there in your state? In which circuit is your state located? Which other states are in your circuit?
11. If you hear that "cert." has been denied in a case, what does that mean?
12. In the federal system, what are the "inferior courts"?

Pages 125 through 133

13. Describe a typical state court system. How is your state court system similar to or different from the "typical" state system?
14. True or false: In every state, the highest appellate court is called the supreme court.
15. How are state judges selected? How does that differ from how federal judges are selected?

16. Jurisdiction refers to the power a court has to hear a case. Define each of the following types of jurisdiction:
    a. general jurisdiction
    b. limited jurisdiction
    c. original jurisdiction
    d. appellate jurisdiction
    e. exclusive jurisdiction
    f. concurrent jurisdiction
17. What are the two major grounds for gaining federal court jurisdiction?
18. Other than judges and lawyers, what other court personnel are you likely to encounter in a courtroom? What are their functions?

WEB EXERCISES

1. At *www.oyez.org,* you can hear U.S. Supreme Court arguments, take a virtual tour of the Supreme Court building, or learn more about the Supreme Court justices.
   a. Watch this eight-minute Supreme Court video: *c-span.org/video/?c4756134/supreme-court-oral-arguments.* How did the speakers describe the oral argument?
   b. Watch this eight-minute Supreme Court video: *c-span.org/video/?c4552963/opinion-writing-announcement.* You may have heard the saying that there is no good writing—only good rewriting. According to the speakers, how many times might one of the justices redraft an opinion?
2. Go to the National Center for State Courts at *ncsc.org,* and then, under "Information and Resources," click on "Connect to state court websites." Find your state and then answer the following questions:
   a. Does your state publish the opinions from its highest appellate court? If so, how far back is the coverage?
   b. What are the names of your state's trial courts? Are there courts for specialized jurisdiction as well as general jurisdiction?
   c. What are the names of your court(s) of appeals?
   d. Many states have a description of their court system on their website. Does yours? Explore the court websites for your state and create a chart of your state court system.

Chapter 6

Civil Litigation and Its Alternatives

Discourage litigation. Persuade your neighbors to compromise whenever you can. As a peacemaker the lawyer has superior opportunity of being a good man. There will still be business enough.
Abraham Lincoln

Chapter Objectives

After reading this chapter, you should be able to:

- Explain the advantages and disadvantages of litigation, mediation, and arbitration.
- Describe the three basic stages of litigation.
- Explain the importance of subject matter and personal jurisdiction.
- Discuss the functions of the complaint, answer, and summons.
- Compare and contrast a motion to dismiss with a summary judgment motion.
- List the main methods used in discovery, including electronic discovery.
- List the steps in a typical trial.

INTRODUCTION

Settlement
The resolution of a dispute between parties independent of the rendering of a final decision by a trial or appellate court.

Litigation is the process of using the courts to settle disputes. In this chapter, we provide an overview of the litigation process, including the procedural steps involved in initiating, trying, and appealing civil cases. Litigation can be a very expensive, stressful, and lengthy process. The party that loses a lawsuit rarely pays the legal fees of the prevailing party. Because of this, most civil litigation cases settle.[1] **Settlement** can occur prior to the filing of the lawsuit, any time prior to trial, during trial, or even after trial. Because of the time, expense, and uncertainty of the litigation process, various alternatives to litigation, such as arbitration and mediation, are commonly used. The alternative approaches are known collectively as **alternative dispute resolution (ADR)**.

Alternative dispute resolution (ADR)
Techniques for resolving conflicts that are alternatives to full-scale litigation. The two most common of these are arbitration and mediation.

To help illustrate the procedures used to settle civil disputes, we will again refer to the hypothetical situations involving Donald Drake (first discussed in Chapter 1) and Diane Dobbs (introduced in Chapter 3) to illustrate litigation and its alternatives. You will recall that Drake witnessed the death of his grandson, Philip, when he was struck by the car driven by Wilma Small. Ms. Diane Dobbs was the waitress who was fired when she announced to her boss that she was pregnant.

Case 1: The Distressed Grandfather (Continued)

After researching the law and gathering additional facts, lawyer Harper met with Drake a second time to discuss their various options, including proceeding with a lawsuit or first trying an alternative method for resolving his case.

A. ALTERNATIVE DISPUTE RESOLUTION (ADR)

We begin with a discussion of ADR techniques because they are designed to be used either prior to or instead of litigation. You should keep in mind, however, that in real life, actions may not proceed in such a straightforward manner. Although informal negotiations may begin the moment a dispute arises, there is no set order in which the parties are required to proceed. They may decide to file a complaint immediately, initiating the litigation process, but then suspend their litigation efforts while trying to resolve the dispute through arbitration or mediation. Should those efforts fail, the parties may then pick up where they left off in the litigation process. A variation of ADR may be required prior to trial in some jurisdictions. At other times, however, the parties may turn first to an

---

[1] For a nuanced article on civil settlement rates, the American Judges Association has published a study, "A Profile of a Settlement" by John Barkai, Elizabeth Kent, and Pamela Martin, found at *aja.ncsc.dni.us/courtrv/cr42-3and4/CR42-3BarkaiKentMartin.pdf* (last accessed May 24, 2020).

ADR process and then proceed with initiating a lawsuit only if that process fails. Finally, parties may have signed a contract agreeing to the sole remedy of arbitration long before a dispute arises. Therefore, as you read this chapter, keep in mind that the various forms of ADR, including informal negotiations, mediation, and arbitration, can occur at any time, from before formal litigation has begun to well after a lawsuit has been filed and the litigation process is underway.

In comparison to litigation, ADR is designed to resolve conflicts more rapidly and at a lower cost. It can take many forms, ranging from very informal negotiations, which usually begin as soon as a dispute arises and may not end until the final appeal has been filed, to the more formal approaches of mediation and arbitration, which require the involvement of a neutral third party as either a mediator or arbiter.

The main difference between mediation and arbitration is that in mediation, the third party acts as a facilitator who tries to help the parties reach their own resolution. In arbitration, the third party is a decision maker who acts much as a judge would at a bench trial.

To encourage greater use of ADR, Congress enacted legislation in 1998 requiring each U.S. district court to establish and implement programs to offer ADR to litigants. Nearly all of the U.S. courts of appeals have also established mediation programs to assist parties in resolving their appeals. Similarly, many state and local court systems have also incorporated ADR, especially in the area of family law, where the parties are often required to participate in formal mediation regarding issues of child custody and visitation.

NETNOTE

If you are interested in learning more about various forms of ADR, there are several websites you can visit, including the American Arbitration Association, the Mediation Information and Resource Center, the ABA Section on Dispute Resolution, and the College of Commercial Arbitrators. The ABA Journal online has a list of ADR blogs.

1. Mediation

In **mediation,** a neutral third party attempts to guide the disputants toward a compromise that is voluntarily accepted by both sides. Mediation is based on the premise that the best solution is one that the parties themselves devise, rather than having one imposed on them. The mediation process is designed to help the opposing parties view themselves as collaborators working toward a compromised solution rather than as combatants out to "win" at any cost.

The mediator helps the disputants identify the issues that divide them and explore potential solutions that would be acceptable to both parties. If the mediation is successful, the mediator will draft a written agreement for the parties to

Mediation
An ADR mechanism whereby a neutral third party assists the parties in reaching a mutually agreeable, voluntary compromise.

sign. Once signed, this agreement becomes a court-enforceable contract. If they do not reach an agreement, the parties can simply walk away from the mediation and seek other approaches to resolving their differences.

While mediation is normally seen as a process involving voluntary cooperation between the parties, many states are now imposing "mandatory mediation" in selected types of disputes. It is "mandatory" in the sense that both parties are required to engage in a formal mediation process before a court will hear the case. If the mediation process fails, the parties can continue with the court proceedings.

Generally, some types of cases are better suited for mediation than others. Mediation is particularly useful in situations where the parties will have to deal with each other in the future, such as child visitation issues after a divorce or a dispute between neighbors. In these situations, it is hoped that the mediation process will not only resolve the current situation, but also improve the partici-pants' interpersonal and conflict management skills as they continue to deal with each other in the future.

Some situations do not lend themselves to mediation, such as in situations involving domestic violence. Not only may the contact during mediation between the abuser and the victim result in further violence following the media-tion session, but the victim may perceive the mediation session itself as another form of abuse. Further, as mediation works best when the parties are of fairly equal bargaining power, it is not as effective in situations of abuse, where the victims often perceive themselves as powerless against the abuser.

2. Arbitration

Arbitration
An ADR mechanism whereby the parties submit their disagreement to a third party, whose decision is binding.

In 1924, Congress passed the Federal Arbitation Act to encourage arbitration in civil matters. Unlike mediation, in **arbitration,** the neutral third party has the authority to render binding decisions even if the parties do not agree with that result. Whereas a mediator is a facilitator, an arbitrator plays a role more similar to that of a judge. Arbitrators follow a much simpler set of procedures than do judges, however, and arbitration does not require as much time or expense as litigation. Generally speaking, both parties must agree in advance to accept the arbitrator's decision, and a dissatisfied party may not challenge it in court except on very limited grounds, such as arguing that the award was obtained by fraud.

The business community strongly supports arbitration because it is viewed as a faster and less expensive means of settling disputes that arise in the course of doing business. It is a common practice for businesses to include arbitration clauses in their contracts. Under these clauses, the parties are legally bound to refer disputes over the interpretation of a contract to arbitration rather than take them to court. In addition to saving time and money, arbitration often allows a company to settle a dispute without attracting the public attention that may accompany a lawsuit because arbitration often includes confidentiality clauses.

Arbitration does have its critics, though. Many complain that arbitration is acquiring too many of the disadvantages of litigation regarding cost and time spent, without retaining the benefits of litigation (i.e., the ability to use discovery to uncover facts known only to the other party and the possibility of appealing an unfavorable decision).

In the field of labor law, arbitration is often used as a way of avoiding strikes. Sports fans are familiar with the role that arbitration has played in determining the salaries of baseball players. Public employees are often required to use arbitration when state law prohibits them from striking.

As mentioned above, arbitrators are not required to apply the same procedures and rules of evidence that judges must use, something that the professional football player Adrian Peterson learned when he attempted to challenge an arbitration ruling that upheld the decision by the National Football League (NFL) to suspend and fine him. The NFL had acted after Peterson was charged with "reckless or negligent injury to a child" in connection with his allegedly having beaten his four-year-old son with a switch. After the arbitrator upheld the league's decision, Peterson sued in federal court, alleging that the charge against him and the arbitrator's ruling violated the due process clause of the U.S. Constitution. He based his argument on the fact that the NFL had applied a new disciplinary rule to him that had not been in effect at the time of the incident with his son. In rejecting these claims, the Court of Appeals emphasized that the NFL Players' Association had agreed to the arbitration procedures, and that the statute governing labor arbitration did not allow rulings to be vacated on grounds of lack of "fundamental fairness."[2]

As it turns out, the pregnant waitress, Dobbs, was not a member of a union. If she had been, then there would have been a collective bargaining agreement with her employer, and it is likely that she could have filed a formal grievance. The union representative would then have attempted to negotiate a resolution of her dispute with management. If those negotiations were not successful, most likely the collective bargaining agreement would have included a mandatory arbitration clause that would require Dobbs to submit her grievance to arbitration.

Some employers require that their employees sign an agreement that provides that all employment disputes will be resolved through arbitration. Although Dobbs did not sign such an agreement, in *Epic Systems Corp. v. Lewis*,[3] the U.S. Supreme Court upheld the validity of such compulsory arbitration clauses.

The #MeToo Movement, however, has had an impact on companies requiring employees, as a condition of employment, to sign confidential arbitration agreements for any future sexual harassment claims. Concerns that confidential arbitration of sexual harassment claims fail to adequately protect employees from sexual predators has changed company policy and the laws of several states. A number of employers, including Google and Facebook, voluntarily ended private arbitration clauses in their employment contracts. In February 2018, the attorney generals of all 50 states signed a letter to the U.S. Congress asking that legislation be enacted to end mandatory arbitration of sexual harassment claims.[4] In 2019, the House of Representatives passed the Forced Arbitration Injustice Repeal (FAIR) Act,[5] which would end forced

---

[2] NFLPA v. NFL, N. 15-1438 (August 4, 2016).
[3] 138 S. Ct. 1612 (2018).
[4] The letter can be found on the website of the National Association of Attorneys General (NAAG), *www .naag.org/naag/media/naag-news/ags-to-congress-help-employees-with-sexual-harassment-claims-in-the -workplace-access-the-courts.php* (last accessed May 25, 2020).
[5] H.R. 1423, 116th Cong. (2019).

arbitration in employment, consumer, civil rights, and antitrust disputes. This legislation is illustrative of the growing concerns regarding potential abuses in arbitration and the movement toward limiting its use.

3. Role of Paralegals in ADR

Because arbitrators and mediators do not have to be lawyers, experienced paralegals may be able to qualify for such positions if they have the right mix of formal training and experience in the substantive field in which they wish to work. Some states, such as Texas, have extensive programs to train mediators in many areas in which disputes can arise between individuals. In Texas, nonlawyer mediators are frequently used, but in some states, it is much less common for nonlawyers to be used as mediators.

Even if paralegals are not working as mediators, their assistance in mediations is often critical. Their involvement in ADR closely parallels the functions that paralegals serve in traditional litigation. They assist in gathering and preparing information that will be presented to the mediator or arbitrator. They help make administrative arrangements for the ADR proceedings and schedule expert and lay witnesses. They also prepare clients and other witnesses for what to expect in the ADR process. Following a decision, they will often prepare documents required as part of the settlement.

Case 1: The Distressed Grandfather (Continued)

Drake's lawyer prefers to use a form of ADR whenever possible, as it may save her clients time, stress, and expense. Also, if there is a chance for an ongoing relationship between the parties, mediation, because it is less adversarial than litigation or arbitration, may help to preserve that relationship.

However, Small's lawyer has indicated that his client is not interested in using ADR. It is his position that because Drake was not Philip's parent, there is no legal basis for making Small responsible for his injuries.[6] Therefore, Drake's lawyer informed him that they had no choice but to proceed with formal litigation.

DISCUSSION QUESTIONS

1. If you were involved in a dispute, which ADR method would you prefer, and why?

2. Do you think either mediation or arbitration would be appropriate to resolve Drake's case? Why or why not?

When ADR methods fail, the parties may decide to proceed to litigation. The process of litigation is the subject of the next section.

---

[6] See the discussion of standing later this chapter on page 144.

B. LITIGATION

Both the federal and state courts have published their particular rules under names such as the Federal Rules of Civil Procedure, the Federal Rules of Evidence, Massachusetts Rules of Civil Procedure, and Illinois Criminal Law and Criminal Procedure. Most state rules are quite similar to those used in the federal courts.

In both federal and state courts, litigation has three basic stages: pretrial, trial, and appeal. Take a few moments to study Figure 6-1, which provides an overview of the litigation process. Refer to it as you proceed with the remainder of this chapter to help you keep track of the various stages.

1. The Pretrial Stage

However, before this can occur, the lawyer must handle some preliminary matters:

- whether a legal basis for the suit exists,
- who should be sued,
- in which court the case should be brought,
- whether the statute of limitations has expired, and
- whether any administrative agency must be consulted before filing suit.

Once those issues have been resolved and a determination to sue has been made, the lawsuit enters the pleadings stage. The **pleadings** are the documents that each side files with the court and serves on the other side to commence the lawsuit. In order to narrow the issues, either party may file **pretrial motions**. Finally, the parties will engage in **discovery**, an attempt by both sides to gather as much information as possible. The end result of this process may be a negotiated settlement, a court determination to dismiss the suit, or a decision to proceed to the trial stage.

a. Preliminary Matters

The decisions as to these preliminary matters are not always easy to make and may involve extensive factual and legal research in order to determine the best course of action. Paralegals are often assigned the task of locating and analyzing statutes, court rules, and cases that are relevant to these decisions. In addition, they may be called upon to engage in factual investigation, such as tracing corporate ownership or locating parties and witnesses to the suit.

(1) Legal grounds for the suit

As you will recall from Chapter 1, not every problem is a legal problem for which the courts can provide a remedy. Therefore, before a lawyer can initiate a lawsuit, she or he must be convinced that the client has a valid cause of action—that is, based on the law and the facts, the client's claim is sufficient to support a lawsuit. This determination involves answering two questions affirmatively. First, does the lawyer believe that there are sufficient credible facts to support the plaintiff's position? Second, does the lawyer believe that there is a valid legal theory to support the claim?

In determining whether a client's position is supported by credible facts, lawyers must review relevant documents and interview witnesses. In some

PRACTICE TIP

Keep a copy of your state's rules of civil procedure and rules of evidence, along with the federal rules. Add to this set any local trial court rules. These can all be found at *uscourts.gov/rules-policies/current-rules-practice-procedure*.

Pleadings
The documents that begin a lawsuit—generally, the complaint and the answer.

Pretrial motion
A motion brought before the beginning of a trial, either to eliminate the necessity for a trial or to limit the information that can be presented at the trial.

Discovery
The modern pretrial procedure by which one party gains information from the adverse party.

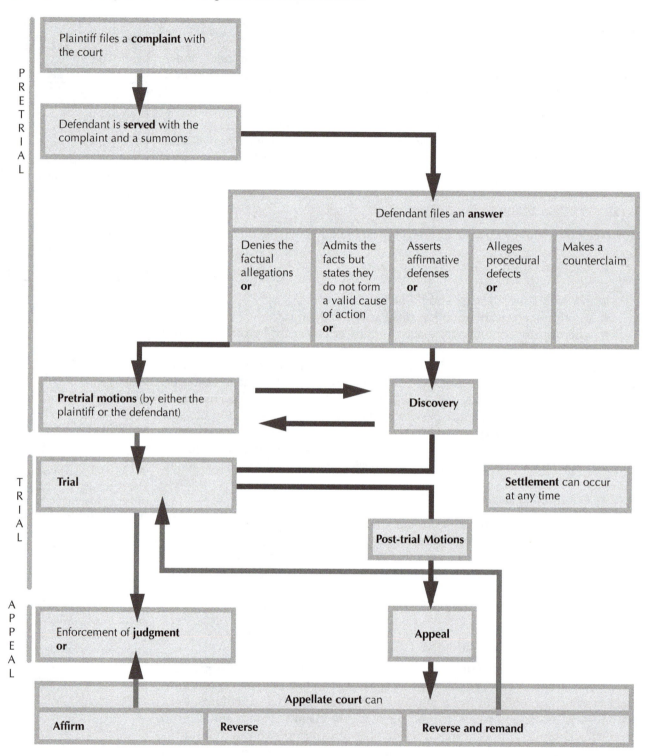

Figure 6-1   Civil Procedure

PRACTICE TIP

A paralegal generally performs several tasks at the beginning of any lawsuit, including the following:

- Collecting contact information for the client and all potential litigants so that a conflict of interest check can be performed to ensure that no one at the law firm has represented or spoken to any of the other litigants;
- Sending a fee agreement that delineates the scope of engagement and the agreed-upon fee;[7]
- Setting up a **tickler system** to list and monitor all of the deadlines in the case, including statutes of limitations;
- Creating a file to collect all recording/tickler deadlines, evidence, records, pleadings, correspondence, pleadings, and discovery;
- Creating a trial notebook; and
- Creating a settlement brochure (as an option). Prior to the filling of any complaint, the lawyer may request a settlement brochure evaluating the case and delineating the liability and damages of the opposing party. Presented as a story, it explains why the plaintiff is likely to win the lawsuit. Settlement brochures can be written; however, they can also be provided in video form, sometimes referred to as a "legal settlement documentary."

PRACTICE TIP

Once the client has signed the fee agreement, paralegals should begin putting together a trial notebook. Gathering this information from the beginning of the representation can help at all stages of litigation — from settlement negotiations to trial. For directions about how to put together a trial notebook, go to *blumberg.com/downloads/TrialNotebook.pdf*.

Tickler system
A calendaring system that records key dates and important deadlines.

practice areas, including worker's compensation and family law, lawyers will ask for access to the client's social media accounts. They may assign a paralegal to do much of the background research needed to determine whether there are credible facts and a valid legal theory to support the claim.

If lawyers file lawsuits without first conducting a reasonable investigation regarding the facts of the case, they may be subject to court-imposed sanctions. For example, under Rule 11 of the Federal Rules of Civil Procedure, if a judge determines that a lawyer has not conducted a reasonable inquiry into the facts and law or has filed suit for an improper purpose, then the judge may impose monetary sanctions on the lawyer and on the parties that lawyer represents. If a party is represented by a lawyer, Rule 11 also requires that the lawyer sign the pleadings, written motions, and other papers. Paralegals are never authorized to sign these documents.

Ethics Alert

---

[7] Of course, if the firm chooses not to proceed, then the appropriate document to prepare would be a non-engagement letter. A non-engagement letter should include a sentence informing the client that in order to be able to continue pursuing the claim with another lawyer, the client should act immediately so as not to lose the right to sue.

Even if there are legal grounds for proceeding with a lawsuit, not all legal solutions are worth the cost. For example, no matter which side wins, both parties usually remain responsible for paying their own lawyer's fees. Therefore, lawyers should speak to their clients about the amount that they can expect to recover if they win the lawsuit, minus any expenses and lawyer fees. Clients should also be told that there is never a guarantee that they will win their claim, no matter how strong their case appears to be. Even when clients pay their lawyers on a contingency fee basis so that the lawyers recover a percentage of the award plus costs, plaintiffs may end up losing money if the costs outweigh their portion of the award.

PRACTICE TIPS

Recommendation 1: Once the lawyer has identified the cause of action, looking at your state's Pattern Jury Instructions can help you assist your supervising lawyer in determining what the lawyer will need to prove to win the lawsuit. Once that information has been identified, it is helpful to create a list of those elements and of ideas about what is necessary to prove them.

Recommendation 2: Paralegals often interview witnesses. Every time the paralegal interviews a potential witness, the paralegal should type up the witness's statement and ask the witness to sign it. Once a witness statement is in the form of a notarized, signed document, it increases the likelihood that the witness's testimony on the stand will be consistent with that in the initial interview. People tend to tell interviewers what they think that person wants to hear. By capturing statements in this way, it is unlikely that the story will change at trial. If a witness is not willing to sign an affidavit, then it may be necessary to do additional research to support the client's claim.

Recommendation 3: Facts can change as the case develops. A story often has two sides, and when clients first meet with a lawyer, they usually only present one—theirs. If at some point it becomes clear that the facts do not support a client's claim, the lawyer may direct that a disengagement letter be sent to the client.

---

(2) Parties to the suit

Lawsuits can involve just one plaintiff and one defendant or multiple plaintiffs and defendants. Determining the appropriate parties is one of the first issues that must be resolved before the lawsuit can proceed. The client should provide the lawyer with the names of all of the other potential litigants. Paralegals are often tasked with confirming the legal names of the defendants. If the defendant is a corporation, it is critical to look up the legal corporate name. The secretary of state of each state maintains a website that allows you to search the legal names of a business incorporated or doing business in that state.

Standing
The principle that courts cannot decide abstract issues or render advisory opinions; rather, they are limited to deciding cases that involve litigants who are personally affected by the court's decision.

(a) Standing   You cannot sue someone simply because you do not like something they did or said. In order to sue, you must be able to establish you were personally affected by something the defendant did. This requirement is referred to as **standing.** It is designed to keep courts from deciding abstract issues

or rendering advisory opinions.[8] By requiring the parties to have a vested interest in the outcome, courts benefit from hearing litigants who will vigorously argue their positions.

Why limit lawsuits to people who have been hurt? One reason is that they're likely to marshal the strongest arguments. It brings to mind the old line about the role of the chicken and the pig in furnishing your breakfast: The chicken is involved, but the pig is *committed*. Let chickens file lawsuits against bacon-and-egg combos, and they may lack the motivation to do a good job.[9]

Because of this requirement of standing, persons and organizations cannot file lawsuits simply because they do not approve of a certain governmental policy or some corporation's building project. For example, only persons who have been sentenced to death can challenge the death penalty. If the court determines that the parties do not have standing, it simply dismisses the case without making a determination on the merits.

A classic example of how the requirement of standing affects who can sue occurred in conjunction with the litigation that led up to the famous case of *Brown v. Board of Education*.[10] Although the National Association for the Advancement of Colored People (NAACP) was opposed to the Kansas policy of segregating its public school system, it had no standing on its own to challenge the constitutionality of that policy. Before it could proceed, the organization had to recruit an African-American child who was actually turned away when she attempted to enter an all-white school located in her neighborhood.[11] Eventually, the NAACP was able to find 13 parents and their children who were willing to serve as plaintiffs in the case.

(b) Legal competence The lawyer must also be certain that the parties to a lawsuit are legally capable of suing and being sued. For example, in many states a minor must sue or be sued through a named guardian or "next friend." A **guardian** is someone who has the legal right and duty to take care of another person's property when that person is a child or is otherwise incompetent. A **"next friend"** is not the legal guardian but is a responsible party that the court recognizes as a legitimate representative. Allowing suit by such representatives is an exception to the requirement of standing mentioned above. The guardian or next friend is not suing in his or her own right, but rather as a representative for the child or incompetent person.

(c) Class action lawsuits **Class action lawsuits** allow multiple individuals to come together in a single lawsuit to sue the same defendant for the same type of injury. Class actions promote efficiency by allowing testimony to be heard and issues to be resolved in one large trial rather than repeatedly in a series of individual trials. Also, the use of class actions may allow plaintiffs with individually small claims a chance to recover. Usually, it is not economically feasible for a single plaintiff to pay the legal fees necessary to recover a small amount of damages, but it becomes worthwhile for a lawyer to take the case on a contingency basis when the damages of hundreds or even thousands of plaintiffs are consolidated.

Guardian
A person appointed by the court to manage the affairs or property of a person who is incompetent due to age or some other reason.

"Next friend"
A person who represents the interests of someone in court without being that person's legal guardian.

Class action suit
A lawsuit brought by a person as a representative for a group of people who have been similarly injured.

---

[8] The one exception occurs in some states where courts are authorized to respond to requests for advice from other governmental bodies.
[9] Steve Chapman, *No Decision Sometimes Best Decision*, The Republican, June 22, 2004, at A9.
[10] 347 U.S. 483 (1954).
[11] Paul E. Wilson, *A Retrospective of Brown v. Board of Education: The Genesis of Brown v. Board of Education*, 6. Kan. J.L. & Pub. Pol'y 7 (1996).

Before a class action can proceed, the court must certify that it meets two basic requirements:

1. there must be questions of law or fact common to the class, and
2. the claims of the named class members must be typical of the claims of the class as a whole.

Defendants can object to the validity of proceeding with a class action lawsuit by arguing that either or both of those two requirements are missing. For example, Wal-Mart challenged the validity of a class action brought on behalf of 1.5 million of its employees and former employees. The U.S. Supreme Court agreed with Wal-Mart that the class was too diverse to qualify for class action status.[12] Although they all claimed Wal-Mart had discriminated against them on the basis of their sex, the Court noted that the class members "held a multitude of different jobs, at different levels of Wal-Mart's hierarchy, for variable lengths of time, in 3,400 stores, sprinkled across 50 states, with a kaleidoscope of supervisors (male and female), subject to a variety of regional policies that all differed."[13]

Five years later a group of 3,000 Tyson Foods Inc. employees sued, seeking overtime wages for time they had to spend donning and doffing protective gear, required as part of their job. The Court allowed them to proceed with their class action suit. The Court distinguished *Wal-Mart* on the basis that in *Wal-Mart* the employees were not similarly situated whereas the employees at Tyson Foods were—they worked in the same facility, did similar work, and were paid under the same policy.[14]

DISCUSSION QUESTION

3. Do you agree with the Supreme Court's decision in *Wal-Mart*? Is it fair that Wal-Mart will not have to answer to the thousands of women whose individual claims are too small to justify the costs of litigation? And if the individual women had been able to proceed with a lawsuit, would it have promoted the best use of judicial resources for Wal-Mart to have to defend 1.5 million lawsuits instead of just one large class action suit?

(d) Selecting the appropriate defendants   After having determined who are the appropriate plaintiff or plaintiffs, the lawyer must decide who should be named as defendants. Naturally, the lawyer will choose to sue the person who caused his or her client harm. However, the most logical person to sue may not be worth suing because he or she may not have money to pay the damages that a court might award. This is referred to as being **judgment proof**. If there is more than one possible defendant, the plaintiff will want to make sure to include the one with the deepest pockets, that is, the most assets.

Judgment proof
When the defendant does not have sufficient money or other assets to pay the judgment.

---

[12] Wal-Mart Stores, Inc. v. Dukes, 564 U.S. 338 (2011).
[13] Id. at 359-60.
[14] Tyson Foods v. Bouaphakeo, 136 S. Ct. 1036 (2016).

For example, under a theory known as **respondeat superior,** an employer can sometimes be held responsible for the acts of its employees. Because employers usually have more money than employees, persons injured by an employee will frequently also sue the employer. Similarly, in an automobile accident case, the plaintiff may sue the manufacturer of the auto or the governmental unit responsible for maintaining the roadway.

There are times when a plaintiff cannot sue one potential defendant without including the others as well. This is known as **compulsory joinder.** For example, in a dispute involving a piece of property with three owners, all three would have to be made part of the lawsuit. Where such rules do not apply, the plaintiff may be selective in deciding who should be included in the suit. The defendant, however, may later file a motion to add a defendant that the plaintiff left out.

(3) Selection of the court

The last preliminary issue requires the plaintiff's lawyer to decide in which court to file the lawsuit. From your readings in Chapter 5, you know that lawsuits begin in a trial court and not an appellate court, but which trial court? That will depend on which trial courts have jurisdiction over the type of case that the lawyer will be filing. Recall that **jurisdiction** relates to the power of a particular court to hear a case brought before it. In some cases, the lawyer may have the option of selecting among several different courts and must evaluate the advantages and disadvantages of using one versus the other.

Once it is determined which court has jurisdiction to hear the case, a related issue is the question of **venue,** which determines the specific geographical location of the court that will hear the case. Jurisdiction and venue are related, in that they both deal with which court will hear the case, but they are very different. Once jurisdiction is determined, venue simply relates to which of several courts that have jurisdiction geographically is the most appropriate one. For example, assume that two people signed a contract in Ann Arbor, Michigan. Jurisdiction would be determined by the type of case, the law underpinning the case, and the parties to the contract. Once jurisdiction was established (in this case the state court), then the appropriate geographical area would be selected. In this example, that would likely be the county in which the contract was signed.

In determining whether jurisdiction exists, you must consider both **subject matter jurisdiction** and **personal jurisdiction.** If a court does not have both subject matter jurisdiction and personal jurisdiction, it cannot hear the case.

(a) Subject matter jurisdiction As the term implies, subject matter jurisdiction is determined by the subject matter of the case—that is, by the type of law that is involved. Generally, federal courts can hear only cases relating to federal law (such as federal constitutional or statutory issues) or cases in which the plaintiff and defendant are from different states and the amount in dispute exceeds $75,000. Rule 8 of the Federal Rules of Civil Procedure requires that the lawyer filing a complaint include "a statement indicating why the federal court has jurisdiction to hear the case."

Respondeat superior
The tort theory that an employer can be sued for the negligent acts of its employees.

Compulsory joinder
When a person must be brought into a lawsuit as either a plaintiff or a defendant.

Jurisdiction
The power of a court to hear a case.

Venue
When the court with the power to hear the case has multiple locations, the proper location for the case to be filed and heard.

Subject matter jurisdiction
The power of a court to hear a particular type of case.

Unless barred by a specific federal statute, generally state courts can hear any type of case. Therefore, cases involving diversity of citizenship and more than $75,000 can usually be started in either federal or state court. In deciding which court to choose, a lawyer will consider matters such as filing requirements, deadline dates, the current backlog of cases, discovery procedures, the rules of evidence, and the personalities of the judges. The convenience of the physical location of the court may also be a factor.

Case 1: The Distressed Grandfather (Continued)

Drake's case involves negligence: a matter of state law. Therefore, as the accident happened in Massachusetts, the lawyer, Harper, could bring her lawsuit in a Massachusetts state trial court. However, even though his case does not involve federal law, if the amount in dispute exceeds $75,000, she would also have the option of bringing it in federal court. She could do this under diversity jurisdiction, based on Drake being a resident of Massachusetts and Small, the defendant, being a resident of New Hampshire.

Therefore, in Drake's case, the federal and state courts have concurrent jurisdiction. Harper is free to choose the forum that is most advantageous to her case.

If she elects to sue using a Massachusetts state court, naturally the court will apply Massachusetts law. However, even if she brings the case in federal court, because jurisdiction is based on diversity of citizenship and the accident happened in Massachusetts, the federal court will also apply Massachusetts state law, not federal law.

Personal jurisdiction
The power of a court to force a person to appear before it.

Minimum contacts
A constitutional fairness requirement that a defendant have at least a certain minimum level of contact with a state before the state courts can have jurisdiction over the defendant.

(b) Personal jurisdiction   Personal jurisdiction relates to the court's power to force a person to appear before it—hence the name personal jurisdiction. Generally, for a state court to have personal jurisdiction over a defendant, the defendant must be a resident of that state, be served with process within the state, consent to the lawsuit, or have some **minimum contacts** with it. For example, a state court would have jurisdiction over a nonresident defendant who caused an automobile accident within that state's borders.

States exercise this jurisdiction over nonresidents through "long-arm statutes." Typically, such statutes allow the states to exercise jurisdiction if the subject matter of the lawsuit is a tort the defendant committed within the state, a contract the defendant entered into within the state, or a harm the defendant caused as a result of business conducted within the state. Each of these activities would satisfy the minimum contacts requirement, so long as exercising jurisdiction does not offend "traditional notions of fair play and substantial justice."

Because Drake's accident happened in Massachusetts, the accident supplies the minimum contacts that Massachusetts courts need to hear the lawsuit. Drake may sue Small in Massachusetts.

To better understand this concept of personal jurisdiction, just for a moment assume that the situation had been different, as illustrated in Figure 6-2. Assume that Drake, a Massachusetts resident, had been vacationing in Maine when the accident happened, and assume that Small, a New Hampshire resident, was also vacationing in Maine. Then the issue of personal jurisdiction would

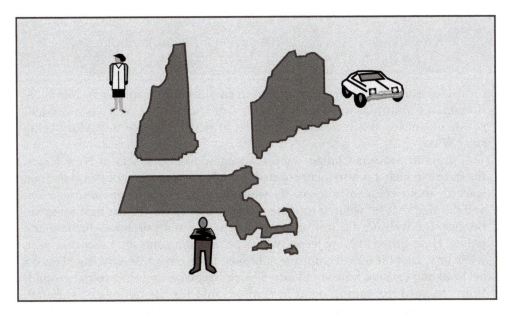

Figure 6-2   Personal Jurisdiction

be much more complicated. As he lives in Massachusetts, Drake would like to commence his lawsuit there. Under these revised facts, however, Small has had no contact with Massachusetts, and as at least minimum contacts are required, Drake would not be allowed to sue her in Massachusetts. He could sue her in New Hampshire because, as a resident of that state, the New Hampshire courts would have jurisdiction over Small. He could also sue her in Maine, as the accident in that state provides the minimum contacts necessary to satisfy personal jurisdiction.

NETNOTE

On the Internet, you can find all sorts of useful information about the courts—everything from their fax numbers to the location of a specific courthouse. To find the address of any state court, a good place to start is at the home page for the National Center for State Courts, *ncsc.org*. The center maintains a complete listing for all 50 states. For information on federal courts, you can visit either the federal judiciary home page or the Federal Judicial Center home page. Finally, the U.S. Supreme Court has its own website, Supremecourt.gov.

Legal Reasoning Exercises

1. Assume that Mary was injured in an automobile accident while vacationing in California. Joe was driving the car that hit her. Mary is a resident of Michigan. Joe is a resident of Florida. In which state(s) may Mary bring suit? Why?

2. Four Seasons Campground rents campground spaces in New Jersey, the state in which it is also incorporated. John Haas, a resident of Pennsylvania, learned about the campsite on its website, *www.fourseasonscamping.com*, and decided that he wanted to lease campground space for the next summer. Because the website did not allow for such seasonal purchases to be made online, Haas drove to New Jersey, where he signed a contract. Later that year, while he was at his leased campsite, a branch fell from a tree, striking Haas on his head and causing him to fall into a brick fireplace, and then to the ground. When he sued the campground in Pennsylvania for the injuries he suffered, the defendant, Campground, filed a motion to have the case dismissed for lack of personal jurisdiction. How do you think the court ruled, and why?

Statute of limitations
The law that sets the length of time from when something happens to when a lawsuit must be filed before the right to bring it is lost.

(4) Statutes of limitations

A **statute of limitations** sets a time limit within which a person can sue. Once that specified time has passed, the person is forever barred from suing. Such statutes vary depending on the type of situation involved. Some statutes of limitations set very short deadlines. For example, a person complaining of discrimination at work has only 180 days to bring a complaint. Other statutes of limitations, such as that for murder, are essentially without limit. Typically, persons have two years from the date of a negligent act to file a lawsuit. Drake is fortunate in that he sought legal advice well within the time frame allowed by the statute of limitations.

NETNOTE

The common statutes of limitations in your state can be found at *statelaws .findlaw.com/*. Click on your state and then click on the link for "Statutes of Limitations."

(5) Exhaustion of administrative remedies

If a person's claim involves matters coming under the jurisdiction of an administrative agency, the plaintiff might have to consult that agency before being allowed to sue in a court of law. Such a requirement is known as the

PRACTICE TIP

Accepting a case a few days before the statute of limitations runs out can be risky. Many lawyers will write a non-engagement letter to such a potential client, letting them know that they are *not* taking the case, that the potential client might have a legal remedy, and that the potential client will need to act quickly to secure another lawyer on their behalf.

exhaustion of administrative remedies. The purpose behind this rule is to give the administrative agency a chance to resolve the problem before the parties resort to a lawsuit.

Once a person has filed a complaint with an administrative agency, that agency usually tries to resolve the issue by getting the parties to reach a mutually agreeable resolution. If those efforts are not successful, the process may proceed to a formal hearing. Such a hearing is similar to a trial, but the rules are relaxed. Instead of a trial court judge, an administrative law judge oversees the proceeding. Usually there is no requirement that the rules of evidence be strictly followed. Some administrative agencies also allow for paralegals and others who are not licensed lawyers to represent people in these administrative hearings. Often, the hearing officer's decision resolves the dispute. However, if one of the parties is dissatisfied with the decision, depending on the agency, that party may have the option either to appeal the decision to a higher body within the agency itself, to appeal the decision to a court, or to start the whole process anew with a lawsuit.

Exhaustion of administrative remedies
The requirement that relief be sought from an administrative agency before proceeding to court.

Caption
The heading section of a pleading that contains the names of the parties, the name of the court, the title of the action, the docket or file number, and the name of the pleading.

Case 4: The Pregnant Waitress (Continued)

In employment discrimination cases, there is a requirement that an employee who has experienced discrimination at work first complain to the state or federal agency that handles such claims before being allowed to proceed with a lawsuit. Therefore, Dobbs's attorney instructed Diane to file a complaint with the local agency handling employment discrimination claims.

After Diane filed her complaint, the state agency conducted an investigation that led it to conclude that there was probable cause to believe she had been fired because of unlawful sex discrimination. After an unsuccessful attempt to resolve the dispute through informal negotiations with the restaurant owner, the agency issued a right-to-sue letter that authorized Dobbs to proceed with a lawsuit.

Drake's case against Small does not raise any administrative law issues. Therefore, Drake's lawyer did not need to involve an administrative agency prior to proceeding to litigation. However, separate from Drake's claims against her, Small may find herself before an administrative agency if the police determine the accident was her fault. For example, she might have to argue before a state licensing agency that her driver's license should not be revoked.

b. Pleadings

The pleadings are the documents that each side files with the court and serves on the other side to commence the lawsuit. Their purpose is to narrow and focus the issues involved. Pleadings begin with a **caption**. The caption must include the names of the parties, the name of the court, the title of the action, the docket or file number, and the name of the pleading.

Exhibit 6-1 shows what the caption would look like in Drake's case. First, the caption would identify Donald Drake as the plaintiff and Wilma Small as the defendant. It would also indicate that the case is being filed in the U.S. District Court for the District of Massachusetts and would leave space for the eventual

PRACTICE TIP

Especially in employment cases, even before seeking an administrative remedy, there may be a contractual or union procedure that must be followed, or else your client may be precluded from pursuing a remedy in court.

UNITED STATES DISTRICT COURT FOR THE DISTRICT OF MASSACHUSETTS

Civil Action, File Number _________

Donald Drake, Plaintiff	}	
v.	}	COMPLAINT
Wilma Small, Defendant	}	

Exhibit 6-1 Caption

Case 1: The Distressed Grandfather (Continued)

After reviewing the facts and the jurisdictional questions involved, Harper has determined that the best court in which to proceed with Drake's case is federal district court. She directs Taylor Kendall, a paralegal, to draft a complaint to initiate the lawsuit.

PRACTICE TIP

Find the specific caption that is required for each of the courts with which you frequently file pleadings. Then use your word processor to create some standard captions.

Complaint
The pleading that begins a lawsuit.

docket number to be entered by the court clerk. The court assigns the number at the time the lawyer files the complaint.

(1) The complaint

The initial document the plaintiff files is logically called a **complaint** because the plaintiff is the person starting the lawsuit, and hence complaining of some behavior. A complaint states the allegations that form the basis of the plaintiff's case.

Note that the complaint contains all of the following:

- a caption listing the names of the parties, the name of the court, the title of the action, and space for the docket file number to be provided by the court;
- all claims and defenses in numbered paragraphs that can be admitted or denied by the defendant(s);
- the basis for jurisdiction;
- the legal grounds for the case;
- the type of relief sought; and
- a request for a jury trial unless the plaintiff wants to waive the right to a jury trial

The requirements for the format and the contents of a federal complaint are spelled out in the Federal Rules of Civil Procedure. A complaint must contain allegations as to why the case falls within the court's jurisdiction, the grounds that form the basis of the plaintiff's case, and the relief desired. If the complaint is to be filed with a state court, the requirements are in the Rules of Civil Procedure for that state.

The body of the complaint consists of the allegations of facts that constitute the cause of action. The federal rules allow for **notice pleading**; that is, the complaint must identify the transaction from which the plaintiff's claim arises. In many states, however, the facts being pleaded must be "ultimate" facts, as opposed to conclusions of law.

In Drake's case, at a minimum, the complaint must include a statement indicating why he believes the federal district court has jurisdiction, a statement showing why Drake has a valid claim against Small, and finally what relief he would like the court to grant him. After considering all of these issues, Kendall drafted the complaint that appears in Exhibit 6-2. Locate each of these items in the complaint.

This sample complaint has only one **count,** or basis for the lawsuit: the negligence of Small. If the facts were different, however, the plaintiff could have alleged more than one basis for his lawsuit. For example, in Drake's case, if he did not know whether Small was simply being careless or had actually intended to hit Philip expressly to cause Drake's suffering, the complaint could include a count for the intentional infliction of emotional distress, as well as one for negligence. This is known as **pleading in the alternative.**

DISCUSSION QUESTION

4. Does it seem fair to you that plaintiffs should be allowed to plead in the alternative? Why or why not?

If a paralegal has drafted the complaint, the supervising lawyer must carefully review and sign it. In some states, there is a final requirement that the client verify the complaint. A **verification** consists of an affidavit signed by the client indicating that he or she has read the complaint and that its contents are correct.

Finally, the lawyer or paralegal will file the complaint with the court, which officially begins the lawsuit. Traditionally, filing pleadings and other legal documents involved delivering a hard copy to the court clerk's office during regular business hours. However, through electronic, or **e-filing,** the federal courts and many state courts now allow pleadings and other documents to be submitted electronically over the Internet.

In the federal courts, it is the **Case Management/Electronic Case Files (CM/ECF)** system that allows for the filing of electronic documents and the maintenance of the case docket. The CM/ECF system uses standard computer hardware, an Internet connection, and a browser, and requires that documents be submitted in **Portable Document Format (PDF).** In addition to allowing lawyers to file their documents over the Internet 24 hours a day, seven days a week, additional benefits include the reduction of paper, photocopy, postage and courier costs, and the ability to receive e-mail notices in CM/ECF cases.

Notice pleading
A method adopted by the federal rules in which the plaintiff simply informs the defendant of the claim and the general basis for it.

Count
In a complaint, one cause of action.

Pleading in the alternative
Including more than one count in a complaint; the counts do not need to be consistent.

Verification
An affidavit signed by the client indicating that he or she has read the complaint and that its contents are correct.

Electronic filing (e-filing)
The filing of court documents over the Internet as electronic files.

Case Management/ Electronic Case Files (CM/ECF)
A comprehensive case management system developed for the federal courts, allowing them to receive electronic filings and to maintain case files accessible via the Internet.

Portable Document Format (PDF)
A format that allows a document to be captured and electronic versions be sent, viewed, and printed consistently across multiple devices and platforms. Federal courts require all documents to be filed in PDF format.

UNITED STATES DISTRICT COURT FOR THE
DISTRICT OF MASSACHUSETTS

Civil Action, File Number _____

Donald Drake, Plaintiff   }
                                 }
         v.   }   COMPLAINT
                                 }
                                 }
Wilma Small, Defendant   }

1. The plaintiff, Donald Drake, is a natural person residing at 56 Bancroft Way, Springfield, Massachusetts.

2. The defendant, Wilma Small, is a natural person residing at 106 Hemingway Lane, Keene, New Hampshire.

3. Jurisdiction of this court is founded on diversity of citizenship. Plaintiff is a citizen of Massachusetts, and defendant is a citizen of New Hampshire. The matter in controversy exceeds, exclusive of interest and costs, the sum of seventy-five thousand dollars.

4. On September 1, 2020, while the plaintiff was walking on the sidewalk along a public way called Bishop Street in Springfield, Massachusetts, the defendant negligently drove a motor vehicle onto the sidewalk where the plaintiff's grandson, Philip Drake, was walking approximately thirty feet ahead of the plaintiff.

5. As a result of the defendant's negligence, the plaintiff's grandson was struck by the defendant's motor vehicle and instantly killed. The plaintiff viewed the entire accident.

6. As a direct result of viewing the death of his grandson, the plaintiff suffered a heart attack, great physical pain, mental suffering, and expenses for medical attention and hospitalization in the sum of one million dollars.

WHEREFORE the plaintiff demands judgment against the defendant in the sum of one million dollars, interest, and costs.

Plaintiff demands trial by jury.

Dated: _____

                                 _____
                                 Pat Harper BBO#098467
                                 333 Main St.
                                 Springfield, MA 01009
                                 413-787-9999

Exhibit 6-2 Complaint

CM/ECF allows courts to make case information immediately available to other parties and the public through the Internet using its Public Access to Court Electronic Records (PACER) program. Litigants receive one free copy of documents filed electronically in their cases, which they can save or print for their files. Additional copies are available to lawyers and the public for viewing or downloading at a minimal cost per page basis.[15] Copies of court opinions, as designated by the authoring judge, are available at no charge.

NETNOTE

A listing of courts accepting CM/ECF filings can be found at *uscourts.gov/ federalcourts/CMECF/Courts.aspx*. To see if your state or local courts accept electronic filings, you can go to the National Center for State Courts' website at *ncsc.org/Topics/Technology/Electronic-Filing/State-Links.aspx*. Information regarding the use of PACER, including a video tutorial can be found at *pacer.gov*.

---

(2) The summons

Before a court will hear a lawsuit, defendants must receive a **notice** that a suit has been filed against them. Courts require such **service** for reasons of basic fairness. A **summons** is a formal notice to defendants named in a lawsuit informing them that a suit has been filed against them and what they must do to respond to the allegations contained in the complaint. A separate summons is made for each defendant, and each summons must have a copy of the complaint attached.

Traditionally, the plaintiff's lawyer arranges to have a copy of the complaint and the summons hand-delivered to a defendant via a **process server.** On some occasions, proper notice could be satisfied by mailing the summons to the defendant's last known address, publishing copies of it in newspapers of general

Notice
Being informed of some act done or about to be done.

Service
The delivery of a pleading, subpoena, or other paper in a lawsuit to another party.

Summons
A notice informing the defendant of the lawsuit and requiring the defendant to respond or risk losing the suit.

Although paralegals may draft pleadings, they may *not* sign them. To do so would constitute the unauthorized practice of law (ULP).

Ethics Alert

---

[15] Anyone can use PACER, but users must first register. Once you start using PACER, you will receive a quarterly invoice. Under the current federal court rules, if your usage is less than $30 for the quarter, the fees will be waived.

UNITED STATES DISTRICT COURT FOR THE DISTRICT OF MASSACHUSETTS

Civil Action, File Number _____

Donald Drake, Plaintiff   }
                    }
        v.   }   SUMMONS
                    }
Wilma Small, Defendant   }

To the above-named Defendant:

    You are hereby summoned and required to serve upon <u>Pat Harper</u> plaintiff's attorney, whose address is <u>333 Main St., Springfield, MA 01009</u> an answer to the complaint which is herewith served upon you, within 20 days after service of this summons upon you, exclusive of the day of service. If you fail to do so, judgment by default will be taken against you for the relief demanded in this complaint.

           Witness _____ Esq,

at _____ the _____ day of _____ 20 _____.

         _____
         Clerk of Court

(Seal of Court)

    This summons is issued pursuant to Rule 4 of the Federal Rules of Civil Procedure.

Exhibit 6-3 Summons

circulation, or delivering it to a corporation's authorized agent. Registered agents can be found in the corporation's articles of incorporation on the secretary of state's website and should be noted and retained in the file when searching for the legal name of the corporation. Some jurisdictions also allow for electronic service in limited circumstances.

Case 1: The Distressed Grandfather (Continued)

    In addition to the complaint, Kendall prepared the summons shown in Exhibit 6-3. This would be served along with a copy of the complaint in order to notify the defendant, Small, of the nature of the claim.

(3)   The answer

Upon receiving the summons, the defendant has a designated time within which to file a formal answer to the complaint. This document is called an **answer** because it contains the defendant's answers to the charges laid out in the complaint. In an answer, a defendant can choose a combination of responses from among the following alternatives:

- deny the facts that the plaintiff says took place,
- admit the facts but assert that those facts do not provide the plaintiff with a legal remedy,
- claim that additional facts give rise to an **affirmative defense,**
- assert that the complaint contains procedural defects, and
- bring a claim of one's own against either the plaintiff or another defendant.

These options are not mutually exclusive.

When reviewing the complaint, notice that each paragraph is numbered, and each alleges only one pertinent fact or concept. In the answer, the defendant will respond to each of the numbered paragraphs.

In addition, if the plaintiff had not asked for a jury trial and the defendant wanted one, the defendant would have to ask for a jury trial in the answer. Otherwise, the right to a jury trial would be considered waived.

While the two basic and most common pleadings are the complaint and answer, there are other options as well, including a **counterclaim** (a counter-suit by the defendant against the plaintiff), a **cross-claim** (a suit by one defendant against another defendant), and a **third-party claim** (a suit by a defendant against someone not originally part of the lawsuit).

Figure 6-3 diagrams one example of how these various pleadings might be used in litigation. Here, Smith sued two defendants, Jones and Brown, by filing a complaint against them. Jones responded with an answer to the complaint and an additional counterclaim against the plaintiff. Brown filed an answer to the complaint, a cross-claim against Jones, and a **third-party claim** against Jim Jackson, someone whom the plaintiff had not named as a defendant in the original complaint.

In Drake's case, it does not appear that Small has any basis for a counterclaim. However, let us suppose the same altered facts laid out above, in which both Drake and Small were driving their own vehicles. If Small had been injured, in addition to alleging that she does not owe Drake any money because of his contributory negligence, she might countersue Drake to try to recover some money from him to compensate her for her own injuries.

One alternative to submitting an answer is simply not to respond at all—that is, not to file any documents with the court. However, the failure to take any action is viewed as an admission of the allegations contained in the complaint and creates a situation in which the plaintiff can seek a default judgment. In a **default judgment,** the judge awards the judgment against the party who fails to appear in court to contest the matter. While the plaintiff must still convince the judge that the claim is legitimate, the defendant has no right to

---

Process server
A person authorized by law to serve legal papers on defendants.

Affirmative defense
A defense whereby the defendant offers new evidence to avoid judgment.

Answer
Defendant's reply to the complaint. It may contain statements of denial, admission, or lack of knowledge and affirmative defenses.

Counterclaim
A claim by the defendant against the plaintiff.

PRACTICE TIP

You can search the web to find sheriffs and others who can perform service of process, but it is much more efficient to keep a current list in your address book or computer database. While all federal district courts now accept e-filings, the states have been slower to abandon the traditional hard copy approach. Many state courts now offer e-filing as an option, however, and some even mandate it.

Figure 6-3   Pleadings

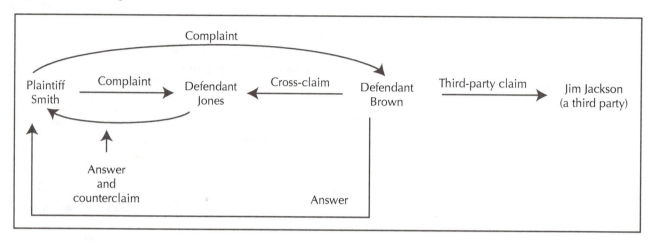

challenge the evidence presented or to present contrary evidence. Although it is possible to have a default judgment set aside, it is a very difficult task.

Small's answer might look like Exhibit 6-4.

c. Pretrial Motions to End Part or All of the Litigation

Sometimes the parties feel they have grounds for having the lawsuit dismissed without a trial. Therefore, in addition to or instead of filing an answer, the defendant may file a motion asking that the court immediately dismiss the case. A **motion** is a written request directed to the court. Under the federal rules, there are two basic motions that can end part or all of a lawsuit: Rule 12 motions, known as motions to dismiss, and Rule 56 motions, known as motions for summary judgment.

(1) Rule 12 motions to dismiss

Rule 12 outlines the basic types of pretrial motions, as well as how they are presented to the court. This rule offers seven options, such as arguing that the court lacks jurisdiction over the subject matter or over the defendant. But probably the most important of the Rule 12 motions is the sixth, commonly referred to as a **12(b)(6) motion.** This motion states that the plaintiff has failed "to state a claim upon which relief can be granted." If the defendant can convince the court that she has a solid foundation for such a motion, then the court will dismiss the complaint. This means that there will be no trial.

In Drake's case, that would mean that no judge or jury will ever hear about the accident or about Drake's injuries. Small's lawyer might very well file such a motion, arguing that, in Massachusetts, trial courts have no right to grant relief to a grandfather who suffers injury upon seeing a grandchild negligently killed.

(2) Rule 56 motions for summary judgment

Another method that lawyers may use to try to end a case before trial is through filing a **Rule 56 motion,** better known generally as a **summary judgment motion.** A lawyer's objective in filing a summary judgment motion is generally the same as that in filing a 12(b)(6) motion—to resolve the case without the need for a trial.

Cross-claim
A claim by one defendant against another defendant or by one plaintiff against another plaintiff.

Third-party claim
A claim by a defendant against someone in addition to the persons the plaintiff has already sued.

Default judgment
A judgment entered against a party who fails to complete a required step, such as answering the complaint.

Motion
A request made to the court.

12(b)(6) motion
A request that the court find the plaintiff has failed to state a valid claim and dismiss the complaint.

UNITED STATES DISTRICT COURT FOR
THE DISTRICT OF MASSACHUSETTS

Civil Action No. 20-483

Donald Drake, Plaintiff   }
                           }
v.   }   ANSWER
                           }
Wilma Small, Defendant   }

First Defense

The complaint fails to state a claim against the defendant upon which relief can be granted, as there is no right to recover for the injuries suffered by a grandparent upon seeing the negligently caused death of a grandchild.

Second Defense

1. The defendant has no knowledge as to the allegations in paragraph 1.

2. The defendant has no knowledge as to the allegations in paragraph 2.

3. The defendant admits the allegation in paragraph 3.

4. The defendant admits that the plaintiff was walking on a sidewalk along a public way called Bishop Street in Springfield, Massachusetts, on September 1, 2020. The defendant denies the allegation of negligence contained in paragraph 4. The defendant is without knowledge or information sufficient to form a belief as to the truth of the remaining allegations contained in paragraph 4.

5. The defendant denies the allegation of negligence contained in paragraph 5. The defendant is without knowledge or information sufficient to form a belief as to the truth of the remaining allegations contained in paragraph 5.

6. The defendant is without knowledge or information sufficient to form a belief as to the truth of the allegation contained in paragraph 6.

Dated: _____

_____
William Smith
886 State St.
Keene, NH 03431
603-787-1111

Exhibit 6-4 Answer

One major difference between the two motions is that when faced with a 12(b)(6) motion, the court must make a determination based only on the facts as alleged in the complaint, and it must assume that those facts are true for purposes of deciding the motion. (If the court denies the motion, all parties treat the facts as once again being in dispute.)

Rule 56 motion (summary judgment motion)
A request that the court grant judgment in favor of the moving party because there is no genuine issue as to any material fact and the moving party is entitled to judgment as a matter of law. It is similar to a 12(b)(6) motion except that the court also considers matters outside the pleadings.

In a summary judgment motion, however, the court will consider additional evidence as presented in documents other than the pleadings, such as depositions, answers to interrogatories, admissions on file, and affidavits. Rule 56 provides that if those documents show that

- there is no genuine issue as to any material fact and
- the moving party is entitled to a judgment as a matter of law,
- then the court will grant the motion and enter judgment for the moving party.

Plaintiffs as well as defendants can bring summary judgment motions. The purpose of a trial is to determine the facts. If the facts are already known, there is no need for a trial, and either side can ask the court to determine that there is no need for a trial and to declare it the winner.

Summary judgment motions can also relate to just part of the case. If a judge grants a partial summary judgment, a trial will be held, but only on the issues still in dispute. For example, assume that during her deposition, Small broke down and admitted that her speeding caused the accident. The court might grant a partial summary judgment in favor of Drake on the issue of liability but still hold a trial on the issue of what caused his heart attack; a combination of old age and poor eating habits or seeing his grandson die in the accident.

To summarize, the most fundamental difference between Rule 12(b)(6) motions and summary judgment motions is that Rule 12(b)(6) motions are based on just the complaint and the law. Summary judgment motions are based on the complaint, the law, and something else. To illustrate, assume in Drake's case that case law held that grandparents cannot sue in a situation such as his. If his complaint stated that he was Philip's grandfather, Small's lawyer could bring a 12(b)(6) motion arguing that the case should be dismissed. If, however, the complaint had not included his relationship to Philip, Small's lawyer could send him a request for admissions. If Drake admitted that he was Philip's grandfather, Small's lawyer could file a summary judgment motion based on the complaint, the law, and a copy of his response in the request for admissions.

P RACTICE T IP

When going to court, bring clean printouts of all cases that the judge may want to see.

(3) Appealing a summary judgment or motion to dismiss

A court's decision to grant a motion to dismiss or a summary judgment is considered a final decision, and as such is appealable. If the losing party convinces the appellate court to reverse the trial court's decision, the case will then be returned to the trial court so that the parties can proceed with the litigation. Having an appellate court reverse the decision to grant a motion to dismiss or a summary judgment motion does not mean that the prevailing party will have won on the merits. All the prevailing party will have won is the right to proceed with the litigation.

Case 1: The Distressed Grandfather (Continued)

Small's lawyer filed a summary judgment motion on the grounds that Small owed Drake, a grandfather, no duty of care. The trial court granted this motion. Harper appealed this decision and convinced the appellate court to reverse the trial court's decision.

By getting the appellate court to reverse the summary judgment motion, Drake has not yet won his case. But he has won the right to continue with the lawsuit from the point at which the motion for summary judgment was granted.

Legal Reasoning Exercise

3. You are a trial court judge. In each case, would you allow a motion to dismiss, grant summary judgment, or order the case to proceed to trial?

a. The law in your state is that a pet owner cannot recover for the emotional distress she suffers from seeing her pet injured or killed. Sam, a German Shepherd, bit Suzy, a toy poodle, killing her. Suzy's owner, Sarah, sued Sam's owner for the emotional distress she suffered in seeing her dog killed. In the complaint, it stated that Suzy was a dog.

b. Assume the same facts as in a., but also assume that in the complaint, Sarah's lawyer did not indicate that Suzy was a dog, merely stating that Sarah suffered emotional distress when she saw Suzy killed. In an answer to a Request for Admissions, however, Sarah admitted that Suzy was a dog.

c. The law in your state is that landowners owe a duty of reasonable care to those invited onto their land, but no duty towards trespassers. Tom went onto John's land. Tom tripped over some garden tools that John had left lying outside on his lawn. Tom sued John for the injuries he suffered. In the complaint, Tom admitted that when he was injured, he was trespassing on John's land.

d. Assume the same facts as in c., but also assume that in Tom's complaint, there was no mention of his being a trespasser. When deposed, Tom admitted that he was injured while trespassing on John's land.

e. Assume the same facts as in c., but also assume that in Tom's complaint, there was no mention of his being a trespasser. When deposed, Tom denied that he was trespassing, and in fact, claimed that he had been invited to John's house to enjoy an evening of playing cards. At his deposition, John denied that he had invited Tom to his house.

f. The law in your state is that an owner of a wild animal is strictly liable for any injuries caused by that animal. Sam kept a pet monkey. One day when his best friend, Jim, came over to his house for lunch, the pet monkey unexpectedly and suddenly attacked Jim, severely injuring him. Everyone agrees to the facts. The only issue is the appropriate amount of money to award Jim to compensate him for his injuries.

d. Discovery

Once the defendant files an answer, each side frequently begins using various **discovery** devices to find out more about the strengths and weaknesses of the other side's case. The purpose of discovery is to help each side find out as much information as possible so that each can fairly evaluate the case and prepare for trial or settlement. The parties seek to discover information about the identification of witnesses, the nature of the testimony that such witnesses can be expected to provide, and the contents of relevant contracts, medical reports, and so forth. Such information is acquired through various discovery tools, including interrogatories, depositions, requests for admissions, motions to produce documents, and motions for physical and mental exams. In addition to making trials run more efficiently, discovery often makes it more likely that the parties can reach an out-of-court settlement.

PARALEGAL PROFILE ||||

Alice Staley
Paralegal
State Farm Insurance Companies

I am employed as a paralegal in the law department of a large insurance company. I work as part of a team with the supervising attorney, our secretary, and defense counsel and claims personnel in managing litigation with allegations of bad faith. I work closely under the supervision of the managing attorneys.

I received my Bachelor of Science in Education degree from Illinois State University before I knew anything about paralegals. After working as a secretary for attorneys who managed litigation at an insurance company, I made the decision to re-enter college and take paralegal classes to better understand my job and the litigation process and vocabulary. Upon completion of the paralegal classes, I was able to move into a paralegal position.

Strong technical skills, critical thinking, attention to detail, good oral communication and writing skills, and a strong work ethic are among my strengths that have helped me with my work. The ability to work independently while being part of a team is important. I bring to my attorneys' attention things that need to be handled that are critical to the matter. I am relied upon to keep track of dates and to complete work in a timely manner without constant monitoring. I take part in conference calls and summarize the record of what is said and the proposed action plan.

Discovery assignments allow me to use my writing skills and critical thinking skills as I draft responses to the discovery and identify and collect corporate documents potentially responsive to the discovery. I work with contacts throughout the company in many departments.

On occasion, I am called on to do research to find similar cases or to obtain information on a case I am working with. Sometimes, I work with company contacts to locate the person who can best assist with responding to what is needed. The job is a mix of day-to-day routine tasks as well as whatever comes up, which usually needs quick action and a response. I have opportunities to learn new skills and grow in my role.

I encourage participation in an internship as part of the paralegal classes. The time I was an intern allowed me to learn new software and the procedures to handle the assigned work. This education about the job increased my skills. I also had a mentor who helped answer many questions and encouraged me to further develop my knowledge.

Paralegals should always strive to improve their skills, learn new things, and work collaboratively with their peers. Participation in professional associations is a great way to increase your expertise and meet others in legal positions.

(1) Interrogatories

Interrogatories are written questions sent by one party in a lawsuit to another party to obtain written answers in return. **Interrogatories** are used to help locate potential witnesses, establish dates, determine a person's medical or financial condition, and inquire about the existence of documentary evidence. Lawyers frequently ask their paralegals to draft interrogatories. A sample of the types of questions that Kendall might draft in Drake's case can be found in Exhibit 6-5.

Interrogatories
Written questions sent by one side to the opposing side, answered under oath.

Note that interrogatories are only sent to parties and may not be served on nonparties. Also, courts usually limit the number of interrogatories that can be sent.

When a law office receives interrogatories directed to its client, the client usually is instructed to write out the answers as fully as possible. A lawyer may then edit these answers and prepare the formal responses, which will be returned to the other party's lawyer. When answers to a firm's interrogatories are received from the other party, a paralegal may help in analyzing and organizing them.

A major advantage of interrogatories is that they are relatively inexpensive to prepare. A major disadvantage is that the answers can be closely reviewed by that person's lawyer or paralegal before they are returned to the party submitting the questions. Other disadvantages include restrictions on the number of interrogatories allowed and on not being able to ask timely follow-up questions.

DISCUSSION QUESTION

5. In addition to the questions raised in the sample interrogatory shown in Exhibit 6-5, what other types of information do you think Kendall attempted to gather through the interrogatories?

(2) Depositions

If a lawyer would like to ask questions of a nonparty, such as the doctor who treated Drake, or would like to ask questions of either a party or a nonparty in person, that lawyer will consider taking a deposition. A **deposition** is sworn testimony that is taken outside the courtroom without a judge being present.

Deposition
The pretrial oral questioning of a witness under oath.

UNITED STATES DISTRICT COURT FOR THE
DISTRICT OF MASSACHUSETTS

Civil Action No. 20-483

Donald Drake, Plaintiff   }

v.   }   PLAINTIFF'S INTERROGATORIES

Wilma Small, Defendant   }   TO WILMA SMALL

[The interrogatories start with fairly standard boilerplate language. Lawyers use the word "boilerplate" to refer to standard language found in a particular type of legal document. In the case of interrogatories, the boilerplate language at the beginning sets out basic information such as to whom the interrogatory answers are to be returned, the deadline for their return, and instructions for answering the interrogatories. This language is then followed by the specific questions.]

1.   State your full name, age, full address, and telephone number.

2.   At the time of the events referred to in paragraphs 4 and 5 of the complaint, did you have a valid driver's license?

3.   Has your driver's license ever been suspended or revoked, and if so, state
     a. When and where it was suspended or revoked;
     b. The grounds upon which the license was suspended or revoked.

. . . .

15. During the 24 hours preceding the events referred to in paragraphs 4 and 5 of the complaint, had you consumed any medicines, drugs, or alcoholic beverages of any type, and if so, state
     a. The type and amount consumed;
     b. The length of time over which the substance was consumed;
     c. The names, addresses, and telephone numbers of every person who has knowledge as to your consumption of the substance.

. . . .

Dated: _____   _____

                                  Pat Harper
                                  333 Main St.
                                  Springfield, MA 01009
                                  413-787-9999

Exhibit 6-5 Interrogatories

Although a judge is not present, there is a court reporter who administers the oath and records the testimony. The format of a deposition is similar to that of a trial, in that one lawyer questions the witness and the opposing lawyer has an opportunity to make objections and cross-examine the witness.

Depositions can be used to preserve the testimony of a witness when that witness may not be available for the trial (as in the case of a physician), or when the lawyer wants to ensure that the story of the individual being deposed cannot be changed. Because a person can be subpoenaed to be deposed, a statement may be obtained from a witness otherwise unwilling to talk to the lawyer or to an investigator. A lawyer is responsible for asking the questions during a deposition.

PRACTICE TIP

Psychological games can often be played regarding the scheduling and holding of depositions. These tactics can involve everything from where the deposition is held to how the room is arranged. If you notice this happening, help your lawyer and client take control. For example, if the chair your client is to sit in has no arms or is otherwise uncomfortable, suggest that the seating arrangement be changed.

The advantages of a deposition over interrogatories are that the deposing lawyer is not limited in the number of questions he or she can ask, the **deponent's** answers are usually more spontaneous, the deposing lawyer can view the demeanor of the person answering the questions, and under certain circumstances, the answers may be used later in a court trial. Because the answers can be used to contradict the deponent's testimony at trial or to show inconsistencies, lawyers often advise their clients to give honest, but not lengthy, answers and to treat the deposition question as they would if they were being questioned while in front of a jury. The major disadvantages are the time and cost involved. At a minimum, a deposition requires the time and presence of both lawyers, a court reporter, and the deponent. Without a special court order, federal rules limit the number of depositions to ten.

Deponent
The person who is being asked questions at a deposition.

Case 1: The Distressed Grandfather (Continued)

The lawyer representing Smith arranged for a deposition of Dr. Gary Booth, one of the doctors who treated Drake after his heart attack.

---

(3) Requests for admissions

A **request for admissions** is a written document that lists statements regarding specific facts for the other party to admit or deny. Once admitted, a matter cannot be contested. The purpose of the request for admissions is to clarify what is not in dispute, and therefore what will not need to be resolved through a trial. Paralegals frequently draft requests for admissions.

Request for admissions
A document that lists statements regarding specific items for the other party to admit or deny.

(4) Requests for documents and physical examinations

The motion to produce documents is used to obtain documents in the possession of one of the parties. Documents in the possession of third parties can be obtained through a **subpoena duces tecum.** The motion for a physical

Subpoena duces tecum
A court order that a person who is not a party to litigation appear at a trial or deposition and bring requested documents.

examination is usually used in personal injury cases or other situations where the health of one of the parties is at issue.

(5) Electronic discovery

Traditionally, discovery requests resulted in the production of one or more boxes of printed documents. However, as law firms and businesses have become more and more computerized, reports, memos, letters, e-mails, voice-mail messages, text messages, and other types of electronic communication are frequently created and then stored in electronic form (e.g., as Microsoft Word, Microsoft Excel, or Adobe Acrobat PDF files). Although these files take far less room to store and are typically easier to send to any interested parties, the trend toward using electronic documents also creates new challenges. For example, some law firms and other businesses employ proprietary software that creates data that cannot easily be read by others.

Electronic discovery (e-discovery)
The process of gaining information from the adverse party when that information is in electronic form, such as e-mails, voice mails, text messages, photographs, spreadsheets, and documents.

Failing to request **electronic discovery** may be grounds for a malpractice lawsuit or an ethics violation. Consider the relatively routine automobile accident case. Liability seems clear—the defendant ran a red light. However, at issue is the amount of damages that the plaintiff suffered. She claims to have ongoing pain and an inability to return to work. But what if, in an e-mail to a friend, she describes spending last weekend water skiing, or better yet, posts a picture of her doing so on her Facebook page? Finding that e-mail or Facebook post could make the difference between winning and losing the case.

PRACTICE TIP

E-Discovery: The Paralegal Perspective
by Suzanne A. Wells, Paralegal
Morrison Mahoney LLP
Springfield, Massachusetts

1. **Meet and Confer Conference:** Do not underestimate the importance of the initial meet and confer conference, which is designed to save time, money, and effort. To prepare an attorney for the conference, review the complaint and any information the parties have shared regarding the people involved and the types of documents available. Create a memorandum listing search terms, the format in which documents will be produced, names of people involved, and time frames. Also confer with the client (get permission first) and list the storage devices available to be searched. Using the memorandum you have prepared, the attorney will only need to circle what is agreed upon in order for the e-discovery process to move to the next step: searching the storage devices.
2. **Document Everything:** This is a good practice for a paralegal no matter what the task, but especially in e-discovery. Paralegals should not perform the actual searches, as the individuals who execute the searches may be required to testify. Instead, paralegals should document the

searches done by the user of the storage device or the network admin-istrator. To document the searches, create a table identifying the date, time, the storage device, the search terms, the number of results, and the number of results that were relevant. Update the table as the searches are performed so the information is accurate. Months later, if opposing counsel contends that documents are missing or a search was not per-formed on a particular storage device; the table will help to determine if a second search needs to be conducted. The table will also assist the paralegal in writing an affidavit to the court to show that a good faith effort was made to search and produce relevant information.

3. **Relevance Review:** Usually, the attorney will review the documents to determine what is relevant. However, if there are a substantial number of files, the attorney may ask the paralegal to narrow it down by catego-rizing the documents:
   a. definitely relevant: communications between the plaintiff and defendant,
   b. not relevant: for example, spam e-mail, such as advertisements that contain the plaintiff's first name, and
   c. possibly relevant: for example, reports to the company president about a similar situation to the one at issue in the lawsuit.

4. **Bates Stamping:** Bates stamp numbering is a useful tool when organizing the thousands of pages generated by e-discovery. Bates stamping assigns a unique, individual number to each page so that out of the thousands of document pages, no two pages have the same number. This makes it easier to locate documents during depositions, hearings, and trials.

5. **E-discovery Companies:** For really complicated systems involving a variety of storage devices (networks, laptop, desktops, mobile phones, archived information, the Cloud), the parties should consider hiring an e-discovery company. E-discovery companies have the technology to perform thor-ough searches quickly and efficiently, as well as special software to assist the attorneys and paralegals in reviewing each file for relevancy.

6. **Good Faith Effort:** It is not possible to collect every electronically stored document. Opposing counsel will say they want everything, but judges, experts, network administrators, and attorneys, including opposing counsel, know it is not possible to produce everything. The key is to make a good faith effort to obtain as much of the relevant electronically stored information as possible.

The greatest challenge facing those engaged in e-discovery is presented by the sheer volume of the electronically stored data, which can be overwhelming. Think how a single e-mail can be duplicated many times when the receiver sends a reply to the sender or forwards the e-mail to others. Hence, a single e-mail can turn into hundreds of "documents." In response to the growing issues associated with e-discovery, in 2006 the Federal Rules of Civil Procedure were amended to clarify how discovery of **electronically stored information (ESI)** should be handled. Many states have made similar revisions (or are in the process of con-sidering revisions) that focus on electronic data.

Electronically stored information (ESI)
Information created, disbursed, or stored in an electronic format.

(6) Preservation of potential evidence

In addition to the very time-consuming process of reviewing and recording useful information found either in hard copy or electronic format, is the problem of simply getting the documents before they have been either shredded or deleted. Federal and state statutes sometimes require businesses to keep certain types of documents for a set period of time, but absent such a restriction, the documents being sought may be lost due to routine, good-faith operations of a document management system. Sanctions may apply for willful alteration or destruction of ESI once there is a reasonable belief that litigation may arise. It is therefore incumbent upon lawyers to inform their clients that as soon as there is a reasonable belief that litigation may be involved, they must preserve all documents, even those they would otherwise routinely delete. This is known as a **litigation hold.** If this is not done, and documents are altered or destroyed, such actions can be seen as **spoliation**, the willful destruction or alternation of relevant documents. Sanctions for spoliation can range from the court ordering additional discovery to setting monetary fines to, in extreme cases, instructing the jury that it can infer that the documents would have been harmful to the party that destroyed them or to dismissing the case altogether.

Once litigation commences, the lawyers must hold a **meet and confer conference,** at which they develop a proposed discovery plan. The plan may include a **claw-back provision.** Assuming that reasonable methods are used to protect confidential material, a claw-back provision gives the parties a way to retrieve confidential information that they may inadvertently give to the other side.

Once the parties and the court agree to a plan, the party required to produce ESI must review the thousands (or even millions!) of documents for relevancy and privilege. Sometimes these records are reviewed manually. Other times, because of the sheer volume of material, computer programs can be written to assist with the process. The relevant documents are then given to the requesting party.

(7) Enforcing discovery rights

The parties to a lawsuit are legally obligated to respond to discovery requests. If a party refuses to respond, the opposing lawyer can file a motion seeking a court order requiring the other side to comply with a valid discovery request. A plaintiff's failure to follow such a court order can result in one of the following sanctions: a prohibition against using certain evidence, a dismissal of some counts, and, on rare occasions, a **dismissal with prejudice** of the entire case. A dismissal with prejudice means that the case cannot be refiled.

On the other hand, there are limits to the materials that each side must supply. If the judge is convinced that discovery attempts have gone beyond the bounds of reasonableness and amount to an undue burden or harassment, the judge can issue a protective order to allow the party to refuse to comply with certain types of discovery requests.

Litigation hold
A requirement that routine alteration or destruction of ESI must stop whenever there is a reasonable belief that litigation may arise.

Spoliation
The destruction or alteration of documents relevant to a case.

Meet and confer conference
In federal court, a mandated conference at which the parties must develop a discovery plan.

Claw-back provision
An agreement whereby privileged documents inadvertently produced can be retrieved.

Dismissal with prejudice
A court order that ends a lawsuit; the suit cannot be refiled by the same parties.

DISCUSSION QUESTION

6. If you were doing the discovery plan for Drake, what methods of discovery would you prefer? Why? Would your answer change if you were representing Small? Why or why not?

e. Settlement or Pretrial Conference

Due in part to the information gained through discovery, most cases settle rather than go to trial. Settlement is a possibility at any time, even before the commencement of a lawsuit, but human nature being what it is, it often seems to happen on the very eve of trial. One method for trying to encourage settlement is the pretrial conference.

Pretrial conferences are informal sessions in which the opposing lawyers meet (usually in the presence of the judge) to discuss the case before it goes to trial. Such conferences focus on the issues to be presented at the trial and encourage the parties to agree to matters that they are not contesting. They also make the trial more efficient and encourage out-of-court settlements. The hope is that as both sides learn more about the strengths and weaknesses of the case, they will be more likely to agree on the probable outcome of a trial, and therefore reach a mutually agreeable accommodation. Such accommodations are encouraged because they serve the public interest by easing the pressure on an overburdened court system.

If the efforts to settle fail, a trial date is set, and various matters related to how the trial will be conducted may be discussed. For example, in a case involving sensitive material a lawyer may make a **motion in limine.** A motion in limine is made to prevent reference to specific information in the presence of the jury. A lawyer might also file a motion requesting that the judge allow inquiry into certain areas during **voir dire,** the portion of the trial during which potential jurors are questioned to determine whether they are fit to serve on a jury.

> **Pretrial conference**
> A meeting of the lawyers and the judge to discuss a case prior to the beginning of the trial.

> **Motion in limine**
> A request that the court order that certain information not be mentioned in the presence of the jury.

> **Voir dire**
> An examination of a prospective juror to see if he or she is fit to serve as a juror on a specific case.

2. The Trial

If the case is not settled, then it proceeds to trial. Even if you have never seen a trial in person, no doubt you have watched enough movies and television shows to have a general feeling for how a trial is conducted. You know that there are opening statements by lawyers, testimony by witnesses, closing statements, and verdicts.

While judges, and sometimes juries, play an indispensable role, lawyers play the most visible (and, many would argue, the most important) role during a trial. Under our **adversarial system,** the lawyers are responsible for presenting all of the relevant facts and arguments needed for a neutral judge or jury to reach a proper decision. It is the lawyer's responsibility to serve the client's interests, and the judge's role is limited to that of a neutral arbitrator of the rules. Within certain limits, it is the lawyer who determines what witnesses to call and what questions to ask.

Although the majority of lawsuits filed never reach the trial stage, the results of those that are tried influence the results of future settlements. For example, some companies compile and publish reports of recently decided personal injury cases in different areas of the country. When parties learn of the amount of damages being awarded in similar cases, they may see the wisdom of settling their case out of court.

> **Adversarial system**
> A system characterized by competing, opposing parties overseen by a neutral decision maker.

PRACTICE TIP

Trial-related paralegal tasks during the trial stage generally include the following:

- delivering all necessary documents, trial notebooks, and exhibits to the courtroom;
- making travel arrangements;
- arranging any special equipment needs;
- serving subpoenas on all necessary parties;
- assisting with voir dire;
- coordinating the attendance of clients and witnesses for testifying;
- handling all documents and exhibits;
- taking notes and observing;
- maintaining contact with the office, court personnel, and witnesses; and
- reviewing the case and presentations for opening and closing statements.

---

a. *The Right to a Jury Trial*

Under the Seventh Amendment to the U.S. Constitution, the right to a jury trial extends to most types of federal civil cases. In contrast, each state has defined for itself the extent to which juries are to be available in state courts. Generally, you will find juries provided for, either by statute or by constitution, in criminal cases and in contractual and tort matters exceeding a specific dollar limit. In all of these cases, the right to a jury trial is an affirmative right. It must be requested in the pleadings or it will be considered waived. In most states, you will not find juries in divorce and probate cases.

The basic function of the jury is to resolve the factual, as opposed to the legal, questions raised in the case. Generally, this comes down to deciding how much credibility to give to the often conflicting testimony of various witnesses. When damage awards are called for, the jury must decide how to measure pain and suffering in terms of dollars and cents. In cases of a bench trial, where a jury is not used, the judge takes over the jury's function in addition to the normal duties of presiding over the trial and resolving the legal questions raised.

Under the common law, a jury consisted of 12 people. However, there is nothing that is constitutionally significant about that number, and 6-person juries have been used in civil cases at both the federal and the state levels. Furthermore, it is not unusual to select 1 or 2 extra jurors as alternates, especially where the trial is expected to last for more than a few days. These alternates sit in the jury box with their fellow jurors throughout the trial and are used as substitutes if regular jurors are unable to continue. An alternate does not participate in the deliberations, however, unless he or she has replaced one of the original jurors.

b. *Jury Selection*

The first formal step in a jury trial is the selection of individual jurors from a pool. The modern trend is to require almost everyone to serve as a juror. In the voir dire process of selecting individual jurors, potential jurors are questioned to determine whether they are fit to serve on the jury for that specific case. For example, a potential juror would be disqualified for having a personal relationship with a party in the case or with one of the lawyers involved. Potential jurors may also be disqualified if they have been exposed to high levels of prejudicial pretrial publicity or if they have been involved in similar lawsuits themselves.

Lawyers use two types of challenges when seeking to prevent specific individuals from serving as jurors. The first is a **challenge for cause,** used when a lawyer wants to convince the judge that something about the person's background or answers demonstrates some type of bias. If the judge agrees, the person will not be seated. The number of such challenges, whether raised or granted, is unlimited. In some well-publicized and highly controversial cases, lawyers have gone through hundreds of potential jurors before arriving at the final 12.

The second is a **peremptory challenge** that allows a lawyer to have a potential juror removed without giving a reason. Peremptory challenges are limited in number. In deciding whether to use one, lawyers must weigh the risk of having to accept a worse juror later if they have exhausted their limited supply of peremptory challenges.

While lawyers need not give a reason for why they used a peremptory challenge, they cannot dismiss jurors based on race. In *Batson v. Kentucky*, the U.S. Supreme Court held that to purposefully exclude members of the defendant's race is to deny defendants their equal protection rights.[16] Most recently, in *Flowers v. Mississippi*,[17] the Supreme Court applied this principle to a case involving a black defendant who had been criminally prosecuted for murder in six separate trials. At his sixth trial, he was found guilty and sentenced to death. He appealed, arguing that the state had engaged in racial discrimination when using its peremptory challenges. The Supreme Court set out what it viewed as the four critical facts that required reversal.

> First, in the six trials combined, the State employed its peremptory challenges to strike 41 of the 42 black prospective jurors that it could have struck—a statistic that the State acknowledged at oral argument in this Court. Second, in the most recent trial, the sixth trial, the State exercised peremptory strikes against five of the six black prospective jurors. Third, at the sixth trial, in an apparent effort to find pretextual reasons to strike black prospective jurors, the State engaged in dramatically disparate questioning of black and white prospective jurors.[18] Fourth, the State then struck at least one black prospective juror, Carolyn Wright, who was similarly situated to white prospective jurors who were not struck by the State. We need not and do not decide that any one of those four facts alone would require reversal. All that we need to decide, and all that we do decide, is that all of the relevant facts and circumstances taken together establish that the trial court committed clear error in concluding that the State's peremptory strike of black prospective juror Carolyn Wright was not "motivated in substantial part by discriminatory intent." In reaching that conclusion, we break no new legal ground. We simply enforce and reinforce *Batson* by applying it to the extraordinary facts of this case.[19]

Challenge for cause
A method for excusing a prospective juror based on the juror's inability to serve in an unbiased manner.

Peremptory challenge
A method for excusing a prospective juror in which no reason need be given.

PRACTICE TIP

Today, some professionals specialize in jury selection analysis. However, if your firm cannot afford such a professional, you can perform many of the same functions by sitting at the counsel table with your supervising lawyer and helping spot potential problems. Make sure to keep track of the peremptory challenges. There are apps that can assist with voir dire, or you can use a paper system. Write a table to add each juror as they are seated, and two numbered lists where you can record the peremptory challenges of each side.

---

[16] Batson v. Kentucky, 476 U.S. 79 (1986)
[17] 139 S. Ct. 2228 (2019)
[18] 145 questions were asked of the 5 black prospective jurors and 12 questions were asked of the 11 white seated jurors.
[19] Flowers, 139 S. Ct. at 2235.

DISCUSSION QUESTIONS

7. Many people argue that lawsuits have become too complex for the average juror. Do you think there are certain types of lawsuits where the jury should be composed only of experts in that field? Should jury trials be eliminated entirely in some areas of the law?

8. Jury experts work under the theory that certain types of people will be likely to favor one side over the other. For example, in a medical malpractice case, a person may lean toward the doctor, while others will favor the patient. Can you think of any groups that you could characterize in this way? Do you think this is a valid approach to choosing a jury? Even if valid, should it be used?

c. Opening Statements

Once the jury is selected, the lawyers make opening statements, in which they outline the evidence they hope to present. The plaintiff's and defendant's lawyers state their theories of the case and describe, from their respective points of view, what allegedly took place and to what they expect the witnesses to testify. The jury is thus presented with a framework for viewing the upcoming testimony.

Because the plaintiff has the burden of proving his or her case, the plaintiff's lawyer presents the first opening argument. In most cases, the defendant's lawyer makes an opening statement immediately following that of the plaintiff's lawyer. At other times, the defense waits until the plaintiff's lawyer has finished presenting the plaintiff's witnesses and exhibits and the defense is about to present its case.

d. Presentation of Evidence

After the opening statements, the plaintiff's lawyer presents evidence in the form of witness testimony and exhibits. The exhibits consist of such things as medical records, accident reports, videos, and photographs. Exhibits can only be introduced through witnesses. For example, accident reports are generally admitted through the officer who wrote the report. Specific rules of evidence dictate what types of evidence can be admitted and the manner in which witnesses can be questioned.

In considering evidence, it is essential to be aware of the difference between facts and opinions. When a witness testifies that he saw the defendant's automobile strike the plaintiff's car broadside, he is testifying about a fact he observed. But when that same witness says the defendant was driving too fast for the icy condition of the road, he is stating an opinion. Generally, only expert witnesses, such as doctors and police officers, can testify as to their opinions, which they have formed based on their expert knowledge.

In conducting the **direct examination** of a witness, a lawyer usually cannot ask leading questions. A **leading question** is one that suggests the answer. For example, "Wouldn't you say the defendant appeared to be very angry at that point in time?" is a leading question.

PRACTICE TIP

When accompanying your supervising lawyer to court, you need to bring three essential items with you: (1) a list of the witnesses, along with their phone numbers (if a witness unexpectedly fails to appear, you can call and try to solve the problem); (2) a pin of the courthouse that you can send as a message to someone's phone or written directions to the courthouse and parking instructions that you can read over the phone to any missing witness; and (3) a cell phone.

Direct examination
The questioning of your own witness.

Leading question
A question that suggests the answer; generally, leading questions may not be asked during direct examination of a witness.

Once the plaintiff's lawyer has completed questioning a witness, the defendant's lawyer may **cross-examine** that same witness. The cross-examination clarifies any potentially misleading statements or half-truths and sometimes attacks the credibility of the witness. For example, the defense lawyer may attempt to bring out possible biases or the inability of witnesses to have seen clearly what they claim to have seen. On cross-examination, a lawyer may ask leading questions; however, the lawyer may not ask questions on a new topic.

Cross-examination
The questioning of an opposing witness.

The defendant's cross-examination is then followed by redirect examination, where the plaintiff's lawyer has the opportunity to ask additional questions of the witness to rehabilitate the witness after the defense's attack on the witness's credibility. These questions cannot be used to raise new subjects or to explore topics that were not covered as part of the cross-examination. The redirect is then followed by an opportunity for recross-examination by the defendant's lawyer, but that must, in turn, be limited to topics raised during the redirect. At that point, the witness is finally excused, and the plaintiff's lawyer then proceeds to call the next witness.

Throughout the process of questioning witnesses and presenting evidence, the lawyers must keep in mind that appellate courts usually require them to raise appropriate objections at the proper times during the trial. Practically, a lawyer will often simply state "Objection" at the point at which the opposing lawyer or a witness makes a remark, without stating the basis for the objection. If it is a common objection and the basis for it is obvious, the judge will rule immediately. If the nature of the objection is not immediately clear, the judge will ask the lawyer to explain the reasons for the objection before either sustaining or overruling it. In some situations, the judge may have the jury removed from the courtroom while the lawyers make their arguments about the objection. After the judge has made a ruling on the objection, the jury will be returned to the courtroom, and the examination of the witness will continue. A lawyer cannot complain later to an appellate court about something that he or she did not complain about at the proper time to the trial judge.

This requirement places additional pressures on the trial lawyer. A careless or incompetent lawyer can simultaneously destroy the client's chances to win at the trial level and to successfully appeal an adverse decision. Lawyers will make objections for the record, even when they do not expect the trial judge to accept them. This is sometimes called "protecting the record" or "making a record for appeal."

After the plaintiff's lawyer has finished calling witnesses and presenting evidence, the defense has its opportunity. Before this occurs, it is not unusual for the defense lawyer to move for a **directed verdict**. This motion requests that the judge end the trial at that point and find in favor of the defendant on the basis that the plaintiff's side failed to meet its obligation of presenting a prima facie case supporting its position. The judge will enter a directed verdict if the judge concludes that the plaintiff's evidence is so weak that even considered in its most favorable light (without considering any rebuttal evidence from the defendant), it is not sufficient as a matter of law to merit a verdict in the plaintiff's favor.

Directed verdict
A verdict ordered by a trial judge if the plaintiff fails to present a prima facie case or if the defendant fails to present a necessary defense.

Case 1: The Distressed Grandfather (Continued)

Drake's lawyer made sure that she presented evidence on each element of negligence. Those four elements are duty, breach, cause, and harm.

It is the plaintiff's responsibility to present a prima facie case. If Harper had inadvertently omitted one of the necessary elements, the court could not find a basis for the negligence claim, and a directed verdict in the defendant's favor would be appropriate.

If the court grants the motion for a directed verdict, the trial is over. However, it is very unusual for a judge to accept a motion for a directed verdict at this point in the trial.

Typically, the judge denies the motion, and the defense lawyer goes on to present his or her witnesses. The same process of direct, cross, redirect, and recross is used. The defense strategy involves presenting evidence that contradicts evidence presented by the plaintiff and possibly attempting to raise a legally accepted defense for that particular type of case.

Once the defendant's case is complete, the plaintiff can ask for a directed verdict on the basis that even if the defendant's evidence is taken in its most favorable light, it would be insufficient to rebut the plaintiff's case. If the judge denies this motion, as is usually the case, the plaintiff can present witnesses who will attempt to rebut the testimony and evidence presented by the defense. After that, either side can again renew its motion for a directed verdict. If these motions are again denied, both sides then give their closing arguments.

DISCUSSION QUESTIONS

9. Do you agree with the rule that only experts should be allowed to state their opinions? Why should it matter if a witness who saw Small stumble just before she entered her car testifies that "Small was drunker than a skunk"?

10. One of the all-time famous leading questions is "So, when did you stop beating your wife?" What is the problem with asking a witness this type of question during direct examination?

e. Closing Arguments

Perhaps the most dramatic part of any trial is the closing arguments. Here, the lawyers review and interpret the evidence in its most favorable light and develop emotional appeals. Closing arguments are their final chance to persuade the jury. Although both the plaintiff and the defendant receive equal time, in some states the plaintiff has the advantage of splitting the time and speaking both first and last. The plaintiff is given this advantage because the plaintiff also has the burden of proving their case.

f. Jury Instructions

Before sending the jury members out to deliberate, it is the judge's responsibility to properly instruct them about the nature of their duties and the requirements of the law. The jury's duty is to determine the facts and then apply the requirements of the law to those facts. However, the jury is composed of a group of lay persons who do not know what the law requires. Therefore, it is the duty of the judge to explain the law in terms the jury can understand.

Rather than starting from scratch and risking reversal for failing to include some key element or for explaining some concept in a misleading way, judges frequently rely on **pattern jury instructions.** These are collections of instructions that have already been tested on appeal in other cases. The lawyers in the case also have the opportunity to submit instructions that they would like to see included. The judge then reviews their submissions and often discusses the issues with the lawyers in chambers before deciding which instructions to give.

Pattern jury instructions
A set of standardized jury instructions.

g. Jury Deliberations, Verdict, and Judgment

Once they have been properly instructed, the jurors retire to a special room where they deliberate in private until they reach their **verdict,** or they report they cannot reach a consensus and the judge declares a **mistrial.** In most cases, the jurors must come to a unanimous agreement regarding the verdict, although some states have provisions for less-than-unanimous verdicts in certain types of cases.

Verdict
The opinion of a jury on a question of fact.

Mistrial
A trial ended by the judge because of a major problem, such as a prejudicial statement by one of the lawyers.

Usually, evidence is presented at the trial regarding the question of liability and the amount of damages. If the jurors find that the defendant is liable, they next consider the amount of damages. In some cases, however, a bifurcated trial is held. During the first phase of such a trial, the jury hears testimony regarding liability and then deliberates on that issue alone. If the jury finds the defendant liable, the trial enters a second stage, in which the jury hears evidence about the nature of the damages. The jury then deliberates regarding the amount of damages to award.

Once a verdict is reached, the court enters its official **judgment** regarding the rights and obligations of the parties involved in the case, and the clerk enters it into the record. Usually, if the losing party does not appeal within a specified time period, the judgment automatically becomes effective. If the losing party does appeal, the court stays the judgment until the appellate court reaches its decision.

Judgment
The decision of the court regarding the claims of each side. It may be based on a jury's verdict.

h. Posttrial Motions

After the verdict has been announced, the losing party has a certain time period within which to file posttrial motions. The most common motions are a motion for judgment notwithstanding the verdict and a motion for a new trial.

The motion for a **judgment notwithstanding the verdict,** also known as a **judgment N.O.V.** (judgment *non obstante veredicto*), is a request to the judge to reverse the jury's decision on the basis that the evidence was legally insufficient to support its verdict. If the judge grants the motion, the case is over and the moving party has won.

A lawyer usually bases the **motion for a new trial** on the assertion that some procedural error has tainted the outcome. The losing party might argue, for example, that some piece of evidence was admitted that should not have been admitted, or that someone made improper contact with a juror on the case. If the court grants the motion, the case has to be retried.

Judgment notwithstanding the verdict (judgment N.O.V.)
A judgment that reverses the verdict of the jury when the verdict had no reasonable factual support or was contrary to law.

Motion for a new trial
A request that the court order a rehearing of a lawsuit because irregularities, such as errors of the court or jury misconduct, make it probable that an impartial trial did not occur.

Exhaustion
The requirement that
appellate courts intervene
only after the trial court
has had an opportunity to
correct its own errors.

Both motions are frequently made but seldom granted. Nevertheless, they are important because they may be necessary to preserve the client's right to appeal to a higher court. The trial court must be given every possible opportunity to correct its own errors before the appellate courts intervene.

3. The Appeal

"I'll take my case all the way to the Supreme Court" is a battle cry that has been echoed by many concerned litigants. No one likes to lose, and there are few lawyers who have not dreamed of arguing a case before the U.S. Supreme Court.

On the other hand, appeals consume time and money. The client's initial desire for appeal often pales because of the costs involved. Cases often settle after the verdict. In fact, they may settle for far less than the verdict because of the time and cost of the appellate process. In addition, the option to appeal may be very limited, or even nonexistent. If the lawyer did not make the correct objections during the trial, or if the client's case did not involve any questions of law, there will be no basis for an appeal.

a. The Timing and Filing of the Appeal

A case cannot be appealed until a final judgment has been entered. A court can grant a final judgment after a jury verdict, but also after a motion to dismiss, a summary judgment motion, a motion for a directed verdict, or one of the post-trial motions. The party wishing to appeal must file a notice of appeal within a specified time period after the final judgment is entered.

Appellate brief
A formal written argument to an appellate court, in which a lawyer argues why that court should affirm or reverse a lower court's decision.

The side bringing the appeal, the appellant, files an **appellate brief,** which explains the facts of the case, lists the relevant statutes and court cases, and then presents legal arguments for overturning the lower court's decision. Then the other side, the appellee, files its brief. Finally, the appellant has the opportunity to file a reply brief in response to the appellee's argument and to any new authorities cited in the appellee's brief.

b. The Scope of the Review

When an appellate court considers a case, it does not conduct a new trial. It simply reviews the official record of the proceedings at the trial court. Moreover, it limits its review to specific appealable issues, for which the party appealing the case must have laid a proper foundation at the trial level.

As you know, appellate courts typically only consider legal issues. Recall that legal issues involve the interpretation and application of the law; factual issues involve the determination of whether a given event took place as alleged.

Sometimes, however, appellate courts are asked to review a trial court's findings of fact. When they do so, it is on a very limited basis. Generally, appellate courts will resolve conflicts in the testimony and questions of the credibility of the witnesses in favor of the trial judge's position. They cannot disregard a trial court's findings of fact unless they determine that the findings were **clearly erroneous.** This means not simply that the appellate court would have found otherwise, but that the appellate court is convinced that the trial court made a mistake, as, for example, when the trial court did not base its findings on sufficient evidence.

Clearly erroneous
The standard used by appellate courts when reviewing a trial court's findings of fact.

However, when an appellate court reviews legal issues, it gives no deference to the trial court's findings but rather makes its own independent review. A legal issue might involve reviewing a trial judge's interpretation of a statute or legal document, such as a will or a lease. Similarly, questions about the nature of the jury instructions and the trial court's decision on the admissibility of evidence present legal issues.

If the appellate court decides that the trial judge made a legal error, it must determine whether that error was prejudicial or merely harmless. Errors are defined as prejudicial when they probably affected the results. **Harmless errors** are errors so minor and peripheral that they had no significant effect on the outcome. Only prejudicial errors are considered to be **reversible errors.**

Harmless error
A trial court error that is not sufficient to warrant reversing the decision.

Examples of harmless errors include (1) a mistake in the pleadings if the facts can be determined at trial; (2) errors in jury instructions, unless there is reason to believe that they actually misled the jury; and (3) the failure to strictly follow the rules of evidence in a bench trial, as it is assumed a judge is unlikely to be affected by incompetent evidence.

Reversible error
An error made by the trial judge that is sufficiently serious to warrant reversing the trial court's decision.

Finally, sometimes an appeal is based upon a challenge to a trial judge's decision as to court procedure or how the case should be managed. Examples include permission to amend a complaint, denial of a request for a continuance, imposition of sanctions for filing an improper pleading, and the awarding of prejudgment interest. Because these types of decisions are generally left to the discretion of the trial judge, appellate courts review them using an abuse of discretion standard. They will reverse a trial court only if the appellant can prove the judge committed a clear error of judgment, lacked the authority to act, or acted with prejudice or malice.

c. Oral Arguments

Depending on the rules of the particular appellate court, the court may hear oral arguments on appeal. During oral arguments, the lawyers present their clients' positions. The court gives the lawyers a limited time to speak, often no more than 20 minutes, and the judges frequently interrupt the lawyers with questions. The purpose of the questioning is to probe weak points in the argument and to explore the implications of the lawyer's line of reasoning.

NETNOTE

The U.S. Supreme Court website makes available all oral arguments made before the Court in audio and transcript form at *supremecourt.gov/oral_arguments/ oral_arguments.aspx*.

d. The Decision and Its Publication

With or without the benefit of oral argument, the judges study the matter until they reach a decision by majority vote. Usually, the case is assigned to one of the judges in the majority to prepare the official opinion of the court. The other judges on the court have the right to prepare either concurring or dissenting opinions. You will recall that in a concurring opinion, the judge agrees with the outcome but disagrees with the reasoning in the official opinion. In a dissenting opinion, the writer disagrees with both the outcome and the reasoning. The court's decision is then published in the appropriate **reporters**, law books that contain all of an appellate court's opinions.

Usually, the appellate decision is either to **affirm** the lower court's action or to **reverse** and **remand** (return) the case to the lower court for reconsideration. Sometimes, based on the nature of the case, a new trial is not needed to supplement the factual record. Then the judges may simply enter a final judgment based on the existing record.

Affirm
When a higher court agrees with what a lower court has done.

Reverse
When the litigants appeal a lower court decision and the higher court disagrees with the decision of the lower court.

Remand
When an appellate court sends a case back to the trial court for a new trial or other action.

e. Further Appeals

Depending on the court structure and the nature of the case, the party that loses at the appellate level may have the option of appealing to yet a higher-level appellate court. The general rule, however, is that there is only one right of appeal. A second appeal to a higher court is usually discretionary rather than a matter of right. The judges on the higher appellate court choose to hear only the cases that they believe have the greatest judicial significance. For example, to have a case heard by the U.S. Supreme Court, the losing party must first petition the Court and request that it grant a writ of certiorari. In support of this request, the applicant will file a written brief. The purpose of the brief is not to argue the merits of the case, but rather to convince the Court to agree to hear the case. Common reasons are the importance of the case for others beyond the immediate litigants and the need to resolve conflicts among the circuits.

For example, for many years, the federal courts of appeals were reaching different results in sexual harassment cases. Some courts of appeals thought such situations were covered by Title VII, while others disagreed. In a federal system, leaving such a conflict unresolved is obviously undesirable, as the outcome of a case would vary based on where it was brought. Eventually, the Supreme Court agreed to hear a case involving sexual harassment, and it resolved the issue by deciding that such situations are covered by Title VII.[20]

If the Court grants the petition for a writ of certiorari, the litigants will then file briefs arguing the merits of the case. However, the Court denies most petitions for certiorari.

Most state courts follow a similar procedure. If the higher appellate court accepts the appeal, the parties file new briefs and the process described above begins all over again.

---

[20]Meritor Savings Bank v. Vinson, 477 U.S. 57 (1986).

PARALEGAL PROFILE

Carolyn Pitts

I work for the lead partner in a 13-attorney law firm in Central Illinois. While the attorneys in our firm practice in a wide range of legal matters, I work exclusively in litigation; mainly on the plaintiff's side of civil law, and in criminal defense. My attorney handles civil matters such as personal injury, workers' compensation, business litigation, and medical malpractice. I do my best to avoid his family law cases.

I really enjoy working in litigation as I have a great deal of variety in my day-to-day activities. For instance, on any particular day, I might be researching and writing either a memorandum for the local court or for my attorney, finding and speaking to an expert for a case, writing an appellate court brief, or speaking with witnesses or potential clients. On a regular basis, for my attorney's review, I will write proposed opinion letters, correspondence to clients, and settlement demand letters to an insurance company or opposing counsel. I draft complaints, read and summarize the medical records of a personal injury client, review the discovery produced by the state in a criminal case, answer discovery requests, and write interrogatories and request to produce that will be sent to the opposing party. I help prepare my attorney to take depositions, collate the appropriate documents he might enter into evidence, and list potential questions he would not want to overlook.

Our clients have turned to me to help them understand the ongoing case, why certain procedures are in place, and what might be the next steps. Of course, my attorney reviews my work before it leaves the office, but it does feel good when he reads something I have written and offers no corrections or changes. We often have law students working for us as law clerks, so I will discuss and review with them their research, preview their memoranda to the attorney, and explain the practical side of working in the field. I have had the privilege of being the "second chair" with my attorney in several medical malpractice trials.

Litigation remains my favorite area of the law because I like the problem-solving aspects of it. There have been times when we have had to develop a new legal theory or adapt an existing concept to fit the particular factual circumstances of a case, and my attorney has enough confidence in my critical thinking skills to bring me in to brainstorm the theories with him, and then to find case law to support the theory. I also find tremendous satisfaction in doing my part to "right the wrongs" of the world, even if it is for only one person at a time.

I have several pieces of advice for students. While computer skills are paramount, my view is that one of the often-overlooked attributes of a valued paralegal is curiosity. Asking "why" or "what if" at every stage of the case can have tremendous payback, both in keeping your skills relevant, as well as in assisting the attorney to achieve the best outcome for the client. My other piece of advice is to become involved in your local and national paralegal associations. I have learned so much from other paralegals and have appreciated how generous so many of them are with their time and talents. I have made lasting connections and friendships with other paralegals through these organizations.

SUMMARY

When people have a dispute they cannot settle themselves, they typically turn to the courts to have a judge or jury settle it for them. This process of using the courts is referred to as "litigation." Because it is such a complex, time-consuming, and expensive way of settling disputes, people are increasingly turning to various forms of ADR.

The most common types of ADR are arbitration and mediation. Increasing numbers of courts are requiring litigants to try different types of mediation before they allow a case to come to trial. Many business contracts include provisions for mandatory arbitration.

In some circumstances, it may be necessary to exhaust administrative remedies prior to filing a lawsuit. Adjudicatory hearings in administrative agencies follow the general outline of a civil trial, but they are less formal and do not involve as many due process protections. A hearing officer presides over the hearing, acting much as a judge would. Although it is relatively easy to get evidence admitted into the record, the hearing officer has a great deal of discretion over the weight given to that evidence. Once all avenues of appeal within an agency have been exhausted, a party can often seek review within the judicial system.

The three main stages of litigation are pretrial, trial, and posttrial. In the pretrial stage, the parties use pleadings, discovery, and pretrial conferences to identify the facts and the legal issues involved in the dispute. The majority of cases are settled "out of court" during this stage.

At the trial stage, the parties present their evidence to either a judge or a jury. The rules of evidence dictate the form in which the evidence must be presented and what types of questions witnesses can be required to answer. Following the trial verdict, the losing party may challenge the trial court's decision in an appellate court.

REVIEW QUESTIONS

Pages 135 through 151

1. What are the most common forms of ADR, and how do they differ from each other?
2. What types of disputes are best suited to resolution through ADR? Which are least appropriate?
3. What do the proponents of ADR see as the advantages of ADR over traditional litigation?
4. What are the three basic stages of civil litigation?
5. What are five common tasks for a paralegal during the pretrial period?
6. What issues have to be considered in deciding who should be sued?

7. How does a class action lawsuit differ from one brought by and on behalf of one individual?
8. If someone says that a particular court does not have jurisdiction over a lawsuit, what is meant by that?
9. What is the difference between jurisdiction and venue?
10. What is the difference between subject matter jurisdiction and personal jurisdiction?
11. What is the purpose of requiring litigants to first exhaust their administrative remedies?
12. How does an administrative hearing differ from a civil trial?

Pages 151 through 158

13. What is the purpose of each of the following pleadings:
    a. the complaint
    b. the answer
    c. a counterclaim
    d. a cross-claim
    e. a third-party claim
14. Under the federal rules, what three items must be included in a complaint?
15. What is a caption?
16. Who must sign all pleadings? Why?
17. What is the purpose of a summons?
18. What are the advantages to e-filing?
19. What is the danger to the defendant in failing to answer a complaint?

Pages 158 through 161

20. What are the grounds for a 12(b)(6) motion, and what is its purpose?
21. What is the difference between a 12(b)(6) motion and a summary judgment motion?

Pages 162 through 169

22. What is the main goal of discovery?
23. What are interrogatories and depositions, and how do they differ?
24. Besides interrogatories and depositions, what are the main discovery tools available to the parties?
25. What is e-discovery, and what basic steps are followed in cases involving it?
26. What special challenges does e-discovery present?
27. What is the purpose of a pretrial conference?

Pages 169 through 176

28. What is the function of the jury?
29. What is a voir dire, and what is its purpose?
30. What are the differences between a challenge for cause and a peremptory challenge, and what is the function of each?
31. What are the limitations to a lawyer's right to use peremptory challenges?
32. What are five common tasks for paralegals during trial?
33. What do lawyers hope to accomplish in their opening statements?
34. Who presents evidence first, the plaintiff or the defendant, and why?
35. When can either side move for a directed verdict? What is the purpose of that motion?
36. What is the difference between a verdict and a judgment?
37. What is the difference between the motion for a judgment notwithstanding the verdict (J.N.O.V.) and a motion for a new trial? Give an example of when each could be used.

Pages 176 through 180

38. Describe the limitations on a litigant's right to appeal.
39. What is the difference between a harmless error and a reversible error?

WEB EXERCISES

1. Use Google (*google.com*) or a search engine of your choice to locate sample civil complaint forms. Two law firms that maintain sample complaints include the Kinsey Law Offices, at *kinseylaw.com* (click on "Free Stuff"), and Miller & Zois, LLC, at *millerandzois.com/sample-personal-injury-complaints.html*. Take a look at a few of the sample complaints. In each, can you spot the information necessary to establish the court's jurisdiction, the facts that gave rise to the lawsuit, and a demand for relief?
2. Visit the College of Commercial Arbitrators' website at *ccarbitrators.org*. Click on the link labeled "Resources," and then click on "Why Arbitrate?" Read through some of the questions and answers. According to this website, when can the decision of an arbitrator be appealed? Compare and contrast the discovery process in litigation as described in this chapter and the discovery process in arbitration as described at this website.

PART

2

Substance of the Law

Chapter 7

Torts

The risk reasonably to be perceived defines the duty to be obeyed.
Justice Benjamin Cardozo

Chapter Objectives

After reading this chapter, you should be able to:

- Explain how intentional torts differ from negligence and strict liability torts.
- List the elements of the prima facia case and common defenses for the torts of battery, false imprisonment, and defamation.
- Apply the elements of negligence to a fact scenario.
- Describe the history and development of product liability law.
- Explain the function of compensatory, punitive, and nominal damages.

INTRODUCTION

In this part of the book, we introduce some of the most important legal terms and concepts dealing with the substance of American law. While only an introduction to a very large and complex body of knowledge, these chapters should give you a useful framework for understanding the basic areas of civil and criminal law and for acquiring the vocabulary needed for legal research.

Previously, we discussed the basic differences between civil law and criminal law. Civil law can be divided into a wide variety of specialty areas. However, most of these specialty areas involve the application of basic principles that originated in torts, contracts, or property law. In this chapter, we focus on tort law.

Tort
Harm to a person or a person's property.

A tort can occur when someone injures you, slanders your reputation, or damages your property. A **tort** is defined as a private wrong (other than a breach of contract) in which a person or property is harmed because of another's failure to carry out a legal duty. In most instances, this legal duty is an obligation to refrain from taking actions that harm others. Occasionally, a duty will consist of an affirmative obligation to act.

An important difference between tort and criminal law is that not every tort qualifies as a crime. But some acts, if done intentionally, can lead to both a criminal prosecution and civil litigation. If the government considers the act to be a public wrong, it will classify that harmful act as a crime and prosecute the offender. If convicted, the defendant is usually punished by fine or imprisonment. When a fine is levied, it goes into the government treasury. On the other hand, the victim of a tort must pursue a remedy by initiating a civil law suit. If successful in proving that a tort has been committed, usually the result is a monetary award paid directly to the plaintiff.

Restatement of the Law of Torts, Second
An authoritative secondary source, written by a group of legal scholars, summarizing the existing common law, as well as suggesting what the law should be.

Tort law is generally court-made law. Therefore, looking to prior cases for similar situations plays an important role in any analysis of a tort problem. In addition, the courts frequently look to an authoritative secondary source, the **Restatement of the Law of Torts, Second.** Drafted by a group of legal scholars, this resource summarizes the existing common law rules in a set of black letter principles. At times, instead of simply "restating" the law, the drafters also included their vision of what tort law should become. Although the Restatement is a secondary source and is therefore only persuasive authority, you will frequently see courts citing to it and even formally adopting some of its provisions.

Despite its ancient roots, tort law has never been static. One area of tort law that is undergoing rapid change is that involving injuries to participants and bystanders at sporting events. Consider the following and how, what started out as an afternoon of fun ended up being a day of tragedy.

Case 8: The Mishit Softball Game

Dennis Carrai hosted a gathering of family and friends at his home. Among the guests was Maria Judge. At some point, Dennis shouted "who wants to play softball?" He handed out gloves, a ball, and a metal bat that he had retrieved from his garage. The area available for the field was quite small; the "third base line" was approximately 15 feet from the house, running parallel to the side of the unenclosed porch. Maria, along with several other guests, was sitting in a chair on the porch, with her back to the game.

Dennis admonished the batters to "bunt" rather than taking full swings in order to reduce the distance a batted ball might travel. Nonetheless, a batted ball flew in the direction of the house, landing on the porch roof. One of the guests laughed, commenting to Dennis that he hoped his homeowner's insurance policy premium was paid. The ball had narrowly missed hitting a skylight on the porch roof. The game continued and a short time later, one of the players hit a foul line drive toward the porch, where it struck Maria on the back of her head, causing her serious injury.

As you read, think about:

- whether Dennis had a duty to stop the game once the first ball landed on the roof;
- what role Maria played in her own injury; and
- the consequences for backyard sports if a court were to find Dennis liable for Maria's injury.

While tort law is still predominately court-made law, legislatures are playing an increasingly active role. For example, both Congress and state legislatures have enacted "tort reform" statutes, with the purpose of modifying some of the perceived abuses of the tort system. One example is legislation to place limits on the amount of damages that can be awarded in certain types of tort cases.

Torts have traditionally been classified into three major categories: intentional acts, negligence, and strict liability. See Figure 7-1. In any one of these three areas, the person who commits the tort is known as the **tortfeasor**.

Figure 7-1 Degrees of Fault

When people intentionally seek to violate a duty toward others, their purposeful conduct is classified as an **intentional tort**. Those who commit intentional torts are subject to punitive damages in addition to compensatory damages. If John intentionally drives his car into Jill's car, damaging her car and injuring Jill, John has committed an intentional tort. As we will see later in this chapter, John's motive (reason) for hitting Jill's car is irrelevant. All that matters is that he intended to do so.

When the harm occurs as a result of a careless act done with no conscious intent to injure anyone, the act is classified as **negligence**. Negligent actors are subject to compensatory damages but not to punitive damages. If the reason John's car struck Jill's was not because he had intended to do so, but because he had carelessly taken his eyes off the road to adjust his radio, John's behavior may be classified as negligent.

There are times when, for policy reasons, the defendant is held responsible even though the defendant did not act negligently nor intentionally to harm the plaintiff. These are classified as **strict liability** torts. Strict liability is usually limited to situations involving an ultrahazardous activity, such as dynamiting, or the manufacture or sale of a potentially dangerous product. For example, if the reason John ran into Jill's car was because his brakes failed, the car manufacturer may be held strictly liable.

Finally, it is important to realize that the law does not provide for compensation for all injuries. There are true accidents, when either no one is at fault or the fault rests solely with the person injured. In those situations, the injured party cannot recover damages.

A. INTENTIONAL TORTS

An **intentional tort** occurs whenever someone intends an action that results in harm to a person's body, reputation, emotional well-being, or property. Almost any harm that you can imagine, if caused intentionally, can be classified as an intentional tort. Torts we will discuss in this section include assault and battery, false imprisonment, defamation, invasion of privacy, the intentional infliction of emotional distress, and trespass to either land or personal property.

In order to prove that an intentional tort occurred, the plaintiff must prove each of that tort's elements. The defendant then has the opportunity to raise any defenses. The primary defenses available in intentional tort cases are consent, self-defense, defense of third parties, and various types of privilege.

As we will see, one set of facts can give rise to more than one type of intentional tort. In addition, many intentional torts are also crimes. Consider the following fact scenario.

Case 9: The Abused Spouse

One day, John Bloom, a lawyer, asked his paralegal, Sally Green, to sit in on an initial client interview. Bloom introduced Green to the client, June Day, and explained to Day that Green was a paralegal. Day told them the following story:

June Day has been living with David Day for the past five years. While their marriage has never been a happy one, Mrs. Day never thought of divorce until last night. Mr. Day came home very late from an adult co-ed softball game. Mrs. Day said it was obvious that he had been drinking. They soon got into a verbal fight. Among other things, Mr. Day yelled at Mrs. Day that he had told her boss she had been skimming money from the company's petty cash drawer. Mrs. Day had never done any such thing. He also told her that he had received a call earlier in the day from the local hospital, telling him that Mrs. Day's mother had been admitted following a massive heart attack. (Later, Mrs. Day found

out that this was not true, but at the time she believed her husband and became very upset.) The fight escalated, and Mr. Day began waving his baseball bat in front of Mrs. Day. Mrs. Day said that she was not frightened, as Mr. Day had never hit her, and she did not believe he would do so then. In fact, she turned her back on him and started to leave the room. He then yelled at her and, before she could turn around, hit her on the back of her arm with the bat, breaking her arm. Mrs. Day then fled to the bathroom, locking the door behind her. She remained in the bathroom for over two hours until she felt it was safe to leave. She found Mr. Day asleep on the living room couch. She fled to a neighbor's, who drove her to the hospital. The next morning Mrs. Day returned home to find Mr. Day gone, as well as her purse. There was a message on the answering machine from her boss saying that she was fired.

While June Day is contemplating divorce proceedings, her more immediate concern is to learn what actions she can take to compensate her for her broken arm, emotional distress, missing purse, and lost job.

1. Assault and Battery

Assault
An intentional act that creates a reasonable apprehension of an immediate harmful or offensive physical contact.

Battery
An intentional act that creates a harmful or offensive physical contact.

In the scenario you just read, Mr. Day waved a baseball bat in front of Mrs. Day. She was not frightened and, in fact, turned her back on him, at which point he hit her on the arm, breaking it. Do you think Mrs. Day suffered from either an assault or a battery? An **assault** occurs when someone reasonably fears that he or she is about to suffer a harmful or offensive physical contact. A **battery** is the intentional harmful or offensive physical contact. While we usually think of assault and battery as one tort, in reality they are two torts. They can be present together, as, for example, when Tom first waves a fist in front of Sam's face and then proceeds to punch Sam in the nose. However, there can also be an assault with no battery whenever there is the threat of a battery but no ensuing physical contact. And there can also be a battery with no assault, as, for example, when the person being attacked does not see the threat of physical contact before it actually occurs. In the case of Mrs. Day, there probably was no assault. However, there clearly was a battery when Mr. Day hit her with the baseball bat, breaking her arm.

For both assault and battery, the contact does not actually have to be physically painful. It simply must be harmful or offensive. Thus, an unwanted kiss from a stranger could qualify as an offensive contact. Also, the defendant need not actually do the touching if the defendant set the action in motion, such as by throwing a rock or ordering a dog to attack.

For a battery to occur, the touching must be intentional, not accidental. The following case involves a friendly backyard touch-football game that unfortunately ends in injury. While reading the case, decide whether you think the plaintiff should have been allowed to succeed on her claim of battery. Keep in mind that if in jumping up to retrieve the ball, the defendant accidentally knocked the plaintiff, no battery has occurred. The defendant's intent was to grab the ball, not to touch the plaintiff. However, if the defendant deliberately ran into the plaintiff, a battery will have occurred. Note that the plaintiff does not need to prove that the defendant meant to cause her harm — only that the defendant intended to touch her. The extent of her injury only goes to the amount of damages she can collect, not to whether a battery occurred.

Knight v. Jewett
3 Cal. App. 4th 1022, 275 Cal. Rptr. 292 (1990)

FACTS: Kendra Knight and a group of friends, including Michael Jewett, gathered at a friend's home to watch the Super Bowl football game. During half-time, they decided to play a game of coed touch football. Knight and Jewett were on different teams.

About five minutes after the game started, Jewett ran into Knight. Knight asked Jewett not to play so rough and reminded him that the only player that was supposed to be "touched" was the one with the ball. On the next play, one of Knight's teammates caught the ball and ran down the field. Jewett, in pursuit of the ball, came from behind Knight and knocked her down. Knight put her arms out to break the fall and Jewett ran over her, stepping on her right hand, injuring her little finger, necessitating multiple surgeries, and eventually amputation.

During her deposition, Knight was asked: "Do you believe that Mr. Jewett was trying to step on your hand?" Her answer: "No."

RULE: Battery consists of an intentional act that creates a harmful or offensive physical contact.

ISSUE: Whether a battery occurred, which requires an intentional harmful contact, when in the midst of a backyard touch football game, a player runs into and steps on another player causing serious injury but does so without any intent to cause harm.

HOLDING: No, there was no battery.

REASONING: A requisite element of assault and battery is intent. Here, however, there is no evidence that Jewett intended to injure Knight or commit a battery on her. In her deposition, Knight even stated that she did not believe Jewett had the intent to step on her hand or injure her. Without the requisite intent, Knight cannot state a cause of action for assault and battery.

The trial court was correct in granting summary judgment to the defendant.

CASE DISCUSSION QUESTIONS

1. What role do you think Knight's deposition played in the court's reasoning?

2. Do you think the court should have taken into account Jewett's knocking down Knight even though she was not in possession of the ball?

3. The record indicated that Knight had previously played touch football and frequently watched football games on television. Do you think the result would have been different if Knight had never watched football or played touch football prior to her accident?

If an injured plaintiff is able to prove that a battery occurred, the defendant is given the opportunity to raise defenses. For example, in the case of the touch football game, the defendant might argue that the battery was excused because the other player, by agreeing to play the game, had consented to such contact. Other available defenses include self-defense, defense of others, and sometimes defense of property. For self-defense and defense of others to be valid, the plaintiff must reasonably believe that a threat exists and then must use only as much force as is necessary to stop that threat. Self-defense, for example, could be used as a valid defense if Eric threatened Mark with a loaded gun and Mark defended himself with a knife. However, if Eric was unarmed and had only yelled a threat, it would not be a valid self-defense for Mark to stab Eric with a knife.

2. False Imprisonment

False imprisonment
Occurs whenever one person, through force or the threat of force, unlawfully detains another person against his or her will.

False imprisonment occurs whenever one person, through force or the threat of force, unlawfully detains another person against his or her will. Issues of false imprisonment most frequently arise in situations in which store employees seek to detain suspected shoplifters or employers wish to detain and interview employees they suspect of unlawful activities. The plaintiff must actually be confined, with no means of escape. For example, leaving someone alone in an unlocked office does not constitute false imprisonment.

The most common defense to false imprisonment is that the defendant was justified in restraining the plaintiff. For example, many states have enacted statutes to protect merchants who want to question a suspected shoplifter. Usually, these statutes provide that a shopkeeper may detain a suspected shoplifter only if the shopkeeper can show probable cause to justify the delay and then may detain the suspected shoplifter only for a reasonable time and in a reasonable manner.

As you can imagine, because of the way these three statutory requirements are worded, each has given rise to a great deal of litigation. For example, consider the following situation. Assume that Martha, a young mother, entered the QuickMart store carrying her small child in an infant seat that she had purchased two weeks previously. The seat had cat hairs, food crumbs, and milk stains on it, as well as a large QuickMart price tag that was still attached. She made some purchases, but just before she left the store, a security guard asked her to stop. He pulled out a store badge, showed it to her, and told her to come back into the store, saying that he needed proof that she had purchased the infant seat. When Martha hesitated, the security guard grabbed her by the arm and led her back into the store, stopping just inside the doors. After approximately 20 minutes of heated discussion, the security guard finally told Martha she was free to go.

The first question would be whether Martha could prove that she had been detained through force or the threat of force. Assuming she could do so, the store would argue as its defense, first, that it had probable cause to believe that Martha had stolen something when they saw her about to leave the store with an infant seat that had a price tag attached. Second, they would argue that they detained her in a reasonable manner by asking her to return to the store and then only using force when she resisted. Third, they would argue that their detention of her for 20 minutes was for a reasonable time. What do you think Martha's lawyer would argue in return?

NETNOTE

Increasingly, jurisdictions are charging lower gradations for retail theft if the amount is less than $500, in an attempt to reduce racial bias in the criminal justice system. In 2020, the company Percepta (*Percepta.ai*) was formed; it offers technology that determines if someone is a likely shoplifter based on behavior, in order to reduce the risk of racial profiling in retail.

DISCUSSION QUESTION

1. Under what circumstances should merchants be able to detain a suspected shoplifter?

3. Defamation

Whether it is oral (slander) or written (libel), **defamation** consists of the publication of false statements that cause harm to a person's reputation. The first element, publication, means that someone other than the plaintiff and the defendant must read or hear the defamatory comments. The offending material cannot harm someone's reputation if it is never seen or heard by a third party. Second, and perhaps most important, the defamatory material must be false. No matter how damaging the information, a tort of defamation has not been committed if the statement was true. As to the third element, the plaintiff must show that the publication of this false information damaged his or her reputation. This is usually established by showing that the plaintiff lost a job, a contract, or something else of value as a result of people having read or heard the defamatory material.

A special set of rules applies in situations where the alleged victim of the defamation is a public official or a "public figure." In *New York Times Co. v. Sullivan*, the U.S. Supreme Court stated that a public official cannot recover for defamation "relating to his official conduct unless he proves that the statement

Defamation
The publication of false statements that harm a person's reputation.

was made with 'actual malice'—that is, with knowledge that it was false or with reckless disregard of whether it was false or not."[1]

The application of this rule was widened to cover "public figures" in 1974.[2] To qualify as a public figure, a person must either have achieved widespread fame or notoriety or be someone who became well known through involvement in a public controversy.

Note that "actual malice" does not mean acting with evil intent. Rather, it simply means the plaintiff must show that the defendant either knew the material was false but went ahead and published it anyway or acted with a "reckless disregard" for whether or not it was true. The courts take into consideration such factors as the nature of the news being reported, the historical trustworthiness of the source of the information, and the time constraints publishers are under to meet a deadline.

Ethics Alert

A famous movie star comes to your office seeking representation in what sounds like a very exciting defamation lawsuit against the local newspaper. Your boss is about to begin the initial interview when you remember that his partner represented the newspaper last year in a contract dispute that it had had with its paper supplier. You alert your boss. While disappointed in having to turn down the case, he appreciates your pointing out this potential conflict of interest to him.

DISCUSSION QUESTIONS

2. Why should it be harder for a "public figure" to collect damages for defamation? Where should the courts draw the line as to who is categorized as a "public figure"?

3. When using social media sites, many people are quite casual about what they say, often posting material that could be viewed as unpleasant, offensive, or critical of others. Under what circumstances do you think someone could be sued for defamation based on comments made on Twitter or Facebook?

4. An interesting issue is whether presidential candidates can be sued for lying during elections. Read the discussion found at *www.quora.com/Can-presidential-candidates-get-sued-for-lying-to-the-general-public-during-elections*. Do you think that candidates should be able to be sued for lying? Who should be able to bring the lawsuit? What damages could a court award?

[1] New York Times Co. v. Sullivan, 376 U.S. 254, 279 (1964).
[2] Gertz v. Welch, 418 U.S. 323 (1974).

4. Invasion of Privacy

The tort of **invasion of privacy** covers a variety of different situations. They include

1. disclosure,
2. intrusion,
3. appropriation, and
4. false light.

Invasion of privacy
An intentional tort that covers a variety of situations, including disclosure, intrusion, appropriation, and false light.

Disclosure and intrusion best fit our common concept of what would be an invasion of privacy. **Disclosure** is the publicizing of embarrassing private affairs, and **intrusion** is the unjustified intrusion into another's private activities. Examples of intrusion include a neighbor eavesdropping and a photographer hounding a movie star by following that person everywhere he or she goes. **Appropriation** is defined as the unauthorized exploitative use of one's personality, name, or picture for the defendant's benefit. For example, Johnny Carson sued a Michigan corporation for renting and selling "Here's Johnny" portable toilets. The corporation acknowledged that "Here's Johnny" was the introductory slogan for *The Tonight Show* and in fact coupled the phrase with a second one, "The World's Foremost Commodian." The court determined that the defendant unfairly appropriated Carson's identity and used it for the sale of its products.[3] Finally, **false light** involves the use of a picture or some other means to infer a connection between the person and an idea or a statement for which the individual is not responsible.

In cases involving invasion of privacy, truth is not a valid defense. For example, it is not considered acceptable to publicize that someone is having an affair with his or her neighbor, even if it is true. However, "newsworthiness" is a valid defense. If the material is of legitimate public interest—for example, the mayor having an affair with a member of city council—then its publication is considered to be privileged unless it was done with malice. That is why it is so difficult for movie stars to prove this tort against tabloids and gossip columnists. Finally, as with other intentional torts, consent is a defense.

DISCUSSION QUESTION

5. Politicians often use music at their speaking events, such as rallies. The politician may have purchased the right to use the music through broad blanket licenses or venue licenses, but this may not always be the case. What arguments could artists make for appropriation when a politician with whom they do not agree uses their songs?

5. Intentional Infliction of Emotional Distress

Traditionally, plaintiffs could recover for their emotional distress only if that distress were caused by another tort, such as battery or false imprisonment. An

---

[3] Carson v. Here's Johnny Portable Toilets, Inc., 698 F.2d 831 (6th Cir. 1983).

exception to that general rule occurs with the tort of **intentional infliction of emotional distress**, which allows plaintiffs to recover for emotional distress, even absent another type of injury. This tort of intentional infliction of emotional distress is sometimes referred to as the "tort of outrage." In order to ensure that such claims are valid, most courts have placed severe restrictions on what the plaintiff must prove, such as requiring that the intentional act that causes the emotional distress be extreme and outrageous and the emotional distress suffered be severe. Some courts add that the emotional distress must be so severe that it results in physical injury.

DISCUSSION QUESTION

6. What constitutes "extreme and outrageous" conduct is obviously a troubling issue, as is how debilitating emotional distress must be to be seen as "severe." Consider the facts of *Harris v. Jones,* 380 A.2d 611 (1977). The plaintiff sued his employer (General Motors) and one of his supervisors, H. Robert Jones. Jones knew that the plaintiff suffered from a speech impediment that caused him to stutter. Jones also knew that the plaintiff was very sensitive about his disability. According to the opinion, "Jones approached Harris over 30 times at work and verbally and physically mimicked his stuttering disability. . . . As a result of Jones's conduct Harris was 'shaken up' and felt 'like going into a hole and hide.'" However, the court concluded that Harris's humiliation was not so intense as to meet the requirement of being severe. Do you agree?

6. Harm to a Person's Property

Intentional torts can also involve harm to property. The tort of **trespass to land** occurs whenever someone enters or causes something to enter or remain on the land of another without permission. **Trespass to personal property** occurs when someone harms or interferes with the owner's exclusive possession of the property but has no intention of keeping the property. For example, if your neighbor intentionally lets your dog loose, hoping it will never return, your neighbor has committed the tort of trespass to personal property. **Conversion** involves the taking of someone else's property with the intent of permanently depriving the owner. It is the civil side of theft.

Legal Reasoning Exercise

1. Review Case 9: The Abused Spouse. Do you think that David Day committed any intentional torts?

7. Other Intentional Torts

In the previous sections, we briefly introduced you to some of the more commonly used intentional torts. You should know, however, that there are other intentional torts that for space considerations, we simply could not include in this discussion. In fact, there is an intentional tort to cover most types of harmful behavior. For example, three torts that are designed to provide protection against misuse of the legal system include false arrest, malicious prosecution, and abuse of process. Fraud and inducing a party to breach a contract are torts related to business dealings. Figure 7-2 summarizes the elements and defenses of the most common intentional torts.

PRACTICE TIP

Does the other side claim that it was snowing on the date of the accident? Check it out by getting climatological data through your local airport, newspaper archives, television station records, or the Internet.

B. NEGLIGENCE

The most common tort actions involve **negligence.** Negligence is a failure to act reasonably under the circumstances. It is the basis for such diverse personal injury lawsuits as those arising out of traffic accidents, slip and fall cases, and malpractice actions.

PRACTICE TIP

When an accident occurs, keep in mind that the media are often the first on the scene, even well before the police or the ambulances. Check to see whether local news personnel were there, and whether they have it all on video.

---

1. The Elements of Negligence

To be found negligent, a person must have acted unreasonably under the circumstances. More specifically, the courts look to the following four elements to establish negligence:

1. The defendant must owe a duty to the plaintiff to act reasonably, and
2. the defendant must have breached that duty,
3. thereby causing
4. the plaintiff harm.

Prima Facie Case	Defenses
Assault 1. an intentional act 2. that creates a reasonable apprehension of 3. an immediate harmful or offensive physical contact	1. consent 2. self-defense 3. defense of others 4. sometimes defense of property
Battery 1. an intentional act 2. that creates a harmful or offensive physical contact	
False imprisonment 1. an intentional act 2. that caused confinement or restraint 3. through force or the threat of force	1. consent 2. justification (e.g., shopkeeper's statute)
Defamation 1. publication 2. of false statements 3. that cause harm to reputation	1. truth 2. privilege
Invasion of privacy covers a variety of different situations, including 1. disclosure 2. intrusion 3. appropriation 4. false light	1. consent 2. newsworthiness
Intentional infliction of emotional distress 1. an intentional act 2. that is extreme and outrageous 3. and causes 4. severe emotional distress	1. consent
Trespass to land 1. someone enters or causes something to enter or remain 2. on the land of another 3. without permission	1. consent 2. private necessity 3. public necessity
Trespass to personal property 1. interference with the owner's exclusive possession 2. of personal property	1. rightful retention (e.g., under a mechanic's lien) 2. necessity
Conversion 1. taking 2. personal property 3. of another 4. with the intent of permanently depriving the owner	

Figure 7-2   Summary of Intentional Torts

a. Duty

The law imposes a duty to act with "due care," defined as how a "reasonably prudent person" would act in the same situation. If the person has some specialized type of training, such as a medical degree, then that individual is expected to act not just as a reasonable person would act, but also as a reasonable person with medical training would act. What legal duty you owe to others also varies depending on your relationship to that other person. The closer and more direct the relationship, the greater the likelihood that a court will find a duty. For example, a doctor clearly has a duty to use due care in treating her patients. However, does the doctor also owe a duty to the patient's family? For instance, if the doctor failed to diagnose a contagious disease and the patient transmitted that disease to his wife, should the wife be able to sue the doctor?

Legal Reasoning Exercises

2. By late February 2020, the cruise ship industry knew that passengers and crew were spreading COVID-19 on its ships. Krystina Black boarded a cruise ship in California for a one-week trip to Mexico on March 10, 2020. While she was on board the ship, Black and several passengers and crew came down with flulike symptoms and were confined to their cabins. The ship was denied entry to any of the ports in Mexico or California and was forced to remain at sea for two weeks past the original date that it was scheduled to return to California. Black was then quarantined in California for another two weeks. She requires continuing therapy because of lung damage and missed a month of work. Can the cruise line be held liable? What factors might be considered in determining whether the cruise line is liable?

3. A grocery store sponsored a float in a parade. As the float traveled down the street, employees threw candy to the crowd. Children running to collect the candy injured a spectator. Develop an argument for why the spectator should be allowed to sue the grocery store.

b. Breach

In order to determine if someone has breached the duty of due care, the court considers all the circumstances and measures the defendant's actions by an objective standard. That is, the court considers what a reasonable person would have done. In the case of professional liability, the standard is what a reasonable professional would have done. Therefore, in cases involving defendants who are being sued for professional malpractice, normally the plaintiff will be required to call an expert witness to testify as to the professional standard of care and how in the expert's opinion the defendant breached that standard. For example, in a case involving alleged medical malpractice by a pediatric oncologist, the plaintiff would call as an expert witness a doctor specializing in the field.

Negligence per se
Violation of a statute as proof of negligence.

If a defendant's actions violated a statute that was designed to protect the public, some states will hold that this violation of the statute is **negligence per se**, meaning that simply violating the statute is enough to prove that the defendant was negligent. In other states, violation of such a statute is only evidence of negligence and can be rebutted.

Res ipsa loquitur
"The thing speaks for itself"; the doctrine that suggests negligence can be presumed if an event happens that would not ordinarily happen unless someone was negligent.

Another concept that a plaintiff can sometimes use to show negligence is the doctrine of **res ipsa loquitur**—whose name literally means "the thing speaks for itself." Res ipsa loquitur applies in those situations where the event ordinarily would not have happened unless someone was negligent, the cause of the injury was under the defendant's exclusive control, and the injury was not due to the plaintiff's actions. For example, elevators usually do not drop, panes of glass usually do not fall out of windows, and planes do not crash absent someone's negligence. In those types of situations, the court will assume that the defendant was negligent without the plaintiff having to prove the precise nature of that negligence.

Ethics Alert

A personal injury practice can become very hectic. Missed deadlines are always a constant worry. In fact, one of the major causes of legal malpractice claims is the failure to meet a deadline. To avoid such problems, develop a tickler system. The tickler system should be computerized, as well as supplemented with a manual method.

c. Cause

To be found liable, the defendant's actions must be the cause of the plaintiff's injuries. There are two types of causation: but for and proximate. Under the "but for" standard, it is necessary to establish that if the defendant had not acted, the plaintiff would not have been injured. This is also known as the **actual cause,** or cause in fact.

Actual cause
This is measured by the "but for" standard: But for the defendant's actions, the plaintiff would not have been injured; also known as "cause in fact."

The second prong of the requirement that the defendant's actions "cause" the injury is known as **proximate cause**. For a defendant's actions to be considered the proximate cause, a natural and continuous causal sequence must be shown between action and harm that is unbroken by any efficient intervening cause. In deciding cases in which determining the proximate cause is a key issue, the courts frequently wrestle with unforeseeable consequences and intervening forces. For example, the courts are sometimes faced with chain-reaction situations in which a person's actions lead to an event that in turn leads to several other events that eventually impact other people. Is everyone along the chain to be held responsible under the theory that but for their actions no injury would have happened, or is it more just to say that only those actors most immediately involved in the injury should be held responsible?

Proximate cause
Once actual cause is found, as a policy matter, the court must also find that the act and the resulting harm were so foreseeably related as to justify a finding of liability.

This notion of proximate cause is not really about cause at all, but rather represents a policy decision that at some point, a defendant will not be held responsible for every consequence of every action. Just as a pebble thrown into a pond sends out ripples of ever-decreasing strength, every action sends out repercussions of ever-decreasing importance. At some point, we say that the consequences are too remote from the original action to hold the actor responsible.

In the following case, do you think the railroad should have been held liable for Palsgraf's injuries?

Palsgraf v. Long Island Railroad Co.
248 N.Y. 339, 162 N.E. 99 (1928)

FACTS: Ms. Palsgraf was standing on a railroad platform waiting for her train to arrive. Meanwhile on a different track, a man was running, trying to catch a train that had just started to move. A guard pushed him from behind, and the man successfully boarded the train, but dropped his package, which unbeknownst to the guard, contained fireworks. The fireworks exploded and the shock of the explosion knocked over some heavy scales, striking Ms. Palsgraf, seriously injuring her.

RULE: For negligence to occur, unreasonable behavior must cause foreseeable harm.

ISSUE: Should the railroad be liable for negligence, which requires unreasonable behavior that causes foreseeable harm, when Ms. Palsgraf's injuries occurred after an employee pushed another customer on a track distant from where Ms. Palsgraf was standing?

HOLDING: No, the railroad should not be held liable for the injuries Ms. Palsgraf suffered.

REASONING: Negligence is only negligence if the unreasonable actions are directed at the plaintiff. In this case, while it may have been negligent to push a person onto a moving train, the unreasonable behavior was directed towards the man, not Ms. Palsgraf, who was standing a distance away. Also, there were no markings on the package to indicate its contents. The guard could not have foreseen that his actions would cause harm to anyone other than the man he pushed. "The risk reasonable to be perceived defines the duty to be obeyed . . . Here there was nothing in the situation to suggest to the most cautious mind that the parcel wrapped in newspaper would spread wreckage through the station." Case dismissed.

CASE DISCUSSION QUESTIONS

1. Why did the majority hold that the railroad had not committed negligence as to Palsgraf's injury? Do you agree?

2. The dissent included the following illustration: "A chauffeur negligently collides with another car which is filled with dynamite, although he could not know it. An explosion follows. A, walking on the sidewalk nearby, is killed. B, sitting in a window of a building opposite, is cut by flying glass. C, likewise sitting in a window a block away, is similarly injured. And a further illustration. A nursemaid, ten blocks away, startled by the noise, involuntarily drops a baby from her arms to the walk." Who out of A, B, C, and the baby, if anyone, should recover from the chauffeur? Why?

Legal Reasoning Exercises

4. Farmer takes a lantern with her to her barn in order to milk her cow and thoughtlessly places it next to the cow, which kicks it over. The barn catches on fire. The fire spreads to the neighbor's field, which also catches on fire. The ensuing group of gawkers, as well as the multiple fire-fighting and police vehicles, blocks traffic for over an hour. As a result, Smith, who is on his way to an important appointment, misses the appointment and consequently is fired.

   a. Should the neighbor be able to sue Farmer for the damage to his field? Why or why not?

   b. Should Smith be able to sue Farmer for his lost job? Why or why not?

5. An alarm company delayed calling the fire department. By the time the firefighters arrived, the fire had advanced to such a stage that one of the firefighters was killed. The firefighter's widow sued the alarm company, alleging its negligent delay in calling in the fire resulted in her husband's death. How do you think the court decided? Why?

6. Do you think a social host should be liable for accidents caused by drivers who obtained alcohol from the social host? Why? For example, consider the following facts. Margaret Davis gave her daughter, a high school student, permission to hold a party. Davis did not keep alcoholic beverages in her home, and there were none on the night of the party. Before the party began, Davis left. During the unchaperoned party, a 17-year-old guest drank beer brought to the party by another guest. While driving home intoxicated, the guest lost control of his car and injured Ruth Langemann. Should Langemann be allowed to sue Davis for her injuries?

d. Harm

The purpose of negligence law is to compensate the plaintiff for any harm suffered. Even if the court finds that the defendant owed the plaintiff a duty of care and breached that duty, if the plaintiff was not harmed, the plaintiff will not be able to recover for negligence.

2. Defenses to Negligence

First, a defense lawyer will attempt to rebut the plaintiff's claim by arguing that no duty was owed to the plaintiff, or that the defendant's action was not the cause of the plaintiff's injuries. If this is unsuccessful, then the defense may raise an affirmative defense. The defense admits that negligence was established, but argues that the defendant should not be held liable because of something the plaintiff did. Traditionally, the two major affirmative defenses were contributory negligence and assumption of the risk. Today, most states have instead adopted a form of comparative negligence.

a. Contributory Negligence

While few states still use the defense of **contributory negligence** in its pure form, it is important to understand that doctrine as it forms the basis for the modern-day defense of comparative negligence. Contributory negligence means that the plaintiff contributed to his or her own injuries.

For example, assume that Sally was crossing the street in a designated pedestrian crosswalk. Playing Pokémon GO, she was looking at her cell phone rather than at the oncoming traffic when Jim, drunk and driving 30 miles per hour over the speed limit, ran her down. Sally was left paralyzed from the waist down. If a judge or jury were to find that Sally was even just 1 percent responsible for her injuries, and Jim 99 percent responsible, under a theory of contributory negligence, she would receive nothing. That is because whenever contributory negligence is found, the defendant is relieved of all liability, no matter how great the defendant's negligence and how slight the plaintiff's contributory negligence. This seemingly unfair result is what led to the development of comparative negligence.

Contributory negligence
Negligence by the plaintiff that contributed to his or her injury. Normally, it is a complete bar to the plaintiff's recovery.

NETNOTE

The Internet contains many sources for medical information. For example, you can find current medical news at *medscape.com*, and several websites have free online medical dictionaries. Note that the Internet does not post results in the order of credibility, but rather based on algorithms that sometimes include payments by companies to appear higher on the list. Therefore, the first items listed may not be the most reliable. Medical information can be particularly fraught with false information.

b. Comparative Negligence

All but a handful of states have eliminated the doctrine of contributory negligence and substituted **comparative negligence**. Under comparative negligence, negligence is measured in terms of percentages, and damages are distributed proportionately. There are two alternative theories of comparative negligence:

1. Under pure comparative negligence, a plaintiff can recover actual damages less a percentage, calculated as the amount of negligence attributable to the plaintiff.
2. Under modified comparative negligence, a plaintiff's recovery is reduced by the percentage of his or her own negligence, but the plaintiff is barred from recovering anything if the plaintiff's negligence is greater than the defendant's. In some states, this means that the plaintiff's negligence can be no more than 50 percent, and in others, 51 percent.

Comparative negligence
A method for measuring the relative negligence of the plaintiff and the defendant, with a commensurate sharing of the compensation for the injuries.

Returning to our example of Sally and Jim, under either approach to comparative negligence, Sally would receive a damage award reduced by 1 percent. Assume, however, that a jury found her 60 percent responsible (after all, she was not looking where she was going!) and Jim only 40 percent responsible. In a pure comparative negligence state, she would recover 40 percent of her damages. In a modified comparative negligence state, she would recover nothing.

DISCUSSION QUESTION

7. Is your state a comparative negligence state or a contributory negligence state? If a comparative negligence state, does your state follow pure comparative fault or modified comparative fault? What does that mean if you are representing the plaintiff in a car accident who is 50 percent at fault for the accident in which she or he was injured?

c. Assumption of the Risk

Assumption of the risk
Voluntarily and knowingly subjecting oneself to danger.

Another affirmative defense involves the concept of **assumption of the risk**. Unlike contributory and comparative negligence, which are judged by the reasonable person standard, assumption of the risk uses a subjective standard. This means the plaintiff must voluntarily and knowingly assume the danger. That is, he or she must actually understand the risk. For example, when people choose to attend a baseball game, they assume the risk of being hit by a foul ball.

Under the traditional view, assumption of the risk, like contributory negligence, was a complete bar to recovery. Today, many states have eliminated assumption of the risk as a separate defense, having subsumed it under the defense of comparative negligence. This eliminates the proof problem of having to prove what the plaintiff was actually thinking and the problems of categorizing specific behavior as either negligence or assumption of the risk. For example, if you get into a car being driven by someone you know is intoxicated, is that an unreasonable act on your part (contributory negligence) or assumption of the risk (knowingly subjecting yourself to a dangerous situation)? In those states that have subsumed assumption of the risk under comparative negligence, it does not matter how you categorize the actions. The plaintiff's recovery can be reduced either if it can be shown that a reasonable person would have acted differently or if the plaintiff actually knew and voluntarily assumed the risk.

Exculpatory clause
A provision that purports to waive liability.

An example of an express assumption of the risk is the signing of a waiver of liability. Such waivers are frequently called **exculpatory clauses** because their purpose is to relieve tortfeasors of liability. In certain circumstances, the courts have upheld such waivers, particularly when the parties have fairly equal bargaining power and the event involves inherent danger, such as skydiving or mountain climbing. Increasingly, however, courts are refusing to enforce such waivers. Sometimes the refusal is based on the public policy argument that the parties had very unequal bargaining power. Other times, the courts have invalidated such waivers by requiring specific language or by finding an ambiguity and construing the language against the drafter. In addition, the courts usually disallow exculpatory clauses in cases of gross negligence.

Legal Reasoning Exercise

7. Alack joined a local health club. He signed a two-page, single-spaced contract that included the following language:

> Member assumes full responsibility for any injuries, damages or losses and does hereby fully and forever release and discharge [the health club] from any and all claims, demands, damages, rights of action, or causes of action, present or future . . . resulting from or arising out of the Member's . . . use or intended use of said gymnasium or the facilities and equipment thereof.

One day while he was exercising, the handle of a rowing machine disengaged from the weight cable and smashed into Alack's mouth. It was discovered that the machine's handle was not connected with the necessary clevis pin, and that the health club did not require periodic inspections of its equipment. If you were representing Alack, how would you argue that the release would not bar him from suing the health club for its negligent failure to maintain the rowing machine?

8. Mrs. Jones filled out a contract at a local stable for riding lessons for her 6-year-old daughter, Alice. The contract included an exculpatory clause stating that horseback riding is an inherently dangerous activity, and that the stable could not be held liable for any injuries. Alice was put on a horse known for being high-spirited, nicknamed "Killer" because of his erratic behavior. Alice was injured during one of her lessons when Killer, for no apparent reason, bucked and threw Alice to the ground. Do you think that this waiver would bar her from suing the stable?

d. Immunities

Defendants may also argue immunity as a defense. For policy reasons, certain defendants, even though negligent, are immune from suit. Traditionally, immunity meant a complete bar to recovery. Recently, however, the courts have been reexamining many immunities and in some instances limiting their effect or even eliminating them entirely. For example, the doctrine of charitable immunity has also been abolished or limited in most states.

The doctrine of sovereign immunity prohibits suits against the government without the government's consent. It can be traced back to the concept of the divine right of kings and the idea that the king could do no wrong. In modern times, federal and state governments have passed legislation that modifies this concept. For example, at the federal level, Congress has enacted the Federal Tort Claims Act (FTCA).[4] Under that statute, someone can sue the government for harm caused by a government employee's negligence. However, the statute prohibits suits against the government for an employee's intentional tort, partly

---

[4] 28 U.S.C. §1346 (B) (2020).

Plaintiff's Prima Facie Case	Defenses
1. The defendant must owe a duty to the plaintiff to act reasonably, and 2. the defendant must have breached that duty, 3. causing (i.e., being both the cause in fact and the proximate cause) 4. the plaintiff harm.	1. **Contributory negligence** The plaintiff fails to use due care; traditionally, this has been a complete bar to the plaintiff's suit. Most states have abandoned contributory negligence and have adopted comparative negligence. 2. **Comparative negligence** The plaintiff fails to use due care; the plaintiff's negligence is compared to the defendant's negligence, and damages are reduced accordingly. 3. **Assumption of the risk** The plaintiff knowingly and voluntarily subjects himself or herself to danger; traditionally, this has been a complete bar to the plaintiff's suit. Today, assumption of the risk has been eliminated in many states that have adopted comparative negligence. 4. **Immunity** This complete bar to a lawsuit is based on policy considerations, such as preventing suits between family members and protecting charitable organizations.

Figure 7-3   Negligence Summarized

because it is not seen as fair that the government should have to pay for an employee's intentional bad acts. Of course, the injured party could still sue the employee. A second limitation is that the government will not be responsible if what the employee did is considered to have resulted from a discretionary function. These limitations are a cause for much litigation, as it is often difficult to determine whether a particular action is the result of negligence or an intentional act, or whether the action falls within a "discretionary function." Similarly, on the state and local levels, governmental acts are often protected from suit if the public employee's action involved basic policy choices.

The elements of negligence, as well as the defenses, are summarized in Figure 7-3.

3. Reckless Behavior

In between the two main categories of torts, intentional torts and negligence, is an area of liability variously described as gross negligence, or willful or wanton behavior, or **recklessness.** While there is a great deal of confusion as to the exact meaning of these terms, all three imply a *conscious* or knowing disregard of an unreasonable and substantial risk of serious bodily harm to another. While the person may not wish to cause harm, he or she is aware of the potential for harm and proceeds anyway, indifferent to the consequences. Unlike negligence, which requires merely unreasonable behavior, recklessness requires a "conscious choice."

That said, the courts have not been able to clearly define recklessness, and it is decidedly difficult to know where negligence ends and recklessness begins and, in turn, where reckless behavior ends and intentional behavior begins. For example, if a golfer carelessly forgot to check to see if anyone was in the vicinity before taking a shot, that might be negligence. However, if that golfer had looked, had seen a person in the line of sight, had yelled a warning, and then had taken a shot anyway before the person had a chance to move, some courts would find the behavior to have been reckless, but others would still see it as merely negligent. Finally, if the golfer was angry at another golfer and deliberately aimed his shot at the other player, intending for the ball to hit her, then the golfer's actions would amount to either an intentional tort or recklessness.

You may be asking: But why does it matter? First, it matters because the standard that the court chooses to apply—negligence, recklessness, or intent—may well determine whether the plaintiff can recover anything. It is more difficult to prove recklessness than negligence, and more difficult to prove intent than recklessness. Therefore, if the court requires a finding of recklessness, but the plaintiff only has evidence showing that the defendant acted in a careless manner, the plaintiff will lose. An example is sports injuries that occur during an athletic event when one participant harms another participant. Because some contact is inherent in most sports, and because they do not want to discourage vigorous competition, most courts will apply the recklessness standard to such situations. If an injured player can only show that the other player acted carelessly, with no conscious desire to harm, then the injured player will not be able to recover.

Second, the plaintiff may wish to introduce evidence that the defendant's actions went beyond negligence and involved some level of conscious intent, so as to constitute reckless or intentional behavior, in order to raise the possibility of recovering punitive damages. Finally, several courts have held that if the plaintiff can show that the defendant acted recklessly or intentionally, the plaintiff's contributory negligence cannot be used as a defense.

Recklessness
Disregarding a substantial and unjustifiable risk that harm will result.

Legal Reasoning Exercises

8. An amateur soccer game was played between high school–aged players. Julian Nabozny was a goalie. David Barnhill was a forward for the opposing team. David was known for being a very rough player, having acquired

more penalties than any other player on the team. Rather than cautioning David to play a clean game, David's coach urged all his players to play as hard as they could and to "go for the kill."

During the game, David kicked Julian in the head while Julian was in possession of the ball. Contact with a goaltender while he is in possession of the ball is a violation of rules set by FIFA (the International Association Football Federation, soccer's international governing body), which governed the contest.

When Julian's dad saw David kick his son in the head, he jumped out of his chair, rushed onto the field, and hit David in the chin with his fist, breaking David's jaw.

Another parent, Mike Bishop, also rushed onto the field. Afraid that Julian might be hurt further, he scooped him up and carried him off the field. Unfortunately, when David had kicked Julian, he had broken his neck. When Mike picked him up, the movement caused compression in Julian's spinal cord, leaving him permanently paralyzed from the waist down.

a. Julian wants to sue David, the other player. In his complaint, which tort theory is Julian's lawyer most likely to allege, and what will he have to prove for Julian to be successful?

b. Julian also wants to sue the coach. In his complaint, which tort theory is Julian's lawyer most likely to allege, and what will he have to prove for Julian to be successful?

c. Finally, Julian wants to sue Mike, the parent who "helped" him. In his complaint, which tort theory is Julian's lawyer most likely to allege, and what will he have to prove for Julian to be successful?

d. For the court to allow David to recover against Julian's dad, on what tort theory will David's lawyer rely?

9. Return to the fact situation with which we opened. Have your thoughts changed about whether Maria should be able to sue Dennis for the injuries she suffered? What arguments do you think her lawyer would make? What counterarguments would you expect Dennis's lawyer to raise?

C. STRICT LIABILITY

Strict liability
Liability without having to prove fault.

Negligence and intentional torts result in liability because the defendant was at fault. In the former, the fault is a result of carelessness, and in the latter, it is intentional. When the concept of **strict liability** is applied, however, liability is imposed even though the defendant is not at fault. The courts impose liability for the policy reason that, as between the defendant and the injured plaintiff, the defendant is in a better position to absorb the costs of the injury. The courts have applied the doctrine of strict liability in two situations: those involving inherently dangerous activities and products liability.

1. Inherently Dangerous Activities

When persons engage in activities that are inherently dangerous, they may be responsible for any injuries that result, even though the activities may be carried out in the safest and most prudent way possible. A classic case is the use of dynamite in blasting. The rationale for finding strict liability in such cases is that blasting as a business carries with it extreme risks that cannot be guarded against. Therefore, as between a for-profit company that chooses to engage in blasting and an innocent person harmed by the results of the blasting, the company should be held accountable, with the damages to be absorbed as part of the costs of doing business. Of course, any company engaging in such dangerous activities would be wise to purchase liability insurance. In addition to such dangerous business activities as using or storing explosives, courts have frequently found the owners of wild animals, and in some jurisdictions even pet dogs, strictly liable for injuries that the animals cause.

2. Products Liability

When a product proves to be defective, an injured party can sue under any one of three theories: negligence, breach of warranty, or strict liability. Which theory to use depends on the facts of the case.

Products liability
The theory holding manufacturers and sellers liable for defective products when the defects make the products unreasonably dangerous.

Negligence would be the appropriate theory if the plaintiff has proof of a manufacturing defect or a design defect. For example, a hockey helmet with cutouts around the ears that allows penetration of a hockey puck is arguably defectively designed. Also, a failure to warn of a danger known to the manufacturer but probably unknown to the user would form the basis for a negligence suit.

There are times, however, when a product is defective (i.e., it is unreasonably dangerous for use in the ordinary manner), and it caused an injury, but the plaintiff cannot point to any one act of negligence that caused the defect. In those cases, the plaintiff might rely either on a warranty theory—the product failed to meet the buyer's expectations for a safe product—or on a tort strict liability theory—the product was defective.

For example, assume that you purchase a new car. One week later, as you are driving home from work, your brakes fail, and because you were unable to slow your car, you run off the road and end up in a ditch. Luckily, you are able to escape before your car bursts into flames. Because of the fire damage, there is no way to pinpoint the exact cause of the brake failure. As brand-new cars are supposed to have brakes that work, obviously the brakes were defective. However, you cannot prove the exact cause of the defect. Under negligence theory, you would be out of luck because you cannot not prove the precise negligence that caused the defect. However, under strict products liability, you simply have to prove that the dealer sold you the car in a defective condition that was unreasonably dangerous.

NETNOTE

The Consumer Product Safety Commission has a website, *www.cpsc.gov,* where you can find information on recalls and unsafe products.

The law of strict products liability was heavily influenced by the 1965 passage of Section 402A of the Restatement of the Law of Torts, Second. Under Section 402A, a manufacturer or seller is liable if it sells a defective product that harms a consumer and that defect made the product unreasonably dangerous. Unlike other provisions of the Restatement, Section 402A was not really a restatement of existing law. Rather it was the American Law Institute's vision of what the law should be. When it was passed, it had little support. Over the years, that has changed, and today Section 402A has been adopted by many state courts and legislatures.[5]

Product misuse
When the product was not being used for its intended purpose or was being used in a dangerous manner; it is a defense to a products liability claim, so long as the misuse was not foreseeable.

A plaintiff's contributory negligence is usually not considered a defense to strict liability. However, assumption of the risk and **product misuse** may be. For a manufacturer to assert the affirmative defense of product misuse, the manufacturer must prove that the product was not being used for its intended purpose or was being used in a dangerous manner that could not reasonably have been foreseen by the manufacturer. However, even if a plaintiff misuses a product, if that use is foreseeable, the manufacturer may be liable for a design defect. For example, in one case a young child opened a stove door in order to step on it in an attempt to reach a shelf located above the stove. Although a stove clearly is not meant to be used as a stepping stool, the court held that this misuse was foreseeable and could have been avoided by a different design.

Legal Reasoning Exercise

10. A 15-year-old threw a two-and-a-half-pound piece of concrete from an overhead pass. It went through the windshield of the truck that Barbara Collins was driving. As a result, she suffered severe brain injuries. She sued the manufacturer of the truck, under a theory of strict product liability, claiming that the windshield was defective because its penetration resistance was inadequate. In turn, the truck manufacturer argued that the juvenile's criminal conduct was a superseding cause that relieved it of liability. Who do you think has the better argument, and why?

D. REMEDIES AND THE CHOICE OF WHOM TO SUE

The most common form of remedy that a plaintiff seeks in a tort action is the awarding of some form of damages. Because employers have "deeper pockets" (i.e., more resources to pay a large damage award), a plaintiff will often seek those damages from an employer rather than, or in addition to, the employee when hurt by an employee's negligence.

---

[5] Restatement (Second) of Torts § 402A has been updated by Restatement (Third) of Torts § 402A, but very few states have adopted that update.

Under the doctrine of **respondeat superior**, a Latin term translated as "Let the master answer," the extent to which an employer is held accountable for the acts of a worker depends on three factors. First, was the worker an employee or an independent contractor? An employer is generally not responsible for the negligent actions of an independent contractor unless the contractor is engaged in an ultrahazardous activity, such as dynamiting. Second, if the worker was an employee, did she or he act negligently? If the employee was not negligent, then the employer cannot be held responsible. Third, at the time of the injury, was the employee engaged in work of the type that the employee was hired to perform? This last question requires an assessment of whether the employee was working within the "scope of employment" or, as the courts so quaintly put it, whether the employee was "on a frolic of the employee's own."

Respondeat superior
The tort theory that an employer can be sued for the negligent acts of its employees.

Keep in mind that the doctrine of respondeat superior binds employers who are lawyers, too. If a paralegal fails to perform a necessary task, such as filing a document as requested by the lawyer, the paralegal's negligence will be attributed to the lawyer, who could then be found liable in a malpractice action.

Ethics Alert

Once the plaintiff has decided whom to sue, the plaintiff may seek one of three types of damage awards: compensatory, punitive, and nominal. In addition to or instead of damages, the plaintiff may ask for an injunction. An injunction is a court order directing the defendant to do a specific act or to cease doing a specific act.

Compensatory damages (sometimes referred to as "actual damages") are awarded to compensate the plaintiff for the harm done to him or her. In a tort action involving harm to a person, that might mean the cost of medical bills, lost time from work, and pain and suffering.

Punitive damages, also called "exemplary damages," are designed to punish the defendant. Typically, they are awarded only for intentional torts, when the court determines that the tortfeasor deserves an additional punishment beyond just compensating the plaintiff for the harm done to him or her. Punitive awards are granted in very few cases, and the court is more likely to find that punitive damages are appropriate when the harm involves personal injury as opposed to mere property damage.

Finally, **nominal damages** are awarded when a right has been violated, but the plaintiff cannot prove any monetary harm. For example, a trespasser may have caused no harm to the land, but the landowner would still be entitled to a nominal award.

DISCUSSION QUESTION

8. Should fast-food restaurants be required to pay punitive damages for serving their coffee at a temperature that they know to be hot enough to

seriously burn someone if the coffee is spilled on them? What if, after numerous complaints and injuries, other restaurants in the area reduced the temperature of their coffee, but one fast-food chain did not, and the coffee caused third-degree burns on a customer, requiring skin grafts? If so, what would be the appropriate measure of punitive damages?

SUMMARY

A tort is a private wrong that causes harm to a person or property. Torts are generally classified as involving intentional acts, negligence, or strict liability. Intentional torts occur whenever someone intends an action that results in harm. Examples include assault and battery, false imprisonment, defamation, invasion of privacy, intentional infliction of emotional distress, and trespass. Negligence involves a breach of duty that causes harm. Cause includes both actual cause and proximate cause. Strict liability includes both ultrahazardous activities and products liability, where an unreasonably dangerous defective product is sold. Finally, in a limited number of situations, such as those involving contact sports, the courts will apply a recklessness standard. Recklessness involves a conscious decision to proceed despite a substantial and unjustifiable risk that harm will result.

Tort law is constantly evolving. The courts are still developing new torts to cover changing societal views as to what should be protected. Examples include the torts of wrongful life or birth and battered woman's syndrome.

Finally, in bringing a tort action, a plaintiff is generally seeking either an injunction or damages. Damages can take the form of a compensatory, punitive, or nominal award.

REVIEW QUESTIONS

Pages 185 through 191
1. How can the same set of facts result in both a tort and a crime? Will every tort also create criminal liability?
2. What are the elements of assault? Of battery?
3. How can there be an assault and no battery? A battery without an assault?
4. What are the elements of false imprisonment?
5. When does a shopkeeper have a valid defense to a detained person's allegation of false imprisonment?

Pages 191 through 195
6. What are the elements of defamation? The defenses?
7. In *New York Times v. Sullivan*, what limitation did the Supreme Court put on the ability of public figures to sue the press?
8. Assume Robin Barker dictates a letter to her secretary. The letter is addressed to Wanda Jones. In the letter, Barker tells Jones that she thinks Jones is a thief.

The secretary types and mails the letter to Jones. Can Jones sue for defamation? What element is arguably missing?

9. How do the torts of defamation and invasion of privacy differ?
10. What must a plaintiff prove to win a case of intentional infliction of emotional distress?

Pages 195 through 206

11. What are the four basic elements of a negligence claim?
12. When might the court find that a defendant was negligent per se?
13. Explain the doctrine of res ipsa loquitur.
14. What is the difference between "but for" causation and proximate cause?
15. Describe the three basic affirmative defenses to negligence. How do they differ from each other?
16. What is the doctrine of sovereign immunity? What types of lawsuits does it prevent?
17. How is recklessness defined? How does it differ both from intentional conduct and negligence?

Pages 206 through 210

18. What are the two situations where a court might apply the doctrine of strict liability?
19. Describe the three theories that a plaintiff can use to sue a manufacturer when harmed by that manufacturer's product.
20. What are the three basic types of damages that a plaintiff can recover in a tort action, and what is the purpose of each?

WEB EXERCISES

1. Use Google, *google.com*, or go to *socialhostliability.org* to research the social host law in your state. Do you agree that adults providing alcohol to minors (even their own children) should be held liable if the minor hurts himself or another person? Also, should social hosts be subject to criminal prosecution?
2. Now for the lighter side of the law. Go to *dumbwarnings.com*. Do you agree that all of the warnings listed are "dumb," or do you think that they serve a purpose?

Chapter 8

Criminal Law

We can have as much or as little crime as we please,
depending on what we choose to count as criminal.
Herbert L. Packer

Chapter Objectives

After reading this chapter, you should be able to:

- List the basic classifications of crimes.
- Discuss the differences between *actus reus* and *mens rea* and how they are relevant to the prosecution's case.
- Identify the elements of a crime.
- Identify the most common defenses asserted in criminal cases.
- Discuss the death penalty and mandatory sentencing.

INTRODUCTION

Both torts and crimes involve acts that harm individuals. But in tort law, those harmful acts are treated as "private wrongs," while in criminal law, they are treated as offenses against the state. A **crime** is therefore defined as an act that is prohibited by the legislature, prosecutable by the government, and carries a punishment of a fine, imprisonment, or even death.

Hardly any aspect of our legal system is as dynamic as the study of crime and criminals. Reacting to the fears and concerns of society, this field of law changes rapidly. In this chapter, we will discuss types of criminal behavior, common defenses, and the nature of punishment. Then, in chapter 9, we will discuss the procedures used to investigate and prosecute violations of criminal law.

Crime
An activity that has been prohibited by the legislature as violating a duty owed to society; it is prosecutable by the government, with the possibility of punishment of a fine, imprisonment, or even death.

In the criminal law field, you will typically find paralegals working in prosecuting attorneys' offices, for public defenders' offices, and for private defense lawyers. In these offices, they are involved in reviewing police reports and statements of witnesses, drafting documents such as discovery requests and motions, interviewing potential witnesses, researching legal issues, arranging for expert witnesses, helping to evaluate potential jurors, organizing documents for trial, helping prepare witnesses, keeping them informed as to when they will be called to testify, and taking notes during the trial. Many prosecutors use paralegals to work with crime victims. Paralegals may assist victims with investigations, preparation for trial, and writing of impact statements.

Paralegals may also be used by judges to do legal research related to the motions that have been filed and requests for jury instructions. When they work for lawyers doing appellate work, they are frequently called upon to digest the record and help draft appellate briefs. Finally, paralegals are sometimes employed within the penal system as prison librarians. They may also serve as probation or parole officers and may work in prerelease or day-reporting programs, which help inmates make the transition from incarceration to the outside world.

Ethics Alert

While paralegals may act as a type of advocate, paralegals may not dispense legal advice to the victims and should always be supervised by a lawyer.

Case 10: The Cyberbully

Billy Love, 16 years old, was crushed when Janet Looker, another 16-year-old whom he had been dating, told him she had found a new boyfriend and no longer wanted to date him. When he saw her hanging around with Eric Manley, the star quarterback on their high school football team, he got really depressed and began to obsess over Janet.

At first, he left notes in Janet's locker and sent her e-mails and text messages begging her to take him back. When she ignored his messages and continued to hang out with Eric, Billy sent messages warning her that bad things would happen to her if she kept dating Eric. Janet called him and begged him to leave her alone. Instead, Eric used Facebook to post a topless picture of her and some explicit text messages, which she had sent him while they were still dating.

Janet was so mortified that she purposely took an overdose of pills she found in her mother's bathroom medicine cabinet. Fortunately, her parents discovered what she had done in time to rush her to the emergency room, and doctors were able to save her life. The emergency room staff reported Janet's failed suicide attempt to the local police department.

As you read this chapter, think about the types of laws that either Billy or Janet may have violated, and what, if any, charges a prosecutor could bring.

A. SOURCES OF CRIMINAL LAW

Although some behavior might be considered morally or ethically wrong, it is important to understand that nothing is a crime unless the law makes it one. That is, no act is a crime unless the legislature has written a statute explicitly prohibiting that behavior.

By putting our criminal laws in statutory form, we provide all citizens with written notice as to what behaviors may result in prosecution and punishment. This notice helps contribute to **due process** as it is guaranteed to all citizens through the Fifth and Fourteenth Amendments to the U.S. Constitution.

Although the principles of due process require the federal government and each of the states to set out their criminal laws in written form, there is no requirement for uniformity among the states. Thus, while lotteries or casino gambling may be legal in some states, they may be illegal in others.

In 1956 the American Law Institute assembled a group of law professors and practicing lawyers to attempt to simplify U.S. criminal law by creating a **Model Penal Code,** which would be adopted in all 51 jurisdictions. However, this hoped-for uniformity was never achieved. While many of the provisions of the Model Penal Code have been adopted and incorporated into the laws of various states, the Code itself has not led to a uniform set of criminal laws. Significant variations continue to exist among the state criminal codes.

Due process
The principle, guaranteed by the Fifth and Fourteenth Amendments to the U.S. Constitution, that notice and a hearing must be provided before depriving someone of property or liberty.

Model Penal Code
The American Law Institute's proposal for a uniform set of criminal laws; it is not the law unless adopted by a state's legislature.

PRACTICE TIP

In examining both the definition of the crime and the authorized punishment, be sure to check the date of the offense against the effective dates of the statutes governing the alleged criminal act. If the law has been changed, the governing statute is the one that was in effect at the time that the crime was committed.

B. CLASSIFICATION OF CRIMES

As discussed in Chapter 4, crimes are usually classified on the basis of the type of harm done and the nature of the punishment imposed. Serious crimes are classified as **felonies,** and they are generally punishable by a year or more in a state prison. **Misdemeanors** are thought to do less harm and therefore carry a lesser punishment—incarceration in a local jail for less than one year, a fine, or performing some type of public service.

Sometimes the same basic activity, such as drug possession, can be either a felony or a misdemeanor depending on the drug and the quantity involved. For example, while possession of a small quantity of marijuana might be classified as only a misdemeanor, possession of a large quantity of heroin would certainly qualify as a felony. Legislators determine whether a given act is to be considered a felony or a misdemeanor at the time that they enact the statute making it a crime.

Most criminal behavior is defined by state law. Federal criminal law tends to focus only on those crimes that involve federal property or interstate activities. There are situations in which a single act could be prosecuted as either a federal or a state crime, or both. One notorious example is that of Terry Nichols, who was tried twice, first in federal court and then in state court, for his role in the 2000 bombing of a federal building in Oklahoma City that resulted in the death of 168, including 19 children. In federal court he was tried and convicted of conspiring to build a weapon of mass destruction and of involuntary manslaughter, resulting in a sentence of life without parole. The state of Oklahoma then put him on trial for first-degree murder, seeking the death sentence. Nichols was also convicted in state court, and the judge ordered Nichols to serve 161 consecutive life terms without the possibility of parole.

The Model Penal Code and the criminal codes of most states are organized into groups on the basis of the type of harm caused to society. Offenses involving physical harm to a person are considered more serious than offenses involving damage to someone's property. Figure 8-1 illustrates how some of the more familiar crimes are classified as harm to the person, harm to habitations and property, harm to society's health and safety, or crimes against the government itself.

Harm to Persons	Homicide crimes	
	Murder	
	Manslaughter	
	Negligent homicide	
	Other crimes against persons	
	Assault	
	Battery	
	Child abandonment	
	Kidnapping	
	Rape	
	Robbery	
	Stalking	
Crimes Against Habitations and Property	Arson	Receiving stolen property
	Burglary	Shoplifting
	Forgery	Theft
		Trespass
Crimes Against the Public Health, Safety, or Decency	Alcohol offenses	Drug offenses
	Child pornography	Obscenity
	Disorderly conduct	Prostitution
Crimes Affecting Governmental Functions	Bribery	
	Perjury	
	Treason	

Figure 8-1   Classifications of Crime Based on Harm

NETNOTE

The U.S. Department of Justice maintains statistics about crimes and victims, as does the University of Michigan through its National Archive of Criminal Justice Data (NACJD) project at *www.icpsr.umich.edu/NACJD/archive.html*.

1. Offenses Against the Person

Offenses against the person include various types of homicides, kidnapping, and acts involving the infliction of bodily harm or a threat to inflict bodily harm. The most serious of these offenses, a **homicide,** is the killing of one human being by another. The circumstances under which the killing takes place and what the defendant was thinking at the time of the killing determine whether it was a first-degree murder, manslaughter, negligent homicide, or not a crime at all.

Also related to the taking of human life are laws criminalizing suicide. The Model Penal Code includes the felony of "Causing or Aiding Suicide." It occurs when a person purposely causes another to commit **suicide** by "force, duress or deception," and the same act is a misdemeanor where "force, duress or deception" are not present.

Notice that in addition to criminalizing *causing* another person to commit suicide, most states have also criminalized the act of *assisting* someone who plans to commit suicide. For instance, the Illinois law on suicide prohibits persons, including medical professionals, from providing "the physical means by which another person commits or attempts to commit suicide, or participates in a physical act by which another person commits or attempts to commit suicide."[1] In contrast, Oregon's "Death With Dignity Act" provides that a person who has been "determined by the attending physician and consulting physician to be suffering from a terminal disease, and who has voluntarily expressed his or her wish to die, may make a written request for medication for the purpose of ending his or her life in a humane and dignified manner."[2] **Battery** is a wrongful physical contact with a person that entails some injury or offensive touching. An **assault** is conduct that places another person in reasonable apprehension of receiving a battery. **Kidnapping** is similar to the tort of false imprisonment, in that it involves unlawful confinement. However, in most states, the victim must also be moved. **Robbery** is a theft of personal property in circumstances that involve either the infliction of serious bodily injury or the threat of such injury.

Stalking and intimidation are relatively new crimes that are now included in many state criminal codes. **Stalking** is the act of following another person or placing them under surveillance when these actions place that person

Suicide
The deliberate termination of one's own life.

---

[1] 720 ILCS 5/12-34.5 (Westlaw 2020).
[2] Ore. Rev. Stat. §127.805 (Westlaw 2020). Eight states and the District of Columbia now allow assisted suicide, including California, Colorado, Hawaii, Maine, New Jersey, and Oregon. And Montana's Supreme Court held that the state's laws do not prohibit assisted suicide.

in reasonable apprehension of bodily harm, sexual assault, confinement, or restraint. **Intimidation** involves putting someone in fear, usually of physical harm to themselves or another person they know. The goal is to force the person to do something or to refrain from doing something because of the fear that the intimidation causes. Witness intimidation is a classic example. Other crimes similar to intimidation include coercion, extortion, and duress.

Increasing concerns about protecting minors from online bullying or harassment have led states to enact "cyberbullying" laws that explicitly include electronic forms of communication within more traditional stalking or harassment laws. In the absence of these more specific statutes, prosecutors can usually still bring charges under the more general laws on stalking and intimidation.

The prosecutor in Case 10 might charge Billy with both stalking and cyberbullying. Prosecutors will often charge with more than one crime if the facts of the case meet all of the elements of both crimes. The jury can choose to find the defendant not guilty, guilty on all charges, or guilty on just some of the charges.

2. Crimes Against Habitations and Property

Crimes against habitations and property involve harm to or the taking of another's property without consent. Under the common law, **arson** was defined as the malicious burning of the house of another. Modern statutes have generally enlarged the definition to include the burning of any structure, not just dwellings, and to include the arsonist's own home if the intent was to collect on an insurance policy.

Despite frequent misuse of the term, burglary is not synonymous with theft. **Burglary** involves breaking into and entering a building with the intent of committing a felony. That felony could be theft, but it also could be some other felony, such as rape.

Theft, also known as **larceny**, is the act of "stealing" (i.e., taking property without the owner's consent). Traditionally, theft required the taking of tangible personal property. Today, however, legislatures have created laws that also criminalize activities involving intangible property such as the taking or altering of computerized information.

Another crime against property is that of receiving stolen property. For a defendant to be found guilty, the state must prove that the property was stolen, that the defendant knew the property was stolen, and that the defendant knowingly had the stolen property in his or her possession. **Forgery** involves the alteration or falsification of documents with the intent to defraud. **Trespass** is an unauthorized intrusion or invasion of the premises or land of another.

3. Crimes Affecting Public Health, Safety, and Decency

Crimes affecting the public health, safety, and decency cover a wide variety of crimes, ranging from alcohol and drug abuse to obscenity and prostitution. This is one of the most controversial areas of the criminal law. As "victimless crimes," many of the laws in this category are criticized for interfering with basic civil liberties. Offenses covering alcohol and drugs include the possession, use, and sale of these substances. Some drugs are totally outlawed, while others can be sold or possessed only when prescribed by a licensed physician. Alcohol regulation can range from the establishment of a minimum drinking age to complete prohibition. Prostitution involves participation, or offering to participate, in sexual activity for a fee, and obscenity regulations restrict the availability of sexually explicit books, magazines, movies, videos, and live performances.

DISCUSSION QUESTIONS

1. What criteria should be used in determining when something should be considered a crime? For example, what, if any, so-called victimless crimes should be decriminalized?

2. Federal prosecutors successfully prosecuted top executives of the opioid maker Insys for racketeering. The company paid medical professionals to prescribe medically unnecessary pain medication. In addition, scores of doctors, nurses, pharmacists, and other medical professionals were found to have distributed opioids in extraordinarily large quantities, often with no legitimate medical purpose. Brian Benczkowski, head of the Justice Department's criminal division, told reporters that "when medical professionals behave like drug dealers, the Department of Justice is going to treat them like drug dealers."[3] Drug companies often use aggressive sales tactics to get medical professionals to prescribe their drugs. When, if ever, do you think such tactics should lead to criminal prosecution? Do you believe that medical professionals sometimes behave like drug dealers when prescribing opioids?

4. Crimes Affecting Governmental Functions

Crimes affecting governmental functions include bribery, perjury, and treason. Historically, **bribery** involved offering something of value to a public official that, if accepted, would cause that public official to act in such a way as to violate the public trust. Today, there is also commercial bribery. **Perjury** involves knowingly making a false statement while under oath. **Treason** consists of either attempting to overthrow the government or betraying the government to an enemy of the United States, traditionally defined as a country or organization with which the United States is at war. Although it is a very serious crime, and in fact is the only crime defined in the U.S. Constitution, it is also difficult to prove. Only one person has been indicted for treason since 1954.[4]

There are other actions that can affect government functions. In 2013, two associates of New Jersey governor Chris Christie decided to punish one of the governor's political opponents by closing access lanes to the George Washington Bridge for "traffic studies." That bridge is one of the world's busiest and the closure caused enormous traffic jams. They were tried and convicted of wire fraud and other federal charges for lying about their reasons for closing traffic. The convictions were appealed. The U.S. Supreme Court ruled that while the decision to close the lanes was an abuse of power, it was not a federal crime. "Under

---

[3] Sadie Gurman and Sara Randazzo, *Dozens of Medical Professionals Charged in Opioids Sting*, WALL ST. J., (Apr. 18, 2019), *www.wsj.com/articles/dozens-of-medical-professionals-charged-with-illegally-prescribing-opioids-11555533761*.

[4] The National Constitution Center provides a common interpretation of the Treason clause, as well as a for/against debate.

settled precedent, the officials could violate those laws only if an object of their dishonesty was to obtain Port Authority's money or property."[5]

DISCUSSION QUESTION

3. Assuming that the defendants' actions in closing the George Washington Bridge did not fit the elements of the crime with which they had been charged, but were nonetheless unethical, do you think the Court should still have upheld their conviction? Why would convicting someone under those circumstances be problematic? How could the legislature make certain that this type of action would lead to a conviction in the future?

C. ELEMENTS OF A CRIME

Actus reus
A wrongful act.

In order for a crime to take place, someone with a "guilty intent" (**mens rea**) must commit a "guilty act" (**actus reus**) that causes specified harmful results.

1. Actus Reus

The Model Penal Code and every criminal statute in every jurisdiction require the defendant to do some act to be found guilty of a crime. This act, referred to as the actus reus of the crime, must be voluntary. The act in itself need not do any harm. For example, just possessing some substances, such as an illegal drug, may be a sufficient action to satisfy the actus reus.

Consider the following crimes from the Illinois Criminal Code.

720 Ill. Comp. Stat. 5/18-1 Robbery

(a) A person commits robbery when he or she takes property, except a motor vehicle covered by Section 18-3 or 18-4, from the person or presence of another by the use of force or by threatening the imminent use of force.

720 Ill. Comp. Stat. 5/18-2 Armed Robbery

(a) A person commits armed robbery when he or she violates Section 18-1 while he or she carries on or about his or her person or is otherwise armed with a dangerous weapon.

Therefore, to be found guilty of robbery in the state of Illinois, a defendant must

1. take property, except a motor vehicle,
2. from the person or in the presence of another
3. by the use of force *or*
4. by threatening the imminent use of force.

A prosecutor must prove all portions of the statute (1, 2, and either 3 or 4) before the defendant may be found guilty. These individual portions, referred

---

[5]Kelly v. United States, 140 S. Ct. 1565, 1568 (2020). Justice Kagan went on to write "the realignment of the toll lanes was an exercise of regulatory power—something this court has already held fails to meet the statutes' property requirement."

to as the elements, include the actus reus of this crime—the taking of property. A defendant would be found not guilty if the prosecutor failed to prove any part or element of the statute or if the finder of fact had a reasonable doubt about any part of the prosecutor's proof.

The more serious offense of armed robbery shares all of the elements of the robbery statute plus the added actions or elements of

5. carrying on or about his or her person or otherwise being armed
6. with a dangerous weapon.

Because all the robbery elements are contained in the armed robbery statute, robbery is called a **lesser included offense** of armed robbery. Typically, a defendant may be charged with both crimes, but if found guilty of the more serious offense, the lesser included offense usually will be dismissed.

Sometimes something happens that prevents the criminal from completing the crime. Therefore, because there is no required actus reus, the defendant cannot be charged with having committed that crime. Such attempts, however, can form the basis for a separate conviction. Such attempts are classified as **inchoate crimes**. To be found guilty of an attempt, the state must prove the defendant intended to commit the crime and that the defendant did some overt act in furtherance of that intent that went beyond mere preparation. For example, the Model Penal Code lists several acts that indicate an intent to commit the crime, such as "possession of materials to be employed in the commission of the crime, which are specially designed for such unlawful use or which can serve no lawful purpose of the actor under the circumstances."[6]

Lesser included offense
A crime whose elements are contained within a more serious crime. For instance, theft is a lesser included offense of robbery.

Inchoate crimes
An attempted crime.

Legal Reasoning Exercise

1. Review the robbery and armed robbery statutes from the Illinois Criminal Code. What crimes were committed under the following circumstances if they happened in Illinois?

a. Martin waited until the bartender turned her head. Then he slipped $10 from the cash register into his pocket.

b. Kamil used a crowbar to break the lock securing a bicycle and stole it while the owner was in the grocery store.

c. David drove his car behind a woman walking on the side of the road. When she stopped for the light, David reached out of the car window and grabbed her purse. The set of knives that David just won while playing bingo was on the front passenger seat of the car.

d. After everyone left the party, Rosie took a fur coat that had been left behind, hid it in a shopping bag, left the apartment, and pushed the doorman as she left the building.

[6] Model Penal Code §5.01(2)(c).

Solicitation
Encouraging someone to commit a crime.

Conspiracy
An agreement to commit an unlawful act.

Two other inchoate crimes are solicitation and conspiracy. **Solicitation** involves requesting or encouraging someone to commit a crime. For example, if a wife encourages her boyfriend to kill her husband, she could be found guilty of the crime of solicitation. **Conspiracy** involves an agreement between two or more persons to commit an unlawful act. The state must show that they intended to enter into an agreement and that they had the specific intent to commit some crime. Unlike an attempt, where mere preparation is not enough of an overt act to satisfy the actus reus requirement, in many states, preparation is sufficient to prove conspiracy. In others, the defendants must take substantial overt steps to be found guilty.

2. Mens Rea

Mens rea
Criminal intent.

The **mens rea**, the nature of a person's intent, is also a critical factor in the definition of most crimes. The difference between innocently bumping into someone on a crowded street and the commission of the crime of battery depends for the most part on the state of mind of the person who initiated the contact. In order for the act to be considered a crime, there has to be evidence of a "guilty mind."

Mens rea is critical in distinguishing one crime from another. The same act and the same result can constitute different crimes based on the intent of the criminal. For example, murder, voluntary manslaughter, involuntary manslaughter, and reckless homicide all involve the taking of a human life. They differ primarily in terms of the intent of the person responsible for the killing. In the following case, the court grappled with whether there was sufficient evidence to find that a young woman had the appropriate mens rea to be charged with involuntary manslaughter.

Commonwealth v. Carter
474 Mass. 624, 52 N.E.3d 1054 (2016)

FACTS: Michelle Carter, 17, was charged with involuntary manslaughter. The prosecution alleges that she encouraged 18-year old Conrad Roy to commit suicide. On the afternoon of July 13, 2014, a police officer found the deceased in his truck, parked in a store parking lot. The medical examiner ruled the death a suicide and concluded that Conrad had died after inhaling carbon monoxide.

Prior to his death, Michelle and Conrad and exchanged hundreds of text messages which revealed that Michelle knew of Conrad's depressed state and a prior suicide attempt. Most of their text messages focused on suicide. Michelle encouraged Conrad to kill himself, when and how to do it, and chastised him when he delayed doing so. She repeatedly told him, "You just have to do it."

After his death, she erased the text messages, lied to police about the content of her conversations with him, and sent the following text message to a friend: "Conrad's death is my fault like honestly I could have stopped him I was on the phone with him and he got out of the truck because it was working and he got scared and I fucking told him to get back in."

RULE: Involuntary manslaughter is an unlawful killing unintentionally caused by wanton and reckless conduct involving a high degree of likelihood that substantial harm will result to another."

ISSUE: Whether the evidence was sufficient to warrant the return of an indictment for involuntary manslaughter where the defendant's conduct did not extend beyond words.

HOLDING: Yes, words alone, if sufficient to overcome the will of another, can constitute wanton and reckless conduct sufficient to warrant the return of an indictment for involuntary manslaughter.

REASONING: It was apparent that the defendant understood the repercussions of her role in the victim's death. The jury had sufficient evidence to support a finding of probable cause that the defendant's conduct (1) was intentional; (2) was wanton or reckless; and (3) caused the victim's death.

Here, the particular circumstances of the defendant's relationship with the victim may have caused her verbal communications with him in the last minutes of his life to carry more weight than mere words, overcoming any independent will to live he might have had. It his final moments, Conrad had gotten out of his truck, expressing doubts about killing himself. Michelle commanded him to "get back in." He obeyed, returned to the truck, closed the door, and succumbed to the carbon monoxide. The coercive quality of that final directive was sufficient in the specific circumstances of this case to support a finding of probable cause.

CASE DISCUSSION QUESTIONS

1. Do you agree that Michelle's actions were sufficient to justify an indictment for involuntary manslaughter?

2. Have you ever been in a situation, either on the sending or receiving end, of a string of text messages that caused, if not physical, strong emotional harm? Do you think such "talk" should be criminalized?

Under the common law, intent was divided between general and specific intent. If the defendant intended to act only, without regard to causing the results of the act, then the defendant had general intent. If the defendant did the act and intended to cause the harm that resulted from the act, then the defendant possessed specific intent. For example, many states divide murder into first- and second-degree murder. To be found guilty of first-degree murder, state statutes often require that the defendant's actions be "willful, deliberate, and premeditated." As such, first-degree murder is a specific intent crime. That is, the defendant must not only intend to do the act, such as shooting a gun, but also intend that the victim die.

The Model Penal Code abandoned the use of general and specific intent. Compare the ways in which criminal homicide, murder, manslaughter, and negligent homicide are defined in the Model Penal Code.

Offenses Involving Danger to the Person
Article 210. Criminal Homicide

Section 210.1   Criminal Homicide

(1) A person is guilty of criminal homicide if he purposely, knowingly, recklessly or negligently causes the death of another human being.

(2) Criminal homicide is murder, manslaughter or negligent homicide.

Section 210.2   Murder

(1) Except as provided in Section 210.3(1)(b), criminal homicide constitutes murder when

(a) it is committed purposely or knowingly; or

(b) it is committed recklessly under circumstances manifesting extreme indifference to the value of human life. Such recklessness and indifference are presumed if the actor is engaged or is an accomplice in the commission of, or an attempt to commit, or flight after committing or attempting to commit robbery, rape or deviate sexual intercourse by force or threat of force, arson, burglary, kidnapping or felonious escape.

Section 210.3 Manslaughter

(1) Criminal homicide constitutes manslaughter when:

(a) it is committed recklessly; or

(b) a homicide which would otherwise be murder is committed under the influence of extreme mental or emotional disturbance for which there is reasonable explanation or excuse. The reasonableness of such explanation or excuse shall be determined from the viewpoint of a person in the actor's situation under the circumstances as he believes them to be.

(2) Manslaughter is a felony of the second degree.

Section 210.4   Negligent Homicide

(1) Criminal homicide constitutes negligent homicide when it is committed negligently.

(2) Negligent homicide is a felony of the third degree.

As you can see in the definition for criminal homicide, the Model Penal Code divides intent into four categories: purposeful, knowing, reckless, and negligent.

When the defendant's acts are **purposeful**, they are specifically intended by the defendant. The defendant must desire to cause the harm that resulted from the actions taken. For example, the defendant shoots a gun with the intent to harm one particular person. This is the highest level of intent, and when found, the defendant usually pays the highest price.

If the judge or jury finds that the defendant acted **knowingly**, the defendant knew or had reason to know that harm would be caused, even if the specific harm was not the defendant's objective. For example, a defendant who shoots a gun into a crowded room would know that the action would cause harm, even though the defendant was unaware that the action would harm one particular victim.

A defendant is said to have acted **recklessly** when he or she disregards a substantial and unjustifiable risk that harm will result from that action. For example, the defendant shoots a gun into the air while walking through a park at night, and the bullet strikes a person sitting on a bench. The defendant's intent is said to be **negligent** when he or she simply fails to be aware of that substantial and unjustifiable risk. For example, negligence could be found if, when cleaning a gun, a defendant forgets to check the bullet chamber, accidentally pulls the trigger, and shoots someone.

Purposeful

Intending to cause a specific harm.

Knowingly

Not intending to cause a specific harm, but being aware that such harm would be caused.

Reckless

Disregarding a substantial and unjustifiable risk that harm will result.

Negligence

The failure to act reasonably under the circumstances.

As we mentioned earlier, not all states have chosen to follow the Model Penal Code, and that is certainly true of its classification of mental states into the four categories of purposeful, knowing, reckless, and negligent. For example, instead of defining murder as a homicide committed purposely or knowingly, states often define first-degree murder as a homicide done willfully with premeditation, deliberation, and malice; and second-degree murder as an intentional killing that was not premeditated.

Frequently, states also deviate from the Model Penal Code's definition of manslaughter and instead categorize it as either voluntary or involuntary. **Voluntary manslaughter** is usually defined as an intentional killing that is partially excused either by extenuating circumstances, such as provocation, or by the defendant's raising what is known as an imperfect defense. For example, if the defendant committed homicide believing he or she was acting in self-defense when in reality there was no imminent danger, then the mistaken belief as to the existence of a threat may serve to reduce the charge from murder to manslaughter. For **involuntary manslaughter**, the defendant must not have intended to cause the death but must have done so by acting recklessly. In sum, it is important to check the specific language of the statutes in your state, so that you can see precisely how the degree of culpability varies depending on the defendant's mental state.

As you might suspect, without a direct statement from the defendant that explains what he or she was thinking at the time of the incident, proving mental state is a difficult task. To deal with this problem, the law generally assumes that people know the probable consequences of their acts. Therefore, a person who strikes another is presumed to have intended the infliction of harm, in that such a result naturally flows from hitting another.

Also, during a criminal trial, the judge or the jury is allowed to draw **inferences**. After looking at the facts of the case presented during the trial, including any statements and actions of the defendant and other prosecution or defense witnesses, the jury is allowed to reach a conclusion about the defendant's intent and to draw an inference about the defendant's state of mind, as well as what most likely occurred. For example, in *Commonwealth v. Gilbert*,[7] a man was charged with having murdered his roommate by beating her with his cane. He told the police that she had died from an overdose of painkillers. Based on the testimony that the victim had been beaten, that there were no traces of any painkillers found during the autopsy, that the victim and the defendant had been having difficulties, and that the defendant was the only individual in the apartment at the time of the victim's death, the court held that it was reasonable for the jury to conclude he had deliberately premeditated his roommate's death and hence was guilty of first-degree murder.

Voluntary manslaughter
The unlawful killing of another human being with malice.

Involuntary manslaughter
The unlawful killing of another human being through criminal negligence or recklessness.

Inference
A conclusion reached based on the facts given.

---

[7] 637 N.E.2d 46 (Mass. 1996).

Legal Reasoning Exercise

2. Apply Article 210 of the Model Penal Code to each of the following situations. What crimes, if any, have been committed?

a. Sam, a hired assassin, pulls out a gun and points it at Mary's head. He pulls the trigger, the bullet strikes Mary in the temple, and she is killed instantly.

b. Janet, to protest what she views as the increasing decadence of modern society, leaves a bomb in an empty adult movie theater. Later that night, the bomb goes off and kills the janitor, who was cleaning the theater.

c. Rita accompanies John while he robs a store owner at gunpoint. The gun goes off, and the owner is killed by the gunshot.

d. Five boys are playing a game of "Russian roulette," in which they pass a partially loaded gun (one of the six chambers contains a live bullet) around the circle. Each player takes a turn spinning the cylinder, pointing the gun at his head, and pulling the trigger. When Dan takes his turn, the gun goes off, and he dies instantly.

e. After leaving a bar, Ralph and Sam started arguing in the parking lot. Both had been drinking, and they began to fight. Ralph threw the first punch, but Sam soon retaliated, by pulling out a gun and pistol-whipping him in the head. Ralph was overcome by rage, grabbed Sam around the neck, and flung him to the pavement. As a result of his injuries, Sam died.

f. Marjorie owned a 130-pound dog. On more than 30 occasions, the dog had lunged, snapped, and growled at people or physically attacked other dogs. One day, in the hallway of her apartment building, the dog broke away from her and attacked and killed a neighbor. Marjorie did not call 911 for help, never asked after the attack about the victim's condition, and returned to the scene of the attack, not to assist the dying victim but to find her keys.

g. A passenger in an automobile fires a pistol into the driver's-side window of a tractor trailer in an adjacent lane. The bullet strikes the driver in the head and kills him.

h. A robber who knows that he has been infected with the human immunodeficiency virus (HIV) rapes one of his robbery victims. As a result of the rape, his victim also becomes infected with HIV.

D. PARTIES TO THE CRIME

Principal
The person who actually commits a criminal act.

When more than one person commits a crime, the perpetrators may be classified as principals, accomplices, or accessories. The person who commits a criminal act is a **principal** in the first degree. A principal in the second degree, sometimes also referred to as an **accomplice**, assists the principal in the first degree during the commission of the crime, for example, by driving the get-away car. An **accessory before the fact** is someone who assisted in the preparation of the crime, but was not present during the crime. Finally, an **accessory after the fact** is someone who aided the principal after the commission of the crime. When it comes to punishment, principals of any degree and accessories are generally all treated the same, although in the past accessories after the fact have not been punished as severely as principals and accessories before the fact.

Accomplice
A person who assists the principal with the crime or with the preparation of the crime; also referred to as an "accessory."

Accessory before the fact
A person who assisted in the preparation of the crime, but was not present during the crime.

Accessory after the fact
A person who aids the principal after the commission of the crime.

Legal Reasoning Exercise

3. Your firm represents Jimmy Jones. He and his best friend, Bobby Smith, are both 20-year-old high school dropouts. They have held several part-time jobs in the past but are currently unemployed. Last Saturday night, Jimmy and Bobby, along with their friend Doris, were restless with nothing to do. Bobby then had a brainstorm, and what started out as a frolic has since ended in a nightmare for Jimmy.

For "fun" and money, the three decided to hold up the local convenience store. Doris volunteered the information that the only person on duty at that time of night would be an elderly gentleman who would give them no trouble. Shortly before leaving for the store, Doris had a change of heart and told the other two that she would not be coming along.

Neither Jimmy nor Bobby owns a gun. Unbeknown to Jimmy, Bobby decided to take along his kid brother's very realistic-looking water pistol. When they got to the store, no customers were present. Jimmy and Bobby went up to the counter and demanded that the clerk hand over the money in the cash register. When the clerk simply stared at them, Bobby pulled out the water pistol, which had been concealed under his jacket. He said, "Hand over the money, old man, or I'll spray you with acid." Actually, the gun only had water in it. The clerk, who was an elderly, overweight man, began to perspire and shake. He placed the money on the counter. Then he suddenly clutched his chest and fell to the floor. Bobby grabbed the money and ran from the store.

Although very frightened by the turn of events, Jimmy decided to stay and try to help the clerk. He called the police, telling them to send an ambulance right away. When the police arrived, Jimmy turned himself in. Unfortunately, on his way to the hospital, the store clerk died.

   a. With what crimes do you think Bobby could be charged?
   b. What would be the major weaknesses in the prosecution's case?
   c. Do you think Doris could be convicted of any crimes? If so, which ones?
   d. What about Jimmy?

E. DEFENSES

Complete defense
A defense that, if proven, relieves the defendant of all criminal responsibility.

Partial defense
A defense that reduces a crime to a lesser included offense.

Alibi defense
A defense requiring proof that the defendant could not have been at the scene of the crime.

In some circumstances, the law excuses persons from criminal responsibility if they have what the law considers to be a valid excuse for their actions. The alibi and insanity defenses are perhaps the best known. Other criminal defenses include ignorance or mistake, intoxication, duress, necessity, and entrapment.

If believed by the judge or jury, some defenses are **complete defenses** to a crime, and the defendant will be found not guilty. **Partial defenses** may reduce a crime to a lesser included offense.

1. Alibi Defense

An **alibi defense** is one in which the defense attempts to show that the defendant could not have committed the crime because the defendant was in a specified place at a specific time that would make it impossible for him or her to have committed the crime. For example, if four witnesses testify that they were playing poker with the defendant at a home on the east side of town, then the defendant could not have been the person who robbed a liquor store on the west side of town at that time.

2. Ignorance or Mistake

We have all heard that ignorance of the law is no excuse. Generally, that is true. On the other hand, ignorance or mistake as to facts can form the basis for a defense if it can be shown that the defendant's ignorance or mistake negated the requisite mens rea. For example, if you left a classroom with a classmate's textbook, thinking it was your own, you would be mistaken as to the fact of ownership. Therefore, you could not be prosecuted for theft, as you did not have the required mens rea, the intent to steal the property of another.

3. Status of the Offender

Infancy, insanity, and intoxication are referred to as "status defenses." They all involve excusing people from the criminal consequences of their actions because their status or condition renders them incapable of formulating the required element of mens rea.

a. Children

Under the common law, children under the age of 7 were conclusively presumed to be incapable of forming criminal intent, while there was a rebuttable presumption that those between the ages of 7 and 14 were not capable of forming such intent.

The juvenile court system was created to provide an alternative to the regular "adult courts" for dealing with youths who are accused of acts that would be considered crimes if they had been committed by adults. Technically, those who are diverted into these alternative courts are adjudged to be

PRACTICE TIP

Depending on your jurisdiction, the defendant may have the burden of raising defenses and proving them. Check to determine who has the burdens of production and proof. In many jurisdictions, defenses must be alleged prior to the start of the trial.

Juvenile Courts
Special courts established to deal with juveniles who commit crimes or status offenses, or who are adjudged to be abused or neglected.

juvenile delinquents, do not have a "criminal conviction" on their record, and are usually required to take part in various types of treatment options such as counseling, special classes, or community service.

In some cases, particularly those where the juvenile is older and commits a very serious crime, such as rape or murder, a state may have processes to remove the accused from the juvenile court and authorize adult criminal prosecution. Some state statutes do not allow removal at all, some states allow removal, and some states have mandatory removal under specific circumstances.

In addition to being held responsible for any adult crimes they might commit, juveniles can also be found liable for so-called status crimes. These cover activities, such as truancy, running away from home, and alcohol consumption, that are criminal only when committed by juveniles.

DISCUSSION QUESTION

4. If children engage in criminal behavior, how old do you think they should be before being treated the same as adults? Do you think that answer should change based on the crime committed?

PRACTICE TIP

Jurisdictions differ greatly on how children should be treated when they commit acts that would be crimes if committed by adults. Carefully check a young person's age at the time the offense was committed, and do the research necessary to determine when a child perpetrator can be treated as an adult.

---

b. Mental Illness

The **insanity defense** is based on the assertion that the defendant is incapable of forming the requisite mens rea. While most jurisdictions have the insanity defense, there is disagreement among the states and the federal circuits about the standard that should be used to determine insanity. The three most common alternatives are the M'Naghten test, the irresistible impulse test, and the Model Penal Code Substantial capacity test. These tests are summarized in Figure 8-2.

When the **M'Naghten test** is used, a defendant is not considered guilty of the crime if, at the time of committing the actus reus, the defendant was suffering from a defect or disease of the mind and could not understand whether the act was right or wrong. Under the M'Naghten test, a defendant will be found sane if he or she knew that a certain action was wrong but could not stop from taking that action. Therefore, some jurisdictions have both the M'Naghten standard and a variation of what is commonly known as the **irresistible impulse test**. With this test, the focus is on the defendant's ability to control his or her own actions.

Juvenile delinquent
A minor, usually under the age of 18, who commits acts that would be considered crimes if committed by adults or who commits status offenses, such as underage drinking or truancy.

Insanity defense
A defense requiring proof that the defendant was not mentally responsible.

M'Naghten test
A test that provides that the defendant is not guilty due to insanity if, at the time of the crime, the defendant suffered from a defect or disease of the mind and could not understand whether the act was right or wrong.

> ## M'Naghten or "Right from Wrong" Test
>
> "[T]o establish insanity sufficient to relieve the defendant of guilt, it must be proved that, at the time of the commission of the act, the defendant was laboring under such a defect of reason, from disease of the mind as not to know the nature and quality of the act he was doing, or if he did know it, that he did not know that what he was doing was wrong." *M'Naghten's Case,* 8 Eng. Rep. 718, 722 (1843).
>
> ## Irresistible Impulse Test
>
> One is not guilty by reason of insanity if it is determined that the defendant has a mental disease that kept the defendant from controlling his or her conduct.
>
> ## Substantial Capacity Test (Model Penal Code)
>
> (1) A person is not responsible for criminal conduct if at the time of such conduct, as a result of mental disease or defect, he or she lacks substantial capacity to appreciate the criminality (wrongfulness) of his or her conduct or to conform that conduct to the requirements of law.
>
> (2) The terms *mental disease* and *mental defect* do not include an abnormality manifested only by repeated criminal or otherwise antisocial conduct.

Figure 8-2   Insanity Tests

Substantial capacity test
Part of the Model Penal Code; a test that provides that the defendant is not guilty due to insanity if, at the time of the crime, the defendant lacked either the ability to understand that the act was wrong or the ability to control the behavior.

If a mental disease robs the individual of control over his or her conduct, the person is not guilty by reason of insanity.

The drafters of the American Law Institute's Model Penal Code developed a third test, which combines elements of the other two. This test is known as the **substantial capacity test**. It requires that the defendant "appreciate," rather than "know," the wrongfulness of his or her actions. Under the two options provided in this test, defendants can lack either the ability to understand that their acts were wrong or the ability to control their behavior. Although the complete Model Penal Code has not been widely adopted, this section has been accepted as the test for insanity in a majority of the states.

The difficulty of successfully using the insanity defense is demonstrated in a Texas case involving Andrea Yates, a mother who confessed to having drowned her five young children in the bathtub because she heard voices telling her to kill them in order to "save them from Satan."[8] The case was tried in a state that still followed the M'Naghten "right from wrong" test. So, to prove insanity, the defense had to show not just that the mother was mentally ill, about which there was no dispute, but also that she was not aware what she had done was wrong. In a three-week-long trial, the defense called psychiatrists, relatives, and friends as witnesses to testify that Yates suffered from severe postpartum depression. The prosecution countered by arguing that Yates's prompt action in reporting the drowning to the police established that she did know what she had done was

---

[8] "Jury to Decide Yates' Sentence," *USA Today,* March 14, 2002, p. 3A.

wrong. The jury apparently agreed with the prosecution that she was not legally insane and convicted her of murder. She was sentenced to life in prison and sent to a prison psychiatric ward to receive treatment for her mental illness.It is also possible that the jury found her guilty, not because they thought she was sane when she drowned her children, but because they were afraid that a "not guilty by reason of insanity" verdict would have resulted in her being released from state custody. What the jury did not know, because by Texas statute[9] they could not be told, is that even a "not guilty by reason of insanity" verdict would most likely have resulted in her immediate involuntary commitment to a mental institution.[10] When a trial ends in a verdict of "not guilty by reason of insanity," the defendant is absolved of any criminal responsibility but is often civilly committed to a mental health facility for treatment. And unlike a finding of guilt that results in a fixed sentence, a finding of "not guilty by reason of insanity" can result in defendants being committed for an indefinite term, potentially for life, until they are deemed to no longer be a threat to themselves or society. As a result of both the difficulty of proving the defendant was insane at the time the crime was committed and the uncertain result, the insanity defense is rarely used. Studies have shown that it is alleged in less than 1 percent of all criminal cases.

Legal Reasoning Exercise

4. Emanuel Jones had been on medication for several years to stop the voices he heard in his head. He recently stopped taking his medication because it made him feel sleepy. Five days ago, during a visit with his best friend, Sam, Emanuel became angry and confused. He attacked Sam with a golf club and chased him from room to room as he tried to escape. He hit Sam several times with the golf club, and Sam died as the result of the wounds he sustained.

Working as a member of the defense team, apply each of the three tests for insanity to each of the following to determine whether this defendant might succeed with an insanity defense.

a. Emanuel walked out of the house and stopped at a nearby restaurant for a hamburger. When the waiter asked him how Sam was, Emanuel replied that he thought Sam was at home sleeping.

b. Before leaving the house, Emanuel put the golf club and his bloody clothes in the bathtub and filled the tub with water. He changed his clothes and ran home.

c. When the police questioned Emanuel the next day and asked him about Sam, he replied, "I killed him. He'll be back tomorrow."

---

[9] Tex. Code Crim. Proc. art. 46.03(1)(e) ("The court, the attorney for the state, or the attorney for the defendant may not inform a juror . . . of the consequences to the defendant if a verdict of not guilty by reason of insanity is returned.").

[10] In fact, that is what eventually happened in the Yates case. A Texas appeals court reversed Yates's conviction based on improper expert testimony and ordered a retrial. At the second trial, the jury found her not guilty by reason of insanity, and she was involuntarily committed to a mental health facility.

d. When the police questioned Emanuel the next day and asked him about Sam, he replied, "I killed him. I tried to stop, but he just kept laughing at me."

e. Several weeks after the incident and his return to his medication, Emanuel expressed great grief and guilt over the death of Sam.

Consider the same facts as a member of the prosecution team. Do you come to the same conclusions?

DISCUSSION QUESTION

5. Do you think anyone should ever be found not guilty on the basis of insanity? If so, under what circumstances?

c. Intoxication

Intoxication defense
A defense requiring proof that the defendant was not able to form the requisite mens rea to commit a crime due to intoxication.

The third defense of this type is the **intoxication defense**. In some jurisdictions and under some circumstances, being under the influence of drugs or alcohol is considered a valid defense if the intoxicating substance interfered with the defendant's ability to form the required mens rea. Although intoxication cannot be used as a defense for charges involving reckless behavior (such as drunk driving or criminal damage to property), it can generally be used as a defense for crimes requiring a specific intent, such as murder.

4. Duress and Necessity

Duress
A defense requiring proof that force or a threat of force was used to cause a person to commit a criminal act.

Because one of the fundamental principles of criminal law is that criminal behavior must be the result of a voluntary act, the law recognizes both duress and necessity as legitimate defenses. If a defendant can establish that the criminal act was committed because he or she was forced to carry it out, that individual is not held accountable for the criminal act.

The Model Penal Code defines **duress** as coercion through "the use of, or a threat to use, unlawful force against his person or the person of another, which a person of reasonable firmness in his situation would have been unable to resist." Therefore, if someone held a gun to your head and forced you to commit a criminal act, you would be entitled to use the defense of **duress**.

Necessity
A defense requiring proof that the defendant was forced to take an action to avoid a greater harm.

The **necessity** defense is similar to the duress defense except that the force is exerted by nature rather than by another person. For example, you may be forced to trespass across a neighbor's yard to escape a fire in your home. In addition, this defense may be used in a more general way to exonerate otherwise criminal conduct when a person believes that such conduct is necessary to avoid a greater injury. An example would be where a motorist chooses to crash an automobile into a building in order to avoid hitting a child who runs into the street.

5. Entrapment

Entrapment
A defense requiring proof that the defendant would not have committed the crime but for trickery or inducement by law enforcement officers.

The defense of **entrapment** arises when a defendant believes that he or she was tricked or led to commit a crime by a law enforcement agency when the defendant would not have committed the crime without the government's enticement. It is not entrapment if the government agents provide a person with the opportunity to commit a crime that he or she was already contemplating. The key is whether the defendant had a predisposition to commit the crime before the government agents contacted the person.

6. Self-Defense

One of the most frequently used defenses in criminal trials is **self-defense**. When asserting a variation of this defense, a person admits that they did something which is normally illegal—such as shooting another person—in order to protect themselves from being harmed by the person who was shot.

In most jurisdictions the justification of self-defense can also be applied to a person's right to protect another person if the threat of bodily harm is immediate and that the amount of force used is reasonable. You may also act against another person in defense of property, but many states do not authorize the use of deadly force to protect property because they value human life over property—even when the human life in question is trying to steal that property. However, deadly force is permitted if a home intruder is attempting to do great bodily harm.

Self-defense
The justified use of force to protect oneself or others.

PRACTICE TIP

The most important part of using or disproving a defense is to research the elements of the defense carefully. It is especially important to look at past cases where the defense has already been asserted. Then you will know which defenses are available in your jurisdiction and which defenses the courts tend to favor.

Generally, the right to use force is valid only so long as the following conditions are met:

- The person claiming self-defense must not have been the initiator of the violence;
- The threat of bodily harm must be immediate;
- The amount of force used must be no more than is reasonably necessary to repel the attack; and
- **Deadly force** can only be used when the danger faced includes fear of serious bodily injury or death.

Deadly force
A force that would cause serious bodily injury or death.

Once the threatening party ceases the threatening behavior, the right to self-defense disappears.

This right to defend oneself does not extend to all people at all times. In fact, it does not even extend to all people who find themselves in dangerous positions. Most jurisdictions include a **retreat exception** to the right to self-defense. This doctrine of retreat generally requires a person in danger to get away from the danger or give up possessions before resorting to the use of deadly force. If

Retreat exception
The rule that in order to claim self-defense, there must have been no possibility of retreat.

Castle doctrine
The defense that one can use deadly force if necessary to protect one's home and its inhabitants.

Stand-your-ground laws
Statutes that allow citizens to use deadly force without attempting to retreat, even when they are threatened outside their homes.

the victim can avoid danger but chooses instead to use deadly force, that victim may be prosecuted for any crime committed. However, potential victims need not retreat if they are in their own homes, known as the **Castle doctrine**, or if retreating would create additional danger for them.

Since 2005, a number of states have extended the right of self-defense by enacting so-called **stand-your-ground laws,** which allow citizens to use deadly force without attempting to retreat, even when they are threatened outside their homes. These laws give citizens a right to use deadly force, so long as they reasonably believe that they are facing a threat of death or bodily harm.

These laws first received national media attention when George Zimmerman, a "neighborhood watch" volunteer in Florida, shot and killed Trayvon Martin, an unarmed black teenager. Rather than heeding police directives to back off and let them handle the "suspicious" teenager, Zimmerman followed him. According to Zimmerman's account of the incident, Martin confronted him and then physically attacked him. Zimmerman told police that he shot Martin because he feared for his life. Because Martin died before police arrived, and there were no eyewitnesses, prosecutors were not able to present enough evidence to convince a jury to convict Zimmerman. Following Zimmerman's acquittal, the Florida legislature considered but rejected a bill to repeal the stand-your-ground law.

Florida has had a number of cases since the Zimmerman case. All have been difficult to prosecute because the statute uses a subjective standard regarding threat of death or bodily harm rather than an objective standard. Therefore, the jury can acquit a defendant if it finds the defendant was actually fearful of death or bodily harm, even if no reasonable person would have felt threatened. The Florida legislature has made it even more difficult to prosecute by passing a 2017 amendment to the statute that shifts the burden to the prosecutor to prove that the defendant was not acting in self-defense rather than the defendant having to prove that he or she was acting in self-defense.[11]

The so-called **battered spouse syndrome** is a variation on self-defense that does not require the defendant to have been in immediate danger at the moment of the attack if it can be established that the defendant had been the victim of repeated attacks and did not believe escape from future attacks was possible. However, not all states have been willing to accept this defense, as the defendant's actions usually are not taken in the face of "imminent" death or great bodily harm. The effects of the battered spouse syndrome may be used, however, to reduce the charge from murder to manslaughter.

A final variation on self-defense relates to the special exemptions given to law enforcement and military personnel to take actions that are required as part of their official duties. Soldiers killing enemy soldiers in battle and police officers killing an escaping felon fall under the category of justifiable homicide. Special

---

PRACTICE TIP

Not all jurisdictions accept the battered spouse syndrome as a defense. Research your jurisdiction's law to determine whether this defense is available to defendants or whether the time is right in your jurisdiction for a new defense to be tested.

Battered spouse syndrome
A form of defense that is sometimes allowed when someone has been the victim of repeated attacks, even when that victim is not in immediate danger.

---

[11] Fla. Stat. § 776.032(4)(2019). "In a criminal prosecution, once a prima facie claim of self-defense immunity from criminal prosecution has been raised by the defendant at a pretrial immunity hearing, the burden of proof by clear and convincing evidence is on the party seeking to overcome the immunity from criminal prosecution."

guidelines apply to the use of **deadly force**, which is defined as a force that would cause serious bodily injury or death. Thus, while a police officer could justifiably shoot a person who is shooting at him or her, that officer could not shoot a purse snatcher running away down an alley.

If law enforcement officers exceed the appropriate use of force, the governmental units for which they work are subject to civil lawsuits. Historically, it has been difficult to discipline or prosecute for such actions.

The Black Lives Movement began in response to the Trayvon Martin shooting and expanded to protest the use of excessive force by the police against Black men and women. In August, 2014, a white police officer shot Michael Brown, Jr., an 18-year-old Black man, suspected of shoplifting. Numerous witnesses saw the shooting, but gave conflicting testimony as to what they observed. Some said Mr. Brown was standing still with his hands raised, while others said he was charging the officer in a threatening way. The evidence indicated that the officer had fired a total of 12 shots (two from within his squad car and the other ten from outside the car). Evidence also showed that Mr. Brown did not have a gun or a knife. After hearing the conflicting testimony and reviewing the physical evidence, a local grand jury chose not to bring criminal charges against the officer. That decision was followed by both peaceful protests and destructive riots.

Since then, there have been a number of other cases. On May 25, 2020, George Floyd, a Black man arrested under suspicion of using a counterfeit bill, died after a police officer pressed his knee against Floyd's neck and three other officers watched as George Floyd told them he could not breathe. All four officers were charged. One with second-degree murder, third-degree murder, and manslaughter. The rest were charged with aiding and abetting second-degree murder and manslaughter.

Earlier that year, in March 2020, police, delivering a no-knock warrant, knocked down Breonna Taylor's apartment door, shot and killed her. As a result of the prosecutor recommending the relatively minor charge of wanton endangerment, and that to just one of the three officers involved, no other indictments were brought by the grand jury.

In rare instances, police officers have been convicted for killing civilians. For example, in 2017, the police were called to investigate an underage drinking party. When the police approached, the teens scattered. A police officer shot five times into one of the cars. Fifteen-year-old Jordan Edwards, sitting in the front passenger seat, was fatally shot in the head. The officer was found guilty of murdering an unarmed person.

DISCUSSION QUESTIONS

6. As noted in the discussion of stand-your-ground laws, George Zimmerman consciously put himself in danger by following Trayvon Martin even though police had told him not to do so.

    a. To what extent do you think this should have made a difference in the outcome of his trial?

    b. Do you think the law should be modified so as not to apply in situations where people put themselves in danger?

7. In another incident in Florida, Curtis Reeves, a 71-year-old man, shot and killed Chad Oulson during an argument over Oulson's texting in a movie theater. Witnesses reported that Oulson, threw a bag of popcorn at Reeves. Reeves then pulled out a semiautomatic handgun from his pocket and shot Oulson. The police report noted that during the argument over the texting, no punches were thrown, but the shooter claimed he was "in fear of being attacked" after being struck in the face "with an unknown object."[12]

   a. Do you think Reeves should be able to assert a valid self-defense claim based on his assertion that he was "in fear of being attacked"? Why or why not?

   b. In this case, the shooter was a retired police officer. Do you think this fact helps or hurts his use of the stand-your-ground law? Why?

   c. Why does the 2017 amendment to Florida's "stand your ground" law make it harder to prosecute someone in a shooting incident? Do you think that the amendment defense should be retroactive?

8. In June 2020, protesters marched through a gated community and past the home of a St. Louis couple. The couple stood outside their home and brandished weapons, a rifle and a handgun, at the protesters. They were each charged with one felony count of unlawful use of a weapon. The couple cited the Castle doctrine as their defense. In Missouri, the Castle doctrine requires that the defendant has to be "reasonably afraid of being in imminent danger." What factors would the court look at in this situation to determine whether the Castle defense is successful?

7. Constitutional Defenses

Two of the most common constitutional grounds for challenging criminal statutes are that they are vague or overbroad or they violate the First Amendment protections of freedom of speech and religion. If a court finds that a statute is unconstitutional, a defendant cannot be legally convicted or punished for violating it.

Void for vagueness
A reason for invalidating a statute when a reasonable person could not determine a statute's meaning.

Overbreadth
A reason for invalidating a statute where it covers both protected and criminal activity.

The due process clauses of the Fifth and Fourteen Amendments can form the basis for a **void for vagueness** or **overbreadth** argument. For example, the Texas stalking statute made it illegal to engage in conduct that is "reasonably likely to harass, annoy, alarm, abuse, torment, or embarrass" someone. The highest Texas criminal appellate court found the statute to be unconstitutionally vague on its face.[13] The overbreadth argument has been used to challenge city ordinances aimed at stopping gang activity. Such ordinances empower the police to order groups of loiterers to disperse if an officer reasonably believes one of the loiterers is a gang member. Obviously, such ordinances have the potential for abuse and for interfering with lawful activities. Therefore, because they cover both criminal activity and protected activity, these ordinances can be challenged as overbroad.

---

[12] "No Bail in Texting Shooting," by William M. Welch, *USA Today*, January 15, 2014, 3A.
[13] Long v. State, 931 S.W.2d 285 (Tex. 1996).

Criminal statutes can also be challenged on the basis that they violate the defendant's First Amendment rights of freedom of religion or freedom of speech. When freedom of religion is used as a basis for challenging a statute, the government must show the law in question is neutral on its face and of general applicability. If this standard is met, the statute is valid even though it may have the incidental effect of burdening a particular religious practice.[14] For example, the U.S. Supreme Court upheld the constitutionality of a statute prohibiting polygamy, even though the Mormon defendant argued that polygamous marriage was part of his religion.[15] However, the Court invalidated a city ordinance prohibiting the ritual sacrifice of animals on the grounds that it was neither neutral on its face nor of general applicability.[16] It was not neutral because it was directed at a specific religious group, the Santerias, and it was not of general applicability because it only applied to the killing of animals in the context of a religious service. If the city had been motivated by legitimate public health concerns, the ordinance would have been applicable to all situations in which animals are killed. The First Amendment protection of freedom of speech can also form the basis for a constitutional challenge. The concept of **content neutrality** plays a critical role in First Amendment cases. For example, in *Texas v. Johnson*, the Supreme Court determined that the state of Texas could not punish someone for symbolic speech, in that case the burning of an American flag, simply because they disagreed with the message being sent.[17]

Content neutrality also plays a role in the Court's treatment of **hate crime** laws. Hate crimes are offenses that are motivated by a hatred of a specific group or category of people, such as racial or religious minorities or homosexuals. In analyzing these types of laws, one needs to distinguish between those prohibiting certain types of **hate speech** and those that enhance the punishment of another underlying crime.

In a case dealing with a form of hate speech, the Court was asked to consider whether a state statute that outlawed cross burning unconstitutionally infringed on protected symbolic speech. The Court held that cross burning by itself could be protected speech. However, if the intent behind the cross burning was to intimidate, the state could constitutionally criminalize that behavior.[18] Therefore, the Court reversed the conviction of a man who had led a Ku Klux Klan rally during which a cross was burned but affirmed that the state could prosecute those who used a cross burning to intimidate, as was done by two men who placed a burning cross in the yard of an African-American family.

Content neutrality
The principle that laws may not limit free expression on the basis of whether the speech's content supports or opposes any particular position.

Hate crime
A crime where the selection of the victim is based on that person's membership in a protected category, such as race, sex, or sexual orientation.

Hate speech
Speech directed at a particular group or classification of people that involves expressions of hate or intimidation.

---

[14] Employment Div. v. Smith, 494 U.S. 872 (1990).
[15] Reynolds v. United States, 98 U.S. 145 (1878).
[16] Church of the Lukumi Balbalu Aye Inc. v. Hialeah, 508 U.S. 520 (1993).
[17] 491 U.S. 397 (1989).
[18] Virginia v. Black, 538 U.S. 343 (2003).

NETNOTE

To learn more about hate crimes, visit the U.S. Department of Justice's page on hate crimes at *justice.gov/hatecrimes*.

In contrast to hate speech laws, the penalty enhancement statutes simply provide for stiffer penalties in situations where the defendant has been found guilty of another crime, such as robbery, but it is proved that the defendant selected the specific victim because of that person's race, religion, or other specified factors.

DISCUSSION QUESTION

9. Some have argued against the adoption of hate crime statutes. They contend that it is the crime itself, not the motive, that should form the basis of punishment, arguing that a person is just as dead if a murder is committed in the course of a robbery gone wrong as during a race riot. How would you answer such critics?

Double jeopardy
A constitutional protection against being tried twice for the same crime.

In addition to challenging the constitutionality of the criminal statute under which they have been charged, defendants can challenge the constitutionality of their prosecution by raising the defense of **double jeopardy**. Relying on the Fifth Amendment, defendants argue that they cannot be prosecuted because they have previously been tried for the same offense. The courts have interpreted the Fifth Amendment protection of not being put twice "in jeopardy of life or limb" as meaning a defendant cannot be tried a second time for the same offense once "jeopardy" attaches. Generally, jeopardy attaches once a jury has been selected. However, the same action can sometimes constitute two different criminal offenses. An act that is prosecuted as a homicide in state court may also be prosecuted as a violation of civil rights in federal court. Furthermore, double jeopardy does not prevent a civil action for damages that arose from the criminal action. Finally, if the defendant appeals a conviction and wins the appeal, the appellate court may remand the case for a new trial.

NETNOTE

To keep up with current topics in criminal law, consider following blogs that discuss national issues, such as CrimProf at *lawprofessors.typepad.com/crimprof_blog/*. Or follow a blog on developments in your state, such as the UNC School of Government's North Carolina Criminal Law blog.

Legal Reasoning Exercise

5. What defense(s) might be available to the following individuals?

   a. The Elliots complained to the police that the son of their next-door neighbor broke their garage windows with rocks. They wanted him arrested. The police went next door to arrest the boy, and they discovered that he is seven years old. They arrested him and brought him to the police station. He was charged with destroying the Elliots' property.

   b. Marcus was arrested for the murder of his cousin Michael. At the time that Michael was killed, Marcus claimed that he was on a business trip 300 miles away.

   c. Every day on the way to school, Rosa pushed Carmen to the ground and stole her lunch. On Tuesday, Carmen hid behind a car on the way to school, and when she saw Rosa walking toward her, she jumped out and hit her. Rosa pushed Carmen to the ground and walked away without taking her lunch.

   d. As Paula walked toward her car after work, she was confronted by Terry, who pointed a realistic toy gun at Paula and demanded that Paula hand over her wallet. Paula took a real gun out of her purse and shot and killed Terry.

   e. After his car was forced off the road, Patrick tried to stop the bleeding on his wife's face. When she passed out, Patrick ran to a nearby home, jumped over the fence, and banged on the front door. When the occupants would not let him in, Patrick broke a window of the house, climbed through, and ran toward the telephone. The homeowner grabbed a rifle and shot Patrick in the back.

   f. During a grocery store robbery, a thief held a gun to a customer's head and demanded that he put all the money from the store safe into a bag, which he did. When the police arrived, they arrested the customer for robbery.

   g. During the last five years of their marriage David beat his wife, Mary, so severely that she was hospitalized four times. About six months after the last beating, Mary stabbed David to death while he was sleeping. She was arrested for murder.

   h. Officer Kaplan responded to an emergency call for a store robbery in progress. When the masked thief shot at the officer, Officer Kaplan shot and killed the thief. The man's family wanted Officer Kaplan charged with murder.

   i. Galen Black, a member of the Native American Church, ingested peyote as part of a religious ceremony held at that church. Peyote contains mescaline, a hallucinogenic drug. Black was arrested for possession and use of an illegal drug.

   j. George Jefferson was tried for murder. After the jury returned a not guilty verdict, George held a press conference and confessed that he had indeed committed the murder. With this new evidence, the prosecutor wants to try George a second time for murder.

F. PUNISHMENTS

Criminal codes establish a range of punishments associated with each type of crime. Often there are significant differences between the possible minimum and maximum. For example, under the Model Penal Code, the sentence for murder can range from one year to life imprisonment. Furthermore, judges often have the power to sentence defendants to **probation**, to give them a conditional discharge, or to suspend a sentence altogether.

1. Capital Punishment

The federal government and the majority of states currently authorize the use of the death penalty. While the states are free to determine for themselves whether to have the death penalty, the Eighth Amendment's prohibition against cruel and unusual punishment places some constitutional limitations as to the type of crime committed and the characteristics of the defendant.

As to the type of crime, it must be one in which the defendant's actions caused someone to die.[19] As to the characteristics of the defendant, the U.S. Supreme Court has held that it is unconstitutional to execute those who were suffering from intellectual disability or who were under the age of 18 when their crimes were committed.[20] Many people believe that the strongest argument against the death penalty is that errors in our criminal justice system have resulted in too many innocent men and women being executed. These wrongful convictions have been caused by a variety of factors, including unethical actions by police and prosecutors, ineffective defense lawyers, biased jurors, and mistaken witness identifications.

DISCUSSION QUESTION

10. What arguments both for and against capital punishment do you find to be most convincing? Why?

2. Mandatory Sentencing

In the 1970s, in reaction to what many saw as a growing crime and drug epidemic, many states and the federal government enacted laws mandating a minimum number of years in prison for specific crimes. Once a defendant pleads guilty or is convicted of committing a particular crime, the trial court judge has no sentencing discretion, even if the mandated minimum sentence does not seem to fit the crime. One result has been the quadrupling of our prison population. The United States now imprisons a higher percentage of its citizens than any other country.[21] Approximately half of the states, as well as the federal government, have enacted "three strikes" or **habitual offender statutes**. Typically, these statutes mandate required prison sentences for third-time offenders. As is true with all mandatory sentencing provisions, these statutes remove a great deal of the sentencing discretion from the hands of judges, and some believe that they

Habitual offender statute
A statute that mandates required prison sentences for third-time offenders.

---

[19] Kennedy v. Louisiana, 554 U.S. 407 (2008).
[20] Roper v. Simmons, 543 U.S. 551 (2005).
[21] *The Week*, "Rethinking mandatory sentencing," p. 11 (September 20, 2013).

can create unfair results in individual cases. For example, a man in California was sentenced to 25 years to life under the state's three strikes law. His crime? Attempting to steal three golf clubs, worth $399 apiece. He challenged the length of his sentence, arguing that the Eighth Amendment's prohibition against cruel and unusual punishment required greater proportionality between the crime and the punishment. In a 5-4 decision, the U.S. Supreme Court disagreed, declaring that such three strikes provisions do not violate the Eighth Amendment.[22]

While the case cited above was an extreme example of the perceived unfairness of a mandatory three strikes law, it illustrates the problems inherent in any proposed solution where one result was designed to fit all situations. While the California law had been enacted to address the problems of violent crimes, it ended up incarcerating many whose third offense was nonviolent. In 2012, California reformed its "three strikes" law so that those who commit a third nonviolent felony would be sentenced to double prison time for that third felony, but only violent felons would face life in prison.

DISCUSSION QUESTION

11. How much discretion should the judge have in sentencing? Why?

SUMMARY

Criminal law defines what behaviors are illegal and what punishments convicted defendants are to receive. Criminal procedure governs how the criminal process works.

Crimes can generally be divided into felonies, crimes that usually involve punishment by incarceration for a year or more, and misdemeanors. For any crime the government must prove that the defendant had the requisite mens rea while committing the actus reus. Common defenses include alibi, ignorance or mistake, infancy, insanity, intoxication, duress, necessity, entrapment, self-defense, and defense of others. In addition, a defendant may challenge a prosecution on the basis of a statute of limitations or the Constitution.

In addition to defining the nature of what constitutes each of the different types of offenses, criminal codes also establish a range of punishments associated with each type of crime.

REVIEW QUESTIONS

Pages 213 through 220
1. Why is no behavior a crime unless the law makes it a crime?
2. What is the Model Penal Code, and what was the intent of its drafters?
3. How are felonies usually distinguished from misdemeanors?

---

[22] Ewing v. California, 538 U.S. 11 (2003).

4. What are the major classifications used for distinguishing among crimes on the basis of the harm done?

Pages 220 through 227
5. What is the actus reus of a crime? What is the mens rea?
6. How do you determine whether one crime is a lesser included offense of another crime?
7. What is an inchoate crime?
8. What is the difference between general intent and specific intent?
9. Define and describe the categories of intent used by the Model Penal Code.
10. What methods, besides a defendant's statements, might a prosecutor use to prove a defendant's state of mind?
11. Who is the principal of a crime? What is the difference between the principal and the accessory to a crime?

Pages 228 through 236
12. What is the difference between a complete and a partial defense?
13. Describe the various tests that have been developed to determine whether a defendant was insane at the time he or she committed the crime.
14. What are the possible results of successfully proving an insanity defense?
15. What is the difference between the duress and the necessity defenses?
16. What does a defendant have to show to prove entrapment?
17. When can a potential victim use deadly force to protect himself or herself?
18. What is the retreat exception to the self-defense doctrine?

Pages 236 through 239
19. When might a statute be challenged for vagueness? For overbreadth?
20. What must the government show when a statute is questioned as violating the defendant's First Amendment right of freedom of religion?
21. What are the two different approaches that states might take to legislate against hate crimes?
22. On what basis might a defendant challenge his conviction under a hate crimes statute?
23. What protections are afforded by the double jeopardy clause?
24. Why is it not double jeopardy for the prosecutor to appeal an intermediate-appellate-level decision?

Pages 240 through 241
25. Who is not eligible to receive the death penalty?
26. What is the basis for a constitutional challenge to the use of the death penalty?
27. What is the purpose of "three strikes" or habitual offender statutes?

‖‖‖ WEB EXERCISES

1. Identity theft is a growing problem. Take the Identity Theft Quiz on the U.S. Department of Justice website at *justice.gov/criminal-fraud/identity-theft/identity-theft-quiz.* What concrete steps do you think you should take to increase your level of protection against identity theft?
2. There is an interesting website, *cyberbullying.us,* that has collected information on cyberbullying and sexting statutes for all 50 states. It also includes editorial blogs. One of these discusses whether criminal prosecution is the best approach. Click on *cyberbullying.us/criminalization-of-cyberbullying/,* and then read the blog. What are the author's main arguments against the criminalization of cyberbullying?

Chapter 9

Criminal Procedure

It is better that ten guilty persons escape
than that one innocent suffer.
William Blackstone (1765)

Chapter Objectives

After reading this chapter, you should be able to:

- Describe the stages of a criminal case, from discovery of a crime through sentencing.
- Explain the difference between reasonable suspicion and probable cause, and when each applies.
- Discuss when a search warrant is required and how one is obtained.
- Discuss the content of and the justification for the *Miranda* warnings.
- Define the exclusionary rule and explain its purpose.

INTRODUCTION

Almost any time you turn on your television, you can see someone's interpretation of how our criminal justice system works, or fails to work. Real-life court cases intertwine in the public's mind with fictitious courtroom battles and send mixed messages. Our criminal justice system raises fundamental questions: How far should police go to capture suspected criminals and to construct cases against

Rules of criminal procedure
Federal and state rules that regulate how criminal proceedings are conducted.

Rules of evidence
Federal and state rules that govern the admissibility of evidence in court.

them? How can criminal defense lawyers represent defendants who they know are guilty? Is it really better to let ten guilty people go free than to have one innocent person sent to jail? Are some innocent persons being sent to jail in spite of all our system's due process guarantees? These are the types of questions that you will encounter in the study of criminal procedure.

The federal and state **rules of criminal procedure** govern everything from investigation and arrest through sentencing and appeals. The federal and state **rules of evidence** regulate what types of evidence can be used in the trial and how it must be presented. The goal of these rules is to protect all of society, even alleged criminals, from unjust prosecutions.

NETNOTE

The FBI maintains a website at *fbi.gov* where you can find a great deal of information, including the "Ten Most Wanted" list.

PRACTICE TIP

To fully evaluate a file for procedural errors, the paralegal should read every word of the file. Do not overlook dates, times, and locations. Even a wrong date on a traffic ticket could make a difference!

Civil and criminal procedure share many similarities, especially at the trial stage. However, there are significant differences as well. For example, whereas civil lawsuits begin with the official filing of the complaint, criminal cases normally begin with the arrest of the accused. Figure 9-1 provides an overview of the stages in a criminal prosecution. Be warned, however, that the details of criminal procedure vary greatly among jurisdictions. For example, only about half the states have a grand jury system. Also, especially for misdemeanors, the stages may be accelerated or even combined. The only mandated uniformity is the U.S. Supreme Court requirement that a probable cause hearing be held within 48 hours after a person is arrested without a warrant.[1] Also, Figure 9-1 assumes that the process continues until there is either a guilty plea or a trial. However, the charges can be dropped at any time. For example, the prosecutor might decide that there is insufficient evidence to file an information, or the grand jury might refuse to indict.

The U.S. Supreme Court has ruled that state, as well as federal, prosecutions must be consistent with the constitutional protections of the Bill of Rights. Therefore, although approximately 95 percent of criminal prosecutions occur in state courts, the U.S. Constitution has a significant impact on how these prosecutions are conducted.

In the next few sections, we will use the fictitious case of *People v. Grant* to illustrate the various stages in a criminal prosecution.

---

[1] County of Riverside v. McLaughlin, 500 U.S. 44 (1991).

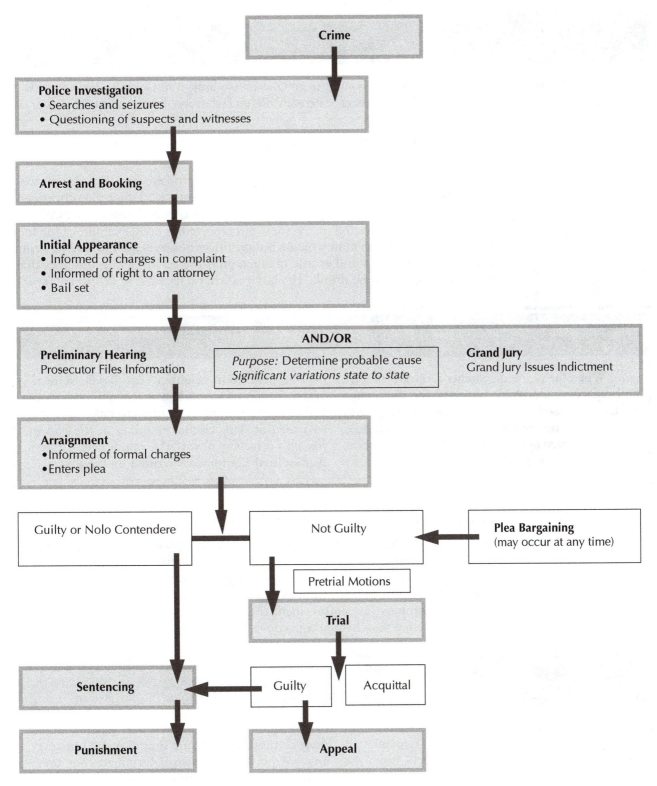

Figure 9-1   Stages of Criminal Procedure

Case 11: *People v. Grant*

When Stephen Joseph returned home at about 10 p.m. on April 30, he discovered that the window of his porch door was broken and someone had taken his stereo, VCR, and television. Joseph called the police.

A. INVESTIGATION OF A CRIME

The criminal process usually begins when a law enforcement officer learns that a crime has been committed or is about to be committed. Either the officer personally observes the crime being committed, or the officer is sent to investigate a crime that either the victim or a witness has reported. A good example of the former would be a situation in which a police officer observes an automobile being driven in a dangerous and erratic manner, pulls the car over, and observes that the driver appears to be drunk. The latter is what happened in *People v. Grant*.

Case 11: *People v. Grant* (Continued)

When the police dispatcher received Joseph's call regarding a possible burglary, she dispatched police personnel to his home. After talking with Joseph, they determined that a crime had indeed been committed and began talking with neighbors and collecting evidence.

A next-door neighbor, Pat Baker, remembered seeing a van parked in Joseph's driveway earlier in the evening. According to Baker, she saw two men in dark clothes standing at the end of Joseph's driveway next to the van. It had "Grant's Audiovisual Equipment" written on the side.

---

1. Discovery of the Crime and Initial Actions Taken

No matter how the crime is originally reported, throughout the investigation process, both federal and state law enforcement officers must conduct themselves in such a way as not to violate constitutional rights set out in the Bill of Rights. The Fourth, Fifth, and Sixth Amendments to the U.S. Constitution impose important restrictions on how law enforcement officials can go about gathering evidence when conducting searches and questioning potential suspects.

Case 11: *People v. Grant* (Continued)

As the police were returning to the station to file a report, they noticed two men in dark clothes walking about ten blocks from the Joseph home. The police turned on their cruiser lights and pulled up behind the men. After briefly questioning the men and patting down their clothes to make sure that they did not carry any weapons, the police determined that these men were late-night joggers and not related to the crime.

In the case of *People v. Grant,* when the police stopped and questioned these late-night joggers, they were conducting what is known as a **stop and frisk.** If the police have a reasonable suspicion that a person has committed or is about to commit a crime, they can stop (detain) that person and ask questions. When circumstances such as the time of day and the number of people in the area justify it, the police can also frisk (pat down the outside of the clothes of the person they stopped) to see if the person is carrying any dangerous weapons.

Note that the police cannot stop and frisk any individual they want at any time they want. An individual may be stopped only when the officer has a reasonable suspicion that the individual has committed, is in the process of committing, or is about to commit a crime. **Reasonable suspicion** must be based on "specific and articulable facts which, taken together with rational inferences from those facts, reasonably warrant that intrusion."[2]

The circumstances of the stop matter. The length of time that the officers detain the suspect cannot be long. The longer the period of time, the closer the court will look at the intrusiveness of the search. The court will also look at the number and the type of questions the police ask. If the questions become detailed or the officers begin to accuse the suspect of committing a crime, then the court may consider the stop too intrusive.

The court will also look carefully at the circumstances of a frisk. Because the purpose of the frisk is to protect the officers and to aid in the detection and prevention of crime, the officers may frisk the suspect only if the officers, based on their experience, believe that the suspect is carrying a weapon. The frisk must take place outside the suspect's clothes. The officers are not allowed to search the inside clothing or pockets of the suspect. If a motorist is stopped, the officer may pat down the areas within the suspect's immediate control, such as the car seat.

In our hypothetical case of *People v. Grant,* the police would argue that they had a reasonable basis to stop and frisk the two joggers:

- The neighbor's description of the men matched their appearances.
- There were two of them.
- They wore dark clothes.
- They were in the neighborhood of the crime late at night.

Stop and frisk
The right of the police to detain an individual for a brief period of time and to search the outside of the person's clothing if the police have a reasonable suspicion that the individual has committed or is about to commit a crime.

Reasonable suspicion
A suspicion based on specific facts; less than probable cause.

2. Searches and Seizures of Evidence and Fourth Amendment Restrictions

Searches of a suspect's home, business, or automobile and seizures of property from those locations are crucial law enforcement tools. Through legal searches and seizures, officers may uncover items that are illegal on their face, such as illegal drugs or weapons. Officers may also locate the fruits of crime, such as stolen property, or the instruments of crime, such as burglary tools, weapons, and plans.

Police and their crime scene investigation units have to be very careful not to compromise the admissibility of evidence. For example, they should not touch

[2] Terry v. Ohio, 392 U.S. 1, 21 (1968).

Chain of custody
A record identifying who had control and access to evidentiary materials from the time they were obtained until the time they are introduced into evidence.

items without gloves nor move anything before pictures can be taken to document the location in which they were found. They must clearly mark any items they take with them and maintain records establishing the **chain of custody**.

The Fourth Amendment begins with a prohibition against "unreasonable" searches of "persons, houses, papers, and effects." It also requires that search warrants be issued only upon a showing of "probable cause" and that these warrants "particularly" describe "the place to be searched, and the persons or things to be seized."

To determine whether a search has taken place, courts evaluate the defendant's expectation of privacy. Some areas, such as a suspect's bedroom closet and the inside of a suspect's refrigerator, clearly raise expectations of privacy. Other areas, such as the license plate of a suspect's automobile and the outside stairs of a suspect's home, are less private. The suspect expects that these areas will be seen by anyone passing by. Therefore, it is not a "search" to write down a speeding car's license plate number.

If police actions do not violate any expectation of privacy, then the Fourth Amendment protection does not apply. However, if individuals have an expectation of privacy, then the police must get a warrant before they can perform a search. For example, if police are looking for evidence that a former bank employee had downloaded customers' credit card information onto a personal computer, then the police would be required to get a warrant before performing a search of the computer's contents.

a. Procedures for Obtaining and Executing Search Warrants

The best way to ensure that the results of a search will be admissible in court is first to have the police or prosecutor go before a judge to obtain a formal **search warrant**. In order to issue the warrant, a judge needs to find that it is supported by **probable cause**.

Search warrant
A court's prior permission for the police to search for and seize property.

In seeking a search warrant, law enforcement agents must:

Probable cause
A belief based on specific facts that a crime has been or is about to be committed; more than a reasonable suspicion.

- list the specific items they expect to find at the location they wish to search (they cannot just look for something that might be incriminating);
- explain how the items they are searching for are connected to criminal activity; and
- convince the judge that there is probable cause to believe the items they seek are located where they intend to search.

Note how this process worked in *People v. Grant*.

Case 11: *People v. Grant* (Continued)

After some investigation, the officers determined that Bruce Grant is the owner of Grant's Audiovisual Equipment. By checking with the motor vehicle department, the police also discovered that the vehicle was registered to Bruce Grant, age 42. When they checked Grant's record, they discovered that he had twice been convicted of stealing audiovisual equipment and selling the stolen goods.

The officers wanted to search the business premises to look for Joseph's missing goods so that they could take those goods, and any other stolen goods, from Grant's place of business to be used against him at a trial.

The officers went to court and told the judge what their investigation had produced. They told the judge exactly what they wanted to search (Grant's place of business and the inside of the van), and they told the judge exactly what they expected to find there (Joseph's stolen items). The judge determined that there was probable cause and issued the warrant to search.

In this case, it would not be appropriate for the officers to simply ask the court for a warrant to search for TV sets because the business could have several TVs for sale that are not the products of the crime. The officers should list the specific brands, models, model numbers (if they are known), and any other specific characteristics of the stolen items. Where the police are looking for illegal drugs, however, they need not be as specific. They can indicate on the warrant that they are looking for heroin because there is no legal heroin that can be found by mistake. The officers should also be as specific as possible about the location, noting street address, apartment number, or level. This not only makes the officers' probable cause stronger but also assists the officers who execute the warrant.

The search warrant must be **executed**—that is, the search must actually be carried out—within a specific period of time. The officers must announce themselves as police officers and execute the warrant during the daytime unless the warrant specifically allows other arrangements. They must inventory and describe in writing all the items they seize, and usually they must give the suspect a receipt.

Execute a warrant
To carry out the provisions of a warrant.

Under special conditions, the courts will sometimes issue **no-knock warrants**, which allow the police to enter without announcing their presence in advance. In order to receive one of these special search warrants, the police must convince the judge that evidence is likely to be destroyed or that the police administering the warrant will be in danger. No-knock warrants are controversial and their use is meant to be a rare exception to the Fourth Amendment's search and seizure requirement. Their legal status in the federal system is unsettled and they are rarely used. However, several states do allow for no-knock warrants. The dangers of no-knock warrants have grown as states have passed stand your ground laws (see Chapter 8), allowing citizens to use deadly force without attempting to retreat if they believe that they are facing a threat of death or bodily harm.

No-knock warrant
A warrant that allows the police to enter without announcing their presence in advance.

In the 2020 Breonna Taylor case, officers went to her apartment to execute a no-knock warrant to search for evidence of drug dealing. Her boyfriend, Kenneth Walker, stated that they heard loud banging on the door and then the door was broken off the hinges. Unaware that the intruders were police officers, Mr. Walker shot his gun once. The officers responded with many shots into the apartment, killing Ms. Taylor. This case illustrates why no-knock warrants are controversial and why it has prompted the federal government and many states to review whether or not no-knock warrants should be allowed.

b. Exceptions to the Warrant Requirement

Although it is always best to obtain a warrant, many searches are conducted without a warrant and are nonetheless valid. Figure 9-2 contains a listing and

Type of Exception	Description of Search	Rationale for Not Requiring a Warrant
Consent search	Search takes place after someone, who has authority to do so, voluntarily agrees to allow law enforcement authorities to search.	Constitutional rights can be voluntarily waived.
In plain view doctrine	Officers see items they believe to be contraband or evidence of a crime when the objects are in plain view and the police are in a place where they have a right to be.	There is no violation of the right to privacy when others can see the items.
Incident to lawful arrest	A search for potential weapons or evidence of a crime that is conducted at the time a person is arrested.	This protects the safety of police and prevents destruction of evidence.
Inventory search	An examination of personal effects or vehicle to document the contents, following an arrest or seizure of a vehicle.	Documentation protects against theft or damage of items while under police control.
Stop and frisk	A "pat down search" of someone the police have stopped to question in surroundings (e.g., a dark alley) where their personal safety might be at risk.	The need to protect the officers' safety outweighs the relatively minor invasion of privacy.
Exigent circumstances	An emergency situation in which there is not adequate time to get a warrant before the evidence could be destroyed or lives could be endangered. (Examples: people are trapped inside a house that is on fire or the police are in "hot pursuit" of a suspect.)	Applies in emergency situations when action is necessary to avoid loss of evidence or to save human life.

Figure 9-2   Exceptions to the Warrant Requirement

brief explanation of the most common exceptions to the requirement that law enforcement authorities obtain a warrant before they conduct a search. Most of these exceptions are based on one of two theories. The first is that the Fourth Amendment is not violated because there is no expectation of privacy (as with the plain view and consent exceptions) or the invasion was minimal (as with the stop and frisk exception). The second is that in order to protect human life or to prevent the destruction of evidence, the police action was reasonable under the circumstances (as with a search incident to an arrest or **exigent circumstances**).

Common exceptions to the requirement of obtaining a warrant are when there is consent to the search, when the seized evidence was in plain view, and incident to an arrest. A **consent to search** occurs when someone, who has authority to do so, voluntarily agrees to allow law enforcement authorities to search a dwelling, car, or business. A warrant is not necessary where proper consent was given, but issues can arise as to whether the person giving consent had the authority to do so.

The **plain view doctrine** holds that law enforcement officers have the right to seize evidence when it is "in plain view." Therefore, if officers observe marijuana growing in containers on someone's front porch, they can seize the plants and use them as evidence against the occupants of the dwelling. And when an officer looks in the driver's window of a car that has been stopped for a minor traffic offense, that police officer can seize a partially filled beer can she observes sitting on the automobile's front seat. However, an officer may not search an automobile without a warrant or in the area immediately surrounding and associated with a home, referred to as the "curtilage," if the evidence is not in plain view from a lawful vantage point.[3]

The exception for a search incident to arrest is based on the need to protect the safety of law enforcement officers and to prevent destruction of evidence. When exigent circumstances exist, police may have no time to obtain a warrant before evidence is destroyed or people are endangered. One example of this is that states are legitimately concerned about drunk driving and the damage it can cause. In addition to conducting field sobriety tests that involve observing the manner in which a driver performs physical tests such as walking a straight line, law enforcement officers rely on the use of breathalyzer tests and blood tests to measure blood alcohol levels and a driver's degree of impairment. All states have some sort of implied consent law that provides for the loss of a driver's license for refusing to take a breathalyzer test, blood test, or urine test after being stopped on suspicion of drunk driving. A number of states have even made refusing to take a breathalyzer test a crime. Two states, Minnesota and North Dakota, have gone further, making the refusal to take a blood test a crime. Noting the difference between requiring a breathalyzer test and a blood test, the U.S. Supreme Court has held that charging a driver with a crime for refusing a breathalyzer test incident to a drunk driving arrest is permitted under the Fourth Amendment. Because of the intrusiveness of the act of taking blood, however, before charging a driver with a crime for refusing a blood test, the Fourth Amendment requires the law enforcement officers to obtain a warrant.[4]

Exigent circumstances
Generally, an emergency situation that allows a search to proceed without a warrant.

Plain view doctrine
A policy that allows police to seize contraband or evidence that is openly visible in an area where they are authorized to be.

DISCUSSION QUESTIONS

1. Which of the following areas do you think should be considered "private" and therefore require a warrant to be searched?
   a. a teenager's bedroom in the parents' home
   b. a garage

---

[3] Collins v. Virginia, 138 S. Ct. 1663 (2018).
[4] Birchfield v. North Dakota, 136 S. Ct. 2160 (2016).

    c. someone's office at his or her workplace

    d. a school locker

    e. garbage that was placed on the curb for roadside pickup

    f. a cell phone

    g. cell-site location data from a cell phone through the phone's wireless carrier

2. Indicate whether you think marijuana could be lawfully seized if its discovery were based on each of the following situations:

    a. Using a helicopter, the police fly over your fenced backyard and see it growing in pots on your back patio.

    b. Standing across the street from your house, the police use binoculars and see it growing inside your sunroom.

    c. Aiming a thermal-imaging device at your house, the police find suspicious "hot spots," indicating the probable presence of marijuana growing within your home.

    d. Using a police dog that has been specially trained to smell marijuana and other illegal drugs, the dog "points" to your briefcase, when

        1) you are walking down the street.

        2) you are walking through an airport.

        3) your briefcase is located in the locked trunk of your car, and you have been stopped for speeding 6 miles per hour over the limit on a major highway.

        4) your briefcase is located in your living room, and the police walked the dog down an interior hallway of your apartment building.

3. While breathalyzer tests can determine the level of alcohol in one's body, such tests cannot be used to detect marijuana and other drugs that can affect someone's driving. Do you think that police should be able to require motorists to provide blood samples whenever they suspect the driver was under the influence of an illegal drug?

Case 11: *People v. Grant* (Continued)

When the search warrant was executed, the police found the stolen items in an unlocked cabinet in the rear of the store. The officers seized the equipment, gave Grant a receipt for the items they seized, and filed a report with the court. The police officers then asked Grant to come to the station to talk to them about the equipment. Grant rode along with them in the back seat of one of the patrol cars.

On the ride to the station, one of the officers asked Grant where he had been on the evening of April 30. He replied that he and his cousin had gone to a movie. The officer then asked him what movie they had seen and what time it had started. Grant said they had gone to an eight o'clock showing of *Avengers: Endgame*. Next, the officer asked him where he had gotten the electronic equipment that they had seized from his store. He replied that he had taken it as a trade-in as part of a sale of a big-screen TV.

When they arrived at the police station, the officers took Grant into an interrogation room and read him his *Miranda* rights. He responded that he did not want to talk to them unless he had a lawyer present. When they gave him a telephone so he could call his lawyer, he told them he wanted a court-appointed lawyer because he could not afford to hire one on his own.

3. Interrogations and Fifth Amendment Restrictions

Police questioning usually takes place at the scene of the crime, or sometimes even in the person's home or office. But for purposes of the Fifth and Sixth Amendments, there is an important distinction between simply addressing questions to victims and witnesses to get background information about a crime, and interrogating suspects to illicit potentially incriminating information linking them to the commission of the crime.

The Fifth Amendment provides for a right against self-incrimination: "no person shall . . . be compelled in any criminal case to be a witness against himself." In the landmark cases of *Escobedo v. Illinois*[5] and *Miranda v. Arizona*,[6] the U.S. Supreme Court ruled that the Fifth Amendment's privilege against self-incrimination and the Sixth Amendment's right to assistance of counsel apply to the interrogation stage, as well as to the trial. The Court reasoned that the right to counsel at trial would not benefit the defendant if the defendant had already confessed before meeting with a lawyer, and the presence of a lawyer during an interrogation would help to ensure that any statements given would be truly voluntary rather than coerced. The famous *Miranda* warnings are designed to notify defendants of their rights and to explain those rights in language that they will understand.

Once the *Miranda* warnings are given, the police cannot interrogate the suspect further unless he or she waives these rights. Note, however, that these rights apply only to testimonial evidence and do not protect a suspect from having to take a breathalyzer test, be fingerprinted, be subjected to a DNA swab,[7] or provide a handwriting sample.

In the hypothetical case of *People v. Grant*, the police read Grant his *Miranda* rights before they began questioning him at the police station. However, they questioned him in the car about his activities on the night of the burglary before they informed him of his *Miranda* rights. Did this questioning in the car constitute an interrogation, and were the police required to have read the *Miranda* rights before they questioned him in the car?

The answers depend on the definition of a **custodial interrogation**. Suspects are in police **custody** when they feel that their freedom has been deprived in a significant way. It does not matter whether the suspects have been arrested (formally charged with a crime), although an arrest would indicate that the suspects are not free to leave. When suspects are in police custody and are questioned by the police, it is difficult, and maybe even frightening, for them to say, "No, thank you," to police questions. Therefore, before beginning this custodial interrogation (questioning of suspects when they feel that their liberty has been deprived), the police are required to tell the suspects about their rights. However, what constitutes "interrogation" is not always clear.

Although suspects have the right not to answer questions during custodial interrogation, this does not mean that they have to remain silent. Suspects may waive their *Miranda* rights as long as they do so voluntarily, knowingly, and intelligently. To determine whether a suspect waived his or her rights, the court

---

Miranda warnings
The requirement that defendants be notified of their rights to remain silent and to have a lawyer present prior to being questioned by the police.
- You have the right to remain silent;
- Anything you say can be used against you in a court of law;
- You have the right to have an attorney present during questioning; and
- If you cannot afford an attorney, one will be appointed for you.

Custodial interrogation
Occurs when law enforcement authorities question a person who has been deprived of his or her freedom in a significant way.

Custody
Occurs when a suspect has been deprived of freedom in a significant way.

---

[5] 378 U.S. 478 (1964).
[6] 384 U.S. 436 (1966).
[7] In Maryland v. King, the U.S. Supreme Court held that "taking and analyzing a cheek swab of the arrestee's DNA is, like fingerprinting and photographing, a legitimate police booking procedure that is reasonable under the Fourth Amendment." 569 U.S. 435, 465-66 (2013).

will look carefully at all the circumstances. The court will consider the educational level of the suspect, language barriers, the existence of a mental condition or impairments, addictions to alcohol or illegal substances, the suspect's prior court experiences, the duration and intensity of the questioning period, and any other facts brought to the court's attention. The prosecution has the burden of proving that the defendant made a proper waiver.

To avoid confusion about whether a suspect received *Miranda* warnings or about whether there were proper waivers of the suspect's rights, law enforcement agencies usually require defendants to sign a card that lists the suspect's rights and asks the defendant questions such as these:

1. Do you understand these rights as they have been explained to you?
2. Understanding these rights, do you wish to speak to me now?
3. Please sign this card indicating that you understand the above information.

In addition to the *Miranda* cards, many police departments videotape or tape-record the suspects as they receive their rights and consider waiving their rights. Then, if the suspects later claim that they did not receive their rights or that they did not understand the waiver of their rights, the police have documentation to show to the court.

If a suspect decides to remain silent, the police cannot continue the questioning and must give the suspect an opportunity to communicate with a lawyer. The police cannot try to continue questioning at a later time unless a lawyer is present. A suspect can waive his or her *Miranda* rights at a later interrogation.

Once in custody, juvenile suspects must also be given their *Miranda* rights, and the age of the suspect must be considered as a factor in determining when the questioning rises to the level of being custodial.[8] In addition to a right to speak to a lawyer, juvenile suspects are given the right to talk to an interested adult, such as a parent or guardian, before deciding to waive their rights. Because of their age, or in some circumstances because of their lack of experience with the criminal justice system, juveniles may need extra help making such important decisions. Just as parents or guardians may help juveniles with other life decisions, the court recognizes that a juvenile needs the extra protection that talking to a trusted adult may provide.

Legal Reasoning Exercise

1. Using the standard discussed in this chapter, did custodial interrogation take place during the following incidents?
   a. A suspect ran up to the police officer and cried, "Help! I killed him. I killed him. I didn't mean to do it!"

---

[8] See J.D.B. v. North Carolina, 564 U.S. 261 131 S. Ct. 2394 (2011) (case remanded for further determination as to whether a 13-year-old student questioned by police in his school's conference room would have felt he was in custody).

b. An officer walked up to a group of boys hanging around a street corner and said, "Hey, guys. What are you doing here?"
c. While at the police station, the suspect explained how he stole the car from the parking lot down the street.
d. As an officer asked questions, the suspect wrote answers on a piece of paper.
e. In the case scenario being used in this chapter, the police questioned Bruce Grant on the ride to the police station.

Case 11: *People v. Grant* (Continued)

On the basis of a witness having reported seeing the Grant's Audiovisual Equipment van and the evidence seized from Grant's store, the police were convinced that Grant had burglarized Stephen Joseph's home. They therefore informed him that he was under arrest and began the process of fingerprinting and booking him.

4. Arrest and Booking

After law enforcement authorities collect enough evidence, they will arrest the alleged suspect and begin the charging process. An **arrest** is the act of legally restraining a person's freedom by taking that person into police custody for the purpose of filing formal charges. A law enforcement officer can make an arrest if he or she either has **probable cause** to believe the person being arrested committed a crime, or the officer has been properly informed that a court has issued a warrant for the individual's arrest.

The **booking** process usually includes taking the defendant's personal information, giving the defendant an opportunity to read and sign a *Miranda* card, and allowing the defendant the opportunity to use a telephone. Additionally, the police may take photographs, or "mug shots," of the defendant for identification purposes. The police may also require the defendant to be fingerprinted. Fingerprints may then be compared to fingerprints found at the scene of the crime or saved to be compared to prints found at future crime scenes. If the defendant is being charged with a serious crime, a DNA swab may also be taken. The defendant is then searched, and his or her belongings are inventoried and stored by the police.

In some jurisdictions, people arrested for less serious crimes may be able to be released on a preset bail schedule or on personal recognizance as soon as the booking process is completed. Others, especially those arrested for felony offenses, will be held in custody until they can appear before a judge.

Probable cause
Not susceptible to a precise definition; a belief based on specific facts that a crime has been or is about to be committed; more than a reasonable suspicion.

Booking
The process after arrest that includes taking the defendant's personal information, giving the defendant an opportunity to read and sign a *Miranda* card, and allowing the defendant the opportunity to use a telephone.

B. THE COURT SYSTEM

A suspect's involvement with the court system begins with the initial appearance and then continues through a series of stages, eventually leading to either a guilty or a not guilty plea. If a guilty plea is entered, the case moves into the sentencing phase. If a not guilty plea is entered, the case is scheduled for trial. Finally, in some situations, either the defendant or the prosecution may appeal the results of a court proceeding.

At any time, this entire process may stop if the defendant agrees to a plea bargain. Rather than going to trial, in over 90 percent of cases, the prosecution and the defense negotiate the defendant's punishment. This negotiation is called **plea bargaining** and can happen at any time in the process. In plea bargaining, the defendant may agree to plead guilty to the crime, or to a lesser included offense of the crime, in exchange for the prosecution's recommendation for a lighter sentence. The judge may consider the results of the plea bargain but is not required to accept it. A defendant has the right to effective assistance of counsel throughout the plea bargaining process.[9]

Prosecutors are willing to make these types of bargains for a variety of reasons. Because most prosecutors' offices are understaffed and overworked, plea bargaining provides a way to more efficiently manage their workloads and produce high conviction rates. Many prosecutors are willing to settle for a sure conviction on the record with at least some jail time for the defendant rather than risking an uncertain conviction for the sake of longer jail time.

Plea bargaining
A process whereby the prosecutor and the defendant's lawyer agree for the defendant to plead guilty in exchange for the prosecutor's promise to charge him or her with a lesser offense, drop some additional charges, or request a lesser sentence.

DISCUSSION QUESTION

4. How might you respond to your neighbor who says the judicial system is "falling apart" because of plea bargaining?

1. Formal Charges, Bail, and Initial Appearances

After an individual has been placed in custody, the law requires that he or she be brought before a judge or magistrate without unnecessary delay. At this initial appearance the defendant must be told of the charges, be advised of the right to counsel, and have bail set.

Case 11: *People v. Grant* (Continued)

The following morning, Grant was taken to court to have bail set and to determine if he was qualified to have a public defender appointed. At this initial appearance, the judge told Grant of the charges being brought against him, set bail at $5,000, and denied his request for a public defender because he appeared to have enough assets in his business to be able to afford to hire his own lawyer.

His case was then bound over to the grand jury to determine if there was sufficient evidence to proceed to trial.

Bail
Money or something else of value that is held by the government to ensure the defendant's appearance in court.

Bail is money or something else of value, such as a deed to real property, held by the government to ensure the defendant's appearance in court for further proceedings. The Eighth Amendment includes a prohibition against "excessive bail." Thus judges are expected to set bail at an amount of money

---

[9] See Lafler v. Cooper, 566 U.S. 156 (2012); Missouri v. Frye, 566 U.S. 134 (2012).

that will make it too costly for the defendant to skip town, but yet not be "excessive." In deciding what this amount should be, judges will often consider such things as having a job or owning a home in the community. In many states, a bail bondsman will post the money for defendants who do not have ready access to the amount required for bail.[10]

Persons can also be released prior to the trial date on a **personal recognizance bond** by giving their personal promise to appear in court when instructed to do so. These defendants are indebted to pay a specified amount if they fail to fulfill the conditions of the bond.

At the initial appearance, a defendant who cannot afford the services of a private lawyer will usually have either a public defender or a member of the private bar appointed to provide representation. Most courts have developed local guidelines that take into consideration the income and assets of the defendant, as well as the nature of the offense.

Lawyers do not have to be provided in all misdemeanor cases, but indigent defendants cannot be given jail sentences unless they either were provided with counsel or waived their right to such representation.

Personal recognizance bond
A defendant's personal promise to appear in court.

Case 11: *People v. Grant* (Continued)

Two weeks later, the grand jury heard testimony from the police officers who had taken the report of what had been stolen from Joseph's home and had interviewed the witness about seeing the Grant's Audiovisual Equipment truck there. It also heard from the officer who was involved in executing the search warrant and had heard Grant say that he had been watching *Avengers: Endgame* at the local theater that night. In addition to describing the goods they had seized, the officer reported that when he checked with the local theaters, he discovered that none had been showing *Avengers: Endgame* on April 30. The grand jury never heard any testimony from Grant.

The grand jury then followed the prosecuting attorney's suggestion and indicted Bruce Grant for possession of stolen property, selling stolen property, and larceny.

---

2. Grand Juries and Preliminary Hearings

The Fifth Amendment requires that "[n]o person shall be held to answer for a capital, or otherwise infamous crime, unless on a presentment or indictment of a Grand Jury. . . ." The members of a **grand jury** determine if probable cause exists to believe that a crime has been committed and that the defendant committed it. Note, however, that this requirement of a grand jury is one of the few constitutional guarantees that has not been incorporated by the Fourteenth Amendment due process clause, and therefore it does not apply to the states. Today, some

Grand jury
A group of people, usually 23, whose function is to determine if probable cause exists to believe that a crime has been committed and that the defendant committed it.

---

[10]The bondsman receives a fee from the defendant for posting the amount of money the judge has set for bail. The fee is to compensate the bondsman for taking the risk that the money posted will be forfeited to the court if the defendant does not appear when he or she is supposed to do so. If the defendant does appear, the funds posted will be returned to the bondsman. If the defendant "skips town," the bondsman may hire a "bounty hunter" to find and bring the person back.

states require grand juries; others allow the prosecutor the option of using one; and some do not use grand juries at all.

If the majority of grand jury members conclude that adequate evidence has been presented, they return an **indictment.** The federal government and most states that use grand juries follow the common-law format of having 23 persons serve during a term and requiring at least 12 votes for an indictment.

Historically, grand juries were thought to be a protection against arbitrary governmental prosecutions because they required prosecutors to obtain approval from a group of ordinary citizens before forcing someone to undergo the expense and ordeal of a trial. Today, however, many advocate abolition of the grand jury system on the basis that they increase costs to taxpayers while failing to check prosecutorial abuses.

When grand juries are not used, a prosecutor files an information and a preliminary hearing is held. An **information,** like an indictment, sets out the formal legal charges against a specifically named individual.

At the **preliminary hearing,** the prosecutor must present sufficient evidence to convince the judge that there is probable cause to believe the named individual committed the crimes for which he or she is being charged. Thus, it serves as an alternative to the grand jury as a check on prosecutorial discretion.

Finally, some states require neither a preliminary hearing nor a grand jury indictment for misdemeanors. After the initial court appearance, the prosecutor can simply file the information.

3. Arraignments

Case 11: *People v. Grant* (Continued)

Grant was released from custody after posting his bond, and he arrived at his arraignment with a private lawyer he had hired. The judge informed him that he had been charged with possessing stolen property, selling stolen property, and committing larceny. Following his lawyer's advice, Grant pleaded not guilty and demanded a jury trial. The judge accepted his plea and assigned the case to the next jury calendar.

At this point, Grant's lawyer filed a motion to require the state to turn over police notes regarding interviews with witnesses. She also moved to suppress the statements her client had made in the back of the police car about his activities on the night of the crime.

Indictment
A grand jury's written accusation that a given individual has committed a crime.

Information
A prosecutor's written accusation that a named individual has committed a crime.

Preliminary hearing
A hearing where the prosecutor must present sufficient evidence to convince the judge that there is probable cause to believe the named individual committed the crimes for which he or she is being charged.

Arraignment
A criminal proceeding at which the court informs the defendant of the charges being brought against him or her and the defendant enters a plea.

At an **arraignment,** the court informs the defendant of the charges contained in the indictment or the information. The judge then asks the defendant to answer the charges by pleading guilty or not guilty. At this stage, defendants represented by counsel are highly unlikely to plead anything but not guilty. Their lawyers will have told them to wait until they go through the discovery process and have the opportunity to engage in plea bargaining.

But if the defendant wishes to plead guilty, the judge must ensure that the defendant understands the nature of the charge, the minimum and maximum sentences prescribed by law, and that entering a guilty plea waives the right to a trial and to confront and cross-examine witnesses. If the court determines that

Case 11: *People v. Grant* (Continued)

After several continuances pushed back the original court date, the judge announced that he would tolerate no further delays in the case, and both lawyers needed to be ready to begin the trial on January 10. Shortly before Christmas, Grant's lawyer called the assistant prosecutor that had been assigned to the case to discuss the terms of a possible plea bargain.

The prosecutor offered to drop the larceny charges if Grant would plead guilty to possession of stolen property. Grant's lawyer then proceeded to inquire as to what the prosecutor would recommend for jail time if her client accepted this offer. When the prosecutor said five years, she countered with one year. The prosecutor then laughed and said that his absolute minimum offer was four years. She responded that she would discuss the offer with her client, but she doubted he would accept. When she discussed the matter with Grant, he told her he would rather take his chances with a trial.

the defendant is voluntarily pleading guilty, usually the court will ask the prosecution to recommend a sentence. The judge may either pronounce the sentence at that time or set a specific time for a sentencing hearing at some later date. If the defendant enters a not guilty plea, a tentative date is set for the trial based on whether the defendant requests a jury trial or a bench trial.

PRACTICE TIP

Many prosecutors and defense teams create checklists of possible pretrial motions and attach them to each case. Using a checklist helps the parties evaluate all the possible motions. By including the criteria for each motion on the checklist, the parties can save valuable time during strategy meetings.

A seldom used alternative to pleading either guilty or not guilty is to plead **nolo contendere**. This Latin phrase means "no contest." With a nolo contendere, plea, a defendant neither admits nor denies the charges. He or she simply agrees that if the case went to trial, the prosecution would have sufficient evidence to prove its case beyond a reasonable doubt. This plea is not considered an admission of guilt and so cannot be used later against the defendant at a civil trial. However, for purposes of the arraignment, the case proceeds as though the defendant had pleaded guilty.

Nolo contendere
A defendant's plea meaning that the defendant neither admits nor denies the charges.

4. Discovery, Pretrial Motions, and the Exclusionary Rule

As in civil proceedings, the parties in a criminal case have an opportunity to use various discovery devices to avoid "trial by ambush." The defense generally has a right to discover all the evidence that the prosecution intends to use at trial, including such things as the names, addresses, and statements of persons that

Inculpatory evidence
Evidence that suggests the defendant's guilt.

Exculpatory evidence
Evidence that suggests the defendant's innocence.

the prosecution intends to call as witnesses; transcripts of any electronic surveillance; and physical evidence, such as a gun, a knife, illegal drugs, or the results of scientific tests. In addition to turning over **inculpatory evidence**, which suggests the defendant's guilt, the prosecution is required to produce **exculpatory evidence**, which suggests that the defendant did not commit the crime. If the prosecution refuses to provide discovery to the defense, the defense team may file motions to compel the evidence and ask the court to force the prosecution to supply the evidence. The prosecution, in turn, has a right to have the defendant appear in lineups, give handwriting samples, provide names and addresses of people who will be called as defense witnesses, and provide results of laboratory and medical reports to be used as evidence.

Legal Reasoning Exercise

2. Would the prosecution consider the following items to be potentially inculpatory or exculpatory? Could this evidence be potentially inculpatory *and* exculpatory?
  a. The fingerprints of a second person on the murder weapon
  b. A statement that the defendant gave to the police shortly after the arrest disclosing the location of the missing body
  c. Samples of hair and skin found at the scene of the crime

The most common **pretrial motions** relate to facilitating the discovery process and preventing certain types of evidence from being used at the trial. Figure 9-3 lists the motions that you are most likely to encounter. Note, however, that not all of these are available in every jurisdiction. You need to check local court rules to determine the availability and format of specific motions. Usually, motions are accompanied by a memorandum of law, analyzing how the courts have decided similar motions in past cases and arguing how the motions should be decided in this case.

It may be considered legal malpractice not to file a motion to suppress evidence when that motion has a probability for success. Any time there is a search, the defense lawyer should carefully evaluate the file to determine whether these motions are required.

Motion to suppress
A request that the court prohibit the use of certain evidence at the trial.

Success in winning a **motion to suppress**, the first type of motion listed in Figure 9-3, could mean the difference between winning or losing the entire case. Such a motion is a request to have the court prohibit the use of certain evidence at the trial. If the evidence is excluded, then the prosecution may not be able to prove its case.

Type of Motion	Goal	Rationale
Motion to suppress	To eliminate all or some of the evidence against the defendant	Without evidence, the state cannot meet its burden of proof. Evidence obtained during an illegal search and seizure, or other improper behavior, may be suppressed.
Motion to dismiss	To dismiss all or some of the charges against the defendant	The best way for the defense team to win is to get the case (or at least a few charges) dismissed before subjecting the defendant to the dangers of trial.
Motion to compel	To force the opposition to provide evidence that has been refused	There is no more trial by ambush. The prosecution must disclose inculpatory *and* exculpatory evidence.
Motion to sever	To try multiple defendants at separate trials	If several defendants are tried together, they may be deprived of certain defenses that point to another defendant as more culpable, and the jury may be overwhelmed and confused about what evidence pertains to each defendant. Through this motion the court attempts to eliminate undue prejudice.
Motion to bifurcate	To isolate the charges against a defendant and try each charge at a separate trial	If the jury would be misled by alternative charges, the defendant would benefit by defending against one charge at a time. Prejudice and unfairness are considered proper grounds under most circumstances.
Motion for a bill of particulars	To force the prosecution to provide specific information regarding the case	The defense team is entitled to know the details of the case with as much specificity as possible.
Motion to sequester witnesses	To keep witnesses out of the court-room until after they testify	The testimony of one witness or the questioning tactics used by the attorneys may influence the testimony of witnesses yet to testify. Keeping witnesses outside the courtroom may help keep their testimony pure.

Figure 9-3   Typical Pretrial Motions

Type of Motion	Goal	Rationale
Motion to recuse	To remove a particular judge from a case	If a judge knows a victim or defendant in a case, pulblicly voices an opinion about the outcome of the case, or otherwise has a conflict of interest, the judge should step down, and another judge should proceed.
Motion for funds	To allow indigent defendants access to funds from the state	An indigent defendent has the same legal needs for trial preparation as a wealthy defendant. Money may be made available through the court for expert witnesses, scientific tests, or other investigatory needs.
Motion for change of venue	To achieve an impartial jury panel through a request for a change of the location for trial	Sometimes a defendant cannot get a fair trial in the location where the crime was committed. Pretrial publicity or local prejudice may inhibit justice.
Motion to continue	To change the date of trial, usually to postpone to a later date	The parties may require more time to prepare or to allow witnesses to travel to the trial. Attorneys, witnesses, or the defendant could fall ill. When the trial cannot proceed as scheduled, this motion should be filed. Motions of this type, if not abused, are usually allowed.
Motion in limine	To make evidentiary and trial decisions prior to the beginning of trial	Some decisions, such as the order of witnesses, the scope of examination or cross-examination, and the admission of certain documents, may be decided by the parties prior to the start of trial. This speeds up the trial process and avoids bickering in front of the jury.
Motion for a view	To let the jury visit the scene of the crime	A viewing can give the jury members a better understanding of the crime scene than they could otherwise gain from witness testimony alone.

Figure 9-3   Typical Pretrial Motions (*continued*)

Motions to suppress are based on what is known as the **exclusionary rule**. Under the terms of the exclusionary rule, evidence that has been obtained in violation of an individual's constitutional rights cannot be used against that individual in a criminal trial. For example, if police interrogate suspects without first informing them of their *Miranda* rights, the confession cannot be used in court. The U.S. Supreme Court applied the exclusionary rule in federal cases in 1914 and then in 1961 extended its application to state courts.

The application of the exclusionary rule does not invalidate the arrest or prevent the defendant from being convicted on the basis of independent evidence. Nor does it prohibit officers from later conducting legal searches and gathering additional evidence as long as that evidence was gathered without the aid of knowledge gained from the tainted evidence that was suppressed. Nevertheless, the exclusionary rule does make law enforcement's job more difficult, and police may not be able to gather enough evidence to obtain a conviction. In these cases the application of the exclusionary rule does in fact result in guilty persons going free.

Furthermore, if illegally obtained evidence in turn leads to the discovery of other evidence (such as the location of stolen property), that evidence is likewise inadmissible under the doctrine known as the **fruit of the poisonous tree doctrine**. Any evidence that is directly derived from an illegal search or illegal interrogation is inadmissible against the defendant by virtue of being tainted by the original illegality. If the tree (the primary evidence) has been poisoned from the illegal search, then all the fruit (collateral or additional evidence) must also be suppressed. The exclusionary rule, which remains one of the most controversial aspects of constitutional law, applies to state as well as federal court cases.

Exclusionary rule
A rule that states that evidence obtained in violation of an individual's constitutional rights cannot be used against that individual in a criminal trial.

Fruit of the poisonous tree doctrine
Evidence that is derived from an illegal search or interrogation is inadmissible.

Legal Reasoning Exercise

3. Suppose that someone fired a bullet through the floor of an apartment into the apartment below. The police entered the shooter's apartment looking for the shooter, for other weapons, and possibly for victims. While they were in the apartment, the police discovered weapons and a stocking cap. The police also noticed stereo equipment and, suspecting it was stolen, recorded the serial numbers. In order to read all the numbers, the police moved some of the equipment. When the police headquarters notified the police that the equipment was stolen, the police officers seized it.

a. If you worked for the defense team, what arguments would you make to convince the court to suppress the evidence?

b. If you worked for the prosecution, what arguments would you make to convince the court that the search was legal?

c. Which side has the most persuasive arguments?

5. Competency to Stand Trial

Separate from the issue of mental competency at the time the crime was committed is the question of whether, at the time of trial, the defendant is mentally competent. If the defense argues that the defendant cannot understand the legal process or assist with the defense by, for example, talking about the case with the lawyer or testifying meaningfully at trial, the court will hold an evidentiary hearing to determine competency, and the trial cannot begin until the court determines the defendant is mentally competent.

6. The Right to a Jury Trial

The Sixth Amendment to the U.S. Constitution creates a right to trial by an impartial jury in federal criminal cases. The due process clause of the Fourteenth Amendment applies the right to a trial by jury to defendants in state criminal actions who face possible incarceration of six months or more.[11]

The U.S. Constitution requires that criminal juries at the federal level consist of 12 members and that their verdicts be unanimous. The U.S. Supreme Court has ruled that six-member juries are permissible at the state level,[12] as are less-than-unanimous verdicts.[13] It is left to the states to select which of these options they wish to use.

One of the most frequently misunderstood principles of the jury system is the concept of being tried before a jury of one's peers. This does not mean that the jury must consist of a group of people who are similar to the defendant. Rather, the jury simply must be broadly representative of the community in which the trial takes place. Perhaps the most problematic aspect of jury selection is the goal of selecting an "impartial jury." The criminal courts rely on the same jury selection process used in civil cases. As discussed in Chapter 6, the courts rely on voir dire questioning and both peremptory challenges and challenges for cause to eliminate jurors who have biases or prior experiences that could affect their ability to be impartial. Other options include either a change of venue or a change of venire. The former involves moving the location of the trial to another area where potential jurors are unlikely to have read or heard about the case, while the latter option holds the trial in the area where the crime was allegedly committed but imports jurors from another community. If a criminal defendant does not trust any of these options, the only remaining choice is to waive the right to a jury trial and to choose a bench trial, with the judge serving as both the fact finder and the presiding officer.

DISCUSSION QUESTIONS

5. In 2013, Dzokhar Tsarnaev and his brother, Tamerlan, set off two pressure cooker bombs near the finish line of the Boston Marathon. The bombing killed 5 individuals and left 280 others injured. Tamerlan was killed while being apprehended by police, but Dzokhar was arrested and put on trial.
    a. Do you think you could be an impartial juror in the accused bomber's trial? Why or why not?
    b. In a memorandum in support of their motion for a change of venue from Boston, defense lawyers claimed that 85 percent of the 1,373 people

---

[11] Baldwin v. New York, 399 U.S. 66 (1970).
[12] Apodaca v. Oregon, 406 U.S. 404 (1972).
[13] Williams v. Florida, 399 U.S. 78 (1970).

who had completed prospective juror questionnaires either believed their client was guilty or had some self-identified connection to the case. The federal judge handling the case denied the defendant's motion. Do you think he made the correct decision? Why?

6. In situations where the prosecution may ask the jury to return a verdict that includes a possible death sentence, potential jurors can be questioned about their views on capital punishment and can be excused for cause if they indicate that they are unwilling to impose the death penalty for religious or moral reasons. The catechism of the Roman Catholic Church states that the death penalty should not be used when "non-lethal means are sufficient to defend and protect people's safety from the aggressor." Should all Roman Catholics automatically be excluded from being jurors in capital cases? Why or why not?

7. The Trial

There are few, but very important, differences between civil and criminal trials. The major difference is that the prosecutor in a criminal case must bear the burden of a higher standard of proof, beyond a reasonable doubt, as opposed to preponderance of the evidence. The defense is not required to put the defendant, or any other witnesses, on the stand. If the defendant chooses not to testify, the prosecution cannot comment or otherwise draw attention to it during any part of the trial.

The prosecution goes first, presenting all the information necessary to meet its burden of proof beyond a reasonable doubt. Through witnesses and the introduction of evidence, the prosecution attempts to prove each element of each charge. With cross-examination of the prosecution's witnesses, the defense attempts to discredit their testimony.

When the prosecution has completed its case, it "rests." At that time, in most jurisdictions, the defense may make a **motion to require a finding of not guilty** for some or all of the charges. Outside of the hearing of the jury, the defense may argue that the prosecution failed to meet its burden and that the court should remove the case from the jury by finding the defendant not guilty. The judge looks at the evidence presented and evaluates it in the light most favorable to the prosecution. If the judge grants this defense motion, the defendant can be found not guilty of the individual charges or the entire case. If the judge does not allow this motion, the jury returns and resumes hearing the case.

As mentioned above, the defense is not required to put witnesses on the stand. If the defense does call witnesses, the defense examines and the prosecution cross-examines each witness, again with an eye toward credibility.

Once the defense has rested its case, the defense may renew the motion for a required finding of not guilty. This time the judge looks at the motion in the light most favorable to the defendant. If the motion is allowed, the case never goes to the jury for a verdict. If the motion is denied, the lawyers deliver their closing arguments to the jury. The judge then informs the jurors of the law that they need to know to make their decision, which is called **charging the jury**. Once they are charged and sworn to do their duty, the jury members are released from the courtroom to deliberate. They may bring any items entered into evidence into the jury room with them to help them decide, and they can come back into the courtroom to ask questions.

Motion to require a finding of not guilty
A defense request that the court find the prosecution failed to meet its burden and that it remove the case from the jury by finding the defendant not guilty.

Charging the jury
After both sides have presented their final arguments, the judge's instructions to the jury on the meaning of the law to be applied to the facts of the case.

PRACTICE TIP

Prepare Your Case for Trial

Concentrate on preparing as much as possible in advance of trial to avoid last-minute confusion and to reduce last-minute stress.

Organize your materials: Many lawyers and paralegals find it helpful to prepare a trial notebook that contains all the documents they may need during the trial. Include reports, statements, documents to be entered into evidence, the names and addresses of potential witnesses, some sample questions, and clean copies of all statutes and court opinions used to support motions and memoranda of law. Organize them for easy access.

Subpoena all witnesses: Even witnesses you believe are anxious to testify should be summonsed and required to attend.

Prepare the defendant and witnesses for trial: Remember, however, that you may not supply the answers, and witnesses should testify only to their own personal knowledge. You may also want to review documents, such as police reports and witness or defendant statements, so that the witnesses can remember what they might have said or done at earlier stages of the proceedings.

Prepare Yourself for Trial

Read the case file from start to finish, including all motions and all supporting law.

Make a list or a file of all motions filed by each party and the outcomes of the motions. The lawyers or the judge may forget what was actually decided as the result of any motion.

Make a list of all potential witnesses, their addresses, and their telephone numbers. Keep one copy of the list in the file, and keep one copy with you in case you must contact witnesses in a hurry.

Prepare explicit directions to the courthouse for potential witnesses, and carry them with you in case witnesses get lost on the way. Decide with the lawyers before trial whether to provide taxi assistance for expected witnesses.

Wear clothes that reflect your important position at trial. Conform to local customs and habits. Remember that the jury can see you as easily as you can see them. And they can hear you, too. Avoid impatient or disappointed gestures, comments, or facial expressions, and even avoid expressions of delight or gloating. Also, remember that the judge and the jurors may be in the courthouse halls or on the courthouse steps prior to trial and could even be in the same parking garage. Be aware of them at all times, and consider yourself to be "in trial" from the minute you leave for court.

Never talk to the press or to anyone about the trial, your client, or even your own role at trial. Do not talk to your client in the presence of strangers. Do not respond to the comments of others.

Nothing can describe the waiting period while the jury is deliberating. It is too late to change anything, too soon to know whether your strategy worked. Many lawyers spend this time discussing possible outcomes with their clients or evaluating their trial performances. There is no set length of time that a jury can deliberate and no special process that a jury must follow. If the defendant is found not guilty, the case is over. If the defendant is found guilty, then the case moves into the sentencing phase.

DISCUSSION QUESTIONS

7. Criminals are guaranteed a jury of their peers. If you were on trial for a criminal offense, what factors would you consider when trying to select a jury of your peers? Is there really such a thing?

8. "It is better that ten guilty persons escape than that one innocent suffer" is an often-quoted legal expression by William Blackstone in 1765. Do you agree or disagree?

8. Sentencing

With the exception of capital punishment cases, where statutes frequently give the defendant the option of having the jury decide if the death penalty should be imposed, the jury usually has no role to play in the sentencing process. Once the jury has found the defendant guilty of a specified crime, the judge is responsible for determining what the sentence will be.

Following a conviction for serious crimes, a separate sentencing hearing is usually held, at which evidence can be presented "in aggravation and mitigation." At such a hearing both the prosecution and the defense have an opportunity to present evidence that was not relevant to whether the defendant committed the crime but is relevant to the nature of the punishment that is to be imposed. The judge also receives a pre-sentence report, which reviews the defendant's criminal record, work record, family background, and other factors considered relevant in determining the appropriate punishment. Some states provide for **victim impact statements**, in which the victim of the crime describes how it negatively affected his or her life and the lives of family members.

Victim impact statement
A written or oral statement made by the victim of the crime (or the family members of a deceased victim) that is presented at the sentencing hearing.

9. Appeal

Criminal defendants who wish to appeal a conviction must file the appropriate post-trial motions, usually accompanied by a notice of appeal within a specified time period. While the Fifth Amendment protection against double jeopardy prevents prosecutors from appealing an acquittal, it does not prevent them from appealing the dismissal of a case on technical grounds or a lower appellate court ruling to a higher court.

10. Writ of Habeas Corpus

If the deadline for appeal has expired or the appeal was unsuccessful, lawyers sometimes file a petition for a writ of habeas corpus as a sort of "back door" way to get a client's case reconsidered. A petition for a **writ of habeas corpus** is a prisoner's request that a court review the legality of his or her imprisonment.

Writ of habeas corpus
A court order to produce the person detained; designed to give a neutral judge an opportunity to review the charges, in order to ensure there is a lawful basis for the incarceration.

Executive clemency
The power of the president or a governor to pardon, reduce, or delay a sentence.

Pardon
An executive action that cancels a conviction for a crime and the penalty associated with it.

Commutation
An executive action that lessens the penalty for a crime without changing the fact of conviction.

Reprieve
An executive action that temporarily postpones the punishment until some future time where another authority can review the sentence.

In practice, the vast majority of petitions for a writ of habeas corpus are filed in federal court by incarcerated state prisoners who have been convicted of committing a state crime, such as murder. The basis of their petition is the argument that the state violated their Constitutional right to due process during their arrest, trial, or incarceration. For example, a defendant could argue that his trial lacked fundamental fairness because the judge was biased against him or his lawyer was incompetent.

11. Petitions for Executive Clemency

After having exhausted all other avenues, the only remaining option for convicted criminals involves filing a petition for clemency with the governor for state offenses or the president for federal offenses. Clemency can come in a variety of forms, including a full **pardon**, a **commutation**, which is a reduction of a sentence, or a **reprieve**, which is a temporary stay. Many states utilize a formal Board of Pardons to review applications for executive clemency and then make recommendations to the governor on those requests.

The case of Sara Kruzan provides a good example of the use of executive clemency. At the age of 17, she was convicted of first-degree murder for killing the man who had forced her into a life of prostitution when she was only 13 years old. She was sentenced to life imprisonment without parole. In 2011, California governor Arnold Schwarzenegger commuted her sentence to 25 years with the possibility of parole. Because of what had happened to her at such a young age, Sara's case had received a great deal of publicity and was therefore unique. Normally, however, the odds of a petition for executive clemency proving successful are not very good.

DISCUSSION QUESTION

9. In a 1991 trial in the Georgia criminal courts, Troy Davis was convicted of murder and sentenced to death for the 1989 death of a police officer. At the trial, several witnesses stated they saw Davis shoot the officer. No gun was found, and no physical evidence tied Davis to the murder. Davis then began a series of appeals and habeas corpus actions based on affidavits from ten witnesses in the case in which they recanted their testimony and claimed that police had coerced them into falsely implicating him. The Georgia Board of Pardons and Paroles received more than 663,000 signatures on petitions to spare his life, and such prominent people as Jimmy Carter, Pope Benedict XVI, and Desmond Tutu publicly supported his appeals. After a last-minute appeal to the U.S. Supreme Court was denied, he was executed by lethal injection in 2011.

   a. What does this case indicate about the efficiency of the criminal justice process?

   b. What does this case indicate about the ability of the system to reach a "just" result?

   c. To what extent do you think a pardon and parole board or a governor should consider petitions from members of the public in determining whether to grant clemency?

SUMMARY

The rules governing criminal procedure begin with the criminal investigation and continue in force through trial and any possible appeal. The Fourth Amendment requires that all searches and seizures be reasonable. The court-crafted exclusionary rule provides that any evidence unlawfully seized may not be used in court against the defendant. The Fifth Amendment protects defendants against self-incrimination, and the Sixth Amendment guarantees a right to an attorney. While every defendant has a right to a trial, most cases end through a negotiated plea bargain.

If a trial does occur, the prosecution bears the burden of proving guilt beyond a reasonable doubt. The defense lawyer is not required to put the defendant, or any other witnesses, on the stand. If the defendant chooses not to testify, the prosecution cannot comment or otherwise draw attention to the defendant's silence.

If the jury finds the defendant guilty, the judge is usually responsible for determining what the sentence will be. Most state statutes give the judge a broad range of discretion between a minimum and a maximum sentence for the crime.

Criminal defendants have the right to appeal a conviction. However, due to the Fifth Amendment protection against double jeopardy, the government cannot appeal an acquittal. A prosecutor can appeal the dismissal of a case on technical grounds or a lower appellate court ruling to a higher court.

REVIEW QUESTIONS

Pages 243 through 252
1. What is a stop-and-frisk search?
2. What is the difference between reasonable suspicion and probable cause? Why does it matter?
3. Why does the court consider the suspect's expectation of privacy when evaluating a search?
4. What is a warrant?
5. List some specific facts that must be included when police officers apply for a warrant to search a suspect's home.
6. What is a no-knock warrant?
7. What exigent circumstances may allow the police to search without a warrant?

Pages 253 through 255
8. What are the *Miranda* warnings, when are the police required to give them, and under what circumstances might a defendant waive them?
9. What extra protection do juveniles usually get when they are given their *Miranda* rights?

Pages 255 through 265
10. What might a defendant expect to occur during booking?
11. What are the differences between a guilty plea and a plea of nolo contendere?

12. Discuss the purpose of each of the following motions:
    a. to sever
    b. to bifurcate
    c. to sequester witnesses
    d. to recuse
    e. for change of venue
    f. in limine
13. How do motions to suppress affect the prosecution's case against defendants?
14. What is the exclusionary rule?
15. If the following facts are true, what pretrial motions might a defense lawyer file on behalf of the defendants?
    a. All the local papers have reported that the judge on the case used to be married to the victim.
    b. Each of the two defendants claims that the other defendant was the sole assassin.
    c. The defendant, who was represented by a public defender, needs to conduct an independent drug evaluation, especially since the defendant alleged the green, leafy substance was oregano bought to add spice to spaghetti sauce.
    d. Four of the seven witnesses prepared to testify at trial are related by blood or marriage.
    f. The police stopped the defendant for speeding and then proceeded to search the glove compartment, in which they found a bag of heroin.

Pages 265 through 269
16. Describe the basic steps that occur in a criminal trial.
17. Why is there no requirement that the defendant take the stand?
18. What is the purpose of charging the jury?
19. What is a writ of habeas corpus? When is it usually used?

‖‖‖ WEB EXERCISES

1. There is a wealth of information on the Federal Bureau of Investigation website. You can even play games. Explore the site and click on "News," and then on the right side of the box, labeled "More News & Information," click on "Video." Select a video. Which one did you watch? What did you learn?
2. Congress established the National Constitution Center in Philadelphia to disseminate non-partisan information about the Constitution at *constitutioncenter.org*. The center has created an online interactive Constitution, with links to articles from selected scholars presenting opposing points of view for each of the Constitution's provisions. Read the description of the Fourth Amendment and accompanying articles. Which of the articles did you find more persuasive? What did you learn?

Chapter 10

Contract Law

*A contract has, strictly speaking, nothing to do with
the personal, or individual, intent of the parties. . . .
If . . . it were proved by twenty bishops that either
party, when he used the words, intended something
else than the usual meaning which the law imposes
upon them, he would still be held.*
Judge Learned Hand

Chapter Objectives

After reading this chapter, you should be able to:

- Describe the purpose of the Uniform Commercial Code (UCC).
- Differentiate between the requirements for a valid gift and a binding contract.
- Apply the basic requirements of a contract to a factual situation.
- List the most common defenses to a contract formation.
- Discuss possible remedies available in a breach of contract case.

INTRODUCTION

Contracts are involved in almost every aspect of our lives, from day-to-day commercial transactions to corporate mergers—from purchasing and financing a home to insuring that home, automobile, life, or health. A **contract** is simply an agreement, oral or written, that can be enforced in court. Contract law sets out the basic elements that must be present for an agreement to be considered legally

Contract
A legally enforceable agreement supported by consideration.

271

enforceable. It also spells out when the court will excuse one of the parties for not living up to that side of the agreement. In sum, contract law reflects society's values regarding what promises we think should be kept and what excuses we will allow.

Case 12: Who Owns the Watch?

Sally, a paralegal student, had often told her friend Jill how much she admired Jill's Mickey Mouse watch. Last Monday, as the two were walking to class, Sally noticed that Jill was wearing a different watch and asked her about it. Jill replied that at her birthday party yesterday, her boyfriend gave her this new watch. "In that case," Sally inquired, "would you be interested in selling your Mickey Mouse watch to me?" Jill replied, "I paid $200 for it, but because we are friends, I will sell it to you for $100 and will bring the watch with me tomorrow." Sally said, "Great; it's a deal."

When Sally said, "it's a deal," what do you think she meant? Do you think she realized she may have been forming a binding contract? In this chapter, we will explore when a statement like Sally's constitutes a legally enforceable contract and the circumstances under which a court will enforce it.

Contract law has strong common-law roots, and in areas that do not deal with the business world, the common-law rules still govern. However, if a contract involves a business setting, then you may also have to consult legislation, in the form of the **Uniform Commercial Code (UCC)**. The UCC is a series of model statutory provisions drafted by prominent legal scholars. It was developed with the intent that states would voluntarily incorporate these provisions into their own statutes, thus providing a uniform set of legal principles that would facilitate commercial transactions among persons in different states.

Although all states, as well as the District of Columbia, have adopted the UCC entirely or in part, it is not a federal law. That would require its enactment by Congress. The terms of the UCC are valid only if they have been adopted by the state. In addition, while most states have adopted the UCC as it was originally written, each state has the option of changing the terms. Therefore, when dealing with the UCC in a specific state, be sure to check that state's precise wording.

Uniform Commercial Code (UCC)
Originally drafted by the National Conference of Commissioners on Uniform State Law, it governs commercial transactions and has been adopted by all states, entirely or in part.

PRACTICE TIP

Even though it is called the Uniform Commercial Code, always check your state statutes. States are free to modify the UCC as they see fit.

NETNOTE

The UCC, as revised through 2012, can be found on the Internet at *law.cornell .edu/ucc*. You can also find Uniform Commercial Codes by state. Make sure that you know what version governs your contract.

The UCC was specially developed to make the commercial world more uniform and efficient, and there are special rules that apply only to merchants.

A merchant is simply someone who routinely deals in the goods that are the subject of the contract. Unlike a consumer, a merchant's obligation of good faith includes "honesty in fact and the observance of reasonable commercial standards of fair dealing in the trade." UCC §2-103(b). Therefore, merchants are expected not only to deal honestly but also to be aware of the normal business practices for their trade.

The UCC is divided into ten articles (Ssee Figure 8-1). In this chapter, our discussion will focus on Article 2. Article 1 sets forth general provisions, such as definitions that apply to the entire UCC. Article 2 deals with the sale of goods. Note that while Article 2 of the UCC applies to some contract situations, it does not apply to all of them. For example, it does not apply to real estate or employment contracts because neither involves the "sale of goods."

Whenever you are faced with a contract situation, first ask yourself: does the situation involve a contract for the sale of goods? If the answer is yes, then ask whether either or both of the parties can be classified as a merchant. If yes, then be sure to check the special provisions that apply only to merchants. Finally, keep in mind the UCC's overall commitment to ensuring that all parties act in good faith and in such a way as to promote the expansion of commerce. See Figure 8-2 for a breakdown of how to handle these questions.

Article 1	General Provisions
Article 2	Sales
Article 2A	Leases [New]
Article 3	Commercial Paper
Article 4	Bank Deposits and Collections
Article 5	Letters of Credit
Article 6	Bulk Transfers
Article 7	Warehouse Receipts, Bills of Lading, and Other Documents of Title
Article 8	Investment Securities
Article 9	Secured Transactions
Article 10	Effective Date and Repealer

Figure 10-1 The Uniform Commercial Code

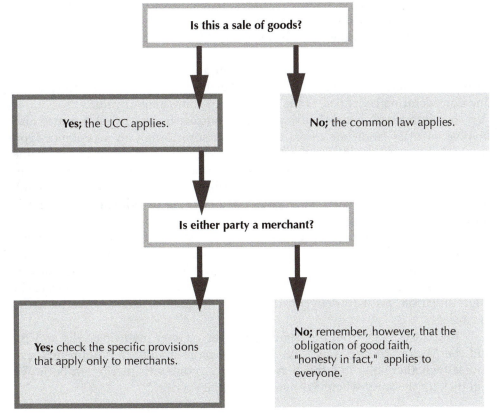

Figure 10-2   Does Article 2 of the UCC Apply?

You will discover that contract law is very rule-bound. That is, to become an expert in contract law, you must master a vast array of technical rules. Our brief overview of contract law in this chapter is designed to help you understand the basic concepts that lie behind these rules so that you will be able to recognize a contract law problem when you are faced with one and be able to undertake research in this area.

One of the most common contracts you will find in a law firm is the fee agreement. As the only parties to the contract are the client and the lawyer, a paralegal cannot establish the fee agreement. In addition, any attempt by a paralegal to set fees is considered the unauthorized practice of law (UPL).

A. THE ELEMENTS OF A BINDING CONTRACT

A contract can be either oral or written, but in order to be considered valid, each of its three key elements must be present:

1. An offer must be made,
2. an acceptance must be given, and
3. something of value must be exchanged (consideration).

Some writers list only two elements: an agreement and consideration. In such formulations, an agreement is defined as both an offer and an acceptance, and consideration is defined as the exchange of something of value.

It is important to clearly distinguish a contract from a gift. A gift may also involve an offer (someone offers to give you something), an acceptance (you respond that you would like the gift), and the passage of something of value (the gift itself). The difference is that in a gift situation, the consideration is one-sided. Only one of the parties receives something of value. On the other hand, in a contract situation each party gives up something of value. Because of this difference, a contract is completed and binding on both parties once the parties have reached their agreement. However, a gift is not completed until the thing of value is actually delivered. This difference becomes important if one of the parties tries to take back a promise. In a contract situation, the taking back of the promise creates a right in the other party to sue for breach of contract. In a gift situation, prior to delivery of the gift, the giver is free to take back the promise.

Recall the story from the beginning of the chapter involving Sally and Jill and the Mickey Mouse watch. As you learn more about what happened, ask yourself whether you think this presents a gift, a contract situation, or both. We will pick up the story where Sally said "Great; it's a deal."

Case 12: Who Owns the Watch? (Continued)

Unnoticed by Sally and Jill, Mike had over-heard the conversation. "Wait," Mike said, "I have always wanted a Mickey Mouse watch. I will give you $150 for the watch." Jill thought about it for a moment and then turned to Sally and said "Gosh; I'm sorry, Sally, but I'm afraid that unless you can match Mike's offer, I will have to sell the watch to him." Sally replied that she could not raise her offer.

Mike, feeling a bit guilty, told Sally that on Tuesday, when he got the Mickey Mouse watch, he would no longer need his current watch and would give it to Sally. The next day, Jill sold her watch to Mike. Mike, however, had a change of heart and refused to give his old watch to Sally. Sally is understand-ably upset by this turn of events. Does she have any legal rights against either Jill or Mike?

Sometimes in analyzing contract situations, it is helpful to diagram them. The arrow indicates something of value passing from one party to the other.

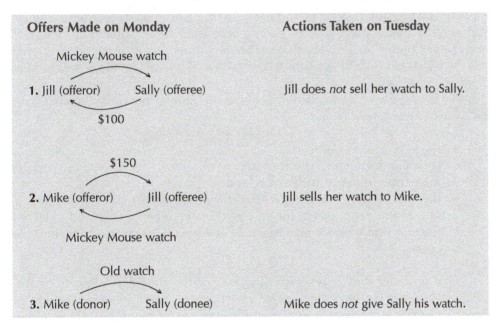

Offers Made on Monday	Actions Taken on Tuesday
Mickey Mouse watch **1.** Jill (offeror) ⟷ Sally (offeree) $100	Jill does *not* sell her watch to Sally.
$150 **2.** Mike (offeror) ⟷ Jill (offeree) Mickey Mouse watch	Jill sells her watch to Mike.
Old watch **3.** Mike (donor) → Sally (donee)	Mike does *not* give Sally his watch.

Looking at the first situation between Sally and Jill, we see there was an agreement to exchange something of value. Recall that to form a binding con-tract, there must be an agreement to sell (Jill said she would sell the watch for $100 [an offer] and Sally said, "I agree" [an acceptance]); also, something of value must be exchanged (Sally was going to give $100 in return for the Mickey Mouse watch). Therefore, Sally and Jill had a binding contract. By selling the watch to someone else, Jill is in breach of contract. Sally is entitled to the benefit of her bargain. However, it is unlikely that the court would order Jill to sell the watch to Sally. Such an order for specific performance occurs only when the item is unique. Instead, Sally would be entitled to money damages. In this case, she can purchase a similar watch, and if it costs more than the $100 that she had agreed to spend for Jill's watch, she can recover the difference.

The second situation illustrates a fully executed contract. Mike made an offer, Jill accepted, and they agreed to exchange something of value. A binding contract was formed. Then when they fulfilled their promises, the contract was fully executed.

In the third situation, involving Sally and Mike, there was no contract. Sally did not agree to exchange anything with Mike. Mike simply offered to give Sally his old watch. For a gift to be complete, however, delivery must occur. Because Mike never handed Sally the watch, there was no completed gift, and Sally has no rights to Mike's watch.

The courts treat these situations so differently because in a contract negotiation, both parties give up something of value. In the last situation, however, the transaction is one-sided. Because gift givers receive nothing in return, they should be allowed time to reconsider up until actual delivery. The delivery then provides proof that there was the intent for a gift to occur.

1. Offer

Offer
In contract law, an indication of a firm desire to enter into an agreement that is sufficiently definite that once accepted, a contract is formed.

An **offer** is a promise to do something (e.g., to sell a product or provide a service) that is conditioned on the other party's promising to do something in return (e.g., to pay money or provide some other type of goods or services). The offer sets the parameters of the agreement and gives the other party the power to bind them to a contract.

To be considered valid, the terms of the offer must contain a reference to at least the following four items:

1. the parties to the contract,
2. the subject matter of the contract,
3. the nature of the consideration, and
4. the time for performance. (When the time for performance is very important to the parties, as in the case of the sale of perishable fruit, then the time for performance may be stated along with the phrase "time is of the essence.")

One problem that arises with this stage of the contract is that of distinguishing between a true offer to enter into a contract and a mere statement of intent to begin negotiations. For example, assume Sam says, "I am thinking of selling my car. What would you give me for it?" If John replies, "I will give you $750 for it," Sam has made only a statement of intent, not an offer. John's reply is the offer, and it is up to Sam whether he wants to accept or not. When a person asks, "Will you buy?" or says, "I plan to sell," this also gives rise to the inference that the person was only beginning the process of negotiation but was not yet ready to be bound by the statements. Similarly, ads are usually not viewed as offers because their terms are too indefinite to constitute an offer. The following case, however, presents an interesting exception to that rule. As you read the case, look for what differentiated this ad from the usual ad.

Lefkowitz v. Great Minneapolis Surplus Store, Inc.
251 Minn. 188, 86 N.W.2d 689 (1957)

FACTS: A store published the following advertisement in a Minneapolis newspaper:

"Saturday 9 A.M.
1 Black Lapin Stole Beautiful, worth $139.50
$1.00 First Come First Served"

On Saturday, Mr. Lefkowitz was the first to arrive at the store. He demanded the stole and offered to pay the sale price of $1. The store refused to sell him the stole.

RULE: For a binding contract to arise from an advertisement, the advertisement must be clear, definite, and explicit, and leave nothing open for negotiation; if so, it constitutes an offer, acceptance of which will complete the contract.

ISSUE: Whether the advertisement was sufficiently clear, definite, and explicit to constitute an offer when it stated the object to be sold, the quantity, value, and selling price.

HOLDING: Yes, in this particular case, the advertisement constituted an offer, and so when accepted, created a binding contract.

REASONING: The store contended that a newspaper advertisement offering items for sale at a named price is an invitation for an offer of sale. If the customer accepts the offer, the store may reject it or even change the terms of the offer. Only if the store accepts the customer's offer is a binding contract formed.

However, the store's advertisement for the sale of the Lapin fur was not simply an invitation to bid, it was an offer. It was clear, definite, and explicit, and left nothing open for negotiation. Mr. Lefkowitz successfully managed to be the first one to appear. Once he offered the stated price, he accepted the store's offer. At that point, all of the requirements for a binding contract were complete, and Mr. Lefkowitz was entitled to the stole. Judgment for Mr. Lefkowitz.

CASE DISCUSSION QUESTIONS

1. Why did the court hold that there was a binding contract for the black Lapin stole?

2. What do you suppose Lefkowitz actually won as a result of this lawsuit?

3. The previous week, the store had published this advertisement:

"Saturday 9 A.M. sharp
3 Brand New Fur Coats Worth to $100.00
First Come First Served $1 Each"

The store also refused to sell Lefkowitz one of the fur coats. In this instance, the court agreed with the store that there was no binding contract. What do you think was the basis for their reasoning in differentiating the two situations?

As you just saw in the *Lefkowitz* case, it is important that the terms of the offer be definite so that a court can fashion a remedy and so that there is sufficient evidence that a bargain has been struck. For example, assume that Sam says, "I want to sell my car," and John replies, "Done!" There is no contract because neither knows the price.

The UCC has made some major changes in this area of the law. Under the UCC, a contract can be formed even if there are missing terms, so long as the quantity is specified. The missing terms are supplied by the UCC itself. For example, a missing price term becomes a reasonable price. UCC §2-305(1).

Finally, the offer must be communicated to the offeree. Usually, this last requirement does not present any problems except in the case of rewards. Some courts have held that if a person fulfills the terms of a reward—for example, returning a lost dog to its owner—without knowing beforehand of the reward, that person cannot claim the reward, as it was never communicated to him or her.

Legal Reasoning Exercise

1. DotTV posted the Internet domain name *golf.tv* on its website, to be sold to the highest bidder. Je Ho Lim submitted the highest bid: $1,010. DotTV sent an e-mail to Lim congratulating him on winning the bid and concluded with the statement: "See ya on the new frontier of the Internet!" Shortly thereafter, DotTV sent a second e-mail stating that they were releasing Lim from his bid and that the prior e-mail had been sent in error. DotTV then publicly offered the domain name with an opening bid of $1 million. Was Lim's bid an invitation or an offer? Why does it matter? Do you think Lim or DotTV won the lawsuit?

2. Acceptance

Acceptance
In contract law, an act by the offeree indicating agreement to be bound to the contract.

The second element of a valid contract is **acceptance**. The UCC explicitly states that an offer can be accepted either by sending notification of such acceptance or by performing the act requested. If Alice offers to pay Bruce $10 for Bruce's bicycle, Bruce's acceptance can take the form of making a telephone call stating that he will sell her the bicycle, or by delivering the bicycle to her. UCC §2-206(b).

Mirror image rule
The requirement that the acceptance exactly mirror the offer or the acceptance becomes a counteroffer.

If the offeree decides to accept, then the **mirror image rule** requires that the acceptance exactly mirror the offer. The offeree cannot add new terms or vary the original terms. If he or she attempts to do so, the acceptance becomes a counteroffer. A **counteroffer** takes away the power of the offeree to accept the original offer. For example, if John states, "I accept; please send a written contract," then there is an acceptance. However, if John says, "I accept if you send a written contract," then there is no acceptance because John has added an additional term to the contract.

Counteroffer
A return offer rejecting an offer from the other party in the negotiations and replacing it with a new offer.

The UCC has made some major changes to the mirror image rule. Basically, the UCC states that if the parties intend to make a contract, then the use of additional or different terms in the acceptance will not prevent the contract from being formed. This provision recognizes that often the parties will assume they have made a contract and will act on that assumption even if the offer and acceptance do not match in every detail.

3. Consideration

The third element of a valid contract is **consideration**. It is defined as the exchange of something of value. The consideration can be money, services, goods, or anything else that is a benefit to one party or a detriment to the other. The key is that something of real value has to be exchanged by both parties. In other words, a contract must be distinguished from a gift. When a person promises to give something without expecting to receive anything in return, that promise does not constitute an enforceable contract.

At times, it may appear as though something of value has been exchanged when in actuality it has not. For example, if someone promises to hire you and pay you "what you are worth," the phrase is so vague as to make the promise illusory. In addition, if someone makes a promise because he or she feels morally obligated to do so but receives nothing else in return, there is no consideration. For example, assume that Julie is friends with Martha. Martha feels ill but does not have a doctor. Julie takes Martha to her doctor. Once Martha is cured, she refuses to pay the doctor bill. Julie may feel morally obligated to pay the bill because she took Martha to the doctor, but she is under no contractual obligation to do so.

Also, past consideration will not support a contract. Assume that I volunteer to take care of your cat while you are away on vacation. When you return, if you are very pleased with the job I have done and offer to pay me for my services, no contract has been formed. I have already done my job, and there is no new consideration for me to give in return for your promise. Finally, if someone is under a preexisting duty to act, performing that duty cannot serve as the consideration for a new contract. If your house is on fire and you offer a firefighter $2,000 to put out the fire, you will be under no obligation to pay the money. The firefighter is already under a preexisting duty to put out the fire.

Generally, the court will not look into the adequacy of the consideration. Simply put, the court does not care if you made a poor bargain. The philosophy behind freedom of contract is that you are free to make any bargain you like, even a bad one. In addition, if people could sue to get out of their contractual obligations every time it turned out they had made a poor bargain, the courts would be flooded with lawsuits. Finally, the security of being able to rely on contractual performance would be gone.

Consideration
Anything of value; it must be present for a valid contract to exist, and each side must give consideration.

B. CONTRACT INTERPRETATION

Sometimes even though it is clear that there is an offer, acceptance, and consideration, thus forming a valid contract, the parties disagree about the legal effect of the contract's terms. This is often due to the innate ambiguity of the English language. When such differences in interpretation arise, the parties may turn to the courts for assistance.

When asked to interpret ambiguous language, the courts usually begin by trying to give the words their plain or commonsense meaning. When that is not possible, the court will try to see if the meaning of the words can be deciphered from the parties' intent as expressed in the contract. The court may also apply commonly accepted definitions from the relevant industry or business. Finally, the court may interpret the language so as to favor the party who did not draft the contract.

Legal Reasoning Exercises

2. Hurricane season often spawns a number of high-profile lawsuits over the interpretation of standard homeowner insurance policies. Such policies are contracts between the insured homeowner and the insurance company to cover damage to the insured's home and furnishings. These policies typically cover damage from high winds but exclude water damage. However, when hurricanes hit shore, they usually combine high winds, heavy rain, and sometimes even tidal waves. Which of the following types of damage do you think should be considered wind damage if they follow a hurricane?

   a. During the hurricane, a limb broke off a tree and damaged the roof.
   b. During the hurricane, water came into the insured's house through windows that had been blown out by the hurricane's winds.
   c. Rain from the hurricane caused a nearby river to overflow its banks, and floodwaters covered the first-floor carpet.
   d. Rain from the hurricane overwhelmed the local sewer system and caused water to back up into the insured's basement.
   e. A beach house was knocked off its foundation by the tidal wave that accompanied the hurricane.

Now assume that a homeowner's policy explicitly excluded "water damage" and defined that term as "(1) flood, surface water, tsunami, seiche, overflow of a body of water, or spray from any of these, whether driven by wind or not; (2) water or sewage from outside the residence premise's plumbing system that enters through sewers or drains, or water which enters into and overflows from within a sump pump, sump pump well, or any other system designed to remove subsurface water which is drained from the foundation." Which, if any, of the types of damage listed above would be excluded from coverage under the terms of the policy?

3. Mr. Phan lost control of his vehicle, veered off the road, and hit a telephone pole. If nothing more had occurred, he would have survived the accident. However, the trauma of hitting the pole caused Phan to have a heart attack. He died on the way to the hospital. Prior to the accident, Phan had never suffered from any heart ailments. His widow attempted to collect on his life insurance policy that provided for double coverage in the case of accidental death. There was an exclusion, however, if death was the result of physical illness. The insurance company refused to pay the accidental

death benefits, and his widow sued. If you were the trial judge, how would you rule?

4. When the Panera Bread Co. bakery-café chain moved into the White City Shopping Center, it signed a lease containing a clause that prevents the center from renting to another "sandwich" shop. When the shopping center management later rented space to a Qdoba's Mexican Grill, Panera took the matter to court, claiming that Qdoba's burritos, tacos, and quesadillas were sandwiches.

    a. The key issue in this case involved interpretation of the term "sandwich," but that term was not defined in the lease. How do you think the judge should go about determining whether burritos, tacos, and quesadillas were sandwiches?

    b. Based on your own common understanding of the term, how would you define a "sandwich"?

5. Many commercial rental agreements include a "force majeure" clause, also known as an "act of God" clause. This is meant to protect businesses when an unforeseeable event outside of their control keeps them from being able to pay their rent. A restaurant being forced to close because of the effects of a hurricane would be one example of the circumstances in which the force majeure clause might be invoked. What are the best arguments that a fine-dining steak house could raise to enforce a force majeure clause if all the restaurants in a state were closed for dining for two months because of COVID-19?

C. DEFENSES IN CONTRACT CASES

Once the plaintiff has proven the existence of an offer, acceptance, and consideration, the defendant can raise various defenses. Those defenses include an argument that one or both of the parties lacked contractual capacity, the contract should not be enforced because it is illegal or because it violates public policy, there was no true genuineness of assent because of fraud, mistake, or undue influence, the product was defective in violation of the seller's warranties, or in some situations that the proper format was not followed, as, for example, with those contracts that must be in writing.

1. Lack of Contractual Capacity

The parties to a contract can be either people or corporations. However, an individual may be considered incapable of contracting if that person is a child, is mentally incompetent or is under the influence of drugs or alcohol.

If one of the parties is a minor, the contract may be **voidable** by the minor. Therefore, the terms of the contract are enforceable against the adult party to the contract, but not against the minor party. The one exception is that minors are liable for necessaries, such as housing, food, and clothing. Minors can disaffirm the contract for necessaries, but they must pay the reasonable value of the good or services they received.

Voidable
A valid contract that can be set aside at the option of one of the parties.

The next case graphically illustrates how dangerous it can be for an adult to deal with minors.

Quality Motors, Inc. v. Hays
216 Ark. 264, 225 S.W.2d 326 (1949)

FACTS: Johnny Hays brought this suit to disaffirm his purchase of a Pontiac automobile and recover the purchase price of $1,750 from defendant Quality Motors, Inc.

Sixteen-year-old Johnny went to Quality Motors, Inc., to inspect and test a Pontiac car. The salesman raised the question of Johnny's age and told him he could not sell the car unless the purchase was made by an adult. Johnny left and returned shortly with Harry Williams, 23 years of age, whom he met in the parking lot. Johnny then gave to Quality Motors, Inc., a cashier's check for $1,800 which was made payable to him, in payment for the car. A bill of sale was made to Harry Williams. The salesman then recommended a Notary Public who could prepare the necessary papers for transferring the title of the car to Johnny, and drove the two boys to town for this purpose. Williams transferred the title, and the salesman delivered the Pontiac to Johnny at Arkansas State College

When Johnny's father learned of his son's purchase, he immediately called one of the owners of Quality Motors, Inc. and demanded that they take the car back. They refused to do so. He then took the car from his son, stored it in a hangar, and tried on three more occasions to get the dealership to agree to the return of the car. One month later, Johnny found the car keys, took the car, and was involved in an accident. Again the father called asking the dealership to take back the car. Again they refused. Shortly thereafter, Johnny took the car again and was involved in a second, more serious accident, making it undriveable.

RULE: A minor may disaffirm his contracts, except those made for necessaries, and recover the consideration paid upon returning the consideration received.

ISSUE: Whether a minor in disaffirming a contract can recover the full amount of the consideration he paid when what he can return no longer has any value.

HODLING: Yes, a minor may disaffirm a contract, recover the full amount of consideration paid, and be required to return only whatever he still has in his possession.

REASONING: The dealership argues that Johnny should be liable for damages to the car which occurred while he was driving it, after he had slipped the car from its storage place. In order for the dealership to prevail, it must prove that Johnny was guilty of conversion in taking the automobile. Conversion is the exercise of control over property in violation of the rights of the owner. In advancing this argument appellant is in an inconsistent position. Until this court decrees return of the car and recovery of the consideration paid, Johnny still has title to the car. One cannot be liable for conversion in taking your own property.

The dealership knowingly and through a planned subterfuge sold an automobile to a minor. It then refused to take the car back. Even after the car was wrecked once, they still refused. The dealership's loss is the direct result of its own acts. Johnny may disaffirm the contract and recover the amount of the purchase price.

CASE DISCUSSION QUESTIONS

1. What does the court say is the general rule about the right of minors to disaffirm contracts?

2. What should this dealer have done differently?

3. As with the case you just read, in order for a minor to disaffirm a contract, some states simply require the return of the goods, no matter their condition. Others require that the adult be compensated for any loss due to damaged goods. Which approach do you think is better?

Mental incompetence can also cause a contract to be voidable, a situation analogous to that of minors. As is true with minors, the incompetent person remains responsible for the reasonable value of necessaries. However, if someone has been adjudged mentally incompetent and the court has appointed a guardian to handle the incompetent's affairs, then that individual is without the capacity to make contracts. Instead of being merely voidable, any contract the incompetent individual tries to make is **void**. Only the guardian can enter into valid contracts.

Void
A contract that is invalid even if it is not repudiated by either party.

Intoxication is rarely used successfully to void a contract. The courts look with disfavor on this defense because the condition is self-inflicted. However, if the defendant can show the intoxication prevented him from understanding the import of his actions, a court might find that there was no meeting of the minds.

DISCUSSION QUESTION

1. What do you think the age limit should be for being able to enter into contracts? What was your rationale for picking that age?

2. Lack of Genuine Assent

Another basis for challenging a contract is to assert that the parties never reached a true meeting of the minds regarding the terms of the contract. This is referred to as "lack of genuineness of assent." A court will not enforce a contract if one of the parties can convince the court that fraud, mistake, undue influence, or duress interfered with a mutual understanding of the terms.

a. Fraud

In order to prove fraud, it must be demonstrated that the other party made intentional misrepresentations or intentional nondisclosures of material facts during the course of the negotiations. Furthermore, it must be shown that the defendant did not know of the fraud and had no way to find it out. Note that the misrepresentations must be material and that they must be made regarding a factual statement, not merely opinion or sales puffery. It is expected that the reasonable person engaged in contract negotiations will realize that he or she should not rely on opinions or on overblown sales statements that are obviously made simply as part of the sales pitch. However, in certain circumstances, the opinion of an expert can be viewed as a fact when it is reasonable to rely on the expert's opinion and the other party has no independent means of testing the statement's validity.

Legal Reasoning Exercise

6. During an episode of the television program *Antiques Roadshow*, an elderly man brought an antique vase for the host to value. On air, the host

looked over the vase and stated that she thought it was worth $200. After the show, the host purchased the vase for $200 and sold it a week later to a collector for $20,000. Would this be considered fraud? Why or why not?

b. Mistake

Mistakes about facts can sometimes form the basis for rescinding a contract. If the mistake is bilateral, then both parties had a different concept of what was to be included in the contract. Therefore, there never was a meeting of the minds, and the failed contract can be rescinded by either. The classic case that illustrates this principle took place in England in 1864. A buyer purchased a shipment of cotton from a seller, the cotton to be shipped on the *Peerless*. Unknown to either party, there were two ships named the *Peerless*, one to depart in October and one in December. The buyer was thinking of the ship destined to leave in October, and the seller the one in December. Consequently, the seller did not ship the cotton until December. By that time, though, the buyer no longer needed the cotton. The court held that because there never was a "meeting of the minds" as to which ship was intended, no contract had been formed and the buyer was not obligated to pay for the cotton.[1] Usually, however, if the mistake is unilateral and only one party is mistaken, both parties are bound. The only exceptions are if the other party knew or should have known of the mistake and if the mistake was the result of a mathematical error.

Keep in mind that we are talking only about factual mistakes. Mistakes as to the value of the subject matter can never be the basis for rescission. For example, assume that Joan contracts to sell her diamond ring to Bertha. Both think the ring is worth about $500, and they set $500 as the contract price. Later, Bertha has the ring appraised and is delighted to learn that it is actually worth $5,000. Joan cannot ask to have the contract rescinded on the ground that she was mistaken as to the value of the diamond. On the other hand, if Joan had contracted to sell what she thought was a zirconium ring to Bertha and then, upon appraisal, it turned out to be a diamond ring, some courts could see that as a mutual mistake as to a fact and allow the contract to be rescinded.

c. Undue Influence

Undue influence
When one party is in a position of trust and misuses that trust to influence the actions of another.

Claims of **undue influence** are generally limited to situations in which there is a special fiduciary relationship between the parties. The party who is in a position of trust misuses that trust to influence the actions of another. Situations alleging undue influence are frequently brought by family members against caretakers of the elderly or ill.

---

[1] Raffles v. Wichelhaus, 2 Hurl. & Co. 906, 159 Eng. Rep. 375 (Ex. 1864).

d. Duress

A contract is also not valid if it was agreed to under duress rather than as a result of a truly voluntary action. The actions of the second party must be sufficient for the court to find that the first party was forced into the agreement. Duress is difficult to prove because the defendant must show that the pressure exerted was so great as to overwhelm his or her ability to make a free choice.

3. Illegal Contracts and Those That Violate Public Policy

Contracts can also be declared unenforceable if they are found to be either illegal or against public policy. A contract involves illegality if it calls for behavior that violates the criminal law, such as robbery, gambling, or prostitution. Contracts for an illegal purpose are void and cannot be enforced by either party.

An example of a contract that may be unenforceable because it is contrary to public policy is a **covenant not to compete,** also known as a "noncompete agreement." This is an agreement whereby an employee agrees not to work for one of the employer's competitors, or the seller of a business agrees not to compete with the new owners by establishing a similar business in a geographically competitive area. By their very nature, such agreements are against public policy because they may restrict the right of an individual to earn a living or they tend to decrease competition. However, they can also be a form of necessary business protection. For example, if a pharmaceutical company expends a great deal of time and money training a chemist, the company will want the chemist to sign a noncompetition clause, promising not to work for another pharmaceutical plant for a certain amount of time after leaving employment with the first company. The courts are generally willing to enforce that type of covenant, so long as it is tied to employment or to the sale of a business and its terms call for a reasonable time and within a reasonable geographic area.

As you will recall from our earlier discussion of inadequate consideration, normally courts will adhere to the theory of freedom of contract and will not inquire into the fairness of a bargain. Therefore, if you agree to the terms of such a one-sided contract, most likely you will be bound by its terms. Indeed, the majority of contracts are **adhesion contracts** in that the parties are of unequal bargaining power, the contract terms are drafted by the party with the greater power, and there is no opportunity to negotiate. Two examples of such typical contracts include a contract to purchase a cell phone app, and by clicking through the terms or a contract to purchase a new flat-screen TV by signing a standard-form contract. However, when a contract is formed between two parties of very unequal bargaining power and the result is so one-sided as to be oppressive and grossly unfair, the court may view this as an unconscionable, unlawful adhesion contract.

This determination is very fact specific and depends on a review of the contract. The court may hold that the contract is unconscionable and refuse to enforce it. Generally, a contract is considered **unconscionable** if, in the context of the general commercial practices and under the specific circumstances in which the contract was made, it is so one-sided as to be oppressive and grossly unfair. For example, if a poor, illiterate person were to purchase a

Covenant not to compete
A promise not to compete within a given geographic area for a specific time period; also known as a "noncompete agreement."

Adhesion contract
A contract formed where the weaker party has no realistic bargaining power. Typically, this form of contract is offered on a "take it or leave it" basis.

Unconscionable contract
A contract formed between parties of very unequal bargaining power where the terms are so unfair as to "shock the conscience."

$300 freezer, agreeing to pay 24 monthly installments of $50 each, the seller would net a $900 profit (24 × $50 = $1,200 – $300 = $900). The court might find the agreement to be so unfair as to "shock the conscience" and declare it unenforceable.

Be aware that what courts and legislatures view as violating public policy can change over time. For example, some recently enacted statutes prohibit confidentiality clauses in mandatory arbitration agreements if the case involves sexual harassment. The public policy rationale given is the chilling effect that confidentiality clauses can have on addressing sexual harassers in the workplace and the difficulty that it can cause in identifying repeat offenders.

DISCUSSION QUESTION

2. There has been a movement in recent years to limit the ability of employers to force new employees to sign noncompete clauses. Do you think this is something that should be decided by state legislatures or left to the courts to evaluate on a case-by-case basis?

4. Warranties

Warranty
A guarantee, made by the seller or implied by law, regarding the character, quality, or title of the goods being sold.

A common defense raised in the sale of consumer goods is that of breach of warranty. The consumer argues that he or she should not be required to pay for the item purchased because it failed to perform as expected. A **warranty** is a statement or representation, made by the seller as part of the contract of sale or implied in law, regarding the character, quality, or title of the goods being sold. If such warranted facts later prove to be untrue, the buyer is relieved of his or her obligations under the contract and the seller must compensate the buyer for any losses incurred as a result of the misrepresentation.

Under the terms of UCC §2-314, if a merchant is the seller, any contract of sale automatically includes an "implied warranty of merchantability," an unspoken promise that the goods being sold will be usable for the ordinary purpose for which they were sold.

Implied warranty of fitness
An implied promise that the goods being sold will satisfy a special purpose.

When a more specialized use of the goods is communicated to the seller during the course of negotiations, an **implied warranty of fitness** is also created. UCC §2-315. This is a warranty regarding the fitness of the goods for that special purpose. For example, if you go to a hardware store and ask the clerk for electrical wiring and say nothing more, the wire will be warranted for its usual purpose of carrying household current. If instead you want the wire for outside use, you tell the clerk your special purpose, and you rely on the clerk's expertise in picking out the wire, then there will be an implied warranty of fitness for that particular purpose.

Express warranty
An express warranty or promise created by an affirmation of fact or a promise made by the seller, a description of the goods sold, or a sample or model provided that forms the basis of the bargain.

In addition to these implied warranties, a contract can create **express warranties**. UCC §2-313. The term *warranty* or *guarantee* does not have to be used in order for a warranty to be created. However, the seller's conduct or statements must have been communicated to the buyer so that the warranty becomes part of the "basis of the bargain." UCC §2-313(1). Express warranties can be created by an affirmation of fact or a promise made by the seller; a description of the goods being sold, including technical specifications and blueprints; or a sample

Type of Warranty	Created by	Excluded by
Implied warranty of merchantability	the sale of goods by a merchant. The goods must be fit for their ordinary purpose.	language that includes the word *merchantability* or a disclaimer that includes the word *merchantability* or phrases such as "as is" or "with all faults." If in writing, it must be conspicuous.
Implied warranty of fitness	a seller ■ knowing the particular purpose the buyer has in mind *and* ■ being aware that the buyer is relying on the seller's expertise.	a writing that is conspicuous.
Express warranty	■ an affirmation of fact or a promise made by the seller, *or* a description of the goods being sold, including technical specifications and blueprints, *or* a sample or model *and* ■ that becomes a basis of the bargain.	words or conduct tending to limit or negate the warranty so long as such interpretation is reasonable.

Figure 10-3   Warranties Summarized

or a model provided. A mere expression of opinion as to the value of an item is considered "puffing" and does not constitute a warranty.

Warranties may be excluded or modified by disclaimers. UCC §2-316. In many states, however, merchants are limited in their ability to exclude or modify the implied warranty of merchantability when the sale is to a consumer. For each type of warranty, Figure 10-3 summarizes how it is created and what actions a seller must take to exclude the warranty.

DISCUSSION QUESTION

3. When should a buyer be able to rely on a salesperson's claims? What standards do you think should be used in drawing a line between so-called puffery and fraud?

5. Lack of Proper Format—Writing

Statute of frauds
A statutory requirement that in order to be enforceable, certain contracts must be in writing.

Even though many oral contracts are legally enforceable, it is always wiser to put them in writing because when disputes arise, it often comes down to one person's word against the other's. In addition to the fact that it simply makes sense to reduce any important contract to writing, all states have a statute known as the **statute of frauds**, which requires certain types of contracts, such as those involving transfer of real estate, to be in writing in order to be enforceable. The purpose of such statutes is to ensure that there will be reliable evidence of important or complex matters. If the contract is of the type that requires a writing and there is none, the contract is unenforceable.

Ethics Alert

A lawyer should always be very careful to explain a contingency fee arrangement with the client. Generally, the client is responsible for any court costs and other expenses, and the law firm receives a percentage, commonly 33 percent, of any settlement or court award. Smith, a lawyer, has never seen any need to put this arrangement in writing. Do you see any problems with her approach?

Generally, the types of contracts that must be in writing fall into one of the following categories:

- contracts involving land, including fixtures, and documents dealing with land, such as mortgages and leases;
- contracts that cannot be performed in one year;
- collateral contracts, those that involve a secondary as opposed to a primary obligation, unless the main purpose is to secure a personal benefit;
- promises made in consideration of marriage, such as prenuptial agreements; and
- contracts for the sale of goods valued at $500 or more.

Legal Reasoning Exercise

7. Jonathan Shattuck thought he had a deal to buy a house for $1.825 million. Using e-mail, Shattuck and the seller had settled on the price. The last e-mail from the seller stated:

> Once we sign the P&S (purchase and sale agreement), we'd like to close ASAP. You may have your lawyer send the P&S and deposit check for 10 percent of purchase price ($182,500) to my lawyer. I'm looking forward to closing and seeing you as the owner of 5 Main Street, the prettiest spot in Marion Village.

Before the buyer's lawyer had a chance to draw up the P&S agreement, the seller informed Shattuck that he was not going to follow through on the deal, as he had another buyer who was willing to pay $1.96 million. His argument is that there is no signed writing binding him to the deal. How do you think the court decided? Why?

PRACTICE TIP

When drafting contracts, follow these basic rules:

- Use simple language. If you cannot understand what you are saying, no one else will be able to either.
- Be consistent in the terminology you use. If you once refer to the subject as the "car," do not refer to it later as the "automobile."
- Do not feel as though you have to reinvent the wheel. The careful and thoughtful use of forms and boilerplate language can save you many drafting hours.

When reviewing contracts:

- Check to see if all of the essential terms are there: parties, subject matter, consideration, and time for performance.
- Check to see for any inconsistencies or ambiguities.
- Make sure that none of the clauses contradicts another.

D. REMEDIES FOR BREACH OF CONTRACT

When one party fails to live up to the terms of a contract, a variety of remedies may be available to the other party, including going to court to seek either specific performance or monetary damages. **Specific performance** is a court order that the breaching party live up to the terms of the agreement. Specific performance gives the contracting party exactly the item for which the contract was formed. However, specific performance can be used only in situations where there is no alternative comparable product available, or when money alone is an inadequate remedy. Examples of when specific performance is appropriate are usually limited to items such as rare antiques or land.

> **Specific performance**
> When money damages are inadequate, a court may use this equitable remedy and order the breaching party to perform his or her contractual obligations.

Because specific performance is possible only if dollars are inadequate, courts are far more likely to award damages. Damages in contract cases are classified as compensatory, consequential, incidental, and nominal. Punitive damages are not allowed in a contract action.

The purpose of **compensatory damages** is to place the injured party in the same position that party would have been in had the contract been performed; that is, their purpose is to give the injured party the "benefit of the bargain."

> **Compensatory damages**
> Money awarded to a plaintiff in payment for his or her actual losses.

In calculating compensatory damages, courts frequently use the following formula:

Promised performance minus actual performance minus mitigation plus expenses (incidental damages)

For example, if John agrees with Bill to sell Bill his watch for $500, but Bill only pays $300, John can sue Bill for $200. If Bill had paid nothing and simply reneged on the deal, John could have sold the watch to someone else and could have recovered the difference between that price and the contract price, along with any expenses incurred in finding the new buyer (incidental damages).

On the other hand, if John refuses to sell the watch, then Bill has two options. First, he can try to find another watch. The UCC calls this finding of substitute goods **cover**. Then his damages are the cost of the substitute watch minus the contract price. For example, if Bill finds a similar watch but has to pay $700, his damages are $200. Alternatively, he can decide to forgo a new watch. In that case, his damages would be the difference between the market price and the contract price.

The principle of **mitigation of damages** requires the nonbreaching party to take reasonable steps to limit his or her damages. For example, assume that Mary signs a 12-month lease for an apartment but in month 6, she accepts a new job out of state. She notifies her landlord that she does not intend to rent the apartment for the remainder of the term. The landlord can sue Mary for the amount remaining on the lease, but will also be required to mitigate the damages. Generally, this means that the landlord must try to rent Mary's apartment for the 6 months remaining on the lease. If the apartment is rented, the amount of that rent would reduce the amount that Mary owes. She would, however, also be liable for what it cost her landlord to find the new renter for the apartment.

Consequential damages arise out of special circumstances that must be foreseeable to the other party. Typically, this is handled by notifying the other party of any such circumstances. The classic case setting forth this rule is an English case from 1854.[2] The Hadley family ran a flour mill. Their crankshaft broke, and they gave it to Baxendale to deliver to a foundry for repair. Baxendale promised to deliver the shaft the next day. However, it was not delivered for several days. Despite the common practice, the Hadleys did not have an extra crankshaft, so they were forced to keep the mill closed for those extra days. Because the Hadleys had not notified Baxendale of their lack of a spare crankshaft, he could not be held liable for their lost profits.

As in tort actions, **nominal damages** are sometimes awarded when there has been a breach, but no provable damages.

In order to avoid having to litigate damage issues, some contracting parties put **liquidated damages** clauses in their contracts. Such clauses specify what will happen in case of breach. Such clauses are valid if two requirements are met. First, the amount of damages must be difficult or impossible to calculate.

Cover
Finding substitute goods.

Mitigation of damages
The requirement that the nonbreaching party take reasonable steps to limit his or her damages.

Consequential damages
Also called special damages. Indirect damages that must be foreseeable to be recovered.

Nominal damages
A token sum awarded when liability has been found but monetary damages cannot be shown.

Liquidated damages
The result of a provision in a contract that specifies what will happen in case of breach.

---

[2] Hadley v. Baxendale, 9 Exch. 341, 156 Eng. Rep. 14 (1854).

Second, the amount must bear a reasonable relationship to the true loss and not be seen as a penalty clause. Liquidated damages clauses are frequently found in building contracts. For example, a university that contracts to build a new science building and anticipates that the science building will be completed by the first day of the fall semester will suffer damages if the building fails to be completed on time. But how would the damages be calculated? There would be serious inconveniences for faculty and students, as well as potentially increased costs associated with moving. Classes might need to be rescheduled to accommodate a move at midsemester. Both parties could agree that there would be a cost associated with a late completion date, but neither side can anticipate what those exact costs would be. A liquidated damages clause acknowledges those increased costs by allowing the parties to agree on an estimate of the costs when the contract is signed.

In situations when the judge finds that the parties imperfectly expressed themselves or that without changes, the contract could not be lawfully enforced, the court may rewrite the contract. This is an equitable remedy known as **reformation.** For example, assume that a covenant not to compete is included in a sale of a business. While it is limited geographically to one county, its duration is for ten years. The court might reform the contract so that the duration is for a shorter period of time.

Reformation
An equitable remedy whereby the court rewrites a contract.

E. ALTERNATIVES TO ENFORCEABLE CONTRACTS: PROMISSORY ESTOPPEL AND QUASI-CONTRACT

Sometimes even when the requirements for a contract are not met, a court will find one of the parties liable under a theory of quasi-contract or promissory estoppel. Quasi-contracts can occur even though there was no agreement between the parties, if one of the parties nonetheless benefits. Promissory estoppel can be applied even though no final agreement had been reached if one of the parties relied on a promise to its detriment. In either case, keep in mind that if either of these theories apply, it means no one was in breach of contract because there was no contract. Therefore, the application of either of these theories is quite rare and can require quite a bit of creativity on the part of a lawyer.

1. Quasi-Contract

Quasi means "as if." Therefore, a **quasi-contract** is not a real contract, but the situation is treated "as if" there were one. Usually, a quasi-contract situation arises when there is no agreement, but in order to avoid unjust enrichment, the court orders the party that benefited to pay. For example, in an emergency, an injured party might not be able to ask for assistance. Therefore, there could be no agreement between the injured person and the doctor. However, once the doctor gives medical aid, it would be unjust to let the patient benefit without compensating the doctor. This is an example of a court using its equitable powers to do what it views as fair in order to avoid allowing one side to be unjustly enriched.

Quasi-contract
A scenario in which there is no agreement, but both parties treat it as though one existed. Although no actual contract was formed, the courts will fashion an equitable remedy to avoid unjust enrichment.

DISCUSSION QUESTION

4. A man hired a roofing company to put a new roof on his house. The roofing crew mistakenly switched two of the numbers in the address and put the new roof on the wrong house. Would the courts treat the scenario where the roof replaced was old and obviously in need of repair differently from the scenario where the roof that was replaced was obviously new?

2. Promissory Estoppel

Promissory estoppel
Occurs when the courts allow detrimental reliance to substitute for consideration.

Sometimes people rely on promises to their detriment, but they cannot sue for breach of contract because while promises were made, they were not definite enough to amount to consideration. Nonetheless, some courts think it would be unfair not to compensate the person who relied on the promise. In that situation, the promisor is estopped, or prevented, from revoking his promise. This is known as **promissory estoppel,** or "detrimental reliance." For the courts to find a case of promissory estoppel:

1. a promise must be made with the intent to induce action,
2. it must do so, and
3. the court must believe that it would be unjust not to enforce the promise.

Assume that an elderly relative induces you to give up your job in order to care for her with the promise of being remembered in her will. Her promise would not fulfill the requirements of valid consideration, as her promise of remembering you in her will is too indefinite to be enforceable. If, however, you give up your job and care for your relative for a number of years, the court might view your detrimental reliance on her promise as a substitute for consideration and enforce her promise to pay.

The Wisconsin Supreme Court was one of the first to adopt the theory of promissory estoppel as an alternative to a breach of contract action. In the case of *Hoffman v. Red Owl Stores, Inc.,*[3] Hoffman and his wife engaged in extensive negotiations with agents of the Red Owl grocery store chain in an attempt to obtain a Red Owl franchise, only to "have the rug pulled out from under them." The agents had originally promised the Hoffmans that for $18,000, they could establish a store. The figure was then changed to $24,100. Relying on further promises that the deal was about to go through, and at the urging of the Red Owl representatives, Hoffman sold his own grocery store to raise the necessary money. While waiting to be placed in his new store, he began working the night shift at a local bakery. Finally, the Red Owl representatives said it would take $34,000 to close the deal. At that point, Hoffman informed them that he could not afford to go through with the proposal. Hoffman then sued Red Owl for the damages he had incurred in relying on the promises of its representatives.

Because the negotiations had never gotten far enough for the parties to establish the precise terms of the contract, such as the size, layout, and design of the store, Hoffman was not able to sue on a breach of contract theory. He also could not sue for fraud. There was no evidence that the Red Owl representatives

---

[3] 133 N.W.2d 267 (Wis. 1965).

intended to misrepresent the facts. Relying instead on the doctrine of promissory estoppel, the court stated that each of the following questions must be answered in the affirmative:

1. Was the promise one which the promisor should reasonably expect to induce action or forbearance of a definite and substantial character on the part of the promisee?
2. Did the promise induce such action or forbearance?
3. Can injustice be avoided only by enforcement of the promise?[4]

The court noted that the first two questions are issues of fact for the jury to decide. The third question, however, involves a policy decision that must be made by the court. In the Hoffmans' case, the court concluded that "injustice would result here if plaintiffs were not granted some relief because of the failure of defendants to keep their promises which induced plaintiffs to act to their detriment."[5]

SUMMARY

A contract is an agreement that can be enforced in court. The basic elements of a contract are offer, acceptance, and consideration. The most common defenses are lack of contractual capacity, illegality, violation of public policy, lack of genuineness of assent, breach of warranty, and the statute of frauds. Sometimes even when the requirements for a contract are not met, a court will find one of the parties liable under a theory of quasi-contract or promissory estoppel.

Third parties can attain contractual rights either through assignment or delegation or through being an intended beneficiary. A plaintiff bringing a contract action may be under a duty to mitigate damages and is usually seeking specific performance or compensatory or consequential damages.

While many contracts are still controlled by the common law, contracts for the sale of goods are generally governed by Article 2 of the UCC. The UCC was drafted by a group of legal scholars with the hope of making commercial law more unified among the states. Most of the UCC's provisions apply to everyone, but some sections contain specific rules that apply to merchants only. Under the UCC everyone is under the obligation to act in good faith.

REVIEW QUESTIONS

Pages 271 through 279
1. How do the courts determine if the UCC governs a contract situation?
2. What are the three basic elements of a valid contract claim?

---

[4] Id. at 275.
[5] Id.

3. What are the four basic elements that every offer should contain?

4. Juan says to Jim, "I would like to sell my watch to you." Jim replies, "Great. I will be happy to give you a fair price for it." Has a contract been formed? Why?

5. Sally offers Tom a job as a paralegal, saying she will pay him "what he is worth." Tom accepts. Has a contract been formed? Why?

6. Janet says to Joan, "I am eager to sell my antique vase to you." Joan says, "Would you consider $400 for it?" Has a contract been formed? Why?

7. We Growum, a garden center, places the following advertisement in the Sunday paper:

Spring Planting Sale
Lilac bushes $20

On Tuesday, John goes to the garden center. All the lilac bushes have been sold. He sues for breach of contract. Will he succeed? Why?

8. What is the name of the rule that states that the acceptance must completely agree with the terms of the offer?

9. How has the UCC changed the mirror image rule?

Pages 279 through 281

10. John volunteers to take care of Sam's pet rabbit while he is away on vacation. When Sam returns, he is very pleased with the good care John gave his rabbit and tells him that he is going to pay him $50. When John arrives the next day to receive his money, Sam said that he has changed his mind. Is Sam under a contractual obligation to pay John for the care of his rabbit? Why?

11. Anna Sacks was an employee of the Ajax Company for 37 years. The president of the company told her that (in consideration for her outstanding service) when she retired, the company would pay her $200 per month for life. Two years later, she retired and began receiving the payments. Shortly thereafter, the company was sold, and the new president refused to continue the payments, arguing that there had never been a valid contract between Ms. Sacks and the company. How do you think the court resolved the case?

Pages 281 through 289

12. Name the major defenses to a contract action.

13. Jim, who is 16 years old, buys a stereo from Circuit Playground. Jim takes the stereo to the beach and ruins it when it becomes filled with sand. Jim takes it back to the store and demands the return of the money he paid for the stereo. Will the store have to refund his payment?

14. Mark and Bill are sitting at a bar drinking. They discuss the possibility of Mark selling Bill his watch for $50. Bill leaves, but Mark remains and continues to drink. Two hours later Bill calls Mark and offers him $5 for the watch. Now very intoxicated, Mark mutters, "Whatever." The next day, Mark has no memory of the phone call. Will the court enforce this arrangement? Why?

15. Sara offers to sell her "car" to Janet for $800. Janet thinks that Sara means her 1978 VW Beetle and agrees. But Sara was thinking of her 1970 VW van. Has a contract been formed? Why?

16. A law firm requires all new lawyers to sign an agreement that states that if they leave the firm for any reason, they will not work for another law firm or open their own practice within a 50-mile radius for two years. How do you think the court would treat such an agreement? Why?

17. What is the difference between a warranty of merchantability and an implied warranty of fitness? How do both of those differ from an express warranty?

18. Joan offers to buy Bill's sailboat for $2,000. Bill agrees and asks Joan to put it in writing. Joan leaves an e-mail message for her secretary, stating that she wants him to draft a contract stating that she agrees to buy Bill's sailboat for $2,000. The next day, Joan changes her mind. If Bill sues for breach of contract, will he succeed? Why?

Pages 289 through 291

19. Martha contracts with Sam, a noted concert pianist, to take a series of ten music lessons. After the second lesson Sam is offered the opportunity to go on a world tour. He contacts William, a lesser-known pianist, to take over his lessons. Martha is upset. Does she have any grounds to complain?

20. When is specific performance an appropriate remedy?

21. What is cover?

22. What are consequential damages?

23. Sara Smith is a struggling young artist. Recently, however, she was "discovered" when an art dealer saw one of her paintings hanging in a local art gallery. The art dealer contracted with Sara to hold a major showing of her work in six months, November 1. Under the contract, Sara was to show no fewer than ten original paintings. In preparation for the show, Sara contracted with Paint Masters, Inc., for four cases of her favorite oil paints to be shipped no later than July 1. Sara heard nothing more from Paint Masters, Inc., until September 1, when one case arrived. Sara attempted to find the same paint from other sources but was able to procure only one more case, at $200 more than she had contracted to pay Paint Masters. Because of the delay in shipment, Sara was able to complete only six paintings, and the show was canceled. Sara would like to sue Paint Masters, Inc., for the lost profits she would have received from her heightened recognition had the show gone as planned, for the money she had to spend on alternative paints, and for punitive damages to teach Paint Masters a lesson. Please evaluate Sara's situation.

24. Kate contracts with Bennett to buy 100 guitars at $300 each. Kate hopes to resell the guitars for $400 each. When the time for delivery arrives, Bennett refuses to deliver the guitars. Kate then spends $100 in phone calls trying to obtain an alternative supplier. Finally, she finds substitute guitars, but she has to pay $350 each for them. She saved $50, however, because in her contract with Bennett, she was going to have to pay for shipping, whereas in her new contract, the seller paid the shipping. How much is Kate owed in compensatory damages?

Pages 291 through 293

25. For each situation, determine whether you think it should be covered by traditional contract law, quasi-contract, or promissory estoppel.

    a. Jeffrey owned a 125-acre plot of land. He agreed to sell it to his daughter for $200,000. They put their complete agreement in writing and set a day for the closing, but when that date arrived, Jeffrey refused saying he had decided to sell the land to someone else. His daughter sued and asked the court to order her father to sell the land to her. What theory do you think her lawyer used?

    b. Jeffrey owned a 125-acre plot of land. He frequently told his daughter that he wanted her to have it and agreed to her constructing a house on the land. She acquired a $200,000 mortgage and built her house, with her father doing a substantial part of the building work himself. However, he never gave her the title to the land, and several years later, they had a falling-out. She sued, asking the court to force her father to give her the title or to reimburse her for the $200,000 she expended in building the house. If the court were to help her, what theory do you think it would use?

c. John is in a car accident and is rushed, bleeding and unconscious, to the hospital. His wallet was lost in the accident, so there is no way to contact any relatives. He needs immediate surgery or he will die. The surgery is performed, and John recovers completely. When he gets the hospital bill, however, he refuses to pay, saying that he never agreed to the surgery. The hospital sues. What theory do you think it should use to try to recover its money?

WEB EXERCISES

1. Team up with a classmate and decide on the terms for a basic contractual arrangement. For example, assume that your classmate wants to go into the used textbook business. Agree to sell her your used law textbooks at the end of the semester. Be sure to decide on all of the basic terms, such as price, condition of the books, time of delivery, etc. Then go to *lawinsider.com,* look at "Browse the Cases" or "Browse the Contracts," and complete the contract using the terms of your agreement.

2. Take advantage of the wealth of material on the Internet placed there by those who want to make learning about contracts fun. One professor has even created songs to help you remember basic contract principles. Go to YouTube and search for songs by "Profblaw," such as the "Statute of Limitations Song." On YouTube, you will also find videos and cartoon clips demonstrating various contract principles. Find the clip where Lucy convinces Charlie Brown to try to kick the football that she is holding by giving him a "signed document." When she fails to live up to the terms of the "signed document," is she in breach of contract? Why or why not?

Chapter 11

Specialized Practice Areas

Most of them (lawyers), in time, do find their practice narrowed to a special line of chores; they have become specialists by default.

Everett C. Hughes

Chapter Objectives

After reading this chapter, you should be able to:

- Describe the different types of legal entities that a business can take, and identify the advantages and disadvantages of each type.
- Compare the three basic types of bankruptcy proceedings.
- Define real and personal property.
- Discuss the main forms of intangible property rights.
- Discuss intestate versus testate succession.

INTRODUCTION

Upon completing law school and passing a state bar exam, lawyers are licensed to practice in all areas of the law. Some spend their entire career working in a general practice. Others end up specializing in just one or two areas of the law. Still another career pattern involves going to work for a business corporation or government agency.

Most paralegals follow similar career paths. Your first job may have you doing work involving a variety of different areas of the law or only one narrow area of the law.

While high-profile litigators get the most public attention, most lawyers engage in a transactional practice. They spend little, if any, time in a courtroom, and they focus on helping clients buy houses, draw up wills and contracts, and file required documents with governmental agencies. Paralegals who work with lawyers primarily engaged in a transactional practice will assist in gathering information relevant to the transaction and integrating that information into standardized forms. They may also be involved in filing these documents, physically or electronically. In addition to the tasks just mentioned, paralegals working with lawyers involved in litigation may help develop trial notebooks and exhibits, and they even sit at the counsel table during trials.

In the past four chapters, we have focused on three main areas of law: torts, including personal injury and products liability; criminal law and procedure; and contracts. In this chapter, we discuss a variety of additional specialty areas, including business organizations, employment, bankruptcy, administrative law, immigration, real estate, intellectual property, estate and probate, and family law. Our focus will be on giving you the basics of the substantive law in each area, as well as an overview of what you could expect to be doing as a paralegal working in that field of law.

A. BUSINESS ORGANIZATIONS

Take a few minutes to review the following hypothetical case involving four friends who are interested in starting a new business.

Case 13: The Four Friends

Four friends—Alice, Betty, Claire, and Dan—meet once a week to play bridge. During the course of one such meeting, they began discussing the possibility of going into business together. Alice, who is 30 years old, is currently working as a baker for FreshStuff Bakeries, earning $22,000 a year. She loves her work but has long dreamed of opening her own bakery. She even has a name picked out—We BakeUm Fresh. Unfortunately, she is a single parent raising two small children and does not feel she can afford to invest any of her approximately $5,000 in savings into such a business. Her friends, however, think that they may be able to help.

Betty, a 62-year-old retired schoolteacher, just won $150,000 in the state lottery. In addition, she has $80,000 in retirement savings. Enjoying her retirement, she does not want anything to do with the day-to-day running of a business. However, assuming that her money would not be at risk, she would be willing to invest up to $100,000 in a business.

Claire, a 20-year-old college student, recently inherited a small, two-story building, worth $125,000, in the downtown area that could easily house a bakery. She would be too busy with classes to help run the business, but she would be willing to let the others use her building to house the bakery.

Finally, Dan is 25 years old. He currently works odd jobs for a local landscaping company. However, he feels that he is a born salesperson and manager. Of the $10,000 he has in savings, he feels he could contribute up to $5,000 toward the business. He would love to quit his current job, at which he earns $19,000 a year, to serve as the bakery salesperson and manager.

Type of Business	Sole Proprietorship	Partnership	Corporation	Limited Liability Company	Limited Liability Partnership
Number of Owners	One	Two or more	One or more	Usually one or more	Two or more
Taxation	Single	Single	Double	Single	Single
Liability	Unlimited	Unlimited	Limited to capital contribution	Limited to capital contribution	Usually limited to capital contribution; sometimes liable for business debts and for own negligent acts
Ease of Formation	Very easy; nothing to file except "DBA" certificate if using fictitious name	Very easy; formed by partners' oral or written agreement; no filing required except for "DBA" certificate if using fictitious name (can also be established by partners' words or conduct—partnership by estopppel)	File articles of organization; pay annual fee; elect board of directors and officers; hold annual meetings; keep corporate records; use designation such as Corp. or Inc.	File certificate of organization; pay annual fee; use designation such as LLC	Register with the state; pay annual fee; use designation such as LLP
Managed by	Sole owner	Partners	Board of directors and officers	Manager (either an owner or a nonowner) or the owners	Usually the partners

Figure 11-1   A Comparison of the Basic Types of Business

If the four friends decide to go into business together, they will confront many basic legal issues, but the first will be to decide what form they would like their business to take. The three classic forms of business organizations are (1) sole proprietorship, (2) partnership, and (3) corporation. In the mid-1990s, the limited liability company (LLC) and the limited liability partnership (LLP) emerged as hybrids, offering the benefits of both the partnership and the corporate form. Figure 11-1 summarizes the major features of each business type.

A **sole proprietorship**, the most common form of business organization, is a business formed by a single owner. They are the simplest to start and maintain, requiring a minimum of paperwork and expense. However, all the owner's personal assets, regardless of whether they are related to the operation of the business, are available to satisfy business-incurred debts. For example, if the business is not able to pay its debts, in addition to seizing the assets of the business, creditors can take the business owner's home, automobiles, jewelry, or any other personal assets. Also, the owner of a sole proprietorship is often limited in funding to his or her own resources. One of the most common reasons for changing from a sole proprietorship to a partnership or corporate form is the need for additional capital to finance the business's expansion.

Under the Uniform Partnership Act, a **partnership** is defined as "an association of two or more persons to carry on as co-owners of a business for profit." As with a sole proprietorship, partnership assets are only taxed once as personal income to the partners.

NETNOTE

You can find business ownership information, such as the names of the resident agent and the corporate officers, at various places on the Internet, including *www.westlaw.com* (Westlaw), *www.lexis.com* (Lexis), and many state government websites.

The major disadvantage to doing business as a partnership is that every partner assumes liability for the actions of every other partner. And as with a sole partnership, personal assets can be taken to pay for business liabilities.

Each partner is responsible for the acts of all the other partners because each partner is an agent for the partnership. An **agent** is someone who has the power to act in the place of another. A **principal** is a person who permits or directs another person, the agent, to act on his or her behalf, subject to the principal's direction and control. When an agent is authorized to act in the principal's place, the acts of the agent become binding on the principal. Therefore, each partner's acts bind the partnership as a whole.

In order to protect their personal assets, some business owners turn to the corporate form. A **corporation** is a business entity formed by an association of stockholders. A corporation can sue, be sued, own property, and make contracts in its own name. In a corporation, the investors have the advantage of being owners without having to assume any liability beyond the cost of their individual shares. While this limitation on liability may be important in the context of lawsuits, it may be somewhat illusory when it comes to seeking credit because banks and other creditors often require shareholders in small corporations to provide personal guarantees to secure loans. Another benefit of the corporate form is the perpetual existence and transferability of shares. Unlike a partnership, it has a

Agent
Someone who has the power to act in the place of another.

Principal
A person who permits or directs another person to act on the principal's behalf.

continuing life of its own that is not affected by the death of a stockholder or the exchange of shares of stock.

The major disadvantages of a corporation are the necessity for following certain formalities in order to ensure that the business will be viewed as a corporation and the "double taxation" involved. The corporation's profits are taxed at the corporate level before dividends are distributed to shareholders. A "dividend" is a distribution of the corporate profit as ordered by the directors. The shareholders then are taxed again on the dividends they receive.

Limited Liability Corporations (LLC) and **Limited Liability Partnerships (LLP)** are particularly attractive to small businesses. These forms are created by statute and offer the best of two worlds—the limited liability that is afforded by the corporate form and the single taxation that occurs in a partnership. Limited liability means that the members cannot be sued for the negligent actions of their partners. However, as is true with corporate limited liability, it cannot protect them from their own personal conduct. Professional partnerships, such as law firms, appear to be gravitating more toward the LLP form. Because this form is essentially identical to a general partnership, except for obtaining the benefits of limited liability, law firms can easily make the change to an LLP limited liability partnership with minimal disruption of the firm's internal workings.

Legal Reasoning Exercises

1. Write a memorandum analyzing the advantages and disadvantages of each of the four major business forms in light of the needs of Alice and her friends. Be sure to take into account the special life situation of each person and how that would affect that person's choice of business form.

2. Assume that Alice and her friends have decided to form a partnership. Draft a partnership agreement that will best satisfy all the parties' needs.

3. The four friends in our previous scenario successfully create We BakeUm Fresh. Sixth months after they open their bakery, six customers develop food poisoning after eating there and sue the bakery. What liability would each of the friends have if they were partners? How would their liability be different if they had formed either a sole proprietorship or a corporation?

Another important category of organizational structure is the "not for profit" category. This category applies to legally recognized organizations that do not earn profits for "owners." All of the money earned by or donated to a not-for-profit organization must be used for pursuing the organization's charitable objectives. If they meet various federal and state requirements, they are often exempt from various types of taxes.

A lawyer who works with business entities often first helps them decide which business form works best for them. If they choose the partnership form, a common task is the drafting of a partnership agreement. If instead they choose the corporate form, a lawyer will perform many tasks ranging from preparing the initial articles of incorporation and bylaws for a new enterprise, to handling corporate mergers, reorganizations, and bankruptcies. They may also handle registration and reporting requirements required by secretary of state offices and the Federal U.S. Securities and Exchange Commission (SEC). Lawyers use these same organizational structures to carry on the practice of law. Lawyers working in a "private practice" are most often self-employed in a sole proprietorship, are partners in one of the various partnership forms, shareholders in a legal corporation, or are employed as "associates" in a law firm operating as a partnership or legal corporation. They may also operate as employees of business organizations such as financial institutions, insurance companies, manufacturing corporations, trade associations, nonprofits, or governmental agencies.

Paralegals working in this area often research corporate information and prepare various corporate records and reports. They are also frequently assigned to monitor government legislation and administrative regulations that impact the corporation's business.

B. EMPLOYMENT AND LABOR LAW

Employment and labor law addresses the legal rights of workers and their employers. It involves the application of contract law principles covered in Chapter 10 and federal and state labor regulations. It includes disputes regarding wages; hours; unlawful termination; child labor; workplace safety; workplace injury and disease; family and related leave; pension and benefit plans; the right to unionize; regulations of and negotiations with union employees; sexual harassment; discrimination based upon race, gender, age, and disabilities; and government civil service systems.

Employees, who work without the benefit of a union contract, are considered to be employees "at will." Under traditional interpretations of the **at-will doctrine**, employers have been free to fire their employees for a good reason, a bad reason, or no reason at all, so long as that reason does not conflict with specific statutes to the contrary. For example, if a paralegal reports late for work, the employer is free to fire that employee, even if this is the first instance of late arrival.

In recent years, however, some courts have begun to give at-will employees more protection. In some cases where employers have established employee handbooks that spell out various personnel procedures, the courts have required those employers to follow their own rules. In addition, a few courts have stated that employers owe employees an implied covenant to act in good faith. Finally, many courts have found a public policy exception that prevents an employer from firing an employee when the employer's actions are seen as harming not only the employee, but also society as a whole. Examples include an employer firing an employee for asserting a legally guaranteed right, such as applying for worker's compensation; for doing what the law requires, such as reporting for jury duty; and for refusing to do an unlawful act, such as committing perjury. This is a rapidly changing area of the law, so you should expect to see the rights of employers to freely fire at-will employees come under increased judicial scrutiny in the coming years.

In addition to those rights given to "at-will" employees by the courts, both the federal and state legislatures have enacted many statutory protections, including worker's compensation laws, antidiscrimination laws, and laws to protect the health and safety of workers. Lawyers working in this area must become conversant with the statutory provisions, as well as the regulations issued by administrative agencies that have been established to enforce these laws.

One of the most important of these federal laws protecting employees from discrimination is Title VII. Until 1964, it was perfectly legal for private employers to discriminate against current and potential employees based on their race, sex, or national origin. Congress dramatically changed this with the passage of Title VII of the Civil Rights Act of 1964. With the passage of the Civil Rights Act, Congress hoped to stop all forms of discrimination, whether in voting, education, public accommodations, or employment. The legislature expanded Title VII with the Pregnancy Discrimination Act of 1978, and the U.S. Supreme Court has interpreted this statute to forbid discrimination based on sexual orientation.[1] Title VII of the Civil Rights Act of 1964 deals specifically with employment. It states that

> [i]t shall be an unlawful employment practice for an employer (1) to fail or refuse to hire or to discharge any individual, or otherwise to discriminate against any individual with respect to his compensation, terms, conditions, or privileges of employment, because of such individual's race, color, religion, sex, or national origin.[2]

Race, color, religion, sex, and national origin are known as protected categories. Title VII does not mean that an employer can never make an employment decision adverse to a member of a protected class. For example, an employer can refuse to hire an African American because that person lacks the skills required for the job, withhold a woman's promotion because of a bad attendance record, or fire a Muslim because that employee was caught embezzling company funds. The key is the reason behind the employer's actions. A negative action against a member of a protected class is unlawful only when the action was taken because that person is a member of a protected class.

The most difficult part of the typical employment discrimination case is the determination of the employer's true motivation behind the allegedly discriminatory action. While some employers may admit to discriminatory motives, most employers will claim that their decisions were based on legitimate considerations, such as educational credentials or work record.

In Title VII, Congress also established the Equal Employment Opportunity Commission (EEOC) and delegated to it the task of developing regulations to more specifically delineate what is unlawful behavior. It also provided that persons who feel they have been discriminated against must first file claims with the EEOC or a similar state agency, before taking their cases to court.

NETNOTE

The EEOC home page is located at *www.eeoc.gov*.

Two other important federal statutes that provide employees protection are the Age Discrimination in Employment Act (ADEA), which prohibits

---

[1] Bostock v. Clayton County, Georgia, 140 S. Ct. 1731 (2020).
[2] 42 U.S.C.S. §2000e-2(a) (2020).

discriminating against individuals 40 years of age or older, and the Americans with Disabilities Act (ADA), which prohibits employers from discriminating against those with a physical or mental impairment who are otherwise qualified to perform a job with reasonable accommodations.

Lawyers practicing employment and labor law might represent an individual employee, a group of employees, job applicants, a union, union employees, government workers, a large or small business or organization, a government agency, or interest groups. Paralegals are often used to monitor changes in the government regulations affecting health and safety regulations, employee benefits, and labor relations. Paralegals working on worker's compensation cases gather information about the extent of workers' injuries and the context in which they were received. Because these cases are handled by administrative agencies rather than by the courts, paralegals in some states are authorized to represent clients at hearings.

C. DEBT COLLECTION AND BANKRUPTCY PRACTICES

Most businesses are involved in a variety of commercial transactions that include borrowing money, buying supplies, selling and shipping products, and collecting debts. Some lawyers either work directly for companies trying to collect what they are owed by people or businesses that have not been paying their bills. Some companies have their own internal collections department, while others turn their claims over to outside "collection agencies." Collections lawyers represent the creditors in suits they file in court. When possible, they seek to recover property that was used to secure the debt. The debtor may seek relief from its financial obligations through a **bankruptcy proceeding.**

Bankruptcy proceeding
A process governed by federal law whereby a debtor unable to pay its debts seeks protection.

Bankruptcy law is governed by the U.S. Bankruptcy Code. The Code has three major goals. The first is to preserve as much of the debtor's property as possible. The second is to determine how to divide the debtor's assets fairly between the debtor and the creditors. And the third is how best to divide the creditors' share fairly among the creditors. To effectuate these goals, the Code has three options:

- **Chapter 7 liquidation:** The debtor must sell its assets to pay the creditors, and the business ends. Typically, there are not enough assets to pay all of the creditors everything that they are owed. However, once the debtor's assets have been distributed, the creditors have no rights to any of the debtor's future earnings.
- **Chapter 11 reorganization:** Under this option, the debtor develops a plan whereby it can stay in business. Typically, the plan calls for some immediate payments to creditors with promises to make future payments as the business continues to operate. This is the type of bankruptcy proceeding that you probably have read about involving major airlines and other large businesses.
- **Chapter 13 consumer reorganization:** Limited to individuals, this type of proceeding lets the debtor keep most of his or her assets in exchange for promising to make future payments out of a regular source of income.

Lawyers who work in this area find themselves applying a variety of laws in addition to the Bankruptcy Code, including contract law, the Uniform Commercial Code (UCC), and various consumer protection statutes. Depending upon the size of the businesses, it will either employ its in-house lawyers to do this type of legal work or retain the services of outside counsel. In addition to representing businesses, lawyers may focus on representing individuals who have bad debt problems or consumer complaint issues.

This is another area of law that makes widespread use of paralegals to research and identify the assets and liabilities of corporations and individuals. Paralegals also arrange for appraisals and draft appropriate notices, petitions, schedules, pleadings, agreements, judgments, and liens.

DISCUSSION QUESTION

1. We BakeUm Fresh was forced to close for two months during the COVID-19 pandemic. The partners were able to renegotiate their rent with their landlord, rewrite contracts with vendors, and get a small business loan from the federal government. They purchased several tables to serve food outside and invested in a better website to make it easier for customers to buy goods using curbside delivery. Their cash flow is getting better, but their creditors are starting to pressure them for payment. What type of bankruptcy would best meet the bakery's needs?

D. ADMINISTRATIVE LAW

Administrative law affects our lives every day. It governs everything from how drug companies label their products to the amount of pollution that a power plant can release into the atmosphere. Specifically, administrative law occurs on both the state and federal level and is what governs the creation and then the running of government agencies, such as the Food and Drug Administration (overseeing drug labels) and the Environmental Protection Agency (maintaining pollution controls). Agencies on the federal level are created by Congress and on the state level by state legislatures, or even town councils. Agencies must act within the specific powers granted to them by the governmental entity that created them, the U.S. Constitution, and the particular state's constitution.

Lawyers specializing in administrative law advise clients regarding the legal duties imposed by these administrative agencies and represent their clients in seeking various licenses and permits or responding to alleged violations. When dealing with agencies such as the Environmental Protection Agency, the Federal Communications Commission, the Occupational Safety and Health Administration, or a state insurance commission, the clients are usually business corporations. When dealing with agencies such as the Immigration and Naturalization Service, the Internal Revenue Service, or a state workers' compensation board, the clients are more likely to be individuals.

Many lawyers and paralegals are also employed by the agencies themselves to conduct investigations, prepare complaints, and represent the agency in legal proceedings. In the following Paralegal Profile, Maryann Brunton, describes her work as an administrative compliance officer.

PARALEGAL PROFILE

Maryann K. Brunton
Compliance Officer
Massachusetts Commission Against Discrimination

The Massachusetts Commission Against Discrimination (MCAD) is an administrative agency that investigates and prosecutes complaints of discrimination by people who charge they have been discriminated against based on their race, color, religion, national origin, ancestry, sex, sexual orientation, age, or disability. The commission hears complaints in the areas of employment, housing, places of public accommodation, education, credit, services, and mortgage lending. My job is to investigate these complaints and to enforce the state and federal laws and regulations regarding unlawful discrimination.

Once a complaint is filed with the commission, an investigation is initiated. The investigation entails written submissions filed by the parties regarding their respective positions. As part of the investigative process, I draft interrogatories and requests for production of documents, hold investigative conferences whereby the parties present their legal arguments, conduct witness interviews, conduct on-site visits, and draft affidavits.

The education I received as a paralegal student has equipped me with the knowledge and training I use every day to carry out my responsibilities as a compliance officer. Although the job is at times difficult, it is also rewarding. I have the opportunity to investigate and obtain evidence when individuals have been subjected to egregious harassment and discrimination. The education I received as a paralegal student has enabled me to pursue a career where I can help to correct some of society's injustices.

Some agencies have provisions that allow paralegals to provide formal representation in administrative hearings. For example, the section of the federal regulations governing representation of parties at Social Security Administration hearings explicitly allows for persons other than lawyers to provide representation if they are "capable of giving valuable help" in connection with the claim.[3]

E. IMMIGRATION LAW

Immigration law deals with the application of the policies and procedures related to the entry into the United States of non-U.S. citizens and their legal

---

[3] 20 C.F.R. §404.1705 (2020).

status while they are in the country. It also involves the application processes and procedures involved with naturalization of foreign nationals who wish to become U.S. citizens.

Immigration lawyers and paralegals may be part of a regular law office or work directly for nonprofit groups that advocate for immigrants and refugees where they assist clients with all aspects of immigration law. They also work for the U.S. Citizenship and Immigration Services.[4] Due to the complexity of the law and the frequency of updates and changes, many choose to specialize in subcategories of immigration law such as asylum or refugee law, business immigration law, or criminal and deportation defense.

PRACTICE TIP

Knowing a second language is beneficial for practicing immigration law in law firms representing individuals seeking to work or stay in the United States. Knowing a second language typically is not needed for practicing immigration law with corporations seeking visas for foreign skilled workers.

F. PROPERTY LAW

Property is usually thought of as being a tangible object, such as a house or an automobile, which is "owned" by an individual, a corporation, or a government. However, in its broadest sense, the legal concept of property includes any valuable right or interest that belongs to a person. Property can include promissory notes and admission tickets to concerts or sporting events. There are also circumstances under which a person can have a "property interest" in a job, an idea, or a reputation.

Property
A tangible object or a right or ownership interest.

Property law affects everyone; it affects renters as well as homeowners. It also involves personal property, such as cars and jewelry; and intellectual property, such as books, movies, and computer software.

There are two basic types of property: real property and personal property. **Real property**, also referred to as "real estate," consists of land and whatever is growing on or built on that land. It includes not only the houses, garages, sheds, and other types of buildings that are on the land, but also everything that is permanently attached to those buildings, such as light fixtures, plumbing fixtures, and built-in shelves.

Real property
Land and items growing on or permanently attached to that land; also known as "real estate."

---

[4] In 2003, in response to the 9/11 terrorist attacks, the U.S. Department of Homeland Security was created, and it absorbed the U.S. Immigration and Naturalization Department and U.S. Customs Service. It then created three new agencies under its aegis: the Bureau of Customs and Border Protection, the Bureau of Citizenship and Immigration Services, and the Bureau of Immigration and Customs Enforcement.

Personal property
All property that is not real property; also referred to as "chattel."

All property other than real property is classified as **personal property**, which sometimes is also referred to as "chattel." Personal property is often classified as being either tangible or intangible. **Tangible property** consists of goods that can be touched and moved, such as automobiles, jewelry, clothing, and television sets.

Intellectual property is personal property that cannot be touched, such as a stock certificate or a patent. While you can certainly touch the piece of paper that documents the stock ownership or the awarding of the patent, it is not the paper itself that has value. The term **intellectual property** is used to cover intangible assets such as trademarks, copyrights, and patents that are the product of someone's intellectual creation, which we will discuss in more detail below.

Intellectual property
Intangible assets that are created by someone's intellectual activity, such as trade secrets, copyrights, patents, and trade or service marks.

1. Real Estate Practice

Lawyers specializing in property law provide a good example of a transactional law practice. They spend most of their time drafting the various legal documents involved in buying and selling real estate and rarely enter a courtroom.

State laws and local practices vary with respect to the point at which, and the degree to which, lawyers become involved in the typical sale of a piece of real estate. If the sale is being financed through a bank or other financial institution, that financial institution will have the key legal documents reviewed by their own lawyers.

Title search
An examination of documents recording title to the property to ensure that the owner has clear title to the property.

If an agreement is reached, the buyer arranges for financing and the seller arranges for a **title search**, and sometimes title insurance. These arrangements are often handled by a paralegal working for the seller's lawyer. Title companies, which specialize in providing these services, typically employ paralegals as well as lawyers.

Real estate closing
A meeting at which the buyer and the seller and/or their representatives sign and deliver a variety of legal documents to finalize the sale and transfer of property.

When the buyer or seller is using a lawyer, that person will usually be present at the **real estate closing,** where the buyer and the seller or their representatives sign and deliver a variety of legal documents to finalize the sale and transfer of the property. Paralegals often play a major role in drafting the documents signed and exchanged at the closing. They often assemble the required information from financial institutions and government records.

Deed
A legal document that formally conveys title to property to the new owner. In most sales, a warranty deed is used.

The most important part of the closing is the delivery of the **deed**. The deed is the legal document that formally conveys title to the property to the new owner. In most real estate transactions, the buyer has a mortgage. Typically, the buyer will provide twenty percent of the purchase price in cash and borrow the rest from a bank. The deed will be held by the bank until the mortgage is paid off. In most sales, a warranty deed is used. With this type of deed, the seller, also known as the "grantor," promises clear title to the property, one that has no encumbrances or other defects.

Ethics Alert

While some state and local jurisdictions allow paralegals to assist clients at real estate closings without the lawyer also being present, most require the physical presence of the supervising lawyer. The rationale for such restrictions is that the paralegal would be engaging in the unauthorized practice of law (UPL) if the paralegal attempted to explain the legal consequence of the documents being signed or to negotiate a last-minute change in any of the terms of the agreement.

Besides helping people buy and sell homes and commercial buildings, lawyers practicing in this area also draw up rental agreements and construction contracts. They may also help developers obtain the proper building permits and zoning waivers. Paralegals working for real estate lawyers typically draft closing documents and coordinate schedules with everyone involved in the closings. They may also work for the title companies that research and ensure the validity of the deed.

2. Intellectual Property

Traditionally, land was the greatest measure of a person's wealth. Today, the rights to use various types of technologies, to perform popular music, to distribute best-selling books, and to use popular symbols can be worth as much or more than owning a particular tract of land. These are all examples of what is known as **intellectual property**. The law protects intellectual property when there is a concrete manifestation of an idea. The practice of intellectual property law deals mainly with trade secrets, patents, copyrights, trademarks, and service marks.

Trade secrets and patents are closely related, in that they both protect the manufacture or use of physical products. Whereas a **trade secret** is knowledge about how a product is made, a **patent** gives its owner the right to exclude others from making, using, or selling his or her invention. An example of a trade secret would be knowledge of the ingredients and their proportions that make up the herbs and spices in Kentucky Fried Chicken. Examples of inventions that have been patented include the autofocus camera lens, automatic intermittent windshield wipers, and Amazon's "1-Click" payment method.

Patent
A right to exclude others from making, using, or selling one's invention.

Copyrights give authors, composers, and artists the right to control, with certain limitations related to "fair use," the use of their writings, musical performances, and artistic creations. A **trademark** is a distinctive symbol or set of words that identify a product with a specific manufacturer. Familiar examples include "Coke," "Jell-O," and "Like a good neighbor, State Farm is there." The law gives the registered holders of these trademarks and service marks the right to control their use. A **service mark** is a distinctive symbol or set of words that identify a service with a particular service provider. Some examples of service marks include United Airlines and its phrase "Fly the friendly skies."

Copyright
An author's or artist's right to control the use of his or her works.

Trademark
A name, combination of letters or numbers, or logo that identifies a particular product.

Many companies hold both trademarks and service marks, such as McDonald's. McDonald's has a trademark for the goods that it sells, such as hamburgers and French fries, and it also holds service marks such as "I'm lovin' it," as a restaurant serving customers.

Service mark
A mark used to identify a service-oriented business.

If a client desires to protect a copyright, patent, trademark, or service mark, lawyers and paralegals first research the existence of previous copyrights, related patents, and similar trademarks and service marks. If they do not find any that conflict, they will assist their client in preparing and filing the forms needed to register these rights with the appropriate government agencies. If someone else already holds those rights, they will sometimes assist their client in negotiating with the holder to be able to use those rights.

While it is usually quite clear if others are illegally trespassing on your land, it is not always easy to know or prove that others are infringing on your rights to your intellectual property. This can occur if others incorporate your invention in their product, include your melody in their song, or use your picture to help sell their product. To help ferret out such illegal use, intellectual property owners often hire specialists to surf the Internet, monitor advertisements in magazines, and scrutinize the broadcast media to identify people or businesses infringing on their copyrights, trademarks, etc. Lawyers then follow up with official cease-and-desist letters to the offending parties. To protect trade secrets, companies usually give only limited access to key information and have their employees sign contracts containing special provisions regarding the need to keep all trade secrets confidential.

To learn more about what paralegals working in the area of intellectual property do, read the following Paralegal Profile of Deb Monke.

PARALEGAL PROFILE

Deb Monke
Intellectual Property Administrator
State Farm Insurance Companies

As an Intellectual Property Administrator for one of the nation's largest insurance companies, I spend much of my time working with employees in many different areas of the company to ensure compliance with company guidelines regarding the use of trademarks in advertisements and brochures. This often involves meetings, conference calls, and e-mails with the brand group, creative services, and marketing. As brand liaison for the department, I help the brand group develop an understanding of the proper usage of trademarks and further develop our brand program.

Another major part of my job involves trademark, copyright, and to a lesser extent, patent registrations and infringement matters. In this context I review items involving potential infringement of State Farm's intellectual property and send out cease-and-desist letters. I am often in contact with retained counsel regarding the registration of foreign marks or an infringement matter I may have sent them for handling.

My administrative duties include delegating and coordinating the intellectual property workflow to a legal assistant, an intellectual property technician, a secretary, and occasionally a legal assistant intern.

In order to qualify for my current position, I needed a bachelor's degree, formal paralegal training, and several years of paralegal experience in this area of law. In addition to having completed the requirement for becoming a Certified Legal Assistant, I also successfully completed the Intellectual Property Specialty exam offered by National Association of Legal Assistants (now called NALA: The Paralegal Association). I attend seminars and read journals to keep up with the changes in intellectual property.

My membership in NALA has proven to be very helpful. In addition to its certification program, I have benefited from the continuing legal education courses I have taken and my experiences serving on various committees and the board of directors, and finally from my two terms as president. These activities have improved my knowledge of the paralegal profession and my management skills. I am also involved in the International Paralegal Management Association, the International Trademark Association, the Illinois State Bar Association, and the Central Illinois Paralegal Association.

My paralegal career has been very enjoyable and rewarding. I particularly like my job because it is intellectually challenging, I am given a great deal of freedom in managing my duties, and I work with creative people.

For students considering this profession, make sure you participate in an internship, quickly establish a mentoring relationship once you begin working, keep your skills up with the changes in technology and the law, and make sure you join associations.

Legal Reasoning Exercise

4. Assume that you have invented a new type of baby stroller that can be converted into a portable crib, and you created an app to keep track of the number of minutes that a baby naps each day. You also have a home business, making and selling your "secret recipe" chocolate chip cookies. For each of the following, determine which type of intellectual property protection is appropriate: trademark, copyright, patent, trade secret, or nothing.

    a. The step-by-step instructions for how to manufacture your stroller
    b. Your idea for a tire that would never go flat
    c. The instruction booklet you give to purchasers of your strollers
    d. The distinctive mark you emboss on your strollers
    e. The lyrics to a song you create for a TV commercial advertising your stroller
    f. The recipe for your cookies
    g. The programming of your app
    h. The name of your app
    i. The concept of keeping track of the number of minutes that a baby naps each day
    j. The cute baby images in your app
    k. The organization of your app

G. ESTATE PLANNING AND PROBATE

Another example of a transactional law practice involves lawyers helping clients plan how they want to transfer their real and personal property to their surviving relatives, friends, and charities upon their deaths. They do this by drafting wills and trust agreements designed to pass on their real and personal property in the most efficient and cost-effective way. If a person died **intestate**

Intestate
The status of a person's estate when that person died without leaving a valid will.

(i.e., without a will), the property is distributed according to the special procedures and formulas set out in state statutes. These laws may not correspond to how the deceased wanted to dispose of the estate. For this reason, as well as to take advantage of potential tax savings, it is preferable to have an up-to-date will.

NETNOTE

The Uniform Probate Code has been adopted by 18 states. You can access the text of the code as it has been adopted by each of those states by going to *law.cornell.edu/uniform/probate.html.*

In judging the validity of a will, the courts focus on three factors: whether the testator was an adult, usually 18 or older; his or her testamentary capacity; and whether the testator voluntarily executed the will. As to the second requirement of testamentary capacity, all that is required is that the testator know what he or she owns, what he or she wants to do with that property, and the "natural objects of the testator's bounty" (i.e., the testator's spouse and other close relatives). Finally, based on the third criterion, a court can invalidate a will if it finds that due to fraud or undue influence, the testator did not voluntarily sign the will.

In addition to drafting a will that directs how the decedent's property should be distributed at death, most lawyers recommend the creation of several documents relating to situations in which a living person is temporarily or permanently unable to act, such as being in a coma or an advanced stage of dementia. These documents consist of a **durable power of attorney** for financial affairs, and a **durable health care power of attorney** for medical affairs. Both authorize someone, usually a close relative, to make either financial or medical decisions for the individual

A **living will** is a document containing instructions for the person who holds the power of attorney, as well as for health care professionals and family members, regarding what end-of-life health care measures the individual would or would not want if no longer capable of communicating those desires.

Lawyers who draft wills are also likely to be involved in the process of probating wills after the person has died. **Probate** is a formal legal procedure for distributing a deceased person's assets under a judge's supervision. The judge's role is to ensure that the deceased's bills get paid and that the remaining assets are distributed according to the provisions of a valid will. Probate lawyers represent clients in these hearings.

Many states have adopted an "informal probate," alternative process that allows for the distribution of the deceased's assets without the necessity of having formal court proceedings. To avoid "formal probate," it is usually necessary to have an uncontested will, no ownership of real property, and personal property assets below a set amount.

Durable power of attorney
A document that gives someone else power to act for you if you become incapacitated and unable to handle your financial matters on your own.

Durable health care power of attorney
Also known as a health care proxy or medical power of attorney, a document that gives someone the power to make health care decisions for you if you become incapacitated and cannot make those decisions yourself.

Living will
A document expressing a person's end-of-life health care wishes; also known as a "medical directive."

Probate
The legal process for settling an estate after a person has died.

Lawyers and paralegals involved in estate planning and probate usually work for private law firms and banks. A major part of the paralegal's work involves gathering and organizing financial information for lawyers to review and then incorporating personal and financial information into standardized language used in wills and trust documents. In addition to working for private law firms and banks, paralegals working in the probate field are also employed by probate courts. In these settings they assist administrators and executors by collecting and inventorying the deceased's assets, arranging for appraisals, helping locate and notify heirs, and completing and filing probate and tax forms.

PRACTICE TIP

Avoid these witnesses: the elderly and casual acquaintances who may disappear and therefore not be available to testify should the need arise.

It is a common practice for paralegals and other office staff to act as witnesses to a will. However, states vary on the subject of whether a paralegal can supervise the execution of a will. The Connecticut Bar Association recommends against it, while Colorado favors it, and many states do not address the issue at all. The rationale for such restrictions is that the paralegal would be engaging in UPL if the paralegal attempts to explain the legal consequence of the documents being signed.

H. FAMILY LAW

A family law practice involves an interesting mix of litigation and transactional law, along with a combination of civil and criminal law. Sometimes referred to as "domestic relations law," the field involves laws governing marriage, annulment, separation, divorce, paternity, adoption, guardianship, custody, support, child abuse, and child neglect.

It is also one of the most dynamic areas of the law. For example, in recent years, the very notion of what constitutes a family has changed. No longer can we limit our definition of a family to a husband, a wife, and children. Today, a family might mean an unmarried mother and her children; a single father and his children; a mother, her children, and a stepfather; or a mother, her child, and her female spouse.[5]

Family law also illustrates the inability of the courts to solve basic social problems. The breakdown of the traditional family, advances in medical science,

---

[5] In 2015, the U.S. Supreme Court declared "that same-sex couples may exercise the fundamental right to marry. No longer may this liberty be denied to them." Obergefell v. Hodges, 135 S. Ct. 2584 (2015).

and changing societal mores are all pressing the courts with increasingly complex issues that can be only imperfectly resolved within the legal arena. Family law decisions go to the very heart of what we feel is important. For example, should the best interests of the child or the rights of a natural parent govern the outcome of a custody dispute?

Because state statutes and the court decisions interpreting those statutes dominate family law, there is a great deal of variation from one state to the next. However, while state law is the principal source of family law, the federal government has enacted legislation in certain areas of family law, such as those laws assisting states with the collection of child support and trying to prevent divorced or separated parents from kidnapping their own children and taking them across state lines.

Such things as who can be married, how marriages take place, the property rights of marital partners, how marriages are dissolved, and how children are adopted are governed by civil law, while criminal statutes can cover child and spousal abuse.

Paralegals working in this area of the law are often engaged in meeting with clients. They gather financial information in preparation for divorce or separation proceedings. Paralegals also draft petitions, discovery requests, separation agreements, and other court documents in regards to divorce and child custody proceedings. As with criminal law, family law raises a number of emotional issues, and the client is often unhappy no matter the results. But family law can also involve happy events, such as marriage and the adoption of children.

NETNOTE

"Concerned over making decisions about abused and neglected children's lives without sufficient information, a Seattle judge conceived the idea of using trained community volunteers to speak for the best interests of these children in court. So successful was this Seattle program that soon judges across the country began utilizing citizen advocates." This program is now known as Court Appointed Special Advocates (CASA). To learn more about CASA and how to train as a volunteer, go to its national website at *nationalcasa.org*.

SUMMARY

Lawyers can work in a variety of different specialty areas. Therefore, the prepared paralegal will have a basic working knowledge of the substantive law in many of those areas as well.

Dealing with business clients requires an understanding of the different forms that a business can take: sole proprietorship, partnership, corporation, or limited liability partnership or company. Those working in the area of employment law must be familiar with state and federal statutes, including Title VII of the Civil Rights Act of 1964, prohibiting discrimination based on race, color, religion, sex, or national origin; the Age Discrimination in Employment Act (ADEA), prohibiting discrimination based on age; and the Americans with Disabilities Act (ADA), prohibiting discrimination based on disability.

Bankruptcy can involve a Chapter 7 liquidation, Chapter 11 reorganization, or Chapter 13 consumer reorganization. Some lawyers, including those working in the area of immigration law, specialize in practicing before administrative agencies. Some agencies authorize paralegals to appear as representatives at adjudicatory hearings.

Property law deals with ownership rights in real and personal property, including intellectual property. The major types of intellectual property are patents, trade secrets, copyrights, trademarks, and service marks.

Estate planning involves the analysis of a person's future financial needs and ways to ensure that desires regarding distribution of assets will be accomplished after death. A will is the most common estate-planning tool. End-of-life planning also involves the creation of advance directives, such as living wills.

Family law includes laws governing marriage, annulment, separation, divorce, paternity, adoption, guardianship, custody, support, childcare, abuse, and neglect. There is a great deal of variation in family laws from one state to the next.

Those who work in litigation will find more of their time devoted to investigating and compiling facts in preparation for a potential trial while those in more transactional settings may have more client contact and duties involving the drafting of important documents. However, no matter in which of these specialty areas a paralegal works, the basic skills needed for factual and legal research, along with good communication skills, are essential requirements.

REVIEW QUESTIONS

Pages 297 through 305
1. What are the basic differences between a transactional and a litigation law practice?
2. What are the four basic forms of business organizations, and what are the main advantages and disadvantages of each?
3. What is the most common reason for changing from a sole proprietorship to a partnership or a corporation?
4. Why might forming an LLC be preferable to forming either a partnership or a corporation?
5. What is employment at will?
6. What protections are afforded an employee by Title VII? The ADA? The ADEA?
7. What are the main purposes of the Federal Bankruptcy Code?
8. Describe the three types of bankruptcy proceedings available to a debtor.

Pages 305 through 315

9. Name some areas governed by administrative regulations.
10. In what types of offices do lawyers and paralegals specializing in immigration law work?
11. Define the two basic types of property.
12. What is intellectual property, and what is it meant to protect?
13. What does it mean to say someone died intestate?
14. Why is it not a good idea to die without a will?
15. What is the purpose of a living will? A durable health care power of attorney?
16. Name four areas covered by family law.

WEB EXERCISES

1. Go to the website of the secretary of state's office in the state where you live. Look up the documents that you must file to create a corporation. Create a list of questions that you would need to ask a client seeking to form a corporation in order to fill out those documents.

2. The U.S. Patent and Trademark Office maintains a website through which you can learn more about trademarks, copyrights, and trade secrets. Start by going to *uspto.gov*.
   a. First, search to see which trademarks have been claimed. In the middle of the home page, click on "Trademark Basics: Start Here." Read the basic information provided and follow up on any links that are of interest to you, such as the link to the booklet "Basic Facts About Trademarks." Then, return to the home page and click on the link to TESS, the online Trademark Electronic Search System. Choose the "Basic Word Mark (New User)" form and then search for any well-known trademark, such as "Nike" or "Chicago Bulls." You may have to click on several of the search results before seeing the symbol as well as the words that have been trademarked. What was the trademark for which you searched? What did you find?
   b. Now contrast the treatment of trademarks with that of patents. Return to the home page, and on the left side under "Patents," click on "Search." Use the "Quick Search" link to locate information on conduit benders. Scan through the list and then click on the link for "Reciprocal Conduit Bender." Read the sections labeled "Background of the Invention" and "Summary of the Invention." Based on the information contained in these two sections, briefly explain what a conduit bender is and how the inventor's product differs from those that had been patented before his.

3. Use FindLaw or a general search engine such as Google to see if your state has enacted a statute authorizing businesses to form an LLP. (If you would like to use FindLaw, start at *findlaw.com/casecode*. Scroll down on the screen, and under "State Resources," select your state and then click on the link to the state's statutes.) If your state has enacted a statute authorizing LLPs, find the provision that specifies the designation, such as LLP, that such a business must use. Why do you think states typically require the use of a specific designation showing that a business is being run as an LLP? In your state, are partners in an LLP shielded from liability for their own acts of negligence, or only for the acts of the other partners?

PART 3

Legal Analysis and Research

Chapter 12

Finding and Interpreting Enacted Law

*A word is not a crystal, transparent and unchanged,
it is the skin of a living thought and may vary greatly
in color and content according to the circumstances
and the time in which it is used.*
Justice Oliver Wendell Holmes

Chapter Objectives

After reading this chapter, you should be able to:

- Apply the general framework for analyzing statutes, administrative regulations, and constitutions.
- Explain the function of citations.
- Discuss why enacted law frequently contains ambiguities.
- Describe the various approaches courts use in the process of interpreting enacted laws.
- Use the IRAC (Issue-Rule-Analysis-Conclusion) format to write a statutory analysis.

INTRODUCTION

In Chapter 1, we gave a brief overview of the process involved in legal reasoning (i.e., applying the law to a set of facts). That law can be found either in enacted law or court-made law (common law). In this chapter we explore the methods used to analyze enacted law. While the emphasis is on analyzing statutes, you can apply the same principles to constitutional provisions and agency regulations. We also discuss a specialized format that is often used for reporting the results of the legal analysis.

Sometimes both **enacted law** and common law may be relevant to a client's situation. Most lawyers, however, begin their legal analysis of a specific legal problem with statutes. They initially focus on statutes because statutes supersede the common law. In addition, reading an annotated statute will alert the lawyer to administrative regulations and court opinions that may also be relevant. (In annotated statutes, in addition to finding the text of the statute, you will find summaries of court decisions that have interpreted the statute, citations to administrative regulations, and cross-references to secondary sources that will help explain or summarize the law.)

Thus if a client has been arrested for murder, a lawyer will start by locating and then analyzing the state statutes on homicide. If a client is seeking a divorce, alimony, and child support, the lawyer will locate and then analyze the state's domestic relations statutes.

While on the surface the process of analyzing enacted law may seem quite simple—just take the words of the relevant law and apply them to the facts—given the inherent ambiguities in much of the English language, this process can actually be quite complicated. Consider the next case that confronted the lawyer, Harper.

Case 14: The Clearance Sale

Last week, Mary Smith, a cellist with the local symphony orchestra, was doing some shopping at Ajax's Country Hardware Store. Mary had gone to Ajax's specifically in response to an ad announcing a clearance sale.

When she got to the store, most of the clearance items were gone, but she did spot one last 50-foot tape measure. Just as she was about to pick it up, another customer grabbed it. Outraged, Mary picked up a hammer that was lying on the counter and told the other customer to hand over the tape measure. The other customer quickly did so, and Mary put the hammer back on the counter.

At home the next day, Mary answered the door to find herself confronted by a police officer who had a warrant for her arrest on charges of carrying a dangerous weapon.

Mary's situation raises two questions—is a hammer a "dangerous weapon," and did picking it up and then putting it back down in the same spot constitute "carrying" it? To answer these questions, you will need to analyze the statute under which Mary is being charged.

A. LOCATING RELEVANT STATUTES

While the emphasis of this chapter is on how to interpret enacted law, before you can interpret it, you have to know how to locate it. In the case of statutes, the easiest way is if you have its **citation.** We discuss techniques for locating relevant statutes when you do not have a citation in Chapter 14.

A statutory citation always includes an abbreviation for the statutory code and a reference to chapter or title and section numbers. Two relatively simple examples of statutory citations are:

> Freedom of Information Act, 5 U.S.C. §552(b)(3) (2018)
> Cannabis Regulation and Tax Act, 410 Ill. Comp. Stat. 705 (2020)

The first citation is to a federal statute. You can tell it is a federal statute because of the abbreviation U.S.C., which stands for "United States Code." The number 5 preceding the U.S.C. designation indicates that the statute is part of Title 5; 552(*b*)(3) is the section number (the symbol § stands for "section"). The second citation is to an Illinois state statute. In each, the date in parentheses refers to when the book was last updated. It does not refer to the date when the statute was enacted.

The United States Code is the official codification of federal statutes; it is printed and distributed by the U.S. Government Printing Office. A **Code** is an arrangement of statutes by subject matter. They can be either annotated or unannotated. For example, the United States Code is unannotated, containing only the statutes themselves. On the other hand, the United States Code Annotated and the United States Code Service are published by West and LexisNexis, respectively. In addition to the text of the laws themselves, these two **annotated** versions of the code have information about the legislative history and references to court decisions that have interpreted the statutes.

Citation
A statutory citation is a formalized method of using abbreviations to identify a location where the text of part of a statute can be found.

Code
A compilation of federal or state statutes in which the statutes are organized by subject matter rather than by year of enactment.

Annotated statute
A privately published statutory code that includes editorial features, such as summaries of court opinions that have interpreted the statutes.

NETNOTE

If you would like additional explanations or a refresher about using Bluebook citations, there are a number of excellent videos on YouTube.

State statutes are also published by West and other private publishers in annotated form. Figure 12-1 lists the most common publications and abbreviations for federal statutes and gives a few examples for state statutes. These abbreviations, as well as those for any statutory compilation, can be found in citation manuals such as *The Bluebook: A Uniform System of Citation*, and the *ALWD Citation Manual*. There are other free citation resources as well, such as the Indigo Book and Cornell's *Introduction to Basic Citation,* but note that

Publication	Abbreviation	Determination
United States Code	U.S.C.	Official codification of federal statutes arranged by subject matter
United States Code Annotated	U.S.C.A.	West's unofficial codification of federal statutes arranged by subject matter with annotations
United States Code Service	U.S.C.S.	LexisNexis's unofficial codification of federal statutes arranged by subject matter with annotations
Alabama Code	Ala. Code	Official codification of Alabama statutes arranged by subject matter
West's Annotated California Code, Business and Professions	Cal. Bus. & Prof. Code	West's unofficial codification of California statutes relating to business and the professions with annotations
General Laws of the Commonwealth of Massachusetts	Mass. Gen. Laws	Official codification of Massachusetts statutes arranged by subject matter.
Massachusetts General Laws Annotated	Mass. Gen. Laws Ann.	West's unofficial codification of Massachusetts statutes arranged by subject matter with annotations

Figure 12-1   Common Publications Containing the Texts of Federal and State Statutes

they are not official sources and do not always agree with the latest Bluebook citation form.

In the "Clearance Sale" case at the beginning of this chapter, Harper, Mary's lawyer, would start with an analysis of the criminal statute that Mary Smith has been charged with violating. In most criminal cases, the arrest warrant will include the citation to the relevant sections of the state's criminal code.

B. STATUTORY INTERPRETATION

Statutes can be quite lengthy, containing many subsections (sometimes called "articles") and cross-references to other statutes. Note in Exhibit 12-1 how the Illinois Domestic Violence Act of 1986 is organized into four articles: General

CHAPTER 750

FAMILIES

ACT 60. ILLINOIS DOMESTIC VIOLENCE ACT OF 1986

ARTICLE I—GENERAL PROVISIONS

60/101. Short title

§ 101. Short Title. This Act shall be known and may be cited as the "Illinois Domestic Violence Act of 1986".

P.A. 84–1305, Art. I, § 101, eff. Aug. 21, 1986.

Formerly Ill.Rev.Stat.1991, ch. 40, ¶ 2311–1.

Title of Act:

An Act concerning domestic violence, amending and repealing certain Acts and parts of Acts herein named. P.A. 84–1305, approved and eff. Aug. 21, 1986.

60/102. Purposes—Rules of construction

§ 102. Purposes; rules of construction. This Act shall be liberally construed and applied to promote its underlying purposes, which are to:

(1) Recognize domestic violence as a serious crime against the individual and society which produces family disharmony in thousands of Illinois families, promotes a pattern of escalating violence which frequently culminates in intra-family homicide, and creates an emotional atmosphere that is not conducive to healthy childhood development;

(2) Recognize domestic violence against high risk adults with disabilities, who are particularly vulnerable due to impairments in ability to seek or obtain protection, as a serious problem which takes on many forms, including physical abuse, sexual abuse, neglect, and exploitation, and facilitate accessibility of remedies under the Act in order to provide immediate and effective assistance and protection.

(3) Recognize that the legal system has ineffectively dealt with family violence in the past, allowing abusers to escape effective prosecution or financial liability, and has not adequately acknowledged the criminal nature of domestic violence; that, although many laws have changed, in practice there is still widespread failure to appropriately protect and assist victims;

(4) Support the efforts of victims of domestic violence to avoid further abuse by promptly entering and diligently enforcing court orders which prohibit abuse and, when necessary, reduce the abuser's access to the victim and address any related issues of child custody and economic support, so that victims are not trapped in abusive situations by fear of retaliation, loss of a child, financial dependence, or loss of accessible housing or services;

(5) Clarify the responsibilities and support the efforts of law enforcement officers to provide immediate, effective assistance and protection for victims of domestic violence, recognizing that law enforcement officers often become the secondary victims of domestic violence, as evidenced by the high rates of police injuries and deaths that occur in response to domestic violence calls; and

(6) Expand the civil and criminal remedies for victims of domestic violence; including, when necessary, the remedies which effect physical separation of the parties to prevent further abuse.

P.A. 84–1305, Art. I, § 102, eff. Aug. 21, 1986. Amended by P.A. 86–542, § 1, eff. Jan. 1, 1990; P.A. 87–1186, § 3, eff. Jan. 1, 1993.

Formerly Ill.Rev.Stat.1991, ch. 40, ¶ 2311–2.

60/103. Definitions

§ 103. Definitions. For the purposes of this Act, the following terms shall have the following meanings:

(1) "Abuse" means physical abuse, harassment, intimidation of a dependent, interference with personal liberty or willful deprivation but does not include reasonable direction of a minor child by a parent or person in loco parentis.

(2) "Adult with disabilities" means an elder adult with disabilities or a high-risk adult with disabilities. A person may be an adult with disabilities for purposes of this Act even though he or she has never been adjudicated an incompetent adult. However, no court proceeding may be initiated or continued on behalf of an adult with disabilities over that adult's objection, unless such proceeding is approved by his or her legal guardian, if any.

(3) "Domestic violence" means abuse as defined in paragraph (1).

(4) "Elder adult with disabilities" means an adult prevented by advanced age from taking appropriate action to protect himself or herself from abuse by a family or household member.

(5) "Exploitation" means the illegal, including tortious, use of a high-risk adult with disabilities or of the assets or resources of a high-risk adult with disabilities. Exploitation includes, but is not limited to, the misappropriation of assets or resources of a high-risk adult with disabilities by undue influence, by breach of a fiduciary relationship, by fraud, deception, or extortion, or the use of such assets or resources in a manner contrary to law.

(6) "Family or household members" include spouses, former spouses, parents, children, stepchildren and other persons related by blood or by present or prior marriage, persons who share or formerly shared a common dwelling, persons who have or allegedly have a child in common,

718

Exhibit 12-1   Illinois Domestic Violence Act of 1986

Provisions, Orders of Protection, Law Enforcement Responsibilities, and Health Care Services. Notice also how the General Provisions article is subdivided into Short title, Purposes—Rules of construction, and Definitions. This last subsection contains definitions of key words used in the statute.

Therefore, the first step in reading and understanding a statute is to pay attention to its overall organizational layout. Here:

Chapter 750 deals with families
Act 60 is the Illinois Domestic Violence Act
Article I contains General Provisions of that act
§103 gives definitions
(1) defines the word "abuse"

When reading statutes, pay careful attention to every word. Some words are especially important. For example, always take note of whether the legislature used a mandatory word, such as *shall*, or a discretionary word, such as *may*. Double-check to see whether the elements of the statute are connected by "and" or "or." If the statute uses "and," each part connected by "and" *must* be satisfied. If the statute uses "or," the parts are alternatives to each other. For example, in the definition of "abuse" notice the use of the word "or." This means that any of those items listed could by itself constitute abuse.

Before deciding how a statute will affect your client's case, you first have to make sure that it was meant to cover your client's legal issue. Assuming it does, then you must break the statute into separable parts, known as "elements," each of which must be satisfied for the statute to apply. Third, you must resolve any ambiguities and apply those elements to your client's facts. Finally, you must conclude as to what you think is the most likely outcome for your client.

NETNOTE

The Library of Congress maintains a "Guide to Law Online." From that page, you can access links to federal and state legal resources.

1. Determine the Statute's Applicability to Your Client's Facts

Once you have found a statute, take a close look at its language and purpose to make sure it does apply to your client's facts. For example, assume your client has a problem with his apartment lease, a type of contract. There is a statute, the Uniform Commercial Code (UCC), which sets out uniform rules governing business relationships. Article 2 deals specifically with contracts. You might wonder if Article 2 applies to your client's problem with his lease. While Article 2 does deal with contracts, it applies only to those contracts that involve "transactions in goods." Therefore, the statute would apply to your client's lease only if an apartment lease qualifies as a "transaction in goods." To find the answer to that question, you would consult the section in Article 2 that defines the most important terms used within the statute. That section defines "goods" as "all things . . . which are moveable." Because an apartment is not moveable, you would conclude that Article 2 does not apply to your client's case.

In addition to analyzing whether the statute's language was intended to cover your client's situation, be sure to check the statute's effective date. Usually, the events of your client's case must have occurred after the statute's effective date for the statute to govern the outcome of your client's case. Occasionally, the legislature will give a statute a retroactive effect, but that is very rare. You must also check to be sure that the statute has not been superseded by a more recent statute.

In our "Clearance Sale" case, the state statute prohibiting the carrying of dangerous weapons is clearly relevant because Mary has been formally charged with violating that statute.

2. Divide the Statute into Its Elements

Assuming you have found a relevant statute, the next step in statutory interpretation is to break the statute down into its elements. A **statutory element** can be defined as a separable part of the statute that must be satisfied for the statute to apply. Another way of stating this is to say that an element is a precondition to the application of the statute.

Statutory element
A separable part of a statute that must be satisfied for the statute to apply.

In Mary's case, she was charged with violating the following statute:

It is unlawful for anyone, other than a police officer, to carry a dangerous weapon.

This statute contains three elements. For Mary to be found guilty,

- she must not be a police officer, and
- she must have "carried"
- a "dangerous weapon."

3. Identify the Issues

Next, you must apply the statutory elements to your client's facts. Sometimes this will be a straightforward process. For example, because the facts state that Mary is not a police officer, the first element of the crime is satisfied. However, sometimes ambiguities will be created either by the statutory language or by the client's facts. For example, it is not clear that Mary "carried" a "dangerous weapon." While she did pick up the hammer, most people think of carrying something as more than just picking it up and then setting it back down in the same place. Similarly, while a hammer could be used to harm someone, most people think of a hammer as a common household tool rather than as a weapon. Therefore, the facts in Mary's case, when combined with the statutory language of two of the elements, create issues:

- whether the hammer was a "dangerous weapon," and
- whether Mary "carried" the hammer when she picked it up and then set it back down in the same place.

Issue
A circumstance when the law is applied to the client's facts and the result is not obvious.

An **issue** arises whenever an element applied to the specific facts fails to give you a clear-cut answer.

When trying to determine whether an element will create an issue, first ask yourself whether you detect any ambiguity in the statute's words. Sometimes the words will seem to have only one possible meaning. However, as we just demonstrated in Mary's case, when you try to apply statutory language to a specific factual situation, often you will find that the language is ambiguous and that it can be interpreted in more than one way.

Ambiguities slip into statutes for several reasons. They can result from sloppy draftsmanship or, more commonly, when the statute is applied to unanticipated circumstances. Remember that when a legislative body formulates a statute, it is setting down general rules that will be applied to a variety of future situations. Trying to lay down rules today for situations that will arise in the future is a difficult task. There are also times when the drafters unintentionally write the ambiguity into the statute when trying to reach a compromise.

When statutes contain ambiguous language, they are open to differing interpretations. Ask yourself which of the possible interpretations makes the most sense. That is, which interpretation do you think would best further the purposes for which the statute was enacted? As we will see in a moment, courts have devised several methods to assist them when they are asked to interpret statutory language. These methods can assist you as well. However, before resorting to reading court opinions that have interpreted the statute, try honing your critical thinking skills by focusing solely on the statutory language, and using your own common sense to try to ferret out a sensible legislative purpose.

One of the most powerful legal reasoning skills that you can acquire is the ability to think creatively and independently about a problem. Develop that skill by working with a statute on its own terms. Develop arguments that you think would best convince a court that the language should or should not be applied to your client's case. Ask yourself, what was the legislature trying to accomplish with the statute, and will that purpose be better fulfilled by saying that an element is or is not satisfied, given the client's particular set of facts?

To help you brainstorm a statute, develop a chart. List the elements, and then under each element, list the facts that you would use to make arguments both for and against satisfying the element. Figure 12-2 is a sample chart that you might develop for Mary's case.

Legal Reasoning Exercise

1. Before the enactment of the following statute, under the common law, a married woman was not allowed to sue in her own name. Instead, the lawsuit was brought in her husband's name. Assume that you have a client who wishes to sue her spouse for negligence. Read the statute. Do you think she will be able to sue her husband? Why?

Mass. Gen. L. ch. 209, §6
> A married woman may sue and be sued in the same manner as if she were sole; but this section shall not authorize suits between husband and wife.

Figure 12-2   Sample Chart of Statutory Elements

Element 1—"to carry"
Element satisfied—moved hammer from counter.

Element not satisfied—did not move it from the building; legislature used specific term of "carry" rather than a broader term, such as "possess."

Element 2—"dangerous weapon"
Element satisfied—a hammer is a heavy, hard object capable of causing physical harm; purpose of legislation is to protect people from physical harm.

Element not satisfied—hammers are normally viewed as tools, not weapons.

At this stage, do not worry about finding the "right" answer. Let yourself feel free to explore all the possible arguments on both sides of each issue. This process of looking at the language of the statute and at the facts of your client's case is an ongoing one. Each time you look at the statute, you may see new ambiguities, and each time you look at your client's facts, you may see new arguments about whether the statute's language applies to your client's facts.

Once you have finished brainstorming, it is time to explore other methods that can help you understand and apply a statute to your client's facts. These methods include searching for statutory definitions to help explain any ambiguous terms and looking to prior court opinions in which your statute or similar statutes have been interpreted.

a. Look for Definitions

When faced with ambiguous wording in statutes, it is a good practice to look to see if key terms, like "dangerous" and "weapon," are defined in some other part of the statute or in a similar statute. Also, some statutes, such as the tax code, give administrative agencies the task of developing more detailed definitions for a statute's general terms. Therefore, it is important to also check administrative regulations for definitions of statutory terms.

In Mary's case, the following could be found in the definitions section of the statute:

The term "dangerous weapon" means a weapon, device, instrument, material, or substance, animate or inanimate, that is used for, or is readily capable of, causing death or serious bodily injury.

But how useful is this definition? If it is interpreted literally, just about anything from a frying pan to an electrical cord could be considered a deadly weapon. Is that really what the legislature intended? As you can see, even definitions can be ambiguous, and hence require further analysis.

b. Look to Prior Court Decisions

Because of the doctrine of stare decisis, judges usually prefer to interpret an ambiguous phrase in a way that is consistent with what other judges have done in similar cases. In addition to looking to decisions from their own state, courts will frequently look to judicial interpretations of similar statutes in other states.

Courts employ various approaches when interpreting statutes. These include looking at the "plain meaning" of the statute, considering legislative history, and using the canons of construction. The judges' own views as to the role of the courts relative to the legislature will also have an impact on how they interpret a statute.

Legislative intent
The purpose of the legislature at the time it enacted the statute.

No matter which method or combination of methods is used, the court's goal is to ascertain the **legislative intent** when the legislature enacted the statute. As Charles Evans Hughes, former chief justice of the U.S. Supreme Court, once put it:

> In the interpretation of statutes, the function of the courts is easily stated. It is to construe the language so as to give effect to the intent of Congress.[1]

The court's objective is to interpret the statute in such a way as to frustrate whatever evil the legislature wanted to prevent or to further whatever positive goals the legislature wanted to achieve.

(1) Plain meaning

Plain meaning
A method for interpreting enacted law in which the key terms are interpreted in light of their dictionary definitions and use in ordinary conversations.

Courts usually begin the process of statutory interpretation by using the **plain meaning** approach. Based on a literal reading of the statute's language, this approach assumes that

- the words used reflect the true intentions of the legislature (that is, they meant what they said); and
- the legislature intended that the words used would be interpreted in light of their common, ordinary meanings.

One problem with this plain meaning approach occurs when there are alternative ways to interpret the same language. For example, assume that the phrase "every wife and mother" is used in a statute. Should you interpret this phrase as applying to all wives and also to all mothers, or just to everyone who is both a wife and a mother?

Another problem arises when there is more than one commonly accepted, ordinary meaning for a term. Return for a moment to the earlier problem with regard to the interpretation of "carrying" when Mary lifted the hammer from the counter. The *American Heritage Dictionary* lists 32 different meanings for the word "carry." One definition involves conveying something from one place to another, while another definition speaks in terms of simply holding something.

---

[1] United States v. American Trucking Assn., 310 U.S. 534, 542 (1940).

Mary's criminal liability will thus depend on which of these two competing definitions the court decides is the common, ordinary meaning.

Occasionally, judges will openly reject the plain meaning approach and ignore the literal meaning of the words in a statute; they do this when they are persuaded that such a reading does not properly reflect the "true intent" of the legislature. For example, assume that a state criminal statute made it a crime for anyone to carry a loaded weapon "in the vicinity" of a public school. If someone were arrested carrying a loaded weapon inside a public school, his lawyer could argue that "in the vicinity" means near but not inside the school. A court would likely reject that argument because it would make little sense for the legislature to convict someone for having a loaded weapon near a school but not for actually having one inside a school.[2]

(2) Legislative history

If the plain meaning approach fails to resolve the issue, judges will turn to other methods to try to determine the legislature's intent when it enacted the statute. This can include looking to current events at the time the statute was enacted, as well as to legislative history.

Legislative history refers to the background documents created during the process of a bill becoming a statute. These documents can include alternative versions of the legislation, proceedings of committee hearings and reports, and transcripts of floor debates. The exact nature of the materials that exist for a particular statute will vary depending on the importance of the statute and the type of legislative body involved. Generally, there is more recorded legislative history for federal statutes than there is for state statutes.

To understand why certain documents form a statute's legislative history, you need to recall the steps that the legislature follows to create a statute. Statutes begin as bills. A legislator introduces a draft of what the proposed law should look like. Before passage, there may be amendments that change various sections of the bill. The pattern that emerges from examining multiple bills and amendments can sometimes provide insight into the legislative intent regarding the final act. The court, for example, would probably not read an act as applying to a particular situation if the legislative history shows that an amendment that would have applied to that situation was defeated.

Before bills are presented on the floor of the legislative body, they are usually sent to a committee. Committees often hold public hearings where interested parties can testify about the proposed law. The proceedings of these committee hearings are published, and the transcript becomes a part of the statute's legislative history. A committee sometimes will issue an official report discussing the nature of the proposed legislation and what it is expected to accomplish. The committee report also becomes part of the legislative history.

When the bill is debated on the floor of the legislative body, proponents and opponents often make statements about what they expect the bill to do or not do. The transcripts of these floor debates are another source of information

Legislative history
The background documents created during the process of a bill becoming a statute. These documents can include alternative versions of the legislation, proceedings of committee hearings and reports, and transcripts of floor debates.

PRACTICE TIP

A legislature often enacts legislation as a reaction to a specific event. Therefore, to gain insight into the legislative thinking at the time, search through archived newspaper reports for major events around the time the legislation was enacted.

---

[2] Based on the case of Adler v. George, 2 QB 7 (1964).

about legislative intent. In determining legislative intent, courts may quote from any of these sources.

When you see a court relying on legislative history, or when you are thinking of relying on it yourself, keep in mind that legislative history should be viewed with an open mind. First, it is frequently incomplete, especially at the state level. Second, it is usually based on what just one or a few of the legislators said, and it is dangerous to make assumptions about why the others remained silent. There is no way of knowing if the other legislators agreed or even knew of the statements. Third, you can usually find history to support opposing points of view.

Legal Reasoning Exercise

2. New York State has a statute governing price gouging. On July 6, 2020, New York amended the definition of the term "goods and services" as follows:

N.Y. Gen. Bus. Law § 396-r

Pre-2020 version: For the purposes of this section, the term consumer goods and services shall mean those used, bought or rendered primarily for personal, family or household purposes.

2020 version: For the purposes of this section, the term goods and services shall include (a) consumer goods and services used, bought or rendered primarily for personal, family or household purposes, (b) essential medical supplies and services used for the care, cure, mitigation, treatment or prevention of any illness or disease, and (c) any other essential goods and services used to promote the welfare of the public.

According to the language of the statute prior to 2020, do you think the definition of "goods and services" would have included price gouging of medical supplies? Why do you think the statute was amended in the summer of 2020?

(3) Canons of construction

Canons of construction
General principles that guide the courts in their interpretation of statutes.

Ejusdem generis
A canon of construction meaning "of the same class."

Another method courts use to deal with ambiguity in statutes is to apply what are known as the **canons of construction**. For example, when a series of specific items is followed by a catchall phrase, such as "and others," the courts may assume that the legislature intended to limit the statute to matters that are like the ones specifically listed. This is known as the principle of **ejusdem generis** (of the same class). Assume that a statute prohibited the outdoor sale of perishables, such as food, drink, beverages, and the like. Does it apply to flowers? You could argue that the legislature did not intend for the statute to cover the sale of flowers, even though they are certainly perishable, as all the items on the list are edible and flowers are not.

Legal Reasoning Exercise

3. Assume that a town council passed the following ordinance:

It shall be unlawful to operate any vehicle on town park paths. Violators will be subject to a $100 fine for the first offense and up to a $500 fine for each additional offense.

The council passed the ordinance in response to citizen complaints about a group of teenagers who had been riding their motorcycles on the paths of the town's parks. Not only are motorcycles noisy, but also the citizens were afraid that one day, an accident would occur and a child walking down one of the paths would be injured.

Following the passage of this ordinance the following four events took place in a town park:

1. For a "lark," two teenagers drove a Jeep Cherokee down one of the park paths.
2. Once a week, the garbage collector backs his truck approximately six feet down one of the park paths to pick up garbage from one of the trash receptacles.
3. A child pushed her doll's baby carriage along a park path.
4. An ambulance drove down one of the park paths to pick up a man who had collapsed in the middle of the park.

Do you think all four of these situations are violations of the law? Before you answer, think about whether you think the town council had each of these situations in mind when they passed the ordinance. Should their intent matter?

A major problem in relying on a canon of construction is that most canons can be negated by yet other canons. For example, when looking at a list, another rule of statutory construction states that the members of that list are only examples and are not meant to be exclusive. Because all the items on the list are examples of perishable items and because flowers are perishable, you could argue that they were not meant to be excluded.

Two general rules of statutory construction are particularly important. First, normally courts **strictly construe** criminal statutes and **statutes in derogation of the common law** (i.e., those that change the common law). When courts strictly construe a statute, they narrow the scope of its coverage. For example, a court interpreting the phrase "dangerous weapon" in the statute dealing with "carrying a dangerous weapon" would say that it does not include hammers. Courts strictly construe criminal statutes because of the severe penalties that defendants face. It is thought to be unfair to make someone suffer criminal sanctions if the legislature did not clearly intend to include

Strict construction
An approach whereby the courts give a statute a narrow interpretation.

Statute in derogation of the common law
A statute that changes the common law.

that particular behavior within the statute. Similarly, courts strictly construe statutes in derogation of the common law because they assume the legislature meant to change the common law no more than was necessary to achieve its purpose.

On the other hand, courts normally give **remedial statutes** a **liberal construction.** When the courts give a statute a liberal construction, they broaden the scope of its coverage. The courts presume that when the legislature is trying to remedy a situation, it does not want its intent thwarted by too narrow an interpretation. An example of a remedial statute is Title VII, the federal statute outlawing discrimination in employment. As we saw earlier, the court liberally construed the term "sex discrimination" to include sexual harassment.

However, even these two basic rules of construction can conflict. For example, what should a court do when interpreting a statute such as one creating a workers' compensation system? Under the common law, if a worker were hurt on the job, that person's only recourse was to sue the employer under tort law. State legislatures created workers' compensation laws so that employers would automatically be required to compensate injured employees. Therefore, it is a statute that both serves a remedial purpose and is in derogation of the common law.

In addition to these formal canons, keep in mind that courts usually also apply the following basic principles of statutory interpretation:

- Statutes should be interpreted to be consistent with the intent of the legislators who enacted them.
- Statutes should be read literally and their words given their "plain" meaning.
- Individual parts of a statute should be interpreted so that they will be consistent with the other parts of the statute.
- Unless the legislative intent is clearly to the contrary, statutes should be interpreted to be consistent with other statutes and with the common law.
- Statutes should be interpreted to be consistent with committee reports, floor debates, and other aspects of the legislative history.

Remedial statute
A statute enacted to correct a defect in prior law or to provide a remedy where none existed.

Liberal construction
An approach whereby the courts give a statute a broad interpretation.

Legal Reasoning Exercises

4. Assume that you represent a client who shipped obscene music CDs from Massachusetts to California. He has been charged with violating a federal criminal statute that prohibits interstate shipment of any obscene "book, pamphlet, picture, motion-picture film, paper, letter, writing, print or other matter of indecent character." Has he violated the statute?

5. Assume that you represent a client who knowingly transported a stolen airplane from Illinois to Oklahoma. He is charged with violating the following federal statute:

National Motor Vehicle Theft Act, 18 U.S.C. §408

Sec. 2. That when used in this Act: (a) The term "motor vehicle" shall include an automobile, automobile truck, automobile wagon, motor cycle, or any other self propelled vehicle not designed for running on rails;

Sec. 3. That whoever shall transport or cause to be transported in interstate or foreign commerce a motor vehicle, knowing the same to have been stolen, shall be punished by a fine of not more than $5,000, or by imprisonment of no more than five years, or both.

Do you think your client should be found guilty? Why?

(4) A note on judicial philosophy

Ultimately, how a particular court interprets a statute will also be influenced by the judicial philosophy of the judge hearing the case. Some judges are strong believers in **judicial restraint** and tend to rely on the plain meaning of the statute, giving it the narrowest, most literal construction possible. They do not view their role as one of second-guessing the legislature. For example, consider the situation outlined in Legal Reasoning Exercise 3 regarding the prohibition against vehicles in public parks. Because an ambulance qualifies as "any vehicle," it would be a violation of the ordinance to drive an ambulance in the park, even if it is being done to save someone's life. Although looking beyond the strict language of the statute might produce a better result, followers of judicial restraint will not do so. It is not their role to correct legislative omissions. Finally, they tend to think that legislative intent is static. That is, the courts should give the statute the meaning that the original drafters of the legislation intended. The meaning of the statute should not change as the needs of society change.

On the other hand, judges who believe in **judicial activism** see the issue of statutory construction a little differently. While they, too, will search for legislative intent, they are more willing to see the need for the meaning of a statute to change over time as society changes. They are also more likely to search for a more general purpose behind the statute, as opposed to a specific intent in the minds of the legislators. For example, rather than applying the literal reading of the ordinance in Legal Reasoning Exercise 3 to an ambulance rescue, they would focus on what they believe to have been the intent behind the ordinance rather than its "plain meaning." While the city council's immediate concern was to ban motorcycles, the broader purpose of the ordinance was to protect life, and prohibiting ambulances on the park paths would clearly be inconsistent with the council's intent.

Judicial restraint
A judicial philosophy that supports a limited role for the judiciary in changing the law, including deference to the legislative branch.

Judicial activism
A judicial philosophy that supports an active role for the judiciary in changing the law.

4. Conclude

You should consider each of the methods we have discussed here when you analyze a statute. At times, these alternative methods may suggest contradictory interpretations. At some point, however, you must reach a conclusion on each issue. Then, based on your resolution of each of those individual issues, you must conclude about the question as a whole.

Returning to the case of Mary and the hammer, assume that you think that Mary possessed a "dangerous weapon," but that she did not "carry" it.

Therefore, one of the statute's elements is not satisfied. Because we have defined an element as a precondition to the applicability of the rule and because one element has not been met, the statute would not apply to Mary's case. She would not be convicted of carrying a dangerous weapon. Of course, a court might not agree with your analysis and might instead find that both elements had been satisfied. If that were to happen, Mary would be convicted.

Keep in mind that often, there is no one right answer. At this stage of learning legal reasoning, developing sound arguments in support of your conclusions is more important than the conclusions you reach.

In summary, the process of analyzing a statute and applying it to a set of facts is as follows:

1. Find the main facts of the client's case.
2. Research the law.
3. Analyze the statutory language.
    a. Determine if a statute is applicable to the client's situation.
    b. Break the statute down into its elements, specifically noting any ambiguous language.
    c. State the issues raised by the specific language of the statute and the specific facts of your case. Analyze the problem.
        (1) Determine how each element applies to the facts, striving to see the arguments that hurt as well as those that help. (*Hint*: Based on our definition of an issue, if you cannot find two sides to the argument, you are probably not dealing with an issue.)
        (2) Think about why the legislature enacted the statute. Thinking about the purpose behind the statute will help you determine how best to interpret ambiguous statutory language.
    d. Given the statute's language and the likely purpose behind the statute, conclude as to the statute's effect on your client's facts.
4. Report the results.

We will begin the discussion of this final step, reporting the results, on page 338.

DISCUSSION QUESTION

1. Which of the various methods that we have discussed—plain meaning, legislative history, or canons of construction—do you think is best suited to finding legislative intent?

Legal Reasoning Exercise

6. Assume that your firm represents Carl Clay. He has been charged with burglary. Briefly, the facts are as follows:

Last Friday, Carl was watching *General Hospital,* his favorite soap opera, when suddenly the TV screen went blank. Nothing he could do would cause it to work.

Unfortunately Carl did not have enough money to buy a new TV. He decided to help himself to someone else's.

He drove to the nearby Sleep Well Motel because he knew that the owners had recently purchased new flat screen TVs. When he got to the motel around 5 p.m., he waited in his car until he saw a woman leave her room, ice bucket in hand. She had left the door to her room slightly ajar. Carl quickly ran to the door, opened it, and saw the TV. He went over to the TV, unplugged it, and picked it up. He was about to leave when the woman unexpectedly returned. Knowing karate, she felled him on the spot and then called the office manager, who, in turn, called the police. The TV, which was purchased for $600 and had a resale price of approximately $400, was returned to its rightful place in the room.

Carl has been charged with violating the following statutes:

General Laws ch. 228, §1
Burglary is defined as the breaking and entering of a dwelling at nighttime with the intent to commit a felony therein.

General Laws ch. 228, §2
Theft of personal property over the value of $500 is a felony.
Theft of personal property of a value less than $500 is a misdemeanor.

    a. Develop a chart listing the elements of each statute.
    b. For each element, determine whether the facts raise an issue.
    c. For each issue, list arguments that both Carl's lawyer and the prosecution would raise. Reach a conclusion on each issue.
    d. Do you think Carl can be convicted of burglary?

C. LOCATING AND INTERPRETING ADMINISTRATIVE REGULATIONS

Legislatures often delegate considerable lawmaking authority to administrative agencies. Therefore, frequently you must look beyond the statutes to administrative regulations that interpret the statute. For example, you may recall from Chapter 3 that Congress enacted a statute prohibiting discrimination in employment on the basis of sex. In that same statute, Congress also created an administrative agency, the Equal Employment Opportunity Commission (EEOC), and gave that agency the power to write regulations interpreting the statute.[3]

Administrative regulations are published in formats that resemble those used for statutes. Federal regulations are published in the **Code of Federal Regulations (C.F.R.).** The C.F.R. is analogous to the United States Code, in that it contains only those regulations that are of a general, permanent nature and are currently in force. The regulations are arranged by agency.

Some states publish codes of regulations that correspond to the C.F.R., in that they contain all the current state regulations and are organized by subject matter. In

Code of Federal Regulations (C.F.R.)
A compilation of federal administrative regulations arranged by agency.

---

[3] C.F.R. §1604.11 (2020).

other states, you must obtain the regulations from each individual agency. At both the state and the federal levels, some private publishers issue loose-leaf reporters that contain administrative regulations in specialized areas such as taxes and labor law.

Citations for administrative regulations follow a form that is analogous to that for statutes. For example:

49 C.F.R. §6.1 (2020)
27 N.C. Admin. Code 01G.0119 (2020)

In the first citation, *C.F.R.* tells you that it is a reference to the Code of Federal Regulations. The number 49 stands for title 49, while §6.1 refers to section 6.1 of title 49. As with statutes, the date in parentheses refers to the last publication date for the book in which the regulation appears, not the date that the regulation was promulgated. The second citation is to a North Carolina regulation.

Administrative regulations have the same basic features as statutes, and they are similarly future oriented. However, they tend to be more detailed than statutes, as their function is to spell out the specifics of the statute. Nonetheless, the basic approaches you use when interpreting statutes can also be used to interpret regulations. In addition, keep in mind that the courts will seek an interpretation that is consistent with the intent of the statute that established and controls the agency in question.

D. LOCATING AND INTERPRETING CONSTITUTIONS

As discussed in Chapter 3, constitutions are at the top of the hierarchy of law because they establish the structure of the government itself, as well as the limitations on the government's power. Therefore, when someone challenges the division of powers among the federal branches of government or between the federal and state governments, that challenge raises a question of federal constitutional law. Also, challenges to the limits of the government's power involve questions of constitutional law. For example, when someone objects to the manner in which government agents have conducted themselves (as in a Fourth Amendment challenge to an allegedly unreasonable search), the courts are called upon to interpret state and federal constitutional law.

1. Locating Constitutions

State and federal constitutions are usually included in the corresponding statutory compilation. For example, the U.S. Constitution can be found in the United States Code, the United States Code Annotated, and the United States Code Service. Similarly, a state statute compilation usually includes a copy of its state constitution, and a few even feature a copy of the U.S. Constitution with annotations to decisions from their own state courts.

Sections of constitutions are cited as follows:

U.S. Const. art. I, §8, cl. 3
U.S. Const. amend. XX, §3
Ill. Const. art. IV, §2(b)

2. Constitutional Interpretation

Just as statutes and administrative regulations contain ambiguous terms, so do constitutions. Indeed, as constitutions use broader and more general terms than do statutes, there is an even greater likelihood that ambiguity will occur. Consider, for example, the following clauses contained in the U.S. Constitution:

> Congress shall have Power . . . to regulate *Commerce* with foreign Nations, and among the several States, and with the Indian Tribes. . . . (Art. I, §8) (Emphasis added.)
>
> Congress shall make *no law* respecting an establishment of religion, or prohibiting the free exercise thereof . . . (Amend. I) (Emphasis added.)
>
> Excessive bail shall not be required . . . nor *cruel and unusual* punishments inflicted. (Amend. VIII) (Emphasis added.)

We have added the italics to some of these words to emphasize their uncertain meaning. Courts have interpreted these and other parts of the Constitution using many of the same approaches we discussed in the section on statutory construction. In addition, a judge's experiences and judicial philosophy can influence how he or she views competing constitutional interpretations.

When faced with an ambiguous word or phrase, some justices favor a historical analysis that attempts to determine what the words meant at the time they were written. For example, under this approach, often referred to as **originalism,** the Eighth Amendment provision against "cruel and unusual punishment" should not be interpreted as prohibiting all forms of capital punishment because capital punishment, an accepted form of sentencing at the time that the Bill of Rights was ratified, would not have been viewed as cruel or unusual.

In contrast, other justices support an approach that views the Constitution as a **living constitution,** sometimes labeled the "evolutionary," or "living law" approach. With this approach, judges first seek to identify the underlying principles reflected in the Constitution. They then interpret any particular provision by applying those basic principles to contemporary conditions. Applying this approach to the question of whether the death penalty is "cruel and unusual punishment," the question would not be how the death penalty was viewed in the eighteenth century, but rather how the modern world views it today, which is less positive.

Finally, as was true of statutory interpretation, some judges strongly believe in judicial restraint, and when the constitutionality of statutory provisions is challenged, they will tend to defer to the other branches of government, especially the legislature. On the other hand, more activist judges view the court's appropriate role as being the final arbiter of what is or is not constitutional.

The terms "judicial activism" and "judicial restraint" are themselves ambiguous, and their meaning often will depend on the outlook of the person using the term. The term "judicial activism" may be applied by some speakers simply because they disagree with a particular outcome. Courts, both liberal and conservative, have been labeled as activist courts. For example, in reaching its conclusion that separate public schools could never be equal, the Supreme Court justices in *Brown v. Board of Education* relied heavily on data supplied by social

Originalism
An approach to constitutional interpretation that narrowly interprets the text of the Constitution in a manner that attempts to be consistent with what most people understood those words to mean at the time that they were written.

Living constitution
A judicial philosophy that seeks to interpret the Constitution in light of existing societal values; also called "evolutionary" or "living law."

scientists rather than on precedent or established law, thereby in effect creating new law. More recently, many argue that the Roberts court usurped the power of the legislature when, in *Citizens United v. Federal Election Commission,* it declared that congressionally enacted limitations on corporate political spending were an unconstitutional restriction on free speech.

In the end, keep in mind that once a court has formally interpreted the meaning of a particular constitutional clause, that court decision takes on precedential value, helping to frame what the Constitution means. Succeeding courts follow the lead of those previous decisions, and gradually a series of cases develops that explains, for example, that despite the literal meaning of the words "no law" in the First Amendment, the government can actually pass some laws restricting freedom of speech, such as obscene materials or libelous statements.

DISCUSSION QUESTION

2. Do you think judges should approach issues of constitutional interpretation differently than how they approach issues of statutory interpretation? Why or why not?

E. WRITTEN ANALYSIS — THE USE OF IRAC

The results of your legal analysis should be put in writing so that they are preserved for future reference by you or by others with an interest in the legal problem. In addition, writing your analysis will force you to rethink the assumptions you have made. Your written analysis will mirror your thought process thus far. That is, you will discuss each issue raised by the statute's elements and the client's facts.

Legal readers do not appreciate reading something that simply reproduces your stream-of-consciousness thinking. A lawyer or judge wants to know four things:

1. what your client's problem (the **issue**) is,
2. what the law (the **rule**) is,
3. how that law will affect your client's case (the **analysis**), and
4. what your answer as to the likely result (the **conclusion**) is.

One widely accepted method for conveying your thoughts in a logical order is known as **IRAC.** IRAC is an acronym for Issue-Rule-Analysis-Conclusion. The IRAC approach is not the only or necessarily always the best approach for every legal issue, but it is an excellent starting point. If you consciously try to write using IRAC, you will find that you will be forced to think about what you are writing and you will be less likely to leave out important information. The result will be better organized and have clearer paragraphs. Figure 12-3 describes each of the IRAC elements.

To see a practical application of the use of the IRAC technique, consider the following problem.

Case 15: The Book Battery

Your client, Mark Brown, was at home one night. He had been studying in bed when he fell asleep. He was awakened when he heard and then saw a stranger in his darkened bedroom. He shouted, and the stranger moved toward the door. Frightened of what the stranger might do next, Mark took one of his heavy law books and threw it at the man's departing back. Unfortunately, the man's spine was broken. Assume that your boss wants you to analyze whether Mark is guilty of committing a criminal battery.

Mark has been charged with violating a criminal statute:

Any person committing an intentional, harmful, unprivileged touching of another shall be guilty of battery.

From our earlier discussions, we know that one of the first steps in analyzing this statute is to break it down into its elements.

Battery is

1. the intentional,
2. harmful,
3. unprivileged
4. touching
5. of another.

The following is a brief description of each of the IRAC elements, with an example of how each would be used to analyze Mark's problem.

1. Issue

Have a topic sentence that states the issue that you will be discussing in that paragraph. This sentence should be brief and clear. It should also contain only

Figure 12-3 Elements of an IRAC Analysis

Issue	Have a topic sentence that states the issue you will be discussing in that paragraph.
Rules	State the rule of law that arguably governs the particular issue in question.
Analysis	Explain how the statutory language and policy behind the statute determine the outcome, given your client's specific facts. Be sure to include arguments both for and against your client's position.
Conclusion	Conclude. State what you think the result will be. Do not leave your reader to decide what the bottom line is. That is why your supervisor asked you to analyze the problem.
Transition	Use a short transition sentence to lead to the next issue that you want to discuss.

one idea: the one to be discussed in that particular paragraph. If there is more than one issue, devote a separate IRAC paragraph to each one.

> The issue is whether Mark Brown can be found guilty of battery.

2. Rule

State the rule of law that arguably governs the particular issue in question. Quote the exact statutory language. If the statute is quite long, quote only the relevant language. Use ellipses[4] to show any omissions. Make sure your omissions do not change the statute's meaning.

> Battery requires "an intentional . . . unprivileged touching of another."

3. Analysis

Explain how the statutory language and policy behind the statute determine the outcome given your client's specific facts. Note the strengths as well as the weaknesses in your client's case. You will be doing your client a great disservice if you only point out the helpful arguments and leave out the harmful ones, and your supervising lawyer may lose confidence in your ability to do legal analysis.

> Because Mark threw a book at a stranger he found in his bedroom, there was a touching. The touching, however, was privileged. The stranger was a trespasser in Mark's house. He awoke Mark from his sleep, thereby frightening him. Mark had a right to defend himself. Although the man had his back turned to Mark and was possibly leaving the room when Mark threw the book at him, it was quite dark in the room. In his half-awake state, Mark could not be held responsible for making a necessary and quick decision to defend himself.

4. Conclusion

Conclude. Do not leave your reader to decide what the bottom line is. That is why you were asked to analyze the problem.

> Therefore, while Mark did touch the stranger, the touching was privileged. Mark should not be found guilty of battery.

---

[4]Ellipses involve the use of three dots, each one separated by a space. If you omit the end of a sentence, use four dots: three to show the omission and one for the period.

If you are discussing more than one issue, use a short transition sentence to lead to the next element you want to discuss. When you put all of the IRAC elements together, the final discussion would look like this:

> The issue is whether Mark Brown can be found guilty of battery. Battery requires "an intentional . . . unprivileged touching of another." Because Mark threw a book at a stranger he found in his bedroom, there was a touching. The touching, however, was privileged. The stranger was a trespasser in Mark's house. He awoke Mark from his sleep, thereby frightening him. Mark had a right to defend himself. Although the man had his back turned to Mark and was possibly leaving the room when Mark threw the book at him, it was quite dark in the room. In his half-awake state, Mark could not be held responsible for making a necessary and quick decision to defend himself. Therefore, while Mark did touch the stranger, the touching was privileged. Mark should not be found guilty of battery.

Some lawyers prefer the CRAC as opposed to the IRAC method. With CRAC you start with the conclusion instead of the issue. If that is what your boss wants, of course, that is what you will do. But for now, it is better to use IRAC. IRAC forces you to support your conclusion with a well-developed analysis. When you start your writing with a conclusion, the answer may seem so self-evident that you will not see any need to justify it with an analysis. However, when you start your paragraph with a statement of the issue and end it with a conclusion, there is all that space in between, just crying out to be filled with an explanation that will convince your reader of how you logically moved from your issue to your conclusion. This will help prevent the most common error in legal writing: stating the rule and simply jumping to the conclusion, with no supporting reasoning. Look at the following paragraph. What is missing?

> The issue is whether Mark Brown can be found guilty of battery. Battery requires both that there be an intentional touching of another and that the touching be "unprivileged." While Mark did touch the stranger, the touching was privileged. Mark should not be found guilty of battery.

After reading this, you would be left wondering: But why? Why was the touching privileged? The writer gave an answer, but not the reasons for that answer. Always double-check your writing to make sure that you are not leaving your reader with any questions about how you reached your conclusion.

If the statute that you are analyzing contains more than one issue, start with an introductory paragraph, also known as a **road map paragraph**, to tell your reader where you will be going. In that paragraph, very briefly outline the facts, the rule, and the issues that you will be discussing. This is not the place to completely retell the client's story. Give just enough of the facts to set the stage. Follow that paragraph with an IRAC analysis of each major issue, using the rest of the facts to make arguments based on the statute's elements.

Road map paragraph
An introductory paragraph listing issues to be discussed in the order they are to be discussed.

Sometimes an issue will be simple enough that you can put all the IRAC elements into a single paragraph. At other times, you may want to divide the IRAC elements into more than one paragraph. For example, you might wish to set out the issue and the rule of law in one paragraph. Then, in the next paragraph, you could include the arguments for one side of the issue. You could follow this with a third paragraph outlining the arguments for the other side and your conclusion on that issue, along with a transitional phrase or sentence to lead into the next issue.

You need to use **transitions** between your issues to help lead your reader from one issue to the next. A transition can be as simple as "The next issue is. . . ." Finally, wrap up your discussion with a **concluding paragraph** that summarizes your analysis.

When using IRAC, remember that each paragraph should contain one, and only one, idea. A paragraph, indeed any written work, is a structure. It should build, grow, and develop toward a denouement. If you cannot discern such a progression in your own work, go back and rework it until you do.

Finally, do not view IRAC as a straitjacket. It is meant not to limit your creative abilities, but simply to provide a structure for your writing.

Exhibit 12-2 is a sample analysis using the IRAC format for the problem of Mary and the hammer, introduced at the beginning of this chapter. We have added the marginal notes to help you locate each of the IRAC elements. When writing a legal analysis yourself, do not include these marginal notations.

Transition
In writing, a technique used to help your reader move from one thought to the next and to see the connections between them.

Concluding paragraph
The final paragraph in a written legal analysis that summarizes the writer's conclusions.

Road map paragraph

Mary is concerned about whether she can be convicted of carrying a dangerous weapon. During an argument with another customer in a local store Mary briefly picked up a hammer from the counter. The statute under which she has been charged makes it unlawful for "anyone, other than a police officer, to carry a dangerous weapon." Because Mary is not a police officer, the first element of the statute is satisfied. However, as Mary only picked up the hammer, there is an issue as to whether she "carried" it. Second, there is an issue as to whether a hammer can be considered a "dangerous weapon."

Exhibit 12-2   Sample IRAC Analysis

Issue 1	As to the first issue of whether her lifting of the hammer constituted "carrying," the statute simply reads that it is unlawful "to carry" a dangerous weapon.
Rule	
Analysis	While in the hardware store Mary did move the hammer from the counter into the air. However, she did not take it from one location to another, such as from the store out into the street. Therefore, while she may have "possessed" the hammer,
Conclusion on issue 1	she cannot be said to have "carried" the hammer. The second issue, however, is not as clear-cut.

Transition

Issue 2	The second issue is whether the hammer should be viewed as a "dangerous weapon."
Rule	The statute does not define "dangerous weapon."
Analysis	A hammer is normally viewed as a tool and not as a weapon. However, being a large, hard object, a hammer certainly has the capacity to become a dangerous weapon. Also, it was only when Mary lifted the hammer and told the other customer to hand over the item that Mary wanted that the other customer did as Mary wished. Because the legislature was probably more concerned about the potential harm that a dangerous weapon could cause than about the specific identity of any particular weapon, the hammer should be seen as a dangerous weapon.
Conclusion on issue 2	

Concluding paragraph

In conclusion, both elements must be satisfied to find Mary guilty. The hammer could be seen as a dangerous weapon, but Mary did not take it from one place to another. Therefore, she did not "carry" it. Because both elements are not satisfied, Mary cannot be found guilty of carrying a dangerous weapon.

Exhibit 12-2   Sample IRAC Analysis (*concluded*)

Legal Reasoning Exercise

7. Apply the principles that we have been discussing in this section to Carl's situation, described in Legal Reasoning Exercise 6, and write an IRAC analysis of his problem.

SUMMARY

Paralegals often assist lawyers by conducting legal research and performing legal analysis. In this chapter, we have discussed the process typically used for analyzing and reporting on statutes, administrative regulations, and constitutional provisions that have a potential impact on a client's case.

The following steps should be followed when analyzing enacted law:

- Gather and analyze the facts.
- Conduct legal research to identify the appropriate legal rules.
- Apply the legal rules to the facts.
- Report the results (usually in writing).

Once you have located a relevant statute, you must analyze it by breaking it into its elements and then applying those elements to your client's facts. When courts are asked to interpret the meaning of statutes, they can use several techniques. For example, they can use a dictionary and a grammar book to give a literal interpretation, they can study committee hearings and floor debates from the legislature to try to ascertain the legislative intent, or they can apply various cannons of construction. A judge's view of the role of courts in interpreting statutes will also influence which method of statutory interpretation is used.

Similar approaches are used with administrative regulations and constitutions. It is important to realize that it is in the area of constitutional law that the courts (particularly the Supreme Court) have the greatest freedom to exercise discretion. This is not only because the meaning of the Constitution is sometimes ambiguous but also because the Constitution is a "living" document. The Supreme Court is thus legitimately able to change its interpretations of constitutional law to meet the needs of a changing society.

Remember that one of the most powerful legal reasoning skills that you can acquire is the ability to think creatively and independently about a problem. Work with a statute on its own terms before turning to other sources, such as court opinions and legislative history, for guidance.

Once you have analyzed the statute, regulation, or constitutional provision, you may be asked to summarize your thinking in writing. One form of written analysis is known as IRAC (Issue-Rule-Analysis-Conclusion).

REVIEW QUESTIONS

Pages 317 through 335

1. When confronted with the need to analyze a specific legal problem, why do lawyers usually begin with a review of statutes?
2. What are the main steps in analyzing a statutory problem?
3. What is a statutory element?
4. How does an issue differ from an element?

5. Why do statutes often contain ambiguous language?
6. What is meant by looking for the plain meaning of a statute?
7. What are the canons of construction? How do courts use them in interpreting statutes?
8. What types of statutes are courts most likely to strictly construe? To liberally construe?
9. What types of documents could make up a statute's legislative history?
10. What are the dangers in relying on legislative history?
11. What type of judge would be more likely to interpret Title VII's prohibition against employment discrimination based on sex to include discrimination based on sexual preference: one who believes in judicial restraint or judicial activism? Why?
12. When reading a statute, why is it important to pay attention to the use of "and" and "or"?

Pages 335 through 338
13. Where can you locate federal regulations?
14. What methods do courts use to interpret constitutional provisions?

Pages 338 through 344
15. What does IRAC stand for, and why does it provide a useful structure for your legal writing?
16. In your analysis section, why is it important to include both the strengths and weaknesses of your client's case?
17. What is the function of a road map paragraph? Of a concluding paragraph?
18. Why is it important to use transitions?
19. We asked you this question at the end of Chapter 1, but we want to ask it again. Why does the study of law involve more than the mere memorization of rules?

WEB EXERCISES

1. Go to *congress.gov* to find the most viewed bills. Browse the bills and find one that might look interesting to you. Read either the summary or the full text of the bill. What is the purpose of the legislation that you selected? At what stage in the process is it? Why is this particular piece of legislation of interest to you?
2. Eugene Kim has produced some helpful videos regarding the use of IRAC.
   a. Go to his video "IRAC with Statutes—Example" at *youtube.com/watch?v=vvWIeH96oLw/*. Why does he think that it is important to complete a quick analysis prior to writing the issue?
   b. Next, go to his video "IRAC with Statutes—Sample Memo" at *youtube.com/watch?v=aFTWKR7F_RY*. What are three important concepts that he addresses in creating the formal analysis using the IRAC method?

Chapter 13

Finding and Interpreting Court Opinions

The picture of the bewildered litigant lured into a course of action by the false light of a decision, only to meet ruin when the light is extinguished and the decision is overruled, is for the most part a figment of excited brains.
Justice Benjamin Cardozo

Chapter Objectives

After reading this chapter, you should be able to:

- Explain the function of a court citation.
- Identify the main elements of a court opinion.
- Contrast mandatory with persuasive authority.
- Distinguish the four basic types of court cases.
- Use case briefing to summarize court opinions.

INTRODUCTION

In Chapter 12, we discussed how to locate and interpret statutes, administrative regulations, and constitutions. In this chapter, we will discuss how to locate and interpret court opinions. The terms "court opinion," "case," and "decision" are synonymous.

As you will recall from Chapter 5, there are two basic types of courts: trial courts and appellate courts. While trial courts determine the facts and apply the law to those facts, appellate courts act as the final interpreters of the law. As such, appellate court opinions serve as precedent for future court decisions. For that reason, you will principally be studying and briefing appellate court decisions. **Case briefing** is a stylized method used to summarize court opinions.

Lawyers and paralegals read and summarize court opinions to help them analyze a client's situation. Assume that a new client has come to the law firm of Darrow and Bryan and recounts the facts given in Case 16.

Case 16: The Teen Bullies

Matt Anderson, a 68-year-old man with a bad hip, was walking with a cane on the sidewalk in front of his house, when he was approached by a group of male high school students. One of these youths said, "Hey, old man, you don't really need that cane." He then knocked the cane from Matt's hand without actually touching any part of Matt's body. The boys then started laughing and ran down the street. As Matt was trying to take a few steps to pick up his cane, he fell and fractured his arm trying to break his fall. Fortunately for Matt, a neighbor saw what happened, rushed out to help him recover his cane, and transported him to the emergency room of the closest hospital. The neighbor was also able to identify the youth who had knocked Matt's cane as 16-year-old Bob Charles. Matt has come to the law firm to see if he can recover for his medical expenses and pain and suffering caused by his fall.

The lawyer, Pat Harper, explains that his injuries would come under an area of law known as "tort law." The specific issue would be whether he had suffered a battery, defined as "an intentional act that creates a harmful or offensive physical contact." While Matt clearly suffered harm, as Bob never touched him, was the harm he suffered a result of "physical contact"? She tells Matt that before she can answer that question definitively, she and her paralegal, Chris Kendall, will need to do some research.

After Matt leaves, Harper asks Kendall to start that research. As tort law is predominately court-made, not statutory, law she asks him to begin his research by looking into prior court opinions with facts similar to Matt's.

Case reporters
Books that contain appellate court decisions. There are official reports and unofficial reporters.

Official report
A governmental publication of court opinions.

Unofficial reporter
A private publication of court opinions—for example, the regional reporters, such as N.E.2d, published by West.

A. LOCATING COURT OPINIONS

Appellate court opinions are published online and in hardbound volumes called **case reporters.** These are sets of books, consisting of hundreds of volumes that contain nothing but appellate court opinions, arranged in chronological order. They are divided into volumes named for the court that rendered the opinions, such as Illinois Reports or United States Reports.

Reporters are generally divided into two categories—**official** and **unofficial.** They are official when published at the direction of state or federal statutes. All others are unofficial. The texts of the opinions published in the unofficial reporters are the same as those in the official ones. What differs are the editorial features, such as case summaries, that the publishers add at the beginning of the unofficial reports. West is the major publisher of unofficial case reporters, and the West National Reporter System covers all appellate court decisions in the 50 states.

The official state reporters use the abbreviated state name, such as Mass. Reports for Massachusetts. West, on the other hand, publishes by region and abbreviates its reporters as follows:

- P., P.2d, or P.3d for the Pacific Reporter
- N.W. or N.W.2d for the North Western Reporter
- S.W., S.W.2d, or S.W.3d for the South Western Reporter
- So., So. 2d, or So. 3d for the Southern Reporter
- S.E. or S.E.2d for the South Eastern Reporter
- N.E., N.E.2d, or N.E.3d for the North Eastern Reporter
- A.2d for the Atlantic Reporter

To locate an appellate court opinion in one of these reporters, the most straightforward method is to start with its citation. In Chapter 14, we will discuss other ways to locate court opinions when you do not have a citation.

At a minimum, a **case citation** to a court opinion will include (1) the names of the parties, (2) the volume and page number of the reporter(s) in which the opinion is published, (3) the court that decided the case (either from the name of the reporter or added to the ending parenthesis), and (4) the date of the case. Here is a typical citation for a state court case:

Callow v. Thomas, 322 Mass. 550, 78 N.E.2d 637 (1948).

Case citation
Information that tells the reader the name of the case, where it can be located, the court that decided it, and the year it was decided.

Each part of the citation is explained in Figure 13-1. Starting at the left, the parties' last names are listed. Always omit the first names and initials of individuals. Muriel Callow and Frederick Thomas become simply Callow v. Thomas. Notice that their names are italicized, as is the small *v.* The *v.* stands for "versus." Case names should be italicized unless a court rule requires underlining.

Figure 13-1 Case Citation

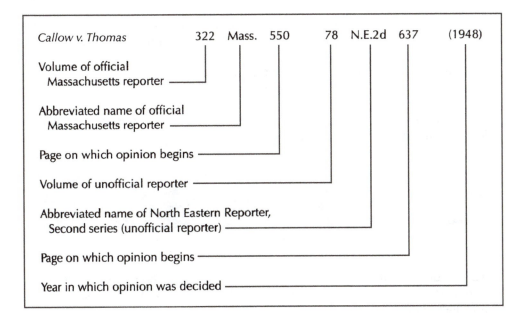

Appellant or petitioner
A person who initiates an appeal.

Appellee or respondent
The party in a lawsuit against whom an appeal has been filed.

The party bringing the appeal (the **appellant** or **petitioner**) is usually listed first, and the opposing side (the **appellee** or **respondent**) is listed second. However, some states follow the practice of listing the name of the original plaintiff first, no matter which party brought the appeal.

When there is more than one party on any side of a dispute, or when several cases have been consolidated, the citation uses only the names of the first parties listed on each side or the first case listed. When the state is a party to a case in its own courts, it is usually listed as *People v.* or *State v.* On the other hand, if a state is a party to a suit in federal court, the case name would include the state name—for example, *Illinois v. Smith.*

After the parties' names, the reporters where the case can be found are listed. Some state court opinions are published in two reporters, the official state reporter and a West unofficial regional reporter. Some state opinions are published only in the West unofficial reporter.

The number immediately in front of the reporter abbreviation indicates the volume in which the case is found. The number immediately after the reporter abbreviation is the page number on which the case begins. Thus, you could find *Callow v. Thomas* either on page 550 of volume 322 of the Massachusetts Reports or on page 637 of volume 78 of the North Eastern Reporter, Second Series.

Following the volume and page numbers of the reporters, the year of the decision appears in parentheses. *Callow v. Thomas* was decided in 1948.

In those cases where the identification of the court is not obvious from the name of the reporter, there will be additional information about the court in parentheses. In the *Callow v. Thomas* citation, you can tell that the Massachusetts Supreme Judicial Court wrote the decision because only Massachusetts Supreme Judicial Court decisions are published in the Massachusetts Reports. If the citation had only been N.E.2d, however, then the abbreviation for the state would have to be included in the parentheses:

Callow v. Thomas, 78 N.E.2d 637 (Mass. 1948).

Wherever you see a citation to a federal district court or court of appeals case, you will see the name of the district or the circuit in the parentheses:

Chambers v. Maroney, 409 F.2d 1186 (3d Cir. 1969).
Brown v. Merkel, 355 F. Supp. 90 (D. Mass. 1990).

This is because you cannot tell simply by the name of the reporter which federal circuit or district court decided the case.

NETNOTE

Most courts post their appellate opinions online. However, do not expect to find most other federal and state opinions older than the early 1990s. To locate appellate court opinions online for your circuit, start by going to *lp.findlaw.com.*

Scroll down, and then click on the link "Cases & Codes." Under "US Courts of Appeals—Opinions & Resources," select your circuit. Follow the same approach to locate court opinions for your state, except go to "State Resources" to select your state. You can also find U.S. Supreme Court opinions dating back to 1760.

Sometimes a writer will refer to a specific part of the court decision where a particular quote appears or where an issue is discussed. This reference to a particular page within an opinion is known as a **pinpoint cite**. In those instances a second page number will appear after the page number on which the case begins. For example, a quotation taken from page 1189 of the *Chambers v. Maroney* decision would be cited as follows:

Pinpoint cite
The reference to a particular page within an opinion.

Chambers v. Maroney, 409 F.2d 1186, 1189 (3d Cir. 1969).

Finally, citations will sometimes include information about the **subsequent case history**. For example:

Subsequent case history
Information about what happened procedurally to the litigation after the case cited. Include this information in a citation.

Telex Corp. v. International Business Machines Corp., 367 F. Supp. 258 (N.D. Okla. 1973), rev'd, 510 F.2d 894 (10th Cir.), cert. denied, 423 U.S. 802 (1975).

This citation indicates that the case was first decided by the U.S. District Court for the Northern District of Oklahoma and can be found on page 258 of volume 367 of the Federal Supplement. The case was then appealed to the Tenth Circuit, where the decision was reversed and reported on page 894 of volume 510 of the Federal Reporter, Second Series. The Supreme Court's decision not to grant certiorari is reported on page 802 of volume 423 of the United States Reports.

B. TYPES OF COURT OPINIONS

Court opinions generally fall into one of four categories:

1. those interpreting and applying enacted law, such as statutes;
2. those deciding the constitutionality of a law;
3. those applying established common-law principles; and
4. those creating new common-law principles.

The first type of opinion, which interprets and applies enacted law, consumes a great deal of the courts' time. As we said in Chapter 12, statutes, administrative regulations, and constitutional provisions often contain ambiguous words and phrases. When interpreting enacted law and attempting to determine legislative intent, the courts rely on the same methods we have discussed: looking at the plain meaning, relying on the canons of construction, examining other parts of the statute, and searching for external evidence, such as legislative history and prior court decisions. Under the doctrine of stare decisis, if previous courts have already interpreted the same or similar language, a court will generally try to reach a decision that is consistent with those earlier interpretations.

A second type of case involves challenges to the constitutionality of a law. Under the power of **judicial review** the courts are responsible for ensuring that all laws comport with the Constitution's requirements. In this type of decision the court's focus is on the intent of the Constitution's framers and the purpose the constitutional provision was meant to fulfill. Then the court determines whether the law in question is consistent with the Constitution's intended purpose.

The third and fourth types of cases involve the common law rather than enacted law. Despite the tremendous growth in statutory law, there are times when no statute covers a litigant's situation. Then the courts rely on the common law, or court-made law. Usually, the court will be faced with a group of prior cases and will use them to form an opinion on the current case. Those cases will be seen as either mandatory or persuasive authority. **Mandatory authority** involves similar facts and law and comes from

1. a higher court
2. in the same jurisdiction.

For state cases, that means higher courts within that state's own court system. Federal courts deciding a case involving state law must follow the interpretations given by that state's courts. Within the federal court system, it means cases from within that circuit and the U.S. Supreme Court.

Persuasive authority consists of the decisions of courts that do not constitute mandatory authority and the writings of legal scholars. It may therefore include primary authority, such as decisions of other state courts, and secondary authority, such as legal treatises or law review articles.

Figure 13-2 shows the hierarchical nature of mandatory authority. A decision handed down by a court is mandatory authority for those courts below it that are connected by an arrow. For example, a federal district court in the First Circuit is required to follow the decisions of the federal court of appeals for the First Circuit. But the decisions of the Second Circuit court of appeals are only persuasive authority for the First Circuit district courts. Likewise, the decisions of state A's highest appellate court are mandatory authority for state A's intermediate appellate and trial courts, but only persuasive authority for state B's courts.

When looking to mandatory authority, unless there is a good reason not to do so, a court will decide a new case based on how courts have held in prior **analogous cases** — that is, cases that involved similar facts and rules of law. If the court decides that the prior cases and the present one are dissimilar on either the facts or the law, the court will **distinguish** the prior cases and reach a contrary decision on the case before it. As you will recall, this process of looking to **precedent**, prior cases, for guidance is known as following the doctrine of **stare decisis**.

At times, however, a court will create new common law. This can occur either because there is no law governing the situation or because the court decides to overrule its own prior decisions. When there is no law covering a situation, the court is faced with an **issue of first impression**. If there are decisions from other jurisdictions, the court may look to those decisions for guidance. In addition, the court may look to secondary authority, such as law reviews and

Judicial review
The court's power to review statutes to decide whether they conform to the Constitution.

Mandatory authority
Court decisions from a higher court in the same jurisdiction involving similar facts and law.

Persuasive authority
Court decisions from an equal or a lower court from the same jurisdiction or from a higher court in a different jurisdiction; also includes secondary authority.

Analogous cases
Cases that involve similar facts and rules of law.

Distinguishable cases
Cases that involve different facts and/or rules of law.

Issue of first impression
An issue that the court has never faced before.

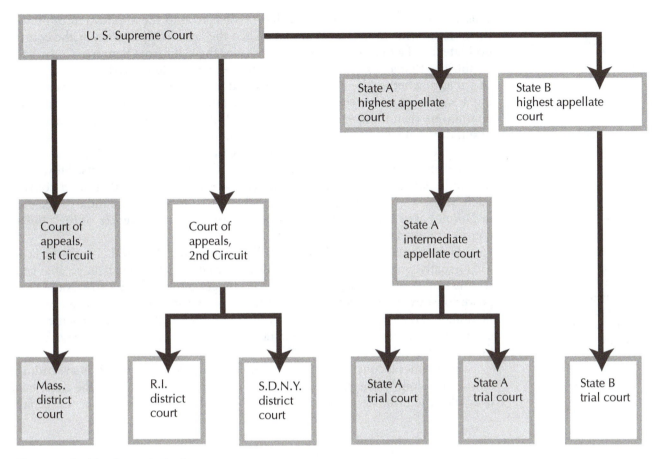

Figure 13-2   Mandatory Authority

treatises. In cases of first impression, the court has the option of creating new common-law rules to cover the situation or refusing to do so and deferring to the legislature. If the court defers to the legislature, it does so because it thinks the case involves an area of law that an elected body can handle better than the courts.

An example of a court deciding to change the current law, thereby creating a new common-law rule, occurred in the 1968 **landmark decision** of *Dillon v. Legg*.[1] Erin Dillon, a young child, was lawfully crossing a road when she was struck by a car being negligently driven by David Legg. As a result of her injuries, Erin died. Erin's mother was standing close by and saw the accident. The law at that time was that bystanders could not recover for the emotional distress they suffered when witnessing an accident. That changed when, in *Dillon v. Legg*, the California Supreme Court created new law by stating that a mother could recover for the emotional injury that she suffered when she saw her child injured. When deciding this type of case, the courts are literally making new law, and at times, this can create quite dramatic and swift changes in the law.

Landmark decision
A court opinion that establishes new law in an important area.

---

[1] 441 P.2d 912 (Cal. 1968).

This can be contrasted with cases that revolve around the application of established legal principles to a set of facts. Then the law slowly evolves as the courts evaluate new fact patterns. For example, once the California Supreme Court had established that a mother could recover for seeing a child injured, questions were raised as to whether the mother actually had to see the accident or whether hearing it was enough, whether other family members could recover, and so on. The courts were then flooded with cases in which the issue was no longer whether a bystander could recover, but rather under what circumstances.

Note that the California Supreme Court's decision in *Dillon v. Legg* became mandatory authority for all lower California state courts. However, it is only persuasive authority in the federal courts and in other state courts. Each of those courts is free to decide whether to follow the standards set out in *Dillon* based solely on each court's view of the persuasiveness of the *Dillon* court's arguments.

Overrule
A decision is overruled when a court in a later case changes the law so that the decision in the earlier case is no longer good law.

Finally, in rare cases, the court will **overrule** precedent and change the law. This usually occurs when the court decides that society's needs have changed so drastically that the old rules should no longer apply. This illustrates the true power of stare decisis. While it normally is a force for stability, it also allows for flexibility and change when the times require it. Figure 13-3 illustrates the various possibilities that a court can pursue when confronted with an issue governed by the common law.

Sometimes a court implies but does not explicitly state that it is overruling a prior decision. When that occurs, it is hard to determine whether the court has overruled the prior decision or merely distinguished it. Conversely, a court may

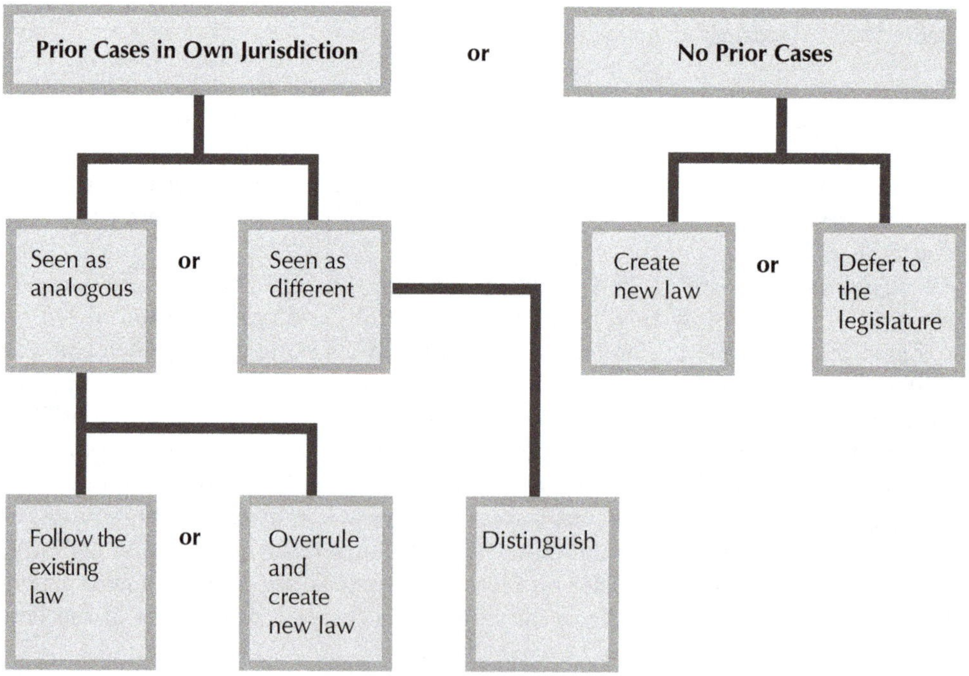

Figure 13-3   Five Routes Open to a Court Faced with a Common Law Problem

state that it is only distinguishing precedent, but it may be implicitly overruling, or at least severely curtailing, the prior court decision. If the court overruled the prior decision, then the legal principle for which that case stood is no longer the law. However, if the court merely distinguished that case from the current one, the prior case's legal principle is still good law.

On a theoretical level, it can be difficult to decide if a court has overruled or merely distinguished a prior case. Because of the nature of our legal system, however, this problem basically disappears in practice. Lawyers are hired to present their client's point of view and therefore will argue that a prior case has been overruled or distinguished based on the needs of their client's position. To some, this may seem disingenuous, reinforcing the popular notion that lawyers are nothing more than hired guns. However, as it is often difficult to state definitively the true meaning of a case, lawyers, who are required to zealously advocate their client's point of view, would be less than ethical if they did not argue for the meaning that best supported their client's position.

In summary, a court can be faced with one of four types of cases:

1. a question regarding the interpretation of enacted law, such as a statute, a constitutional provision, or an administrative regulation;
2. a question regarding the constitutionality of a statute or an administrative regulation;
3. the application of settled law to a new set of facts; and
4. the creation of new law, either because this is a case of first impression or because the court is explicitly or implicitly overruling precedent.

As you read examples of the different types of court opinions included in section D beginning on page 367, notice how the judges are looking for and evaluating precedent. Also note that they have some latitude in how they handle the precedent; at times, they are able to ignore or even overrule it.

Legal Reasoning Exercise

1. For each of the following situations, chose which of the courts listed below could issue decisions that the court would have to follow. Include your reasoning.

- ■ U.S. Supreme Court
- ■ U.S. Court of Appeals for the First Circuit
- ■ U.S. Court of Appeals for the Second Circuit
- ■ U.S. District Court for the District of Massachusetts
- ■ Illinois Supreme Court
- ■ Massachusetts Supreme Judicial Court
- ■ Illinois Court of Appeals
- ■ Massachusetts Appeals Court

> - Illinois Circuit Court
> - Massachusetts Trial Court
>
>   a. The U.S. District Court for the District of Massachusetts hears a case regarding a federal statutory issue.
>   b. The U.S. Court of Appeals for the First Circuit hears a case regarding a federal statutory issue.
>   c. The U.S. Supreme Court hears a case regarding a federal statutory issue.
>   d. A Massachusetts trial court hears a case regarding a Massachusetts state law issue.
>   e. The Illinois Court of Appeals, an intermediate-level appellate court, hears a case regarding an Illinois state law issue.
>   f. The Massachusetts Supreme Judicial Court, the highest appellate court in Massachusetts, hears a case regarding a Massachusetts state law issue.

C. CASE BRIEFING

The word "brief" has several meanings. In this chapter, we use the term "briefing a case" to mean using your own words to make a brief written summary of a court opinion. This is in contrast with an **appellate brief**, which is a formal written argument to an appellate court, in which a lawyer argues why that court should affirm or reverse a lower court's decision.

Appellate brief
A formal written argument to an appellate court, in which a lawyer argues why that court should affirm or reverse a lower court's decision.

1. The Elements of a Court Opinion

Before we discuss briefing, we want to give you a quick overview of what you will normally find in an appellate opinion.

a. Preliminary Material and West Editorial Features

Look at the court opinion *Callow v. Thomas,* beginning on page 384. It is reprinted exactly as it appears in West's North Eastern Reporter. We have added explanatory material in the right and left margins to help you identify the various editorial features that West adds to the opinion.

First, notice that West uses its trademarked key number symbol to separate the cases. Following that are the names of the parties, the name of the court that decided the case, and the dates it was argued and decided. This, in turn, is followed by the **headnotes** and the **syllabus**. The headnotes are short summaries of each of the legal issues decided by the court, but they are not written by the court. They are written by the editors at West. The headnote title and key number (e.g., Husband and Wife, key 205(2)) are cross-references to the West Digest System, which we discuss in more detail in Chapter 14. The syllabus is a summary of the facts and the court's decision.

Below that is a listing of the judges who decided the case and the lawyers involved in the case. The actual opinion itself begins with the name of the judge who drafted the majority opinion.

Headnote
Summary of one legal point in a court opinion; written by the editors at West.

Syllabus
A summary of a court opinion that appears at the beginning of the case.

b. Facts of the Case

Next, you will usually learn about the facts of the case. Facts can be divided into two groups: substantive and procedural.

The **substantive facts** deal with what happened to the parties before the litigation began—that is, why one party is suing the other. **Procedural facts** refer to what happened in the lower courts or administrative agencies, as well as the action taken by the appellate court issuing the opinion. For example, in the trial court, did the plaintiff win after a jury verdict, or did the plaintiff lose on a motion to dismiss?

c. The Body of the Opinion

The bulk of the decision will consist of the court's analysis of the existing law and how it should be applied to the case's facts. A court decision should be analyzed at two different levels: How was the issue settled in this particular case? What general principle of law has been enunciated by the way in which the court resolved this issue? The result that it reaches in this particular case is known as the **disposition**.

The disposition[2] usually consists of **affirming** (approving) or **reversing**[2] (disapproving) the judgment of the lower court. If the lower court's decision is reversed, the appellate court either sends the case back to the lower court for review or substitutes its own judgment for that of the lower court. If the appellate court sends the case back to the lower court, it is with the understanding that the lower court must act consistently with the principles of law that the higher court laid down in its decision.

The impact of the case for future litigants is known as the **holding**. This is the new legal principle established by this court opinion. The holding is the court's answer to the issue and a guide to future courts and litigants in deciding similar cases.

Most written court opinions devote considerable space to justifying the court's holding. A decision can be unanimous, but often not all of the judges agree on the result or the reasons for reaching that result. When this occurs, a **majority opinion** represents the final decision of the court and is binding. In addition, **concurring** and **dissenting opinions** may also be written. In a concurrence, the judge agrees with the result, but not with the reasoning. A judge who writes a dissent disagrees with the majority opinion, both the result and the reasoning. A dissent is not binding and does not represent the law in that jurisdiction.

2. An Overview of Case Briefing

Briefing court opinions serves two purposes. First, and most important, it makes you read the case thoroughly. You have to go back and dig out the essentials, organize them, and state them in your own words. Second, it gives you a permanent, condensed record of each case. You can use your case briefs to refresh your memory without having to go back and reread whole opinions.

---

[2] Do not confuse reversing a decision with overruling. An appellate court reverses a decision when it concludes that a lower court failed to properly apply the law. An appellate court overrules one of its own prior decisions when it determines that the law needs to be changed.

Substantive facts
In a case brief, facts that deal with what happened to the parties before the litigation began.

Procedural facts
In a case brief, facts that relate to what happened procedurally in the lower courts or administrative agencies before the case reached the court issuing the opinion.

Disposition
The result reached in a particular case.

Affirm
A decision is affirmed when the litigants appeal the lower court decision and the higher court agrees with what the lower court has done.

Reverse
A decision is reversed when the litigants appeal the lower court decision and the higher court disagrees with the decision of a lower court.

Holding
The new legal principle established by a court opinion. In a case brief, the court's answer to the issue presented to it; the new legal principle established by a court opinion.

Majority opinion
An opinion in which a majority of the court joins.

Concurring opinion
An opinion that agrees with the majority's result, but disagrees with the reasoning.

Dissenting opinion
An opinion that disagrees with the majority's decision and reasoning.

Be warned: There are almost as many different briefing styles as there are lawyers writing briefs. Everyone develops his or her own favorite method for summarizing a court opinion. Therefore, you should always ask the person for whom you are writing the brief about his or her preferred method. Also keep in mind the purpose for which you are writing the brief. For this course, the principal reason is so that you can learn to analyze and criticize court opinions. Therefore, we will ask you to follow a very structured method, designed to teach you that process. Later, when you are working, your boss may have a very different purpose for asking you to brief cases. For example, your boss may want a factual comparison among a series of cases and so ask you to summarize (brief) only the facts of each case. The bottom line: Follow a briefing style that accomplishes your purpose.

3. Format for a Case Brief

The case briefing method we will be using in this chapter breaks the case into the following elements: (1) case citation, (2) facts—both procedural and substantive, (3) rule, (4) issue, (5) holding, (6) reasoning, and (7) criticism. After you read the opinion once, put the case citation at the top of your paper and list the next six items on the left side of the paper, leaving enough room opposite each for the appropriate information. Reread the opinion and fill in the various items.

Although you list the items in a specific order, you may find yourself filling them in out of order. That is fine. Case briefing is a circuitous process. You will often rewrite one part of your brief as your understanding of that part changes based on your work on other parts. As with any type of writing, thinking and writing are intertwined.

Recall the case of Matt Anderson with which we started the chapter. Assume that Kendall, as part of his research, found the following case. We will use it to illustrate how a case brief is created.

Jim Jones v. Sam Smith
440 Mass. App. Ct. 99, 548 N.E.2d 50
Decided June 4, 1990

The defendant appeals from a judgment for the plaintiff in the amount of $30,000. The plaintiff, Jim Jones, who is blind, was walking on the sidewalk in front of his house, located on Lily Street. He had just returned from classes he was taking at the local community college. A group of youths approached him. One of the youths, 16-year-old Sam Smith, said, "Hey, man, what a cool cane." He then knocked Jim's cane from his hand. In knocking the cane from his hand, the defendant never touched the plaintiff's body. Jim began to search for his cane. While searching, Jim fell over the curb and broke his ankle. We hereby affirm the trial court's decision.

We have long held that an intentional, offensive contact to a person's body constitutes battery. Here the 16-year-old defendant intended to knock the cane from the plaintiff's hand. While the defendant did not actually touch the plaintiff's body, the plaintiff was holding the cane at the time it was knocked away from him. Because the plaintiff was able to go about on his own only with the use of the cane, it was as though the cane were a part of his body. The cane was so closely connected to his person that touching it was tantamount to touching the plaintiff himself. We also note the increased awareness that the legislature has exhibited in recent years for the needs of the disabled.

Affirmed.

a. Case Citation

At the top of a sheet of paper, write the case citation. If this is a case that you are reading for class, you may also want to indicate its page number in your textbook. As we discussed earlier, the citation contains enough information to let the reader know (1) the name of the case, (2) where the reader can locate it, (3) the court that decided it, and (4) the year of decision. For example, this case was between Jim Jones and Sam Smith. The Massachusetts Appeals Court decided the case in 1990. If this were a real case (and not a fictional case we created to illustrate case briefing), you would be able to find it on page 99 of volume 440 of the Massachusetts Appeals Court Reports. You could also find it on page 50 of volume 548 of the North Eastern Reporter, Second Series. Therefore, you cite this case in the following manner.

Jones v. Smith, 440 Mass. App. Ct. 99, 548 N.E.2d 50 (1990).

b. Facts

Include a summary of both kinds of facts: substantive and procedural. Recall that the substantive facts deal with what happened to the parties before the litigation began; that is, why are they suing each other? These are the facts that caused the lawsuit. Be sure to state the relevant facts in your own words rather than copying them directly from the opinion. Omit any facts that you think did not form the basis of the court's decision, but be sure to include all facts that the court relied on in reaching its decision.

When giving the facts, it is always best to be as precise as possible. For example, if the case involves an eight-year-old girl, say so. Do not say that it involves simply a girl or a child. If you give specific details, you can always generalize later. If you start with a generalization, such as that the plaintiff was a child, later you may have difficulties remembering the specifics.

For the procedural facts, be sure to include what happened in the lower court or courts. For example, in the trial court, did the plaintiff or the defendant win? Did the lower court proceedings conclude after a motion or a jury verdict? You should conclude the procedural facts with a statement as to how this court responded by way of disposition; that is, did it reverse, reverse and remand, or affirm the lower court's decision? You will usually find the court's disposition near the end of the opinion, stated in a few words, such as "reversed" or "vacated and remanded."

Some legal writers prefer to put the court's disposition in a separate section rather than including it with the other procedural facts. If you include the disposition with the procedural facts, however, then the reader can see the "whole story" right at the beginning of the brief. Study the following example of a facts section.

> Facts: The plaintiff, Jim Jones, is blind. A group of youths approached him. One of the youths, 16-year-old Sam Smith, knocked Jim's cane from his hand. In knocking the cane from the plaintiff's hand, the defendant never touched the plaintiff's body. In searching for his cane, Jim fell, breaking his ankle. Judgment for plaintiff; affirmed.

First are the substantive facts: who did what to whom. Notice how specific facts that could have changed the outcome of the case are included: Jim is blind; Sam knocked the cane from Jim's hand. However, facts that would not influence the outcome, such as the name of the street down which Jim was walking, are not included.

The last sentence gives the procedural facts. "Judgment for plaintiff" means that the plaintiff won at the trial court level. "Affirmed" means that this court, the court that issued the opinion you are reading, agreed with that result. The amount of the trial court award is not included because it was not an issue in this case. If the parties were disagreeing about the amount of the award, as opposed to whether there should have been an award at all, then it would be appropriate to include it.

c. Rule

Rule
In a case brief, the general legal principle in existence before the case began.

The **rule** is a general legal principle in existence *before* the case began. The court might base it either on prior court decisions or on a statute.

First, explicitly state the area of law, such as burglary. Then give a precise definition of the law in that area: For example, burglary occurs when there is a breaking and entering of the dwelling of another at nighttime with the intention of committing a felony therein. You do not always need to give the complete definition of a rule. For example, if the only issue in the case is whether breaking into a house at 5 P.M. qualifies as nighttime, you would state only the relevant part of the rule: Burglary occurs when there is a breaking and entering at nighttime.

Our sample brief would contain the following statement of the rule.

> Rule: A battery occurs when there is an intentional, offensive contact to a person's body.

Notice how the general area of law, battery, is given first. We will call that the "label." The label is followed by a definition of what constitutes battery.

d. Issue

Phrase this as a "whether" question. The **issue** has two components: first, the rule of law that the court used to resolve the current dispute (section c above) and, second, the specific facts of the case to which the rule of law is being applied (section b above). This is the hardest part of briefing a case. In one sentence you want to let your reader know exactly why the parties are in court. Include facts that make it clear why the issue is an issue; that is, let the reader see what the fight is all about. Modeling your issue after the following formula will assist you in making sure that you have included both the rule and the specific facts in your issue statement:

Whether the defendant is [guilty of or liable for]
(name the general area of law involved—e.g., battery or murder),
which requires that
(give the specific part of the rule at issue—e.g., intended contact or willful intent)
when
(give the specific facts—e.g., the defendant accidentally bumped into the plaintiff).

Keep in mind that this is just a model. There are times when you will need to vary the pattern. Learning to state the issue precisely is a skill you will be working on throughout your legal career; therefore, do not feel discouraged if it seems difficult now.

If a court opinion deals with more than one issue, brief each one separately.

> Issue: Whether the defendant is liable for battery, which requires that there be an intentional, offensive contact to a person's body, when the 16-year-old defendant did not touch the blind plaintiff but did knock his cane from his hand.

Notice how the issue contains both the rule and the specific facts involved in the case. Given the rule of law in existence prior to these parties going to court and given the specific facts of the case, what problem must the court resolve? That is the issue.

Never state your issue as follows: whether or not the trial court erred. Although technically that would be correct, it is not very helpful, as it would be true of all cases; that is, no one would have appealed unless there was an allegation that the court made an error. Remember to include the specific rule of law and the facts involved so that your reader, hearing only your statement of the issue, will know exactly why the litigants were in court.

Finally, be sure to state the issue in an unbiased manner. Do not slant the issue by giving conclusions. Stick to the facts. For example, the following issue is too biased.

Issue
In a case brief, the rule of law applied to the case's specific facts.

> **Example of a biased statement of the issue:**
>   Whether the defendant was negligent, which requires failing to act as a reasonable person, when he got drunk, sped down the highway, and crashed into the plaintiff's car.

To keep it unbiased, you must state the facts underlying your conclusions. And you must include facts that show both sides of the issue.

> **Example of an unbiased statement of the issue:**
>   Whether the defendant was negligent, which requires failing to act as a reasonable person, when he drank one beer, drove 55 mph in a 50-mph zone, and hit the plaintiff's car as he ran a red light.

e. Holding

As stated previously, the holding is the court's answer to the issue. It will be the new version of the rule, a rule that future courts will look to for assistance in deciding similar cases.

If you have given a complete issue statement, technically the holding could be a simple yes or no answer. It is always best, however, to give the holding as a complete sentence. Therefore, include the same elements as you did for the issue statement, except state them as a positive sentence. That is, make sure the holding contains both the rule of law the court was relying on to resolve the dispute and the specific facts of the case.

One of the most difficult aspects of developing the holding is determining how narrow or broad it should be. A **narrow holding** contains many of the case's specific facts, thereby limiting its future applicability to a narrow range of cases. A **broad holding** states the facts in very general terms so that the holding will apply to a wider range of cases. See Figure 13-4.

To be useful, a holding should be broad enough to help courts resolve similar cases. But a holding should not be so broad that it stands for no more than a general legal principle. Learning how to state a holding either very narrowly, by including very specific facts, or very broadly, by stating the facts as generalizations only, is a skill you will acquire over time. For now, state your holdings

Narrow holding
A statement of the court's decision that contains many of the case's specific facts, thereby limiting its future applicability to a narrow range of cases.

Broad holding
A statement of the court's decision in which the facts are either omitted or given in very general terms so that it will apply to a wider range of cases.

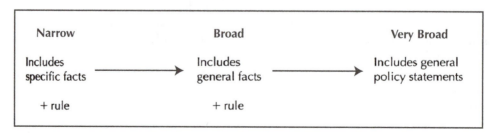

Figure 13-4   Possible Holdings for a Case

narrowly. As with the facts portion of the brief you will find it easier to amend a narrow holding to make it broader than you will to amend a broad holding to make it narrower. However, even with a narrow holding, include only those facts that you think truly affected the court's decision.

> Holding: Yes, the defendant should be liable for battery, which requires that there be an intentional, offensive contact to a person's body, when the 16-year-old defendant did not touch the blind plaintiff but did knock his cane from his hand. (Narrow)
>
> Yes, the defendant should be liable for battery, which requires that there be an intentional, offensive contact to a person's body, when something closely connected to the plaintiff's body was touched. (Broad)
>
> A battery occurs whenever a person's sense of bodily integrity is threatened. (Probably too broad; really a policy statement)

Also be sure to include any possible limitations to the holding. If the court specifically states that its decision covers only a certain set of circumstances, let your reader know that. For example, in a case dealing with a social host's liability for serving alcohol to a minor, a court might relieve the social host of any responsibility but limit its holding to situations where alcohol is not being served for a profit.

Finally, note that the court's procedural answer—reversed, remanded, affirmed, and so on—can never be the holding. That is the disposition. The holding is the statement of the new rule that results from the court's decision.

f. Reasoning

This is an explanation of *why* the court ruled as it did, stated in your own words. The court's reasoning gives you your best clue as to how the court may act in the future in a different but similar situation.

Pinpoint as far as possible the explicit and implicit reasons that the court gave to justify its holding. But do not quote the court's exact language unless the precise phrasing is critical. It will be easier for the reader to understand your summary if it is primarily in your own words.

> Reasoning: While the defendant did not touch the plaintiff's body, the cane was so closely connected to his person that touching it was tantamount to touching the plaintiff himself. (In dicta the court noted the increased awareness in recent years of the needs of persons with disabilities.)

In this section, you may want to note reasoning that is really dictum. **Dictum** (the plural is *dicta*) is language unnecessary to the decision of the case. For example, if the court talks about how it might decide a future case based on different facts, that is dictum. Courts have power to decide only the precise case

Dictum A statement in a judicial opinion that is not necessary for the decision of the case.

with which they are faced. Human nature being what it is, however, judges often cannot resist discussing issues that were not really presented to them. While that part of the opinion will have no effect on the litigants, it could give you a very good clue as to how the court might decide a different case in the future. Dicta, therefore, are often worth noting in your brief.

g. Criticism

PRACTICE TIP

Do not overlook the power of a dissent. It may help you predict the path that the court may take in the next case.

Take a few minutes to think critically about the case. Do you agree with the result? Even if you agree with the result, do you think the court gave the best or only reasons for reaching that result? If the court included a limitation in the holding, what problems do you think that will cause for future litigants?

If there were concurring or dissenting opinions, include a discussion of their reasoning. Remember that a concurring decision is one in which the judge agrees with the majority's result but not with the reasoning. A dissenting opinion is one in which the judge disagrees with both the majority's result and its reasoning. While only the majority opinion represents the court's view, what individual concurring and dissenting judges have to say can influence later courts.

The reason for including a criticism section is to accustom you to thinking critically about court decisions. There will be times when an opinion will harm your client's case, and you will need to argue either that the decision was incorrectly decided or that the reasoning does not apply to your client's case. Practice in thinking critically about court decisions now will prepare you to assist your clients later.

> Criticism: The court left open the question of what constitutes an object so closely connected to a person's body as to be considered a part of it. Because the case involved a blind person, it is unclear whether the court meant to limit future cases to objects used by persons with disabilities, such as canes, hearing aids, and the like, or whether the court meant to include anything closely connected to a person's body, such as clothing.

Do not be discouraged if you find the criticism section one of the most difficult parts of the brief to write. It is the court's job to convince you that it has reached the right result for the right reasons. Therefore, your first reaction may be to simply agree with everything it says. Resist that inclination. Remember that the case would not have been appealed unless someone thought there were two sides to the issue.

Once put together, the entire brief should look similar to the sample brief in Exhibit 13-1. You can find a summary of a case briefing in Exhibit 13-2.

4. Seven Hints for Better Brief Writing

Here are seven hints to help you with your brief writing.

a. Read the Case First, and Then Brief

Do not try to brief the case as you read it for the first time. Read it through, underlining if you wish and making notes in the margins, before you start your brief. When you are reading more than one case on a particular topic, it may save time to first read all of the cases and then begin briefing.

Exhibit 13-1   Sample Brief

Jones v. Smith, 440 Mass. 99, 548 N.E.2d 50 (1990).

Facts: The plaintiff, Jim Jones, is blind. A group of youths approached him. One of the youths, sixteen-year-old Sam Smith, knocked Jim's cane from his hand. In knocking the cane from the plaintiff's hand the defendant never touched the plaintiff's body. In searching for his cane, Jim fell, breaking his ankle. Judgment for plaintiff; affirmed.

Rule: A battery occurs when there is an intentional, offensive contact to a person's body.

Issue: Whether the defendant is liable for battery, which requires that there be an intentional, offensive contact to a person's body, when the sixteen-year-old defendant did not touch the blind plaintiff but did knock his cane from his hand.

Holding: Yes, the defendant should be liable for battery, which requires that there be an intentional, offensive contact to a person's body, when the sixteen-year-old defendant did not touch the blind plaintiff but did knock his cane from his hand.

Reasoning: While the defendant did not touch the plaintiff's body, the cane was so closely connected to his person that touching it was tantamount to touching the plaintiff himself. (In dicta the court noted the increased awareness in recent years of the needs of persons with disabilities.)

Criticism: The court left open the question of what constitutes an object so closely connected to a person's body as to be considered a part of it. Because the case involved a blind person, it is unclear whether the court meant to limit future cases to objects used by persons with disabilities, such as canes, hearing aids, and the like, or whether the court meant to include anything closely connected to a person's body, such as clothing.

---

b. Develop a Workable Style

Develop a briefing style that works best for you. As mentioned above, there is no right or wrong method. However, if your brief is to serve its intended purpose, you must write it in such a way that you can return to it later and easily find the information for which you are looking.

c. Write Based on the Needs of Your Reader

If you are using the brief just as a reference for yourself, abbreviate commonly used terms. For example, use π or P. for plaintiff and Δ or D. for defendant. You may also want to write in phrases rather than complete sentences. If you are writing the brief for another person, however, whether it is your instructor now or your boss later, make sure to ask whether that person wants you to use abbreviations and phrases or prefers that you use complete words and sentences.

Citation goes here

Facts: Provide both the substantive and the procedural facts, including what this court decided.

Rule: This is the rule *before* this case was decided. Include both the label and the definition.

Issue: This is the rule applied to the facts. You may want to use the following format:

Whether the defendant is [guilty of or liable for]
   (name the general area of law involved—for example, battery or murder),
which requires that
   (give the specific part of the rule that is creating the problem)
when
   (give the specific facts; this is not the place for generalizations).

Holding: In a complete sentence, give the court's answer to the issue. If the court puts any limits on its holding, include those limitations.

Reasoning: Include all the major reasons the court gives in support of its decision.

Criticism: Explain what you think is wrong with either the court's holding or its reasoning. If there is a concurrence or dissent, include that reasoning here as well.

Exhibit 13-2   Summary of Case Briefing

d. Cross-reference

Develop a cross-reference system that will allow you to find the court's full discussion of the points you summarized in your brief. For example, you could place numbers in the margin of the case to correspond to the points you discuss in your brief.

e. Paraphrase

Write the brief in your own words. A brief should not be a long series of quotations, so do not copy large parts of the opinion. A brief is your summary of the case, not merely a listing of quotations from it.

f. Use a Dictionary

Make sure you understand every unfamiliar legal term. Initially, you will find the courts using many unfamiliar terms. Do not hesitate to turn to a legal dictionary for help.

g. Use but Do Not Be Misled by the Court's Choice of Terminology

While courts will rarely explicitly label the parts of their opinion using the terms "issue," "holding," "reasoning," and so on, they often use language that provides helpful clues. For example, while not saying "The rule is . . .," they might say something like "The law in this area has long been . . ." Do not be surprised if the court appears to be "mislabeling" various parts of the case. For example, a court might call something its holding when it is really reasoning.

Legal Reasoning Exercise

2. Practice your brief writing skills by briefing the following case.

People of the State of Illinois v. Gary Blair and Jimmy Duncil
52 Ill. 2d 371, 288 N.E.2d 443 (1972)

UNDERWOOD, Chief Justice.

In February 1969, defendant Gary Blair was convicted in superior court of burglary for actions that took place in a carwash. He was sentenced to imprisonment for two to four years. The defendant appealed his conviction, and the intermediate appellate court vacated the judgment of conviction, finding that the carwash structure here involved was not a building as that word is used in the burglary statute. We granted leave to appeal. The statute in part provides:

> A person commits burglary when without authority he knowingly breaks into and enters a building or house trailer with intent to commit a felony or theft therein.

The carwash in question consists of wash bays or stalls completely open at each end (there are no doors), a roof, concrete side walls and floor; attached to the side walls are the washing apparatus and a coin box. The defendant allegedly drove into one of the stalls, washed his car, and then forced open the coin box, took the coins, and fled.

The burglary statute contains no definition of the word "building," and, in the absence of a statutory definition indicating a different legislative intention, the courts will assume that statutory words have their ordinary and popularly understood meanings. In the past, this court has defined a building to be any structure designed for the habitation of men or animals or for the shelter of property. The carwash comes within this definition. It is a structure designed for the shelter and protection of the carwash equipment and the fact that it is not completely enclosed does not necessitate a contrary conclusion.

The judgment of the appellate court is reversed, and the trial court's judgment of conviction for burglary is affirmed.

D. BRIEFING THE VARIOUS TYPES OF COURT OPINIONS

Now that you have experience with the purpose of case briefing, it is time to try your hand with real court opinions. Recall that court opinions generally fall in one of four categories:

1. those interpreting and applying enacted law, such as statutes;
2. those deciding the constitutionality of a law;
3. those applying established common-law principles; and
4. those creating new common-law principles.

The first type of opinion, which interprets and applies enacted law, consumes a great deal of the courts' time. As we said in Chapter 12, statutes, administrative regulations, and constitutional provisions often contain ambiguous words and phrases. When interpreting enacted law and attempting to determine legislative intent, the courts rely on the various methods we have discussed: looking at the plain meaning, relying on the canons of construction, examining other parts of the statute, and searching for external evidence, such as legislative history and prior court decisions. Under the doctrine of stare decisis, if previous courts have already interpreted the same or similar language, a court will generally try to reach a decision that is consistent with those earlier interpretations.

Judicial review
The court's power to review statutes to decide whether they conform to the Constitution.

A second type of case involves challenges to the constitutionality of a law. Under the power of **judicial review,** the courts are responsible for ensuring that all laws comport with the Constitution's requirements. In this type of decision, the court's focus is on the intent of the Constitution's framers and the purpose that the constitutional provision was meant to fulfill. Then the court determines whether the law in question is consistent with the Constitution's intended purpose.

The third and fourth types of cases involve the common law rather than enacted law. Despite the tremendous growth in statutory law, there are times when no statute covers a litigant's situation. Then the courts rely on the common law, or court-made law. Usually, the court will be faced with a group of prior cases and will use them to form an opinion on the current case. Those cases will be seen as either mandatory or persuasive authority.

1. Briefing Cases Involving Statutes

In this section, we will look at two court opinions that illustrate the first two types of cases that courts face: interpreting statutes and ruling on their constitutionality. As you read the two cases, notice the different approaches that the courts take. Remember that when interpreting a statute, the court's only role is to try to divine what the legislature meant when it passed the statute. In the case of questioning the constitutionality of a statute, however, the question is no longer what the words mean, but rather whether the legislature had the power to enact the statute.

a. Interpreting a Statute

Recall the situation from a legal reasoning question in Chapter 12, in which you were asked to apply a federal statute to a situation where a client had been charged with illegally transporting an airplane across state lines. This was the very situation that the Supreme Court had to face in the following case, *McBoyle v. United States.* We have reprinted the *McBoyle* opinion exactly as it appears in the official United States Reports in Exhibit 13-3. The U.S. government pays for the printing and publishing of all U.S. Supreme Court decisions in a series of books called the United States Reports. The opinions are printed and published in chronological order as they are decided. In the margins, we have added labels to describe the different parts of a typical court opinion.

Read and then brief *McBoyle v. United States,* paying special attention to the methods of statutory analysis that the Court relied on in reaching its decision. There is a sample brief following the opinion (see Exhibit 13-4). Wait to look at the sample until after you have briefed the opinion yourself. That way, you will have a better idea as to whether you are on the right track with your case briefing. The sample *McBoyle* brief in the example is just that—a sample. Do not worry if yours does not match the sample exactly. If yours is significantly different, however, reread the prior section on the functions of each part of the brief.

The case name; McBoyle was the petitioner and the U.S. government was the respondent.

McBOYLE v. UNITED STATES.   25

Page in volume 283 of the United States Report where the case begins.

15   Opinion of the Court.

U. S. 192; *Jacob Ruppert* v. *Caffey,* 251 U. S. 264; *Lambert* v. *Yellowley,* 272 U. S. 581.   *Affirmed.*

End of a different decision.

McBOYLE v. UNITED STATES.

This lets you know the court is hearing a case from the Tenth Circuit.

CERTIORARI TO THE CIRCUIT COURT OF APPEALS FOR THE TENTH CIRCUIT.

Docket number and dates the case was argued and decided.

No. 552.   Argued February 26, 27, 1931.—Decided March 9, 1931.

The National Motor Vehicle Theft Act, U. S. C., Title 18, § 408, which punishes whoever transports, or causes to be transported, in interstate or foreign commerce a motor vehicle knowing it to have been stolen, and which defines "motor vehicle" as including "an automobile, automobile truck, automobile wagon, motor cycle, or any other self-propelled vehicle not designed for running on rails," does not apply to aircraft.   P. 26.

43 F. (2d) 273, reversed.

Known as the syllabus, this is a summary of the court's opinion.

Where it is reported that cert, was granted.*

CERTIORARI, 282 U. S. 835, to review a judgment affirming a conviction under the Motor Vehicle Theft Act.

Mr. Harry F. Brown for petitioner.

Petitioner's attorney.

Mr. Claude R. Branch, Special Assistant to the Attorney General, with whom *Solicitor General Thacher, Assistant Attorney General Dodds* and Messrs. *Harry S. Ridgely* and *W. Marvin Smith* were on the brief, for the United States.

Responder's attorneys.

MR. JUSTICE HOLMES delivered the opinion of the Court.

This is where the opinion begins.

The petitioner was convicted of transporting from Ottawa, Illinois, to Guymon, Oklahoma, an airplane that he knew to have been stolen, and was sentenced to serve three years' imprisonment and to pay a fine of $2,000. The judgment was affirmed by the Circuit Court of Appeals for the Tenth Circuit.   43 F. (2d) 273.   A writ of certiorari was granted by this Court on the question whether the National Motor Vehicle Theft Act applies to aircraft.

This is where the Tenth Circuit court's decision is reported.

*This one sentence contains a lot of information. Combined with what you already know about the structure of the federal court system, it gives you the complete procedural history of the case. Start at the end of the sentence and work your way forward. First, we read that McBoyle was convicted. As he was tried in the federal system, his trial and conviction would have occurred in a federal district court. Next the conviction was affirmed. This would have occurred in a court of appeals. In fact, right under the case name we see that the Tenth Circuit court of appeals decided this case. Finally, the U.S. Supreme Court agreed to hear the case by granting certiorari.

Exhibit 13-3   *McBoyle v. United States*   (continues)

26   OCTOBER TERM, 1930.

Opinion of the Court.   283 U.S.

Act of October 29, 1919, c. 89; 41 Stat. 324; U. S. Code, Title 18, § 408.   That Act provides: "Sec. 2. That when used in this Act: (a) The term 'motor vehicle' shall include an automobile, automobile truck, automobile wagon, motor cycle, or any other self-propelled vehicle not designed for running on rails; . . . Sec. 3.   That whoever shall transport or cause to be transported in interstate or foreign commerce a motor vehicle, knowing the same to have been stolen, shall be punished by a fine of not more than $5,000, or by imprisonment of not more than five years, or both."

Section 2 defines the motor vehicles of which the transportation in interstate commerce is punished in § 3. The question is the meaning of the word 'vehicle' in the phrase "any other self-propelled vehicle not designed for running on rails."   No doubt etymologically it is possible to use the word to signify a conveyance working on land, water or air, and sometimes legislation extends the use in that direction, e. g., land and air, water being separately provided for, in the Tariff Act, September 22, 1922, c. 356, § 401 (b), 42 Stat. 858, 948.   But in everyday speech 'vehicle' calls up the picture of a thing moving on land.   Thus in Rev. Stats. § 4, intended, the Government suggests, rather to enlarge than to restrict the definition, vehicle includes every contrivance capable of being used "as a means of transportation on land."   And this is repeated, expressly excluding aircraft, in the Tariff Act, June 17, 1930, c. 997, § 401 (b); 46 Stat. 590, 708. So here, the phrase under discussion calls up the popular picture.   For after including automobile truck, automobile wagon and motor cycle, the words "any other self-propelled vehicle not designed for running on rails" still indicate that a vehicle in the popular sense, that is a vehicle running on land, is the theme.   It is a vehicle that runs, not something, not commonly called a vehicle, that flies.   Airplanes were well known in 1919, when this statute was passed; but it is admitted that they were not mentioned in the reports or in the debates in Congress.

Exhibit 13-3   *McBoyle v. United States*

(continues)

CARBICE CORP. *v.* AM. PATENTS CORP.   27

25   Syllabus.

It is impossible to read words that so carefully enumerate the different forms of motor vehicles and have no reference of any kind to aircraft, as including airplanes under a term that usage more and more precisely confines to a different class. The counsel for the petitioner have shown that the phraseology of the statute as to motor vehicles follows that of earlier statutes of Connecticut, Delaware, Ohio, Michigan and Missouri, not to mention the late Regulations of Traffic for the District of Columbia, Title 6, c. 9, § 242, none of which can be supposed to leave the earth.

Although it is not likely that a criminal will carefully consider the text of the law before he murders or steals, it is reasonable that a fair warning should be given to the world in language that the common world will understand, of what the law intends to do if a certain line is passed. To make the warning fair, so far as possible the line should be clear. When a rule of conduct is laid down in words that evoke in the common mind only the picture of vehicles moving on land, the statute should not be extended to aircraft, simply because it may seem to us that a similar policy applies, or upon the speculation that, if the legislature had thought of it, very likely broader words would have been used. *United States* v. *Thind*, 261 U. S. 204, 209.

Judgment reversed.

The court's decision

CARBICE CORPORATION OF AMERICA *v.* AMERICAN PATENTS DEVELOPMENT CORPORATION ET AL.

CERTIORARI TO THE CIRCUIT COURT OF APPEALS FOR THE SECOND CIRCUIT.

No. 54. Argued January 16, 19, 1931.—Decided March 9, 1931.

1. A patentee can not lawfully exact, as the condition of a license, that unpatented materials used in connection with the invention shall be purchased only from himself. P. 31.

The beginning of the next case

Exhibit 13-3 *McBoyle v. United States (concluded)*

Case Discussion Questions

1. Do you agree with the Court's reasoning and holding in *McBoyle*? Why or why not?

2. Did you notice the similarities between the Court's approach to analyzing a statute and those discussed in Chapter 12? List the methods of statutory interpretation that the *McBoyle* Court used.

3. Why would each of the following not be a correct issue for *McBoyle*?
   a. whether the defendant knew the airplane was stolen
   b. whether the defendant stole the airplane
   c. whether the defendant was guilty
   d. whether the trial court erred

Now that you have read *McBoyle v. United States,* take a close look at how the procedural facts are given in the sample brief shown in Exhibit 13-4. Ask your instructor about his or her preferred method for including the procedural facts. What is given here is a shorthand way of saying that the defendant was convicted. His conviction was affirmed by the U.S. Court of Appeals for the Tenth Circuit. The Supreme Court granted certiorari and then reversed the decision of the court of appeals. For someone versed in the structure of the court system, the method used in the sample brief is quick and to the point. However, when you first start briefing, you may feel more comfortable avoiding abbreviations and writing out each of the procedural steps.

Also notice that the entire procedural story is given, including the final disposition by the U.S. Supreme Court—that is, that it reversed the lower appellate court.

In the reasoning section, notice the use of the verbs "saw," "said," and "stated." Never use language that suggests that the court was emotional about the case. For example, do not say the court "felt" something was so. Say the court "thought," "explained," "discussed," and the like.

The role of the courts in interpreting ambiguous language is to strive to find the meaning that the legislature intended. In this, they are engaged in something of a guessing game, and if they guess wrong, the legislature has the power to amend the statute. For example, sometime after the Supreme Court decided *McBoyle,* the legislature amended the statute to include airplanes within the definition of motor vehicles.

b. Ruling on a Statute's Constitutionality

Most cases decided by state courts cannot be appealed to the U.S. Supreme Court. The major exception is if a federal law is involved. In the following case, because the constitutionality of the state statute was in doubt, the U.S. Supreme Court had jurisdiction to hear it. As you read the Supreme Court's decision in *Texas v. Johnson,* decide whether you agree with the majority, the concurrence, or the dissent.

McBoyle v. United States, 283 U.S. 25 (1931)

Facts: The defendant transported across state lines an airplane that he knew was stolen. He was convicted; aff'd; cert. granted; rev'd.

Rule: National Motor Vehicle Theft Act, Section 3
Whoever transports in interstate commerce a motor vehicle, knowing it to be stolen, shall be punished.

Section 2
A motor vehicle shall include "any other self-propelled vehicle not designed for running on rails."

Issue: Whether the defendant violated the National Motor Vehicle Theft Act, which requires that the defendant transport across state lines a stolen motor vehicle, defined as "any other self-propelled vehicle not designed for running on rails," when he transported a stolen plane across state lines.

Holding: No, the defendant did not violate the National Motor Vehicle Theft Act, which requires that the defendant transport across state lines a stolen motor vehicle, defined as "any other self-propelled vehicle not designed for running on rails," when he flew a stolen plane across state lines.

Reasoning: The Court based its decision on what it saw as the plain meaning of the statute. In support of this view, the Court also looked to other statutes and to other portions of this statute. The legislative history also favored this interpretation, as airplanes were in existence when the statute was enacted and yet no mention was made of them. Also, because this is a criminal statute, the Court said that it should be construed narrowly so as to give any potential defendant fair warning of what was not allowed. Finally, the Court showed great deference to the legislature. The Court stated that it would not extend the statute simply because it might seem to the justices that "a similar policy applies, or upon the speculation that, if the legislature had thought of it, very likely broader words would have been used" (p. 27).

Criticism: The plain meaning approach could also be used to argue that the statute uses the word "including" but does not say "excluding." Therefore, presumably it would cover other "self-propelled vehicles," such as airplanes. Also, it does not stand to reason that the defendant would not have suspected that it was a crime to transport a stolen airplane across state lines.

Exhibit 13-4 Sample Brief

Because a dissent has no effect in the present case, you might wonder why judges bother writing dissents. There are at least three reasons to do so. First, it keeps the majority honest. Because a dissent is being written, the justices in the majority know that what they write can be contradicted. Second, a dissent limits the precedential effect of the opinion. An opinion with a strong dissent does not carry the same weight with future courts as does a unanimous opinion. Finally, there is always the hope that someday a later court will see the wisdom of the dissent and decide to follow that path. Although that hope is not always realized, it can be the motivating force behind continued dissents on such issues as capital punishment. One Supreme Court justice dissented in every capital punishment case, arguing that it always represented cruel and unusual punishment. To date, the Court has not accepted that argument.

We have omitted the footnotes and most of the citations to the cases the Court cites. Also we have greatly condensed the opinion for you. The original was over 30 pages long. The numbers in brackets, such as [*399], refer to the page numbers in the United States Reports.

Texas v. Johnson
491 U.S. 397 (1989)

[*399] Justice BRENNAN delivered the opinion of the Court.

After publicly burning an American flag as a means of political protest, Gregory Lee Johnson was convicted of desecrating a flag in violation of Texas law. This case presents the question whether his conviction is consistent with the First Amendment. We hold that it is not.

I

While the Republican National Convention was taking place in Dallas in 1984, respondent Johnson participated in a political demonstration dubbed the "Republican War Chest Tour." . . . [T]he purpose of this event was to protest the policies of the Reagan administration and of certain Dallas-based corporations. . . .

The demonstration ended in front of Dallas City Hall, where Johnson unfurled the American flag, doused it with kerosene, and set it on fire. While the flag burned, the protestors chanted: "America, the red, white, and blue, we spit on you." . . . [*400] Of the approximately 100 demonstrators, Johnson alone was charged with a crime. The only criminal offense with which he was charged was the desecration of a venerated object in violation of Tex. Penal Code

Ann. §42.09(a)(3) (1989). After a trial, he was convicted, sentenced to one year in prison, and fined $2,000. The Court of Appeals for the Fifth District of Texas at Dallas affirmed Johnson's conviction, 706 S.W.2d 120 (1986), but the Texas Court of Criminal Appeals reversed, 755 S.W.2d 92 (1988), holding that the State could not, consistent with the First Amendment, punish Johnson for burning the flag in these circumstances. . . .

We granted certiorari, 488 U.S. 907 (1988), and now affirm.

II . . .

[*404] The First Amendment literally forbids the abridgment only of "speech," but we have long recognized that its protection does not end at the spoken or written word. While we have rejected "the view that an apparently limitless variety of conduct can be labeled 'speech' whenever the person engaging in the conduct intends thereby to express an idea," United States v. O'Brien, supra, at 376, we have acknowledged that conduct may be "sufficiently imbued with elements of communication to fall within the scope of the First and Fourteenth Amendments," [Spence v. Washington, 418 U.S. 405, 409 (1974) (reversing the conviction of a college student who

displayed the flag with a peace symbol affixed to it by removable black tape)]. . . .

The State of Texas conceded for purposes of its oral argument in this case that Johnson's conduct was expressive conduct, . . . and this concession seems to us as [*406] prudent. . . . Johnson burned an American flag as part—indeed, as the culmination—of a political demonstration that coincided with the convening of the Republican Party and its renomination of Ronald Reagan for President. The expressive, overtly political nature of this conduct was both intentional and overwhelmingly apparent. At his trial, Johnson explained his reasons for burning the flag as follows: "The American Flag was burned as Ronald Reagan was being renominated as President. And a more powerful statement of symbolic speech, whether you agree with it or not, couldn't have been made at that time. It's quite a just position [juxtaposition]. We had new patriotism and no patriotism." 5 Record 656. In these circumstances, Johnson's burning of the flag was conduct "sufficiently imbued with elements of communication," Spence, 418 U.S., at 409, to implicate the First Amendment.

III . . .

The State offers two separate interests to justify this conviction: preventing breaches of the peace and preserving the flag as a symbol of nationhood and national unity. We hold that the first interest is not implicated on this record and that the second is related to the suppression of expression.

A

Texas claims that its interest in preventing breaches of the peace justifies Johnson's conviction for flag desecration. [*408] However, no disturbance of the peace actually occurred or threatened to occur because of Johnson's burning of the flag. . . .

The State's position, therefore, amounts to a claim that an audience that takes serious offense at particular expression is necessarily likely to disturb the peace and that the expression may be prohibited on this basis. Our precedents do not countenance such a presumption. On the contrary, they recognize that a principal "function of free speech under our system of government is to invite dispute. It may indeed best serve its high purpose when it induces a condition of unrest, creates dissatisfaction with conditions as they are, or [*409] even stirs people to anger." . . .

Nor does Johnson's expressive conduct fall within that small class of "fighting words" that are "likely to provoke the average person to retaliation, and thereby cause a breach of the peace." Chaplinsky v. New Hampshire, 315 U.S. 568, 574 (1942). No reasonable onlooker would have regarded Johnson's generalized expression of dissatisfaction with the policies of the Federal Government as a direct personal insult or an invitation to exchange fisticuffs. . . .

[*410] We thus conclude that the State's interest in maintaining order is not implicated on these facts. The State need not worry that our holding will disable it from preserving the peace. We do not suggest that the First Amendment forbids a State to prevent "imminent lawless action." Brandenburg, supra, at 447. And, in fact, Texas already has a statute specifically prohibiting breaches of the peace, Tex. Penal Code Ann. §42.01 (1989), which tends to confirm that Texas need not punish this flag desecration in order to keep the peace. See Boos v. Barry, 485 U.S., at 327-329.

B

[T]he State's claim is that it has an interest in preserving the flag as a symbol of nationhood and national unity, a symbol with a determinate range of meanings. Brief for Petitioner 20-24. According to Texas, if one physically treats the flag in a way that would tend to cast doubt on either the idea that nationhood and national unity are the flag's referents or that national unity actually exists, the message conveyed thereby is a harmful one and therefore may be prohibited. . . .

If there is a bedrock principle underlying the First Amendment, it is that the government may not prohibit the expression of an idea simply because society finds the idea itself offensive or disagreeable. . . .

To conclude that the government may permit designated symbols to be used to communicate only a limited set of messages would be to enter territory having no discernible or defensible boundaries. Could the government, on this theory, prohibit the burning of state flags? Of copies of the Presidential seal? Of the Constitution? In evaluating these choices under the First Amendment, how would we decide which symbols were sufficiently special to warrant this unique status? To do so, we would be forced to consult our own political preferences, and impose them on the citizenry, in the very way that the First Amendment forbids us to do. See Carey v. Brown, 447 U.S., at 466-467. . . .

We are fortified in today's conclusion by our conviction that forbidding criminal punishment for conduct such as Johnson's will not endanger the special role played by our flag or the feelings it inspires. To paraphrase Justice Holmes, we submit that nobody can suppose that this one gesture of an unknown [*419] man will change our Nation's attitude towards its flag. See Abrams v. United States, 250 U.S. 616, 628 (1919) (Holmes, J., dissenting). . . .

We are tempted to say, in fact, that the flag's deservedly cherished place in our community will be strengthened, not weakened, by our holding today. Our decision is a reaffirmation of the principles of freedom and inclusiveness that the flag best reflects, and of the conviction that our toleration of criticism such as Johnson's is a sign and source of our strength. Indeed, one of the proudest images of our flag, the one immortalized in our own national anthem, is of the bombardment it survived at Fort McHenry. It is the Nation's resilience, not its rigidity, that Texas sees reflected in the flag—and it is that resilience that we reassert today.

The way to preserve the flag's special role is not to punish those who feel differently about these matters. It is to persuade them that they are wrong. . . . And, precisely because it is our flag that is involved, one's response to the flag [*420] burner may exploit the uniquely persuasive power of the flag itself. We can imagine no more appropriate response to burning a flag than waving one's own, no better way to counter a flag burner's message than by saluting the flag that burns, no surer means of preserving the dignity even of the flag that burned than by—as one witness here did—according its remains a respectful burial. We do not consecrate the flag by punishing its desecration, for in doing so we dilute the freedom that this cherished emblem represents.

V

Johnson was convicted for engaging in expressive conduct. The State's interest in preventing breaches of the peace does not support his conviction because Johnson's conduct did not threaten to disturb the peace. Nor does the State's interest in preserving the flag as a symbol of nationhood and national unity justify his criminal conviction for engaging in political expression. The judgment of the Texas Court of Criminal Appeals is therefore

Affirmed.

Justice KENNEDY, concurring.

I write not to qualify the words Justice Brennan chooses so well, for he says with power all that is necessary to explain our ruling. I join his opinion without reservation, but with a keen sense that this case, like others before us from time to time, exacts its personal toll. This prompts me to add to our pages these few remarks.

The case before us illustrates better than most that the judicial power is often difficult in its exercise. We cannot here ask another Branch to share responsibility, as when the argument is made that a statute is flawed or incomplete. For we are presented with a clear and simple statute to be judged against a pure command of the

Constitution. The outcome can be laid at no door but ours.

The hard fact is that sometimes we must make decisions we do not like. We make them because they are right, right [*421] in the sense that the law and the Constitution, as we see them, compel the result. And so great is our commitment to the process that, except in the rare case, we do not pause to express distaste for the result, perhaps for fear of undermining a valued principle that dictates the decision. This is one of those rare cases. . . . Though symbols often are what we ourselves make of them, the flag is constant in expressing beliefs Americans share, beliefs in law and peace and that freedom which sustains the human spirit. The case here today forces recognition of the costs to which those beliefs commit us. It is poignant but fundamental that the flag protects those who hold it in contempt.

For all the record shows, this respondent was not a philosopher and perhaps did not even possess the ability to comprehend how repellent his statements must be to the Republic itself. But whether or not he could appreciate the enormity of the offense he gave, the fact remains that his acts were speech, in both the technical and the fundamental meaning of the Constitution. So I agree with the Court that he must go free.

Chief Justice REHNQUIST, with whom Justice WHITE and Justice O'CONNOR join, dissenting.

In holding this Texas statute unconstitutional, the Court ignores Justice Holmes' familiar aphorism that "a page of history is worth a volume of logic." New York Trust Co. v. [*422] Eisner, 256 U.S. 345, 349 (1921). For more than 200 years, the American flag has occupied a unique position as the symbol of our Nation, a uniqueness that justifies a governmental prohibition against flag burning in the way respondent Johnson did here. . . .

[T]he Court insists that the Texas statute prohibiting the public burning of the American flag infringes on respondent Johnson's freedom of expression. Such freedom, of course, is not absolute. . . . In Chaplinsky v. New Hampshire, 315 U.S. 568 (1942), a unanimous Court said: "Allowing the broadest scope to the language and purpose of the Fourteenth Amendment, it is well understood that the right of free speech is not absolute at all times and under all circumstances. There are certain well-defined and narrowly limited classes of speech, the prevention and punishment of which have never been thought to raise any Constitutional problem. These include the lewd and obscene, the profane, the libelous, and the insulting or 'fighting' words—those which by their very utterance inflict injury or tend to incite an immediate breach of the peace. It has been well observed that such utterances are no essential part of any exposition of ideas, and are of such slight social value as a step to truth that any benefit that may be derived from them is clearly outweighed by the social interest in order and morality." Id., at 571-572 (footnotes omitted). The Court upheld Chaplinsy's conviction under a state statute that made it unlawful to "address any offensive, derisive or annoying word to any person who is lawfully in any street or other public place." Id., at 569. Chaplinsky had told a local marshal, "You are a God damned racketeer" and a "damned Fascist and the whole government of Rochester are Fascists or agents of Fascists." Ibid.

Here it may equally well be said that the public burning of the American flag by Johnson was no essential part of any exposition of ideas, and at the same time it had a tendency to incite a breach of the peace. Johnson was free to make any verbal denunciation of the flag that he wished; indeed, he was [*431] free to burn the flag in private. He could publicly burn other symbols of the Government or effigies of political leaders. He did lead a march through the streets of Dallas, and conducted a rally in front of the Dallas City Hall. He engaged in a "die-in" to protest nuclear weapons. He shouted out various slogans during the march, including: "Reagan, Mondale which will it be? Either one means World War III"; "Ronald Reagan, killer of the hour, Perfect example of

U.S. power"; and "red, white and blue, we spit on you, you stand for plunder, you will go under." Brief for Respondent 3. For none of these acts was he arrested or prosecuted; it was only when he proceeded to burn publicly an American flag stolen from its rightful owner that he violated the Texas statute. . . .

[*432] The result of the Texas statute is obviously to deny one in Johnson's frame of mind one of many means of "symbolic speech." Far from being a case of "one picture being worth a thousand words," flag burning is the equivalent of an inarticulate grunt or roar that, it seems fair to say, is most likely to be indulged in not to express any particular idea, but to antagonize others. . . . It was Johnson's use of this particular symbol, and not the idea that he sought to convey by it or by his many other expressions, for which he was punished. . . .

The Court concludes its opinion with a regrettably patronizing civics lecture, presumably addressed to the Members of both Houses of Congress, the members of the 48 state legislatures that enacted prohibitions against flag burning, and the troops fighting under that flag in Vietnam who objected to its [*435] being burned: "The way to preserve the flag's special role is not to punish those who feel differently about these matters. It is to persuade them that they are wrong." Ante, at 419. The Court's role as the final expositor of the Constitution is well established, but its role as a Platonic guardian admonishing those responsible to public opinion as if they were truant schoolchildren has no similar place in our system of government. The cry of "no taxation without representation" animated those who revolted against the English Crown to found our Nation—the idea that those who submitted to government should have some say as to what kind of laws would be passed. Surely one of the high purposes of a democratic society is to legislate against conduct that is regarded as evil and profoundly offensive to the majority of people—whether it be murder, embezzlement, pollution, or flag burning. . . .

I would uphold the Texas statute as applied in this case.

CASE DISCUSSION QUESTIONS

1. Did you notice that more and slightly different facts were brought out by the dissenting justices? This frequently happens. Why do you think the majority did not include all the facts?

2. Were you surprised by the tone of the opinion, especially the way in which the dissent was written? Do you think it is appropriate for U.S. Supreme Court justices to criticize each other? Each other's opinions?

DISCUSSION QUESTION

1. Many U.S. Supreme Court decisions have been decided by a divided court. It is not uncommon to find 5-4 splits. What do you think this does to the public's perception of the power and role of the Court?

2. Briefing Cases Involving the Common Law

So far in this chapter, in addition to learning the basics of case briefing, we have explored the responsibility of courts to interpret statutes and to strike down unconstitutional statutes. In areas where there are no statutory or constitutional issues involved, the courts are free to develop the common law. In dealing with common-law issues much of what the courts do involves areas where the law is well settled. What is not so settled is whether a particular litigant's facts fit within the law. Occasionally, however, the court is faced not with applying the established law to new facts, but with deciding what the common-law rule should be.

To make the process of reading cases more interesting and practical, we will introduce you to a new client and ask you to assist in the evaluation of her case by briefing three court opinions. In the first opinion, *Keller v. DeLong,* the court relies on a long and well-established line of cases to decide liability in a negligence action. In the other two opinions, *Lewis v. Lewis* and *Callow,* the court has the much more difficult task of deciding whether to create a new rule of law to meet society's changing values.

For these final three cases, assume that the paralegal, Chris Kendall, has just received the following memorandum from Pat Harper. The firm is located in Springfield, Massachusetts.

Memorandum

TO: Chris Kendall
FROM: Pat Harper
RE: Miller Intake Interview; Possible Negligence Claim
DATE: March 25, 2020

Last week, Ms. Janice Miller came to our office seeking advice about whether she could sue Mr. George Booth for injuries that she received due to his alleged negligence. She initially presented the facts to me as follows: She and Mr. Booth were cutting firewood. Mr. Booth was using a chain saw, and Ms. Miller was stacking the pieces of wood as Mr. Booth cut them. Neither was wearing safety glasses, although each owned a pair. Ms. Miller explained the omission by saying that they had both thought that they would only be cutting wood for a short time and neither wanted to be bothered by putting on the glasses.

As it turned out, the wood-cutting session took longer than anticipated. After about an hour, both Mr. Booth and Ms. Miller were getting tired. In particular, Mr. Booth complained that he was feeling fatigued and that it was getting harder and harder to hold the saw sufficiently perpendicular to the wood to cut a straight line. Ms. Miller suggested that they quit for the day, but Mr. Booth wanted to cut just a few more pieces. On his next attempt, probably due to his tired condition, he allowed the chain saw to slip slightly so that it hit the log at a slant, slicing off a piece of bark that flew into Ms. Miller's right eye. Unfortunately, the accident has left Ms. Miller totally blind in that eye. Neither she nor Mr. Booth has medical or homeowners' insurance to cover her medical bills, which currently amount to almost $50,000. In addition, Ms. Miller would like to be compensated for her loss of sight, as well as her pain and suffering. I have tentatively attached a value of $400,000 for the former and $150,000 for the latter, for a total possible claim of $600,000.

a. Applying Established Law

Harper first wants to address the issue of whether Booth can be held liable for negligence. Because the injury occurred in Massachusetts, the ideal situation would be to find cases from Massachusetts that have dealt with a similar situation. The only authorities that are binding on a state court are statutes and court opinions from higher courts within that same state. Similarly, in the federal system, the courts are bound only by federal statutes and court opinions from higher federal courts. This constitutes mandatory authority—authority from a higher court within the same jurisdiction dealing with similar facts and legal issues. All else is persuasive authority, and the courts need not follow it. But if the court finds an argument in nonbinding authority persuasive, it may choose to follow it. Researchers usually rely on such persuasive authority when they cannot find any useful mandatory authority because the cases are too old, they go against the client's position, the facts are not sufficiently similar to the client's facts, or when there simply are no prior court opinions dealing with that area of the law.

As it happens, neither Harper nor Kendall could find any Massachusetts cases dealing with a similar issue of negligence. They did, however, find the following New Hampshire court opinion. The bracketed numbers refer to the pages within the Atlantic Reporter, Second Series. As is true in most states, New Hampshire Supreme Court decisions are published in both an official reporter, New Hampshire Reports, and an unofficial reporter, the Atlantic Reporter.

Read and brief *Keller v. DeLong*. Because negligence is a well-established area of the law, most negligence cases, such as this one, involve applying settled principles to new factual situations. Therefore, throughout your brief, make sure that you are very specific about which facts seemed to matter to the litigants and the court.

Keller v. DeLong
108 N.H. 212, 231 A.2d 633 (1967)

Case, for wrongful death. Trial was by the Court (Grimes, J.), without a jury. The Court made findings and rulings in writing and returned a verdict for the defendant. Reserved and transferred by the Presiding Justice upon the plaintiff's exceptions. Exceptions sustained; new trial.

Westcott, Millham & Dyer (Mr. Harold E. Westcott orally), for the plaintiff.

[*634] Wiggin, Nourie, Sundeen, Nassikas & Pingree and Dort S. Bigg (Mr. Bigg orally), for the defendant.

DUNCAN, Justice.

The plaintiff's intestate, a registered nurse who was twenty-eight years of age, died in consequence of injuries suffered at Tyngsboro, Massachusetts at approximately 11:40 P.M. on April 14, 1963, when her automobile, operated by the defendant, collided with a utility pole at the side of the highway. She and the defendant had left Laconia late in the afternoon of the same day. Until shortly before the accident, the decedent had done the driving. A stop had been made at Bow, at which time both parties had some beer to drink. Thereafter they had sandwiches at a restaurant in Concord, and then proceeded toward Lowell, Massachusetts with the decedent at the wheel. At some place near the Massachusetts line, the defendant took the wheel at the decedent's request, and the decedent went to sleep. The accident occurred a few miles from where the defendant commenced to drive.

The Trial Court found "that the sole cause of the accident was the fact that the defendant dozed off to sleep and did not awaken in time to avoid collision with the pole." It further found: "While the defendant had been drinking, the evidence does not convince me that he was unable properly to control the vehicle while awake or that he had difficulty in doing so before dozing off. Neither is it found that after he took the wheel he had any warning that he was going to fall asleep." The Court granted the defendant's request as follows: "After taking over the wheel, Carl DeLong had no advance warning that he was about to doze, but suddenly and unexpectedly dozed at the time of the occurrence of the accident." After reasoning that dozing as a passenger "does not mean that a person cannot keep awake when charged with the responsibility of driving," the Trial Court was "not convinced . . . that in taking over the wheel . . . under all the circumstances was anything different than the ordinary man of average prudence would have done and I therefore do not find the defendant was negligent in doing so."

Under principles which receive general recognition an operator of a motor vehicle who permits himself to fall asleep while driving is guilty of ordinary negligence if he has continued to drive without taking reasonable precautions against sleeping after premonitory symptoms of drowsiness or fatigue. Annot. 28 A.L.R.2d 12, 44 et seq.; *Bushnell v. Bushnell,* 103 Conn. 583; *Bernosky v. Greff,* 350 Pa. 59; *Carvalho v. Oliveria,* 305 Mass. 304. Cf. *Theisen v. Milwaukee Automobile Mut. Ins. Co.,* 18 Wis. 2d 91. . . .

[*635] We are of the opinion that in the case before us, the Trial Court erred in the application of the law to the evidence. The error is best illustrated by the finding made at the defendant's request: "After taking over the wheel, Carl DeLong had no advance warning that he was about to doze, but suddenly and unexpectedly dozed at the time of occurrence of the accident." The effect of this finding, and of the like finding made by the Court of its own motion, was to isolate selected portions of the evidence, in disregard of the evidence upon which the Court found that the defendant had dozed on a "couple of occasions" before he undertook to drive, and was "drowsy just before taking the wheel."

This evidence disclosed ample warning to the defendant that he might fall asleep. It was not disputed that when he took the wheel, the windows of the automobile were closed, and the heater turned on. There was no evidence that he took any precaution to arouse himself before proceeding, whether by walking around the vehicle, opening windows, or reducing the heat. See *Sater v. Owens,* 67 Wash. 2d 699. On the contrary, it appeared that it was the decedent who left the vehicle and walked to the opposite side, to permit the defendant to slide under the wheel without leaving the seat.

Under these circumstances, a finding that "after taking over the wheel" the defendant had "suddenly and unexpectedly dozed at the time of . . . the accident" cannot be sustained. Such an occurrence could not be unexpected in the absence of precaution to prevent it. Thus it was error to judge the defendant's care solely with reference to what occurred after he took the wheel, in disregard of the evidence of "advance warning" which he had just prior thereto. See *Shine v. Wujick,* 89 R.I. 22, 27-28. The plaintiff was entitled to have the defendant's care determined upon a basis of all of the evidence, rather than just what occurred after he took the wheel. See *Murray v. Boston & Maine R.R.,* 107 N.H. 367, 373-374; *Lynch v. Sprague,* 95 N.H. 485, 490. The verdict for the defendant must therefore be set aside.

Exceptions sustained; new trial.

Grimes, J., did not sit; the others concurred.

Case Discussion Questions

1. Will the Massachusetts courts see this case as mandatory or persuasive precedent?

2. What was the rule that both the trial and the appellate court agreed should be applied to the facts?

3. As both the trial and appellate court agreed on the law, what formed the basis of their disagreement? That is, what was the issue on appeal?

Once you have finished briefing a case, the next step is to use that opinion to help you predict how a court will rule in your client's case. If you think the opinion and your client's situation share many similarities, you can assume that a court will decide your client's case as courts have done in the past. If, however, you find many dissimilarities, that could lead you to believe that the court might rule differently than it has in the past. In Chapter 15, we will spend more time on this process of applying court opinions to our client's facts. For now, however, it is important to realize that once you are in the workforce, you will rarely have the luxury of reading cases just for the enjoyment of reading them. You will be reading them to gain insight into how courts have handled similar situations, and hence how they might rule in your client's case.

One method for finding similarities and differences between a court decision and your client's case is to make a chart. First, list all the key facts from the court decision. Then list all the key facts from your client's case. For each fact, note whether it is similar to or different from one of the facts in the prior court decision. Most important, decide if any similarities and differences matter. Then based on your chart make an educated guess as to what a court would do.

Legal Reasoning Exercises

3. Analyze whether, based on the same reasoning used by the *Keller* court, a court would find Booth negligent. (*Note:* The question is not whether Miller was contributorily negligent. Think only about Booth's potential liability.) Recall from Chapter 4 our discussion regarding the importance of distinguishing between a prima facie case and the defenses. Here, you are being asked to focus exclusively on the prima facie case of negligence.

Make a chart in which you list all the ways in which you think *Keller* and Booth's situation are analogous and all the ways in which you think they are distinguishable. (*Hint:* To argue that two situations are analogous, think in general terms. For example, both situations involved a dangerous activity. To argue that two situations are distinguishable, think specifically. For example, *Keller* involved a motor vehicle, while Booth's case involved a chain saw.) Then ask yourself whether the similarities or the differences are more important. If you think the similarities are more important, then you will assume that the court will find Booth negligent. If you think the differences are more important, then you will assume that the court will not find Booth negligent.

4. Recall the case of Matt Anderson from the beginning of the chapter. Analyze whether, based on the *Jones v. Smith* case, you think a court would find Bob liable for Matt's injuries. What similarities do you see between the two cases? What distinctions?

Memorandum

TO: Chris Kendall
FROM: Pat Harper
RE: Miller Intake Interview; Possible Spousal Immunity Defense
DATE: April 15, 2020

There is a development in the Miller situation. It seems that Ms. Miller and Mr. Booth are married. Since the accident, they have been living apart, but they are not legally separated or divorced. This may create a problem for us because to the best of my recollection, I do not believe spouses can sue each other. However, it has been quite a while since I researched that area of the law. Would you please do so for me and report on your findings?[3]

---

b. Creating New Law

We have reproduced the two cases in Exhibits 13-5 and 13-6 exactly as you would find them in the North Eastern Reporter. We have added margin notes to help explain some of the editorial features that West adds.

After reading *Callow* (Exhibit 13-5), try writing a brief. In the procedural history, note that there was no trial in this case. The case was sent from the trial court directly to the Supreme Judicial Court. (This usually happens when the parties agree as to what happened but disagree as to what the law should be.) In your holding, be particularly careful to note any limitations the court places on its holding. View a limitation as a red flag. A limitation is an indication that the court has left some area open that can be resolved only through future litigation.

---

[3] All research materials are contained in your readings. Do *not* do any additional research.

CALLOW v. THOMAS
Cite as 78 N.E.2d 637

Mass.   637

N.E.2d 729, 731. Consequently, no error of fact or of law being made to appear, we cannot modify this provision of the decree.

The matter of allowance of attorney's fees, briefs and expenses in this court will be settled by a separate order of a single justice upon presentation of an itemized list of the expenses.

Decree affirmed.

CALLOW v. THOMAS.

Supreme Judicial Court of Massachusetts.
Middlesex.

April 1, 1948.

1. Husband and wife ⊜205(2)

No cause of action arises in favor of either spouse for a tort committed by the other during coverture.

2. Husband and wife ⊜205(2)

Where either spouse commits a tort upon the other during coverture recovery is denied, not merely because of the disability of one spouse to sue the other during coverture, but because of the marital relationship, no cause of action ever came into existence.

3. Divorce ⊜313

After divorce, no action can be maintained by either spouse for a tort committed by the other during coverture.

4. Marriage ⊜57, 67

Generally an "annulment" is distinguished from a "divorce" in that annulment is not a dissolution of the marriage but is a judicial declaration that no marriage has ever existed, and decree of annulment makes the marriage void ab initio even though the marriage be voidable only at the instance of the injured party. G.L.(Ter.Ed.) c. 207, § 14.

See Words and Phrases, Permanent Edition, for all other definitions of "Annulment" and "Divorce".

5. Marriage ⊜67

Where marriage was voidable and not void and so was valid until set aside by decree of nullity, wife could not after annulment, recover for a tort committed upon her by husband during coverture because of his gross negligence in operation of automobile in which wife was a guest passenger. G.L.(Ter.Ed.) c. 207, § 14.

6. Marriage ⊜67

Where a voidable marriage has been annulled things which have been done during the period of the supposed marriage ought not be undone or reopened after the decree of annulment. G.L.(Ter.Ed.) c. 207, § 14.

Report from Superior Court, Middlesex County.

Action by Muriel Callow against Frederick Thomas for injuries sustained when plaintiff was riding as a gratuitous passenger in an automobile owned and operated by defendant. The case was reported to Supreme Judicial Court without decision.

Judgment for defendant.

Before QUA, C. J., and LUMMUS, DOLAN, WILKINS, and SPALDING, JJ.

M. Harry Goldburgh and J. Finks, both of Boston, for plaintiff.

K. C. Parker, of Boston, for defendant.

SPALDING, Justice.

The plaintiff and the defendant were married in this Commonwealth on August 6, 1944, and thereafter lived together here as husband and wife. On November 9, 1944, while riding as a "gratuitous passenger" in an automobile owned and operated by the defendant, the plaintiff was injured when the automobile, due to the gross negligence of the defendant, ran into a tree. The plaintiff was in the exercise of due care. The accident occurred on a public way in this Commonwealth and the defendant's automobile was registered in accordance with the laws thereof. On June 28, 1945, upon the petition of the plaintiff to annul the marriage because of the defendant's fraud, the Probate Court decreed that the marriage was "null and

---

Margin annotations (left to right):

West key symbol

These are headnotes, so called because they appear at the head of the case. They are written by the editors at West, not by the court. Do not quote them, and do not rely on them.

The bold word or phrase is called a "West topic." There are 414 West topics. The number preceded by a key symbol is called a key number.

Syllabus

Judges hearing the case.

Attorneys of the parties.

This is where the opinion begins.

Each headnote summarizes one legal point. You can find those points in the opinion by locating the bracketed numbers corresponding to the headnote numbers. For example, you can find the points summarized in headnotes 1-3 in one long paragraph beginning at the bottom of the left-hand column on the next page. Headnote 4 is covered in five paragraphs beginning on page 639 of the opinion.

Exhibit 13-5   *Callow v. Thomas*

(continues)

638 Mass.   78 NORTH EASTERN REPORTER, 2d SERIES

void."[1] Two months later the plaintiff commenced this action of tort to recover compensation for her injuries.

The foregoing facts were submitted to a judge of the Superior Court upon a case stated in which it was agreed that no inferences should be drawn. See G.L.(Ter.Ed.) c. 231, § 126. The judge at the request of the parties reported the case to this court without decision. G.L.(Ter.Ed.) c. 231, § 111; Scaccia v. Boston Elevated Railway Co., 317 Mass. 245, 248, 249, 57 N.E.2d 761, "upon the stipulation that if the plaintiff is entitled to recover, judgment shall be entered for the plaintiff in the sum of $3,000, otherwise judgment for the defendant."

The question for decision is whether a wife after the marriage has been annulled can maintain an action against her former husband for a tort committed during coverture. The question is one of first impression in this Commonwealth. Indeed no case in any other jurisdiction has been brought to our attention, and we have found none, in which this question has been presented.

[1-3] That no cause of action arises in favor of either husband or wife for a tort committed by the other during coverture is too well settled to require citation of authority. Recovery is denied in such a case not merely because of the disability of one spouse to sue the other during coverture, but for the more fundamental reason that because of the marital relationship no cause of action ever came into existence.[2] That this is so is revealed by the fact that it has uniformly been held that even after divorce no action can be maintained by either spouse for a tort committed by the other during coverture. Phillips v. Barnet, 1 Q.B.D. 436; Abbott v. Abbott, 67 Me. 304, 24 Am.Rep. 27; Bandfield v. Bandfield, 117 Mich. 80, 75 N.W. 287, 40 L.R.A. 757, 72 Am.St.Rep. 550; Strom v. Strom, 98 Minn. 427, 107 N.W. 1047, 6 L.R.A.,N.S., 191, 116 Am.St.Rep. 387; Lillienkamp v. Rippetoe, 133 Tenn. 57, 179 S.W. 628, L.R.A.1916B, 881, Ann.Cas. 1917C, 901; Schultz v. Christopher, 65 Wash. 496, 118 P. 629, 38 L.R.A.,N.S., 780. There is nothing in our statutes enlarging the rights of married women that can be construed as altering this rule.[3] See Lubowitz v. Taines, 293 Mass. 39, 198 N.E. 320; Luster v. Luster, 299 Mass. 480, 482, 483,

[1] The material portions of the decree are as follows: "On the libel of Muriel Gladys Thomas, of Sudbury, in said county of Middlesex, representing that she and Frederick A. Thomas, now of Lexington, in said county, were joined in marriage lawfully solemnized at Boston, in the county of Suffolk, on August 6, 1944; and that they last lived together in this Commonwealth at said Sudbury; that she now doubts the validity of said marriage for the reason that at the time of said marriage said libellee fraudulently concealed from her the fact that he was afflicted with a contagious disease, thereby practicing a fraud upon her; and praying that said marriage between the said libellant and libellee be annulled and declared void: Said Frederick A. Thomas having had due notice of said libel, objection being made, and after hearing, it appearing to the court that said libellant entered into said marriage in good faith but that said libellee practiced a fraud upon her: It is decreed that said marriage between the said libellant and libellee be and the same hereby is declared to be null and void."

[2] There are, to be sure, instances where one spouse may have a cause of action against the other but cannot enforce it because of the rule prohibiting, with certain exceptions, legal proceedings between husband and wife. See G.L. (Ter.Ed.) c. 209, § 6. Thus in Giles v. Giles, 279 Mass. 284, 181 N.E. 176, it was held that a wife could not maintain a suit in equity against her husband to recover money lent to him before the marriage. But after the parties had been divorced it was held that the suit could be maintained. Giles v. Giles, 293 Mass. 495, 200 N.E. 378. The right to sue was merely suspended during coverture. In Charney v. Charney, 316 Mass. 580, 55 N.E.2d 917, it was held that a wife who, without the intervention of a trustee, had entered into a separation agreement with her husband in New York could not, although the contract was valid by the law of that State, enforce the agreement in the courts of this Commonwealth. Compare Whitney v. Whitney, 316 Mass. 367, 55 N.E.2d 601. See Lubowitz v. Taines, 293 Mass. 39, 198 N.E. 320; Mertz v. Mertz, 271 N.Y. 466, 3 N.E.2d 597, 108 A.L.R. 1120.

[3] In other jurisdictions it has usually been held that statutes removing the common law disabilities of the wife do not

Footnotes can be very important. They are part of the opinion. Always read them.

Exhibit 13-5 *Callow v. Thomas*

(continues)

CALLOW v. THOMAS
Cite as 78 N.E.2d 637

Mass.   639

13 N.E.2d 438. Recognizing the common law rule and the fact that it has not been changed by statute, the plaintiff argues that the decree of nullity "effaced the marriage between the plaintiff and defendant ab initio, and, therefore, at the time of the accident the relationship of husband and wife did not exist."

[4] General Laws (Ter.Ed.) c. 207, § 14, which governs proceedings for annulment, so far as material, reads as follows: "If the validity of a marriage is doubted, either party may file a libel for annulling such marriage. * * * Upon proof of validity or nullity of the marriage, it shall be affirmed or declared void by a decree of the court." In general it may be said that an annulment is to be distinguished from a divorce in that it is not a dissolution of the marriage but is a judicial declaration that no marriage has ever existed. In other words, the decree of annulment makes the marriage void ab initio. Restatement: Conflict of Laws, § 115(1), comment b; Clarke v. Menzies, [1922] 2 Ch. 298; Dodworth v. Dale, [1936] 2 K.B. 503, 511; Mason v. Mason, [1944] N.I. 134; Millar v. Millar, 175 Cal. 797, 804, 805, 167 P. 394, L.R.A.1918B, 415, Ann.Cas.1918E, 184; McDonald v. McDonald, 6 Cal.2d 457, 461, 58 P.2d 163, 104 A.L.R. 1290; Griffin v. Griffin, 130 Ga. 527, 61 S.E. 16, 16 L.R.A.,N.S., 937, 14 Ann.Cas. 866; Henneger v. Lomas, 145 Ind. 287, 298, 44 N.E. 462, 32 L.R.A. 848; Ridgely v. Ridgely, 79 Md. 298, 305,

29 A. 597, 25 L.R.A. 800; Steerman v. Snow, 94 N.J.Eq. 9, 13, 14, 118 A. 696; Jones v. Brinsmade, 183 N.Y. 258, 76 N.E. 22, 3 L.R.A.,N.S., 192, 111 Am.St.Rep. 746, 5 Ann.Cas. 378; Leventhal v. Liberman, 262 N.Y. 209, 211, 186 N.E. 675, 88 A.L.R. 782. See Loker v. Gerald, 157 Mass. 42, 45, 31 N.E. 709, 16 L.R.A. 497, 34 Am.St. Rep. 252; Hanson v. Hanson, 287 Mass. 154, 157, 191 N.E. 673, 93 A.L.R. 701. And this is true even though, as here, the marriage be only voidable at the instance of the injured party. Dodworth v. Dale, [1936] 2 K.B. 503, 511–512; Mason v. Mason, [1944] N.I. 134; McDonald v. McDonald, 6 Cal.2d 457, 461, 58 P.2d 163, 104 A.L.R. 1290; Matter of Moncrief's Will, 235 N.Y. 390, 139 N.E. 550, 27 A.L.R. 1117; Sleicher v. Sleicher, 251 N.Y. 366, 369, 167 N.E. 501, 502.

But the doctrine that such a decree makes the marriage void ab initio has not always been applied unqualifiedly. See Sleicher v. Sleicher, 251 N.Y. 366, 369, 167 N.E. 501, 502.[4] In England, where the question of the effect of a decree of annulment seems to have been considered to a greater extent than in this country, the rule is that such a decree is void for most purposes but not for all. In discussing the effect of such a decree in Mason v. Mason, [1944] N.I. 134, it was said by Lord Chief Justice Andrews, "It is further to be observed that the marriage, after such decree absolute, is void for almost every purpose;

permit her to maintain an action against her husband for a tort committed during coverture. Libby v. Berry, 74 Me. 286, 43 Am.Rep. 589; Bandfield v. Bandfield, 117 Mich. 80, 75 N.W. 287, 40 L. R.A. 757, 72 Am.St.Rep. 550; Strom v. Strom, 98 Minn. 427, 107 N.W. 1047, 6 L.R.A.,N.S., 191, 116 Am.St.Rep. 387; Longendyke v. Longendyke, 44 Barb., N. Y., 366; Lillienkamp v. Rippetoe, 133 Tenn. 57, 179 S.W. 628, L.R.A.1916B, 881, Ann.Cas.1917C, 901; Thompson v. Thompson, 218 U.S. 611, 31 S.Ct. 111, 54 L.Ed. 1180, 30 L.R.A.,N.S., 1153, 21 Ann. Cas. 921. But some statutes have been construed to permit actions in such cases. Johnson v. Johnson, 201 Ala. 41, 77 So. 335, 6 A.L.R. 1031; Brown v. Brown, 88 Conn. 42, 89 A. 889, 52 L.R.A.,N.S., 185, Ann.Cas.1915D, 70; Gilman v. Gilman, 78 N.H. 4, 95 A. 657, L.R.A.1916B, 907. See note in 38 Harv.L.Rev. 383.

4 In that case the defendant was directed by a decree of divorce to pay alimony to the plaintiff "so long as she remains unmarried." Thereafter the plaintiff remarried but the marriage was subsequently annulled on the ground of fraud. Alimony payments ceased at the time of the second marriage. In an action to recover unpaid instalments of alimony it was held that the plaintiff could recover instalments of alimony falling due from the time of the annulment but not for the period during which the second marriage was in force. The court refused to give retroactive effect to the decree of annulment, saying, "The retroactive effect of rescission from the beginning is not, however, without limits, prescribed by policy and justice."

Exhibit 13-5   *Callow v. Thomas*

(continues)

and, speaking in general terms, the only exception to the rule—an exception founded on general equitable principles—may be said to be such transactions as have been concluded and such things as have been done during the period of the supposed marriage. These cannot be undone or reopened after the marriage has been declared null and void" (page 163).

This exception has been recognized in several decisions. Thus in Anstey v. Manners, Gow. 10, the plaintiff, after a sentence of nullity had been pronounced by the Ecclesiastical Court, brought suit against the former husband to recover for necessaries which he (the plaintiff) had supplied to the wife. Some of the necessaries were supplied during the supposed marriage and some were supplied afterwards. In a very brief opinion which is somewhat obscure it was held that the defendant was not liable for debts contracted after the date of the decree. The case has been considered as impliedly holding that the defendant was liable for necessaries furnished prior to that date. See Dodworth v. Dale, [1936] 2 K.B. 503, 512.

In Dunbar v. Dunbar, [1909] 2 Ch. 639, it was held that a completed and executed transaction, namely, an advancement, effected while the plaintiff and the defendant were living together as man and wife, was unaffected by a subsequent decree annulling a marriage which was voidable but not void.

In Dodworth v. Dale, [1936] 2 K.B. 503, it was held that a husband who had obtained an annulment of his marriage on the ground of his wife's impotency and who during the period of his purported marriage had filed tax returns as a married man, could not be compelled to pay additional taxes for that period on the ground that the deductions which he had taken for the support of his wife were improper. The court stated "that what has been done during the continuance of the de facto marriage cannot be undone—cannot be overturned by the operation of law" (page 519).

In Fowke v. Fowke, [1938] Ch. 774, it was held that a decree of nullity granted on the ground of the wife's impotency did not affect a previous deed of separation whereby the husband convenanted to pay the wife an annuity so long as she continued to lead a chaste life. See also P. v. P. [1916] 2 Ir.R. 400; De Reneville v. De Reneville, [1947] A.C.[5]

[5,6] We are of opinion that the exception recognized in these cases is sound and that the present case falls within it. At the time of the accident the parties were husband and wife for all intents and purposes. Had no proceedings been brought to annul the marriage, this status would have endured until the marriage was terminated by death or divorce. In other words, the marriage here was voidable and not void and was valid until it was set aside by the decree of nullity. 1 Bish.Mar. Div. & Sep. §§ 258, 259, 271, 281; Anders v. Anders, 224 Mass. 438, 441, 113 N.E. 203, L.R.A.1916E, 1273; Sleicher v. Sleicher, 251 N.Y. 366, 369, 167 N.E. 501, 502. It is to be observed that this is not a case of a marriage prohibited by law such as a bigamous marriage or one prohibited by reason of consanguinity or affinity between the parties. G.L.(Ter.Ed.) c. 207, §§ 1, 2, 4. Such a marriage is no marriage at all and is "void without a decree of divorce or other legal process." G.L.(Ter. Ed.) c. 207, § 8. While it doubtless is true that a decree of nullity ordinarily has the effect of making a marriage, even one which is voidable, void ab initio, this is a legal fiction which ought not to be pressed too far. To say that for all purposes the marriage never existed is unrealistic. Logic must yield to realities. Public policy requires that there must be some limits to the retroactive effects of a decree of annulment. It was said by Cardozo, C. J., in American Surety Co. v. Conner, 251 N.Y. 1, 9, 166 N.E. 783, 786, 65 A.L.R. 244, "The decree of annulment destroyed the marriage from the beginning as a source of rights and duties * * * but it could not obliterate the past and make events unreal." The better rule, we think, is that in the case of a voidable marriage transactions which have been concluded and things which have been done during

[5] 64 T. L. R. 82.

Exhibit 13-5   *Callow v. Thomas*   *(continues)*

JOYCE v. DEVANEY
Cite as 78 N.E.2d 641

Mass.   641

the period of the supposed marriage ought not to be undone or reopened after the decree of annulment. Applying that principle here, the plaintiff is not entitled to recover. On the day after the accident if the plaintiff had brought suit against the defendant it could not have been maintained, for the marriage at that time had not been declared invalid. The situation was unaffected by the subsequent decree of annulment.

It follows that in accordance with the stipulation judgment is to be entered for the defendant.

So ordered.

JOYCE et al. v. DEVANEY et al.

Supreme Judicial Court of Massachusetts.
Middlesex.
April 1, 1948.

1. Easements ⟸16

The owner of realty may make use of one part of his realty for the benefit of another part in such a way that, on severance of the title, an easement, which is not expressed in the deed, may arise, which corresponds to the use which was previously made of the realty while it was under common ownership.

2. Easements ⟸15

Implied easements, whether by grant or by reservation, do not arise out of necessity alone, and their origin must be found in presumed intention of parties, to be gathered from language of instruments when read in the light of circumstances attending their execution, physical condition of premises, and knowledge which parties had or with which they are chargeable.

3. Easements ⟸15

The creation in deeds of express easements that were unambiguous and definite negatived any intention to create easements by implication, since the expression of one thing is the exclusion of another.

78 N.E.2d—41
MASS.DEC.76–79 N.E.2d—23

4. Easements ⟸17(1)

Where deeds of adjoining lots at time of severance created specific easements shown by plan providing for an 8-foot wide driveway 4 feet of which was to be on each lot, but 10-foot wide driveway was constructed, 8½ feet of which was on defendant's lot, and 1½ feet of which was on plaintiff's lot, there was no implied easement entitling plaintiff to use driveway as constructed, and plaintiff was entitled only to easement expressly set forth in deeds.

———◆———

Appeal from Superior Court, Middlesex County; Goldberg, Judge.

Bill in equity by John J. Joyce and another against John T. Devaney and another to restrain defendants from interfering with plaintiff's use of a common driveway, and for a determination of plaintiff's rights in the driveway, wherein the defendants filed a counterclaim to restrain plaintiffs from trespassing on defendant's land. From an adverse decree, plaintiffs appeal.

Interlocutory decree affirmed and final decree affirmed.

Before QUA, C. J., and LUMMUS, DOLAN, WILKINS, and SPALDING, JJ.

R. B. Brooks, of Boston, for plaintiffs.

M. E. Gallagher, Jr., of Boston, and A. J. Kirwan, of Medford, for defendants.

SPALDING, Justice.

The plaintiffs by this bill in equity seek to restrain the defendants from interfering with their use of a common driveway; they also ask that their rights in the driveway be determined. The answer of the defendants included a counterclaim in which they ask that the plaintiffs be restrained from trespassing on their land. The case was referred to a master whose report, to which there were no objections, was confirmed by an interlocutory decree. The case comes here on the plaintiffs' appeal from a final decree.

We summarize the findings of the master as follows: On April 30, 1931, MacNeil Bros. Corporation, hereinafter called the corporation, acquired for development purposes a parcel of vacant land in West Med-

The beginning
of the next
case.

Exhibit 13-5   *Callow v. Thomas* (*concluded*)

CASE DISCUSSION QUESTIONS

1. In Chapter 12 (Legal Reasoning Exercise 1), we looked at the following statute, which would seem to govern Miller's case. What does the *Callow* court say about it?

> A married woman may sue and be sued in the same manner as if she were sole; but this section shall not authorize suits between husband and wife.

2. What is the difference between a void and a voidable marriage? Do you think the court would have ruled the same way if the marriage had been void? Should such technicalities matter?

3. The result here was the finding that Muriel Callow could not sue her ex-husband. This does not mean that the court thought he was not negligent. Because the court said she could not sue, the court never heard any evidence regarding his behavior that caused his car to run into a tree. Do you think that there should be such absolute bars to even having a case heard? If so, can you think of other situations where the courts should not allow potential litigants to sue each other?

Legal Reasoning Exercise

5. Based on *Callow,* analyze whether you think the doctrine of spousal immunity will bar Miller's claim.

In 1975, the Massachusetts Supreme Judicial Court was asked to change the law regarding parental immunity. A child was hurt when his father allegedly caused an automobile accident. After considering the two major arguments against allowing such suits, the possibility of disrupting the family's peace and harmony and the tendency to promote fraud, the court allowed the child to sue his father. A year later, and 28 years after the Supreme Judicial Court decided *Callow,* the court revisited the issue of spousal immunity in *Lewis,* reprinted here in Exhibit 13-6.

As you read and brief this opinion, ask yourself why the court went to such lengths to explain itself and whether you agree with its reasoning. Pay particular attention to why the court said this was not a matter in which they should defer to the legislature. In the holding section, again be particularly careful to note any limitations the court puts on its holding.

As in *Callow,* there was no trial in *Lewis.* The court granted Mr. Lewis's summary judgment motion. The case then went to the Supreme Judicial Court by way of *direct appellate review.* This occurs when the courts think a case is so significant that the highest appellate court will eventually hear it, no matter how the intermediate court decides. Therefore, to save time, the middle step of going through the intermediate appellate court on the way to the highest court is simply omitted.

Court is not barred by the principle of double jeopardy. Accordingly the defendant's motion is to be denied, and the indictments are to stand for trial in the Superior Court.

So ordered.

Blanche LEWIS

v.

Larry C. LEWIS.

Supreme Judicial Court of Massachusetts, Hampden.

Argued Jan. 8, 1976.

Decided July 9, 1976.

Syllabus

Action was brought by wife against husband for personal injuries sustained in automobile accident. The Superior Court, Moriarty, J., granted defendant's motion for summary judgment, and plaintiff's motion for direct appellate review was allowed. The Supreme Judicial Court, Reardon, J., held that it was open to the Supreme Judicial Court to reconsider common-law rule of interspousal immunity, and that such rule no longer barred wife's action against husband for injuries sustained in automobile accident.

Judgment vacated.

1. Husband and Wife ☞205(2)

Arguments that tort actions between husband and wife would tend to disrupt peace and harmony of family and that such actions would tend to promote fraud and collusion on part of husband and wife for purpose of reaping undeserved financial reward at expense of family's liability insurer are insufficient to justify common-law rule of interspousal immunity.

Headnotes

2. Constitutional Law ☞70.1(11)

Statute which provides that a married woman may sue and be sued in same manner as if she were sole but provides that such statute does not authorize suit between husband and wife except in connection with certain contracts left interspousal immunity rule in its common-law status susceptible to reexamination and alteration by Supreme Judicial Court. M.G.L.A. c. 209 § 6.

3. Courts ☞90(6)

It is within power and authority of court to abrogate judicially created rule and mere longevity of rule does not by itself provide cause for Supreme Judicial Court to stay its hand if to perpetuate rule would be to perpetuate inequity.

4. Courts ☞90(6)

When rationales which gave meaning and coherence to judicially created rule are no longer vital, and rule itself is not consonant with needs of contemporary society, court not only has authority but also duty to reexamine its predecents rather than to apply by rote an antiquated formula.

5. Constitutional Law ☞70.1(11)

Where legislature recognized rule of interspousal immunity but left rule in its common-law form, expressing preference, at least implicitly, that Supreme Judicial Court continue to evaluate usefulness and propriety of rule, it was open to Supreme Judicial Court to reconsider common-law rule of interspousal immunity. M.G.L.A. c. 209 § 6.

6. Husband and Wife ☞205(2)

Wife's action against her husband for personal injuries sustained in automobile accident was not barred by common-law rule of interspousal immunity.

7. Torts ☞5

If there is tortious injury there should be recovery, and only strong arguments of public policy can justify judicially created

Exhibit 13-6   *Lewis v. Lewis*   *(continues)*

LEWIS v. LEWIS   Mass. **527**
Cite as, Mass., 351 N.E.2d 526

immunity for tort-feasors and bar recovery for injured victims.

Morton J. Sweeney, Springfield (Patricia A. Bobba, Springfield, with him), for the plaintiff.

George J. Shagory, Boston (Edward J. Shagory, Boston, with him), for defendant.

Robert M. Fuster, Pittsfield, for Juliette G. Pevoski, amicus curiae, submitted a brief.

J. Norman O'Connor and John D. Lanoue, Adams, for Joseph J. Pevoski, amicus curiae, submitted a brief.

Before HENNESSEY, C. J., and REARDON, BRAUCHER, KAPLAN and WILKINS, JJ.

REARDON, Justice.

This matter raises the question of the continuance in Massachusetts of the doctrine of interspousal immunity. The case originated as a civil action of tort for personal injuries brought by the plaintiff Blanche Lewis against her husband, the defendant Larry Lewis. The defendant's motion for summary judgment was granted, and we allowed the plaintiff's motion for direct appellate review. Blanche Lewis was a passenger in a car owned and driven by her husband on July 27, 1973, when about 9 P.M., on a public highway in the town of Agawam, the car slid on a wet pavement, struck a light pole and rolled over on its side, causing injury to the plaintiff. The motion for summary judgment which was allowed was based on the common law doctrine of interspousal immunity and on the provisions of G.L. c. 209, § 6, as amended by St.1963, c. 765, § 2. In addition to briefs filed by the parties we also reviewed briefs filed by counsel in a case raising a similar question commenced in the Superior Court for Berkshire County. We are thus led to a discussion of the current status of the doctrine of inter-spousal immunity and our opinion relative to the argument here presented by the plaintiff.

The fundamental basis for the common law rule of interspousal immunity was the special unity of husband and wife within the marital relationship. For most purposes the common law treated husband and wife as "a single person, represented by the husband." *Nolin v. Pearson*, 191 Mass. 283, 284, 77 N.E. 890, (1906). See *Butler v. Ives*, 139 Mass. 202, 203, 29 N.E. 654 (1885). This merger of legal identities has been described in the following terms: "By marriage, the husband and wife are one person in law: . . . that is, the very being or legal existence of the woman is suspended during the marriage, or at least is incorporated and consolidated into that of the husband; under whose wing, protection, and *cover*, she performs everything . . . . Upon this principle, of a union of a person in husband and wife, depend almost all the legal rights, duties, and disabilities, that either of them acquire by the marriage." 1 W. Blackstone, Commentaries *442.

Among the many disabilities visited upon a woman once she took her marriage vows was an inability to sue or be sued in her own name. To enforce any right of action for tortious injury to her person her husband had to be joined as a plaintiff; and, furthermore, he was entitled to the proceeds of any judgment obtained. Conversely, to enforce an action against a married woman it was necessary to join the husband as a defendant, and a judgment, if obtained during coverture, became the obligation of the husband. McCurdy, Personal Injury Torts Between Spouses, 4 Vill.L.Rev. 303, 304 (1959). 1 F. Harper & F. James, Torts § 8.10 at 643 (1956).

Within this framework a rule prohibiting suits between husband and wife made some sense. Not only was there the conceptual problem of the single marital entity suing itself but, as a practical matter, the rules of liability would have rendered such suits

Exhibit 13-6 *Lewis v. Lewis*   (continues)

idle exercises. As Dean Prosser pointed out: "If the man were the tort-feasor, the woman's right would be a chose in action which the husband would have the right to reduce to possession, and he must be joined as a plaintiff against himself and the proceeds recovered must be paid to him . . . . If the wife committed the tort, the husband would be liable to himself for it, and must be joined as a defendant in his own action." W. Prosser, Torts § 122 at 860 (4th ed. 1971).

These antediluvian assumptions concerning the role and status of women in marriage and in society which animated and gave support to the common law rule of interspousal immunity were soon perceived as inconsistent with the principles and realities of a progressing American society. Beginning in the middle of the nineteenth century, women's emancipation acts were passed in all American jurisdictions in order to secure to married women their own independent legal identities. See W. Prosser, Torts § 122 at 861 (4th ed. 1971); McCurdy, Torts Between Persons in Domestic Relation, 43 Harv.L.Rev. 1030, 1036–1037 (1930). In Massachusetts, beginning with St.1845, c. 208, the Legislature through a series of enactments now found in G.L. c. 209, §§ 1–13, has moved to recognize and invigorate the legal identity of the married woman. Most of the disabilities which rendered women second class citizens under the common law were removed by these statutes in Massachusetts. They provide inter alia that a married woman may hold and dispose of both real and personal property (G.L. c. 209, § 1), may enter into contracts in her own name (G.L. c. 209, § 2), and may sue and be sued in her own name without joinder of her husband, and without her husband's

being liable for judgments against her (G. L. c. 209, §§ 6, 8). As we recognized as early as 1906 in *Nolin v. Pearson, supra,* 191 Mass. at 285, 77 N.E. at 890, "This remedial legislation has resulted in very largely impairing the unity of husband and wife as it existed at common law." The old order has been changing and the doctrine of the legal unity of husband and wife is no longer a satisfactory foundation on which to base a rule of interspousal tort immunity.[1]

Despite the demise of the unity theory of husband and wife and the enactment of married women's acts, the rule of interspousal tort immunity has survived in Massachusetts and in many other jurisdictions. This court could say in 1948 in very broad and dogmatic terms, "That no cause of action arises in favor of either husband or wife for a tort committed by the other during coverture is too well settled to require citation of authority. Recovery is denied in such a case not merely because of the disability of one spouse to sue the other during coverture, but for the more fundamental reason that because of the marital relationship no cause of action ever came into existence." *Callow v. Thomas,* 322 Mass. 550, 551–552, 78 N.E.2d 637, 638 (1948). Indeed at that time interspousal immunity was the rule in a substantial majority of jurisdictions. However, in the interim there has been a significant trend in other jurisdictions toward abrogating the doctrine. Currently, State jurisdictions are about evenly divided between those which have abandoned and those which have maintained the interspousal immunity rule. Furthermore, among commentators who have considered the topic, criticism of the rule is practically universal. See, e. g., 1 F. Harper & F. James, *supra* at 643–647;

1. What we have said is not to be interpreted as a derogation of the spiritual and emotional unity that many hold as an ideal in marriage. As the Supreme Court of Washington pointed out, "The 'supposed unity' of husband and wife, which serves as the traditional basis of interspousal disability, is not a reference to the common nature or loving oneness

achieved in a marriage of two free individuals. Rather, this traditional premise had reference to a situation, coming on from antiquity, in which a woman's marriage for most purposes rendered her a chattel of her husband." *Freehe v. Freehe,* 81 Wash.2d 183, 186, 500 P.2d 771, 773 (1972).

Exhibit 13-6   *Lewis v. Lewis*   *(continues)*

LEWIS v. LEWIS
Cite as, Mass., 351 N.E.2d 526
Mass. 529

W. Prosser, *supra* at 859–864; McCurdy, Torts Between Persons in Domestic Relation, 43 Harv.L.Rev. 1030 (1930); McCurdy, Personal Injury Torts Between Spouses, 4 Vill.L.Rev. 303 (1959); Comment Tort Liability Between Husband and Wife: The Interspousal Immunity Doctrine, 21 U.Miami L.Rev. 423 (1966); Note, Interspousal Immunity—Time for a Reappraisal, 27 Ohio St.L.J. 550 (1966).

[1] While most jurisdictions recognize that the theory of the legal identity of husband and wife can no longer support the interspousal immunity rule, those courts which have upheld the rule have generally done so on grounds of public policy. The two arguments most frequently advanced in favor of the rule are, first, that tort actions between husband and wife would tend to disrupt the peace and harmony of the family, and, second, that such actions would tend to promote fraud and collusion on the part of husband and wife for the purpose of reaping an undeserved financial reward at the expense of the family's liability insurer. Both of these arguments were considered and rejected in the analogous context of parental immunity in the recent case of *Sorensen v. Sorensen*, —— Mass. ——[a], 339 N.E.2d 907 (1975), decided this term. We refer to our discussion and resolution of these issues in that case. *Id.* at ——–——[b], 339 N.E.2d 907. Suffice it to say that just as we did not find the arguments concerning the preservation of family harmony and the avoidance of family fraud sufficient to justify a rule barring tort suits for personal injuries by a

child against a parent, we are similarly unconvinced by these arguments in the present context of interspousal immunity. We further note that most of the jurisdictions which have rejected the rule of interspousal immunity have considered these very same arguments and found them wanting. See *Self v. Self*, 58 Cal.2d 683, 689–691, 26 Cal.Rptr. 97, 376 P.2d 65 (1962) (intentional torts); *Klein v. Klein*, 58 Cal.2d 692, 694–696, 26 Cal.Rptr. 102, 376 P.2d 70 (1962) (negligent torts); *Brooks v. Robinson*, 259 Ind. 16, 20–22, 284 N.E.2d 794 (1972); *Rupert v. Stienne*, 90 Nev. 397, 401–402, 528 P.2d 1013 (1974); *Immer v. Risko*, 56 N.J. 482, 488–495, 267 A.2d 481 (1970); *Flores v. Flores*, 84 N.M. 601, 603, 506 P.2d 345 (Ct.App.1973) (intentional torts); *Maestas v. Overton*, 87 N.M. 213, 531 P.2d 947 (1975) (negligent torts); *Surratt v. Thompson*, 212 Va. 191, 192, 183 S.E.2d 200 (1971); *Freehe v. Freehe*, 81 Wash.2d 193, 187–189, 500 P.2d 771 (1972).

However, the defendant argues that, unlike the situation prevailing in most other jurisdictions, the rule of interspousal immunity has taken on statutory dimensions in Massachusetts. The argument is based on G.L. c. 209, § 6, as appearing in St. 1963, c. 765, § 2, which provides: "A married woman may sue and be sued in the manner as if she were sole; *but this section shall not authorize suits between husband and wife* except in connection with contracts entered into pursuant to the authority contained in section two" (emphasis supplied).[2] By including the italicized lan-

---

a. Mass.Adv.Sh. (1975) 3662.

b. Mass.Adv.Sh. (1975) at 3674–3683.

2. As to the historical development of G.L. c. 209, § 6, briefly, married women were first given a limited right to sue and be sued in their own names in St.1845, c. 208, which provided for the separate ownership of property by married women and authorized suits by and against married women "in respect to such property." The first mention of tort actions appears in St.1871, c. 312, which

351 N.E.2d—34

provided that a married woman could sue and be sued in tort in the same manner as if she were unmarried but contained no reference to suits by or against her husband. In 1874 the interspousal language we are concerned with in this case was added in substantially the same form as it appears today in G.L. c. 209, § 6. Statute 1874, c. 184, § 3, read: "A married woman may sue and be sued in the same manner and to the same extent as if she were sole, but nothing herein contained shall authorize suits between hus-

---

Exhibit 13-6 *Lewis v. Lewis* (continues)

530 Mass.   351 **NORTH EASTERN REPORTER, 2d SERIES**

guage in the statute, the Legislature, according to the defendant's argument, has chosen to incorporate the rule of interspousal immunity into the statutory law of the Commonwealth and, therefore, this court is without power to abrogate the rule. With this contention we do not agree. The Supreme Court of New Jersey was faced with similar statutory language when called on to reëxamine the doctrine of interspousal immunity in *Immer v. Risko,* 56 N.J. 482, 267 A.2d 481 (1970). New Jersey's Married Persons' Act included the following provision: "Nothing in this chapter contained shall enable a husband or wife to contract with or to sue each other, except as heretofore, and except as authorized by this chapter." N.J.Stat.Ann. tit. 37:2–5 (1968). The court held that this provision did not incorporate the doctrine of interspousal immunity but merely left the common law undisturbed and " 'intact with its inherent capacity for later judicial alteration.' " *Id.* 56 N.J. at 486, 267 A.2d at 483. The court went on to scrutinize the reasons behind the rule of interspousal immunity and abrogated the rule at least with respect to automobile negligence torts.

The Supreme Court of Indiana in abrogating interspousal immunity in the case of *Brooks v. Robinson,* 259 Ind. 16, 284 N.E.

2d 794 (1972), construed a similar statutory limitation to the same effect, holding that the Legislature was not barring tort actions between husband and wife but was preserving the rule of interspousal immunity in its common law form "subject to amendment, modification, or abrogation by this Court." *Id.* at 24, 284 N.E.2d at 798.[3]

[2] With respect to G.L. c. 209, § 6, it was open to the Legislature to take the position that while it did not wish to abolish the common law rule of interspousal immunity neither did it wish to convert the common law rule into a mandate of statutory law. In G.L. c. 209, § 6, it chose apt language to express such an intention. The Legislature apparently recognized the broad scope of the language, "A married woman may sue and be sued in the same manner as if she were sole," and realized that unless some limiting provision were included the statute itself could be construed as authorizing suits between spouses. By making clear that the statute itself does not alter the rule of interspousal immunity, the Legislature closed the path taken by many courts in other jurisdictions in interpreting the broad, general provisions of their married women's acts as in and of themselves removing the barrier of interspousal immunity. See, e. g., *Katzenberg v. Katzenberg,*

---

band and wife." This statutory language was adopted with minor changes in subsequent consolidations and revisions of the laws of the Commonwealth. See Pub.Sts. (1882), c. 147, § 7; R.L. (1902), c. 153, § 6. Finally, in St.1963, c. 765, § 2, the Legislature added the language authorizing interspousal suits on contracts entered into pursuant to G.L. c. 209, § 2, which section was simultaneously amended to authorize such contracts (St. 1963, c. 765, § 1) and now reads, "A married woman may make contracts, oral and written, sealed and unsealed, in the same manner as if she were sole, and may make such contracts with her husband."

3. The court in the *Brooks* case was concerned with the following statutory language of TR. 17(D) of the Indiana Rules of Procedure: "*Sex, marital and parental status.* For the purposes of suing or being sued there shall

be *no distinction* between men and women or between men and women because of marital or parental status; *provided, however, that this subsection (D) shall not apply to actions in tort.*" The court held that this language should not be construed as "anything more than *legislative awareness* of the judicially created doctrine of the common law. The proviso in TR. 17(D) does not purport to abolish tort actions between husband and wife. Rather it merely provides that if any distinction between husband and wife exists in tort actions, such distinction is not removed by the rule as adopted. The 'distinction' which has existed up to the present is, of course, the common law doctrine of interspousal immunity which is, and always has been, subject to amendment, modification, or abrogation by this Court." *Brooks v. Robinson, supra* at 23–24, 284 N.E.2d at 798 (emphasis in the quoted opinion).

Exhibit 13-6   *Lewis v. Lewis*

(continues)

LEWIS v. LEWIS
Cite as, Mass., 851 N.E.2d 526

Mass. **531**

183 Ark. 626, 37 S.W.2d 696 (1931); *Lorang v. Hays*, 69 Idaho 440, 209 P.2d 733 (1949); *Brown v. Gosser*, 262 S.W.2d 480 (Ky.1953); *Gilman v. Gilman*, 78 N.H. 4, 95 A. 657 (1915); *Wait v. Pierce*, 191 Wis. 202, 209 N.W. 475 (1926). On the other hand, G.L. c. 209, § 6, does not directly forbid tort suits between husband and wife. The Legislature could have used language more prohibitory in nature had it been its intention to bar such suits; and its choice of the words, "shall not authorize" cannot be considered inadvertent or accidental. Compare with G.L. c. 209, § 6, the Married Women's Property Act of the English Parliament, 45 & 46 Vict., c. 75, § 12 (1882), which provides that "no husband or wife shall be entitled to sue the other for a tort," and Ill.Rev.Stat. c. 68, § 1 (1973), which provides: "A married woman may, in all cases, sue and be sued without joining her husband with her, to the same extent as if she were unmarried; *provided, that neither husband nor wife may sue the other for a tort to the person committed during coverture*" (emphasis supplied).

In *Frankel v. Frankel*, 173 Mass. 214, 53 N.E. 398 (1899), holding that the enactment of the statutory language now contained in G.L. c. 209, § 6, did not abolish the equitable remedies previously available between husband and wife, this court noted that "[t]he section referred to above does not forbid suits between husband and wife, but simply provides that it shall not be construed to authorize them." *Id.* at 215, 53 N.E. at 398. See *Zwick v. Goldberg*, 304 Mass. 66, 70, 22 N.E.2d 661 (1939). In addition, in *Gahm v. Gahm*, 243 Mass. 374, 375, 137 N.E. 876 (1923), a case decided prior to the amendments to G.L. c. 209, §§ 2, 6, contained in St.1963, c. 765, §§ 1, 2, which authorize contracts between husband and wife and suits on those contracts, the court observed that "[t]he common-law disabilities of married women as to the making of contracts have been removed by statute so that they now can contract and

sue and be sued in the same manner as if single, subject, however, to the limitation that contracts and suits between husband and wife are not permissible but *stand on the same footing as heretofore*" (emphasis supplied). The "footing" which was the basis of the prohibition of suits between husband and wife "heretofore" was the *common law rule* of interspousal immunity. See *Fowle v. Torrey*, 135 Mass. 87, 89–90 (1883). The "shall not authorize" language of G.L. c. 209, § 6, would appear then to be a reference to, not an incorporation of, the common law rule of interspousal immunity. We conclude that the statute has left the rule in its common law status susceptible to reëxamination and alteration by this court.

[3,4] The defendant further argues that even if interspousal immunity is not mandated by statute, a common law rule of such long standing should be abolished, if at all, by legislative and not judicial action. The defendant concedes, as he must, that it is within the power and authority of the court to abrogate this judicially created rule; and the mere longevity of the rule does not by itself provide cause for us to stay our hand if to perpetuate the rule would be to perpetuate inequity. When the rationales which gave meaning and coherence to a judicially created rule are no longer vital, and the rule itself is not consonant with the needs of contemporary society, a court not only has the authority but also the duty to reëxamine its precedents rather than to apply by rote an antiquated formula. Chief Justice Vanderbilt described this interaction between the judiciary and the evolving common law in an oft cited passage from *State v. Culver*, 23 N.J. 495, 505, 129 A.2d 715, 721, cert. denied, 354 U.S. 925, 77 S.Ct. 1387, 1 L.Ed.2d 1441 (1957): "One of the great virtues of the common law is its dynamic nature that makes it adaptable to the requirements of society at the time of its application in court. There is not a rule of the common

Exhibit 13-6 *Lewis v. Lewis*

(continues)

law in force today that has not evolved from some earlier rule of common law, gradually in some instances, more suddenly in others, leaving the common law of today when compared with the common law of centuries ago as different as day is from night. The nature of the common law requires that each time a rule of law is applied it be carefully scrutinized to make sure that the conditions and needs of the times have not so changed as to make further application of it the instrument of injustice. Dean Pound posed the problem admirably in his *Interpretations of Legal History* (1922) when he stated, 'Law must be stable, and yet it cannot stand still.' "

This court has frequently had occasion to effect through its decisions not insignificant changes in the field of tort law. See, e. g., *Sorensen v. Sorensen,* — Mass. — c, 339 N.E.2d 907 (1975); *Mone v. Greyhound Lines, Inc.,* — Mass. — d, 331 N.E.2d 916 (1975); *Diaz v. Eli Lilly & Co.,* 364 Mass. 153, 302 N.E.2d 555 (1973), and cases cited at 166 n. 43, 302 N.E.2d 555. In the *Diaz* case, in rejecting the argument that the court should defer to the Legislature on the question of recovery for loss of consortium, we noted that "the Legislature may rationally prefer to act, if it acts at all, after rather than before the common law has fulfilled itself in its own way." *Id.* at 166, 302 N.E.2d at 563. We are of opinion that this is an especially appropriate comment in the context of this case where the Legislature in G.L. c. 209, § 6, has recognized the rule of interspousal immunity but has left the rule in its common law form, expressing the preference, at least implicitly, that this court continue to evaluate the usefulness and propriety of the rule. We further note that the argument that any change in the doctrine of interspousal immunity should come from the Legislature, not the judiciary, has been considered and rejected in many decisions abrogating the common law rule. See, e. g., *Brooks v. Robinson,* 259 Ind. 16, 22–23, 284 N.E.2d 794 (1972); *Beaudette v. Frana,* 285 Minn. 366, 370–371, 173 N.W.2d 416 (1969); *Rupert v. Stienne,* 90 Nev. 397, 399–401, 528 P.2d 1013 (1974); *Immer v. Risko,* 56 N.J. 482, 487, 267 A.2d 481 (1970); *Flores v. Flores,* 84 N.M. 601, 603–604, 506 P.2d 345 (Ct.App.1973); *Freehe v. Freehe,* 81 Wash.2d 183, 189, 500 P.2d 771 (1972).

[5–7] We conclude therefore that it is open to this court to reconsider the common law rule of interspousal immunity and, having done so, we are of opinion that it should no longer bar an action by one spouse against another in a case such as the present one. We believe this result is consistent with the general principle that if there is tortious injury there should be recovery, and only strong arguments of public policy should justify a judicially created immunity for tortfeasors and bar to recovery for injured victims. See *Morash & Sons, Inc. v. Commonwealth,* 363 Mass. 612, 621, 296 N.E.2d 461 (1973); *Freehe v. Freehe, supra,* 81 Wash.2d at 192, 500 P.2d 771. We have examined the reasons offered in support of the common law immunity doctrine and, whatever their vitality in the social context of generations past, we find them inadequate today to support a general rule of interspousal tort immunity. In arriving at this conclusion we are mindful that the rights and privileges of husbands and wives with respect to one another are not unaffected by the marriage they have voluntarily undertaken together. Conduct, tortious between two strangers, may not be tortious between spouses because of the mutual concessions implied in the marital relationship. For this reason we limit our holding today to claims arising out of motor vehicle accidents. Further definition of the scope of

c. Mass.Adv.Sh. (1975) 3662.

d. Mass.Adv.Sh. (1975) 2326.

Exhibit 13-6   *Lewis v. Lewis*

(continues)

COMMONWEALTH v. LODER   Mass. **533**

Cite as, Mass.App., 351 N.E.2d 533

the new rule of interspousal tort liability will await development in future cases.[4]

It follows that the motion for summary judgment should not have been allowed and that the judgment is to be vacated.

So ordered.

COMMONWEALTH

v.

Robert D. LODER.

Appeals Court of Massachusetts, Middlesex.

Argued May 10, 1976.

Decided July 27, 1976.

Defendant was convicted in Superior Court, Middlesex County, of rape, armed robbery, burglary and the commission of an unnatural and lascivious act, and he appealed. The Appeals Court held that the trial court acted correctly in denying in part defendant's motion to suppress in-court and out-of-court identifications by the victims.

Affirmed.

Criminal Law ⚷339.7(1), 339.8(1)

In prosecution for rape and related offenses, trial court acted properly in refusing to suppress photographic and other pretrial identifications of defendant by victims.

Daniel F. Toomey, Boston, for defendant.

Bonnie H. MacLeod-Griffin, Asst. Dist. Atty., for the Commonwealth.

Before HALE, C. J., and KEVILLE and GOODMAN, JJ.

RESCRIPT.

The defendant appeals under G.L. c. 278, §§ 33A–33G from convictions, after a jury trial, of rape, armed robbery and burglary, and the commission of an unnatural and lascivious act. He claims error in the denial in part, after a voir dire, of his motion to suppress in-court and out-of-court identifications by the victims, a young man and woman. At the time of the crimes the victims were occupying the bedroom of an apartment of the young woman. Two men entered and assaulted them during a period of one and one-half to two hours. The only light in the room came from a street light opposite the window and lights from the park across the street. These dimly illuminated the room. In the course of the episode the young man, despite being nearsighted, was able to view both assailants for a total period of ten minutes. For one minute, the face of the individual, later identified by the victims as the defendant, was only several inches distant from his eyes. The young woman was assaulted by the defendant for approximately thirty minutes. During that time her face was within inches of his face. Later that day the young man selected the defendant's photograph from an array of more than one hundred photographs shown him by the police and the young woman separately selected the defendant's photograph from six to ten

---

Do not overlook this footnote. It is part of the *Lewis* decision.

4. In *Sorensen v. Sorensen,* —— Mass. ——, ——, 339 N.E.2d 907 (1975) (Mass.Adv.Sh. [1975] 3662, 3665), in abrogating parental immunity in automobile tort cases we limited the liability to the extent of the parent's automobile liability insurance coverage. In the present case there is nothing in the record concerning the availability or the amount of the defendant's liability insurance, and we do not refer to insurance as a limiting factor in our holding. We do not interpret the logic (as opposed to the precise holding) of *Sorensen* as turning on the availability of insurance in each case, and we decline to limit liability in interspousal tort actions in such a fashion.

Exhibit 13-6   *Lewis v. Lewis (concluded)*

CASE DISCUSSION QUESTIONS

1. Compare the court's view in *Lewis* regarding the need to defer to the legislative branch with that of the court in *McBoyle*. Those cases, as well as the dissent in *Johnson*, illustrate a constant tension in our system between the elected legislature and the appointed judiciary. While the court will often defer to the legislative branch, there are times when it will not, especially in areas of law not yet touched by legislation. It is then that you will probably see a phrase similar to the one used by the *Lewis* court: "[T]he court not only has the authority but also the duty to reexamine its precedents." Do you think that it is appropriate in a democratic society for a court to wield such power?

2. What exactly did Mrs. Lewis win?

3. On page 529 of the opinion, the court cites *Sorensen v. Sorensen*, a case in which a child wanted to sue his father for negligent driving. By citing this case, the court seems to suggest that the same principles that apply to children suing their parents should apply to spouses suing each other. Do you agree?

Legal Reasoning Exercise

6. Based on *Lewis,* analyze whether you think the doctrine of spousal immunity will bar Miller's claim.

E. THE POWER OF JUDGES TO MAKE NEW LAW

In recent years, some observers, especially conservative politicians, have criticized judges for "making law." arguing that by being "activists," these judges were exceeding their proper judicial role. These critics claim that judges are supposed to stick to enforcing the laws as they were written, rather than changing them to incorporate their own personal political views. But after having read this chapter and Chapter 12, on interpreting and applying the law, you have seen how making law is an inevitable part of a judge's job.

You have seen the extent to which judges exercise discretion when it comes to interpreting ambiguities found in constitutions, statutes, and administrative regulations. And while judges are expected to follow the precedents set in previous cases, they nonetheless retain a great deal of flexibility in terms of what they consider to be mandatory and how they interpret those precedents.

The real conflict is not over whether judges make law, but over the criteria they use in reaching their decisions. In Chapter 12, we explained the basic approaches that judges use for interpreting statutes, regulations, and constitutions. They can apply a literal/plain meaning approach, use various canons of construction, do a contextual analysis, or base a decision on legislative history. These approaches may lead to different results, however, and there is no agreement as to which approach is best. In fact, the same judge may apply different approaches in different cases, and two judges may come to different conclusions even though they are using the same general approach. It is this ability to apply different approaches, coupled with the ambiguity of the materials being analyzed, that provides judges with the wide degree of discretion they have in deciding individual cases.

In this chapter, we have seen the courts taking differing approaches. In *McBoyle,* the Court thought it was bound to narrowly interpret the statute. In *Johnson,* the Court struck down a state statute as unconstitutional. In *Callow,* the court clung to stare decisis, whereas in *Lewis,* the same court chose to remake the law.

How can you know whether a court will take a more liberal or a more conservative view of its role in changing the law? You can never know for sure, but here are some general guidelines. First, remember that all courts, even the U.S. Supreme Court, are bound to follow the Constitution. Therefore, the first question to ask is whether the issue involves a constitutional provision. If it does, then the court has the power to invalidate any statute or common-law principle that is not in conformity with the Constitution.

If no constitutional provision is involved, then the court's only role in statutory cases is to interpret the statute. The court is not free to rewrite the statute to reach a result that it thinks is more just. This is the type of case where the court has the least amount of freedom. (Of course, a determined court can often find ambiguity in the seemingly clearest of language, and thereby "rewrite" the statute.) If there is no constitutional provision and no statute involved, then the court has the most freedom to shape the common law as it deems best to meet the needs of justice. See Figure 13-5.

Figure 13-5   Factors Affecting the Power of a Court to Make New Law

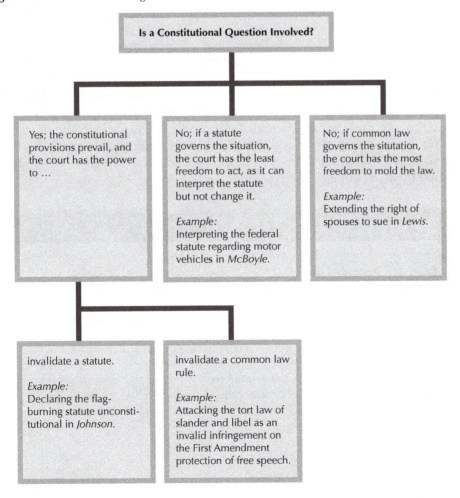

SUMMARY

This chapter has covered how to find and interpret court opinions. The legal significance of a court opinion depends on a variety of factors, including the type of court issuing the opinion and the extent to which it modifies existing precedent. Mandatory authority comes from a higher court in the same jurisdiction.

Court opinions typically follow a standard pattern that includes headnotes (in West editions) and the syllabus (prepared by the court or by West), the facts of the case, the statement of existing law, the issues raised, the decision reached, the reasoning, and, if they exist, concurring and/or dissenting opinions.

The traditional method for summarizing court opinions is known as case briefing. In this chapter we have examined one approach to case briefing that emphasizes the analytical skills that are the focus of this book. Depending on your purpose, however, you or your supervising lawyer may wish to follow another method. There is no one right way to brief. Use the method that best serves your purpose.

We have noted that the pattern of reasoning used depends on the type of issue being decided. In *McBoyle,* the court interpreted a statute, while in *Johnson,* it interpreted the Constitution. *Keller, Callow,* and *Lewis* involved application of the common law.

As you can see from reading the cases in this chapter, the theory of stare decisis plays a vital role in our legal system: While it provides for stability, it also allows for change. It is not always clear what the precedents actually mean and there is wiggle room in determining which ones actually apply in a specific situation.

In Chapter 15, we will discuss how to integrate discussions of statutes and cases into legal arguments. Before that, however, we need to take a more detailed look at how to find the law. Although you may have appreciated how we have thus far supplied you with the statutes and court opinions, you probably have been wondering what you would do if someone asked you to go to a law library and find them for yourself. That is the topic of Chapter 14.

REVIEW QUESTIONS

Pages 347 through 356
1. What are case reporters, and how do official and unofficial reporters differ?
2. What information is included in a typical case citation?
3. What is the difference between mandatory and persuasive authority? Why does it matter?
4. What is the difference between analogizing a case and distinguishing a case?
5. Give an example of when a court decided to overrule precedent and thereby dramatically changed the current law.
6. Why does court-made law generally evolve slowly?
7. What are the four basic categories of court opinions?

Pages 356 through 399

8. List each part of a brief and describe the function of each.

9. Explain the difference between overruling a decision and reversing a decision.

10. Look at each of the following potential case holdings for the *Blair* case. Which one do you think best represents a holding as it should appear in a case brief? Why? What is wrong with the others? Which is the broadest holding? The narrowest?

    a. Yes.

    b. Yes, burglary is committed when someone enters a partially enclosed carwash.

    c. Yes, it is unlawful to enter a partially enclosed carwash.

    d. Yes, the defendant should be found guilty.

    e. Yes, burglary, which requires the entering of a building or house trailer, is committed when someone enters any partially enclosed building designed to protect people or property.

    f. Yes, burglary, which requires the entering of a building or house trailer, is committed when someone enters a partially enclosed carwash.

    g. Reversed.

    h. The trial court's decision was correct.

11. Why is it sometimes important to include the reasoning of concurring and/or dissenting opinions in a case brief?

WEB EXERCISES

1. The web offers many articles with helpful advice about how to brief cases. As you read them, you may find that they vary among themselves, and with the advice provided here, by recommending different or additional categories of information to include. That is to be expected, because as we indicated earlier, there is no one right way to brief cases. Consider the article on how to brief a case at *lib.jjay.cuny.edu/how-to/brief-a-case*. What advice does the author give regarding how to choose the facts when briefing a case?

2. In this chapter, you read the Supreme Court case *Texas v. Johnson*. Before the Supreme Court decides a case, it hears oral arguments. The advocates for each side have just 30 minutes to present their point of view. It is not unusual for a lawyer to have barely started before one of the justices interrupts with a question. To hear the actual argument made in *Texas v. Johnson*, go to *oyez.com/cases/1988/88-155*. There, you will be able to listen to the lawyer for the state of Texas and the lawyer for Johnson as they argue for their clients and attempt to answer the justices' questions. Which lawyer do you think did a better job, and why? What most impressed you about what happens during oral argument?

Chapter 14

Finding the Law

I have found that a great part of the information I have was acquired by looking for something and finding something else on the way.
Franklin P. Adams

Chapter Objectives

After reading this chapter, you should be able to:

- Contrast online with book-based research.
- Identify the six steps of legal research.
- Describe how to locate statutes.
- Describe five methods for finding case law.
- Explain the purpose of doing an online Boolean search.
- Describe how to update your research.

INTRODUCTION

In Chapters 12 and 13, we described how to locate primary authority when you have a citation to enacted law or to a court opinion. In this chapter we will introduce you to other methods for finding both primary and secondary legal materials. One caution: If you feel overwhelmed by the whole researching process, do not despair. Tackling a research assignment can be a daunting experience, and it can take years of experience to become a truly competent legal researcher, but it can be done.

Ever since the 1500s, when law reporters were first introduced, legal professionals have looked to books for answers to their legal questions. Today, most researchers rely on online sources, but the basic steps that you need to take as an effective legal researcher are essentially the same, no matter whether you rely on books or go online. Those basic steps are outlined in Figure 14-1.

To illustrate the steps of legal research, we will follow the process that you might use to research the issue of spousal immunity. Recall the situation of Janice Miller, who was injured while working in her backyard with her husband, George. Because Janice and George lived in Springfield, Massachusetts, we will focus our research on Massachusetts law. However, the principles that we will be discussing can be applied to research in any state. Because the purpose of this chapter is to introduce you to the many researching resources, our journey will be more all-inclusive than would be typical of a normal researching session.

Case 17: The Injured Spouse

Paralegal Kendall received a memorandum from attorney Harper regarding the firm's client, Janice Miller. Miller was injured while working in her backyard with her husband, George Booth. Before the firm can move ahead with a possible lawsuit against Mr. Booth, it needs to conduct research to find out whether spouses can sue each other for tortious injuries.

A. OVERVIEW OF THE RESEARCHING PROCESS

Today, performing online research via the Internet is rapidly becoming the preferred method for conducting legal and factual research. First, if you have an Internet connection and a laptop computer, a tablet, or even a smartphone, the law library becomes instantly portable. Second, the researcher can search for information by citation or by conducting a full-text search. Third, Internet-based research is becoming increasingly cost effective, and sometimes, aside from the cost of the Internet connection itself, even free.

1. Online Versus Traditional Book-Based Legal Research

While the methods that you use to do legal research are essentially the same, whether undertaking research in books or online, there are a few important differences.

First, if your starting point is anything other than a known citation to relevant authority, and you are using books, generally you will start your search in an index, looking for the words that you hope the editors used to describe your problem. If you go online, you will be doing a search for terms that you assume the authors themselves used when writing the legal authority you are seeking (i.e., the legislature for a statute and judges for court opinions).

In books, statutes have indexes located in separate volumes, usually labelled the General Index or something similar. Court opinions, however, are published in chronological order, not by subject matter. Therefore, if you do not know the citation for a court decision applicable to your problem, absent a better way to find relevant court decisions, you would simply have to begin reading court decisions until you stumbled on one that related to your problem. Fortunately, West developed its digest system to help us locate cases more efficiently.

With its digest system, West has organized the law into hundreds of legal topics. Each topic is then subdivided into sections, which West calls "key numbers." The resulting digest is a collection of one-paragraph summaries of court decisions, arranged by subject matter. While the digest is an essential tool for the book-based researcher, it still can be useful to those doing their research online. We describe the West digest system in more detail beginning on page 422.

A second basic difference between online and book-based research is that if you rely on books, then by default, as soon as you select a text, you have also selected a jurisdiction and type of law. For example, if you start with a volume of Massachusetts Reports, you have picked Massachusetts as your jurisdiction and court decisions for the type of law. Online, you can simply type in your search and your results will include all types of law from all 50 states and the federal government. You can then filter your results for jurisdiction and type of law. (However, if you know your jurisdiction and the type of law you are seeking, you can start by putting in those restrictions before running your online search.)

Third, it is easier to move from one resource to the next if you do your research online, as that usually involves nothing more than clicking on links. To accomplish the same result in the books, you need to locate citing references by physically gaining access to the appropriate book. For example, if you find a relevant statute in an annotated code, the editors will include summaries of court opinions. You can easily locate and read those opinions by simply clicking on the provided link. If you are using books, to move from statute to court opinion requires getting up from your desk and searching for the appropriate volume. Then once you have located the case, the court may reference other cases that you would like to read. When using the books, this entails yet another journey to locate the appropriate volume. When online, traveling to a new decision is just a click away.

Finally, a major difference is in the way the materials are kept up-to-date. You can count on commercial online resources, such as Westlaw, LexisNexis, Fastcase, and Casemaker, to be updated on a regular basis, often within 24 hours of a change in the law. Other Internet sources are more variable, and you should always check to see how recently the site has been updated. Books are updated much more slowly. Many books are updated through the insertion of pocket parts. A **pocket part** is a pamphlet that is inserted into a pocket in the back of a book. It contains information that is new since the volume was published. But because pocket parts are usually updated only once a year, the information they contain can be quite out of date.

Pocket part
A pamphlet inserted into the back of a book containing information new since the volume was published.

DISCUSSION QUESTION

1. There is an ongoing debate among educators as to whether, given the widespread availability of online researching tools, there is still a need to teach book-based research techniques anymore. What are some of the pros and cons of knowing book-based research techniques? Do you think it is useful to learn book-based research techniques?

2. Major Online Legal Research Providers

The major law-related Internet-based research providers fall into two general categories. The first type charges a fee for the services. The two best-known and most complete for-fee providers are **Lexis** and **Westlaw.** Two more products, **Casemaker** and **Fastcase,** are available at no extra charge to members of a number of state and local bar associations. CasemakerPro requires an additional fee, and each can be purchased through a subscription service when state and local bar associations do not cover the cost.

All of these platforms allow researchers to perform natural-language searches similar to those done on Google or more complex Boolean searches, which we discuss beginning on page 424.

The second category of law-related Internet-based research providers includes various governmental agencies, educational institutions, and private enterprises. These usually provide both primary and secondary resources at minimal or even no cost.

a. The Major Commercial Databases: Lexis, Westlaw, Casemaker, and FastCase

While there are other commercial research providers, Lexis and Westlaw have historically been the two major competing sources for online legal information. To use either, a law firm must pay a subscription fee. Legal professionals are increasingly using Casemaker and Fastcase because many state and local bar associations have made them free to members.

(1) Coverage

All four services contain databases that include the full text of federal and state court cases, statutes, and administrative regulations, and various specialized legal publications. For example, you can conduct secondary research using legal encyclopedias, the Restatements, bar journals, and law review articles. You can also update your research using a **citator,** which can be used to determine the validity of a law. Lexis includes the online version of Shepard's citations, and the others provide similar services.

(2) Differences between Westlaw and the other services

Perhaps the most significant difference is that in addition to the full text of appellate court cases, Westlaw contains the headnotes and key numbers that appear in West's digest system. This feature can simplify the search process for some users and makes it easier to coordinate the results with materials gathered

Lexis
An online legal database containing court decisions and statutes from the entire country, as well as secondary authority; such as Am. Jur. 2d and A.L.R.

Westlaw
An online legal database containing court decisions and statutes from the entire country, as well as secondary authority; and KeyCite, similar in function to LexisNexis Shepard's online.

Casemaker
An online legal database containing court decisions and statutes from the entire country, as well as secondary authority; and CiteCheck, similar in function to LexisNexis Shepard's citations online.

Fastcase
An online legal database containing court decisions and statutes from the entire country, as well as secondary authority; includes a citation checker and AI Sandbox, using artificial intelligence (AI) to analyze data or documents.

Citator
A resource to help ensure the current validity of a law.

from West's hardbound publications, such as its regional reporters and digests. In Westlaw, you can also search for additional cases on the basis of the West key numbers.

b. Other Internet-Based Resources

Many Internet sites contain legal materials, such as statutes, regulations, and court opinions. The federal government and many state and local governments maintain **websites** where they publish official documents. In addition to the government websites, particularly useful, fairly complete, and (most important) free sites include the Legal Information Institute (Cornell School of Law), FindLaw, the Public Library of Law, the Law Library of Congress, and Google Scholar.

It is often a good idea to begin your research with a free site. You may find just what you need. However, information on free Internet sites is never as complete as the materials accessed through commercial providers. For example, while the coverage of most state court decisions goes back to the 1800s on Lexis and Westlaw, the coverage may extend back only to the mid-1900s on the free sites.

> **PRACTICE TIP**
>
> All four services provide free online training.

> **PRACTICE TIP**
>
> Have a smartphone? Then there is a world of apps just waiting for you to download—everything from legal dictionaries to free access to statutes and case law. Lawyerist (*lawyerist.com*) provides an extensive list of mobile applications, or just go to Google Play on your Android phone or the App Store on your iPhone and do a search for "law" or "legal."

DISCUSSION QUESTION

2. Your firm needs to cut costs, and it has a free Casemaker subscription through its local bar association. Would you advise that they eliminate their Westlaw or Lexis subscription in favor of relying on the free service? Why or why not?

3. Primary Versus Secondary and Mandatory Versus Persuasive Authority

Before we begin discussing the actual researching process, it is important to remember that your goal is almost always to find primary authority. As you will recall from Chapter 13, **primary authority** is the law itself, and **secondary authority** describes and explains the law. Think of an analogy from one of your English classes. Your professor may ask you to read Shakespeare's *Hamlet* (primary authority), but if you have trouble understanding Shakespeare's Old English dialogue, you might also turn to articles that explain the play's meaning (secondary authority).

Primary authority
The law itself, such as statutes and court opinions.

Secondary authority
Information about the law, such as that contained in encyclopedias and law review articles.

In the same way, your main goal in conducting legal research is to look for and find primary authority—that is, court opinions and enacted law (constitutions, statutes, and regulations) governing the situation. But depending on how much you know about the area you are researching, it is often a good idea to start with secondary authority. Secondary authority will provide you with general background information and references to relevant primary authority.

There are also times when secondary authority can prove useful in its own right. For example, both Westlaw and Lexis contain full-text versions of news articles from major newspapers, jury verdicts, secretary of state filings, and asset information. While legal researchers have traditionally relied on primary law sources, these other sources are becoming increasingly important. Because most cases settle and hence never make it to a trial court, let alone an appellate court, you may not be able to find a published court opinion discussing the issue you are researching. For example, assume your client was harmed by a specific product. By searching news articles, you may find that the product manufacturer recently settled a similar case.

While your ultimate goal in conducting research is to find primary authority, not all primary authority is created equal. There is mandatory primary authority and persuasive primary authority. **Mandatory authority** is defined as a statute or court opinion from a higher court in the same jurisdiction. For matters dealing with federal law, that would mean statutes enacted by Congress and court opinions from the relevant circuit court of appeals as well as from the U.S. Supreme Court. Anything from other circuits or the states would be categorized as persuasive only. For states, mandatory authority includes statutes enacted by that state's legislature and court opinions from its appellate courts. Appellate decisions from other states and the federal system could be persuasive, but they would not be binding.

P R A C T I C E   T I P

Recall that in our federal system of government, state courts and federal courts are co-equal partners. Except in matters of federal law, federal court decisions are not mandatory on state courts. Therefore, when a federal court has jurisdiction based on diversity of citizenship and decides a matter of state law, its decision is not mandatory on state trial courts. The federal court is merely guessing as to how state appellate courts would have handled the issue if it had been presented to them.

Notice that while secondary authority is always categorized as persuasive authority, primary authority can be either mandatory or persuasive, depending on the source. Therefore, in our problem involving Miller and Booth, if the accident occurred in Massachusetts, the legal researcher would look primarily to Massachusetts statutes and appellate decisions for guidance, as those would provide the mandatory authority for this situation.

B. THE SIX STEPS OF LEGAL RESEARCH

As outlined in Figure 14-1, there are six basic steps to effective legal research. First, you must define the problem that you have been asked to solve. This includes deciding whether it involves state or federal law, or both, and whether you are most likely to find your answer in a constitutional provision, a statute, an administrative regulation, court opinions, or in a combination of sources.

    Second, if you are not able to answer those questions because you are unfamiliar with the area of law, a good approach is to review some secondary sources for background information and for references to primary law. If, however, you feel comfortable with your knowledge base, you can skip step 2 and go directly to step 3 — brainstorming a list of search terms. Only when you have a complete list should you go on to step 4, actually looking for primary authority. Take your time with this stage. Carefully read and analyze the law you find. How will you be able to decide when you are done and ready to move on (step 5)? Usually,

> **PRACTICE TIP**
>
> When deciding whether to research state or federal case law, remember that even state law issues can end up in federal court under diversity jurisdiction.

Figure 14-1   The Six Steps of Legal Research

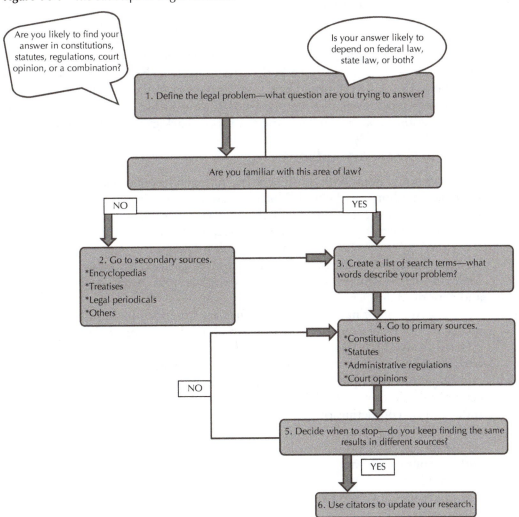

you can stop when you keep finding the same answers no matter what source you consult.

Finally, in step 6, update your research to ensure that what you found is still good law. Below we examine each of these six steps in more detail.

1. Define the Legal Problem

The most important tool that you have in your legal researching arsenal is your ability to think critically. If you do not take the time to think through your problem, then when you go to the library, you will find yourself aimlessly leafing through books. If, instead, you go online, you'll find yourself seduced by the apparent simplicity of typing random search terms into a Google-like interface. But you will retrieve so much irrelevant information that you will be overwhelmed. Instead, force yourself to take the time to analyze the problem critically before you hit the books or log onto your computer.

Try to state the problem you have been asked to resolve in a simple sentence. Sometimes this may be quite easy, as your assignment will include a clear question for you to answer. For example, in our case involving Miller and Booth, we know we have been asked to find out if spouses in Massachusetts can sue each other for tortious injuries. Sometimes, however, you will simply be presented with a set of facts and will have to decide for yourself the areas of law involved.

If the latter is the case, then begin by asking yourself—does the problem involve state law, federal law, or both. Is there likely to be a statute that governs the problem or will you more likely find the answer in the common law? Might an agency's regulations also be involved? If you do not know the answers to these questions, take a step back and read some background information.

2. Go to Secondary Authority

If you are not familiar with the area of law that you have been asked to research, secondary authority is helpful. Not only does it contain general overviews of various areas of the law, but it will also give you citations to primary authority. In this section we discuss various types of secondary authority. If you are looking for a very general overview of the law, then looking in an encyclopedia would be a good place to start. But you can find more focused discussions of specific topics in various sources, such as treatises, restatements, American Law Reports, and periodical articles.

The two major national encyclopedias are **American Jurisprudence Second,** most commonly referred to and cited as **Am. Jur. 2d,** and **Corpus Juris Secundum,** referred to as **C.J.S.** Each is divided into hundreds of separate topics, ranging from abandoned property to zoning and planning, which are then broken down into numerous subtopics. Each subtopic contains a narrative description of the general rules in that area. This is known as **black letter law.** Wherever different states follow conflicting rules, encyclopedias point out the conflict and briefly explain both positions. In addition to this type of general narrative discussion, these encyclopedias provide various cross-references to other secondary sources and citations to relevant court opinions.

In addition to Am. Jur. 2d and C.J.S., which are national in scope, many states have their own state-specific encyclopedias. As with national encyclopedias,

---

PRACTICE TIP

Always think through your proposed researching project before entering the library or going online.

American Jurisprudence Second (Am. Jur. 2d)
A general legal encyclopedia that summarizes the entire body of American law.

Corpus Juris Secundum (C.J.S.)
West's law encyclopedia. Contains cross-references to West digest topics and key numbers.

Black letter law
Generally accepted legal principles.

the textual material is supported by references to court opinions, but with the focus on state law.

Finally, there are also special subject encyclopedias that focus on a single topic, such as contracts or evidence. They bear names like Fletcher's Cyclopedia of the Law of Private Corporations.

Unlike encyclopedias, **treatises** summarize, interpret, and evaluate the law in a specific area. Two well-known treatises are Corbin on Contracts and Wigmore on Evidence.

Restatements, such as the Restatement of Torts or the Restatement of Contracts, are a series of books that summarize the basic principles of common law (i.e., they literally restate the law). As these restatements are written by a group of legal professionals, not judges, they represent a form of secondary authority. However, you will frequently find courts quoting the restatements.

In **American Law Reports Annotated,** you will find only selected topics covered in much more depth than you will find in an encyclopedia. If you find a pertinent A.L.R. annotation, you will have a good overview of the law in that given area. However, because the coverage of A.L.R. is not encyclopedic, there may not be an A.L.R. annotation covering your area.

Law reviews and other types of legal periodicals are still another source for researching the meaning of the law. Law reviews, published by law schools and edited by law students, contain a wealth of thoroughly researched information about specific areas of the law. The lead articles are usually expansive pieces, often written by law professors. A comments or notes section contains contributions of the student editors. Because the law review staffs are traditionally made up of the brightest students, their work has earned a high reputation. Other periodicals are often more specialized and practitioner oriented and also can contain articles of great value.

There are also weekly newspapers devoted to legal topics, both national in scope, such as the *National Law Journal,* and state-specific, such as *Massachusetts Lawyers Weekly.* Not only will these newspapers keep you up to date on current developments in the legal field, but they will frequently provide background information on specific topics.

You can find all of the secondary sources mentioned here both in print and on the two major commercial databases, Westlaw and Lexis; in addition, many of them can be found in Casemaker or Fastcase. Your options for free online secondary resources are more limited. Government websites will often contain background information on their legislative and court systems. On Google Scholar you can search for scholarly articles. However, instead of the full-text of the article, you will often find only an abstract and to read the full article, you will have to pay a fee. A good source for short summaries on many legal topics is the Legal Information Institute's website (*www.law.cornell.edu*).

In terms of citation value, all secondary sources are not created equal. Unless you have absolutely nothing else on which to rely, you should never cite to an encyclopedia. Encyclopedias give you valuable background information, but you should then proceed with your research into primary authority. Also, generally, you should not cite to A.L.R. annotations except when giving general information, such as the number of states that have held a certain way on a particular legal issue.

Treatise
A book that summarizes, interprets, and evaluates the law.

Restatements
A series of books—the Restatements of the Law—summarizing the basic principles of the common law, written by the American Law Institute (ALI).

American Law Reports (A.L.R.)
A source that contains the full text of leading court opinions, followed by a discussion of the issue with references to cases from around the country. Only selected topics are covered, but they are covered in more depth than you will find in an encyclopedia.

Law review
A journal generally published by a law school editorial board or by a bar association. The articles usually contain in-depth analyses of current legal topics.

PRACTICE
TIP

Be warned: Secondary
sources provide only
descriptions of the
author's view of the
law. Never rely only
on a secondary source.
Always read and
analyze the primary
authority yourself.

It is appropriate to cite to other types of secondary authority, especially if they evaluate and analyze the law rather than simply describe it. Of the secondary sources that we have discussed the most authoritative and hence the most valuable to cite are Restatements, law review articles written by known authorities in the field, and treatises. Finally, you can cite to newspaper articles if you cannot find that information in any other source.

Once you start finding references to the same court decisions or statutes in each of the secondary sources you consult, it is time to move on to the next step in the researching process.

3. Create a List of Search Terms

If you research using the books, much of your research will begin with indexes. If you conduct your research using an online source, you will need to type in search terms that hopefully will be contained in the documents you seek. In either case, before you begin, you need to develop a list of words to describe your client's facts and the legal issues.

When creating a list, think of synonyms, antonyms, broader words, and narrower words. For example, in a case involving possible malpractice by a pediatrician, you would certainly think of "pediatrician." A broader term would be "physician." Synonyms would include "doctor" and perhaps "surgeon." An even broader term might be "medical professional" or "practitioner," while narrower terms would include "pediatric oncologist" and "pediatric neurologist."

In analyzing Miller's situation, we can see that the central research issue concerns her ability to sue her husband. Possible words to use include "tort," "negligence," "immunity," "interspousal immunity," "spousal immunity," "spouse," "marriage," "husband," and "wife." Can you think of other words?

It is always best to enter the library or go online with too many rather than too few terms. There is a strange fog that settles on many researchers that prevents them from thinking. If you have thought of only a few words before starting your research and then you do not find them in an index or they do not turn up the results that you expected when you enter them into an online search box, be assured that this mysterious fog will settle in and prevent you from thinking of any alternative approaches. Therefore, brainstorm *before* you begin your research. Assume that you will not be successful on your first try. To handle that eventuality, have a long list of possible alternative search terms.

Legal Reasoning Exercise

1. Last weekend, 10-year-old Eric was exploring and came upon what he thought was a deserted barn. When he climbed up into the loft, he tripped on a loose board and broke his ankle. His parents want to sue the farmer who owns the barn for negligence, even though Eric knew he was trespassing at the time he was injured. What terms would you use to begin researching this problem?

4. Go to Primary Authority

Your ultimate goal in conducting research is to find primary authority: statutes, administrative regulations, and court opinions. If you are unsure as to where to begin, start your research with the statutes. The reason for starting with statutes is that if a statute governs your problem, the courts must follow it. The courts may, of course, interpret the statute, but they cannot ignore it. (This assumes there is no problem with the constitutionality of the statute.) After locating any applicable statutes, you will next read any court opinions that have interpreted those statutes. Finally, you will update your research to make sure the statutes and court opinions you found are still valid.

a. *Finding Statutes*

Each year, as legislatures enact new laws, they are compiled and published in statutory codes. The codes are generally arranged by subject matter. Many states publish an official version of their statutes. In addition, private companies publish the statutes in an annotated version. That is, in addition to the words of the statute, the publishers include editorial features, such as summaries of court opinions that have interpreted the statute. Therefore, it is always best to start your research in an **annotated code**.

Annotated Code
A privately published statutory code includes statutes arranged by subject matter as well as editorial material, such as legislative history and summaries of court decisions interpreting the statutes.

NETNOTE

You can find the text of most state and federal statutes and regulations on government websites. A good place to start your search is at the home page of FindLaw for Legal Professionals at *lp.findlaw.com*. From there, for federal and state statutes and regulations, click on "Cases & Codes." Then, for federal materials, click on "US Code" or "Code of Fed. Regulations." For state statutes and regulations, select your state.

For current information on federal legislation, a good source is *congress.gov*, provided by the Library of Congress.

(1) Starting with the citation

The simplest way to begin statutory research is with a citation to a relevant statute. For example, if you were asked to research the legal validity of spousal immunity in Massachusetts, your boss might know that Mass. Gen. L. ch. 209 §6 governs suits between spouses. Or, while conducting background research, you may have found a statutory reference in one of those secondary sources. In either case, if you have the citation for a statute, you know its chapter and section number.

If you are using the books, you can take that chapter and section number, locate the appropriate volume, and find the statute. Remember that the citation gives chapter numbers, not volume numbers. The chapter numbers are printed on the spine of the statutory code volumes. Using an online source, you can type the citation into an online search box.

You would use this same approach whether looking for a state or federal statute. To illustrate, let's return for just a moment to another case you learned about in Chapter 3. Assume you are representing Diane Dobbs, the waitress whose boss fired her when he discovered she was pregnant. As she wants to sue for sex discrimination under Title VII, which is a federal law, you would begin your research in the federal statutes.

The official publication for the federal statutes is the United States Code (U.S.C.). It is organized by subject matter into fifty titles. Like its official state counterparts, it does not contain summaries of court decisions. It is also only updated every six years. Therefore, most researchers will begin with one of the two private annotated sets: the United States Code Annotated (U.S.C.A.), published by West Group, or the United States Code Service (U.S.C.S.), published by LexisNexis.

The statute that governs unlawful employment practices was enacted as part of the Civil Rights Act of 1964. It is codified in the United States Code in title 42, beginning at section 2000. The first page containing U.S.C.S. §2000e-2, the part of the statute that outlaws certain employment practices, is reproduced in Exhibit 14-1. (The asterisks indicate where we have deleted material for illustration purposes.) As with annotated state codes, in the federal annotated codes, following each statute, there is basic information about the law's legislative history. The United States Code Service also includes cross-references to other sources, including the Code of Federal Regulations. Finally, and most importantly, the annotated codes also include summaries of court decisions.

(2) When you do not have a citation

If you do not know the citation and are doing your research using books, you will have to use the subject matter index for the relevant statutory compilation. For example, returning to Miller's case, which involves Massachusetts law, you could start with the General Index to the Massachusetts General Laws Annotated to find the citation for any statute that might govern our problem. If you are researching online, you would start with search terms that you think would be contained within the statute and type them into the search box. Either approach should lead you to a relevant statute. In Miller's case, that is Mass. Gen. Laws. ch. 209, §6.

PRACTICE TIP

You may find it easier to locate relevant statutes by starting with the index to print volumes rather than going online. In the print indexes, different publishers often use different words to describe the same concept (for example, car instead of motor vehicle). If you have no luck finding index entries in one source, switch to another source, and you may have more success.

EQUAL EMPLOYMENT OPPORTUNITIES   42 USCS § 2000e-2

*   *   *

§ 2000e-2.   Unlawful employment practices

(a) Employer practices. It shall be an unlawful employment practice for an employer—

(1) to fail or refuse to hire or to discharge any individual, or otherwise to discriminate against any individual with respect to his compensation, terms, conditions, or privileges of employment, because of such individual's race, color, religion, sex, or national origin; or

(2) to limit, segregate, or classify his employees or applicants for employment in any way which would deprive or tend to deprive any individual of employment opportunities or otherwise adversely affect his status as an employee, because of such individual's race, color, religion, sex, or national origin.

*   *   *

(July 2, 1964, P. L. 88-352, Title VII, § 703, 78 Stat. 255; Mar. 24, 1972, P. L. 92-261, § 8(a), (b), 86 Stat. 109.)

HISTORY; ANCILLARY LAWS AND DIRECTIVES

References in text:

"The Subversive Activities Control Act of 1950", referred to in subsec. (f) of this section, is Act Sept. 23, 1950, c. 1024, Title I, and appears as 18 USCS §§ 792 note, 793, note prec. 1501, 1507; 22 USCS § 618; 50 USCS §§ 781 et seq., 788 et seq.

Effective date of section:

Section 716(a) and (b) of Act July 2, 1964, provided: "(a) This title [42 USCS §§ 2000e et seq.] shall become effective one year after the date of its enactment.

"(b) Notwithstanding subsection (a), sections of this title other than sections 703, 704, 706, and 707 [42 USCS §§ 2000e-2, 2000e-3, 2000e-5, 2000e-6] shall become effective immediately.".

Amendments:

1972. Act Mar. 24, 1972, in subsec. (a), in paragraph (2), inserted "or applicants for employment"; and, in subsec. (c), in paragraph (2), inserted "or applicants for membership".

CODE OF FEDERAL REGULATIONS

Nondiscrimination requirements, 12 CFR Part 528.

Bureau of Indian Affairs, Department of the Interior; roads of the Bureau of Indian Affairs, 25 CFR Part 170.

Pennsylvania Avenue Development Corporation, Affirmative Action policy and procedure, 36 CFR Part 906.

RESEARCH GUIDE

Federal Procedure L Ed:

12 Fed Proc, L Ed, Evidence, § 33:66.

21 Fed Proc, L Ed, Job Discrimination, §§ 50:1, 16, 85, 127, 144, 176, 270, 275, 480, 488, 558, 576.

33 Fed Proc, L Ed, Trial, § 77:256.

Am Jur:

3A Am Jur 2d, Aliens and Citizens § 2001.

452

Exhibit 14-1   United States Code Service tit. 42, §2000e-2.

(3) Reading an annotated statute

The format for annotated statutes is similar whether you locate them online or in the books. Exhibit 14-2 shows you what you will find once you locate chapter 209, section 6, in West's Massachusetts General Laws Annotated. Under the statute, you will see the heading "Historical Note." The years, such as 1845 and 1902, refer to the years in which the statute was amended. The other numbers, such as "c. 208 §5," refer to the chapter numbers of the statute as it was enacted by the legislature before it was **codified**—that is, placed in the statute books with other statutes dealing with similar subject matter. At the bottom of the page are references to law review articles.

Codification
The process of organizing statutes by subject matter.

Also notice the references on the second page to other resources: the relevant digest topic and key number, C.J.S., M.P.S. (Massachusetts Practice Series), and Westlaw. Finally, at the bottom of the second page, notice the index to the case summaries, called "Notes of Decisions."

On the third page of the exhibit, notice the summaries of cases that have interpreted the statute. One such case is *Lewis*—one of the cases on spousal immunity that you read in Chapter 12. Notice how the citation following the summary for *Lewis* lists the North Eastern Reporter citation first. However, when you cite, you should always give the official citation (in this case Massachusetts Reports) first.

> **PRACTICE TIP**
>
> Always check the pocket part!

b. Finding Agency Regulations

Once you have located a federal or state statute, you should check to see whether any federal or state agency has issued regulations interpreting that statute. Unfortunately, using the books, research into state regulations is often a hit-or-miss affair. Some states have compiled their agency regulations into codes, similar to the statutory codes, complete with a subject matter index. Some states, however, make no attempt to publish all their state regulations in one location. Therefore, researching online may be your best option as many states maintain a government-sponsored website for agency regulations.

On the federal level, administrative regulations are contained in the Code of Federal Regulations (C.F.R.). Like the United States Code, C.F.R. is organized by subject matter into 50 titles. Unfortunately, however, those 50 titles are not the same as those used in the United States Code. Therefore, your first step is to find the correct citation for any applicable regulation. To assist you, the Code of Federal Regulations contains a table of all those sections of the C.F.R. that have been promulgated under the authority of a particular statute.

In order to be as up-to-date as possible, you should also check the latest issues of the Federal Register. The Federal Register is published on a daily basis and contains any newly proposed regulations, as well as any proposed amendments to old regulations.

The Code of Federal Regulations and the Federal Register are also available on commercial databases. Many free cites also include both of these resources.

c. Finding Court Opinions

If you are doing your research in the books, you will find court opinions published in court reporters. Most state court decisions are published in both an official government-published reporter and an unofficial regional reporter, published by West.

The wording of the court decisions, found in West's regional reporters and in the state official reports, is identical. The differences lie in the editorial features. The most useful West editorial feature is the **headnotes** located at the beginning

Headnote
A summary of one legal point in a court opinion on some databases; written by the editors of the database in question.

HUSBAND AND WIFE   **209 § 6**

Who may be appointed trustee, competency, see M.P.S. vol. 22, Lombard, § 1346.

WESTLAW Electronic Research

See WESTLAW guide following the Foreword of this volume.

Notes of Decisions

In general 2
Prior law 1

1. Prior law

Under St.1783, c. 24, § 19, the marriage of a single woman, who was sole administratrix, did not terminate her authority, but made her husband joint administrator with her. Barber v. Bush (1812) 7 Mass. 510.

2. In general

Where A., a married woman, during the lifetime of her husband and before the passage of St.1855, c. 304, deposited in a savings bank a sum of money in her name as "trustee for B," and A., until her death, retained possession of the deposit book, and at times drew out portions of the money, and A.'s executor took possession of the deposit book, charged himself with the amount of the deposit in his inventory, and about two years after her death paid it over to B., who until then had no knowledge of the deposit, the deposit was a part of A.'s estate and was improperly paid to B. Jewett v. Shattuck (1878) 124 Mass. 590.

---

§ 6.   Married woman; power to sue and be sued

A married woman may sue and be sued in the same manner as if she were sole; but this section shall not authorize suits between husband and wife except in connection with contracts entered into pursuant to the authority contained in section two.

Amended by St.1963, c. 765, § 2.

Historical Note

St.1845, c. 208, § 5.   G.S.1860, c. 108, § 8.   P.S.1882, c. 147, § 7.
St.1855, c. 304, §§ 2, 4.   St.1871, c. 312.   R.L.1902, c. 153, § 6.
St.1857, c. 249, § 3.   St.1874, c. 184, § 3.

St.1963, c. 765, § 2, approved Oct. 22, 1963, added the exception.

Cross References

Recovery of money or goods lost at gaming; limitations, see c. 137, § 1.

Law Review Commentaries

Collateral-source rule. William Schwartz (1961) 41 Boston U.L.Rev. 348.

Consortium damages in Massachusetts. John E. Hannigan 21 Boston U.L.Rev. 452 (1941).

Contracts between husband and wife. Frederick M. Hart, 10 Annual Survey of Mass. Law, Boston College, p. 57 (1963).

Equity jurisdiction in Massachusetts, the wife's equity in money advanced to the husband. Frank W. Grinnell (1946) 31 Mass.L.Q. No. 2, p. 47.

Domestic relations, foreign decrees. William J. Greenler, Jr., 6 Annual Survey of Mass. Law, Boston College, p. 74 (1959).

Husband and wife, contract for married woman's services. William J. Greenler, Jr., 3 Ann.Surv.Mass.L. 81 (1956).

Husband and wife tort actions. Monroe L. Inker, 11 Annual Survey of Mass. Law, Boston College, p. 76 (1964).

Interspousal contracts. (1974) 9 Suffolk U.L. Rev. 185.

Interspousal immunity: Application of domiciliary law. Francis J. Nicholson. 13 Annual

351

Exhibit 14-2   Massachusetts General Laws Annotated ch. 209, § 6 (continued)

209 § 6   **DOMESTIC RELATIONS**

Survey of Mass. Law, Boston College, p. 136 (1966).

Interspousal immunity, conflict of laws. Francis J. Nicholson, S. J., 15 Annual Survey of Mass. Law, Boston College, p. 122 (1968).

Law affecting interspousal immunity. Francis J. Nicholson, 11 Annual Survey of Mass. Law, Boston College, p. 91 (1964).

Right of husband to recover for expenses of future medical care of wife. 43 Harvard L.Rev. 661 (1930).

Suits between husband and wife. Harry Zarrow (1957) 4 Ann.Surv.Mass.L. 109.

Wife's liability as husband's surety, disability to sue spouse. Bernard A. Riemer and William E. Hogan, 2 Ann.Surv.Mass.L. 81, 82 (1955).

Written contracts between husband and wife. (1945) 30 Mass.L.Q. No. 4, p. 20.

Library References

→   Husband and Wife ☞203, 204.
      C.J.S. Husband and Wife § 389 et seq.

Comments.

→   Actions between husband and wife, marshalling of assets, see M.P.S. vol. 31, Nolan, § 316.

Antenuptial agreements and contracts, probate, see M.P.S. vol. 23, Lombard, § 1626.

Capacity, husband and wife, defendant's case, the obligation in tort, see M.P.S. vol. 17, Bishop, § 465.

Capacity of parties to contract, see M.P.S. vol. 14, Simpson and Alperin, § 301 et seq.

Capacity to be party, proceedings involving husband and wife, see M.P.S. vol. 9, Nolan, § 155.

Capacity to contract, husband and wife, the plaintiff's case, see M.P.S. vol. 17, Bishop, § 11.

Contracts and suits directly between husband and wife, see M.P.S. vol. 2, Lombard, § 1256.

Contracts between husband and wife, see M.P.S. vol. 3, Lombard, § 2161.

Contracts between husband and wife and trustees, separation agreements, see M.P.S. vol. 2, Lombard, § 1255.

Married women, capacity, contracts, see M.P.S. vol. 14, Simpson and Alperin, § 308.

Married women, capacity, torts, see M.P.S. vol. 14A, Simpson and Alperin, § 1711.

Property and property rights, see M.P.S. vol. 3, Lombard, § 2141 et seq.

Spouse vs. Spouse, actionable tort, see M.P.S. vol. 11, Martin and Hennessey, § 93.

Suits between husband and wife, particular relationships, see M.P.S. vol. 14, Simpson and Alperin, § 771.

Torts between the spouses, see M.P.S. vol. 37, Nolan, § 121.

Forms.

Action by husband against wife to recover savings bank deposit, complaints, pleadings and motions, see M.P.S. vol. 10, Rodman, § 1699.

Agreement between husband and wife, effect of reconciliation, form, see M.P.S. vol. 2, Lombard, § 1306.

WESTLAW Electronic Research

See WESTLAW guide following the Foreword of this volume.

Notes of Decisions

In general 1
Abortions, actions between husband and wife 30
Accounting, equitable proceedings between husband and wife 40
Actions between husband and wife 28–37
   In general 28
   Abortions 30
   Foreign judgments 37
   Marriage settlements 31
   Prior law 29
   Probate proceedings 32
   Professional services 33
   Torts, generally 34

Actions between husband and wife—Cont'd
   Trusts 36
   Vehicular torts, generally 35
Agency, liability of wife 17
Alienation of affections, right of action by wife 9
Burden of proof 55
Clean hands doctrine, equitable proceedings between husband and wife 41
Common law 3
Consortium
   Generally 51
   Right of action by wife 10
Contracts, right of action by wife 6

352

Exhibit 14-2   Massachusetts General Laws Annotated ch. 209, § 6 (*continued*)

rectly, without intervention of a trustee. Charney v. Charney (1944) 55 N.E.2d 917, 316 Mass. 580.

Where, if final and absolute decree of divorce had been entered, remedy of wife to sue at law for alimony awarded would be complete; in action to recover alimony under interlocutory order entered in foreign state, law of forum governed, where laws of foreign state did not appear and under R.L.1902, c. 153, § 6, and St.1910, c. 576, wife could not sue husband in Massachusetts for alimony awarded by interlocutory order. Golder v. Golder (1920) 126 N.E. 382, 235 Mass. 261.

A foreign sister state which by statute conferred jurisdiction upon its courts over nonresidents by service upon them in respective places of their residence within sister states, for causes of action which arose from business transactions within the enacting state, enabled courts of that state to render a judgment against a non-resident husband who entered into and breached a marriage settlement agreement with his wife while they were both domiciled there and where she was still domiciled. Spitz v. Spitz (1965) 31 Mass.App.Dec. 124.

3. Common law

This section which provides that a married woman may sue and be sued in same manner as if she were sole, but provides that this section does not authorize suit between husband and wife except in connection with certain contracts, left interspousal immunity rule in its common-law status susceptible to reexamination and alteration by Supreme Judicial Court. Lewis v. Lewis (1976) 351 N.E.2d 526, 370 Mass. 619.

At common law, one spouse could not sue the other in an action at law. Zwick v. Goldberg (1939) 22 N.E.2d 661, 304 Mass. 66.

At common law, husband, by one action, might recover for wife's personal injuries and expenses and other damage resulting to husband therefrom. Thibeault v. Poole (1933) 186 N.E. 632, 283 Mass. 480.

In the case of Fowle v. Torrey (1883) 135 Mass. 87, the court said: "While the Legislature has removed from a wife many of the disabilities she was under at common law, and has authorized her to hold property as a feme sole, to deal with it as such, and to sue and be sued in relation thereto, it has carefully provided always, in the acts by which this has been done, that nothing therein contained shall be construed as authorizing contracts between husband and wife, conveyances or gifts to each other (except by the husband to a limited amount), or as giving the right to either to sue or be sued by the other. Gen.Sts. c. 108, § 1. Sts.1874, c. 184; 1879, c. 133. Whatever rights

they had in these respects remain as they stood at common law before this legislation commences."

4. Retroactive effect

St.1871, c. 312, providing that any married woman could be sued in an action of tort as if she were sole, and her husband should not be liable to pay the judgment against her in any such suit, did not apply to actions against husband and wife for the wife's tort, begun before the passing of the statute. Hill v. Duncan (1872) 110 Mass. 238.

5. Right of action by wife—In general

By divorce, the marriage was so far suspended that the wife could maintain her rights by suit upon causes which arose after the divorce, and she was to the same extent liable to be sued alone. Chase v. Chase (1856) 72 Mass. 157, 6 Gray 157; Dean v. Richmond (1827) 22 Mass. 461, 5 Pick. 461.

Wife's right to sue "in the same manner as if she were sole" refers both to extent of rights to be established and mode of ascertaining and declaring those rights. Cassidy v. Constantine (1929) 168 N.E. 169, 269 Mass. 56.

In the case of MacKeown v. Lacey (1909) 86 N.E. 799, 200 Mass. 437, 21 L.R.A.,N.S., 683, 16 Ann.Cas. 220, the court said: "The indorsements operated as assignments of the notes to the plaintiff (Hill v. Lewis, 1 Salk. 132; 2 Ames' Cases on Bills and Notes, 100, note 1), and under St.1897, p. 378, c. 402 (Rev.Laws, c. 173, § 4), which was in force at the time of the transfer and of the bringing of the action, the assignee could sue in her own name."

Where a man and woman living in another state came into this commonwealth for the purpose of being married, and were married here, and a few days afterwards, while they were living here at an inn, she wrote to a broker in that state, with whom before the marriage she had deposited property earned by her, to send her a sum of money by an expressman, which the broker did and instructed the expressman to deliver it to her upon her personal receipt; but the expressman delivered it to the husband, who absconded with it, under St.1855, c. 304, she could maintain an action in her own name against the expressman for the money, if she had not authorized her husband to receive it, or held him out as her agent to collect money. Read v. Earle (1859) 78 Mass. 423, 12 Gray 423.

The desertion of a wife by her husband which would enable her to sue, and render her liable to be sued, as a feme sole, should be an absolute and complete desertion by his continued absence from the commonwealth, and a voluntary separation from and abandonment

Exhibit 14-2   Massachusetts General Laws Annotated ch. 209, § 6 *(concluded)*

of each decision. These headnotes summarize the court opinion. But never forget that these are a West editorial feature written by the editors at West. They are not part of the court decision. The decision itself begins with the justice's name who wrote the opinion. These headnotes are also included in court opinions published on Westlaw. Lexis and Fastcase have adopted a similar approach by including headnotes at the beginning of their online opinions.

If you have the full citation to a case, it is relatively easy to locate the text of that case in a reporter. For example, a typical Massachusetts Supreme Judicial Court decision citation would be as follows:

Callow v. Thomas, 322 Mass. 550, 78 N.E.2d 637 (1948).

This citation tells us that the name of the case is *Callow v. Thomas* and that it can be found either in volume 322 on page 550 of the Massachusetts Reports or in volume 78 on page 637 of the North Eastern Reporter, Second Series. To find the case online, you would simply type the volume number, volume abbreviation, and page number into the search box. Either—322 Mass 550 or 78 NE2d 637—would work.

Many free online sites will give you access to recent court opinions if you have the citation. To find cases older than the mid-1990s, however, you may have to use one of the fee-based services.

If you do not have a case citation, there are five different approaches you can use to locate relevant cases. First, as we have already seen, many secondary sources include references to case law. Second, as discussed already, if you know a case interprets a specific statute, you can look up the statute in an annotated version of the statutes and get the citation from that source. Third, if you know at least one party's name, you can use a table of cases to find the full citation or go online, and type the name of the case into the search box. Fourth, you can use a digest to locate relevant cases by their subject matter. Fifth, you can use an online resource, to conduct a search by typing in words that you think would appear in the case. In the following discussion, we examine the last three methods in more detail.

(1) Starting with a name

Often you will remember the name of a case, but not its citation. This is a common problem, and for over a hundred years, West has been providing a solution through its digest system. As mentioned above, a digest contains one-paragraph summaries of court opinions, organized by topic. West publishes such a digest for most states, and included within the digest is a volume entitled "Table of Cases," which lists all of the cases from that state in alphabetical order.

Exhibit 14-3 shows a page from the Massachusetts Digest 2d Table of Cases listing *Callow v. Thomas.* In addition to the citation, you will see a listing of the West topics that are discussed in that opinion. These are the same topics listed at the beginning of the headnotes to *Callow v. Thomas.* This can be very helpful in locating the right case. For example, assume that you are looking for a negligence case called *Callahan v. Somebody.* The Massachusetts Digest Table of Cases lists many *Callahan* cases, but only one with the topic of libel. Notice that the publisher has given you an incomplete citation by omitting the date.

CAMBEX

See Guidelines for Arrangement at the beginning of this Volume

Callahan; Nelson v., CA1 (Mass), 721 F2d 397.—Crim Law 273.1(1), 273.1(4); Hab Corp 85.1(2), 85.2(1), 85.5(4), 90.3(5).

Callahan; Nguyen v., DMass. 997 FSupp 179.—Social S 175.25, 175.30.

Callahan; N.O. v., DMass. 110 FRD 637.—Fed Civ Proc 1559, 1598, 1600(4), 1623, 1653; Mental H 51.5, 486, 487, 490; Witn 184(1), 212.

Callahan; O. v., DMass. 110 FRD 637. See N.O. v. Callahan.

Callahan; Reddick v., DMass. 587 FSupp 880.—Crim Law 1030(1), 1178; Hab Corp 45.3(1.30), 45.3(4).

Callahan; Ricci v., DMass. 646 FSupp 378.—Fed Civ Proc 2397.6.

Callahan; Ricci v., DMass. 576 FSupp 415.—Inj 210.

Callahan; Ricci v., DMass. 97 FRD 737.—Fed Civ Proc 219.

Callahan; Richard v., CA1 (Mass). 723 F2d 1028.—Crim Law 273(4), 273.1(1); Hab Corp 113(12); Homic 234(5), 354.

Callahan; Richard v., DMass. 564 FSupp 511. aff 723 F2d 1028.—Const Law 270(1); Fed Cts 386; Hab Corp 45.1(4).

Callahan; Robinson v., CA1 (Mass), 694 F2d 6.—Crim Law 778(5), 789(13).

Callahan; Setian v., DMass. 973 FSupp 16.—Social S 140.85, 148.1.

Callahan; Sheffield v., DMass. 9 FSupp2d 75.—Social S 140.10, 143.60, 148.15.

Callahan; Shoobridge v., Mass, 39 NE2d 429, 310 Mass 632.—App & E 989; Autos 242(8); Evid 589; Refer 99(4), 99(6).

Callahan; Subilosky v., CA1 (Mass), 689 F2d 7. cert den 103 SCt 1788, 460 US 1090, 76 LEd2d 356.—Const Law 269; Crim Law 938(1); Hab Corp 45.2(4), 45.2(7), 85.2(1).

Callahan v. Superior Court, Mass, 570 NE2d 1003, 410 Mass 1001.—Mand 1, 3(1), 4(4), 31, 176.

Callahan v. Town of Athol, Mass. 188 NE2d 571, 345 Mass 572.—Towns 29.

Callahan v. U.S. I.R.S., BkrtcyDMass. 168 BR 272. See Callahan, In re.

Callahan; Watkins v., CA1 (Mass), 724 F2d 1068.—Crim Law 412.1(4), 667(1); Hab Corp 45.3(1.40), 90.2(6); Homic 8; Witn 2(1).

Callahan v. Westinghouse Broadcasting Co., Inc., Mass. 363 NE2d 240, 372 Mass 582.—Libel 112(2), 124(2); Trial 295(5).

Callahan; Woods v., CA1 (Mass), 172 F2d 179.—Fed Civ Proc 2505; Land & Ten 149; War 210, 220.

Callahan; Young v., CA1 (Mass), 700 F2d 32. cert den 104 SCt 191, 464 US 863, 78 LEd2d 170.—Crim Law 637, 1166.8.

Callahan; Zeigler v., CA1 (Mass), 659 F2d 254.—Const Law 268(5); Crim Law 553, 627.8(6), 627.9(2.1), 1171.8(1); Hab Corp 25.1(8).

Callahan & Sons, Inc. v. Board of Appeals of Lenox. MassAppCt. 565 NE2d 813, 30 MassAppCt 36. See Maurice Callahan & Sons, Inc. v. Board of Appeals of Lenox.

Callan v. Winters, Mass, 534 NE2d 298, 404 Mass 198.—Const Law 93(1); Statut 174; Wills 498.

Callanan, In re. BkrtcyDMass. 190 BR 137.—Bankr 2702.1.

Callanan v. International Fidelity Ins. Co. BkrtcyD-Mass. 190 BR 137. See Callanan, In re.

Callanan v. Personnel Adm'r for Com., Mass. 511 NE2d 525, 400 Mass 597.—Inj 231; Mun Corp 197; Offic 11.7, 11.8.

Calledare v. Sawyer, Mass. 225 NE2d 367, 352 Mass 769.—Theaters 6(19).

Callen; Com. v., MassAppCt. 521 NE2d 861, 26 MassAppCt 920, review den 531 NE2d 1274, 403 Mass 1105.—Autos 144.2(8).

Callender; Com. v., Mass. 673 NE2d 22, 423 Mass 771. See Mendonza v. Com.

Calligaris' Case, Mass. 198 NE 607, 292 Mass 397.—App & E 843(2); Work Comp 2215.

Callinan v. Larsen, MassAppDiv. 1979 MassAppDiv 186.—Judgm 97.

Callow v. Thomas, Mass, 78 NE2d 637, 322 Mass 550, 2 ALR2d 632.—Divorce 313; Hus & W 205(2); Marriage 57, 67.

Callum; Liberty Leather Corp. v., CA1 (Mass), 653 F2d 694.—Fed Civ Proc 839.1, 2146, 2152; Fed Cts 615, 907; Fraud 12, 20, 50, 58(2), 58(3), 58(4); Torts 10(1), 28.

Callum; Liberty Leather Corp. v., DMass. 86 FRD 550.—Fed Civ Proc 2736, 2738.

Calnan; Becker v., Mass, 48 NE2d 668, 313 Mass 625.—App & E 870(5); Equity 417; Labor 107, 109, 114, 122, 127, 763, 769; Plead 8(1), 34(3); Stip 14(3).

Calnan; Weeks v., MassAppCt. 658 NE2d 173, 39 Mass-AppCt 933.—Damag 23; Land & Ten 164(1).

Calore Exp. Co. v. U. S., CA1 (Mass), 351 F2d 596.—Autos 128.

Calore Exp. Co., Inc., In re, DMass. 226 BR 727, opinion after grant of writ 228 BR 338. opinion after grant of writ 228 BR 338.—Atty & C 54; Mand 1, 29, 31, 53.

Calore Exp. Co., Inc., In re. BkrtcyDMass. 199 BR 424.—Bankr 2156, 2671, 2674, 2675, 2679, 2680; Sec Tran 138, 147.

Calvanese v. A. S. W. Taxi Corp., MassAppCt. 405 NE2d 1001, 10 MassAppCt 817.—Autos 244(36.1), 246(1); Pretrial Proc 3; Refer 91, 99(6); Witn 379(10).

Calvanese v. W. W. Babcock Co., Inc., MassAppCt, 412 NE2d 895, 10 MassAppCt 726.—App & E 1067; Damag 166(1); Evid 150, 350, 547, 547.5; Pretrial Proc 383; Prod Liab 54, 83, 97; Sales 1.5; Witn 347.

Calvary Holdings, Inc. v. Chandler, CA1 (Mass), 948 F2d 59.—Fed Civ Proc 2553; Fed Cts 643; Sec Reg 53.15.

Calvert-Distillers Corp.; Jackman v., Mass, 28 NE2d 130, 306 Mass 423.—Courts 91(1); Trade Reg 93, 97, 98, 99, 251, 257, 485, 736.

Calvine Mills, Inc.; Prudhomme v., Mass, 225 NE2d 592, 352 Mass 767.—Neglig 1130, 1173, 1177.

Calvin Hosmer, Stolte Co. v. Paramount Cone Co., Mass. 189 NE 192, 285 Mass 278.—App & E 992, 1050.1(10); Contracts 352(1); Damag 78(6), 175; Evid 213(1), 213(4); Sales 177, 371, 383; Trial 260(9).

Calvo; Com. v., MassAppCt. 668 NE2d 846, 41 MassApp-Ct 903.—Crim Law 982.9(5).

Camacho v. Board of Selectmen of Stoughton, Mass-AppCt, 535 NE2d 1290, 27 MassAppCt 178.—Towns 18, 49.

Camaioni, Case of. MassAppCt. 389 NE2d 1028, 7 Mass-AppCt 927.—Work Comp 1738, 1950.

Camara v. Board of Appeals of Tewksbury, MassAppCt. 662 NE2d 719, 40 MassAppCt 209.—Evid 43(4).

Camara v. Capeto. MassAppCt. 446 NE2d 91, 15 Mass-AppCt 955.—Mun Corp 710.

Camara; Smola v., MassAppCt, 449 NE2d 678, 16 Mass-AppCt 908.—Int Rev 4790; Receivers 29(1).

Camara; U.S. v., CA1 (Mass), 451 F2d 1122, cert den 92 SCt 1513, 405 US 1074, 31 LEd2d 808.—Armed S 20.1(2), 20.8(1), 40.1(7); Crim Law 1031(3), 1115(1), 1186.1; Gr Jury 8.

Camar Corp. v. Preston Trucking Co., Inc., DMass, 18 FSupp2d 112.—Carr 111, 133, 134, 135, 147, 153, 155, 158(1); Evid 351.

Camarra; Bowie v., MassAppDiv, 36 MassAppDec 105.—App & E 192(1); Damag 118; New Tr 74.

Cambara; U.S. v., CA1 (Mass). 902 F2d 144.—Consp 33(1), 47(6); Crim Law 742(1), 1159.2(7), 1166.18.

Cambex Corp.; Greenstone v., CA1 (Mass), 975 F2d 22.—Fed Civ Proc 636.

Cambex Corp.; Greenstone v., DMass. 777 FSupp 88, aff 975 F2d 22.—Fed Civ Proc 636; Sec Reg 60.28(2.1), 60.28(4), 60.28(13).

Exhibit 14-3   Massachusetts Digest, Table of Cases

In any of the commercial databases, if you do not know the citation, but you know one or more of the party's names, you can simply type the name(s) in the search box. If you retrieve more than one court decision, you will have to look through the list to determine which one you are seeking.

To avoid having to look through a long list of retrieved results, it is best to narrow the search as much as possible before you run it. Include other information if you know it, such as the specific court that wrote the decision, a date range, or search terms that you think would be contained within the decision. Otherwise, your search may return so many results that it will be difficult to locate the precise case you are seeking. This may not be much of a problem when one of the party's names is fairly unique, such as in the case of *Callow,* but is a major issue for all of those cases involving a name like *Smith*. As you can imagine, running a search on the word "Smith" in a national database could return thousands of cases.

If you have both the case name and citation, always use the citation. Correctly entered, a citation will usually retrieve just the one case you are seeking.

(2) Using a digest

Digest
A book that contains court opinion headnotes arranged by subject matter.

As mentioned earlier, because cases are printed chronologically as they are decided, not by subject matter, they do not come with an index. However, West, through its digest system, has created what is in effect a super-index to all case law through its topic and key number system. If you located a relevant topic and key number in a digest, you will see one-paragraph summaries of all cases dealing with that topic. Those one-paragraph summaries are in reality the headnotes to be found at the beginning of cases. West editors write the headnotes and then "copy and paste" them into the right digest locations.

Normally, a court decision covers many points of law. The West editors assign each point to a specific topic and key number and then draft a paragraph summarizing what the court says on that point. Therefore, if a given case involves five different points of law, you will find five headnotes at the beginning of the case. Those five headnotes will then be copied and pasted into the relevant digest in five separate locations, under the appropriate topics.

In state digests, West lists the summaries as follows:

- Federal cases that originated in that jurisdiction (if there are any) are listed before state cases.
- The highest courts are listed before the intermediate appellate courts.
- Cases are listed in reverse chronological order, with the newest cases listed first.

PRACTICE TIP

Use headnotes and digest summaries to help you locate relevant opinions. But never quote from or rely on the headnote or digest language. Always read the case for yourself.

For example, Exhibit 14-4 shows a page from the Massachusetts Digest 2d before West recategorized the topic Husband and Wife, key number 205(2) to Marriage and Cohabitation, key number 253. West places headnotes on *all* cases, federal and state. The topic and key number system is the same in all state and federal digests. Therefore, once you know the topic and key number that West uses to categorize a particular legal point, you can go to any of the digests to find relevant cases. For example, if you want to know how another state handles the issue of spousal immunity, you can simply go to the state digest for that state and look under the topic Marriage and Cohabitation, key number 253. Be warned, however: over time as the law has expanded, West has occasionally reworked its

13 Mass D 2d—623   **HUSBAND & WIFE**   ⚯205(2)

For references to other topics, see Descriptive-Word Index

that statute shall not authorize suits between husband and wife. M.G.L.A. c. 209, § 6.
> Patuleia v. Patuleia, 127 F.Supp. 60.

Mass. 1980. Common–law rule of interspousal immunity did not bar action in which it was alleged that husband was in control of premises and responsible for sanding, salting or shoveling after snowstorm, that his failure to do so caused wife to fall, and that she suffered fractures and incurred medical expenses in excess of $2,500.
> Brown v. Brown, 409 N.E.2d 717, 381 Mass. 231.

Mass. 1978. Common-law doctrine of interspousal immunity did not protect husband as host driver from liability to his wife as passenger for injuries sustained in collision and, hence, did not preclude owner and operator of other vehicle, named as defendants in main action by wife, from seeking to recover in third-party action against husband for contribution as a joint tort-feasor. M.G.L.A. c. 231B § 1 et seq.
> Hayon v. Coca Cola Bottling Co. of New England, 378 N.E.2d 442, 375 Mass. 644.

Mass. 1976. Arguments that tort actions between husband and wife would tend to disrupt peace and harmony of family and that such actions would tend to promote fraud and collusion on part of husband and wife for purpose of reaping undeserved financial reward at expense of family's liability insurer are insufficient to justify common-law rule of interspousal immunity.
> Lewis v. Lewis, 351 N.E.2d 526, 370 Mass. 619, 92 A.L.R.3d 890.

Wife's action against her husband for personal injuries sustained in automobile accident was not barred by common-law rule of interspousal immunity.
> Lewis v. Lewis, 351 N.E.2d 526, 370 Mass. 619, 92 A.L.R.3d 890.

Mass. 1974. Supreme Judicial Court had jurisdiction over suit by estranged husband seeking declaratory and injunctive relief against his pregnant wife, who intended to procure an abortion over his objection, as against contention of wife that there was no jurisdiction because of statute relating to suits between husband and wife. M.G.L.A. c. 209 § 6.
> Doe v. Doe, 314 N.E.2d 128, 365 Mass. 556, 62 A.L.R.3d 1082.

Mass. 1959. Purpose of statute to effect that probate court shall have jurisdiction to enforce foreign judgments for support of wife against husband who is resident or inhabitant of commonwealth was to enable wife to enforce in commonwealth a foreign judgment for support against husband, provided he resides in or was an inhabitant of commonwealth but

right to enforce such judgment must be exercised solely in probate court. M.G.L.A. c. 209 § 6; c. 215 § 6.
> Adams v. Adams, 157 N.E.2d 405, 338 Mass. 776.

Mass. 1958. Where bank books and bonds had stood in joint names of husband and wife and husband evidenced intent to give his wife a one half interest in deposits and bonds if she returned to live with him by saying "that they would belong to both equally", wife's interest in deposits and bonds upon return to live with husband was that of a tenant in common, and as such wife could maintain a suit in equity against husband who had converted the property held in common to his own use and by his appropriation of it had finally precluded her from any future enjoyment of it.
> Arsenault v. Arsenault, 148 N.E.2d 662, 337 Mass. 189.

Mass. 1952. A wife had no cause of action against husband for past nonsupport which could be the subject of set-off in proceeding by husband for accounting of his property and business which wife took over upon husband's commitment to hospital as mental patient.
> Peteros v. Peteros, 104 N.E.2d 149, 328 Mass. 416.

Husband was entitled to recover his property or its value and was entitled to an accounting of profits derived therefrom by wife during period husband was committed to hospital as a mental patient, but wife was entitled to credit for her services in operating the business during such period.
> Peteros v. Peteros, 104 N.E.2d 149, 328 Mass. 416.

Mass. 1948. No cause of action arises in favor of either spouse for a tort committed by the other during coverture.
> Callow v. Thomas, 78 N.E.2d 637, 322 Mass. 550, 2 A.L.R.2d 632.

Where either spouse commits a tort upon the other during coverture recovery is denied, not merely because of the disability of one spouse to sue the other during coverture, but because of the marital relationship, no cause of action ever came into existence.
> Callow v. Thomas, 78 N.E.2d 637, 322 Mass. 550, 2 A.L.R.2d 632.

Mass. 1947. Jurisdiction in equity exists to adjudicate conflicting rights of husband and wife concerning property.
> Yurkanis v. Yurkanis, 73 N.E.2d 598, 321 Mass. 375.

Mass. 1945. The fact that parties are husband and wife does not in general enable them to maintain against each other in equity equiv-

---

see Massachusetts General Laws Annotated

13 Mass.Dig.2d—21

Exhibit 14-4   Massachusetts Digest Case Summaries

digest labeling and numbering system. For example, you may have noticed that in *Callow v. Thomas* and *Lewis v. Lewis*, the topic of spousal immunity was categorized as Husband and Wife, 205(2). That topic is now listed under Marriage and Cohabitation, 253.

When working online, if you are using Westlaw, you can also use this digest system to find cases. You simply need to know the number West has assigned to the topic and then do a search using this format—*xkx*—where the first "*x*" is the topic number and the second "*x*" is the key number. So for our case involving spousal immunity, we could type "253k1084" and find every case from the whole country that has dealt with the issue of spousal immunity.

The West system has over 400 topics, arranged alphabetically from #1, Abandoned and Lost Property to #414, Zoning and Planning. For illustration, consider another example. The topic damages has been given the number 115. The key number that relates to expenses is 101, so a search for "115k101" would locate the section in damages that relates to expenses. You can also add words to your search. The search "115k101 /p medical" would retrieve cases dealing with medical expenses.

(3) Online searching

The last method for finding court opinions is to go to an online source and use one of two basic approaches. First, if you are using a commercial database that contains a Google-like search bar and has a natural-language search engine, you can simply type in some terms and view your results. Or you can begin by limiting your search to a particular jurisdiction or type of law, such as cases or statutes. Second, in order to make your search more precise, you can use advanced search techniques that will allow you to include connectors such as *and* and *or* as well as proximity searching.

(a) Performing a Google-like search using a commercial database While this type of searching is very intuitive, especially for those used to doing searches with programs such as Google, you will find that your searches will be most effective if you spend time developing a set of terms before running your search. You would not begin traditional legal research by going to the law library and simply paging through the books in the order that they appear on the shelf. You would first think of key terms to look for in the appropriate legal indexes. Similarly, when you approach the computer terminal, you should already have carefully thought out the nature of the issues and have identified key words or phrases that will become the basis of your computer search. The old computer adage "garbage in, garbage out" is particularly applicable to computerized legal research.

If you find that this first method of researching is not retrieving the precise results you desire, you may want to try more advanced search techniques. Most online resources have this capability, but on some sites, you may have to consult their help screen to find out how to do so.

(b) Searching using advanced search techniques Before the advent of natural-language searches, legal researches accomplished full-text searching by combining their search terms with Boolean operators, such as *or* and *and,* and proximity connectors. You may find that these methods are still useful in order to better focus your search.

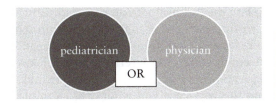

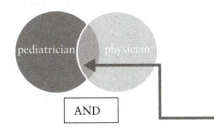

Figure 14-2   Boolean Searching Using "or" versus "and"

There are two basic steps in using the terms and connectors approach. First, you must determine which words best describe the legal issue you are researching. Then you must connect those words.

There are two types of connectors, Boolean (or logical) and proximity. The two most common **Boolean connectors** are "or" and "and." You use "or" to find alternatives, such as "pediatrician **or** pediatric oncologist **or** physician." You use "and" to require that both terms appear somewhere within the opinion: "pediatrician **and** negligence."

> **Boolean connectors**
> Logical connectors, such as "or" and "and," that make key word searches more precise.

You use the word "or" to indicate alternatives. However, in Westlaw, a space also equals "or." Therefore, in Lexis, the search "pediatric oncologist" (not in quotation marks) would find the phrase "pediatric oncologist." In Westlaw the same search would find cases that contained either the word "pediatric" or the word "oncologist." You can always ensure that you are searching for a phrase by including the words in quotation marks: "pediatric oncologist." Figure 14-2 illustrates the difference between searching with "or" and "and."

As indicated above, the use of "and" will require that both terms occur somewhere within the opinion. However, to ensure that the terms are related to each other, you should use a proximity connector, such as "w/s" or "w/p," for

---

PRACTICE TIP

Remember when doing a terms and connectors search that Lexis and Westlaw treat spaces differently. The phrase "probable cause" in Lexis will return documents with the entire phrase, "probable cause." That same search in Westlaw will return documents that have either the word "probable" or the word "cause," creating an impossibly massive number of hit results.

within the same sentence or paragraph. For the "s" or "p," you can also substitute a precise number, such as "w/10," to find two terms that occur within ten words of each other. Some Internet services use the proximity connector "near."

The two most common errors in conducting computerized research are making your search request too general, resulting in hundreds of cases, or making it too narrow, potentially eliminating the very case you want. For example, if you instruct the computer to search for a single key word, frequently you will get back an overwhelming number of cases, with many of them not even relevant to your legal issue. An example of a search that would be too broad is one that searched for the term "negligence" as that search would no doubt return hundreds, if not thousands, of cases. One solution is to substitute narrower terms, such as "legal malpractice." Also, you can search for combinations of terms appearing together within a specifically defined space, such as "assumption" and "risk" appearing together, or "store," "wet," "floor," and "negligent" all appearing within the same paragraph.

The second problem, finding too few cases, usually occurs when too specific a term is used. For example, if you are searching for cases dealing with malpractice by a pediatric oncologist for failure to diagnose leukemia, you could certainly search by typing in "pediatric oncologist." However, if there is a case directly on point but the court referred to the defendant simply as a pediatrician, then you would not find that case. Therefore, you should always enter synonyms. In this example, your search might be for "pediatrician or pediatric oncologist or physician or doctor or surgeon."

In addition to using synonyms, in most computer databases you can also broaden your search by asking the computer to locate any word with a specific root, such as "pediatric." In Westlaw and Lexis, you do this by using the root expander:! (Some Internet services use an asterisk.) If you typed "pediatric!" in either Lexis or Westlaw, you would get cases referring to "pediatric" or "pediatrician." Be careful with root expanders. Entering the search "child!" would get you references to "child" and "children," but it would also retrieve "childish," "childhood," "childlike," and so on.

PRACTICE TIP

When using the terms and connectors method of searching, you will often find yourself with either too few or too many cases.

If you find too few or no cases:

- If you found no cases, the first thing to do is to check your spelling. If you typed "grandfater" when you meant "grandfather," you will get no search results.
- Run your search in a larger database. For example, if you were searching in the database that covered cases from only the state's highest court, expand your search to cases from all of the courts of that state.

- Either eliminate some terms or use less-restrictive terms. Instead of "poodle," search for "dog." Instead of "dog," search for "pet."
- Use less-restrictive connectors. Instead of "w/10," use "w/25." Instead of "w/p," use "and."
- Use more synonyms. Instead of "doctor," use "doctor or physician or surgeon or medical."

If you find too many cases:

- Run the search in a smaller database. If you were looking at all state courts, change to the highest state courts or to all courts in a specific state.
- Add additional terms or use more restrictive terms. For example, change "negligence" to "malpractice" and add the term "legal."
- Use more restrictive connectors. Change "w/p" to "w/s."
- Add a date restriction to find just the most recent cases.

Finally, the computer will allow you to limit your search so that you retrieve only cases decided before or after a certain date or opinions authored by a particular judge. This power to limit your request means that you can perform searches that would be far too time-consuming or even impossible if using book-based research. Imagine trying to use the hardbound reporters to find all cases decided by a particular judge, such as Justice Antonin Scalia, and involving a specific issue, such as freedom of religion. A task that would take hours using only books can be done in seconds using a computerized online service.

5. Decide When to Stop Researching

This can often be one of the most difficult parts of a research assignment. How can you know when to stop? Usually, you will know it is time to stop when you keep finding the same references in different resources. For example, you may find the same court opinion mentioned in an encyclopedia, a state digest, and an annotated code. When looking at more resources no longer gives you new citations to add to your list, stop.

6. Update Your Research

In order to feel confident about your researching results, you must do everything you can to make sure that your results are as up to date as possible. If you do not do this, there will always be the possibility that the statute you have found has been amended or even repealed or that one of the cases you are relying on has been reversed or overruled. Two print-based resources for updating your research are pocket parts and legal newspapers.

However, the main source for updating research, whether online or in the books, is by using a citator. A citator will tell you whether a case you have found is still "good law," meaning that it has not been reversed or overruled. The two best-known citators are Shepard's (both in book and online versions) and KeyCite.

a. Updating in the Books Using Pocket Parts and News Sources

If you have researched exclusively in books and the source you are relying on is organized by subject matter, such as statutes or most secondary authority, then to update what you have found you must be sure to check the pocket part. For statutes, in addition to any statutory changes, the pocket part will include any recent court opinions that have interpreted the statute. If the statute has been amended or repealed in the time since the main volume was printed, and you rely only on the language in the main volume, then you will be relying on law that is no longer valid.

Then update what you found in the pocket part by going online. While pocket parts are often updated only once a year, most commercial online sources update their materials within 24 to 48 hours of any change.[1]

National law journals and newspapers, such as the *National Law Journal*, and state-specific newspapers, such as *Massachusetts Lawyers Weekly*, are also good resources for keeping current with legal changes.

b. Using Citators—Shepard's and KeyCite

Shepardize
Using Shepard's citations to check a court citation to see whether there has been any subsequent history or treatment by other court decisions.

Reverse
A decision is reversed when the litigants appeal the lower court decision and the higher court disagrees with the decision of a lower court.

Overrule
A decision is overruled when a court in a later case changes the law so that its prior decision is no longer good law.

Subsequent case history
Information about what happened procedurally to the litigation after the case was cited. Include this information in a citation.

Researchers began using Shepard's Citations in the mid-1880s. Today most researchers use Shepard's online as part of Lexis or KeyCite, which is part of Westlaw. You can use **citators** to check for the validity of statutes as well as case law, but in this section we will focus on updating case law.

Recall from previous chapters that we say a case is **reversed** when the litigants appeal the decision and a higher court overturns or negates the decision of the lower court. A case is **overruled** when the court in a later case changes the law as it was found in a prior appellate decision. Finally, even if the case has not been reversed or overruled, a later court decision may explain the earlier case in such a way as to change its meaning. It is hard to imagine any more terrible researching nightmare than to turn over the results of your research to someone else and then to have that someone else rely on those results, only to find out that a recent case you did not find invalidates your conclusions. Making sure that your researching results are complete and up to date is vital.

To check the validity of a case, you will want to check to see if there was any **subsequent history** for your case. Not every case has subsequent history, but if it does, this means that there was further litigation between *the same litigants* following the case you read. Subsequent history includes such actions as an appellate court modifying, affirming, or reversing your case.

For example, assume that you find a Massachusetts intermediate appellate court decision that harms your client. You would be delighted if the Massachusetts Supreme Judicial Court (Massachusetts's highest appellate court) reversed that decision, because that would mean the lower appellate court decision is no longer good law. Conversely, you would not be so delighted if the Massachusetts Supreme Judicial Court affirmed the lower court's decision. In either case, you would want to read the decision from the higher appellate court

---

[1] Be wary of governmental websites, however. Often they only include the most recent official statutory compilation without any of the intervening changes. For example, the official United States Code is only updated once every six years.

as it supersedes the lower court decision, and the court may have used reasoning decidedly different from that used by the lower court.

You can also use citators to find out what later courts, deciding cases *involving different litigants*, have had to say about your case. In Shepard's this is called the **treatment** of your case. There are two reasons for looking for treatment. The first is similar to why you search for subsequent history, that is, to see if the legal principle for which your case stands is still good law. The second is to broaden your search by finding other cases that have discussed the same issue raised in your case.

Assume you found a 1985 U.S. Supreme Court decision that harms your client. Things look bleak. But there is always the possibility that in the years since 1985 the U.S. Supreme Court changed its mind regarding the legal issue involved and in a later decision, involving other litigants, overruled that earlier opinion. While this will not affect the outcome of the original case and those original litigants (as subsequent history does), it will have an effect on the precedential value of that case for future cases and future litigants.

Shepard's is available in print format and online. If possible, we recommend that you use Shepard's online. Not only is it much more current, but in many ways it simplifies the process. In fact, many law libraries no longer maintain a subscription for Shepard's in print. To give you an indication of the difficulty that researchers had with the book-based version of Shepard's, we have included a sample page in Exhibit 14-5.

This example assumes that the researcher started with *Callow's* N.E.2d cite. Notice the words NORTHEASTERN REPORTER, 2d SERIES (Massachusetts Cases) that appear centered at the top of the page. Second, find the reference to Vol. 78 in the left-hand corner. This means we have located the right volume number. Next look in the first column for—637—, our page number.

The first citation following—637—is (322Mas550). This is the parallel citation for *Callow*. A parallel citation is a citation to the same case, but in a different reporter. A parallel citation will always be the first reference, and it will always be surrounded by parentheses.

Following the parallel citation are nine citations to other Massachusetts cases.

One of those cases is listed as 315 N.E.2d 528. This is a reference to *Lewis*, and specifically to the page within *Lewis* where the court cited *Callow*. Take a look in the text on page 392, in Chapter 13. This is where we have reproduced page 528 from *Lewis*. Can you find the reference to *Callow*?

If using Shepard's online, links will take you to the precise page on which a court has cited the case you are Shepardizing.

Notice that some of the citations on the Shepard's page are *preceded* by a letter. For example, the first citation under 78 N.E.2d 633 is preceded by the letter "d." A listing of the letters used and what they mean can be found at the beginning of each Shepard's volume. For example, "d" means distinguished and "f" means followed. Three letters are of particular concern: "r" for reversed, "o" for overruled, and "q" for questioned.

When using Shepard's or KeyCite online, the process is much simpler. Starting with the case that you wish to Shepardize, you will see a symbol at the top of the case that will alert you to possible negative or positive history or treatment. This is a tremendous improvement over traditional researching methods. When researching in books, other than possibly noting the date of the case, you have

Treatment
How subsequent cases have affected the case you are Shepardizing. It is sometimes indicated by a one-letter abbreviation before the Shepard's citation.

Vol. 78	NORTHEASTERN REPORTER, 2d SERIES (Massachusetts Cases)			
—629— Wright v Health Commissioner of Boston 1948 (322Mas535) 107NE¹775 157NE228 360NE⁹1060 387NE188 **—633—** Watson's Case 1948 (322Mas581) d 85NE⁶75 88NE³639 102NE⁴415 116NE⁴128 120NE⁴756 127NE⁴193 d 138NE⁴288 138NE³633 138NE⁷751 148NE⁴373 154NE⁴605 155NE⁴790 f 173NE⁴644 232NE⁴927 258NE¹927 363NE⁴1336 373NE⁷1178 408NE⁸894 Cir. 5 186F2d277 **—637—** Callow v Thomas 1948 (322Mas550) 173NE⁴269 178NE⁴283 178NE⁵283 236NE⁴201 351NE²528 373NE⁴358 373NE⁶358 489NE⁴673 574NE⁴405 Cir. 1 504FS⁴654 **—641—** Joyce v Devaney 1948 (322Mas544) 95NE¹175 103NE¹322	115NE¹495 116NE²155 141NE¹516 142NE¹405 146NE²514 165NE¹116 224NE¹224 372NE¹283 372NE⁴283 **—644—** Massachusetts v Hall 1948 (322Mas523) 82NE³10 87NE⁶202 178NE³267 317NE³831 334NE²616 366NE²726 421NE²761 421NE¹764 440NE⁶769 d 595NE¹777 58USLW4925 **—649—** Franklin Square House v Siskind 1948 (322Mas556) 124NE⁵231 183NE⁵291 226NE⁵196 **—651—** Provost's Case 1948 (322Mas604) **—652—** Rosenthal v Maletz 1948 (322Mas586) 80NE⁵15 84NE552 97NE¹⁷171 99NE¹927 d 103NE⁴251 105NE¹248 126NE¹531 129NE¹⁹906 140NE¹⁵646 163NE¹⁰160 170NE⁸839 170NE¹⁸840 247NE¹393 q 342NE¹³717	d 374NE¹⁰350 Cir. 1 331F2d33 97FS¹⁷777 **—697—** Massachusetts v Farrell 1948 (322Mas606) 85NE²451 95NE¹⁸541 109NE¹⁸174 126NE¹⁸808 132NE²⁰303 142NE¹⁰389 182NE¹128 201NE¹⁸832 216NE¹⁸426 226NE¹⁴210 235NE¹⁴800 265NE⁴382 314NE⁴450 326NE⁶714 334NE¹648 337NE711 344NE¹⁸927 348NE¹⁹820 355NE478 363NE⁷1316 370NE⁷1026 370NE¹⁴1026 373NE¹⁴1126 383NE²⁰1121 387NE²164 389NE¹⁰762 402NE⁸1056 402NE⁸1057 f 402NE¹²1060 406NE⁴419 406NE⁴421 417NE⁸980 422NE⁴452 436NE⁸1217 436NE⁸1223 457NE¹²624 471NE⁷1358 487NE⁸1370 504NE¹³615 509NE⁷304 522NE⁶6 547NE944 564NE⁵378 574NE⁷344 576NE¹²711 594NE¹⁴868 23MJ325	**Vol. 79** **—1—** King v Tewksbury 1948 (322Mas668) cc 81NE737 **—2—** Morin v Trailways of New England Inc. 1948 (322Mas744) **—3—** Wagstaff v Director of the Division of Employment Security 1948 (322Mas664) 82NE¹2 84NE¹544 85NE¹780 86NE¹57 89NE¹782 92NE¹253 96NE²862 97NE640 98NE¹362 99NE¹59 106NE³422 117NE¹165 118NE¹774 197NE¹597 344NE²895 382NE²201 454NE⁴95 **—5—** Kubilius v Hawes Unitarian Congregational Church 1948 (322Mas638) 87NE¹214 154NE⁶601 244NE⁴279 244NE⁶279 Cir. 1 735FS⁶1097	**—10—** Royal v Royal 1948 (322Mas662) s 87NE850 j 133NE¹240 **—11—** Seltmann v Seltmann 1948 (322Mas650) 85NE³442 q 146NE²499 294NE¹557 316NE¹763 **—13—** Herald v Rich 1948 (322Mas659) **—15—** Goff v Hickson 1948 (322Mas655) 88NE¹337 89NE³1 91NE⁴235 91NE⁴927 104NE¹495 **—17—** Ryder v Ryder 1948 (322Mas645) 269NE⁸94 412NE⁷917 **—185—** Delgreco v Delgreco 1948 (322Mas706) 145NE²688 215NE³670 **—187—** General v Woburn 1948 (322Mas634) 85NE¹230 86NE¹645 99NE¹43 111NE²671	e 115NE⁵149 129NE¹895 175NE²916 208NE¹234 214NE¹43 252NE¹213 252NE¹896 269NE¹233 438NE⁹1 461NE771 556NE⁴117 **—189—** Connolly v John Hancock Mutual Life Insurance Co. 1948 (322Mas678) 116NE⁴678 129NE¹619 141NE⁴513 141NE⁴726 d 174NE¹38 258NE¹20 Cir. 1 201F2d⁴422 282FS⁴376 **—192—** McCartin v School Committee of Lowell 1948 (322Mas624) 111NE³750 q 184NE³43 217NE¹769 294NE211 d 294NE³212 d 310NE²336 335NE²655 336NE752 356NE³263 378NE²¹376 378NE³¹376 384NE²230 384NE³230 417NE²461 486NE46 486NE³47 **—195—** Owens-Illinois Glass Co. v Bresnahan 1948 (322Mas629) d 110NE²125 142NE²762

318

Exhibit 14-5   Massachusetts Shepard's

no way of knowing whether a case is still good law. But now Lexis Shepard's will alert you to possible negative history or treatment by putting a red stop sign at the top of the case, and similarly Westlaw's KeyCite will attach a red flag symbol. A yellow sign or flag will alert you to the possibility that the case, while not overruled or reversed, has been criticized. Clicking on those symbols will take you directly to the Shepard's or KeyCite results.

You can also type a citation directly into either Shepard's or KeyCite. This will give you a list of cases. By clicking on those cases, you are taken directly to the page on which the court cited your case.

One downside of using citators is that they will only help you find court opinions that have *cited* your decision. If a court simply discusses the same topic without citing your case, you will not find out about that more recent case using a citator.

If a lawyer has access to a commercial service, such as Lexis or Westlaw, and does not use it to update research, that may be grounds for a malpractice action.

C. THE INTERRELATIONSHIP OF RESEARCHING MATERIALS

It may seem that there is a lot to learn about how to conduct legal research—and there is. However, the more researching you do, the more comfortable you will become with the process. Also, always keep in mind one of the major tricks of legal researching: Once you have found *one* relevant authority, you can proceed from there just by following the leads that your first authority gives you. For example, if you start with a citation to a statute, locate that statute using its citation in an annotated set, either in the books or online. With annotated statutes, the editors will have included summaries of court opinions along with the citations for those court opinions, letting you go immediately from statute to court opinion. (And, of course, if you are doing your research online, that is as easy as clicking on the link to the court opinion.) Conversely, if you start with a court opinion that cites a statute, you can use that statutory citation to go immediately from reading the court opinion to the statute.

Legal Reasoning Exercise

2. Assume that you work for a law firm in Pennsylvania. One of your firm's clients, Melba Street, had a pet Yorkie, Sugar, whom she dearly loved. She left the Yorkie one weekend at the local kennel. On Saturday, a new kennel worker accidentally let Sugar loose in the fenced-in yard with Bear, a vicious Siberian Husky. Unfortunately, that was the end of Sugar. Melba would like to sue the kennel for the emotional distress she suffered in having her pet killed.

a. What Google-type search would you construct?

b. What terms and connectors search would you construct to try to find cases that would indicate whether she can recover for her emotional distress?

SUMMARY

The goal of legal research is to find relevant primary authority, court opinions, and enacted law, such as statutes and regulations. Secondary sources, such as legal encyclopedias and law review articles, can provide valuable background information.

The first step in legal research is to define the problem. If you do not know the question you are being asked to answer, you will waste a great deal of time. At this stage, you should also think about whether you want to research federal or state law and whether you want to begin with a statute or court opinion. And if you are unfamiliar with the area of law, consult secondary sources before going any further. Once you have an understanding of your research goal, create a list of search terms. Then it is time to start looking at primary authority. You can stop once you start finding the same answers in different sources. Finally, never forget to update your research by consulting pocket parts and supplements, by checking Shepard's, and by using online resources, such as Westlaw, Lexis, or other Internet-based sources.

REVIEW QUESTIONS

Pages 403 through 408

1. What are four major differences between book-based and online research?
2. What are the two major online legal research providers?
3. What is one limitation of many of the free online legal research websites?
4. What is your main goal when conducting legal research?
5. What is the difference between primary and secondary authority?
6. Your boss represents a client who was injured when his Handy Hardy riding tractor tipped over. You searched through the online sources that contained primary authority but did not find any appellate decisions involving the Handy Hardy riding tractor. In what other types of online databases might you want to search and why?
7. What is mandatory authority?

Pages 409 through 412

8. What are the six basic steps of legal research?
9. In what type of sources can you read general background information on a particular legal topic?
10. How does the A.L.R. differ from an encyclopedia?
11. What is a law review, and what types of articles does it contain?
12. Why do you think the general rule is that it is appropriate to cite to a law review article but not to an encyclopedia?
13. When thinking of terms to use in your search, why is it a good idea to think of as many terms as possible?

Pages 413 through 424

14. When researching primary authority, should you generally begin your research with statutes or court opinions? Why?
15. What makes an annotated statutory code "annotated"?

16. What are five methods for finding a court opinion when you do not know its citation?

17. If you have the citation for a court decision, how do you locate it in the books? Online?

18. If you only know the name of one party to a case, how do you locate it in the books? Online?

19. If you have both the case name and its citation, why should you begin research by using the citation?

20. How are digest summaries and headnotes similar? What is the function of each?

21. Assume that you are researching the topic of whether minors can get out of their contractual obligations and that you have found a New Hampshire case directly on point. That case's third headnote lists the topic as Contracts 211. How would you go about locating a Kansas case dealing with that same issue?

22. Last month, the police saw your client, Bill Johnson, exchange money for a packet of white powder. Without a warrant, the police placed an electronic tracking device on your client's car. The police then followed him to an alley, where he handed the packet to a woman who gave him money in return. They arrested your client for selling illegal drugs. Your boss would like to make a motion to have the evidence excluded by arguing that it was unlawful for the police to put the electronic tracking device on your client's car without a warrant. Assume that in the course of your research, you have found *Commonwealth v. Boven,* 413 Mass. 755, 306 N.E.2d 222 (1986). The headnotes in the North Eastern Reporter, Second Series, appear as follows:

   1. Searches and Seizures [Key] 7(26) Defendant did not have standing to challenge X-ray search of suitcase, where the suitcase belonged to his co-defendant.

   2. Searches and Seizures [Key] 7(10) Utilization of electronic tracking device, without prior court approval, may be justified by probable cause and exigent circumstances.

   3. Criminal Law [Key] 1144.13 On appeal from jury conviction, Court must view evidence, both direct and circumstantial, and all reasonable inferences to be drawn therefrom.

   4. Criminal Law [Key] 696(1) Trial court did not err in failing to grant defense motion to strike testimony of agent, although all of agent's investigatory notes had been destroyed.

      Using the information *from the headnotes,* describe how you would go about finding out whether there are any other court opinions in Massachusetts dealing with the subject of when police officers can place electronic surveillance devices on cars without first obtaining a warrant. Describe the steps you would take in as much detail as possible. Include a description of how you would bring your research up to date.

Pages 424 through 432

23. What is involved in doing a terms and connectors search?

24. You need to find cases dealing with free speech, and using the terms and connectors method, you type in the following search: "free speech" (without quotation marks). How do you think Westlaw and Lexis would differ in the ways they would interpret that search request?

25. When do you know you can stop researching?

26. If you do your search in books organized by subject matter, what should you consult to update your research?

27. What is a citator?

28. What is the difference between saying a case has been reversed and saying it has been overruled?
29. In Shepard's what is subsequent history, and what is the treatment of a case?
30. In Shepard's, to what do the terms "citing case" and "cited case" refer?
31. What advantages are there to using Shepardizing online or KeyCite, rather than using the book-based Shepard's?
32. If you update using a citator, why might you not final all of the relevant cases on your topic?

WEB EXERCISES

1. Team up with one of your classmates. Agree on two or three limited research tasks. For example, you could search your state statutes for a specific law (such as the definition of first-degree murder) or locate a recent court opinion (such as one discussing the tort of intentional infliction of emotional distress). Then one of you should conduct your research using only books and the other only online resources. Keep track of your time and the results you find. Compare your results. Who was more successful? Why do you think that was?
2. Westlaw and Lexis provide very complete coverage of state court opinions. However, they can also be expensive to use. Free sites provide more limited coverage, but have one huge advantage: they are free! Compare:
   ■ FindLaw for Legal Professionals
   ■ Justia
   ■ Google Scholar
   ■ The Public Library of Law
   ■ Your state's official court website
   Which one gives you the most complete coverage of your state's highest appellate court decisions?

Chapter 15

Applying the Law

If you do not know where you are going, it is damnably hard to get there. It is even harder for the instructor to see how you got there.
Karl Llewellyn

Chapter Objectives

After reading this chapter, you should be able to:

- Compare analogous and distinguishable court opinions to a set of facts.
- Develop the ability to select among precedents.
- Apply the IRAC (Issue-Rule-Analysis-Conclusion) format to a written analysis involving court opinions.
- Explain the purpose and list the main sections of an internal law office memorandum.

INTRODUCTION

Written analysis based on court opinions is similar to what we discussed in Chapter 12, on statutory interpretation. Now, however, instead of gleaning the rule from the statutory language and presumed legislative intent, the rule comes from the holding of a court decision or a series of court decisions. Also, now your analysis section will need to be very fact-based as you compare and contrast your client's facts with those of the cases you cite.

Take a few minutes to read over the following factual situation that we will be using to illustrate the techniques discussed in this chapter.

Case 18: The Warrantless Search

The law firm of Murray and Murray has agreed to represent Charles Benson in a criminal case. He has been accused of attempting to pass forged checks.

When Benson met with the lawyer, Caroline Murray, and the paralegal, Anna Hinks, he admitted that he had gone to the drive-up window of a local bank and attempted to cash checks drawn on a non-existent account. The teller, suspecting something was wrong with the checks, refused to cash them and instead called the police.

When the police arrived shortly thereafter, at approximately 1:30 in the afternoon, they found Benson sitting in his car, parked in the bank's parking lot. They arrested him and had his car towed to the station. At the police station, they searched the vehicle without first obtaining a warrant. This search revealed forged checks that had been stuffed in between the seats. Based on that evidence, the prosecuting attorney charged Benson with violating the section of the state's Deceptive Practices Act that covers possession of stolen or fraudulently obtained checks.

Murray hopes she can have the evidence the police found during their search suppressed. She would like to make the argument that the police should have first obtained a search warrant before searching Benson's car. To find out if this is a viable approach, she has asked Hinks to find prior cases and to do an analysis in which she compares them to Benson's situation. In this chapter, we look at how to approach such an analysis.

A. PREDICTING THE OUTCOME IN YOUR CLIENT'S CASE

As a practical matter few people (lawyers and paralegals included) read cases in a vacuum just for the fun it. Usually, they read cases because they are striving to keep current in their area of expertise or because they have a client and need to see whether prior cases will help or hurt the client's situation. In the situation involving Benson, Murray would first search for court opinions that have dealt with the topic of warrantless searches. Her research turns up a number of cases, including *Chambers v. Maroney*, a U.S. Supreme Court opinion. Take a few minutes to read some excerpts from *Chambers v. Maroney* and decide whether you think the holding will help or hurt Benson.

Chambers v. Maroney
399 U.S. 42 (1970)

Mr. Justice White delivered the opinion of the Court.

The principal question in this case concerns the admissibility of evidence seized from an automobile, in which petitioner was riding at the time of his arrest, after the automobile was taken to a police station and was there thoroughly searched without a warrant. The Court of Appeals for the Third Circuit found no violation of petitioner's Fourth Amendment rights. We affirm.

I

During the night of May 20, 1963, a Gulf service station in North Braddock, Pennsylvania, was robbed by two men, each of whom carried and displayed a gun. . . . Two teenagers, who had earlier noticed a blue compact station wagon circling the block in the vicinity of the Gulf station, then saw the station wagon speed away from a parking lot close to the Gulf station. About the same time, they learned that the Gulf station had been robbed. They reported to police, who arrived immediately, that four men were in the station wagon and one was wearing a green sweater. [The station attendant] told the police that one of the men who robbed him was wearing a green sweater and the other was wearing a trench coat. A description of the car and the two robbers was broadcast over the police radio. Within an hour, a light blue compact station wagon answering the description and carrying four men was stopped by the police about two miles from the Gulf station. Petitioner was one of the men in the station wagon. He was wearing a green sweater and there was a trench coat in the car. The occupants were arrested and the car was driven to the police station. In the course of a thorough search of the car at the station, the police found concealed in a compartment under the dashboard two .38-caliber revolvers . . . and certain cards bearing the name of Raymond Havicon, the attendant at a Boron service station in McKeesport, Pennsylvania, who had been robbed at gunpoint on May 13. . . .

II

We pass quickly to the claim that the search of the automobile was the fruit of an unlawful arrest. Both the courts below thought the arresting officers had probable cause to make the arrest. We agree. . . .

In terms of the circumstances justifying a warrantless search, the Court has long distinguished between an automobile and a home or office. [A]utomobiles and other conveyances may be searched without a warrant in circumstances that would not justify the search without a warrant of a house or an office, provided that there is probable cause to believe that the car contains articles that the officers are entitled to seize. . . .

On the facts before us, the blue station wagon could have been searched on the spot when it was stopped since there was probable cause to search and it was a fleeting target for a search. The probable-cause factor still obtained at the station house and so did the mobility of the car unless the Fourth Amendment permits a warrantless seizure of the car and the denial of its use to anyone until a warrant is secured. In that event there is little to choose in terms of practical consequences between an immediate search without a warrant and the car's immobilization until a warrant is obtained.[10]

Affirmed.

---

[10] It was not unreasonable in this case to take the car to the station house. All occupants in the car were arrested in a dark parking lot in the middle of the night. A careful search at that point was impractical and perhaps not safe for the officers, and it would serve the owner's convenience and the safety of his car to have the vehicle and the keys together at the station house.

CASE DISCUSSION QUESTIONS

1. What was the Court's holding?
2. Do you think that holding hurts or helps Benson? Why?

1. Looking for Analogies and Distinctions

In determining the extent to which a court opinion applies to a client's facts, you engage in a process of comparing the facts involved in the prior cases with those of the client's situation. As we have discussed, this process of looking at two decisions and deciding that they are similar is called analogizing. If you find that the two cases are similar, then the doctrine of **stare decisis** will suggest that they should be decided the same way. If they are different in important respects, the prior case is distinguishable and is not applicable to the client's problem.

Learning how to perform legal analysis is one of the most important skills a paralegal can develop. But remember it is a supervising lawyer, and not the paralegal, who determines the legal strategy, signs the documents, and argues in court.

Therefore, after case briefing, the next step is to use the opinions that you have briefed as a basis for predicting the likely outcome in your client's situation. To do that, you must find both the factual similarities (analogies) and the factual differences (distinctions) between your client's situation and that of the prior decision.

The steps that are necessary to evaluate whether a prior decision and a client's case will be seen as essentially similar or dissimilar follow.

a. Determine Whether the Governing Rules of Law and Issues Are the Same in Both Cases

In dealing with Benson's case, the governing rules and issues do appear to be the same as those discussed in *Chambers v. Maroney*. Both involve the admissibility of evidence seized from an automobile. In each case, the defendant was in his car at the time of his arrest, after which the automobile was taken to a police station and was then thoroughly searched without a warrant.

Sometimes you will not be so lucky as to find a case so clearly analogous. For example, you may be dealing in an area where there is no established law. Then you will need to rely on cases in closely related, though not identical, areas of the law, where a logical extension can be made. For example, assume that you were working on a case in which the issue was whether children can sue their parents. If there are no cases in your jurisdiction on parental immunity, you might look to cases on spousal immunity for guidance. Because the rules and issues are not identical, however, you would have to work at convincing the court why the same policies that applied in the prior cases should apply to your case.

b. Decide Which Facts Are the Key Facts in the Prior Case

Key facts are those facts that, if changed, might have caused the court to reach a different result. It is sometimes difficult to determine what these key facts are. To do so, you need to look carefully at which facts the judges emphasize as being important in their written opinions.

Note that in the *Chambers* decision, Justice White specifically mentioned that

- This was a lawful arrest based on probable cause (eyewitness testimony).
- The defendant was suspected of committing armed robbery.
- The defendant was with three other men in a car at the time of his arrest.
- The arrest happened in a dark parking lot in the middle of the night.

■ The evidence of the crime was seized in a warrantless search of the vehicle.
■ The vehicle search took place at the police station.

c. Decide How Those Facts Are Similar to or Different from the Facts of Your Client's Case

To find similarities between the prior decision and the client's situation, think in general terms. For example, both the prior case and your client's situation might involve children who were injured in the daytime. To find distinctions between the prior case and your client's situation, be as specific as possible, within reason. For example, you might find the following differences between your case and the prior case: In your case, the child was 6 years old, but in the prior case, the child was 13 years old. In both cases, the accident happened in the daytime; however, in the prior case, it was at noon on a bright sunny day, and in your case it was at 4:30 in the afternoon on a cold, wintery, overcast day. All these differences might matter. On the other hand, it is irrelevant that the child's name in the prior case was Mark and your client's name is Bill.

Generally, whenever you have a precedent that you like and that you would like the court to apply to your client's situation, you should search for as many similarities as possible between your facts and the key facts in the prior case. For any facts that do differ you must find ways to convince the court that those differences are so insignificant that they do not matter.[2]

On the other hand, if you have a precedent that you do not like, try to find as many differences as possible between the facts in your client's situation and those in the precedent. It is only by thus distinguishing the two situations that you can convince the court it should not apply the precedent to your client's situation. If there are any similar facts, you must argue that they are insignificant and should not affect the court's view that the two situations are fundamentally different.

In Benson's situation, in addition to the similarities to *Chambers v. Maroney* we mentioned above, there are also some key differences:

■ *Chambers* involved the crime of armed robbery (a violent felony) while Benson was arrested for check fraud.
■ In *Chambers,* the car was stopped in a dark parking lot in the middle of the night, whereas police stopped Benson at 1:30 in the afternoon.
■ There were four men in the car in *Chambers,* but Benson was the only occupant of his car.

---

[2] There are times when a difference between two cases actually supports an argument that they should be decided the same way. For example, assume a court found that a store owner who had detained a suspected shoplifter for one hour had acted unreasonably. If, in the next case, the shopkeeper detained a suspected shoplifter for two hours, the facts in the two cases would differ. However, rather than helping the shopkeeper in the second case, the difference actually reinforces the argument that he, too, acted unreasonably.

This is the most important step in legal analysis. If you take the time to note as many analogies and distinctions as possible, most of your work will be done. As a tool to help you find similarities and differences, it is often a good idea to draw a chart. In the chart, explicitly label specific facts as facts that tend to show how the two situations are analogous or distinguishable.

d. Explain Why Those Similarities or Differences Matter

A mere listing of the factual similarities and differences is not enough. You must explain to your reader why particular similarities or differences should affect the outcome of your client's case. For example, assume that a 6-year-old accidentally shot a neighbor's child with his father's hunting rifle. The issue is whether he should be tried for manslaughter. If in the prior case, under similar facts, a 13-year-old child was tried for manslaughter, we would, of course, point to the differences in the children's ages. But do not assume that pointing to differences, even obvious differences, is enough. Explain why a 6-year-old should be treated differently from a 13-year-old.

The similarities between Benson's case and *Chambers* are quite striking. Both involved an arrest based on eyewitness testimony followed by a warrantless search of the defendant's vehicle at the police station. Therefore, Benson's lawyer will try to negate these similarities by finding enough differences to justify distinguishing *Chambers*. What do you think the strongest argument would be?

- The suspects in *Chambers* committed a violent felony, while Benson did not.
- In *Chambers*, the car was stopped in a dark parking lot in the middle of the night, whereas the police stopped Benson on a sunny day in the early afternoon.
- In *Chambers*, the car contained four suspects, whereas Benson was the only occupant of his car.

In looking at the similarities and differences between the two cases, essentially what you are doing is trying to decide on the holding of *Chambers,* that is, what legal principle was established by that case that would govern future cases. Recall from the discussion on case briefing in Chapter 13 that there can be more than one possible "right" holding for a case. A holding can be stated quite broadly—so that it becomes simply a general principle of law—or quite narrowly—so that it is limited to the specific facts of that case.

The lawyers prosecuting Mr. Benson would argue for a broad holding, contending that *Chambers* stands for the principle that whenever the police have the right to conduct a warrantless search of an automobile at the scene of the arrest, they also have the right to conduct such a warrantless search at the police station. Therefore, under that principle established in *Chambers,* the search of Benson's automobile was legal.

Benson's lawyer, on the other hand, would argue for a narrow holding, emphasizing the factual differences between the cases. She would point out that the arrest in the prior case had occurred "in a dark parking lot in the middle of the night," whereas her client had been arrested in the middle of the day. Therefore, she would maintain that *Chambers* stands for the more limited principle that police can conduct a warrantless search of an automobile at the station only when conditions at the scene of the arrest, such as location and time of day, make it unsafe to conduct a search there. Because the police could have safely searched Benson's car in daylight, the *Chambers* decision does not apply to Benson's situation, and hence any evidence found in the illegal search cannot be used against Benson.

This disagreement about the "true" holding of a case occurs not only between lawyers, but also amongst judges. In fact, a good illustration of this can be found in the United States Supreme Court case of *Texas v. White*.[3] This case has facts identical to those of Benson. In the *White* case, his defense lawyers filed a motion to exclude any evidence that had been seized during the warrantless search of his automobile. The trial judge rejected their motion, and a jury convicted White of knowingly attempting to pass a forged instrument.

On appeal, the Supreme Court agreed with the trial judge's decision, upholding the warrantless search at the police station. In justifying its decision, it relied on a broad interpretation of *Chambers*.

> In *Chambers v. Maroney*, we held that police officers with probable cause to search an automobile on the scene where it was stopped could constitutionally do so later at the station house without first obtaining a warrant.[4]

The dissent thought that this was too broad a reading of the *Chambers* case and that its "true" holding made it distinguishable from what had occurred in White's case.

> Only by misstating the holding of *Chambers v. Maroney*, can the Court make that case appear dispositive of this one. The court . . . today extends *Chambers* to a clearly distinguishable factual setting. . . .
> *Chambers* did not hold as the court suggests. . . . *Chambers* simply held that to be the rule when it is reasonable to take the car to the station house in the first place.[5]

So, what's the moral of the story? Do not feel confused if you are not always sure that you are correctly stating the holding of a case. The best you can do is to remember that when faced with a case that is harmful to your client, you should develop a narrow statement of the prior decision's holding so that it is limited to the facts of that case. However, if you have a case that is beneficial to your client, state the holding in broad enough terms so that it will cover both the facts of the prior case and those of your client's case. That is what the government's attorneys succeeded in doing in *Texas v. White*.

2. Selecting Among Precedents

Once you have found and analyzed a number of arguably relevant cases, the next step is to decide which of the cases to emphasize and which to mention only briefly or not at all. In addition to choosing precedents that help over those that

---

[3] 423 U.S. 67 (1975).
[4] Id. at 67, 68.
[5] Id. at 69.

do not, you will focus on **mandatory authority** when possible, rather than on **persuasive authority**. Among mandatory authority, you will usually rely more on cases from the highest appellate court in your jurisdiction than on those from an intermediate-level appellate court.

Other factors that will influence your choice include the age of the case and how close the facts are to your client's facts. Two similar cases are said to be **on point** with each other. If the facts of the two cases are almost identical, they are said to be **on all fours**. You would also rather rely on a unanimous decision or one written by a well-known jurist. Therefore, all things being equal, you would prefer to use

On point
A term used to describe a case that is similar to another case.

On all fours
A term used to describe two cases that are almost identical, with similar facts and legal issues.

1. a case from the highest appellate court in your jurisdiction,
2. that was decided recently,
3. with facts similar to your own,
4. decided by a unanimous court, and
5. written by a well-known and respected judge.

B. THE FORMAT FOR A WRITTEN ANALYSIS

In Chapter 12, we discussed how the IRAC (Issue-Rule-Analysis-Conclusion) format can help you organize your arguments when you write a statutory analysis. Likewise, when writing an analysis based on court opinions, following the IRAC format will help ensure that your writing follows a logical pattern. In addition, you should develop a style that allows you to synthesize the points raised by a group of cases rather than a style whereby you simply report the cases one by one.

1. Using IRAC

The breakdown of each of the IRAC elements, when writing an analysis based on court opinions, is as follows:

ISSUE	Have a topic sentence that states the issue that you will be discussing in that paragraph. This sentence should be brief and clear. It should also contain only one idea: the one to be discussed in that particular paragraph.
RULE	State the rule of law that arguably governs the particular issue in question.
ANALYSIS	Explain how prior court opinions determine the outcome for your client's case. When citing a court opinion, briefly give the facts, holding, and reasoning to demonstrate how and why that case relates to the facts and issues of your own situation. Note the strong parallels (analogies) and the critical differences (distinctions) between the cited opinion and your own situation. Be very specific both when referring to facts from the cited court opinions and when referring to facts from your client's situation. Be sure to explain why you think those similarities or differences matter. Remember that the reasoning in the court's opinion will determine whether a court will see your case and the precedent as fundamentally similar or different.

CONCLUSION Conclude! Do not leave your reader to decide what the bottom line is. That is why your supervisor asked you to analyze the problem.

If your analysis involves more than one issue, use a short transition sentence to lead to the next issue that you want to discuss.

When faced with a fairly simple legal problem, all the IRAC elements may fit into a single paragraph. At other times you may want to divide the IRAC elements. For example, you might wish to set out the issue and the rule of law in one paragraph, the analysis for the plaintiff in a second paragraph, the analysis for the defendant and your conclusion in a third paragraph, and the transitional phrase or sentence in the first sentence of yet a fourth paragraph.

The amount of emphasis that you place on the factual comparisons between your case and the cited cases will vary, however, depending on whether you are working for a change in the law or are dealing with well-established legal principles that require you to analogize and distinguish your client's case relative to existing case law. If you are engaging in the first type of analysis, arguing for a change in the law, then your analysis section will be more policy based.

> If you use information from a dissent in your analysis, *always* tell your reader that it came from a dissent. Failure to do so would seriously mislead your reader as to the correct status of the law.

For example, recall the case of Janice Miller, the woman who was injured when she was working with her husband cutting and stacking wood. If you were representing Miller in 1977, shortly after the Massachusetts Supreme Judicial Court decided that spouses could sue each other but limited their holding to motor vehicle accidents, you would be arguing for a change in the law that would allow suits in any negligence claim. Your analysis would be primarily based not on the factual issues, but on the policy reasons for extending the holding in *Lewis*. Such an analysis might look similar to the following:

Our client, Janice Miller, would like to sue her husband for injuries that she received when they were working together in their backyard cutting wood. She was injured when a piece of wood flew into her eye, due to her husband's alleged negligence in mishandling a chain saw. The current law in Massachusetts is that spouses can sue each other, but only for injuries sustained in motor vehicle accidents. *Lewis v. Lewis,* 351 N.E.2d 526 (Mass. 1976).

Because Miller was not injured in a motor vehicle accident, she may not be allowed to sue her husband. In the *Lewis* decision, the court changed the long-standing rule that spouses could never sue each other for injuries sustained during their marriage by allowing a wife to sue her husband for injuries she received in a motor vehicle accident. However, the court did pointedly limit its holding to such motor vehicle accidents. *Id.* at 532. The court was mindful that "[c]onduct, tortious between two strangers, may not be tortious because of the mutual concessions implied in the marital relationship." *Id.* This is such a case. The spouses were working together on a joint project. This was not the situation where one spouse was solely responsible for the enterprise, as is true when driving a car. If the court were to allow suit in this case, it would open the court system to every injury that occurs when spouses are working together on household chores. Therefore, in acknowledgment of the special unity of marriage, suits between spouses should be limited to situations such as motor vehicle accidents, where one party is solely responsible for the safety of the undertaking. If the court maintains this limitation to injuries that occur during motor vehicle accidents, Miller will not be able to sue her husband.

However, the Supreme Judicial Court has long held that tortious injury deserves recovery. *Id.* While recognizing the spiritual unity of marriage, *id.* at 528, n.1, the court stated that the doctrine of the legal unity of marriage was no longer a sufficient reason to bar such suits. *Id.* at 528. The principal motivating force behind this decision was the "general principle that if there is tortious injury there should be recovery." *Id.* at 532. Similarly, in our case, the husband negligently injured his wife, and spousal immunity should not shield him in a situation such as this one, not involving a motor vehicle accident. As the court itself noted in footnote 4, it is more concerned with the logic of its past decisions rather than precise holdings. *Id.* at 533, n. 4.

Therefore, in keeping with the logic of *Lewis* (i.e., to provide for recovery in cases of tortious injury), the court will most likely extend its holding in *Lewis* to cover any type of tortious injury between spouses. Miller will be able to proceed with her lawsuit against her husband.

The purpose of an analysis is to present the arguments that each side will make and to predict how a court will resolve the issue. In the analysis, you should candidly evaluate both the strengths and the weaknesses of the client's case. An analysis that tells only about the strengths of a client's case will do little good, as a supervising lawyer needs to know not only what arguments to make but also how to combat the arguments that the opposing side will make. As one well-known authority on legal writing stated in the first edition of his hornbook on legal writing:

> Try to put yourself in the position of your opposite number. Ask yourself: If I were he, how would I answer the analysis or argument just made? How would I rebut or distinguish the cases cited? What countervailing arguments could I offer? Minimizing or covering up what may prove to be fatal weaknesses is the worst thing you can do. It is your responsibility to point out where the dangers lie, where the decisive battles are going to be fought.[6]

While it is always nice to turn out to be right in your prediction of how the court will ultimately resolve the issue, it is more important that you fairly present both sides of the issue than that you select the correct result. Remember that until a court resolves the issue, there is no "right answer," just better or worse arguments. As it turns out, the Massachusetts Supreme Judicial Court did not think it was so ridiculous to let a wife sue her husband for failing to salt the front steps. In 1980, in *Brown v. Brown*,[7] a case involving that very fact scenario, the court

---

[6] Henry Weihofen, *Legal Writing Style* 230 (2d ed. 1980).
[7] 409 N.E.2d 717 (Mass. 1980).

expanded the *Lewis* decision to allow spouses to sue each other in all types of negligence cases. As in *Lewis*, the trial court had dismissed the case at the pretrial stage. Therefore, the appellate court was not in a position to determine whether the husband should be found negligent. All the appellate court decided was that the wife had the right to take her case to court and to let a jury hear the facts in order to determine whether her husband should be found liable for negligence.

If your client's case requires you to work not at changing the law, but rather at analogizing or distinguishing the case from existing law, then your analysis will be much more fact based. However, not all factual distinctions and similarities are equally important. Therefore, you will still need to turn to policy arguments to explain why some facts are more important than others. For example, if Miller were to overcome the hurdle of spousal immunity, then the next issue should be whether her husband would be found negligent. Look at the following two possible approaches to analyzing this problem. In the margins of each approach, label each of the IRAC elements. Then decide which approach is better and why.

Approach 1

The issue is whether Booth can be found negligent because of the injuries his wife suffered when Booth allowed the chain saw he was using to slip, slicing off a piece of bark that flew into Ms. Miller's eye. The general rule is that to avoid negligence, a person should take precautions once warned of drowsiness or fatigue. *Keller v. DeLong,* 231 A.2d 633, 634 (N.H. 1967). In *Keller,* the defendant, while a passenger, felt sleepy. Before taking over at the wheel, he did not take any precautions against falling asleep, such as rolling down the windows or turning on the radio. Soon after that, he fell asleep and hit a utility pole, killing his passenger. The court held that the defendant was negligent because he had felt sleepy as a passenger but had taken no precautions before taking over at the wheel. *Id.* at 635. The court reasoned that because the defendant did not take any precautions to avoid the accident, the accident was foreseeable. *Id.*

Unlike the *Keller* case, Booth would argue that the harm to Miller was not foreseeable. There are significant differences between driving a car and operating a chain saw. If someone drives a car negligently, the passengers are just as likely as the driver to be injured. But when using a chain saw, the person most likely to be hurt is the one using it—in this case, Mr. Booth, not Ms. Miller.

However, while the person most likely to be hurt may be the operator of the chain saw, any dangerous instrument, if used carelessly, can easily inflict injury on others. Indeed, that is what happened in this case. As in *Keller,* the defendant was warned of the impending danger. In *Keller,* the driver felt drowsy as a passenger and yet took no precautions before taking over at the wheel. In Booth's case, he told his wife that he was feeling fatigued just before the accident occurred. If anything, the negligence in Booth's case is greater because the defendant felt tired while operating the chain saw, and yet continued to operate it. It would have been a simple matter to have taken a break, but Booth chose to continue with a dangerous activity even while knowing he was fatigued. As in *Keller,* once the defendant is warned of his fatigue, an injury is foreseeable. Therefore, Booth should be found negligent.

Approach 2

Booth's wife suffered injuries when they were working together in their backyard sawing wood. Booth had told his wife that he was feeling fatigued just before the accident happened. In *Keller,* the defendant, while a passenger, felt sleepy. Before taking over at the wheel, he did not take any precautions against falling asleep, such as rolling down the windows or turning on the radio. Soon thereafter, he fell asleep and hit a utility pole, killing his passenger. On its face, that case is easily distinguishable from our own. There are significant differences between driving a car and operating a chain saw. However, both a chain saw and an automobile can cause injuries.

In Approach 1, the writer uses the IRAC format. The paragraph starts with a statement of the issue, followed by the rule that will be applied. The analysis section gives both the holding and the reasoning of a prior court decision, *Keller.* This is followed by two paragraphs comparing and contrasting the facts of the client's case with those of *Keller.* Finally, the writer concludes that Booth should be found negligent. In Approach 2, the writer begins with a statement of the facts without first putting those facts into context by starting with an issue statement. Next, the writer begins a discussion of a prior case without first explaining what the general rule of law is or why the writer is discussing that particular case. For an analysis, the writer simply states that the facts are similar or different, without explaining why the similarities or differences matter. Finally, the writer forgets to conclude. Therefore, Approach 2 fails in its mission to start off with a clear issue statement, explain the current state of the law, apply that law to the client's facts, and conclude.

In sum, when writing an analysis, you may be trying to argue for a change in the law, or you may be working to show how your client's case fits into a pattern of well-established case law. In this latter type of case, however, you should be aware that you are still asking the court to "change the law," even if only in an evolutionary sense, in that after your case, we will know more about exactly what the law means than we knew before the case was decided. Finally, besides analyzing cases, there will be times when, as we discussed in Chapter 12, a statute will govern your problem. In that situation, you will begin with an analysis of the statute itself, but then you will probably add an analysis of any cases that have interpreted the statute. The three legal reasoning exercises at the end of this section will give you practice with each of these three types of analysis.

PRACTICE TIP

Here are some hints for a successful analysis:
- Tell enough about each case so that the reader will not have to read the cases.
- Give both sides of the argument.
- Work with the facts.
- Explain *why* the court should care that the facts are the same or that the facts are different.

2. Synthesizing Cases

When you are doing research, you read cases one at a time and summarize them one at a time. If that is then how you report them to your reader, you have done little more than hand over your case briefs. What you need to do is to synthesize them so that the reader understands what principles of law arise out of reading the series of cases as a unit. The following is an example taken from *Writing and Analysis in the Law*.[8] Read each approach and then decide which you like better and why.

Approach 1

A parent is immune from a tort suit brought by his child if the suit is for negligence and the child is a minor. First, parents are not immune from suits for intentional torts. The Kent Supreme Court has held that parents are not immune from their child's suit for assault, *Brown v. Brown,* and for battery, *White v. White.* But the court has held that parents are immune from a negligence suit brought by his child. *Abbott v. Abbott.* Second, in *Abbott,* the court held that a parent was immune from suit brought by a minor child for negligence. But in *Black v. Black,* the parent was not immune from the negligence suit brought by his 24-year-old son.

Approach 2

The Kent Supreme Court has decided four cases on parental immunity from tort suits by their children. In the first case in 1999, the court decided that a parent was immune from suit for negligence brought by his 12-year-old son.

---

[8] Helen S. Shapo, Marilyn R. Walter, and Elizabeth Fajans, *Writing and Analysis in the Law* 72 (7th ed. 2018). The authors highly recommend this book to any student interested in learning more about legal analysis.

Abbott v. Abbott (1999). However, in the next suit, in 2000, the court held that a parent was not immune from suit for battery brought by a 10-year-old son. *White v. White* (2000). Only a year later in *Brown v. Brown* (2001), the court affirmed that a parent is not immune from suit for assault brought by a 24-year-old daughter. The most recent case on this topic is *Black v. Black,* decided in 2008. In *Black,* the court decided another suit by a 24-year-old against his parent, this time for negligence. The court still decided that the parent is not immune.

Hopefully, you found the first example much easier to understand. The author starts by giving you a frame of reference: There will be two factors determining parental immunity. The author then goes on to discuss each of these factors. In the second example the author simply lists the cases in chronological order. The first approach does a much better job of explaining to the reader the principles for which these cases stand.

Legal Reasoning Exercises

1. In this problem, you need to argue for a change in the law.

Your firm represents Amanda and Sam Baker, grandparents of 2-year-old Brian Baker. Brian was recently injured in a home accident. The 2-year-old stuck a hairpin into an electrical outlet and was severely burned. The parents had not installed safety plugs in the outlets because they felt that the plugs gave a false sense of security. The plugs are easily removed and were not present in many of their friends' homes. The grandparents want to bring a negligence suit on the child's behalf against the parents.

Assume that the accident happened in Massachusetts and that the Massachusetts Supreme Judicial Court has decided the following cases:

■ *Sorensen v. Sorensen* (1975)—A child was injured when his father negligently caused an automobile accident. The court held that children could sue their parents, but limited the holding to motor vehicle cases and limited the recovery to the amount of available insurance. For its reasoning, the court stated that neither the argument that such suits would disrupt the peace and harmony of the family nor the argument that such actions would tend to promote fraud and collusion was valid.

■ *Lewis v. Lewis* (1976)—A wife was injured when her husband negligently caused an automobile accident. The court held that the wife could sue her husband, but limited the holding to motor vehicle cases. The court did not limit the recovery to the amount of insurance, stating: "In the present case there is nothing in the record concerning the availability or the amount of the defendant's liability insurance, and we do not refer to insurance as a limiting factor in our holding. We do not interpret the logic (as opposed to the precise holding) of *Sorenson* as turning on the availability of insurance in each case, and we decline to limit liability in interspousal tort actions in such a fashion." The court cited *Sorenson* with approval as standing for the proposition that such suits would not disrupt the peace and harmony of the family or tend to promote fraud and collusion. Finally, while acknowledging that some actions that would constitute torts between strangers might not constitute torts if committed between spouses, the court based its decision on the general principle that normally there should be recovery for tortious injury.

■ *Brown v. Brown* (1980)—A wife was injured when she slipped on the front steps that her husband had forgotten to salt. The court held that the wife could sue her husband. The court reasoned that while certain behavior between spouses might not be tortious, that was for a trial court to determine at trial, and the case should not be dismissed as a matter of immunity.

Based on the prior case law, develop arguments both for and against the child's being able to sue his parents for negligence.

2. In this problem, you need to show how your case fits with established law.

Your firm represents the Gilberts. Last week, the Gilberts went out to dinner at a fashionable lakeshore restaurant. After dinner, they decided to take a stroll down a boardwalk that leads from the restaurant out onto a pier. The walkway was not lighted. About halfway down the pier, Gilbert stepped on a board that gave way due to dry rot. She fell and was seriously injured. About five years ago, the restaurant, which owns the pier, decided it was too expensive to keep up with the necessary repairs and had done nothing to maintain the pier since. The restaurant owners posted a sign near the entry to the pier that said, "Danger."

Assume that the accident happened in Nebraska and that the Nebraska Supreme Court decided the following case:

■ *Weiss v. Autumn Hills* (1986)—One night, the plaintiff, a tenant in the defendant landlord's apartment building, was walking across the unlighted grassy area adjoining the patio of her street-level apartment. Although there was a sidewalk leading to the parking lot, taking the sidewalk took longer than cutting across the grass, and many people chose this shorter route. The area was eroded due to water falling from a defective rain gutter. The plaintiff stepped in a rut covered by weeds and fell. The landlord was found negligent.

Based on the *Weiss* decision, will your client be able to show that the restaurant was negligent? List all the factual similarities that make you think the restaurant might be negligent. Then list all the factual differences that make you think the restaurant might not be negligent. Decide which of the factual differences or similarities are most important and why.

3. In this last problem, you need to base your analysis on a statute and a case interpreting that statute.

Assume you have a client, Jack Brilliant, who has been charged with violating the National Motor Vehicle Theft Act. Last weekend, a friend of his, Sam Slick, told your client that he had just acquired a new motorboat, but that he did not know how to run it. He asked your client if he would go out for a ride with him on the Connecticut River and show him how to drive the boat. Your client agreed. They left from a marina in Massachusetts and headed south, with your client at the wheel. Soon after they crossed the Connecticut border, they were flagged down by the marine patrol and arrested. Apparently, Sam had stolen the motorboat.

Based on the language of the statute and the *McBoyle* decision, located on page 369, in Chapter 13, what are the arguments that your client should be convicted of violating the National Motor Vehicle Theft Act? What are the arguments that he should not be convicted?

C. INTERNAL OFFICE MEMORANDA

We have been focusing on how to analyze prior court opinions in order to predict how a court will decide your client's case. In a law office setting, your supervisor may ask you to include this analysis within a law office memorandum. A law office memorandum is made up of various sections. The most important section is the discussion section. It is in that section that you include your analysis.

You write a law office memorandum to inform the person to whom it is addressed (usually a lawyer or paralegal supervisor) of what you have discovered. But you will also be creating a concise, permanent record that can be used by you, your supervisor, or someone else working on the same or a similar problem in the future. Such memoranda are usually placed in a permanent file. Later, when the firm has a similar case, lawyers and paralegals can take advantage of the work that has already been done and avoid needless duplication of effort. As we have discussed, in order to fully understand the issues, the analysis section should fairly evaluate both sides. Another reason for this two-sided approach is that someone in your firm representing a client on the other side of a similar issue may later use your memorandum.

As the quotation at the beginning of this chapter suggests, before you start to write, you must have thoroughly thought through the problem. It may be tempting to just sit down and hope that the good thoughts will come to you as you write your memo. Do not fool yourself. It usually does not work that way. Legal analysis is complicated enough in its own right without being further complicated by stream of consciousness writing.

First, think about the problem. Then write an outline. The purpose of the outline is to force you to think through everything you want to say and the order in which you want to say it. To do that, you have to organize your ideas into issues and sub-issues, with some logical progression between issues. Be clear in your own mind why you are citing a particular case or including a specific argument. Ask yourself: how does this idea fit into the general structure of my argument? As you write your outline, many new thoughts probably will come to you. That is the time to organize them into a logical order—not as you write.

1. Format and Content

The degree of detail and the precise elements of a legal memorandum vary from one law office to another (or even from one lawyer within an office to another), but a law office memorandum usually consists of a heading, a listing of the issues raised (called the questions presented), brief answers to those issues, a statement of the facts, a discussion of the law and how it applies to the client's case, and a conclusion. The following outlines how a law office memorandum is ordinarily organized.

a. Heading

Use a traditional "To: From: Re: Date:" format. Identify the person to whom you are directing the memo, yourself, the client's name, the office file number, the memo's subject matter, and the date on which you prepared the memo.

b. Question Presented (Issue)

State the legal issues raised by the facts of the problem in as concrete a fashion as possible; that is, the legal issues should be related to the specific facts of the case. A general legal proposition or abstract question of law will do little to inform your reader of the specific facts and issues involved in your client's specific problem. The issue identification process is similar to that used in case briefs. It contains a general statement of the law and the specific facts to which that law will be applied. You should carefully identify your issues before you begin your research because in writing the memorandum you should organize the analysis section around these issues.

Here are some general guidelines you should follow in formulating the Question Presented section:

1. State the question in terms of the *facts* of the case.
2. Identify the specific narrow legal question raised by the problem's facts.
3. Make sure the reader can understand the question on the first reading.
4. Eliminate all unnecessary verbiage.
5. Only include issues—that is, questions for which there are more than one possible answer.

Following these guidelines serves two purposes: it will ensure that the question informs the reader of the content of this specific memorandum, and it will aid you in your analysis by requiring you to focus on the specific issues of your client's problem. To arrive at such a precise statement, you may have to rewrite the question several times. Do not let that discourage you. If you can write a clear, simple statement of the issue, you will have gone a long way toward understanding how to analyze your client's problem.

c. Brief Answer

The brief answer should be brief. Write a short, specific answer to the question presented. First, give a definite answer. Follow that with a brief statement of the reasons that led you to that conclusion. A good check is to see if you have included a "because" in your answer. Generally, this section should not include restatements of the facts, citations, or argumentation. If you have researched more than one issue, you should write separate question presented and brief answer sections.

d. Facts

State the relevant facts of the legal problem you researched. Begin with a short summary of the general nature of the case, and then continue with a review of the key events in chronological order. As with case briefing, be very specific about the facts. For example, rather than saying that a car was new, give the car's model year; instead of merely stating that a day was cold, provide the day's actual temperature. Do not omit facts that might influence the analysis of the problem. One good practice is to be sure that every fact you refer to in the "Discussion" section is set out in the statement of facts. Conversely, a fact you do not need for analysis is an irrelevant fact and should be omitted. Of course, you may also need to include some facts that are not strictly relevant to the issue to give the reader necessary background information. If you are unsure about how much to include, err on the side of including too many rather than too few facts.

e. Applicable Statutes

If the problem is controlled by a statute, a constitution, or an administrative regulation, quote the relevant language in this section. However, if it is only tangentially related to your main analysis, you may omit this section and quote the necessary language in the "Discussion" section.

f. Discussion

Start your discussion with an introductory paragraph that sets out the issues you will be discussing. Often this can be simply an expanded version of your question presented. The function of this paragraph is to tell the reader what issues you will be discussing and in what order you will be discussing them. This paragraph can also contain background information if your problem involves an area of the law that would not be familiar to most lawyers.

Following your introductory paragraph, use IRAC to help you frame your analysis for each issue. For each case that you cite, decide how much you want to say about it. At one extreme, you can list a bare ruling of law followed by one or more case citations. This is known as a "naked cite" and should be avoided unless you are citing a case only for an undisputed rule of law. At a minimum, always tell the reader why you are citing the case, what its facts were, what it stands for, and how it relates to your case. At the other extreme, you do not have to convince your reader that you read the case by setting forth all the facts. The trick, of course, is to be selective in your statement of the facts of a particular case so that you include only those that show the case's relevance. The discussion of the holding should be similarly limited. Therefore, for each major case you cite, you should tell the reader why you are citing the case (it is the most recent case, the leading case, etc.) and then briefly state the facts, the nature of the case, the holding, and how it applies to your case.

Whatever you do, do not simply give a series of case descriptions. As discussed in the section "Synthesizing Cases," earlier in this chapter, if your supervisor had merely wanted to know what the cases said, she could have read them for herself. Your job is much more difficult. You must analyze those cases and apply them to your client's problem. Your discussion should constantly be shifting back and forth between a discussion of your client's facts and a discussion of how the cases you read relate to those facts.

Similarly, do not give long quotations. Again, if your supervisor had wanted to read the cases, she would not have asked you to do it. Generally, it is better to restate the court's holding in your own words and then to apply that holding to the facts of your case. In that way, you are not simply parroting the court but fulfilling your job of translating the court's language for your reader. The only exception to this rule is if it is important for the reader to see the exact language of the court to understand your analysis.

PRACTICE TIP

Busy people are most likely to read the first and last sentences of a paragraph. They may skip over anything buried in the middle of a paragraph. Therefore, to make sure that you are conveying your main points, go through your analysis reading only the first and last sentences of each paragraph. If when doing so, you realize that you have hidden your main arguments, go back and rewrite until reading just those first and last sentences conveys your main ideas.

Finally, remember that your basic job in writing a memorandum of law is to relate the law to the facts of your case. Keep in mind the famous observation of Justice Oliver Wendell Holmes that "general propositions do not decide concrete cases." Do not engage in extended abstract discussions of the law; instead, devote your energy to applying the law to your facts. One quick method to ascertain the effectiveness of your "Discussion" section is to review it with an eye toward learning the facts of the case. A successful discussion will continually refer to the facts and thus paint a picture, as well as analyze.

In sum, in this section, you should analyze relevant constitutional provisions, statutes, administrative regulations, and court cases. Quote from the key provisions of statutory materials. With cases, state the holdings of relevant cases. Also, discuss the similarities and differences between the facts of the case being cited and the facts involved in the problem being researched. All references to legal authorities should include proper citations. Be sure to report the extent to which intervening court cases have modified any statutes or earlier court opinions. In assessing the strengths and the weaknesses of the client's case, be as objective as possible. Specify which courses of action appear most promising, and when relevant, also identify facts that need to be clarified or additional legal materials that need to be examined.

g. Conclusion

Give a brief review of the most significant conclusions. Do not introduce new ideas or authorities in this paragraph. This final section of the memo should provide a brief and concise summary that points out the strengths and weaknesses of the client's position. It also may include the writer's recommendations for further action, including additional factual investigation and further legal research on specific points.

2. Sample Law Office Memorandum

TO: Latashia Brown, Senior Partner
FROM: Chris Parker
RE: Janice Miller; File No. 17-483
         Possibility of Proving Booth's Negligence
DATE: April 5, 2021

Questions Presented

Issue 1: Whether Booth can be found negligent for failing to take precautions once warned of his fatigue; when Booth stated to Miller that he was tired, he continued to use a chain saw to cut wood, and the chain saw slipped, slicing off a piece of bark that flew into Miller's eye, blinding her.

Issue 2: Whether Miller will be barred from recovering for Booth's negligence if the jury determines that she was negligent in failing to wear a pair of safety goggles.

Brief Answers

Issue 1: Yes, Booth will be found negligent. If someone is fatigued while using a chain saw, it is foreseeable that an injury will occur. Booth was aware of his fatigue but continued to use the chain saw. Therefore, Miller's injury was foreseeable, and Booth was negligent in failing to heed the warning signs.

Issue 2: Miller will not be barred from recovering for Booth's negligence, so long as she was not more than 50 percent responsible for her injuries. However, based on Massachusetts statutory law, the amount that she can recover will be decreased by the percentage of her negligence.

Facts

Last March our client, Janice Miller, was injured in an accident that occurred in her backyard. She and her husband, George Booth, were cutting firewood.

Booth was using a chain saw, and Miller was stacking the pieces of wood as Booth cut them. Neither was wearing safety glasses, although each owned a pair. Miller explained the omission by saying that they had both thought they would be cutting wood only for a short time, and neither wanted to be bothered by putting on the glasses.

As it turned out, the wood-cutting session took longer than anticipated. After about an hour, both Booth and Miller were getting tired. In particular, Booth complained that he was feeling fatigued and that it was getting harder and harder to hold the saw sufficiently perpendicular to the wood to cut a straight line. Miller suggested that they quit for the day, but Booth wanted to cut just a few more pieces. On his next attempt, probably owing to his tired condition, he allowed the chain saw to slip slightly so that it hit the log at a slant, slicing off a piece of bark that flew into Miller's right eye. Unfortunately, the accident has left Miller totally blind in that eye.

Applicable Statutes

Issue 1: There are no statutes that apply.

Issue 2: Contributory negligence shall not bar recovery in any action by any person . . . to recover damages for negligence . . . if such negligence was not greater than the total amount of negligence attributable to the person . . . against whom recovery is sought, but any damages allowed shall be diminished in proportion to the amount of negligence attributable to the person for whose injury . . . recovery is made.

Mass. Gen. L. ch. 231, §85 (2020).

Discussion

The resolution of two issues will determine whether Booth will be found liable for the injuries Miller sustained. The first relates to whether Booth was negligent for continuing to use his chain saw after he acknowledged that he was feeling fatigued. The second is whether Miller will be barred from recovery because of her failure to wear safety goggles.

Issue 1 — Booth's Actions Constitute Negligence

Booth will be found liable for negligently causing his wife's injuries if the injury was foreseeable and Booth did nothing to prevent it. To avoid negligence, a person should take precautions once warned of drowsiness or fatigue. *Keller v. DeLong*, 231 A.2d 633, 634 (N.H. 1967). In *Keller*, the defendant, while a passenger, felt sleepy. Before taking over at the wheel, he did not take any precautions against falling asleep, such as rolling down the windows or turning on the radio. Soon after that, he fell asleep and hit a utility pole, killing his passenger. The court held that the defendant was negligent because he had felt sleepy as a passenger but had taken no precautions before taking over at the wheel. *Id*. at 635. The court reasoned that because the defendant did not take any precautions to avoid the accident, the accident was foreseeable. *Id*.

Unlike the *Keller* case, Booth would argue that the harm to Miller was not foreseeable. There are significant differences between driving a car and operating a chain saw. If someone drives a car negligently, the passengers are just as likely as the driver to be injured. But when using a chain saw, the person most likely to be hurt is the one using it — in this case, Booth, not Miller.

However, while the person most likely to be hurt may be the operator of the chain saw, any dangerous instrument, if used carelessly, can easily inflict injury on others. Indeed, that is what happened in this case. As in *Keller,* the defendant was warned of the impending danger. In *Keller,* the driver felt drowsy as a passenger and yet took no precautions before taking over at the wheel. In Booth's case, he told his wife that he was feeling fatigued just before the accident occurred. If anything, the negligence in Booth's case is greater because the defendant felt tired while operating the chain saw and yet continued to operate it. It would have been a simple matter to have taken a break, but Booth chose to continue with a dangerous activity even while knowing he was fatigued. As in *Keller,* once the defendant is warned of his fatigue, an injury is foreseeable. Therefore, Booth should be found negligent.

Issue 2—Miller's Contributory Negligence Will Reduce Her Damages

The second issue is whether a jury, finding that Miller failed to use reasonable care by not protecting her eyes with safety glasses, would bar her from recovering. A jury finding of contributory negligence will not bar a plaintiff from recovery so long as her negligence "was not greater than" the defendant's negligence. Mass. Gen. L. ch. 231, §85 (2017). Therefore, so long as the jury finds that Booth's negligence was at least 50 percent of the reason for Miller's injury, she will not be barred from recovery.

However, the statute also provides that "any damages allowed shall be diminished in proportion to the amount of negligence attributable" to Miller's actions. For example, if the jury were to decide that Miller's own actions contributed 25 percent to her injuries and that her damages are $400,000, she would be able to recover $300,000. Therefore, so long as the jury finds that Miller's actions contributed 50 percent or less to her injuries, she will be allowed to recover for her injuries, with the total damages reduced by the amount of her contributory negligence.

Conclusion

On the first issue, regarding Booth's failure to stop using the chain saw after experiencing warning symptoms of fatigue, he will be found negligent. Once he felt tired, an accident was foreseeable, and Booth was negligent in continuing to use a dangerous tool, such as a chain saw. On the second issue, regarding Miller's failure to use safety goggles, if the jury determines that her contributory negligence did not cause more than 50 percent of the harm, then she will still be allowed to recover, but her damages will be reduced by the amount of her negligence.

SUMMARY

The purpose of analyzing court opinions is to try to predict the outcome of your client's case. The process involves searching for analogies and distinctions between prior court opinions and the facts of your client's situation. Generally, to find analogies, you will think in general terms, while to find distinctions, you will think as specifically as possible about the facts. Legal analysis also involves selecting among available precedents based on such factors as the court that decided the case, the age of the case, and the number of factual similarities or differences between that case and your own.

In writing an analysis, the deductive model—major premise (rule of law), minor premise (facts), and conclusion—can provide a structure for your argument. Another method is to rely on IRAC. Finally, whenever you are analyzing more than one case, you are engaging in synthesis, the process of integrating the concepts you find in the cases so that the reader can appreciate the principles of law that arise from seeing the series of cases as a unit.

REVIEW QUESTIONS

1. Why is it important to find both analogies and distinctions between your client's facts and the facts of prior cases?
2. Why is it not enough simply to list the similarities and differences between your client's facts and the facts of prior cases?
3. What factors help determine whether you should use a particular case in support of your client's position?
4. Assume that you have been asked to write an analysis of whether a client is guilty of murder. The case occurred and will be tried in California. List the following in order from most to least authoritative. Explain your choices.
   a. A 1995 Illinois Supreme Court decision, with facts similar to your client's facts, in which the defendant was found not guilty of murder.
   b. A 1989 law review article that surveys all of the murder statutes in the 50 states.
   c. A 1980 California Supreme Court decision, with facts similar to your client's facts, in which the defendant was found guilty of murder.
   d. A 1990 California intermediate court decision, with facts similar to your client's facts, in which the defendant was found guilty of manslaughter.
   e. A California state statute defining murder and manslaughter.
   f. A section from Am. Jur. 2d explaining the differences between murder and manslaughter.
   g. A 1995 California Supreme Court decision on breach of warranty in automobile sales.
5. What does it mean to say a case is on all fours?
6. What is the relationship between deductive reasoning and legal reasoning?

WEB EXERCISES

1. *Scribes* is an online journal produced by the American Society of Legal Writers. Find volume 16 online and click on Gerald Lebovits's article "Legal-Writing Myths." Read through the article. Myth 10 is "No one cares how you cite, so long as your citation can be found." Why doesn't the author believe that myth? Do you agree with his analysis? Why or why not?

2. In Legal Reasoning Exercise 1, we asked you to think about how a court might resolve the issue of whether a child should be allowed to sue a parent for harm the parent negligently causes. Using a free resource, such as FindLaw, *lp.findlaw .com,* or the Public Library of Law, *lol.org*, conduct a search to see if your state's appellate courts have issued any decisions within the last five years concerning parental immunity. If yes, how did the court resolve the issue? If no, conduct a similar search in Massachusetts. You should find a case from 2004, in which the court had to decide if a child could sue her mother for her mother's negligent driving that resulted in an accident leading to the plaintiff's premature birth and subsequent related injuries. Did the court allow the child to sue her mother?

PART  4

Paralegals and the Work World

Chapter 16

Interviewing

Life is not so short but that there is always time enough for courtesy.
Ralph Waldo Emerson

Chapter Objectives

After reading this chapter, you should be able to:

- Understand basic communication techniques for conducting effective interviews with clients and witnesses.
- Discuss how ethnic, racial, and gender differences can affect communication.
- Identify the types of locations and physical surroundings that are most conducive to conducting effective interviews.
- Describe the types of notes that should be taken during an interview and what should be included in a written report that would go into a case file.

INTRODUCTION

Resolving legal conflicts involves applying general principles of law to a specific set of facts. Therefore, a lawyer needs to know not only the law, but also the factual details of the client's situation in order to be able to advise the client on a specific course of action. These facts begin to emerge in the initial client interview and then are developed further as part of the case preparation process. In this chapter, we will look at how paralegals gather facts through client and witness interviews. In Chapter 17, we will take a closer look at gathering facts through documentary evidence and from personal observation.

Paralegals can be involved in several types of interview situations. These situations can include the initial client interview, follow-up interviews with the client (either in the office or in the field), and field interviews with both friendly and hostile witnesses. In this chapter we will use the case of Donald Drake, which we introduced in Chapter 1, to illustrate interviewing techniques.

Case 1: The Distressed Grandfather (Continued)

Approximately one year ago, Drake and his six-year-old grandson, Philip, were walking down a residential road on their way home from visiting one of Philip's friends. Philip was walking on the sidewalk approximately 30 feet in front of Drake. Suddenly a car sped past Drake, seemingly went out of control, jumped the curb, and hit Philip. Drake ran to Philip's side, but it was too late. Philip had been killed instantly. The driver of the car, Wilma Small, was unhurt.

At the time of the accident, Drake's only concern was for the welfare of his grandson because he himself was clear of the danger. Naturally,

Drake suffered a great deal of mental pain and shock because of seeing his grandson killed. While being driven home from the accident, he suffered a heart attack that necessitated a lengthy hospital stay.

One year later, he still does not feel completely recovered and often suffers from nightmares, reliving the accident and his grandson's death. Drake has decided to approach the Darrow and Bryan law firm to see if he can sue Small to recover for his hospital bills, for his pain and suffering, and for the emotional distress that he felt upon seeing his grandson killed.

A. COMMUNICATION SKILLS

To be an effective interviewer, you must have strong verbal communication skills. You must be able to relate well to other people, read their reactions, and adjust to their situations and their moods. Perhaps most important, you must be able to put others at ease and win their confidence.

1. Communication as a Two-Way Street

It is quite possible for two people to receive different messages from the same set of words and gestures. The authors of a book on communication problems report having seen the following sign in a lawyer's office:

> I know you believe you understand what you think I said, but I am not sure you realize that what you heard is not what I meant.[1]

This sign points out a common communication problem—the listener is not getting the message that the speaker has intended to convey.

Communication is a two-way street: You have an obligation to make sure that you understand what the other person is saying. But you also must ensure

---

[1] G. Nierenberg and H. Calero, *Meta-talk* 16 (1975).

that the other person understands what you are saying. Be very conscious of the words, expressions, and gestures you use, as well as the reactions they evoke.

Make sure that you are using plain English, not legalese. It is important to watch for signals that could indicate that the people to whom you are talking does not understand what you are saying. The person to whom you are speaking may not let you know or even be aware that their understanding of what you are saying differs from what you mean. This may occur because they do not realize there is a difference between what you said and what they understood, or because they are too embarrassed to tell you they did not understand the terminology you used. In those cases, go back and restate the message in different terms.

2. Active Listening

Active listening involves the process of signaling that you are really listening. This is accomplished by

1. using verbal and nonverbal clues,
2. paraphrasing, and
3. reflecting the client's feelings.

Active listening
The process of signaling that you are really listening, accomplished by using verbal and nonverbal clues, paraphrasing, and reflecting the client's feelings.

Not only does active listening show the person being interviewed that you are listening, but it conveys a sense of empathy, that you not only hear but also understand what the other person is trying to convey. It also gives the interviewee an opportunity to correct you if you did not correctly interpret what the interviewee said.

You can use a number of verbal and nonverbal clues to convey that you are listening and that the person interviewed should continue with his or her story. These include head nods and short, nonintrusive expressions such as "And?" "Could you tell me a bit more about that?" and even "Um-hm."

Paraphrasing involves repeating, in a shortened, revised form, what the interviewee has just finished saying. It has two purposes:

- ■ It shows the client that the interviewer is listening and trying to understand what the client is saying.
- ■ It provides a mechanism for ensuring that the person conducting the interview correctly understood what the client said.

For example, if a client relates a rather involved conversation with a bill collector, the interviewer might respond: "So the bill collector threatened to get you fired if you didn't pay by Tuesday. Is that right?" Be careful with this, however. Shortening an involved conversation to one sentence might leave the client viewing you as brusque and unfeeling.

In addition to using paraphrasing to reflect the interviewer's perception of the facts, you should use it to acknowledge the client's emotions. A reflection of feelings demonstrates that you have been listening closely and understand the feelings the client has expressed. The goal is to communicate an understanding of how the client feels—a sense of empathy. It is not necessary to show acceptance for the person's feelings—just that those feelings are respected.

Thus, after listening to a client describe an incident at a party where her husband made derogatory remarks about her, the interviewer might comment, "My goodness, that must have been difficult for you." However, do not become so overcome by the client's plight that you lose your professional distance. There is a fine balance between showing acceptance and keeping your objectivity.

When using either the paraphrasing or the reflection of feelings technique, deliver the feedback in a tentative tone of voice. This offers the interviewee a chance to respond by (1) affirming that the stated understanding is correct, (2) correcting what was a false understanding on your part, (3) elaborating further on the topic, or (4) using some combination of the first three. These techniques show the interviewee that you are listening and encourage him or her to correct any misunderstandings.

If you are beginning to think that listening is hard work, you are right. It is easy to become so overcome with empathy for the client's plight or so wrapped up in trying to get all of the answers for your intake form that you simply neglect to listen to what the client is telling you. While good interviewing skills come mostly with practice, the techniques discussed here can help you develop the art of listening.

3. Nonverbal Communication

Good listening skills involve more than simply hearing what is being said. It is essential to watch, as well as listen. As Alfred Benjamin has written in an excellent book on interviewing skills:

> Listening requires, first of all, that we not be preoccupied, for if we are we cannot fully attend. Secondly, listening involves hearing the way things are being said, the tone used, the expressions and gestures employed. In addition, listening includes the effort to hear what is not being said, what is only hinted at, what is perhaps being held back, what lies beneath or beyond the surface. We hear with our ears, but we listen with our eyes and mind and heart and skin and guts as well.[2]

Pay attention to nonverbal communication. Nonverbal messages can be either conscious or unconscious and either intentional or unintentional. A smile is both intentional and conscious. A quivering voice is usually conscious yet unintentional.[3]

Nonverbal behavior plays an important role in the feedback process. Just as the client sends nonverbal cues to the interviewer, so too the interviewer sends nonverbal cues to the client. The paralegal therefore must remain conscious of nonverbal behavior and the effect it has on the client. For example, crossing your arms, leaning back, or frowning might convey hostility. On the other hand, a relaxed posture while leaning forward generally conveys a positive attitude.

4. The Influence of Ethnic, Racial, and Gender Differences

Because an interviewer's ability to establish rapport and trust with the person being interviewed is critical to the success of the interview, cultural and gender

---

[2]A. Benjamin, *The Helping Interview* 46 (3d ed. 1981).
[3]Id. at 67.

difference can present special challenges. For example, it is often suggested that one facilitator to good communication is the use of direct eye contact. Yet, in some cultures, direct eye contact between strangers is interpreted as rudeness. The more you can educate yourself about racial, cultural, and gender differences, the better off you will be.

One way to put the person being interviewed at ease is to refer to that person by their preferred gender. For some clients it is very clear, but it is increasingly possible to meet with transgender clients or clients who prefer not to identify strictly as male or female or simply prefer that you use gender neutral language. If you are not clear about an interviewee's preference, simply ask "what pronouns do you use?" For a period of time, the singular "they" was not considered to be grammatically correct, but it is now preferred in the *APA Style Manual* (developed by the American Psychological Association and used in the social sciences), the *MLA Handbook* (developed by the Modern Languages Association and used in the language arts and the humanities), the *Chicago Manual of Style,* and the AP (Associated Press) style guide in instances where either an individual states a preference or where the gender of a person is unknown.[4]

It is also important that you not treat people on the basis of stereotypes associated with their background. For example, after you have interviewed dozens of clients with landlord-tenant disputes, you may start to think in terms of stereotyped categories. You may then begin to assume that simply because something happened one way in a similar case, it happened the same way in the present case. Having categorized the current case, you may fail to hear what the interviewee really says. Experience with similar cases may also have created some bias on your part. For example, if you have interviewed a series of so-called "deadbeat" dads (i.e., fathers who are unwilling to support their children), you may unconsciously begin to view all noncustodial fathers as "deadbeats." However, the person you are interviewing may be willing but simply unable to provide support. The best approach to interviewing is to be yourself and to let your own personality come through. Be especially careful, however, not to appear condescending or patronizing. Listen, document, and empathize, but do not judge. Always treat the interviewee with respect.

DISCUSSION QUESTIONS

1. Active listening is an important part of effective communication skills. However, some argue that it is inappropriate to use active listening during client interviews because it interjects too much emotion into what should be a professional setting. Do you agree?

2. What, if any, cultural or gender differences do you think exist with respect to verbal and nonverbal communications? To what extent should they affect one's interviewing style?

---

[4] For more detail about the history of the use of the singular "they," you can refer to "A Brief History of the Singular 'They,'" at Oxford University Press, *public.oed.com/blog/a-brief-history-of-singular-they/* (last accessed July 29, 2020).

Only a lawyer can establish the lawyer–client relationship and negotiate the fee agreement. As the *People v. Mitchell* case in Chapter 2 illustrated, there may be an issue of whether the lawyer–client privilege has been established if the initial interview is conducted solely by a paralegal.

B. INITIAL CLIENT INTERVIEWS

Having discussed the general communications skills involved in conducting any good interview, we now move on to interviews that are conducted as part of the legal process. While our focus will be on the initial client interview, much of this discussion is also relevant to witness and follow-up client interviews.

The two main goals of an initial client interview are

- to obtain information that is legally relevant, complete, and reliable; and
- to establish a relationship of trust with the client so that the client will feel sufficiently comfortable to convey the needed information.

You may not always be able to attain the first goal for any number of reasons, such as limited time for the interview or lack of knowledge of a particular area of the law. Nonetheless, at a minimum, you should leave the interview with enough information to enable your supervising lawyer to decide whether the firm should accept the case and formally establish the client–lawyer relationship. You should also have a sufficient understanding of the facts to be able to begin working toward an appropriate solution to the client's problems, including deciding what further investigation needs to be done either to corroborate the client's story or to fill in gaps in the client's account.

1. Lawyer and Paralegal Roles

Law firms follow any one of three possible approaches regarding the presence of paralegals at the initial client interview. In Drake's case, the law firm preferred to use a paralegal–lawyer team. In others, the preference is to have a paralegal meet with the client first to collect a considerable amount of information about the client's problems before a lawyer meets with the client personally. Finally, there are some law offices where the lawyers prefer to handle the initial interview alone.

For example, a lawyer will usually conduct the initial client interview (with or without a paralegal) in order to recruit the person being interviewed as a client. On the other hand, in a public defender's or legal aid office, it is common for paralegals to conduct the initial interviews on their own.

2. Prior to the Interview

Ideally, before the interview, the prospective client will have sent information using a form on your website, or through e-mail, or mail, that can provided the firm with basic information to determine whether or not there is any potential conflict of interest. If there is such a conflict, a nonengagement letter should be sent. If there is no conflict, of interest, an interview may be scheduled. In some cases, the client will not fill out a form until in the office, and a potential conflict can be identified in the minutes leading up to an interview; in other cases the client will have sent information using a form on your website, via e-mail, or mail.

If there is some time before the initial interview, send the potential client an e-mail or letter in which you confirm the time of the appointment and provide directions about how to sign into a virtual meeting, or how to find the office and where to park. If the meeting is to be held virtually, make sure that you have the client's telephone number in case there are problems with audio or with connecting with the client. This can make the difference between an easy transition in case of a glitch or leaving the prospective clients with the belief that communication with your firm is too difficult for your firm and that they should seek representation elsewhere.

Include in this initial communication letter should also include a checklist of documents and other relevant information to be brought to the interview, such as a list of the key dates and names and contact information of witnesses, insurance companies, health care providers, and relevant others. For estate planning and probate matters, the client should be asked to bring a list of assets, insurance and bank account numbers, deeds, specific bequests, and guardians' names and addresses. If you would like to have the information before the interview, enclose a self-addressed, stamped envelope to make it easy for the client, or send the questions and or ask for a response electronically or through a form on your website. Make certain that you make clear that the individual is not yet your firm's client.

Case 1: The Distressed Grandfather (Continued)

When Drake appeared for his first appointment at the law office of Darrow and Bryan, the receptionist notified the lawyer, Harper, that Drake had arrived. Harper then went to the reception area, where she greeted Drake by name, shook his hand, and escorted him to a conference room. When they arrived in the conference room, the paralegal, Kendall, was there waiting for them. Harper introduced Drake to Kendall and explained that Kendall was one of the firm's paralegals and would be joining them for the interview.

DISCUSSION QUESTION

3. What are some ethical issues connected with communicating with a client over the Internet?

3. Location and Setting of the Interview

Communication can be facilitated or impeded by something as simple as where the interview takes place and the seating arrangements that are used. It is best to

conduct interviews in a comfortable, quiet, and private location. The right surroundings help establish good rapport and avoid distractions.

There is no one right seating arrangement, but be aware that the one that
you choose will send a message. Which one you choose will depend on how you
want the other person to perceive you, who that other person is (new client,
established client, hostile witness, etc.), and why that person has come to the
firm (ax murderer or elderly gentleman seeking tax advice, for examples).

Figure 16-1 shows the basic seating arrangements available in most offices.
In the traditional arrangement, the lawyer sits behind a large, imposing desk, reinforcing the authority image. The client sits on the other side of the desk—usually
in a chair that is lower than that of the interviewer. Traditionally, such a seating
arrangement is thought to intimidate clients and make them uneasy. However,
there may be times when you want that extra authority that such a seating
arrangement can provide, such as when meeting with a representative from the
opposing side of a case. Once you have established a good working relationship,
you might then consider one of the other possible seating arrangements.

At the opposite end of the spectrum from the authority image evoked by
arrangement A, arrangement D strikes a very casual tone. The interviewer leaves
the desk behind and uses chairs placed around a low table of some sort. This
arrangement places you and the interviewee on an equal level, at a distance that
facilitates personal communication. It also has the advantage of providing comfortable eye contact; it allows the two parties either to look directly at each other
or to easily glance away at a 90-degree angle. A major disadvantage is that it will
be more difficult for you to take notes. In effect, you will have to balance a note
pad on your knee. Also, it may convey too casual an image to a client who, after
all, has probably come to the law firm seeking serious help.

When you have no need for a show of authority and yet do not want to
convey too informal an image, arrangement B provides a good compromise. This
positioning of client and paralegal offers the same advantages as to distance and
eye contact as arrangement D. It also provides the interviewer with a large surface on which to take notes.

Finally, arrangement C, while conveying an image of equality, can be quite
awkward for both you and the interviewee. The positioning of the chairs does

Figure 16-1 Alternative Seating Arrangements for Interviews

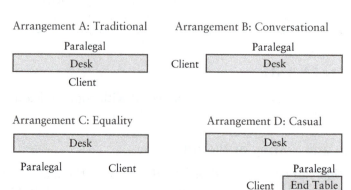

not allow for any but direct eye contact, and the full body is exposed. Note-taking is also quite awkward, and there is no way to hide any notes you might not want the interviewee to see.

Remember that the location of the interview is also important if you are meeting virtually. You will want to make sure that you are in a quiet and professional-looking environment with an appropriate backdrop, and that you have eliminated any distractions. Check your headset, microphones, and video call software prior to meeting with the client to ensure the best-quality conversation. Troubleshoot potential issues prior to the meeting and have a number of solutions for each. For example, if the computer audio is not working, make sure that you have the client's telephone number.

PRACTICE TIP

In situations where an interview involves highly emotional issues, it is good to keep tissues nearby. You may also want to offer water or suggest a short break. Acknowledge that you are asking difficult questions and remind the client why you need to do so.

DISCUSSION QUESTION

4. Have you ever experienced a glitch in a virtual meeting? If so, how was the problem resolved? Whether or not you have actually experienced one, troubleshoot various virtual meeting issues and create a chart of possible ways to fix those issues.

4. Starting the Interview

If possible, greet the client in the reception room and escort the client to the interview location. This will help the client feel welcome. It also helps preserve other client confidences that a wandering client might accidentally overhear. If the meeting is virtual, make sure that you are a few minutes early to the meeting and that you can quickly resolve any technical issues. Make sure that you are making the client feel welcome and comfortable with the technology.

Whenever a paralegal is present at an initial client interview, as part of the introduction process the attorney or paralegal should give a brief explanation of the paralegal's role. The person being interviewed has a right to know who the interviewer is and that the interviewer is not a lawyer. The paralegal's role should be described in relatively simple, positive terms. For example: "I am a paralegal, not an attorney. My job involves gathering the basic facts for (attorney's name). I will be working with him/her on your case."

Once the client is seated and comfortable, if it seems appropriate, you can begin by engaging in some small talk about the weather or the parking situation until the client feels relaxed enough to move on to the nature of the problem. If after some awkward periods of silence, the client seems to have trouble discussing the specific situation, you can then initiate the conversation with an open-ended inquiry, such as "Well, Mr./Ms. . . . what is it that brings you in to see us?"

Case 1: The Distressed Grandfather (Continued)

As Drake entered the office, he seemed somewhat shaky and ill at ease. Because Harper knew that Drake was coming to see them about a matter related to his grandson's recent death, she felt it best not to spend too much time on small talk. So, after asking if she could get Drake a cup of coffee or tea, and explaining that the paralegal, Kendall, would be taking notes so that they would have an accurate record of their meeting, she started by saying, "Mr. Drake, I understand you have come to see us regarding an accident that involved your grandson. In what way would you like us to help you?"

---

5. Taking Notes

Note-taking is essential in most legal interviewing situations. Although some people claim that it can be distracting, it shows clients that you are taking very seriously what they have to say. You cannot afford to rely on memory until you can write up the interview at a later time. If you do not take good notes, you will need to call the client back to fill in the gaps. This irritates the client and needlessly increases the client's billable hours. On the other hand, too much note-taking will mean that you will miss what the client is saying and make the client feel like an object.

There are many ways to take notes. Some interviewers take handwritten notes on a legal pad (if the interview is taking place in an office) or a smaller, pocket-sized notepad (if the interview is taking place in someone's home, front step, etc.) and type them into a computer file shortly after the interview. Others use programs for taking handwritten notes on tablets or notepads that will then transcribe them into their firm's preferred format. Another common method is to type. If you are very adept at entering your notes directly into a laptop or tablet, you may prefer to save time by skipping the handwritten stage. However, be aware that if you are typing, you may have a harder time maintaining eye contact, and the person you are interviewing may find this process more distracting.

Regardless of which technique you use for recording your notes, it takes a lot of practice to develop the skill of being able to take notes and listen at the same time. One time-saving technique is to use abbreviations, such as "W." for "witness." But make sure that you can interpret your handwriting or abbreviations later. Another method that can help is always to put the same type of information in the same place, such as all potential witness names in the upper-right corner of your notepad. This is also where a checklist can prove to be invaluable. Not only will a checklist cut down on the amount of writing that you will have to do, but also it will keep you on track. Some offices create preprinted forms containing information that is needed in the initial interview. But be careful that you do not rely so heavily on the checklist that you fail to follow up on possibly fruitful areas of inquiry.

PRACTICE TIP

Starting off with some very narrow factual information, such as the client's address and phone number, can sometimes be of great assistance, especially in the case of a nervous client (or a nervous interviewer!). However, as soon as the client appears to be at ease, switch to a series of open questions.

---

6. Asking the Right Questions

In order to get the information you need, it is important to ask the right questions. This is done not only by focusing your questions on the topics that are important to the case, but also by wording your questions in a way that will draw out the information you need. Always keep in mind that you are helping a client reach her or his objectives, and make sure that you understand what those objectives are.

A question can take many forms: open, closed (yes-no and narrow), and leading. **Open questions** such as "How did the accident take place?" focus the interview without greatly limiting the freedom of the respondent. On the other hand, **closed questions** are by their nature very specific and usually demand very short or yes-no answers: "What color was the car that hit you?" "How far in advance did you see it coming?" "Was the sun shining in your face at the time?"

It is generally good to start the interview with open-ended questions, in order to discover what the person being interviewed thinks is important, and then to follow up with closed questions to clarify information deemed to be important to the case. Clients are frequently much more forthcoming with information when asked open, rather than closed questions.

Compare the information given below by the client in response to the different forms of questions from the paralegal:

Open questions
Broad questions that put few limits on the freedom of the respondent.

Closed questions
Specific questions that usually demand very short or yes-no answers.

Interview No. 1

Paralegal: Did you receive a written eviction notice?
Client: Yes.

Interview No. 2

Paralegal: How did you find out that you were going to be evicted?
Client: The landlord came up to me around 7 o'clock in the evening while I was sitting on the front porch with some other residents. He yelled something

about my being a no-good troublemaker because I was always complaining to the city inspections department. Then he stuck this eviction notice in my hand and stomped off.

In addition, asking only a series of narrow questions may lead the client to answer only the specific questions you ask, thereby causing you to miss valuable information. A further danger is that you may find yourself concentrating so hard on framing the next question that you fail to listen to what the client is saying. Therefore, start the interview with an open-ended question so that the client can describe the problem independently, and not in response to specific questions.

Once you have elicited the general story through broad, open questions, it is time to move to the second stage of the interview: clarification and verification. During this stage, you can use the active listening techniques discussed earlier to keep the conversation going, to elicit more detail, and to confirm that you have accurately heard what the client has said. Ask questions to clarify areas of ambiguity and help the interviewee tell the story. This approach of starting with broad questions and then progressively narrowing the inquiry is sometimes referred to as the "funnel approach," as illustrated in Figure 16-2.

Leading question
A question that suggests the answer.

Avoid **leading questions** because leading questions suggest the answer. For example, after hearing Drake's story, Kendall should not ask, "To have caused such long skid marks, Mrs. Small was probably speeding, wasn't she?" Leading questions are dangerous because they put words in the client's mouth—words that might not otherwise have been there. In trying to give you the answers that they think you want, clients may unconsciously "misremember" the facts. Also, leading questions may cut off what would otherwise be a more helpful and detailed discussion of the event.

It is especially important to limit the use of "why" questions to circumstances in which the motivation behind an act is really important to the case. This is because a seemingly innocuous inquiry, such as asking why a person was at a bar that night, can appear as though you are disapproving of the interviewee's actions. "Why" questions may put the interviewee on the defensive and

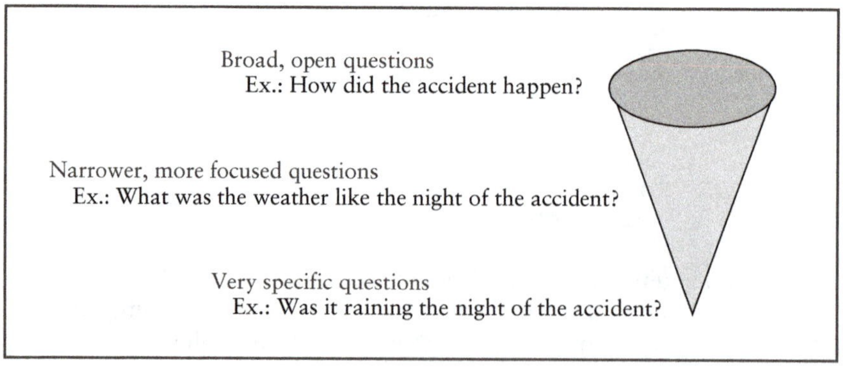

Broad, open questions
Ex.: How did the accident happen?

Narrower, more focused questions
Ex.: What was the weather like the night of the accident?

Very specific questions
Ex.: Was it raining the night of the accident?

Figure 16-2   The Funnel Approach

erode the relationship of trust that you are trying to build. This is especially true where matters of values and judgment are involved. On the other hand, there are times where questions such as "Why did you move out of your apartment?" or "Why did you dispute the charges?" are critical to the understanding of the case.

If the client states a conclusion about some person or event, probe to find the specific observations on which that conclusion is based. Distinguish exactly what the client said or heard personally from what he or she learned second-hand. If the client simply conveys to you what someone else told him or her, you may be obtaining inadmissible hearsay evidence. **Hearsay** testimony is usually not admissible because it is, in effect, someone giving secondhand information. If possible, get the name of the person with the firsthand information so that you can interview that person.

Hearsay
Testimony or evidence introduced in court regarding what someone said out of court for the purpose of establishing the truth of what was said.

Using legal jargon can unintentionally lead paralegals into the unauthorized practice of law (UPL). The more you use it, the more the client will ask you to explain what it means, and the more likely it is that you will eventually pass over that forbidden line into UPL.

Finally, as you are asking your questions, be sure to keep legal jargon out of the conversation. Law is a foreign language that you are rapidly mastering, but your clients may have an entirely different understanding of the legal terms you use. For example, most people assume that burglary is stealing, but as you know from your studies, it means breaking and entering a building at nighttime with the intent to commit a crime—an act that could be, but does not necessarily have to be, theft. Therefore, whenever possible, avoid legal terminology.

Case 1: The Distressed Grandfather (Continued)

After having obtained basic information such as Drake's date of birth, Social Security number, physical and e-mail addresses, phone number, place of employment, health insurance carrier, and details of the accident, Kendall asked about the extent of Drake's injuries, any prior medical history, especially involving any heart problems, and his relationship to his grandson (were they close; did they live in the same household; did they see each other daily, weekly; etc.). After Harper and Kendall had listened to Drake's story

with few or no interruptions, Harper told Drake that she would like to start at the beginning again, but that this time, she would stop him occasionally with specific questions in order to help them fill in the details.

For example, Harper pursued the following line of questioning: "Mr. Drake, you said that you and your grandson had started out on your walk because it was such a nice day. Could you tell me a bit more about what the weather conditions were?" Then Harper asked a series of narrow questions, focusing on the details regarding the specifics of the weather that day.

When trying to obtain more details about a subjective condition such as pain, it is sometimes helpful to suggest the use of analogies. Therefore, Harper also asked Drake to think back to other situations in which he had been hurt and to describe any that were similar.

DISCUSSION QUESTION

5. If you were interviewing Drake, what other areas would you want to ask him about? Create an initial interview form that you think would prove helpful in a personal injury case, such as Drake's, with a short list of questions in each area.

PRACTICE TIP

A good interview checklist can help you keep focused on the necessary facts when you might otherwise have a tendency to get sidetracked.

---

7. Concluding the Interview

Near the end of the interview, you should summarize your understanding of the client's problem to give the client a chance to add any information that may have been overlooked and to correct any misunderstandings you may have. You might also ask the client a very general question, such as, "Is there anything else about this incident that I haven't asked about and that you think I should know?" This sometimes elicits important information, but sometimes not. This is also the time to double-check to make sure you have all of the necessary identifying information, such as the client's phone numbers and addresses, name and phone number of his current physician, and so on.

Before the client leaves the office, the lawyer must explain the firm's policy regarding the payment of fees and expenses. In addition, most firms will ask the client to sign a retainer agreement. A **retainer agreement,** is a written contract that outlines the lawyer's duties and the client's obligations regarding payment, on either an hourly or a contingency fee basis, as well as the client's responsibility regarding costs and expenses. Standard retainer agreements are usually stored as word-processing templates, with all of the variable information left blank. With a keyboard merge, the word-processing program stops at each place where the paralegal or secretary needs to insert specific client information.

Before leaving, the client should also be informed of what, if any, follow-up will be necessary. Do documents need to be brought in? Should another appointment be scheduled? When should the client expect to hear from the firm? To ensure that you remember to give the client all of the necessary follow-up instructions, it is helpful to make a checklist for the client. For example, on the

Retainer agreement
A contract that outlines the lawyer's duties and the client's obligations regarding payment, on either an hourly or a contingency fee basis, as well as the client's responsibility regarding costs and expenses.

checklist, you can remind the client to bring certain items to the next appointment, to start a journal detailing how the client's daily activities have been curtailed by his or her injuries, and to begin keeping copies of all medical bills.

Once these steps have been completed, collect, or make arrangements to collect, copies of all the relevant legal documents. Photocopy and return them to the client as soon as possible. If the client needs to sign authorization forms so that the firm can obtain medical or employment records, explain the purpose of the forms to the client and have the client sign them. Alternatively, the forms can be given to the client along with a self-addressed, stamped envelope so that they can be easily mailed back to the firm. Exhibit 16-1 illustrates a typical release form.

It is also important at this stage to remember the ethical prohibitions that apply to a paralegal's role. Clients often attempt to elicit advice and opinions about their cases from paralegals, but paralegals are not allowed to give legal advice. Also, clients should not be given false expectations about the outcomes of their cases by either the lawyer or by the paralegal. If things do not turn out as hoped, not only will you have a disappointed client, but also you may have a potential malpractice claim as well. Finally, do not get trapped by questions that place you between the lawyer and the client. For example, it is not uncommon for a client to ask the paralegal, "Do you think the lawyer really can help?"

Darrow & Bryan
Attorneys at Law
333 Main St.
Springfield, MA 01009
413-999-9999

AUTHORIZATION

To: Dr. George Boothby

I hereby authorize you to release a copy of my medical records to Pat Harper of Darrow & Bryan, or her representative. This authorization is effective immediately and remains in effect until I revoke it in writing.

_____*Donald Drake*_____

Donald Drake
79 Sycamore Lane, South Hadley, MA 00107
D.O.B. 4/27/29
S.S.N. 364-77-8948

Witnessed by me this _4th_ day of _May 2021_.

_____*Chris Kendall*_____

Exhibit 16-1 Sample Release

Even though a client may pressure you with repeated requests of "Please, just tell me. What would you do if you were in my position?" remember that only the client can decide on the appropriate course of action for himself or herself. No matter how much you may empathize, you simply are not in the client's position and so cannot decide for the client.

Case 1: The Distressed Grandfather (Continued)

After she had gathered all the information that she thought she would need to decide on whether to take his case, Harper summarized what she understood to be the critical facts and asked if there was any additional information they had overlooked.

After Drake said no, there was not, Harper told him that the firm would be happy to file a personal injury complaint on his behalf on a contingency fee basis if a search of their client database revealed no conflicts of interest. She then went on to explain how the firm's contingency fee worked and briefly explained the possible legal problems that might be encountered in his case. When Drake indicated that he wanted the firm to take his case, she asked him to sign a retainer agreement.

DISCUSSION QUESTIONS

6. What do you think is the most important goal to accomplish during the initial client interview: to establish a good rapport with the client or to gather all of the essential facts? Why?

7. What are the advantages and disadvantages of having a paralegal rather than the lawyer conduct the initial interview with a client?

8. When meeting clients or witnesses for the first time, you must be sure that they understand your role as a paralegal. At the same time, you do not want to send the message that you are "only the paralegal." Can you think of ways other than that described in the text to accomplish that goal?

8. Postinterview Follow-Up

As soon as possible after the interview, review the notes that you took during the interview, and summarize them in a form that can be understood by your supervising lawyer. These notes, along with the copies that were made of relevant documents, should then be placed in the appropriate office file, whether in hard copy or electronic format. A more formal approach is to write a follow-up memorandum addressed to the lawyer or to the file. Such a memo should include the date and time of the interview, basic background information on the client (name, address, Social Security number, etc.), information on the reason the client is seeking legal advice, a list of tasks that need to be completed for the client, a notation as to what the client was asked to do next, any record of lost business or wages, and the total medical bills to date.

It is also good practice to always follow office appointments with a brief letter to the client. After a brief introduction stating that the lawyer or paralegal enjoyed meeting with the client, the body of the letter should include the following information:

- You were in the office on . . .
- We discussed . . .
- You decided . . .
- I will . . . by this date
- You will . . . by this date
- We'll meet on . . . to do . . .

Enclose a self-addressed and stamped envelope to make it easy for the client to return the information requested. For Drake, Kendall drafted the letter in Exhibit 16-2, on the next page, for Harper's signature.

If a client decides not to retain the firm or the firm decides not to accept the case, you should still send a follow-up letter documenting that fact. The letter should contain basic information regarding the date of the interview and whether the client stated that he or she would not be retaining the firm or the firm declined to accept the case. Many lawyers also include a statement regarding the statute of limitations on the claim.

In conclusion, the initial client interview consists of three major stages. First, you must consider the location of the interview and gather as much information as possible before the interview. Second is to conduct the actual interview itself. Third, you must follow through by sending the client a follow-up letter and summarizing the interview for your files. Figure 16-3 summarizes the three interviewing stages.

A. Before the Interview
   1. Consider the best place to meet, including accommodating any special needs of the client.
   2. Gather all information you can before the interview.
B. During the Interview
   1. Use the funnel approach: Start with open questions, and then use various forms of narrow questions to gather detail and clarify ambiguities.
   2. Use active listening.
   3. Do not judge the client.
   4. Be aware of how racial, cultural, and gender differences between you and your client may affect your ability to communicate.
   5. Give the client a checklist outlining the next steps the client should take.
C. After the Interview
   1. Send the client a follow-up letter.
   2. Summarize the interview.
   3. Develop an investigation plan.

Figure 16-3 Interviewing Stages

> Darrow & Bryan
> Attorneys at Law
> 333 Main St.
> Springfield, MA 01009
> 413-999-9999
>
> May 9, 2021
>
> Mr. Donald Drake
> 79 Sycamore Lane
> South Hadley, MA 00107
>
> Dear Mr. Drake:
>
> It was a pleasure meeting with you last Friday. At that time we discussed the accident last September when your grandson was killed and you suffered a heart attack. We decided that before proceeding to file a lawsuit, we should first engage in some legal and factual investigation. To assist us with that investigation you agreed to furnish us with the names, addresses, and phone numbers of all physicians who have treated you within the last ten years. We will also plan to meet again here in the office on July 19, at 2:00 p.m. By that time, we will have had an opportunity to engage in some preliminary legal research to better assess the likelihood of the court's willingness to consider your case.
>
> Thank you again for retaining our firm. If you have any questions or have a need to contact us before your next appointment, please feel free to call either myself or my paralegal, Chris Kendall, at the above number.
>
> Sincererly,
>
> *Pat Harper, Esq.*
>
> Pat Harper, Esq.

Exhibit 16-2   Follow-Up Client Letter

No matter how productive the initial interview is, it often is necessary to gather additional facts from the client. So long as you accomplished the second goal of establishing a relationship of trust with the client, you can easily do so by having the client return to the office, by going to the client's home or office, or by using the telephone or e-mail.

Your supervising lawyer may also ask you to develop an investigation plan based on what you have learned. This investigation plan could include interviewing witnesses and gathering documentary and physical evidence. In the next section of this chapter, we will discuss witness interviews. In Chapter 17 we will discuss the process of gathering physical and documentary evidence.

DISCUSSION QUESTION

9. Elsa Brown met with a lawyer, Jacob Jones, about an injury that she sustained at work. After about half an hour of discussion, Brown said that she would have to think it over before deciding whether to retain the firm. Jones wrote a quick memo summarizing their discussion and filed it. He never heard from Brown again and took no action on her case. What ethical problems do you think the lawyer may have created for himself?

C. INTERVIEWING WITNESSES

After completing the initial client interview, the lawyer and the paralegal should have a basic understanding of the facts of the case and the client's goals. It is important to remember, however, the client seldom knows all of the relevant facts and sometimes has an inaccurate perception of the facts that are remembered. Therefore, the lawyer or paralegal will need to verify the client's rendering of the facts and fill in any gaps. One way to do this is to interview witnesses. In addition to providing key testimonial evidence regarding disputed facts, witnesses can also identify other witnesses and other sources of evidence that can help you prove your case.

1. Types of Witnesses

When a witness gives testimony in a legal proceeding, a distinction is made between lay witnesses and expert witnesses. We will address the reasons for this distinction more fully in Chapter 17, when we discuss the rules of evidence. For now, it is important to understand that **lay witnesses** are "regular people" who do not have any special expertise on the subject on which they are testifying and are limited to testifying about what they personally observed. **Expert witnesses,** on the other hand, must possess some special knowledge that goes beyond what the average person would possess, and they are allowed to give an opinion as to what may have happened or what might have caused it to occur, even when they were not present to personally observe the event in question. For example, in a medical malpractice case, a doctor might be asked to testify as to whether the surgeon who operated on the plaintiff followed good medical practice when he failed to remove what appeared to be a benign tumor. Paralegals may be called upon to locate, interview, or help prepare both types of witnesses.

Lay witness
A witness who has not been shown to have any special expertise and is limited to testifying about what was personally observed.

Expert witness
A witness who possesses skill and knowledge beyond that of the average person and is allowed to speculate about what caused something or how it happened.

2. Locating Lay Witnesses

During the initial interview, the client should be asked to supply as much information as possible about both the identities and the possible locations of relevant witnesses. Depending on the type of event involved, check police reports, newspaper articles, social media posts, and other Internet resources, such as online photos and videos, for information about possible witnesses, as well as details about the event.

It may also be important to find documentation of an accident scene and details about an accident. Do not forget that the media are often the first on the accident scene. Search for newspaper archives to find articles that provide any reports of the accident. There may also be photos and even videos. If possible, locate and interview eyewitnesses as soon after the incident as possible. The longer the delay is, the more difficult it will be to find them and the less likely it is that they will accurately remember the incident.

Whenever there is a chance that someone who lives or works nearby may have seen or heard something related to the event in question, check with the occupants of all nearby buildings. In investigating an event that took place at a particular intersection at a particular time, observe and record the license numbers of automobiles that go through that intersection at approximately the same time every day. There is a good chance that the drivers of some of those vehicles may have seen at least something relevant to the event in question. Sometimes the search for witnesses may also involve posting a notice in the area, or even taking out an advertisement in a local newspaper.

Occasionally, you will have a witness's name but will be unable to locate that person because the address is either missing or incorrect. When this occurs, you should use Internet searches, including social media sites, people search engines, or voter registration records. Other databases include Whitepages.com and Facebook, as well as telephone books and city directories. If the person has moved, landlords, utility companies, neighbors, and relatives often know the person's new address. If you have a phone number, a reverse directory is especially useful.

3. Locating Expert Witnesses

Although expert witnesses may be used in almost any type of case, they are most likely to be found in products liability and professional malpractice cases. An expert is usually needed to testify about the generally accepted practices and standards of that industry or profession. For example, in products liability cases, the plaintiff must show that there was a defect in the design or manufacture of the product in question. To qualify as an expert in a products liability case, an engineer must demonstrate sufficient technical familiarity with the general type or class of product or equipment under consideration. He or she must also be able to demonstrate knowledge of the pertinent industry at or before the date of manufacture of the product and often must have conducted appropriate tests with the product in question.

In many cases, the law firm you work for may already have established relationships with expert witnesses used in previous cases. If your supervising lawyer wants to broaden the search, you should look for advertisements in legal newspapers and journals. You can also review specialized/technical journals to find the names of experts in the relevant field. Another approach is to check trade association websites.

In addition to their general academic credentials (e.g., a medical or engineering degree from a respected university), you want to match the person's specialization with the facts in your case. For example, a family doctor would not be the best choice to discuss a gynecological problem. While the person's availability and their fees are certainly relevant, the most important qualification is that individual's ability to present his or her knowledge in an understandable way to the jury.

> **PRACTICE TIP**
>
> Just prior to trial, require experts to update their curricula vitae and their publications lists to catch any recent accomplishments and avoid any new problems.

It is good to contact expert witnesses early enough for them to give advice as to the types of factual material that you should be gathering. In fact, in some cases, such as medical malpractice, you will need the services of an expert to help determine whether your client even has a viable cause of action.

4. Setting Up Appointments

On occasion, it is best to appear at the witness's doorstep without advance notice. This is particularly true when there is reason to believe that the person might rehearse a story with someone else. Generally, however, it is best to make advance arrangements to ensure that the time available is adequate and convenient for the witness. You need the witness's cooperation, so you should make every effort to accommodate the witness's needs.

5. Reluctant and Hostile Witnesses

Generally speaking, you should attempt to interview **hostile witnesses** first. Statements from such adverse witnesses can indicate problem areas that your lawyer may have when preparing the case and can provide clues for the type of information needed to impeach that testimony.

     The conventional wisdom dictates that interviewing a hostile witness is one of those situations mentioned earlier, where it is sometimes better to interview the witness without making an appointment in advance. Such a strategy reduces the chance that the witness will carefully rehearse a story before your arrival. However, in this context, we are using the term "hostile" in the legal sense, to mean a witness who simply is not in favor of your client's position. Such a strategy might place you in danger if the witness is truly hostile. If there is any chance that the witness could prove to be hostile in the conventional sense of being potentially violent, showing up unannounced and alone may be the last thing you want to do, as that might place you in danger. In any event, be prepared for any eventuality because you probably will have only one opportunity to talk to the hostile witness.

     When witnesses appear to be reluctant to cooperate, attempt to determine the cause for this reluctance: Are they friends of the other party or the victim? Do they fear some sort of retaliation? Are they simply afraid of being called to testify at the trial stage? Point out that by giving a statement now, they may be able to avoid having to testify at a trial.

> **Hostile witness**
> A witness who shows bias or hostility toward the party that asked her or him to testify; also known as an "adverse witness."

6. Location of the Interview

Whereas initial client interviews are usually held in the lawyer's office, there is no standard practice for interviewing witnesses. Besides using a law office conference or interview room, witness interviews can take place in the witness's home, or even at the witness's place of work. There may be instances where it is necessary to meet virtually. Using the telephone or meeting virtually are the least expensive methods, but unless the nature of the information to be provided is routine and unlikely to be contested, it is best to meet the witness in person. Not only may the witness be more willing to talk to you in person, but you will be given a better opportunity to assess the witness's credibility.

     One way of making sure that you inconvenience witnesses as little as possible is to offer to come to them rather than asking them to come to your office.

PRACTICE TIP

While investigating away from the office, always be mindful of personal safety issues for yourself and your witnesses.

This is especially appropriate in the case of those who may have a physical disability, the very young, and the very old. As with client interviews, whatever location you choose, make sure that it is a relatively private setting where interruptions can be minimized. If possible, the interview should take place out of the presence of friends, family, or co-workers. One exception to this rule is when a young child is being interviewed, if having a parent present helps put the child at ease. It is always possible, however, that children may be willing to tell the interviewer something that they would not tell their parents. Another exception is the situation in which an interpreter is needed because the witness cannot speak English.

7. Interview Format

When starting a witness interview, be sure to explain who you are and your role in the investigation. From Chapter 2, recall that it is unethical to ever misrepresent yourself. And, once again, courtesy can be your best ally. The witness is probably busy and would much rather be doing something other than helping you. Therefore, you want to assure the witness that you appreciate the time that the witness is giving you.

While you will have to provide certain background information to set up the interview and establish your credibility, it is essential that you not give away vital information about the client's case during the course of the interviews. This admonition is especially true when dealing with insurance company representatives and parties that are closely allied with the opposing party.

Case 1: The Distressed Grandfather (Continued)

While talking to an insurance agent, the agent told Kendall how awful it must have been for Drake to have suffered a heart attack so soon after his first one. Kendall was about to reply, "Yes, especially as after his first attack, the doctor told him he should stop smoking." But he suspected that the agent was bluffing, with no actual knowledge of any prior heart attack, and wisely said nothing.

As with client interviews, begin the witness interview with open questions. Then employ the same types of feedback mechanisms discussed earlier in this chapter—giving nonverbal encouragement, paraphrasing, and reflecting feelings. As the interview progresses, use closed questions to extract the essential details.

As you conduct the interview, carefully evaluate the person's potential strengths and weaknesses as a witness in the courtroom: How convincing will the witness be on the witness stand? Will the witness be able to follow the questions easily, or will the witness become confused? If the interviewee was an eyewitness or overheard something, you may want to subtly test the witness's eyesight or hearing. If a witness wears eyeglasses, it is wise to determine the type of prescription and whether the eyeglasses were worn at the time of the incident about which the person will be testifying.

Make sure that you record the actual events witnessed—the facts—as opposed to the opinions the witness formed based on those facts. While lay witnesses are often allowed to testify as to opinions that are formed in everyday life—the man was staggering and reeked of alcohol; therefore, he was intoxicated—do not rely on it. Be sure that you have the facts—exactly what the witness means by "staggering," and how the witness knows the man reeked of alcohol (distance from the man, prior familiarity with the smell of alcohol, etc.).

When interviewing friendly witnesses, be especially careful not to use leading questions, and guard against the witness who embellishes the truth to win approval or help a friend. Finally, do not forget to ask the witnesses if they know of anyone else who could provide information.

If an adverse witness has consulted with a lawyer, that lawyer probably told the witness not to say anything to an investigator. And if any witness has retained a lawyer, remember that the rules of ethics forbid you from talking to that witness at all. All communications must be with the witness's lawyer.

8. Taking Statements from Witnesses

As with interviewing clients, it is helpful to use a checklist, such as is illustrated in Figure 16-4. At the end of the interview, some interviewers ask for a formal statement. Having a witness sign an affidavit makes it more likely that the testimony given is accurate. This statement cannot be used as direct evidence at the trial, but it can be used to refresh the witness's memory. It may also form the basis for impeaching a hostile witness's testimony by demonstrating that the testimony given in court is inconsistent with statements that the witness made in the earlier statement. (*Note:* As we will discuss in more detail in Chapter 17, this type of out-of-court statement does not violate the rule against hearsay because the statement is being offered not to prove its truth, but rather to impeach the witness. In other words, it does not matter whether the witness was telling the truth then or telling the truth now. All that matters is that at some point, the witness lied.) However, many lawyers would prefer that you only summarize the interview. A verbatim statement may not be protected by the lawyer–client work product privilege. This would mean that the opposing side could obtain it as a part of a discovery request.

> **PRACTICE TIP**
>
> When going out on investigations, bring a good supply of business cards. They provide a form of identification and set a professional tone. Also, you can leave them with witnesses with a reminder on the back that they should contact you if they recall additional information.

> If the opposing party is represented by a lawyer, you may not speak with that party without that lawyer's permission.
>
> *Ethics Alert*

The first section of your statement should supply as much information as possible about the witness. In addition to such items as name, address, and phone number, it should include information about employer, relatives, professional group memberships, social clubs, and even hobbies. Most of this information

1. *Identity of the witness*
   Name
   Age, sex, and marital status
   Occupation and employer
   Residence, business, e-mail addresses, and phone numbers
   Organizational affiliations and other items that will help locate the person in the future, such as children and their ages and schools
2. *Identification of the accident*
   Date, day of the week, time
   Location of the accident
   Type of accident
   Identification of parties involved (drivers, passengers, etc.)
   Were parties traveling as part of their job?
   Description of vehicles involved (owner, make, model, color, year, license number, serial number)
   Identification of potential witnesses
3. *Detailed description of the scene of the accident*
   Description of streets and highways
       Direction
       Width
       Number of lanes
       Grade
       Speed limit
       Traffic controls
       Type and condition of surface
   Weather conditions
   Buildings and other objects that could obstruct one's view
4. *Detailed description of the accident*
   Direction and speed of vehicles, pedestrians
   Status of traffic signals
   Evasive action
   Point of impact (on roadway and on each vehicle)
   Final resting place of vehicles
   Skid marks and debris
   Statements made
   Location of witnesses
5. *Bodily injuries (for each person injured)*
   Part of body injured
   Extent of injury
   Nature of treatment (ambulance, hospital, doctor)
   Nature of disability
   Occupation and salary
   Preexisting medical problems
6. *Property damage*
   To vehicles, to buildings, etc.

Figure 16-4   Interviewing Checklist

is simply for the purpose of making it possible to locate the witness in case the person moves prior to the trial. This first section also should include the date and location where the statement was given. If others are present during the interview, mention that as well.

The heart of the summary is the description of whatever it is that the witness observed. Usually, you will want to present the events in chronological order. In addition to describing the events themselves, it is important to have the witness carefully describe the environment in which those events took place. Thus, in an automobile accident case, ask the witness to describe such matters as the weather and the existence of any temporary obstructions to a driver's view.

DISCUSSION QUESTION

10. You are interviewing a witness who observed an automobile accident. He was sitting in his car waiting for a red light when he saw your client's car hit from the rear. What questions might you ask to find out as much as you can from the witness as to exactly what happened?

SUMMARY

The key to successful interviewing is the development of good communication skills. Good communication is a two-way street that requires active listening and attention to nonverbal as well as verbal signals. Be extremely cautious about approaching an interview with preconceived ideas and biases, and be conscious of ethnic, racial, and gender differences in communication styles.

Interviews should take place in a comfortable and quiet location in which there will be privacy and no interruptions. The seating arrangement should be one that facilitates personal communication rather than one that intimidates the person being interviewed.

Begin the interview by explaining the paralegal's role in terms that the client will understand. Then use open questions to give the client the opportunity to describe the problem in his or her own terms. Ask narrower questions in order to clarify areas of ambiguity and to assist the client who becomes bogged down or forgets a train of thought. Gentle encouragement to talk, paraphrasing, and reflections of feelings are useful techniques for keeping the interview moving ahead constructively. Above all, do not be judgmental. Listen, record, empathize, but do not judge.

When bringing the interview to an end, it is wise to summarize your understanding of what the client has said in order to ensure accuracy and to give the client a chance to add information that might have been overlooked. Collect copies of all relevant documents and have the client sign appropriate authorization forms. Immediately afterward, review your notes from the interview and write your summary while the matter is still fresh.

Interviewing witnesses requires the use of many of the same communication skills as those used in client interviews. In cases that lend themselves to the use of expert witnesses, identify appropriate individuals and enlist their support. These experts then can be used as resources for the investigation, as well as witnesses at the trial.

At all times, remember that paralegals are representatives of the firm. Act in a professional and courteous manner. Using common courtesy is one of the most effective ways to get the cooperation of clients as well as others.

REVIEW QUESTIONS

Pages 461 through 466

1. What is meant by saying that communication is a "two-way street"?
2. What is active listening, and why is it important?
3. Give some examples of nonverbal communication.
4. How are the interviewer's and the client's race, ethnicity, and gender related to the interviewing process?

Pages 466 through 479

5. What is the first step that a law firm should take prior to a client interview?
6. What are the two main goals of the client interview?
7. How can the seating arrangement impede or facilitate conversation?
8. What are some special considerations that you should take into account in a virtual interview?
9. What are the advantages and disadvantages of open questions? Of closed questions?
10. Describe the funnel approach to interviewing.
11. Generally, why is it not a good idea to use leading questions when interviewing clients?
12. Why should the interviewer avoid the use of "why" questions?
13. When interviewing clients or witnesses, why is it important to find out the facts that support the client's or witness's conclusions?
14. When interviewing clients and others, why is it generally a good idea to keep legal jargon out of the conversation?
15. What should be done at the end of a client interview?
16. After meeting with a client, what information should you include in a follow-up letter?
17. What should you include in a letter that you send to a potential client who decides not to retain the firm?

Pages 479 through 486

18. How does an expert witness differ from a lay witness?
19. What are the most common means of locating lay and expert witnesses?
20. In what types of cases are you most likely to need expert witnesses?
21. Why do many lawyers prefer witness statements in summary form only?
22. What types of information should be included in a summary of a witness statement?

WEB EXERCISES

1. Locate online the Expert Institute's article, "10 Tips for Effectively Questioning an Expert Witness." What are some of the differences in the way that you question a witness on direct examination as opposed to during a cross-examination? Do you agree? Why or why not?

2. The New York State court system has an online document titled "Credibility of Witnesses," which lists a series of questions that a judge should ask a jury at the end of a trial before they begin deliberating over their verdict. Read through the list. Do you agree with the list? Do you think that any items on the list may unfairly hurt the credibility of a witness? Why or why not?

Chapter 17

Evidence and Investigations

*I think there is no sense in forming an opinion
when there is no evidence to form it on.*
Recollections of Joan of Arc

Chapter Objectives

After reading this chapter, you should be able to:

- Explain the purpose of the rules of evidence.
- Describe the advantages and disadvantages of physical, documentary, and testimonial evidence.
- Distinguish among direct, circumstantial, cumulative, and corroborative evidence.
- Explain the difference between lay and expert witnesses.
- Plan and carry on an investigation involving both real and documentary evidence.

INTRODUCTION

In Chapter 16, we saw how lawyers and paralegals first learn about the facts of a case from their client at the initial interview. Unfortunately, you cannot assume that everything the client tells you is correct. While not intentionally lying, they may have misunderstood what actually happened. Furthermore, the client may not even be aware of other facts that are important to their case.

In this chapter we discuss the actions law firms take to check the accuracy of what the client tells them, and to seek out a more complete understanding of all of the relevant facts. Before we do so, however, we need to provide some background on the nature of different types of evidence and the rules governing how these various forms of evidence can be used in court.

We will continue following the case of Donald Drake.

Case 1: The Distressed Grandfather (Continued)

In Drake's case, the paralegal, Kendall, did not think there would be much physical evidence. The car had been so badly damaged in the accident that it had been towed to a junkyard and demolished for scrap. However, there was a wealth of documentary evidence that he needed to collect, including all of the medical records beginning with Drake's ambulance ride to the hospital, the hospital records themselves, and his treating physician's notes. Other documentary evidence included the police report made at the scene of the accident and the certification from the registry of motor vehicles that Wilma Small was indeed the owner of the car she was driving. Kendall was also busy organizing potential testimonial evidence from Drake, the police officers who were at the scene, eyewitnesses to the accident, Drake's treating physician, and a medical expert who could give testimony on how severe emotional distress can cause heart attacks.

A. RULES OF EVIDENCE

Rules of evidence
Federal and state rules that govern the admissibility of evidence in court.

Evidence
Information that can be presented in a court of law as proof of some fact.

Fact
An actual incident or condition; not a legal consequence.

Simply put, the **rules of evidence** govern the admissibility of evidence (documents, physical objects, and testimony) in court proceedings. These rules exist at both the federal and state levels and are typically developed by special committees of lawyers and judges, approved by the Supreme Court, and then adopted in statutory form by the legislature. Because there is some variation among the states and from the Federal Rules of Evidence, you should always research the specific rules that apply to your state courts.

You need to be familiar with these rules in order to focus your efforts on properly collecting information that can be used in court. **Evidence** is defined as information that can be presented in a court of law as proof of some fact, and a **fact** is defined as an actual incident or condition that is distinguished from its legal consequence. For example, a plaintiff's assertion that the defendant ran a red light is an alleged fact. The plaintiff's assertion that the defendant's running a red light constituted negligence is a legal conclusion or consequence.

While you do not have to be an expert on every esoteric aspect of the rules of evidence, you should have a basic understanding of the general principles behind them. This knowledge should affect the manner in which you gather and preserve information. The following provides a general overview of some of the most important principles reflected in the rules of evidence.

NETNOTE

You can locate the Federal Rules of Evidence at several locations. One good website is run by Cornell Law School at *law.cornell.edu/rules/fre*.

Form of Evidence	Examples
Real or physical evidence	A knife; a gun; a shoe
Documentary evidence	A contract to purchase refrigerators; an apartment lease
Testimonial evidence	On the stand, John says, "I saw Jim shoot Joe."
Judicial notice	Christmas falls on December 25.

Figure 17-1   Forms of Evidence

1. Forms of Evidence

Evidence is usually categorized into one of four distinct forms: real or physical evidence, documentary evidence, testimonial evidence, and judicial notice. **Real or physical evidence** is any tangible object, like a knife or a gun. **Documentary evidence** consists of records, contracts, leases, wills, and other written instruments. In addition to hard copies, you may find this evidence can be found as a file on a computer hard drive or in the cloud, or as a posting on a social network site. **Testimonial evidence** consists of the description of events that a witness testifies to under oath in a legal proceeding. Before real and documentary evidence can be introduced, testimonial evidence is often used to establish the foundation or background information necessary to introduce and **authenticate** the evidence.

Sometimes through a process known as **judicial notice,** a judge will formally recognize something as being a fact without requiring the lawyers to prove it through the introduction of other evidence. In effect, the judge acknowledges that the information is so well known that specific proof is not required. For example, a judge might take judicial notice of the fact that August 19, 2020, fell on a Wednesday, or that a city lies within a particular county. However, if a fact goes to your cause of action, do not rely on judicial notice. Be prepared to prove all of the facts. For example, if it is necessary to show that an accident happened on a public way, get the documents to prove both where the accident happened and that the place was a public way. These various forms of evidence are summarized in Figure 17-1.

DISCUSSION QUESTION

1. Which type of evidence (testimonial, documentary, or physical) do you think is the most reliable? Which is the least reliable? Describe the potential advantages and disadvantages of each.

2. What are some potential problems with finding evidence on social networking platforms? How reliable is that evidence compared to traditional testimonial or documentary evidence?

2. Types of Evidence

Evidence can also be classified in terms of its being direct, circumstantial, cumulative, or corroborative.

Direct evidence is evidence that is directly linked to the event that must be proven. For example, a witness's testimony that "I saw the defendant shoot the victim" is direct evidence. **Circumstantial evidence**, on the other hand, provides information from which an inference can be drawn. A police officer who did not

Real or physical evidence
Any tangible object, like a bloody glove.

Documentary evidence
Consists of records, contracts, leases, wills, and other written instruments, saved as hard copy printouts, computer files on a hard drive or in the cloud, or as a posting on a social network site.

Testimonial evidence
Consists of the description of events that a witness testifies to under oath in a legal proceeding.

Authenticate
To establish that the document being presented is what it is claimed to be.

Judicial notice
When a judge formally recognizes something as being a fact without requiring the lawyers prove it through the introduction of other evidence.

Direct evidence
Establishes a direct link to the event that must be proved.

Circumstantial evidence
Indirect evidence, used to prove facts by implication.

Type of Evidence	Example
Direct	On the witness stand, John says, "I saw Jim shoot Joe."
Circumstantial	A police officer testifies he saw skid marks on the pavement.
Cumulative	The fifth witness in a row testifies he saw Jim at Jake's Donut Shop at the same time the murder was occurring on the other side of town.
Corroborative	Janet from Security-Is-Us authenticates a surveillance tape taken at Jake's Donut Shop showing Jim entering the shop at the same time the murder was occurring on the other side of town.

Figure 17-2 Types of Evidence

witness the crime, but who testifies that the defendant was found with powder burns on his hands consistent with having fired a weapon, provides **circumstantial evidence.** While the powder burns do not directly prove that the defendant shot the victim, they do create a possibility that he did. There is no requirement that any of the evidence admitted be direct evidence. Sufficient circumstantial evidence can be enough to find liability in a civil case or to convict a defendant in a criminal case.

Cumulative evidence

Evidence that does not add any new information but that confirms facts that already have been established.

Corroborative evidence

Evidence that supports previous testimony but that comes in a different form.

Cumulative evidence is evidence that does not add any new information but that confirms facts that already have been established. For example, if two people both testify that they saw the defendant make a phone call, the second witness would be providing cumulative evidence. Such evidence may be excluded if, in the court's opinion, it will add nothing to what has been already presented. In most trials, the quality of the evidence is more important than the quantity. A single unbiased eyewitness carries more weight than a series of witnesses who have inherent biases or who tell conflicting stories. The concept of **corroborative evidence** is very similar, in that it also supports previous testimony. The difference is that corroborative evidence comes in a different form. For example, cell phone company billing records can be introduced to support a statement by a witness that he made a phone call to a certain party on a certain date. Figure 17-2 summarizes the various types of evidence.

3. Relevance and Materiality

Relevancy

Determined by whether the evidence leads one to logically conclude that an asserted fact is either more or less probable.

Material fact

A fact on which the outcome of the case depends.

Before any information can be introduced as evidence, it must be shown to be relevant. Irrelevant evidence can never be admitted. To qualify as **relevant evidence,** the evidence must be both material and probative. First, to be material, the evidence must relate to a fact on which the outcome of the case depends. Second, to be probative, the evidence must make that fact more or less probable than it would be without that evidence.

To illustrate these principles, assume that your firm represents a person injured in an automobile accident,[1] and your firm's theory of the case is that the other driver was at fault. The fact the firm wants to prove is that the other driver was exceeding the speed limit at the time of the accident. A bill of sale for the car could prove the date it was purchased. However, the bill of sale should not

---

[1] This hypothetical is based on a problem from Christopher B. Mueller & Laird C. Kirkpatrick, *Evidence Under the Rules* (7th ed. 2011).

be admitted as evidence as it does not relate to an issue in the case. That is, if ownership of the car is not disputed, then the date of purchase is irrelevant and hence not a material fact. On the other hand, any evidence regarding the speed of the car would be material, as it is directly related to who was at fault. Whether or not it is also probative depends on a number of factors.

Legal Reasoning Exercise

1. Assume that a lawyer wants to prove that the mail carrier left mail in the mailbox at 67 Dressel Avenue. She calls the following witnesses:

■ Mrs. Baker, who lives at that address, testifies that at 11 a.m., she went to the mailbox, found mail, and brought it into her house.
■ Mr. Baker testifies that he checked the mailbox when he left for work at 9 a.m., and it was empty.
■ Mrs. Brown, a next-door neighbor, testifies that at 9:30 a.m., she saw two sets of footprints in the snow in the Baker yard. One set led up to the mailbox, and one set led away.
■ Mr. Grimes, who lives across the street, testifies that he saw the mail carrier put mail in the mailbox at 9:15 a.m.
■ Mr. Smith, another neighbor, testifies that he saw the mail carrier put mail in the mailbox but is not sure of the time.
■ Mrs. Williams, a relative of the Bakers, testifies that she was walking down the street that morning and saw the mail carrier delivering mail to the house next door, at 69 Dressel Avenue.
■ Ms. Murray, the mail carrier's supervisor, testifies that he left the post office at 8 a.m. with mail for everyone on Dressel Avenue, and that late in the afternoon, he returned with an empty mailbag.

Label each piece of testimony as direct, circumstantial, cumulative, or corroborative testimony.

In the case of eyewitness testimony, the probative value of that testimony will depend on what the witness claims to have seen, when the witness saw it, and where he or she was at the time it was seen. If a witness testifies that the other driver had passed him going "at least 90 miles per hour" about 20 minutes before the accident occurred, do you think the judge would rule that testimony admissible? While the speed of the driver *at the time of the accident* is clearly relevant, how relevant is the speed of the driver *20 minutes before the accident*? While the driver's speeding 20 minutes earlier does not prove speeding at the time of the accident, the requirement of relevancy is a very low standard, only requiring that the evidence have "any" tendency to make the fact more or less probable. Thus the judge would probably allow the testimony, on the basis that the driver's speeding 20 minutes earlier could make it more probable that speeding also occurred at the time of the accident.

Note, however, that the relevance standard only relates to the admissibility of the evidence, not to how much weight the judge or jury must give it. The opposing lawyer will cross-examine the witness and argue that what the witness observed was too far removed in time from the accident to allow for any inference that the driver continued to speed. Without other evidence, such as photographs of skid marks at the scene of the accident, this evidence alone may not be sufficient to convince the jury that the other driver was speeding at the time of the accident.

To summarize, for evidence to be admissible, it must be relevant. But it does not have to bear the entire weight of proving a fact. It must simply have some tendency to make the fact more or less probable. It is for the jury to decide whether that evidence, along with other evidence introduced, supports the existence of the fact that the lawyer is trying to prove.

There are a few circumstances that could lead a trial judge to refuse to admit evidence even if it is relevant.[2] A trial judge can exclude relevant evidence if its probative value is substantially outweighed by a danger of

- unfair prejudice,
- confusing the issues,
- misleading the jury,
- undue delay,
- wasting time, or
- needlessly presenting cumulative evidence.

The evidence's probative value must be substantially outweighed by any prejudicial or other negative effect. Thus, trial judges have a great deal of discretion in determining whether to exclude relevant evidence. For example, in a murder case, a defendant may want to exclude autopsy pictures as unfairly prejudicing the jury. But in reality, all negative evidence prejudices the jury. So the question becomes whether the autopsy pictures are more important for proving a fact in dispute (such as the type of weapon used) or are more likely to simply inflame the jury so that it cannot rationally weigh the evidence.

4. Competency

Competency
Relates to the ability of a witness to testify; generally, the witness must be capable of being understood by the jury, must understand the duty to tell the truth, and if a lay witness, must give testimony based on personal knowledge.

In addition to being relevant, the evidence must be **competent.** With respect to oral testimony from a witness, it must be established that the witness can be understood by the jury (possibly through an interpreter), understands the duty to tell the truth, and in the case of a **lay witness,** is testifying to personal knowledge regarding the particular matter about which he or she is called to testify. The first two factors usually involve the age or mental condition of the witness. The third involves the meaning of hearsay evidence.

Lay witness
A witness who has not been shown to have any special expertise.

5. Hearsay and Its Exceptions

Hearsay
Testimony or evidence introduced in court regarding what someone said out of court for the purpose of establishing the truth of what was said.

In nontechnical terms, **hearsay** is secondhand information. It is someone in court testifying to what someone said out of court for the purpose of establishing the truth of what was said. Imagine, for example, a situation in which Paul was walking down Main Street when he saw a car, driven by Betty, drive through a red light. Later that day, Paul told his wife Sally about what he had seen. Sally would not be allowed to testify about what Paul told her. She did not see

---

[2] Fed. R Evid. 403.

Betty drive through the red light. The person with the firsthand information who should be on the stand testifying is Paul. We want Paul on the stand so that he can be questioned and evaluated by the trier of fact as to his credibility. This includes needing to know whether he is being truthful and whether he had the ability to accurately report what he thought he saw.

Not every out-of-court statement is hearsay. To be hearsay, the statement must be offered to prove the truth of the matter stated. One prime use of out-of-court statements is to impeach the credibility of a witness. Imagine that right after an accident, an eyewitness told a police officer that he saw a red car run the stop sign. On the witness stand, that same witness testifies that the car was blue. The witness's prior out-of-court statement about the color of the car can be introduced not to prove its color, but to show that the witness is unreliable.

Another twist involves admissions by party-opponents. According to the Federal Rules of Evidence, even though an out-of-court statement by a party opponent is hearsay, it is to be treated as nonhearsay. That is, a party's own statements, offered against the party, can be admitted for their truth, and yet they are not considered to be hearsay. Usually, the statement is harmful to the person who made it, but that is not a requirement.

Also, even though evidence remains labeled as hearsay evidence, it may be admissible under one of many exceptions. One set of exceptions relates to when the **declarant,** the person who made the statement, is not available to testify—for example, when the declarant is dead. The second set of exceptions covers a wide range of other circumstances in which it is thought that the nature of the statement itself indicates its trustworthiness. Such exceptions include excited utterances (the witness testifies: "I heard a bystander say, 'Oh, no, she just ran over that boy!'"), business records, and statements regarding the declarant's mental, emotional, or physical condition (the witness testifies: "I heard Mr. Drake say, 'My heart is pounding.'").

One way of understanding why some hearsay evidence is allowed while other hearsay evidence is not is to first assume the witness is truthfully recounting what the witness heard. The only question is: assuming the statement was really made, do we need any further information to evaluate its worth? In the example above, we would want to ask Paul how he knew it was Betty that he saw. How well did he know Betty? Does he wear glasses? Was he wearing them when he thought he saw Betty? In some cases, however, we can assume that the declarant's statements are trustworthy without the need for further examination. For example, if Sally were also to say, "Paul said that it was very cold out that night," cross-examination of Paul as to why he thought it was cold out is probably not necessary.

Declarant
The person who made a statement.

Legal Reasoning Exercise

2. Hearsay is defined in Rule 801 of the Federal Rules of Evidence as a statement, other than one made by the declarant while testifying at the trial or hearing, offered in evidence "to prove the truth of the matter asserted." A statement is not hearsay if it is an admission by the opposing party and the statement is offered against the opposing party's interests.

Ms. Small has been sued for negligently causing the death of Philip Drake in a motor vehicle accident. Evaluate each of the following statements as to whether they would be admissible or inadmissible as hearsay.

a. John just testified that Philip was still alive when the police arrived. When the lawyer asked him how he knew that, he said, "Because the poor little guy had just whispered in my ear, 'Why did that lady in the red car run me down?' "

b. Mary testified, "John told me just yesterday all about how he saw Mrs. Small's car jump the curb and run over Philip."

c. The first police officer at the scene is on the witness stand. When asked, he testifies that he interviewed John at the scene, and John told him that he saw Small's car jump the curb and run down Philip.

d. A bystander who was at the scene of the accident testifies that right after the accident, he heard Small cry out, "Oh, no, I can't afford another speeding ticket."

Figure 17-3 lists some of the more common hearsay exceptions that are found in the Federal Rules of Evidence. Remember these are hearsay statements that the court allows to be heard as evidence of the truth of the matter stated. This is to be contrasted with the rule mentioned earlier allowing out-of-court statements for impeachment purposes.

6. Fact Versus Opinion

Always keep in mind the difference between fact and opinion. A witness who testifies that he saw the defendant's automobile strike the plaintiff's car broadside is testifying about a fact he observed. But when that same witness states that the defendant was driving too fast for the icy condition of the road, he is stating an opinion.

Generally, everyone is allowed to testify to personal knowledge about basic facts of life. Lay witnesses (regular witnesses who have not been shown to have any special expertise) can give opinions on such subjects as the speed of moving vehicles, the similarity of a person's voice or handwriting to that of someone's voice or handwriting with which they are familiar, and whether or not a person is angry or intoxicated. In order to be allowed to venture such opinions, the trial judge must be satisfied that

1. lay witnesses testify only to facts "of which [they] have personal knowledge,"[3] and
2. if stating an opinion or conclusion (such as that the red sticky substance was blood), that the matter must be one about which they have personal experience or it is within the range of common experience.[4]

As an example of personal experience, consider the case in which a federal judge properly allowed two lay witnesses who were heavy amphetamine users to testify that a substance was amphetamines. The judge, however, should not

---

[3] Fed. R. Evid. 602.
[4] Fed. R. Evid. 701.

FRE 803(1) Present sense impression	The declarant describes the event as it is being perceived.	The bystander said, "It is raining."
FRE 803(2) Excited utterance	The declarant responds to a startling event.	The bystander said, "The driver of that car is out of control!"
FRE 803(3) Then existing mental, emotional, or physical condition	The declarant describes his or her feelings, state of mind, or physical condition.	The driver of the car said, "I feel dizzy."
FRE 803(4) Medical diagnosis or treatment	The declarant's statements were made for the purpose of medical diagnosis or treatment.	A physician testifies, "Mr. Drake told me he often suffered from heart pain."
FRE 803(6) Records	Various records, including business records, public records, vital statistics, and marriage certificates, are admissible.	Mr. Drake's hospital records are introduced.
FRE 804(b)(1) Former testimony	Former testimony under oath is admissible if the declarant is unavailable.	At a deposition, a witness to the accident stated, "I saw the defendant's car jump the curb and hit the little boy." The witness has since died. The deposition testimony is admissible.
FRE 804(b)(2) Dying declaration	Statements made when the declarant thought he or she was dying are admissible if the declarant is unavailable.	A witness at the scene heard Mr. Drake say, "I saw that woman's car run down my grandchild." If Mr. Drake died before trial, the witness could testify as to what Mr. Drake said.
FRE 804(b)(3) Statement against interest	Statements made by the declarant that are against that person's financial interests or that would expose the declarant to civil or criminal liability are admissible if the declarant is unavailable.	The day after the accident Mrs. Small told her neighbor, "I just looked down at my map for a minute, and the next thing I knew I realized my car had left the road." If Mrs. Small were to refuse to testify, the neighbor could testify as to what Mrs. Small said.
FRE 807 Statements not otherwise covered	If a statement does not fall under a specific exception but it relates to a material fact, it is more probative than any other evidence, and the interests of justice so dictate, it may be admitted.	

Figure 17-3 Hearsay Exceptions

have allowed another witness to make such an identification because she had no experience with amphetamines.[5] An example of conclusions that are within the range of common experience was provided by a case from Tennessee, in which the court noted that a lay witness could testify that a substance appeared to be blood, but that a witness would have to qualify as an expert before he could testify that bruising around the eyes indicates skull trauma.[6]

---

[5] United States v. Westbrook, 896 F.2d 330, 336 (8th Cir. 1990).
[6] State v. Brown, 836 S.W.2d 530, 550 (1992).

Expert witness
A witness who possesses skill and knowledge beyond that of the average person.

According to Rule 702 of the Federal Rules of Evidence, an **expert witness** is someone who is "qualified as an expert by knowledge, skill, experience, training, or education." For the purposes of giving testimony, it is vital to understand that a witness is not an expert, no matter how impressive the credentials, unless the lawyer first lays a foundation to prove the witness's expertise to the court and the court then accepts the person as an expert.

Case 1: The Distressed Grandfather (Continued)

In Drake's case, the paralegal, Kendall, was hard at work developing the expert witness list. This list included Drake's treating physician, as well as other doctors hired to look at his records and give their opinion as to the cause of his heart attack and his prognosis. Kendall knows that in each case, the lawyer will first have to convince the court of the doctor's expertise, so he has asked each of them to prepare an extensive curriculum vitae, which he will then review with the lawyer.

PRACTICE TIP

Keep curricula vitae of all experts on file in a central location for use on future cases.

While jurors are usually impressed by the amount of formal education that a witness has, and are especially impressed when the witness has authored books or articles on the subject, formal education itself is not a requirement for being an expert witness.[7] For example, a burglar could testify as an expert witness on the techniques for breaking and entering, so long as the court made a ruling that the burglar was an expert witness. Without establishing his expert status, the burglar could testify regarding locks and various security devices as to which he has personal knowledge. However, he could not testify as to whether the security was breached in that particular case unless he was first qualified as an expert.

If the expert witness has personal knowledge of the facts on which the opinion is based (as in the case of a physician who has treated an injury personally), the expert can testify about that opinion directly. If the expert has no such personal knowledge (as in the case of a physician who did not treat an injury personally but is called to give an expert opinion on this injury's ramifications), the lawyer must present the witness with a series of hypothetical questions. These hypotheticals ask the witness to express an opinion on the basis of the information provided by the lawyer during the questioning.

Authentication
Proof that the evidence is what it is said to be.

Lay a foundation
The process of providing the qualifications of a witness or properly identifying and authenticating evidence so that it can be introduced.

7. Authentication

Before physical and documentary evidence can be introduced into evidence, it must be **authenticated**. This is done by having a witnesses, who has personal information about the item, identifying the item in question, explaining its use, and in some cases, establishing a chain of custody. This is known as **laying a foundation**.

If the right questions are not asked and the proper authentication is not made, the court will not accept the evidence. For example, in order to properly authenticate physical evidence, the investigator should be asked whether

---

[7] F. Bailey and H. Rothblatt, *Fundamentals of Criminal Advocacy* 123 (1974).

he or she (1) kept the object in his or her exclusive personal control from the time it was found until the time it is presented in court, (2) maintained a complete record of everyone involved in the chain of possession (i.e., everyone who handled the object from the time it was found to the time it was presented in court), or (3) marked the object in a way that will make it easily distinguishable at a later time.

Legal Reasoning Exercise

3. Determine whether you think the following testimony would be allowed in Drake's case. If not, state the appropriate objection.

a. An eyewitness stated, "I heard the brakes squeal, and then the car jumped the curb. To my horror, I saw the car hit a little boy."

b. A second eyewitness testified, "That red car was going at least 80 miles an hour just before it swerved onto the sidewalk."

c. Small's husband is on the stand. He is asked what, if anything, Small told him about how the accident occurred.

d. The plaintiff's lawyer wants to show a video taken of Drake's heart valve repair, necessitated by his heart attack.

e. The plaintiff's lawyer wants to introduce color pictures of the grandchild, taken at the accident scene, showing the boy crushed under the front wheels of the defendant's car.

f. The defendant's lawyer wants to introduce a sketch of the accident scene that he drew based on the statements given to him by his client.

Because of the ease with which digital photographs can be altered and the existence of technology to create **deepfakes** in audiovideo files, there has been some concern about how to ensure that only unaltered photographs, audio, and video are admitted as evidence. However, the basic decision as to whether to admit a photograph (or a video) is the same whether it was taken using film, a digital camera, or a smartphone. In order for a photograph to be admitted as evidence, a witness has to testify that the photograph accurately represents the scene depicted.[8] There is no need for the person who took the photograph to testify. The witness must simply be able to testify that the photograph is a true and accurate representation of the image it contains.[9] The question of whether a digital photograph has been altered is handled through the normal process of the opposing lawyer conducting a thorough cross-examination to ascertain whether the evidence has been altered.[10]

Deepfake
An audiovisual file that has been altered, usually using off-the-shelf artificial intelligence tools, so that the file appears to be unaltered.

[8] Fed. R. Evid. 901(a); see also *United States v. Mojica*, 746 F.2d 242, 245 (5th Cir. 1984) (establishing that the Federal Rules of Evidence merely require "evidence sufficient to support a finding that the matter in question is what its proponent claims.").
[9] Id.
[10] See Brian Barakat & Bronwyn Miller, *Authentication of Digital Photographs Under the "Pictorial Testimony" Theory: A Response to Critics*, Fl. Bar J., July/August 2004, at 38.

Best evidence rule

The rule requiring that the original document be produced at trial.

Written documents must also be authenticated. According to the **best evidence rule,** the original document itself usually must be produced at the trial. Proper testimony must establish that the document presented is in fact what it is purported to be. Under some circumstances, however, a copy may be considered admissible. Public records (official governmental documents, as well as private deeds and mortgages that are officially recorded with the government) can be presented through the use of certified copies. In addition to presenting a copy showing an official seal and signature, an affidavit from the record's custodian usually is presented explaining what the record shows and attesting that it is an accurate copy of the one on file.

Copies of private papers may be allowed when the original has been lost or destroyed, is in the hands of an adverse party who has refused to produce it, or is in the hands of a third party who is outside the jurisdiction of the court's subpoena power.[11] In cases where the original is so voluminous that it is impractical to produce it in its entirety, the litigant is allowed to produce a summary.[12]

The best evidence rule also means that when witnesses are called to explain a document, that document should already have been introduced. The witness should not be asked to describe a document not in evidence because as the rule suggests, the best evidence of a document is that document itself. Sometimes you will notice lawyers forgetting this rule when you see them trying to get a witness to testify to the contents of a document rather than introducing the document itself.

Legal Reasoning Exercise

4. A father took a cell phone video of his children and posted it on Facebook. In the background of the 45-second clip, you can see the accident in Drake's case and the 30 seconds leading up to the incident. Is the video admissible? How would you authenticate the video?

B. INVESTIGATIONS

Investigations are a critical part of case preparation. The goal of factual investigations is to find admissible evidence that will establish the facts necessary to prove the client's case. At times, this can mean having to study what may be quite boring and repetitious details. But at other times, it can be exhilarating and very satisfying work.

A good investigator must be systematic, but must also show creativity, imagination, and resourcefulness. As with client interviewing, good communication skills are essential for interviewing potential witnesses and other persons

---

[11] Fed. R. Evid. 1004.
[12] Fed. R. Evid 1006.

who can help you establish the facts of your case. Finally, good investigators must be able to maintain an open mind. Approach each situation without any preconceived ideas or notions. Never assume anything, and be careful of reaching conclusions that cannot be supported by the facts.

PRACTICE TIP

Lawyers will often require that clients provide user names and passwords for all of their social media accounts. This is especially true in family law and employment law cases. Paralegals may be tasked with checking these sources for any postings that could cast doubt on the client's credibility.

---

1. Planning an Investigation

Case 1: The Distressed Grandfather (Continued)

After ending his interview with Drake, Kendall met with Harper, and they developed a checklist of the information that they wanted Kendall to gather based on what they would have to prove to win a negligence claim against Small. First on the list was anything they could find to establish her negligence. This included locating witnesses and documentary evidence, such as the police report, that could show that she was speeding immediately prior to the accident, that Philip was on the sidewalk when the car hit him, and that there were no defects in the operation of the automobile. Second, they needed to be able to prove that seeing his grandson's death is what actually caused Drake's heart attack. For that, Kendall would first obtain all medical and hospital records. However, it was likely that they might also need an expert witness to testify that the heart attack was more likely than not caused by seeing the accident. Finally, they needed evidence to prove Drake's injuries. Again, they would rely heavily on medical records, but other witnesses, including Drake himself, could also provide evidence of the pain and suffering caused by the heart attack and the pain and suffering from seeing his grandson die.

Generally speaking, the legal system is a slow-moving process in which delays and continuances are common. For example, it is not uncommon for a period of four to five years to pass between the time of an accident and the eventual courtroom resolution of the negligence and damages issues that arose from the accident. But accident scenes change. Witnesses' memories fade. Witnesses move. Broken parts are repaired or discarded. Injuries heal. Therefore, factual investigation should begin as soon as possible.

The process of factual investigation begins with the development of an investigation plan that outlines the types of information needed and the methods for obtaining it. The first step in planning an investigation is to determine what evidence already exists in the firm's files. Then you have to develop a strategy for getting other information. Much information can be learned by collecting documents, such as medical and police records. You may also need to conduct additional interviews with the client, interview key witnesses, or visit the scene of an accident.

a. Identifying Needed Facts

Before beginning the investigation, it is important to discuss the theory of the case with the supervising lawyer. For example, if your firm is representing a criminal defendant, you must know the elements of the crime. If your client wants to sue for a personal injury, you will need to know what must be proven to establish a cause of action in a negligence case. You must gather evidence on each element of the case for which your side has the burden of production; otherwise, the other side may move to have the case dismissed.

PRACTICE TIP

Once the lawyer has identified the cause of action for a lawsuit, looking at pattern jury instructions can help you assist the lawyer in determining what will be needed to win the lawsuit. That information can then be incorporated into the theory of the case and used to develop the list of evidence to be gathered.

Lawyers frequently develop a primary theory for their cases, such as negligence, and also alternative theories, such as fraud or another intentional tort, that they might pursue. In addition, the opposition may have yet different theories of the case. Your supervising lawyer may want you to gather evidence relevant to all these alternatives.

To help organize the investigation, you may find it useful to begin by chronologically listing the events that the client described. Then attempt to identify evidence that either substantiates or contradicts the client's description of each event. This analysis provides a basis for identifying additional information that you will have to gather. For example, for each event on the list, identify witnesses who may have observed it or documents that might substantiate it.

Look for any gaps within this sequence of events. Is it possible that something else could have taken place at that same time? Are there key details that the client cannot remember? Is there something that one would expect to have happened that did not? What was the mental state of the people involved? Who was responsible for creating the conditions that may have contributed to the events that took place? For each gap found, you must identify possible sources of information that could help complete the picture.

b. Developing a Coordinated Plan

The second part of any investigation plan should identify who will be responsible for carrying out each task specified in the plan. Paralegals are often assigned the tasks of contacting outside investigators (if they are needed) and expert witnesses.

Once you and your supervising lawyer have identified the types of information you will need, consider how you might gather it quickly and relatively inexpensively. Often, it is cheaper to gather facts informally before litigation is even started rather than waiting until later, when you may have to rely on the more formal discovery process. For example, think about whether you can take advantage of investigative work that has already been done by law enforcement agencies and insurance company claims representatives. Then consider how additional evidence should be gathered. Most likely, you will be expected to gather documentary evidence and interview possible witnesses. If there is also a need to gather physical evidence, then it may be necessary to hire a private investigator.

DISCUSSION QUESTION

4. Recall the case from Chapter 3 of Diane Dobbs, the waitress who was fired for being pregnant. If you were put in charge of investigating her case, what types of evidence would you look for, and how would you go about collecting it?

2. Gathering Physical Evidence

Generally, the tasks of collecting real evidence (such as a piece of glass found at the accident scene) and going to the scene of the accident should be left in the hands of professional investigators. Similarly, any diagrams or charts should be developed by a professional, such as an expert in accident reconstruction. This is especially true when the case is likely to go to trial or when the case is potentially worth a significant amount of money. Leaving this work to the professional investigator is for practical as well as ethical reasons. If the paralegal is the one who develops the diagram, then the paralegal may be called to the stand to authenticate it. It is much more credible to have a "neutral" investigator testifying than the firm's employee.

It is important that paralegals consult with their supervising lawyers, regarding what they need to do in order to properly preserve the evidence they gather and the supportive information that will be needed to authenticate that evidence at trial.[13] In criminal cases and those involving accidents or damage to property, it is important to visit the scene and to view the damaged property. Because conditions change over time, it is desirable to observe them as soon as possible. If possible, visit the scene at the same time of the day as the matter being investigated took place and under similar weather conditions. Not only will you get a better perspective on how the accident might have happened, but also you might meet people who frequent that area at that particular time of day and witnessed the accident.

a. Taking Photographs and Videos

Photographs are one of the most effective means of gathering and preserving information. While you may want to consider hiring a professional

---

[13] For more information on this process, see the section entitled "Authentication," earlier in this chapter.

photographer, you should also keep a camera in your office. There will be times when a professional photographer will not be available, and waiting for one will not be possible or practical. For example, soft-tissue injuries in particular disappear quickly. You may also want to visit the scene of the accident to observe and photograph anything that might help you reconstruct how the accident happened.

P R A C T I C E T I P

Whether you use your smartphone or digital camera to take photographs, keep each client's images on a separate SD card in order to protect each client's confidentiality.

At times, a still picture will not be sufficient. For example, in a personal injury suit brought because the plaintiff has been paralyzed, the plaintiff's lawyer may want to show a "one day in the life of . . ." type of video in order to make the jury more aware of the full implications of the plaintiff's injuries.

b. Preparing Diagrams

In addition to taking photographs of the scene of an accident, it is often useful to make diagrams. Keep in mind, however, that there is a difference between the diagrams you will draw to help you and the witnesses you interview visualize the scene and those that your lawyer will be allowed to introduce as evidence at trial.

Even if you are creating a diagram only for your own use, record the distances between key points as accurately as possible. Carefully measure everything, from the width of the street to the location of any traffic signs.

If there is any possibility that the diagram will be used as an exhibit at trial, remember that the diagram cannot be introduced as evidence unless it can be shown to accurately represent the accident scene. The science of accident reconstruction is becoming more sophisticated every day, including the use of computerized reenactments. To properly present such evidence and exhibits, your firm should consider whether it needs to hire a qualified expert to prepare the evidence and to testify at trial. The success of civil litigation often depends on the quality of the experts hired.

3. Obtaining Documents

Depending on the nature of the case, various kinds of documentary evidence may be needed. For example, in personal injury actions the injured party's medical records become an important factor. In a products liability suit information about safety records and industry standards is usually vital to its outcome. Likewise, in many cases, information about a company's corporate structure and financial position can be a key element. Fortunately, this sort of information is usually readily available if you know where to look for it. Often, it is simply a matter of going to the right office and asking for it. At other times, you may need a release form signed by your client or a subpoena.

When gathering documentary evidence, it is essential to also gather the supporting information that will be required to authenticate the documents should the case go to trial. One common way to authenticate a document is to have a witness, in a position to know, testify as to the document's authenticity. For example, a hospital records custodian could testify as to the authenticity of the plaintiff's medical records. In some cases, you may be able to avoid having to call a witness by using another method of authentication. For example, the other side may agree to stipulate as to the document's authenticity. If that is not possible, you may be able to get a signed affidavit from the record keeper and have the document certified through that means.

a. Private Documents

Many of the most critical documents used in lawsuits such as medical reports, internal studies, memos, and e-mails, are not available to the general public. Obtaining access to them typically requires the use of release forms or subpoenas.

(1) Medical records

In personal injury and industrial accident cases, the paralegal will need to have the client complete the appropriate release form and then send that form to hospitals and doctors' offices. Medical records can supply information on the diagnosis (the nature and extent of the illness or injuries), the treatment (the drugs, surgery, and so forth used to control or alleviate the condition), and the prognosis (the long-term effect of the condition, including the need for further treatment). Many states have statutes that prescribe what you must do to obtain them and get them admitted. Therefore, it is important to check to see whether your state has any statutes that govern how to obtain medical records. Figure 17-4 lists the various types of medical records you may want to review.

Figure 17-4   Medical Records

Hospital Records
    Admissions form
    History and physical
    Progress notes
    Physician orders
    Lab, X-ray, and ancillary service reports
    Operative report
    Consultant's report
    Discharge summary
Physician's outpatient notes and letters

If your client was hospitalized, the hospital itself will usually be the best source for information. In order to be accredited by the Joint Commission on Accreditation of Hospitals, hospitals must maintain a complete set of patient records that conform to the commission's specific standards. Private physicians also keep detailed records of the patient's visits. When records are requested for a lawsuit, many physicians will send copies of those records or will dictate a letter based on their notes.

Hospital records usually begin with an admissions form, which gives personal data, including date and place of birth, marital status, occupation, religion, former names, relatives, and insurance carrier. At the same time, the doctor is performing a history and physical examination. Based on that and any initial lab work, the doctor formulates an initial plan for the patient. Exhibit 17-1 provides an example history and physical for Drake's case. The subsequent hospital records include the daily observations of temperature, blood pressure, pulse rate, and skin condition; other observations as required based on the patient's condition; and orders of the physician regarding laboratory tests, medications administered, consultations requested of other doctors, and diagnostic tests.

If an operation was performed, an operative report by the surgeon is included that describes the type of surgical procedure used and what was observed about the patient's condition during the operation.

The discharge summary reviews the patient's condition on admission, progress while in the hospital, results of diagnostic procedures used, condition of the patient on release, any medication that was prescribed for the patient to be taken at home, and a follow-up plan for the patient's post-hospital treatment.

As you can see from Exhibit 17-1, medical reports contain a great deal of technical terminology that is difficult to understand without a medical background. Extremely useful resources that you can consult to help you decipher medical records include a good medical dictionary or an online medical dictionary like the one found on webmd.com; the Physician's Desk Reference (referred to as the PDR), which lists and describes all prescription drugs; and an anatomy book that identifies the parts of the body, refers to the functions of these parts, and discusses the ramifications of injuries to them. There are also books explaining medical terminology that are written specifically for lawyers. In cases that present unique medical issues, your firm may also want to consider hiring the services of a legal nurse consultant or other medical experts. Finally, if your firm does a great deal of personal injury litigation, you might consider taking a medical terminology or health law course.

PRACTICE TIP

Create a template for any of the standardized letters that you routinely use for such things as requests for medical records and releases. These templates should include all of the information that never varies, with blank spaces or merge codes inserted as placeholders for the client-specific information that will be different each time you use the letter.

MERCY HOSPITAL

HISTORY AND PHYSICAL FORM

PATIENT NAME: Donald Drake
DATE ADMITTED: September 1, 2021

HISTORY

CHIEF COMPLAINT: chest pain, rule out MI
HISTORY OF PRESENT ILLNESS: This 68-yr-old gentleman was brought to the ER by ambulance around 10 am after suffering crushing substernal chest pain, diaphoresis nausea, and weakness. At the time of onset he had been supervising the play of his 5-yr-old grandchild when the child was struck by a passing car. As EMTs were summoned by a passerby, the grandfather tried to revive the child. Help arrived very soon, and EMTs took over treatment and transport to the hospital. Within minutes the patient began having the above-mentioned symptoms and felt very weak and collapsed to the ground. He was still breathing and had a pulse but was unconscious. Another ambulance was summoned, and the patient was brought to hospital ER. At his arrival he was again conscious with oxygen running at 6 liters and Ringer's Lactate at 150 cc/hr. He was immediately evaluated by the ER physician, and the on-call cardiologist was called. The patient was stable at this point with a presumed inferior MI based on EKG and lab findings and was transported to the ICU for further management.
PAST MEDICAL HISTORY: Allergies, Illnesses, Operations, Tobacco, and Alcohol: None.
Family History: Father died at 81 of coronary disease and diabetes. Mother died at 87 of "old age." He has two sons both in good health and 5 grandchildren also in good health except for the above-mentioned accident victim. His wife is alive and well with no current medical problems. Social History: He lives with his wife and two dogs on a farm. He is a retired toolmaker.

PHYSICAL EXAM

Alert 68-yr-old male in mild distress with persistent anterior chest wall pain. Temp 98.0, pulse 98, resp 28.

HEART: Early mild bilateral cataracts. Otherwise neg. exam with normal EOM and clear fundi.
NECK: Non-tender with no masses or enlarged thyroid. No adenopathy. Oropharynx is clear with good dental hygiene. No dentures.
CHEST: Normal breath sounds, no extra sounds. No shortness of breath or wheezing.
ABDOMEN: Neg exam, no masses, rebound guarding. Normal bowel sounds.
NEURO: Alert and oriented times 3. CN intact. No upper or lower extremity sensory or motor deficits. Reflexes 2+ symmetrical.
LABS: Initial Labs show small Q waves in II, III, and AVF and elevated ST segments in the anterior chest leads. CPK is elevated with MB fraction in the abnormal range. CBC, electrolytes, and chem screen are all in the normal range.
ASSESSMENT: Acute inferior MI.
PLAN: MI management, continued care of his cardiologist.

Exhibit 17-1 Sample History and Physical Examination Section of Hospital Record

(2) Internal e-mails and reports

Electronically stored documents, such as internal reports, e-mails, voice-mails, text messages, and information located on social network sites, can be very useful in cases involving product liability and fraud. Plaintiffs' lawyers will typically file e-discovery motions to obtain them.

As we discussed in Chapter 6 on civil litigation, many courts are now developing rules regarding e-discovery. There are many problems connected with e-discovery that we can mention only briefly here, including developing a plan for handling the sheer volume of the electronic documents, determining how to eliminate duplicate copies, deciding how to segregate and protect confidential and protected documents, and establishing a method for retrieving such documents if they are inadvertently released. To further complicate matters, electronically stored information can be created by a wide variety of software programs, making its retrieval difficult, especially if the document was created with a version of a program that is no longer readily available.

To adequately handle all of the issues connected with electronically stored materials, it may be necessary for the law firm to hire information technology experts. A technologically savvy paralegal can play a vital role as a liaison between such technology experts and the supervising lawyer.

PRACTICE TIP

Never write on, punch holes in, or staple an original document.

b. Public Documents

Often government documents can be quite helpful. City building departments have information on building construction plans and safety inspections. Coroners' offices have autopsy and inquest reports. County recorders' offices have information on mortgages, bankruptcies, trusts, and judgments. License bureaus have all sorts of background information on license holders. The secretary of state's office in the relevant state and the federal Securities and Exchange Commission (SEC) have extensive data about the structure and financial position of corporations.

While the law differs from one state to the next, the general rule is that the public has a right to inspect public records during reasonable business hours. The right to inspect such documents carries with it the right to make copies. For a nominal service fee, most offices will provide you with photocopies of the documents you need. At the federal level the Freedom of Information Act requires each agency to make various records available to the public. Exceptions are allowed, however, for such matters as defense and foreign policy secrets, trade secrets, confidential commercial or financial information, personnel and medical files, and investigatory files compiled for law enforcement purposes.

PRACTICE TIP

First, check to see if you can find the agency information you seek online. If not, then call before you go as some governmental agencies do not allow public access on certain days. Obviously, if you go that day, it will simply waste your time. Also, find out who at the agency can best help you, and make sure that he or she has the documents you need. Then go to the agency as soon as possible before your newly discovered contact person has a chance to forget you and the purpose of your mission.

Two state offices most commonly used by paralegal investigators are the secretary of state's office and the agency responsible for licensing occupations. The secretary of state's office maintains a list of all foreign and domestic corporations registered to do business in the state, as well as other business entities. For example, it can provide information as to the official legal names of corporations; the nature of the business the corporation is engaged in; and the names and addresses of its registered agent, its board of directors, and its officers.

PRACTICE TIP

If the person being sued is required to obtain some form of licensing, such as an electrician or a beautician, start your investigation with the state licensing board. Not only can you find out the requirements for licensure, but also you may find that the person being sued allowed his or her license to lapse. You may also learn of other complaints pending against that person—a tremendous incentive to the other side to settle the case early.

The county courthouse also provides a wealth of very useful information. In the office for the registry of deeds you can find information about who owns certain real estate in the county, as well as who holds the mortgages and various liens on the property. You can find additional information on liens in the clerk of the court's office. In the assessor's office, you can find information about who pays the taxes on the property and whether any delinquencies exist.

Nongovernmental groups such as trade associations and public interest groups also issue reports that are available to the public. In products liability cases, you will need to obtain copies of the relevant industry standards established by both government agencies and voluntary associations. While the courts of different states vary with regard to their treatment of the admissibility of such codes, the modern trend seems to favor their use.

PARALEGAL PROFILE

William R. Matlock
Litigation Paralegal

I work in a law firm with seven attorneys, six paralegals, and five secretaries. Almost all our work is in the area of personal injury, but our firm also handles other tort cases, such as employment discrimination and medical malpractice, as well as some real estate work, workers' compensation, and social security and disability claims. If you were to ask me what a typical day is like, I would have to say that it is impossible to describe a typical day. No two days are ever alike, and I have never been bored.

The way most of our clients come to us is through an initial phone contact with an attorney. The attorney will then ask the client to come to the office. Often after the attorney handles the initial interview, I will then meet with the client, take pictures if the client has suffered injuries or property damage, and have the client sign all necessary release forms.

The next step I am involved in is the factual investigation of the case. That can include photographing the accident scene, obtaining all of the documents, such as medical records, getting police reports, and interviewing witnesses. I encourage witnesses to speak with me by letting them know that if they help us now, they may not have to appear later for a deposition or for court. However, if they choose not to speak to me, we will subpoena them. But even when I need to appear firm, I always remain respectful and cordial. The case then moves on to a separate department where they try to reach a settlement. One of the most satisfying aspects of the job is seeing a settlement check come in and knowing that the hard work and time I put in to a case helped to settle it. If the case doesn't settle, then it comes back to me to start the litigation process, and I draft the pleadings, such as the complaint and motions. (I enjoy asking interrogatories far more than answering them!)

I use the computer all the time for drafting my documents. In addition, our firm has an Internet account that allows us to do online legal research. I also use the Internet to do searches to find information on corporations and their agents as well as to track down witnesses by using a phone number, address, or any other information I have.

What I like best about my job is the variety—the number of different things I do. In addition to client interviews, document drafting, and investigative work, I assist at depositions and occasionally with arbitrations. One of the unique features of our firm is that we own a twin-engine airplane, and we will use it, for example, to take photos through a telephoto lens of an intersection that was the scene of a motor vehicle accident. Aerial photos are intrinsically interesting. We frequently blow them up to poster size to use as an exhibit for a trial or arbitration hearing.

To do this job well, you have to have compassion and be willing to be patient with clients who would rather be doing anything else than answering what they view as very intrusive interrogatory questions. You have to be able to talk but also be able to listen to people. Attention to detail is crucial, especially when drafting documents; I proofread everything two or three times even after I spell check because the documents I send out have to look perfect. It is the best way to let the other side know that we are professionals.

4. General Empirical Information

In the process of investigating a specific case, such things as what the weather was like on a particular day or the side effects of specific drugs may be relevant to the case you are working on. This type of information is generally readily accessible through the Internet. Online databases can lead you to summaries or the full text of articles in periodicals and journals, books, news stories, and scientific and technical reports. (We discussed Lexis and Westlaw, the two most prominent legal databases, in Chapter 14 on legal research.) When seeking this type of information, public libraries and reference librarians can be extremely helpful. Many libraries subscribe to specialized databases that are not available to the public without first purchasing a costly subscription.

5. Reporting the Results of the Investigation

It is important that paralegals record not only the results of their investigations and analysis, but also the sources of the information and how they gathered it. The supervising lawyer may want one comprehensive report or, in longer, more complex matters, a series of interim reports.

In the report's "Analysis" section, isolate each factual question about which there is some dispute. For each one, detail all aspects of the evidence (testimonial, physical, and documentary) that relate to that specific issue. Note any factors that may affect a witness's credibility, such as being hard of hearing or having a surly manner.

Although you should try to present this information in a concise manner, it is important that it be complete. An item might appear to be insignificant at the time the report is being prepared, but it may become extremely important at some later date. Attach any relevant statements, diagrams, and photographs.

SUMMARY

In both civil and criminal suits, there is usually more of a dispute over what actually took place (the facts) than there is about the meaning of the law. Although on occasion both sides may stipulate to a particular description of the facts, the major part of the lawyer's energy goes toward convincing the court to adopt the client's view of the facts rather than the opponent's contrary view.

A good paralegal, therefore, should be a skilled fact finder. At times, a paralegal is personally involved in the investigative process. At other times, when the initial investigative work is done outside the law office, the paralegal is frequently used to coordinate the information gained from these outside sources and to prepare it for presentation in the courtroom. In either case, it is important to understand the basic concepts and techniques that go into conducting investigations.

To as great an extent as possible, strive to collect information in a form that is admissible in a court of law. Developing a basic understanding of the rules of evidence and what constitutes relevant and competent evidence will assist you in determining what evidence to gather.

Begin the investigation as soon after the incident as possible. Physical surroundings change, witnesses' memories fade, and injuries heal. Time is particularly important if you are investigating an automobile accident or similar event in which the physical evidence is likely to change or disappear.

Facts can be obtained through a number of sources, including interviews of clients and witnesses; documentary evidence, such as police reports, hospital and doctor records, employment records, contracts, and photographs; and personal observation, from visiting an accident scene or examining the condition of an apartment.

||| REVIEW QUESTIONS

Pages 489 through 500

1. How do courts determine what types of information can be used and what the lawyers must do in order to get evidence admitted?
2. Define each of the following: real or physical evidence, documentary evidence, testimonial evidence, and judicial notice.
3. Define each of the following: direct, circumstantial, cumulative, and corroborative evidence.
4. What is the requirement for finding that evidence is relevant?
5. What is hearsay, and under what circumstances is hearsay evidence admissible?
6. Under what circumstances can a lay witness give opinion testimony?
7. Before a person can testify as an expert witness, what must happen?
8. How does the testimony of an expert differ from that of a lay witness?
9. What must be done to properly authenticate real evidence?
10. What impact does the best evidence rule have on the presentation of evidence?

Pages 500 through 512

11. What is the goal of a factual investigation?
12. Before beginning the investigation, why is it important to discuss the theory of the case with the supervising lawyer?
13. Why might it sometimes be more appropriate to hire a professional, independent investigator rather than relying on the firm's employees?
14. What is e-discovery, and what particular challenges does it present?

||| WEB EXERCISES

1. On the Internet, there are many articles on the exploding world of e-discovery. One good place to start is at *technology.findlaw.com,* where you will find not only articles on e-discovery, but also an eDiscovery Guide. Another good source for information on e-discovery is YouTube. On that site, you can find one particularly well done video at *youtube.com/watch?v=CZNNZMO_7sE&t=59s* entitled "What Every Businessperson Should Know About E-Discovery." Watch the video and note the many steps involved in the e-discovery process.
2. Nikolai Pozdianakov with vDiscovery, a Manhattan-based provider of eDiscovery services, has an engaging video at *youtube.com/watch?v=xCMsNguFkGQ&t=4s* entitled "Mobile Device Collection—eDiscovery FAQ," in which he lists information that his firm needs when asked to provide e-discovery from a mobile device. What are four pieces of information that he wants to obtain before his forensic team starts mobile device collection?

Chapter 18

Computers and Case Management

*A man may as well open an oyster without
a knife as a lawyer's mouth without a fee.*
Barten Holyday

Chapter Objectives

After reading this chapter, you should be able to:

- Explain why it is important for a law firm to run a conflict check before accepting a new client.
- Identify the types of specific information that law offices collect in a case file.
- Discuss how law offices handle calendaring, timekeeping, billing, and case management.
- Describe the advantages of using an integrated case management program.
- Contrast a structured with a full-text database.

INTRODUCTION

In the past, legal documents, lawyers' letters and notes, billing and payment records, and other documents were all kept in paper files. Today, while many firms still maintain backup hard copies of important documents, most rely on computers to store their case information in a digital format. This has made it cheaper to copy, store, search, analyze, and share the information that lawyers need to serve their clients more efficiently and effectively.

Large firms often maintain their own information technology (IT) department to select, set up, and maintain their computers, computer software, and computer networks. Sole practitioners and small firms may subscribe to software packages that include 24/7 tech support from the company selling each specific product. Others rely on the knowledge of an in-house "techie" lawyer or paralegal to help them make hardware and software choices.

Cloud computing revolutionized the way that law firms purchase software and store data. With cloud computing the software programs or data are stored on a remote server rather than on a specific computer located within the law firm. Users access these programs and data over the Internet through a desktop, laptop, tablet, or smartphone. This means that lawyers and paralegals have 24/7 access to their programs and data, no matter where they are. Lawyers and paralegals can work on a case from the beach as easily as from the office computer. Cloud computing has allowed the lawyers and paralegals at some law firms to work entirely remotely. Some of these virtual law firms have no physical presence and may only rent a conference room for a day when it is necessary to meet with a client in person. And, even for law firms that still maintain traditional office space, this ability to work virtually allowed them to continue assisting their clients during the COVID-19 pandemic.

Ethics Alert

A law firm must consider security and confidentiality issues before storing client data in the cloud.

In this chapter, we will provide an overview of how advances in law office computer applications have affected how paralegals perform their case management functions. **Case management** is about handling the information involved in a case within the law office. All documents and case materials must be organized so as to allow for the easy, fast, and accurate retrieval of information. While some firms still accomplish these tasks by relying principally on paper files and records, computers make the whole process much more manageable, especially in any case involving more than just a few basic documents.

Case management functions include:

Case management
Handling the flow of information involved in client cases.

- running conflict checks,
- setting up and maintaining the client file, containing background information on the client and the case, and a record of actions taken,
- entering key dates, such as filing deadlines and court dates, into a calendar or "tickler system,"

- preparing correspondence, pleadings, and other documents,
- recording time charges and sending out bills, and in some cases, managing litigation documents.

To help explain how this process works, we will follow Kendall, the paralegal, as he manages the case file for Donald Drake.

Case 1: The Distressed Grandfather (Continued)

At the end of their interview, Kendall escorted Drake to the door and then sat at his computer to enter key information from the interview. Next, he used his computer to do a conflict check to ensure that the firm had never represented Wilma Small or anyone related to her.

A. PERFORMING A CONFLICT CHECK

Before a law firm can accept someone as a new client, it must perform a conflict check. To maintain client confidentiality and to avoid any breach of the fiduciary duty of client trust and loyalty, lawyers cannot accept any case that would involve either a personal conflict or a conflict with a prior client. In an increasingly litigious society, conflict checks are becoming more complex. Thus, when a new file is opened, not only the names of the adverse parties, but also any other entities connected with the case, must be cross-referenced with other law firm records.

Especially in small firms, it may be tempting to assume that it is possible to do a mental conflict check. But the best approach is to realize that memories are fallible and all conflict checking should be done through a computerized system that faithfully records all client names and related parties. Also, once the conflict program has been run, firms frequently double-check for conflicts by circulating memos within the firm to inform all lawyers and paralegals of the firm's new clients.

Conflict check
The process of ensuring that there is no conflict of interest between the firm's current or past clients and a potential new client.

B. SETTING UP A CLIENT CASE FILE

Once a person is formally accepted as a client, a paralegal or a member of the clerical staff will set up a **client file**. The first step in this process is usually that of assigning the file a coded number rather than the client's name. This client number is used to help preserve client confidentiality. A numbering system can include such information as the date when the file was opened and a code for the matter type. An indication of the specific matter is included as a law firm can represent a client in more than one matter, such as in both a divorce and a personal injury.

Most client files contain:

1. background information on the client (including addresses, phone numbers, and billing arrangements);
2. correspondence between the firm and either the client or other outside parties connected to the case;

3. internal office memoranda (including research memos prepared in connection with the case);
4. copies of all pleadings related to the case;
5. copies of relevant documents, such as contracts, leases, medical reports, and laboratory reports; and
6. notes by lawyers and paralegals working on the case.

Usually, copies of correspondence, contracts, leases, and other documents are scanned into Portable Document Format (PDF) files or imported as a word processing document. Depending on office practices, a backup set of the hard copies may also be kept.

PRACTICE TIP

If you are the person responsible for maintaining the case file, as the case progresses, always get the full name of any insurance or opposition representative who contacts you, and always take notes recording the substance of the conversation and place them in the file. You should also have an organized way for keeping an ongoing narrative of all the phone calls you have made and received in which you record the substance of all conversations. If you are not around to provide an update, your supervising lawyer can still locate the needed information.

Many law firms use dedicated case management software. With such programs, it is possible to store all of the case's basic information, correspondence, legal documents, and pleadings in one linked system. There are many software programs dealing with one or more aspects of case management.

Case 1: The Distressed Grandfather (Continued)

Kendall really appreciates that he never has to search for anything related to Drake's case, because it is all stored in one location and all of the relevant items are linked to each other.

While the case is still open or shortly before it is closed, many law firms evaluate the various work products, such as complaints, motions, and memoranda of law as to their future usefulness. Legal research can be time-consuming, and there is nothing to be gained from duplicating work that already has been done. Rather than beginning from scratch, it would be more efficient if a lawyer or a paralegal could review work that someone else had done on a similar topic or problem. Therefore, if a document might serve as a valuable starting point for future work, the document is placed in the firm's work product files.

After the firm's involvement in a matter is completed, a file clerk or secretary officially closes the file. Some materials in the file are returned to the client, some are discarded, and some remain as part of a permanent file.

C. CALENDARING AND DOCKET CONTROL

The failure to meet deadlines is a leading cause of malpractice claims. Therefore, every law office needs a reliable way to keep track of and give advance warnings of important dates.

Probably the most important date is the statute of limitations. If a lawsuit is not filed within the time limits established by the statute of limitations, clients may be barred from going to court. Other important dates include deadlines for filing responses to complaints and motions. Every time a motion is filed or an answer is received, another time period begins, and another deadline approaches. To monitor these important dates, lawyers develop docket control systems, commonly referred to as **tickler systems**.

Tickler system
A calendaring system that records key dates and important deadlines.

Although a tickler system can be as simple as writing important dates on a desk calendar, most law firms use some electronic form of tracking their important events. Many rely on generic programs, such as Microsoft Outlook or Google Calendar, but law office–specific software programs can be much more powerful. For example, they can automate a whole series of events, based on a set of rules that the user sets up, so that any specific steps required prior to a certain event can be automatically entered. For example, a computer can generate dates for all of the steps that must be completed prior to a real estate closing or in litigation for each stage of a court-imposed tracking system.

These programs will also automatically calculate dates that occur a certain number of days before or after any given date. They can add reminders at any interval you like prior to the deadline itself. If you should have to change a deadline, the reminders connected to that deadline will automatically change as well. Then, if you fail to complete a task, most programs will keep reminding you of the missed deadline until you mark the task as completed. They also allow the entering of such recurring events as weekly staff meetings or the boss's birthday.

Case 1: The Distressed Grandfather (Continued)

In addition to doing a conflict check and setting up a case file, Kendall entered the date of Drake's next appointment and a list of tasks, such as obtaining the medical records with reminder dates; and most important, the relevant statute of limitations, into the calendaring function in his case management system.

The key to the success of any tickler system is making someone responsible for routinely checking on what needs to be done and circulating that information with sufficient advance notice to the relevant lawyer or paralegal. Some paralegals also keep a paper calendar of important dates to make sure that there is a redundant system and that all deadlines are met.

D. DOCUMENT AUTOMATION

Lawyers and paralegals create a lot of documents—letters, contracts, settlement agreements, pleadings, and research memos, to name only a portion of the volume of written work produced in the average law firm. Much of this can be based on work already created for another client. For example, when drafting a complaint, many lawyers and paralegals will first look for a similar complaint that the firm has filed in the past and then adapt it to the new case. This is fine, and it can save a lot of time, so long as it is done properly.

The incorrect, but common, method is to pull up the old document and then simply delete the information unique to the prior case, such as the client's name, and replace it with information from the current case. This method, however, can create ethical problems. It is easy to miss one of the references to the prior case, so that suddenly, in a complaint involving Donald Drake, a reference to Sam Jones, a prior client, appears. A second problem is the need to reenter information instead of just typing it once. For example, in a typical case, the client's name will appear repeatedly in correspondence, court pleadings, and other documents. It is much better to type the name once and then have a computer automatically insert it in multiple locations. Many case management programs, such as Abacus, have this ability as do dedicated document assembly programs. There are also a number of cloud-based programs for document automation.

Case 1: The Distressed Grandfather (Continued)

Harper asked Kendall to draft a complaint in Drake's case. Kendell has created a form for pleading captions using his firm's document automation software. The program shows up as a tab in his word processing program.

To use it, he just has to follow three steps. First, he had already created a basic pleading caption. But instead of inserting any specific client's information, he created fields to hold the information, which will vary with each client. It takes time to set up a caption template and the relevant questions to ask, but once this shell is created, it makes creating captions much easier and less time-consuming. For instance, when Kendall is inputting data for a new client, he will simply have to answer a series of questions that he has already created. The form will look something like this:

Label	Question	Answer
Plaintiff	Who is the plaintiff?	
Defendant	Who is the defendant?	
Title	What is the title for this pleading?	
Case number	What is the civil action number?	

The document automation software will then insert those answers into the form. Most document assembly programs are quite smart and can be programmed to enter data using correct capitalization, such as all caps for the pleading title, and the correct/preferred pronouns for people.

Kendall fills in the information for Drake's case without answering the question regarding the civil action number, as he does not yet have it, creating the following caption. The placeholders have been replaced by the unique information in Drake's case. (When printed, the shading will not appear.)

UNITED STATES DISTRICT COURT
DISTRICT OF MASSACHUETTS

Civil Action No.

Donald Drake, Plaintiff	}	
v.	}	COMPLAINT
Wilma Small, Defendant	}	

The creation of a caption is a very simple demonstration of what document automation programs can accomplish. Think about how much time would be saved by only having to type a client's name once in documents such as contracts or wills, where the name might appear many times.

NETNOTE

"Unless you still ride to work on a horse, and draft one character at a time with a quill, it's time you start using your computer . . . as a computer instead of as a 1950 typewriter." (Quotation from TheFormTool)

E. TIMEKEEPING AND BILLING

As the quotation at the beginning of this chapter somewhat drolly suggests, to lawyers and paralegals, time is money. In order for a law firm to prosper, not only must it provide quality legal services to a sufficient number of clients, but it must also bill and receive payment for those services. To accomplish this, lawyers and paralegals must keep track of the time that they spend on a case. This must be followed by a timely and detailed bill to the client. Studies have shown that the longer the time lapse between the time the legal service is rendered and the time the bill is received, the less likely it is that the client will pay. Using a computerized timekeeping and billing program is the best method to ensure that there is an efficient method for recording time spent and generating bills in a timely fashion.

1. Alternative Fee Structures

In any law firm, the discussion of fees is an essential element of the initial client interview. Depending on the nature of the case and whether the representation is for a plaintiff or a defendant, lawyers use various methods to bill for their own and their paralegals' time.

Retainer agreement
A contract that outlines the attorney's duties and the client's obligations regarding payment, on either an hourly or contingency fee basis, as well as the client's responsibilities regarding costs and expenses.

Before starting work on a case, the law firm will draft a written agreement between the law firm and the client regarding the client's obligations as to the payment of fees and expenses. This is known as a **retainer agreement**. The firm may also ask the client to pay an amount of money, a **retainer,** as a kind of down payment against future fees and expenses. The firm must deposit such advances in a special client's trust fund and cannot withdraw any of the funds until they have been earned as fees or spent on expenses. All unused funds must be returned to the client at the conclusion of the case.

Retainer
An advance or down payment that is given to engage the services of a lawyer.

The most common billing methods include the following:

■ fixed fee,
■ contingency fee, and
■ hourly fee.

a. Fixed Fees

Fixed fee
A set charge for a specific service, such as drafting a simple will.

Consumers generally pay a set fee for a particular product or service. For example, a physician typically charges a set amount for a routine office call or a specific surgical procedure. Lawyers also price some of their services in this manner, charging a fixed fee. This is especially true for routine tasks, such as drawing up a simple will, incorporating a small business, or handling an uncontested divorce. In many areas, real estate closing fees are also billed in this manner.

When **fixed fees** are used, it is to the firm's advantage to delegate as much work as possible to paralegals because they typically cost the firm less than lawyers. The decreased overhead that results from such delegation to paralegals should result in higher profits, a reduction in the established fee, or both. A fee reduction not only benefits consumers of legal services, but also improves the firm's competitive position in the marketplace.

b. Contingency Fees

Contingency fee
A fee calculated as a percentage of the settlement or award in the case.

Under a **contingency fee** arrangement, the client does not pay the lawyer anything by way of fees unless the plaintiff collects some sort of award or settlement. However, in most states, the client is still responsible for all expenses. If the plaintiff does collect some sort of award or settlement, then the lawyer's fee will be calculated as a percentage of the damage award and paid from those funds when the plaintiff receives them. It is common for the law firm to receive 33 percent if a case is settled before it goes to trial, 40 percent if it goes to trial, and 50 percent if the case is appealed.

The plaintiff's lawyer in a personal injury suit and lawyers doing collections work are usually hired on a contingency fee basis. On the other hand, this type of fee structure is usually prohibited in divorce and criminal actions. Although percentage fees used to be common in real estate and probate work, the trend in those areas has been to use fixed fees and time charges, respectively.

The use of a contingency fee raises a number of significant issues. Proponents argue that contingency fee agreements allow some clients to bring cases who could not otherwise afford to do so. However, a contingent fee also reduces the amount of the client's award. If the award represents the amount the jury or judge thought adequate to compensate the client for pain and suffering, medical expenses, lost earning capacity, and disfigurement, then any reduction in that award leaves the client without adequate compensation. Also, as the size of the recovery (and hence the size of the fee) increases, the gap widens between what the lawyer would have recovered if charging on an hourly basis and what the lawyer actually recovers based on a contingency fee basis.

In some states, these concerns have been addressed by placing a cap on the amount of contingent fee awards in certain types of cases, such as medical mal-practice, so that as the award increases, the lawyer's percentage decreases. For example, a lawyer might recover 40 percent of any award under $150,000, but only 25 percent of any amount of an award that exceeds $500,000.

As with fixed fees, it is economically advantageous for a law firm to del-egate as much work as possible to paralegals. Such delegation reduces costs without affecting the fees received from the case.

c. Hourly Basis

Many legal fees are based on **hourly rates** rather than on percentages or fixed charges. This is particularly true for litigation defense and corporate work. Hourly charges vary depending on whether the work is done by a paralegal, an associate, or a senior partner. The hourly fee may also vary based on the type of activity. For example, court appearances usually command a higher rate than out-of-court work. The client's best interests are served by having less complex matters delegated to paralegals and paying top dollar only for the matters that require the expertise and experience of a senior partner.

Hourly rate
A fee based on how many hours lawyers or paralegals spend on the case. Different hourly rates are often charged for different lawyers and paralegals within the firm, based on their seniority and experience.

The hourly fees established by the firm reflect its overhead costs, the income expectations of its partners, and the fees charged by competing law firms. Part of the amount collected for an hour of paralegal time pays the para-legal's salary, part pays for office space and secretarial services, and part is the firm's profit.

Both lawyers and clients have attacked the acceptability of billing by the hour. When firms bill by the hour, there is tremendous pressure on lawyers and paralegals to increase their **billable hours.** A number of reports by the American Bar Association have documented a slow shift away from hourly billing, driven by both client demand and lawyer preference.

Billable hours
The number of hours, or parts of an hour, that can be charged to a specific client.

> Hourly billing generally rewards inefficiency and tends to lead lawyers away from employing technological solutions. To meet the new demands that continue to evolve, implementing alternative billing models and technological solutions will ensure the ability to maintain a competitive edge without losing clients.[1]

---

[1] American Bar Association, *2019 Lawyer Wellbeing TechReport* (2019).

DISCUSSION QUESTIONS

1. From the perspective of the client, what are the advantages and disadvantages of using a contingency fee structure?

2. In what ways do you think the various methods of billing affect how willing lawyers are to delegate significant legal work to paralegals?

2. Time and Expense Records

No matter which fee system is used, a law office must maintain adequate time and expense records. If the firm charges an hourly rate for its services, it must document those charges. In cases where a court may order the payment of lawyers' fees, a specific accounting must be made of the time actually spent on the case by different legal personnel. Even when there is a flat fee, the firm needs to have a record of the time spent on the case so that it can determine whether or not it has set its rates at levels that will produce a reasonable profit. In addition to recording the time spent, the firm must keep track of and bill the client for the firm's expenses, such as photocopying, computerized legal research, and postage.

Several systems are used for recording how the time is spent. Many lawyers and paralegals use specialized computer software, some use simple software apps, and others may simply write down their time on a ledger or on notecards. No matter which system is used, throughout the day, the timekeeper (whether lawyer or paralegal) must record everything done on a client's case, typically in six-minute intervals. Although that may seem like an awkward number, it represents one-tenth of an hour and thus simplifies calculation of bills.

Each time record must indicate the date, the name of the client, a description of the nature of the work performed, the initials of the timekeeper, and the time spent on the project. To speed data entry, codes are frequently used for recording services performed. For example, TF stands for *t*elephone call *f*rom; LR, *l*egal *r*esearch; FR, *f*actual *r*esearch; P, *p*reparation of, and so on.

PRACTICE TIP

Record your time as close to when you do the work as possible. If you wait until later, you may find that it is impossible to make an accurate record. This could result in overbilling the client (an obvious ethical problem) or underbilling (a disservice to your firm). Profitable law firms cannot afford to make a regular practice of billing for less time than is actually spent on a case.

As in other areas of law office administration, specialized computer software has been developed to automate the reporting and integration of this data into the firm's billing and cost accounting systems. Typically, these systems allow the timekeeper (the lawyer or paralegal) to directly enter time into the computer, so that the information is automatically linked to a specific case. The computer can also automatically take the time spent and multiply it by the user's hourly rate to arrive at the amount to bill the client.

At whatever intervals the firm and client have agreed upon, the computer software then totals the entire amount owed and prepares an itemized bill. Some systems can also prepare staff paychecks and calculate various partners' contributions to the income of the firm.

Case 1: The Distressed Grandfather (Continued)

Each time Kendall sat down at his computer to work on Drake's case, he first started Abacus and turned on its automatic timer so that it would accurately record how much time he was spending. Whenever his was interrupted, he would turn off the timer, and then start it again when he resumed his work.

By now, you will have noticed that integrated programs like AbacusLaw can perform many case management functions: conflict checks, client contact information, docket control, and timekeeping. This integrated approach is one of the strengths of modern computerized case management programs.

PARALEGAL PROFILE

Angela Ellis Wilde
Paralegal/Legal Forms Manager on the Content Specialist Team
Smokeball

I work for Smokeball, a case management software company for lawyers and their staff. Our clients range from sole practitioners to 15-user firms. Smokeball assists attorneys by organizing all relevant contact information, case information, documents, and e-mails into one digital file. We create individual data files for every case and help attorneys avoid the need for paper files. Our content team is made up of paralegals and attorneys where we use our knowledge and experience of the law to build and maintain the software. My work is a marriage of law and technology.

In addition to case management software, Smokeball has established an extensive forms library where we compile and create legal forms from across the United States. I am responsible for building, compiling, and maintaining Smokeball's Forms Library. Our software integrates with Microsoft Office, specifically Outlook and Microsoft Word. The integration with Word allows me to automate forms with the data already stored in the software. Our clientele spans across the United States, making it imperative to have an understanding of the rules for each jurisdiction. Doing so ensures the forms are properly automated and are legally compliant.

Along with my research on what forms our clients need in a specific area of law I, along with my staff, develop and convert forms to a specific and uniform format. All of our forms must run through the same process of conversion to ensure all forms maintain a consistent look and structure in the software. Once our forms are converted, automated, and published in the software, we must ensure the forms remain up to date in accordance with local rules and statutes. This requires staying current on legislative and judicial changes and making changes as statutes and case law evolve.

I love what I do because no two days are alike, I am exposed to new areas of law, different court structures, and new laws across the United States. I owe the success in my career to achieving my paralegal certificate and gaining unmeasurable experience working in law firms. I was even lucky enough to be the senior paralegal on a personal injury case where we won a $67 million verdict for our client. It is important to remain current, so I actively participate in paralegal committees and regularly attend seminars regarding a variety of different areas of law.

Your knowledge and skills as a paralegal are transferable across many career paths. Becoming a paralegal doesn't mean your only option is to work for a law firm. I took my experience and converted into a technology company — additionally I am also a licensed real estate broker. If you are considering a career in legal services, I cannot stress enough the importance to always network, build relationships, stay informed, and keep your skills sharp. Remember, it is not always what you know, but who.

F. COMPUTERIZED LITIGATION SUPPORT PROGRAMS

Case 1: The Distressed Grandfather (Continued)

During the course of his investigation, Kendall collected numerous documents. As he collected each document, he entered a summary of it into his computer program. This enabled him to sort and search through the information contained in those documents. For example, he could easily sort all of Drake's medical records by date in order to create a chronology of his medical treatment.

Cases that involve litigation provide their own special challenges. As such a case progresses through formal discovery activities, such as interrogatories and depositions, as well as more informal investigation undertakings, a great deal of documentary and witness testimony is generated. To organize such a large volume of information so that any item can be retrieved easily, many firms are turning to computerized litigation support systems. These can be based on a structured database, a full-text database, or a combination of the two.

A **structured database** consists of fields into which the paralegal can enter specific information, such as a client's contact information or a summary of a key document, along with its date, author, and other relevant information. Many law firms use a Microsoft Excel spreadsheet for this purpose. This works well

Structured database
A computerized database that contains key information about the content of documents, such as medical records.

for the entry of objective data, such as the dates a client visited a doctor, but not as well for subjective data, such as a summary of a doctor's report. To be able to see the entire original document, such as the doctor's report, it would be best to use a full-text database.

In a **full-text database**, the entire document, such as a medical record or deposition transcript, is entered into the computer. This allows for searching for any word or phrase contained in the document. Some law firms use the best of both worlds with programs that allow for a structured database that then can be linked to the full text.

The primary advantages of creating a database are as follows:

Full-text database
A computerized database that contains the full text of documents, such as court opinions or depositions.

- The speed and ease with which information can be retrieved. Rather than walking to the file room and searching through file drawers to locate the precise document required, you can find and easily view the document on your computer.
- The number of people who can view the same document at the same time from different locations. With paper files, the number of people who can view a document at any one time is limited to the number of copies that have been made. However, when an electronic database is available on a computer network, multiple users can read the same document at the same time. Network users can have either read-only access, which allows them to view but not alter the document, or read/ write access, which allows the user not only to read, but also to make changes in the document.
- The ease with which you can add or modify information in the file. In a structured database, you enter summary information such as the date of a document, its author, and a brief description of its contents. If you discover that any of the information you entered is not correct, it is a simple matter to edit your entry.
- The decreased amount of physical space required for records storage.
- Finally, the search capabilities of database programs allow you to locate that proverbial needle in the haystack. For example, assume that you remember that a deponent mentioned that your client had seen a psychiatrist or psychologist. That information had not seemed important at the time, but now your supervising lawyer wants to know who said it and in what context. Unfortunately, you do not remember which deponent made that statement, and there were eight deponents who collectively created over a thousand pages of deposition testimony. Using a full-text system, you can type in a search such as "psych*." The * is known as a "wildcard," and it tells the program to search for all words that begin with the letters "psych." Within seconds, the program would search through those hundreds of deposition pages and produce a list of all the question-answer pairs that contain any variation of a word beginning with "psych," such as "psychiatrist" or "psychologist." You could then print out those question-answer pairs so that your supervising lawyer could see the context in which the word "psychiatrist" or "psychologist" was used.

SUMMARY

Case management involves the handling of the information involved in cases within the law office. All documents and case materials must be organized so as to allow for easy, fast, and accurate retrieval. While there are variations among offices, the same basic types of files will be kept in most law offices. These include client files, work product files, tickler systems, and timekeeping and billing records.

Sophisticated software programs have greatly increased office automation. This has reduced the number of clerical personnel needed to operate a law office and has opened new opportunities for paralegals to increase their effectiveness. Integrated programs that combine the ability to manage conflict checks, client information, timekeeping, and docket control are particularly useful. Litigators dealing with massive amounts of information can also benefit from litigation support programs.

REVIEW QUESTIONS

Pages 513 through 517
1. What is "cloud" computing?
2. What is case management?
3. What is the purpose of performing a conflict check? Why is a computerized conflict check more reliable than manual methods?

Pages 517 through 519
4. Why should client files not be labeled with the client name?
5. What might a typical client file contain?
6. What is a tickler system, and why is it important? What are the benefits of a computerized tickler system over a manual system?
7. Why is it not a good idea to simply reuse old documents for a different client's case?
8. What are the advantages of using a document assembly program?

Pages 519 through 524
9. Why is it important for paralegals to record the time they spend?
10. Why is it important to bill a client promptly once work is completed?
11. Describe the three traditional billing methods. Give an example of when each type of billing method is most commonly used.
12. What are the problems with hourly billing?
13. What are the problems with contingency fee billing?

Pages 524 through 526
14. What are the advantages of computerized litigation support programs?
15. Describe the differences between a structured and a full-text database.

WEB EXERCISES

1. Google "legal case management software reviews," and take note of how many reviews are available. Based on reading at least three of these reviews, which programs appear to be the most popular? What makes them popular?

2. Watch the YouTube video "How to Choose a Law Practice Management System (Lens #29)," produced by Lawyerist at *youtube.com/watch?v=fFdK6SHdoaU*. On their website, find their page on law practice management software and compare software. Choose one of the software programs and find an online video about that product. What are the pros and cons of the software that you chose? Is there a type of law that would work best with the software that you chose?

Appendixes

Appendix A

The Constitution of the United States

We the People of the United States, in Order to form a more perfect Union, establish Justice, insure domestic Tranquility, provide for the common defense, promote the general Welfare, and secure the Blessings of Liberty to ourselves and our Posterity, do ordain and establish this Constitution for the United States of America.

Article I

Section 1. All legislative Powers herein granted shall be vested in a Congress of the United States, which shall consist of a Senate and House of Representatives.

Section 2. The House of Representatives shall be composed of Members chosen every second Year by the People of the several States, and the Electors in each State shall have the Qualifications requisite for Electors of the most numerous Branch of the State Legislature.

No Person shall be a Representative who shall not have attained to the Age of twenty five Years, and been seven Years a Citizen of the United States, and who shall not, when elected, be an Inhabitant of that State in which he shall be chosen.

Representatives and direct Taxes shall be apportioned among the several States which may be included within this Union, according to their respective Numbers, which shall be determined by adding to the whole Number of free Persons, including those bound to Service for a Term of Years, and excluding Indians not taxed, three fifths of all other Persons. The actual Enumeration shall be made within three Years after the first Meeting of the Congress of the United States, and within every subsequent Term of ten Years, in such Manner as they shall by Law direct. The Number of Representatives shall not exceed one for every thirty Thousand, but each State shall have at Least one Representative; and until such enumeration shall be made, the State of New Hampshire shall be entitled to chuse three, Massachusetts eight, Rhode-Island and Providence Plantations one, Connecticut five, New-York six, New Jersey four, Pennsylvania eight, Delaware one, Maryland six, Virginia ten, North Carolina five, South Carolina five, and Georgia three.

When vacancies happen in the Representation from any State, the Executive Authority thereof shall issue Writs of Election to fill such Vacancies.

The House of Representatives shall chuse their Speaker and other Officers; and shall have the sole Power of Impeachment.

Section 3. The Senate of the United States shall be composed of two Senators from each State, chosen by the Legislature thereof, for six Years; and each Senator shall have one Vote.

Immediately after they shall be assembled in Consequence of the first Election, they shall be divided as equally as may be into three Classes. The Seats of the Senators of the first Class shall be vacated at the Expiration of the second Year, of the second Class at the Expiration of the fourth Year, and of the third Class at the Expiration of the sixth Year, so that one third may be chosen every second Year; and if Vacancies happen by Resignation, or otherwise, during the Recess of the Legislature of any State, the Executive thereof may make temporary Appointments until the next Meeting of the Legislature, which shall then fill such Vacancies.

No Person shall be a Senator who shall not have attained to the Age of thirty Years, and been nine Years a Citizen of the United States, and who shall not, when elected, be an Inhabitant of that State for which he shall be chosen.

The Vice President of the United States shall be President of the Senate, but shall have no Vote, unless they be equally divided.

The Senate shall chuse their other Officers, and also a President pro tempore, in the Absence of the Vice President, or when he shall exercise the Office of President of the United States.

The Senate shall have the sole Power to try all Impeachments. When sitting for that Purpose, they shall be on Oath or Affirmation. When the President of the United States is tried, the Chief Justice shall preside: And no Person shall be convicted without the Concurrence of two thirds of the Members present.

Judgment in Cases of Impeachment shall not extend further than to removal from Office, and disqualification to hold and enjoy any Office of honor, Trust or Profit under the United States: but the Party convicted shall nevertheless be liable and subject to Indictment, Trial, Judgment and Punishment, according to Law.

Section 4. The Times, Places and Manner of holding Elections for Senators and Representatives, shall be prescribed in each State by the Legislature thereof; but the Congress may at any time by Law make or alter such Regulations, except as to the Places of chusing Senators.

The Congress shall assemble at least once in every Year, and such Meeting shall be on the first Monday in December, unless they shall by Law appoint a different Day.

Section 5. Each House shall be the Judge of the Elections, Returns and Qualifications of its own Members, and a Majority of each shall constitute a Quorum to do Business; but a smaller Number may adjourn from day to day, and may be authorized to compel the Attendance of absent Members, in such Manner, and under such Penalties as each House may provide.

Each House may determine the Rules of its Proceedings, punish its Members for disorderly Behaviour, and, with the Concurrence of two thirds, expel a Member.

Each House shall keep a Journal of its Proceedings, and from time to time publish the same, excepting such Parts as may in their Judgment require Secrecy; and the Yeas and Nays of the Members of either House on any question shall, at the Desire of one fifth of those Present, be entered on the Journal.

Neither House, during the Session of Congress, shall, without the Consent of the other, adjourn for more than three days, nor to any other Place than that in which the two Houses shall be sitting.

Section 6. The Senators and Representatives shall receive a Compensation for their Services, to be ascertained by Law, and paid out of the Treasury of the United States. They shall in all Cases, except Treason, Felony and Breach of the Peace, be privileged from Arrest during their Attendance at the Session of their respective Houses, and in going to and returning from the same; and for any Speech or Debate in either House, they shall not be questioned in any other Place.

No Senator or Representative shall, during the Time for which he was elected, be appointed to any civil Office under the Authority of the United States, which shall have been created, or the Emoluments whereof shall have been increased during such time; and no Person holding any Office under the United States, shall be a Member of either House during his Continuance in Office.

Section 7. All Bills for raising Revenue shall originate in the House of Representatives; but the Senate may propose or concur with Amendments as on other Bills.

Every Bill which shall have passed the House of Representatives and the Senate, shall, before it become a Law, be presented to the President of the United States: If he approve he shall sign it, but if not he shall return it, with his Objections to that House in which it shall have originated, who shall enter the Objections at large on their Journal, and proceed to reconsider it. If after such Reconsideration two thirds of that House shall agree to pass the Bill, it shall be sent, together with the Objections, to the other House, by which it shall likewise be reconsidered, and if approved by two thirds of that House, it shall become a Law. But in all such Cases the Votes of both Houses shall be determined by Yeas and Nays, and the Names of the Persons voting for and against the Bill shall be entered on the Journal of each House respectively. If any Bill shall not be returned by the President within ten Days (Sundays excepted) after it shall have been presented to him, the Same shall be a Law, in like Manner as if he had signed it, unless the Congress by their Adjournment prevent its Return, in which Case it shall not be a Law.

Every Order, Resolution, or Vote to which the Concurrence of the Senate and House of Representatives may be necessary (except on a question of Adjournment) shall be presented to the President of the United States; and before the Same shall take Effect, shall be approved by him, or being disapproved by him, shall be repassed by two thirds of the Senate and House of Representatives, according to the Rules and Limitations prescribed in the Case of a Bill.

Section 8. The Congress shall have Power To lay and collect Taxes, Duties, Imposts and Excises, to pay the Debts and provide for the common Defence and general Welfare of the United States; but all Duties, Imposts and Excises shall be uniform throughout the United States; To borrow Money on the credit of the United States; To regulate Commerce with foreign Nations, and among the several States, and with the Indian Tribes; To establish an uniform Rule of Naturalization, and uniform Laws on the subject of Bankruptcies throughout the United States; To coin Money, regulate the Value thereof, and of foreign Coin, and fix the Standard of Weights and Measures; To provide for the Punishment of counterfeiting the Securities and current Coin of the United States; To establish Post Offices and post Roads; To promote the Progress of Science and useful Arts, by securing for limited Times to Authors and Inventors the exclusive Right to their respective Writings and Discoveries; To constitute Tribunals inferior to the supreme Court; To define and punish Piracies and Felonies committed on the high Seas, and Offences against the Law of Nations; To declare War, grant Letters of Marque and Reprisal, and make Rules concerning Captures on Land and Water; To raise and support Armies, but no Appropriation of Money to that Use shall be for a longer Term than two Years; To provide and maintain a Navy; To make Rules for the Government and Regulation of the land and naval Forces; To provide for calling forth the Militia to execute the Laws of the Union, suppress Insurrections and repel Invasions; To provide for organizing, arming, and disciplining, the Militia, and for governing such Part of them as may be employed in the Service of the United States, reserving to the States respectively, the Appointment of the Officers, and the Authority of training the Militia according to the discipline prescribed by Congress; To exercise exclusive Legislation in all Cases whatsoever, over such District (not exceeding ten Miles square) as may, by Cession of particular States, and the Acceptance of Congress, become the Seat of the Government of the United States, and to exercise like Authority over all Places purchased by the Consent of the Legislature of the State in which the Same shall be, for the Erection of Forts, Magazines, Arsenals, dock-Yards, and other needful Buildings; — And To make all Laws which shall be necessary and proper for carrying into Execution the foregoing Powers, and all other Powers vested by this Constitution in the Government of the United States, or in any Department or Officer thereof.

Section 9. The Migration or Importation of such Persons as any of the States now existing shall think proper to admit, shall not be prohibited by the Congress prior to the Year one thousand eight hundred and eight, but a Tax or duty may be imposed on such Importation, not exceeding ten dollars for each Person.

The Privilege of the Writ of Habeas Corpus shall not be suspended, unless when in Cases of Rebellion or Invasion the public Safety may require it.

No Bill of Attainder or ex post facto Law shall be passed.

No Capitation, or other direct, Tax shall be laid, unless in Proportion to the Census or enumeration herein before directed to be taken.

No Tax or Duty shall be laid on Articles exported from any State.

No Preference shall be given by any Regulation of Commerce or Revenue to the Ports of one State over those of another; nor shall Vessels bound to, or from, one State, be obliged to enter, clear, or pay Duties in another.

No Money shall be drawn from the Treasury, but in Consequence of Appropriations made by Law; and a regular Statement and Account of the Receipts and Expenditures of all public Money shall be published from time to time.

No Title of Nobility shall be granted by the United States: And no Person holding any Office of Profit or Trust under them, shall, without the Consent of the Congress, accept of any present, Emolument, Office, or Title, of any kind whatever, from any King, Prince, or foreign State.

Section 10. No State shall enter into any Treaty, Alliance, or Confederation; grant Letters of Marque and Reprisal; coin Money; emit Bills of Credit; make any Thing but gold and silver Coin a Tender in Payment of Debts; pass any Bill of Attainder, ex post facto Law, or Law impairing the Obligation of Contracts, or grant any Title of Nobility.

No State shall, without the Consent of the Congress, lay any Imposts or Duties on Imports or Exports, except what may be absolutely necessary for executing it's inspection Laws: and the net Produce of all Duties and Imposts, laid by any State on Imports or Exports, shall be for the Use of the Treasury of the United States; and all such Laws shall be subject to the Revision and Control of the Congress.

No State shall, without the Consent of Congress, lay any Duty of Tonnage, keep Troops, or Ships of War in time of Peace, enter into any Agreement or Compact with another State, or with a foreign Power, or engage in War, unless actually invaded, or in such imminent Danger as will not admit of delay.

Article II

Section 1. The executive Power shall be vested in a President of the United States of America. He shall hold his Office during the Term of four Years, and, together with the Vice President, chosen for the same Term, be elected, as follows:

Each State shall appoint, in such Manner as the Legislature thereof may direct, a Number of Electors, equal to the whole Number of Senators and Representatives to which the State may be entitled in the Congress: but no Senator or Representative, or Person holding an Office of Trust or Profit under the United States, shall be appointed an Elector.

The Electors shall meet in their respective States, and vote by Ballot for two Persons, of whom one at least shall not be an Inhabitant of the same State with themselves. And they shall make a List of all the Persons voted for, and of the Number of Votes for each; which List they shall sign and certify, and transmit sealed to the Seat of the Government of the United States, directed to the President of the Senate. The President of the Senate shall, in the Presence of the Senate and House of Representatives, open all the Certificates, and the Votes shall then be counted. The Person having the greatest Number of Votes shall be the President, if such Number be a Majority of the whole Number of Electors appointed; and if there be more than one who have such Majority, and have an equal Number of Votes, then the House of Representatives shall immediately chuse by Ballot one of them for President; and if no Person have a Majority, then from the five highest on the List the said House shall in like Manner chuse the President. But in chusing the President, the Votes shall be taken by States, the Representation from each State having one Vote; A quorum for this purpose shall consist of a Member or Members from two thirds of the States, and a Majority of all the States shall be necessary to a Choice. In every Case, after the Choice of the President, the Person having the greatest Number of Votes of the Electors shall be the Vice President. But if there should remain two or more who have equal Votes, the Senate shall chuse from them by Ballot the Vice President.

The Congress may determine the Time of chusing the Electors, and the Day on which they shall give their Votes; which Day shall be the same throughout the United States.

No Person except a natural born Citizen, or a Citizen of the United States, at the time of the Adoption of this Constitution, shall be eligible to the Office of President; neither shall any Person be eligible to that Office who shall not have attained to the Age of thirty five Years, and been fourteen Years a Resident within the United States.

In Case of the Removal of the President from Office, or of his Death, Resignation, or Inability to discharge the Powers and Duties of the said Office, the Same shall devolve on the Vice President, and the Congress may by Law provide for the Case of Removal, Death, Resignation or Inability, both of the President and Vice President, declaring what Officer shall then act as President, and such Officer shall act accordingly, until the Disability be removed, or a President shall be elected.

The President shall, at stated Times, receive for his Services, a Compensation, which shall neither be increased nor diminished during the Period for which he shall have been elected, and he shall not receive within that Period any other Emolument from the United States, or any of them.

Before he enter on the Execution of his Office, he shall take the following Oath or Affirmation: "I do solemnly swear (or affirm) that I will faithfully execute the Office of President of the United States, and will to the best of my Ability, preserve, protect and defend the Constitution of the United States."

Section 2. The President shall be Commander in Chief of the Army and Navy of the United States, and of the Militia of the several States, when called into the actual Service of the United States; he may require the Opinion, in writing, of the principal Officer in each of the executive Departments, upon any Subject relating to the Duties of their respective Offices, and he shall have Power to grant Reprieves and Pardons for Offences against the United States, except in Cases of Impeachment.

He shall have Power, by and with the Advice and Consent of the Senate, to make Treaties, provided two thirds of the Senators present concur; and he shall nominate, and by and with the Advice and Consent of the Senate, shall appoint Ambassadors, other public Ministers and Consuls, Judges of the supreme Court, and all other Officers of the United States, whose Appointments are not herein otherwise provided for, and which shall be established by Law: but the Congress may by Law vest the Appointment of such inferior Officers, as they think proper, in the President alone, in the Courts of Law, or in the Heads of Departments.

The President shall have Power to fill up all Vacancies that may happen during the Recess of the Senate, by granting Commissions which shall expire at the End of their next Session.

Section 3. He shall from time to time give to the Congress Information of the State of the Union, and recommend to their Consideration such Measures as he shall judge necessary and expedient; he may, on extraordinary Occasions, convene both Houses, or either of them, and in Case of Disagreement between them, with Respect to the Time of Adjournment, he may adjourn them to such Time as he shall think proper; he shall receive Ambassadors and other public Ministers; he shall take Care that the Laws be faithfully executed, and shall Commission all the Officers of the United States.

Section 4. The President, Vice President and all civil Officers of the United States, shall be removed from Office on Impeachment for, and Conviction of, Treason, Bribery, or other high Crimes and Misdemeanors.

Article III

Section 1. The judicial Power of the United States shall be vested in one supreme Court, and in such inferior Courts as the Congress may from time to time ordain and establish. The Judges, both of the supreme and inferior Courts, shall hold their Offices during good Behaviour, and shall, at stated Times, receive for their Services a Compensation, which shall not be diminished during their Continuance in Office.

Section 2. The Judicial Power shall extend to all Cases, in Law and Equity, arising under this Constitution, the Laws of the United States, and Treaties made, or which shall be made, under their Authority; — to all Cases affecting Ambassadors, other public Ministers and Consuls; — to all Cases of admiralty and maritime Jurisdiction; — to Controversies to which the United States shall be a Party; — to Controversies between two or more States; — between a State and Citizens of another State; — between Citizens of different States; — between Citizens of the same State claiming Lands under Grants of different States, and between a State, or the Citizens thereof, and foreign States, Citizens or Subjects.

In all Cases affecting Ambassadors, other public Ministers and Consuls, and those in which a State shall be Party, the supreme Court shall have original Jurisdiction. In all the other Cases before mentioned, the supreme Court shall have appellate Jurisdiction, both as to Law and Fact, with such Exceptions, and under such Regulations as the Congress shall make.

The Trial of all Crimes, except in Cases of Impeachment, shall be by Jury; and such Trial shall be held in the State where the said Crimes shall have been committed; but when not committed within any State, the Trial shall be at such Place or Places as the Congress may by Law have directed.

Section 3. Treason against the United States, shall consist only in levying War against them, or in adhering to their Enemies, giving them Aid and Comfort. No Person shall be convicted of Treason unless on the Testimony of two Witnesses to the same overt Act, or on Confession in open Court.

The Congress shall have Power to declare the Punishment of Treason, but no Attainder of Treason shall work Corruption of Blood, or Forfeiture except during the Life of the Person attainted.

Article IV

Section 1. Full Faith and Credit shall be given in each State to the public Acts, Records, and judicial Proceedings of every other State. And the Congress may by general Laws prescribe the Manner in which such Acts, Records and Proceedings shall be proved, and the Effect thereof.

Section 2. The Citizens of each State shall be entitled to all Privileges and Immunities of Citizens in the several States.

A Person charged in any State with Treason, Felony, or other Crime, who shall flee from Justice, and be found in another State, shall on Demand of the executive Authority of the State from which he fled, be delivered up, to be removed to the State having Jurisdiction of the Crime.

No Person held to Service or Labour in one State, under the Laws thereof, escaping into another, shall, in Consequence of any Law or Regulation therein, be discharged from such Service or Labour, but shall be delivered up on Claim of the Party to whom such Service or Labour may be due.

Section 3. New States may be admitted by the Congress into this Union; but no new State shall be formed or erected within the Jurisdiction of any other State; nor any State be formed by the Junction of two or more States, or Parts of States, without the Consent of the Legislatures of the States concerned as well as of the Congress.

The Congress shall have Power to dispose of and make all needful Rules and Regulations respecting the Territory or other Property belonging to the United States; and nothing in this Constitution shall be so construed as to Prejudice any Claims of the United States, or of any particular State.

Section 4. The United States shall guarantee to every State in this Union a Republican Form of Government, and shall protect each of them against Invasion; and on Application of the Legislature, or of the Executive (when the Legislature cannot be convened), against domestic Violence.

Article V

The Congress, whenever two thirds of both Houses shall deem it necessary, shall propose Amendments to this Constitution, or, on the Application of the Legislatures of two thirds of the several States, shall call a Convention for proposing Amendments, which, in either Case, shall be valid to all Intents and Purposes, as Part of this Constitution, when ratified by the Legislatures of three fourths of the several States, or by Conventions in three fourths thereof, as the one or the other Mode of Ratification may be proposed by the Congress; Provided that no Amendment which may be made prior to the Year One thousand eight hundred and eight shall in any Manner affect the first and fourth Clauses in the Ninth Section of the first Article; and that no State, without its Consent, shall be deprived of its equal Suffrage in the Senate.

Article VI

All Debts contracted and Engagements entered into, before the Adoption of this Constitution, shall be as valid against the United States under this Constitution, as under the Confederation.

This Constitution, and the Laws of the United States which shall be made in Pursuance thereof; and all Treaties made, or which shall be made, under the Authority of the United States, shall be the supreme Law of the Land; and the Judges in every State shall be bound thereby, any Thing in the Constitution or Laws of any State to the Contrary notwithstanding.

The Senators and Representatives before mentioned, and the Members of the several State Legislatures, and all executive and judicial Officers, both of the United States and of the several States, shall be bound by Oath or Affirmation, to support this Constitution; but no religious Test shall ever be required as a Qualification to any Office or public Trust under the United States.

Article VII

The Ratification of the Conventions of nine States, shall be sufficient for the Establishment of this Constitution between the States so ratifying the Same. Done in Convention by the Unanimous Consent of the States present the Seventeenth Day of September in the Year of our Lord one thousand seven hundred and Eighty seven and of the Independence of the United States of America the Twelfth.

ARTICLES IN ADDITION TO, AND AMENDMENT OF THE CONSTITUTION OF THE UNITED STATES OF AMERICA, PROPOSED BY CONGRESS, AND RATIFIED BY THE LEGISLATURES OF THE SEVERAL STATES, PURSUANT TO THE FIFTH ARTICLE OF THE ORIGINAL CONSTITUTION

Amendment I [1791]

Congress shall make no law respecting an establishment of religion, or prohibiting the free exercise thereof; or abridging the freedom of speech, or of the press; or the right of the people peaceably to assemble, and to petition the Government for a redress of grievances.

Amendment II [1791]

A well regulated Militia, being necessary to the security of a free State, the right of the people to keep and bear Arms, shall not be infringed.

Amendment III [1791]

No Soldier shall, in time of peace be quartered in any house, without the consent of the Owner, nor in time of war, but in a manner to be prescribed by law.

Amendment IV [1791]

The right of the people to be secure in their persons, houses, papers, and effects, against unreasonable searches and seizures, shall not be violated, and no Warrants shall issue, but upon probable cause, supported by Oath or affirmation, and particularly describing the place to be searched, and the persons or things to be seized.

Amendment V [1791]

No person shall be held to answer for a capital, or otherwise infamous crime, unless on a presentment or indictment of a Grand Jury, except in cases arising in the land or naval forces, or in the Militia, when in actual service in time of War or public danger; nor shall any person be subject for the same offence to be twice put in jeopardy of life or limb; nor shall be compelled in any criminal case to be a witness against himself, nor be deprived of life, liberty, or property, without due process of law; nor shall private property be taken for public use, without just compensation.

Amendment VI [1791]

In all criminal prosecutions, the accused shall enjoy the right to a speedy and public trial, by an impartial jury of the State and district wherein the crime shall have been committed, which district shall have been previously ascertained by law, and to be informed of the nature and cause of the accusation; to be confronted with the witnesses against him; to have compulsory process for obtaining witnesses in his favor, and to have the Assistance of Counsel for his defence.

Amendment VII [1791]

In suits at common law, where the value in controversy shall exceed twenty dollars, the right of trial by jury shall be preserved, and no fact tried by a jury, shall be otherwise reexamined in any Court of the United States, than according to the rules of the common law.

Amendment VIII [1791]

Excessive bail shall not be required, nor excessive fines imposed, nor cruel and unusual punishments inflicted.

Amendment IX [1791]

The enumeration in the Constitution, of certain rights, shall not be construed to deny or disparage others retained by the people.

Amendment X [1791]

The powers not delegated to the United States by the Constitution, nor prohibited by it to the States, are reserved to the States respectively, or to the people.

Amendment XI [1798]

The Judicial power of the United States shall not be construed to extend to any suit in law or equity, commenced or prosecuted against one of the United States by Citizens of another State, or by Citizens or Subjects of any Foreign State.

Amendment XII [1804]

The Electors shall meet in their respective states and vote by ballot for President and Vice-President, one of whom, at least, shall not be an inhabitant of the same state with themselves; they shall name in their ballots the person voted for as President, and in distinct ballots the person voted for as Vice-President, and they shall make distinct lists of all persons voted for as President, and of all persons voted for as Vice-President, and of the number of votes for each, which lists they shall sign and certify, and transmit sealed to the seat of the government of the United States, directed to the President of the Senate; — the President of the Senate shall, in the presence of the Senate and House of Representatives, open all the certificates and the votes shall then be counted; — The person having the greatest number of votes for President, shall be the President, if such number be a majority of the whole number of Electors appointed; and if no person have such majority, then from the persons having the highest numbers not exceeding three on the list of those voted for as President, the House of Representatives shall chuse immediately, by ballot, the President. But in chusing the President, the votes shall be taken by states, the representation from each state having one vote; a quorum for this purpose shall consist of a member or members from two-thirds of the states, and a majority of all the states shall be necessary to a choice. [And if the House of Representatives shall not chuse a President whenever the right of choice shall devolve upon them, before the fourth day of March next following, then the Vice-President shall act as President, as in case of the death or other constitutional disability of the President. — The person having the greatest number of votes as Vice-President, shall be the Vice-President, if such number be a majority of the whole number of Electors appointed, and if no person have a majority, then from the two highest numbers on the list, the Senate shall choose the Vice-President; a quorum for the purpose shall consist of two-thirds of the whole number of Senators, and a majority of the whole number shall be necessary to a choice. But no person constitutionally ineligible to the office of President shall be eligible to that of Vice-President of the United States.

Amendment XIII [1865]

Section 1. Neither slavery nor involuntary servitude, except as a punishment for crime whereof the party shall have been duly convicted, shall exist within the United States, or any place subject to their jurisdiction.

Section 2. Congress shall have power to enforce this article by appropriate legislation.

Amendment XIV [1868]

Section 1. All persons born or naturalized in the United States, and subject to the jurisdiction thereof, are citizens of the United States and of the State wherein they reside. No State shall make or enforce any law which shall abridge the privileges or immunities of citizens of the United States; nor shall any State deprive any person of life, liberty, or property, without due process of law; nor deny to any person within its jurisdiction the equal protection of the laws.

Section 2. Representatives shall be apportioned among the several States according to their respective numbers, counting the whole number of persons in each State, excluding Indians not taxed. But when the right to vote at any election for the choice of electors for President and Vice-President of the United States, Representatives in Congress, the Executive and Judicial officers of a State, or the members of the Legislature thereof, is denied to any of the male inhabitants of such State, being twenty-one years of age, and citizens of the United States, or in any way abridged, except for participation in rebellion, or other crime, the basis of representation therein shall be reduced in the proportion which the number of such male citizens shall bear to the whole number of male citizens twenty-one years of age in such State.

Section 3. No person shall be a Senator or Representative in Congress, or elector of President and Vice-President, or hold any office, civil or military, under the United States, or under any State, who, having previously taken an oath, as a member of Congress, or as an officer of the United States, or as a member of any State legislature, or as an executive or judicial officer of any State, to support the Constitution of the United States, shall have engaged in insurrection or rebellion against the same, or given aid or comfort to the enemies thereof. But Congress may by a vote of two-thirds of each House, remove such disability.

Section 4. The validity of the public debt of the United States, authorized by law, including debts incurred for payment of pensions and bounties for services in suppressing insurrection or rebellion, shall not be questioned. But neither the United States nor any State shall assume or pay any debt or obligation incurred in aid of insurrection or rebellion against the United States, or any claim for the loss or emancipation of any slave; but all such debts, obligations and claims shall be held illegal and void.

Section 5. The Congress shall have the power to enforce, by appropriate legislation, the provisions of this article.

Amendment XV [1870]

Section 1. The right of citizens of the United States to vote shall not be denied or abridged by the United States or by any State on account of race, color, or previous condition of servitude.

Section 2. The Congress shall have the power to enforce this article by appropriate legislation.

Amendment XVI [1913]

The Congress shall have power to lay and collect taxes on incomes, from whatever source derived, without apportionment among the several States, and without regard to any census or enumeration.

Amendment XVII [1913]

The Senate of the United States shall be composed of two Senators from each State, elected by the people thereof, for six years; and each Senator shall have one vote. The electors in each State shall have the qualifications requisite for electors of the most numerous branch of the State legislatures.

When vacancies happen in the representation of any State in the Senate, the executive authority of such State shall issue writs of election to fill such vacancies: *Provided,* That the legislature of any State may empower the executive thereof to make temporary appointments until the people fill the vacancies by election as the legislature may direct.

This amendment shall not be so construed as to affect the election or term of any Senator chosen before it becomes valid as part of the Constitution.

Amendment XVIII [1919]

Section 1. After one year from the ratification of this article the manufacture, sale, or transportation of intoxicating liquors within, the importation thereof into, or the exportation thereof from the United States and all territory subject to the jurisdiction thereof for beverage purposes is hereby prohibited.

Section 2. The Congress and the several States shall have concurrent power to enforce this article by appropriate legislation.

Section 3. This article shall be inoperative unless it shall have been ratified as an amendment to the Constitution by the legislatures of the several States, as provided in the Constitution, within seven years from the date of the submission hereof to the States by the Congress.

Amendment XIX [1920]

The right of citizens of the United States to vote shall not be denied or abridged by the United States or by any State on account of sex.

Congress shall have power to enforce this article by appropriate legislation.

Amendment XX [1933]

Section 1. The terms of the President and the Vice President shall end at noon on the 20th day of January, and the terms of Senators and Representatives at noon on the 3d day of January, of the years in which such terms would have ended if this article had not been ratified; and the terms of their successors shall then begin.

Section 2. The Congress shall assemble at least once in every year, and such meeting shall begin at noon on the 3d day of January, unless they shall by law appoint a different day.

Section 3. If, at the time fixed for the beginning of the term of the President, the President elect shall have died, the Vice President elect shall become President. If a President shall not have been chosen before the time fixed for the beginning of his term, or if the President elect shall have failed to qualify, then the Vice President elect shall act as President until a President shall have qualified; and the Congress may by law provide for the case wherein neither a President elect nor a Vice President shall have qualified, declaring who shall then act as President, or the manner in which one who is to act shall be selected, and such person shall act accordingly until a President or Vice President shall have qualified.

Section 4. The Congress may by law provide for the case of the death of any of the persons from whom the House of Representatives may chuse a President whenever the right of choice shall have devolved upon them, and for the case of the death of any of the persons from whom the Senate may chuse a Vice President whenever the right of choice shall have devolved upon them.

Section 5. Sections 1 and 2 shall take effect on the 15th day of October following the ratification of this article.

Section 6. This article shall be inoperative unless it shall have been ratified as an amendment to the Constitution by the legislatures of three-fourths of the several States within seven years from the date of its submission.

Amendment XXI [1933]

Section 1. The eighteenth article of amendment to the Constitution of the United States is hereby repealed.

Section 2. The transportation or importation into any State, Territory, or Possession of the United States for delivery or use therein of intoxicating liquors, in violation of the laws thereof, is hereby prohibited.

Section 3. This article shall be inoperative unless it shall have been ratified as an amendment to the Constitution by conventions in the several States, as provided in the Constitution, within seven years from the date of the submission hereof to the States by the Congress.

Amendment XXII [1951]

Section 1. No person shall be elected to the office of the President more than twice, and no person who has held the office of President, or acted as President, for more than two years of a term to which some other person was elected President shall be elected to the office of President more than once. But this Article shall not apply to any person holding the office of President when this Article was proposed by Congress, and shall not prevent any person who may be holding the office of President, or acting as President, during the term within which this Article becomes operative from holding the office of President or acting as President during the remainder of such term.

Section 2. This article shall be inoperative unless it shall have been ratified as an amendment to the Constitution by the legislatures of three-fourths of the several States within seven years from the date of its submission to the States by Congress.

Amendment XXIII [1961]

Section 1. The District constituting the seat of Government of the United States shall appoint in such manner as Congress may direct: A number of electors of President and Vice President equal to the whole number of Senators and Representatives in Congress to which the District would be entitled if it were a State, but in no event more than the least populous State; they shall be in addition to those appointed by the States, but they shall be considered, for the purposes of the election of President and Vice President, to be electors appointed by a State; and they shall meet in the District and perform such duties as provided by the twelfth article of amendment.

Section 2. The Congress shall have power to enforce this article by appropriate legislation.

Amendment XXIV [1964]

Section 1. The right of citizens of the United States to vote in any primary or other election for President or Vice President, for electors for President or Vice President, or for Senator or Representative in Congress, shall not be denied or abridged by the United States or any State by reason of failure to pay poll tax or other tax.

Section 2. The Congress shall have power to enforce this article by appropriate legislation.

Amendment XXV [1967]

Section 1. In case of the removal of the President from office or of his death or resignation, the Vice President shall become President.

Section 2. Whenever there is a vacancy in the office of the Vice President, the President shall nominate a Vice President who shall take office upon confirmation by a majority vote of both Houses of Congress.

Section 3. Whenever the President transmits to the President pro tempore of the Senate and the Speaker of the House of Representatives his written declaration that he is unable to discharge the powers and duties of his office, and until he transmits to them a written declaration to the contrary, such powers and duties shall be discharged by the Vice President as Acting President.

Section 4. Whenever the Vice President and a majority of either the principal officers of the executive departments or of such other body as Congress may by law provide, transmit to the President pro tempore of the Senate and the Speaker of the House of Representatives their written declaration that the President is unable to discharge the powers and duties of his office, the Vice President shall immediately assume the powers and duties of the office as Acting President.

Thereafter, when the President transmits to the President pro tempore of the Senate and the Speaker of the House of Representatives his written declaration that no inability exists, he shall resume the powers and duties of his office unless the Vice President and a majority of either the principal officers of the executive department or of such other body as Congress may by law provide, transmit within four days to the President pro tempore of the Senate and the Speaker of the House of Representatives their written declaration that the President is unable to discharge the powers and duties of his office. Thereupon Congress shall decide the issue, assembling within forty-eight hours for that purpose if not in session. If the Congress, within twenty-one days after receipt of the latter written declaration, or, if Congress is not in session, within twenty-one days after Congress is required to assemble, determines by two-thirds vote of both Houses that the President is unable to discharge the powers and duties of his office, the Vice President shall continue to discharge the same as Acting President; otherwise, the President shall resume the powers and duties of his office.

Amendment XXVI [1971]

Section 1. The right of citizens of the United States, who are eighteen years of age or older, to vote shall not be denied or abridged by the United States or by any State on account of age.

Section 2. The Congress shall have power to enforce this article by appropriate legislation.

Amendment XXVII [1992]

No law, varying the compensation for the services of the Senators and Representatives, shall take effect, until an election of representatives shall have intervened.

Appendix B

Fundamentals of Good Writing

*I have made this letter longer than usual, only because
I have not had the time to make it shorter.*
Blaise Pascal

INTRODUCTION

How you say something is often as important as what you say. No matter how insightful and intelligent your thoughts are, if your writing is filled with misspellings and grammar errors, the reader will very likely discount the value of what you are saying. In legal writing, good writing is especially important because people's fortunes often rest on what a lawyer or a paralegal has written. In legal writing, therefore, it is simply too costly to write in any style other than one that is clear, concise, and grammatically correct.

To be an effective writer, follow these simple rules:

Rule 1	Develop a clear, readable writing style that is appropriate for the audience to whom it is directed. This partly depends on an awareness of the ways in which legal writing differs from more informal writing and speech.
Rule 2	Always use good grammar and proper punctuation. The law is a profession of words. Precision is necessary in order to make certain that the meaning of each sentence you write is clear and unambiguous. If you do not follow the basic conventions of correct spelling and grammar, the meaning of your writing may not be clear and that could have profound legal consequences.

Rule 3   Carefully proofread what you have written. Take advantage of any spell-checking or grammar programs associated with the word-processing software you use, but do not rely on these programs alone. A spell checker will not find correctly spelled but misused words. For example, a spell checker would find nothing wrong with this sentence: "The witness recounted the hole story."

Rule 4   Write and rewrite and then rewrite again. There is no such thing as good writing, only good rewriting. For those of you who suffer from writer's block, this is actually good news. Sometimes people are afraid to start writing because they assume what they initially write will be the final product. It is not.

This appendix is designed to help you improve the style and technical quality of your writing so that your work will be as professional looking as possible.

PART I: GRAMMAR

Good legal writing starts by being good writing, period. Therefore, to rate as good legal writing, the document must follow the normal rules of grammar and punctuation. The following suggestions should help you correct the most common grammar errors.

A. USE PROPER SENTENCE STRUCTURE

Using proper sentence structure will make your writing easier to comprehend. Proper sentence structure means using simple sentence construction, avoiding sentence fragments and run-ons, and using parallel constructions.

1. Use Simple Sentence Construction

Whenever possible, stick to simple sentences. Legal writing is hard enough to read without complicating it further through long, convoluted sentences. Follow these guidelines:

a. Use normal sentence order

Unless there is a good reason to do otherwise, follow normal sentence order: noun, verb, object.

b. One thought per sentence

Have one main thought in a sentence.

c. Limit sentences to 25 words

Vary the sentence length but the average sentence should be no longer than 25 words.

d. Use tabulations

Divide long sentences using **tabulations**. If the items are complete sentences, use the following format:

1. Begin each item with an uppercase letter.
2. End each item with a period.

If the items are not complete sentences, use the following format:

1. a lowercase letter at the beginning of each item,
2. a semicolon or comma after each item, and
3. an "or" or "and" before the last item.

e. Avoid intrusive phrases

Do not let phrases or clauses intrude between the subject and verb. These **intrusive phrases** disrupt the sentence's logical flow and make it difficult for the reader to follow what is being said.

> **Example:**   The interrogatories sent to our client and received by him at his home three days ago force us to reformulate our defense strategy.

A total of 14 words separate the subject, *interrogatories*, from the verb, *force*. This writing style creates several problems. First, until the reader reaches the verb, he or she must wait in suspense as to what is going on with the subject, the interrogatories. Second, the reader must process the new information contained in the intrusive clause while remembering that the main point of the sentence relates to the interrogatories.

If you find yourself writing particularly long sentences, check to see whether your reader may get lost between the beginning and the end. If so, you may have inserted intrusive phrases between your subject and verb. There are two solutions. First, you can simply divide the sentence and create two sentences.

> **Revised:**   Three days ago our client received interrogatories. The interrogatories force us to reformulate our defense strategy.

The other solution is to take the intrusive phrase out of the middle and put it at the beginning or the end.

> **Revised:**   Sent to our client and received by him at his home three days ago, the interrogatories force us to reformulate our defense strategy.

2. Avoid Sentence Fragments

An obvious corollary to the rule that you should use simple sentence construction is the requirement that you write in sentences. A sentence contains a subject and a verb and can stand alone as a complete thought. A sentence can be a single independent clause, two independent clauses joined with a coordinating conjunction, or an independent and a dependent clause.

> **Example:** The man yelled for help.
> (independent clause)
>
> The man yelled for help, and the police came running. (two independent clauses)
>
> Even though the man yelled for help, no one came to his assistance. (dependent clause followed by independent clause)

Sentence fragment
An incomplete sentence.

Sentence fragments are incomplete sentences and cannot stand alone. One type of sentence fragment is the phrase with no verb.

> **Example:** The doctor in white. (Did what?)

Another type of sentence fragment is the prepositional phrase standing alone.

> **Example:** By six o'clock. (What will happen?)

To correct the first type of fragment, insert a verb.

> **Revised:** The doctor in white *said* that I could go home.

To correct the second type of fragment, attach the prepositional phrase to the rest of the sentence.

> **Revised:** By six o'clock *we should have heard from the doctor.*

NETNOTE

To find online exercises on run-ons, fragments, and more, go to Grammar Bytes!.

Dependent clause
A clause that contains a subject and a verb but that cannot stand alone, as it does not contain a complete thought. A dependent clause always begins with a subordinating conjunction.

The most common type of sentence fragment is the **dependent clause** standing alone. The writer thinks she has written a complete sentence when she has not. The dependent clause does contain a subject and verb, but it cannot stand alone and make sense, as it does not contain a complete thought. When you read a dependent clause that is standing alone, it is as though you are waiting for the other shoe to drop.

> **Example:** Although the defense attorney asked for a finding of not guilty. (What
> happened?)

Dependent clauses always begin with what is known as a **subordinating conjunction:** *after, although, as, because, before, even though, if, since, unless, when,
where, whereas,* and *while.* To correct a sentence fragment created by a dependent clause standing alone, drop the subordinating conjunction and turn the
dependent clause into an independent clause, or add an independent clause.

> **Revised:** The defense attorney asked for a finding of not guilty. (subordinating
> conjunction dropped)
> Although the defense attorney asked for a finding of not guilty, the jury
> brought in a guilty verdict. (independent clause added)

Subordinating conjunction
Dependent clauses always
begin with subordinating
conjunctions: *after,
although, as, because,
before, even though, if,
since, unless, when, where,
whereas,* and *while.*

3. Avoid Run-On Sentences (Fused Sentences and Comma Splices)

The **run-on sentence** is the opposite of the sentence fragment. Instead of being
half a sentence, it is actually two sentences. It can occur either as a comma splice
(two independent clauses joined by a comma) or as a fused sentence (two independent clauses with no separating punctuation).

> **Example:** The man yelled for help, the police came running. (comma splice)
>
> The man yelled for help the police came running. (fused sentence)

Run-on sentences can be corrected in any of the following ways:

> **Revised:** The man yelled for help. The police came running. (divided into two
> sentences)
> The man yelled for help, and the police came running. (two independent
> clauses joined by a comma and a coordinating conjunction)

Run-on sentence
Two sentences written as
one. It can occur either
as a common splice (two
independent clauses joined
by a comma) or as a fused
sentence (two independent
clauses with no separating
punctuation).

As seen above, a comma and a coordinating conjunction can join two independent clauses. **Coordinating conjunctions** include *and, but, for, nor, or,* and *yet.*
However, you cannot use conjunctive adverbs to join two independent
clauses. Examples of **conjunctive adverbs** are *also, consequently, furthermore,
however, moreover, nevertheless, then,* and *therefore.*
A very common error is to try to use *however* or *therefore* to join two independent clauses. Do not do it.

Coordinating conjunction
A coordinating
conjunction can join
two independent clauses;
examples include *and, but,
for, nor, or,* and *yet.*

Conjunctive adverbs
Examples include *also,
consequently, furthermore,
however, moreover,
nevertheless, then,* and
therefore. These should
not be used to join two
independent clauses.

> **Incorrect:** The holding in the *Lane* decision would appear to be against our client,
> however, we do have one counterargument.
>
> **Revised:** The holding in the *Lane* decision would appear to be against our client. We
> do, however, have one counterargument.

4. Use Parallel Construction

Parallel construction
Using the same grammatical structure for clauses or phrases that bear the same relationship to some major idea.

Clauses or phrases that bear the same relationship to some major idea should have parallel grammatical structure. When writing lists, be particularly careful about not drifting into variations that lack **parallel construction.**

Incorrect:	The boy ate, he went horseback riding, and he was swimming.
Revised:	The boy ate, went horseback riding, and swam.
Incorrect:	My objections are that the complaint was filed late, no valid cause of action, and the wrong defendant.
Revised:	My objections are that the complaint was filed late, that it does not contain a valid cause of action, and that the plaintiff has sued the wrong defendant.

B. USE THE PROPER VERB TENSE

In legal writing there are two common problems with verb tense: making inappropriate shifts between verb tenses and using present tense for events that happened in the past. The first problem, inappropriate shifts, occurs when a writer begins describing an event in one tense but then, perhaps realizing the wrong tense is being used, switches to another tense. When proofreading, be sure to check for this potential problem.

To correct the second problem, inappropriately using present tense, remember that past tense should always be used for actions that happened in the past. In legal writing these include

1. the facts that make up your client's story,
2. the events that occurred in the cases you read, and
3. what the court said in those cases.

Incorrect:	1. In *Bennett,* Mrs. Brown runs home . . .;
	2. In *Bennett,* a woman sues . . .; and
	3. In *Bennett,* the court holds that. . . .
Revised:	1. In *Bennett,* Mrs. Brown ran home . . .;
	2. In *Bennett,* a woman sued . . .; and
	3. In *Bennett,* the court held that. . . .

But use present tense when describing a rule of law.

Incorrect:	In *Bennett,* the court held that minors *were* allowed to void contracts that they have signed.
Revised:	In *Bennett,* the court held that minors *are* allowed to void contracts that they have signed.

C. MAKE SURE PRONOUNS AND ANTECEDENTS AGREE

When you do not want to use a noun, you use a **pronoun** as a substitute. In the following sentence *Mary* is the noun and *her* is the pronoun.

> **Example:** Mary reviewed her testimony with her attorney.

Because a pronoun (*hers, her, his, him, it, its, them, their, theirs*) substitutes for a noun that has preceded it, the noun is known as an **antecedent**. The pronoun and its antecedent must match as to gender and number. When you are writing about people in general, there are several ways to write a sentence without using gendered language. One way is to make the pronoun plural.

> **Example:** The new computer user may find, after many attempts at installing the software by themselves, that they need help.

Sometimes you can correct this by making the noun plural.

> **Example:** New computer users may find, after many attempts at installing the software by themselves, that they need help.

Another possibility is to drop the pronoun.

> **Example:** The new computer user may find, after many attempts at installing the software, that help is needed.

Finally, you may need to resort to a "he or she," "his or hers," "her or him," or "they or them" combination.

> **Example:** The new computer user may find after many attempts at installing the software that he or she needs help.

D. PUT MODIFYING WORDS CLOSE TO WHAT THEY MODIFY

Misplaced modifiers are a very common problem. Sometimes the result is merely humorous, as in the following example:

> **Example:** The college has all the money from students deposited in the bank.

Obviously, the college has deposited the money and not the students. Other times, however, a misplaced modifier could cause serious interpretation problems, and even litigation. Consider the following example, taken from a lease provision:

> **Example:** If through no fault of Tenant, the apartment becomes uninhabitable, Landlord shall be notified immediately to provide alternative dwelling.

Does this mean that the landlord must be notified immediately or that the landlord must provide an alternative dwelling immediately? In this last example, the word *immediately* is referred to as a squinting modifier because you cannot tell if the writer means for it to modify the word that precedes it or the word that follows it. Frequently, this happens with the placement of the word *only*.

> **Example:** You may talk with the witness only today.

Does this mean that you can talk with the witness but not with anyone else, such as the defendant, or does this mean that you can talk to the witness today only? Depending on what you mean, you could rewrite the sentence as follows:

> **Example:** You may talk with only the witness today.

You may talk with the witness today only.

E. AVOID PUNCTUATION PROBLEMS

One area of grammar that may seem the most boring and useless is the area of punctuation. Nothing could be further from the truth. There are too many cases where a comma, or the lack of one, has been the focus of litigation. One example should suffice to emphasize the importance of being careful with punctuation. A will contained the following provision:

> I bequeath and devise my entire estate, both personal and real, . . . in equal shares, absolutely and in fee to my cousin, the said Walter Cassidy; Robert Jamison and William Stivers, tenants on my farm; George E. Smith, who rents my property on Bland Avenue, Shelbyville, Kentucky; and the Kentucky Society for Crippled Children.[1]

Jamison and Stivers argued that they should each receive one-fifth of the bequest. The other three beneficiaries argued that the two men should share one-fourth. Semicolons separated each of the other beneficiaries, whereas Jamison and Stivers were not separated. How would you decide this case? The court awarded the two men one-fifth each. Was the court correct? Only the dead testator knows for sure.

---

[1] Cassidy v. Vanattas, 242 S.W.2d 619, 620 (Ky. App. 1951).

1. Use the Serial Comma

As suggested above, the punctuation problem that gets more attorneys and para-legals into trouble than any other is the one regarding the **serial comma**. In a series of three or more items, use a comma after each item until you reach the final conjunction.

Serial comma
In a series of three or more items, use a comma after each item until you reach the final conjunction.

Incorrect:	The boy swam, ran and played.
Revised:	The boy swam, ran, and played.

By always including that final comma, you will never have to face the following interpretation problem:

Sally went to the bookstore to buy book covers in green, red, blue and yellow.

Does this mean she bought three covers: one green, one red, and one blue and yellow? Or did she buy four book covers: one green, one red, one blue, and one yellow?

2. Do Not Use a Comma with Compound Verbs or Between a Subject and Its Verb

Do not use a comma with compound subjects, verbs, or objects. Also do not let a comma separate your subject and its verb. Legal writers most often mis-punctuate compound verbs.

Incorrect:	The boy ran, and fell down.
Revised:	The boy ran and fell down.

3. Use Commas to Set Off Phrases Containing Nonessential Information

Grammarians say that we must set off **nonrestrictive phrases** with commas. What that means is that if the sentence would make sense without the phrase, the phrase is nonrestrictive (i.e., nonessential) and should be set off with commas.

Nonrestrictive phrase
A phrase that is not essential to the sense of a sentence; it should be set off with commas.

Incorrect:	In the leading case *Dillon v. Legg* the court held that a mother can recover for emotional distress.
Revised:	In the leading case, *Dillon v. Legg*, the court held that a mother can recover for emotional distress.

The sentence would retain its meaning and still make sense without the phrase *Dillon v. Legg*.

Restrictive phrase
A phrase that contains
essential information; it
should not be set off with
commas.

A **restrictive phrase** contains essential information.

Incorrect:	All students, who do not register on time, must pay a $20 late fee.
Revised:	All students who do not register on time must pay a $20 late fee.

Without the phrase "who do not register on time," the sentence reads: "All students must pay a $20 late fee." The phrase contains essential information, the absence of which alters the sentence's meaning. Therefore, it should not be set off with commas.

Example of restrictive:	Courts that recognize spousal immunity usually base their decision on a desire to promote family harmony. (Only some courts recognize spousal immunity.)
Example of nonrestrictive:	Courts, which are forums for justice, decide cases based on the facts presented to them. (All courts are forums for justice.)

As a general rule of thumb, use *that* with restrictive phrases and *which* with nonrestrictive phrases.

4. Forming the Possessive

To form the possessive for singular nouns, use *'s* unless the noun ends in an **s** and it would make the possessive hard to pronounce.

Example:	child's Bob's James's witness's

Traditionally, however, you should drop the *s* after the apostrophe with some proper names that both end in **s** and have an internal *s* sound.

Example:	Jesus' life

To form the possessive for plural nouns, use *'s* for nouns that do not end in **s** but only an apostrophe for those that end in *s*.

Examples:	children's witnesses'

5. Combining Quotation Marks with Other Punctuation

Periods and commas always belong inside the closing quotation mark.

Examples:	The court stated that "the case should be remanded for a new trial." The court stated that "the case should be remanded for a new trial," and then it reprimanded the prosecuting attorney for his delay tactics.

Semicolons and colons always belong outside the closing quotation mark.

> **Example:** The court stated that "the case should be remanded for a new trial"; the court also reprimanded the prosecuting attorney for his delay tactics.

When they are part of the quotation, place dashes, question marks, and exclamation points inside the closing quotation mark.

> **Example:** The attorney asked his client, "Should we proceed?" before entering the courtroom.

Otherwise, place those marks outside the closing quotation mark.

> **Example:** Did the court state that "the case should be remanded for a new trial"?

PART II: STYLE

> **Accident Report**
>
> The party of the first part hereinafter known as Jack . . . and . . . The party of the second part hereinafter known as Jill . . . Ascended or caused to be ascended an elevation of undetermined height and degree of slope, hereinafter referred to as "hill." Whose purpose it was to obtain, attain, procure, secure, or otherwise gain acquisition to, by any and/or all means available to them a receptacle or container, hereinafter known as "pail," suitable for the transport of a liquid whose chemical properties shall be limited to hydrogen and oxygen, the proportions of which shall not be less than or exceed two parts for the first mentioned element and one part for the latter. Such combination will hereinafter be called "water." On the occasion stated above, it has been established beyond reasonable doubt that Jack did plunge, tumble, topple, or otherwise be caused to lose his footing in a manner that caused his body to be thrust into a downward direction. As a direct result of these combined circumstances, Jack suffered fractures and contusions of his cranial regions. Jill, whether due to Jack's misfortune or not, was known to also tumble in similar fashion after Jack. (Whether the term, "after," shall be interpreted in a spatial or time passage sense, has not been determined.)[2]

Like the author of *The Legal Guide to Mother Goose*, many view legal writing as ponderous and laden with unnecessary verbiage and redundancies. However, that does not have to be true of what you write. Besides following

---

[2] *The Legal Guide to Mother Goose* 7-11 (Don Sandburg trans., 1978).

the basic rules of grammar, there are various techniques you can use to increase the clarity and effectiveness of your writing. These techniques include avoiding long paragraphs, using transitions, being concise by eliminating unnecessary words and introductory phrases and by saying it only once, and avoiding the passive voice. This section concludes with some special techniques peculiar to legal writing.

A. AVOID LONG PARAGRAPHS

Of course, there is no mechanical rule as to paragraph length. Nonetheless, if you find you have written a paragraph that is over half a page in length, consider whether it is too long. Check to be sure that you have only one major idea in the paragraph.

Trying to develop more than one theme in each paragraph can confuse the reader and require her or him to reread the paragraph. A good check is to go back over your document and see whether you can find a topic sentence in each paragraph that states the theme for that paragraph. Then, reading just those sentences from each paragraph, you should be able to follow your argument as it develops throughout your document.

NETNOTE

At the site *guidetogrammar.org,* you can find help organized by level: word and sentence, paragraph, and paper.

B. DO NOT BURY YOUR POINTS

A common error is to start a paragraph with "In the case of. . . ." This is a poor writing style for two reasons. First, a reader pays the most attention to the first and last sentences of a paragraph. Therefore, you should place your most important points there rather than burying them in the middle of the paragraph. Second, if you simply start your paragraph with a case description, you have failed to tell the reader why the case is relevant. No one (or at least no one we know) enjoys reading about case law in the abstract. In order to be interested in what you have to say about a given case, the reader must first understand why it is relevant. Lead off with a sentence or clause that will help the reader understand why you will be discussing the next case. At a minimum let the reader know that it is the leading case, the only case, the most recent case, or the like, and place the case citation at the end of the sentence.

Incorrect:	In *Bennett v. Bennett*, 186 N.E.2d 85 (Mass. 1988), the plaintiff sued to have a contract set aside, arguing that she was only 16 years old when she signed it. All students who do not register on time must pay a $20 late fee.
Revised:	Several cases have dealt with the issue of whether a contract can be set aside if one of the parties was a minor when the contract was signed. For example, in one recent case the plaintiff sued to have the contract set aside, arguing that she was only 16 years old when she signed it. *Bennett v. Bennett*, 186 N.E.2d 85 (Mass. 1988).

C. USE TRANSITIONS

The type of case introduction in the prior example is one form of **transition**. Transitions help your reader follow the flow of your argument. They provide the link from where you have been to where you are going. On the simplest level, transitions can indicate a sequence: "The first point to be made is . . . . The second point to be made is. . . ." On a more sophisticated level, transitions artfully tie together the preceding thought and the one that follows. Assume a writer has written a paragraph analyzing *Bennett v. Bennett* and the paragraph concludes with the following sentence:

Transition
In writing, a technique used to help your reader move from one thought to the next and to see the connections between them.

> The court therefore held that as the plaintiff was only 16 at the time she signed the contract, the contract should be set aside as void.

The next paragraph could pick up on the theme presented in the first paragraph by beginning with the following sentence:

> Because Margaret was only 15 at the time of the contract's formation, her position that her contract should be set aside is consistent with that of the court in *Bennett*.

D. BE CONCISE

A taxpayer testified, "As God is my judge, I do not owe this tax." The judge answered, "He's not, I am; and you do."[3] While this may be an extreme example of brevity, it is always a good idea to write concisely so as not to bore your reader. But it is particularly important for lawyers to do so.

One major reason for being as concise as possible is that every unnecessary word serves as a source of potential ambiguity. If you write "null and void" instead of simply "void," you raise the issue of whether there is a difference between something that is only "void" and something that is both "null and void."

---

[3] Judge J. Edgar Murdock of the United States Tax Court, quoted in Brison v. Commissioner of Internal Revenue, T.C. Memo 1983-01, 11.

Second, those who read an attorney's or paralegal's writing are usually very busy people. Judges, other lawyers, and clients have little time to waste. They want to hear what you have to say and be done with it.

You should remember three guidelines when reviewing something you have written: Eliminate unnecessary words, remove unnecessary introductory phrases, and say it once. By following these guidelines you can condense your writing without sacrificing any of the content.

1. Eliminate Unnecessary Words

There are many compound word combinations that you can replace with a single word. Here are some examples:

At this point in time	Now
At that point in time	Then
Notwithstanding the fact that	Although
There is no doubt but that	Doubtless
The reason why is that	Because
The fact that	(Usually no replacement necessary)

> **Incorrect:** Because of the fact that John shot the victim, he will be found guilty.
> **Revised:** Because John shot the victim, he will be found guilty.

Finally, there is the attorney's favorite word: **clearly**—as in "Clearly the defendant was negligent." Either the defendant was or was not negligent. Saying the issue is clear will not make it so. In fact, this word often acts as a red flag, raising the reader's suspicions. After all, if you have to bootstrap your argument with words such as *clearly*, perhaps your argument is not that clear.

2. Remove Unnecessary Introductory Phrases

Phrases such as "It is interesting to note that . . ." and "It should be noted in this connection that . . ." are unnecessary filler. When writing a first draft, these phrases are often just what the writer needs to make the pen start moving across the page (or to cause the words to start appearing on the computer monitor). Use these phrases for that purpose, but then go back and strike them out. A good test is this: If the sentence makes sense without the introduction, cross it out.

3. Say It Once

If you find phrases such as "in other words" sprinkled throughout your writing, check to make sure that you are not engaging in some unnecessary duplication. Often a writer will finish a sentence and then think of a better way to say the same thing. We all have doubts now and then about just how clear our points are. Therefore, when this better approach occurs to us, instead of recognizing it as the better alternative we leave in both sentences. Instead try to combine the two approaches, or simply pick the better one and drop the other.

E. AVOID THE PASSIVE VOICE

Use the active voice whenever possible. The **passive voice** is a weaker form of writing. In the passive voice the subject is acted on, but it is often unclear who is doing the acting.

Passive voice
A form of writing where the subject of the sentence is being acted on; opposite of active voice.

> **Examples:**   The ball was thrown by Mary. (*passive voice*)
> The ball was thrown. (*passive voice with actor missing so that it is unclear who threw the ball*)
> The ruling was made by the trial judge that the defendant was guilty. (*passive voice*)
> The ruling was made that the defendant was guilty. (*passive voice with actor missing so that it is unclear who made the ruling*)

Such ambiguity has its place in legal writing but only if you plan it.

The best clues that you are using the passive voice are the "by" construction, as in the first and third examples ("by Mary," "by the trial judge") and the absence of the actor entirely, as in the second and fourth examples.

Active voice is just that—active. In the **active voice** the subject of the sentence acts.

Active voice
A form of writing where the subject of the sentence does the acting; opposite of passive voice.

> **Examples:**   Mary threw the ball.
> The trial judge ruled that the defendant was guilty.

Avoid the passive voice whenever possible. Usually, because of the "by" construction, it adds needless weight to your writing through the addition of useless words. When, to solve that problem, the writer omits the "by" construction, ambiguity often results. Consider the following lease provision, and try to determine who must report what to whom:

> When conditions affecting the habitability of the rental property are discovered, they must be promptly reported and failure to do so shall constitute a material breach of this lease.

Does the landlord have to report defects to the tenant, or does the tenant have to disclose conditions that affect the habitability to the landlord? Perhaps each party must disclose such conditions to the other party. Ambiguity such as this is an open invitation to a lawsuit.

The third reason for avoiding the passive voice is that it is a less powerful form. This becomes particularly important to the legal writer in advocacy writing, but it is something to keep in mind for any form of writing.

There are times when the passive voice is appropriate. But you must know when those times are and then use the passive voice by design and not by inadvertence. Specifically, there are four occasions when you may wish to use the passive voice:

1. When the writer wants to highlight the action instead of the actor.

> **Example:**   The man had been murdered.

2. When the actor is unknown.

> **Example:**   The dead body had been left in the woods.

3. When the writer wants to state a general principle.

> **Example:**   All people are created equal.

4. When the writer wants to disassociate the actor from the statement.

> **Example:**   The victim was robbed.
> **Not:**   Our client robbed the victim.

F. SPECIAL RULES FOR LEGAL WRITING

As we mentioned at the beginning of this appendix, good legal writing is simply good writing. If you possess a clear, understandable style, you are well on your way to being a good legal writer. However, because you will be writing about the law and the legal system, you need to know a few special rules.

1. Avoid Legalese

Avoid the temptation to use "legalese," archaic legal terminology, to impress your reader. Several states have passed legislation requiring that all legal documents be written in plain English. Although many attorneys are still resisting the plain English movement, you should avoid legalese whenever possible.

Whenever you find yourself tempted to use legal sounding words, such as *wherefore*, *aforesaid*, and especially *said*, ask yourself if there is a less stilted English word that can serve your purpose better. Consider the following example, and ask yourself whether the word *said* adds anything or actually creates ambiguity:

> **Example:**   The defendant was seated inside a station wagon. Parked next to him was a Corvette. Said car was green.

Usually, words such as *said* only give the illusion of precision and bog down the writing with heavy-sounding legal words.

2. Make the Court and Not the Court Opinion the Actor

You can avoid another common writing error if you remember that inanimate objects cannot act. Always make the court and not the court opinion do the holding.

> **Incorrect:** *Lewis* held that. . . .
> **Revised:** The court in *Lewis* held that. . . .

3. Avoid Unnecessary Variation

If you have written "the car" four times in a paragraph, you may be tempted to switch to "the motor vehicle." Avoid the temptation. You may leave your reader wondering if you are talking about both a car and a motor vehicle. As this example illustrates, variation can cause serious interpretation problems if your reader thinks you mean to refer to two separate objects when you mean to refer to only one.

4. Do Not Use the First Person

The generally accepted rule in legal writing is to avoid using the first person. You want the emphasis to be on what you are saying and not on the fact that it is you who is saying it. Whenever you find yourself starting a sentence with a phrase such as "I think the court will hold that . . .," go back and delete the first two words. Because you are the author, the reader already knows that these are your thoughts and no one else's. The reader also knows that there is no way that you can be one hundred percent certain of what you write. Therefore, there is no need to soften the certitude with which you write by inserting "I think."

The one time when you can use the first person is when you are referring to one of your firm's clients, as in "Our client wishes to settle." However, even in that case some purists would prefer to use the client's name, as in "Ms. Brown wishes to settle."

5. Do Not Use Contractions

Legal writing is formal writing, and in formal writing there is no place for contractions. Contractions are acceptable only when you are writing an informal note for someone within the firm or, depending on the policy of your firm, occasionally a letter to a client.

6. Do Not Ask Your Reader Questions

It is your job to provide answers, not to ask your reader questions. There is nothing more annoying than to be reading someone's legal analysis only to be stopped by a series of questions.

> **Example:** The court in *Lewis* held that liability is limited to automobile accidents. Will that court extend its holding to our client's facts? Will the court limit its holding to exclude our client's facts?

The reader will probably be thinking, "I don't know. That's what I'm paying you to tell me." When you find yourself posing questions, simply rephrase them as issues.

Revised:	The court in *Lewis* held that liability is limited to automobile accidents. That raises the issue of whether the court will extend that holding to our client's facts or limit it to the facts of Lewis.

7. That Case/This Case

That case
A case that you are citing.

This case
Your client's case.

The convention is to refer to a cited case as **that case** and to your client's case as **this case**.

Example:	The court in *Lewis* held that liability is limited to automobile accidents. In that case the husband had been driving and the wife was a passenger when the accident occurred.

8. Written Numbers Versus Numerals

There are times when you should write out numbers as opposed to using numerals. Many attorneys prefer the older, more formal approach of writing out all numbers from zero to ninety-nine, but a more modern approach is to use numerals for all numbers higher than ten. In addition, you should write out:

■ any round number, such as one hundred; and
■ any number that begins a sentence.

In footnotes you follow the same rules except you write out only the numbers zero through nine. When you have a series of numbers in a sentence, some of which you should write out and some of which you should give as numerals, use all numerals.

Example:	There were 2 attorneys, 40 witnesses, and 105 documents.

9. Do Not Eliminate the Articles *A*, *An*, and *The*

Leaving out articles makes your writing choppy and hard to follow. This style probably comes from students mistakenly thinking that their writing will appear more "lawyerly" if they adopt a headnote style of writing.

Incorrect:	A person injured in fall from automobile parking floor to ground below while seeking shelter from rain was at most gratuitous or bare licensee.
Revised:	A person injured in *a* fall from *an* automobile parking floor to *the* ground below while seeking shelter from *the* rain was at most *a* gratuitous or bare licensee.

PART III: CORRECT WORD USAGE

Correct word usage simply means choosing the correct word to say exactly what you mean. At times this may require you to consult a dictionary or thesaurus. The following is a list of the most commonly misused words.

And/Or	There is much debate as to whether the *and/or* combination is acceptable. Many writers believe it is cumbersome and requires the reader to do too much work to understand its meaning. For example, in the phrase "the husband and/or the wife," the reader must translate that to mean the husband, the wife, or both. Therefore, many writers prefer it to be written just that way.
Because/Since	*Because* denotes a causal relationship. *Since* refers to time. Using *since* to also denote a causal relationship can cause ambiguity.

> **Examples:** Because he admitted his guilt, he has been held without bail. (The reason he is being held without bail is that he admitted his guilt.)
>
> Since he admitted his guilt, he has been held without bail. (Since the time he admitted his guilt, he has been held without bail.)

Court/court	Unless it starts a sentence, the word *Court* stands for the U.S. Supreme Court. Use *court* when referring to other courts.
Have/Of	In speech it often sounds as though someone is saying "of" when it really is "have." In writing, always use *would have, could have, should have*, not *would of, could of, should of*.
Its/It's	*Its* is a pronoun. *It's* is a contraction for *it is*.

> **Examples:** The car wobbled on its loose axle.
>
> It's a beautiful day.

That/Which	*That* is used for restrictive or essential phrases.

> **Example:**   He went to the store that was around the corner to buy some bread.

The phrase "that was around the corner" describes which store and is essential for identifying the store.

> **Example:**   He went to George's Grocery, which was around the corner, to buy some bread.

The phrase "which was around the corner" simply further describes the store that was already clearly identified as George's Grocery. Therefore, it provides nonessential information.

Their/There/They're

Their is a possessive pronoun. *There* represents a place. *They're* is a contraction for *they are*.

> **Example:**   They're going to their house. Once they are there, they will have supper.

Which/Who

Use *which* for things and *who* for people.

Who's/Whose

Who's is a contraction for *who is*. *Whose* is a possessive pronoun.

> **Examples:**   Who's going to the store?

Whose jacket is this?

Your/You're

Your is a possessive pronoun. *You're* is a contraction for *you are*.

> **Example:**   You're going to have to finish your report.

||| SUMMARY

Good legal writing starts with good writing. Follow the basic rules of grammar by using proper sentence structure, avoiding sentence fragments and run-on sentences, and using parallel construction. Also use the proper verb tense. Make sure your pronouns agree with your antecedents. Put modifying words close to what they modify, and be aware of common punctuation problems.

While you are encouraged to develop your own style, you should follow certain style guidelines. Avoid long paragraphs, and be careful that you do not bury your points in the middle of your paragraphs. Use transitions between paragraphs. Be concise by eliminating unnecessary words and phrases. Because the active voice is stronger, use it whenever possible. And when engaged in legal writing, do not fall into the trap of using legalese. Keep the court and not the court opinion the subject of your sentences. Avoid unnecessary variation and the use of the first person. In formal writing do not use contractions, and do not ask your reader questions. Be aware of the differences between "that case" and "this case." Know when to use numerals and when to write numbers out. Finally, do not write like a headnote editor. Include the articles — *a*, *an*, and *the*.

REVIEW QUESTIONS

Pages 543 through 550

Correct the following sentences.

1. On any given day a paralegal can be asked to perform any of the following tasks, to interview clients, research in the library, drafting of documents, filed pleadings, or writing client letters.
2. The complaint, which contains theories based on both tort and contract law, alleging that the product was defective, was filed with the wrong court.
3. Even though the attorney made a long-winded and impassioned plea to the jury at the end of the trial.
4. The attorney made a long-winded and impassioned plea to the jury at the end of the trial the jury found the defendant guilty.
5. In *Jones,* a child is injured by his father's negligence. The court decides that children were able to sue for parental negligence.
6. Even though a criminal defendant may engage in plea bargaining, they still may receive a different sentence from the judge.
7. The judge, denied the plaintiff's request, ordered a new trial and set the new trial date.
8. All paralegals, who are members of the local paralegal association, have access to the job bank information.
9. He went over to Bob Browns house where he saw the Browns collection of stamps.
10. The witness stated that "I ran away from the accident", and he testified that he was "scared".

Pages 550 through 563

Correct the following sentences.

11. In *Black* the court held that only involuntary intoxication could be a defense to the formation of a contract. (first sentence in a paragraph)
12. It is interesting to note that notwithstanding the fact that the defendant was found guilty, at that point in time clearly the defendant still felt his attorney had done a good job of defending him.
13. The decision by the jury to convict the defendant surprised no one.

14. In *Jones v. Warner* the court felt that only those who were involuntarily intoxicated could be excused from their contractual obligations.

15. Said court also stated that two beers wouldn't be sufficient to prove intoxication.

16. Will the court in our case say that four beers are sufficient to prove intoxication? Would six be enough? What of two whiskeys?

17. There are five cases that deal with intoxication.

18. Defendant driving car after drinking five beers was found to be intoxicated.

19. The plaintiff can bring suit for negligence against the city for injuries he sustained in the accident. Even though his contributory negligence may bar him from recovery.

20. The woman was frightened by a man she described as seedy, it was only after she struck him with a rock that she discovered he was an undercover police officer.

21. During an autopsy, looking for the cause of death, the deceased is examined by the pathologist.

22. The new computer system offers four advantages for our firm:
    1. it includes 15 software packages
    2. the warranty extends to 160 days
    3. provides a full-scale training program
    4. state-of-the-art features are included.

23. The enclosed forms should be completed by you no later than August 15.

24. The depositions proved to be very revealing, however, our client has decided to settle.

25. *Dillon* holds that under certain circumstances a bystander may recover for emotional distress.

WEB EXERCISES

1. An excellent way to increase your ability to write in clear, grammatical sentences is to test yourself using online programs. Grammar Bytes! is full of humor and is one of the best. Start by going to *www.chompchomp.com*. On the home page, under "Exercises," click on "Test your grammar knowledge here." Then try your hand at any of the interactive exercises. The ones on "Comma Splices & Fused Sentences" and "Fragments" are particularly worth doing.

2. Many words in the English language can be confusing. Go to *lousywriter .com*. Scroll down and click on "Confusing English Words." Choose a set of words (e.g., "affect" and "effect") and write a paragraph incorporating each of the words.

✣ Appendix C

NetNotes

ALTERNATIVE DISPUTE RESOLUTION (ADR)

American Arbitration Association (*adr.org*)

The ABA Section on Dispute Resolution (*americanbar.org/dispute*)

The College of Commercial Arbitrators (*ccarbitrators.org/*)

The Mediation Information and Resource Center (*mediate.com*)

BLOGS

Find legal blogs at *legalblogs.findlaw.com*.

BUSINESS INFORMATION

The Electronic Data Gathering, Analysis, and Retrieval (EDGAR) system—Go to *sec.gov/edgar*.

From the Equal Employment Opportunity Commission (EEOC), *eeoc.gov*, you can find information on the following:

- Age Discrimination in Employment Act
- Americans with Disabilities Act
- Civil Rights Act of 1964

From the Department of Labor, *www.dol.gov*, you can find information on the following:

- Employee Retirement Income Security Act (ERISA)
- Fair Labor Standards Act

- Family and Medical Leave Act
- Federal Worker's Compensation Law

National Labor Relations Act (*nlrb.gov*)

Occupational Safety and Health Administration (*osha.gov*)

Secretary of State—there are online links to each state's secretary of state at *e-secretaryofstate.com.*

Uniform Commercial Code—Go to *uniformlaws.org/acts/ucc.*

COMMERCIAL ONLINE PROVIDERS

Casemaker (*casemakerlegal.net*)

Fastcase (*fastcase.com*)

Findlaw (*findlaw.com*)

Findlaw for Legal Professionals (*lp.findlaw.com*)

LexisNexis (*lexis.com*)

Westlaw (*westlaw.com*)

COURT SYSTEM

For federal court information, go to either the federal judiciary home page (*uscourts.gov*) or the Federal Judicial Center home page (*fjc.gov*).

Go to the National Center for State Courts (ncsc.org) for information on specific state courts under "Information & Resources." Find visual representations of state court structures at *courtstatistics.org.*

Information on Public Access to Court Electronic Records (PACER), including a video tutorial, can be found at *pacer.gov.*

For information on the U.S. Supreme Court, go to *supremecourt.gov*. You can hear oral arguments at *oyez.com.*

CRIMINAL LAW

The U.S. Department of Justice has a robust website with information relevant to federal crimes, as well as statistics about crimes and victims, at *justice.gov.*

The Federal Bureau of Investigation (FBI) maintains a website at *fbi.gov*.

The University of Michigan maintains statistics about crimes and victims through its National Archive of Criminal Justice Data (NACJD), found at *icpsr.umich.edu/icpsrweb/content/NACJD/index.html*.

A blog on current topics in criminal law can be found at CrimProf (*lawprofessors.typepad.com/crimprof_blog/*).

OTHER GOVERNMENT SITES

Congress—Both the House and Senate maintain websites at *house.gov* and *senate.gov*.

The EEOC home page is located at *eeoc.gov*.

The U.S. Department of Justice website is located at *usdoj.gov*.

The U.S. Patent and Trademark Office website is located at *uspto.gov*.

The White House's website is *whitehouse.gov*.

GRAMMAR

Grammar Bytes! at *chompchomp.com*.

Help with grammar at *guidetogrammar.org/grammar*.

LEGAL ETHICS

The ABA Model Rules of Professional Conduct and information about developments in legal ethics and links to the states' Rules of Professional Conduct or Code of Professional Responsibility and to their ethics opinions can be found at *americanbar.org*.

NALA's Code of Ethics and Professional Responsibility (*nala.org*).

NFPA's Model Code of Ethics can be found at NFPA's home page (*paralegals.org*).

To view the ABA Model Guidelines on the Utilization of Paralegal Services, go to *americanbar.org/groups/paralegals*.

A blog about developments in legal ethics can be found at *bernabepr.blogspot.com/*.

LEGAL SEARCH ENGINES

There are various search engines that can assist you with your Internet legal research. One that has been designed specifically for legal research is *findlaw.com*.

ORGANIZATIONS

American Association for Paralegal Education (AAfPE)—*aafpe.org*.

American Bar Association (ABA)—*americanbar.org*.

International Paralegal Management Association (IPMA)—*theipma.org*.

NALA: The Paralegal Association (NALA)—*nala.org*.

National Federation of Paralegal Associations (NFPA)—*paralegals.org*.

Vote Smart—*votesmart.org*.

PRIMARY MATERIAL

For cases and codes, start at *lp.findlaw.com* and click on "Cases & Codes."

- For U.S. Supreme Court opinions dating back to the 1800s—select "US Supreme Court."
- For federal appellate court opinions—select your circuit.
- For state court opinions—select your state.
- For federal statutes and regulations—select the U.S. Code or the Code of Federal Regulations.
- For state statutes and regulations—select your state.
- Current information on federal legislation—A good source is *thomas .loc.gov*, provided by the Library of Congress.

A good source of current information on federal legislation is *regulations.justia .com*.

The following documents can be accessed from *archives.gov*.

- The Declaration of Independence
- The Constitution
- The Bill of Rights

Congress established the National Constitution Center in Philadelphia to disseminate nonpartisan information about the Constitution. It has created an online interactive Constitution at *constitutioncenter.org*.

TORTS

Consumer Product Safety Commission—*cpsc.gov*.

Expert witnesses can be identified by going to *lp.findlaw.com* and click on "Find an Expert."

Medical information—You can find current medical news at *medscape.com*.

UNIFORM LAWS

Various uniform laws governing various areas of the law can be found at *law.cornell.edu*. This website includes information on the following:

- Uniform Commercial Code
- Uniform Probate Code
- Uniform Child Custody Jurisdiction Act
- Uniform Interstate Family Support Act
- Uniform Premarital Agreement Act
- Uniform Marriage and Divorce Act

Glossary

Abstract   A condensed history of the title to real property, which includes the chain of ownership and a record of all liens, taxes, or other encumbrances that may impair the title.

Abuse of process   Misusing the criminal or civil court process.

Acceptance   In contract law, an act by the offeree indicating agreement to be bound to the contract.

Accessory   A person who assists the principal in the preparation of the crime; also known as an **accomplice**.

Accessory after the fact   A person who aids the principal after the commission of the crime.

Accessory before the fact   A person who assisted in the preparation of the crime, but was not present during the crime.

Accomplice   A person who assists the principal with the crime or with the preparation of the crime; also known as an **accessory**.

Accord and satisfaction   An accord is an agreement to do something different from that which was originally promised. The satisfaction is the performance of the accord.

Acknowledgment   A formal declaration of a signature before a public official.

Acquit   To determine that a criminal defendant is not guilty of the crime with which he or she is charged.

Active listening   The process of signaling that you are really listening, accomplished by using verbal and nonverbal clues, paraphrasing, and reflecting the client's feelings.

Active voice   A form of writing in which the subject of the sentence does the acting; the opposite of **passive voice**.

Actual cause   This is measured by the "but for" standard: But for the defendant's actions, the plaintiff would not have been injured; also known as **cause in fact**.

Actual damages   See **Compensatory damages**.

Actus reus   A wrongful act; along with **mens rea** (bad intent), a required element of any crime.

Adhesion contract   A contract formed where the weaker party has no realistic bargaining power. Typically, this form of contract is offered on a "take it or leave it" basis.

Adjudicatory hearing   A mechanism through which parties to a dispute can present arguments and evidence about their case to an administrative law judge.

Administrative law   Rules and regulations created by administrative agencies.

Administrative law judge   See **Hearing officer**.

Administrative regulations   Rules, regulations, orders, and decisions created by administrative agencies under their authority to interpret specific statutes.

Administrator/Administratrix   A person appointed by the court to carry out the directions and requests of someone's will.

ADR   See **Alternative dispute resolution (ADR)**.

Advance sheets   The first printing of a court decision before it appears in a hardbound reporter.

Adversarial system   A system characterized by competing, opposing parties overseen by a neutral decision maker.

Adverse possession   A transfer of real property rights that occurs after someone other than the owner has had actual, open, adverse, and exclusive use of the property for a statutorily determined number of years.

Adverse witness   See **Hostile witness**.

Affinity   Persons related to the decedent by marriage.

Affirm   A decision is affirmed when the litigants appeal a lower court decision and the higher court agrees with what the lower court has done.

Affirmative action plan   A temporary plan designed to remedy past discrimination by using race or sex as a "plus factor" in employment settings or admission to educational programs.

Affirmative defense A defense whereby the defendant offers new evidence to avoid judgment.

Agency adoption An adoption in which a licensed agency assumes responsibility for screening adoptive parents and matching them with available children.

Agent Someone who has the power to act in the place of another.

Alibi defense A defense requiring proof that the defendant could not have been at the scene of the crime.

Alien corporation A corporation formed in another country.

Alimony Financial support and other forms of assistance required to supply the "necessities" of life; also known as **maintenance** or **support**.

Alternative dispute resolution (ADR) Techniques for resolving conflicts that are alternatives to full-scale litigation. The two most common of these are **arbitration** and **mediation**.

American Association for Paralegal Education (AAfPE) A national organization of paralegal programs that promotes high standards for paralegal education.

American Bar Association (ABA) A national voluntary organization of lawyers.

American Bar Association approval A voluntary process; approval by the American Bar Association (ABA) indicates that a paralegal program meets its standards.

American Jurisprudence Second (Am. Jur. 2d) A general legal encyclopedia that summarizes the entire body of American law.

American Law Reports (A.L.R.) A source that contains the full text of leading court opinions, followed by a discussion of the issue with references to cases from around the country. Only selected topics are covered, but they are covered in more depth than you will find in an encyclopedia.

Amicus curiae Someone who, with the court's permission, intervenes in litigation, usually on appeal, to influence the decision; also known as a **friend of the court**.

Analogize To find similarities between two situations.

Analogous cases Cases that involve similar facts and rules of law.

Annotated code A privately published statutory code that includes statutes arranged by subject matter as well as editorial material, such as legislative history and summaries of court decisions interpreting the statutes.

Annotated statutes See **Annotated code**.

Annotations Editorial features, such as court decision summaries and references to other sources of information, added by the editor to assist the researcher.

Annulment A legal (or religious) judgment that a valid marriage never existed.

Answer The defendant's reply to the complaint. It may contain statements of denial, admission, or lack of knowledge and affirmative defenses.

Antecedent When a pronoun (*hers, her, his, him, it, its, them, their, theirs*) substitutes for a noun that has preceded it, the noun is known as an antecedent.

Antenuptial agreement See **Prenuptial agreement**.

Anti-heart-balm statute A law that prohibits lawsuits for such things as breach of a promise of marriage, alienation of affection, and seduction of a person over the legal age of consent.

Appeal To ask a higher court to review the actions of a lower court.

Appealable issues Questions that can form the basis for an appeal.

Appellant or petitioner The party in a lawsuit who has initiated an appeal.

Appellate brief A formal written argument to an appellate court, in which a lawyer argues why that court should affirm or reverse a lower court's decision.

Appellate courts Courts that determine whether lower courts have made errors of law.

Appellate jurisdiction The power of a higher court to review and modify the decision of a lower court.

Appellee or respondent The party in a lawsuit against whom an appeal has been filed.

Appropriation An intentional unauthorized exploitive use of another person's personality, name, or picture for the defendant's benefit.

Arbitration An ADR mechanism whereby the parties submit their disagreement to a third party whose decision is binding.

Arraignment A criminal proceeding at which the court informs the defendant of the charges being brought against him or her and the defendant enters a plea.

Arrest Occurs when the police restrain a person's freedom and charge the person with a crime.

Arrest warrant A court order directing the arrest of a person.

Arson The malicious burning of the house or property of another.

Articles of incorporation The primary document needed to form a corporation.

Artisan's lien The right to retain an interest in property until a worker has been paid for his or her labor.

Assault An intentional act that creates a reasonable apprehension of an immediate harmful or offensive physical contact.

Assigned counsel A private lawyer paid by the state on a contractual basis to represent an indigent client.

Assignee A person to whom contract rights are assigned.

Assignment The transfer by one of the original parties to the contract of part or all of his or her interest to a third party.

Assignor　A person who assigns contract rights.

Assumption　In logic, a belief that justifies one in arguing a conclusion.

Assumption of the risk　Voluntarily and knowingly subjecting oneself to danger.

At-will employment　When an employee has not signed a formal contract with the employer governing the employment relationship.

Attachment　In secured transactions, a process that gives the creditor rights against the debtor when the creditor either possesses collateral from the debtor or has a signed **security agreement.**

Attorney　A lawyer; a person licensed by a court to practice law. This term is often used to refer to a job title.

Attorney-client privilege　A rule of evidence that prevents a lawyer or a paralegal from being compelled to testify about confidential client information.

Attorney general　The chief legal officer of the federal or a state government.

Attorney work product　Materials prepared by an attorney or paralegal in anticipation of litigation.

Authenticate　To establish that the document being presented is what it is claimed to be.

Authentication　Proof that the evidence is what it is said to be.

Bail　Money or something else of value that is held by the government to ensure the defendant's appearance in court.

Bailee　The party taking temporary control of personal property during a bailment.

Bailiff　An officer of the court who is responsible for maintaining order in the courtroom.

Bailment　A temporary transfer of personal property to someone other than the owner for a specified purpose.

Bailor　The owner of the personal property that is being temporarily transferred as part of a bailment.

Bankruptcy judges　Appointed for set terms, judges who handle bankruptcy matters.

Bankrupty proceeding　A process governed by federal law whereby a debtor unable to pay its debts seeks protection.

Bates stamping　Assigns a unique, individual number to each page so that out of the thousands of document pages, no two pages have the same number.

Battered spouse syndrome　A form of defense that is sometimes allowed when someone has been the victim of repeated attacks, even when that victim is not in immediate danger.

Battery　An intentional act that creates a harmful or offensive physical contact. Can form the basis for either a tort or a criminal action.

Bearer paper　A document that has written on its front a statement that it is payable to cash or payable to the bearer, or has a signature on the back, causing it to be indorsed in blank.

Bench trial　A trial conducted without a jury.

Beneficiary　The person named in a will, insurance policy, or trust who receives a benefit.

Bequest　Also known as a **legacy**; a gift of personal property in a will.

Best evidence rule　The rule requiring that the original document be produced at trial.

Beyond a reasonable doubt　The standard of proof used in criminal trials. The evidence presented must be so conclusive and complete that all reasonable doubts regarding the facts are removed from the jurors' minds.

Bilateral contract　A contract where a promise is exchanged for a promise.

Bill　A proposed law as presented to a legislature.

Billable hours　The number of hours, or parts of an hour, that can be charged to a specific client.

Bill of Rights　The first ten amendments to the U.S. Constitution.

Black letter law　Generally accepted legal principles.

Bluebook　A book originally written by a group of law students to provide a uniform method for citations in law reviews; contains detailed rules for all forms of citation.

Board of directors　The group responsible for the management of a corporation.

Boilerplate　Standard language found in a particular type of legal document.

Bona fide occupational qualification (BFOQ)　A defense to an overt discrimination claim, alleging that the qualification is necessary to the essence of the business operation.

Booking　The process after arrest that includes taking the defendant's personal information, giving the defendant an opportunity to read and sign a *Miranda* card, and allowing the defendant the opportunity to use a telephone.

Boolean connectors　Logical connectors, such as "or" and "and," that make key word searches more precise.

Bribery　Offering something of value to a public official with the purpose of influencing that official's actions.

Brief　Either a short written summary of a court opinion or a written argument presented to a court. See **Appellate brief.**

Brief answer　In a law office memorandum, the brief answer gives the reader a short, specific answer to the question presented.

Broad holding　A statement of the court's decision in which the facts are either omitted or given in very general terms so that it will apply to a wider range of cases.

Burden of production   The necessity to produce some evidence, but it need not be so strong as to convince the trier of fact of its truth.

Burden of proof   The necessity of proving the truth of the matter asserted.

Bureau of National Affairs (BNA)   A private publishing company that publishes legal materials, including United States Law Week.

Burglary   Breaking into and entering a building with the intent of committing a felony.

"But for" standard   See **Actual cause.**

Buyer in the ordinary course of business   Someone who buys a product in good faith and without knowledge that someone else has a security interest in the goods.

Canons of construction   General principles that guide the courts in their interpretation of statutes.

Capital crime   A crime for which the death sentence can be imposed.

Caption   The heading section of a pleading that contains the names of the parties, the name of the court, the title of the action, the docket or file number, and the name of the pleading.

Case briefing   A stylized method for summarizing court opinions.

Case citation   Information that tells the reader the name of the case, where it can be located, the court that decided it, and the year it was decided.

Case of first impression   A type of case that the court has never faced before.

Case history   Either prior or subsequent procedural history of the case cited.

Casemaker   An online legal database containing court decisions and statutes from the entire country, as well as secondary authority; and CiteCheck, similar in function to LexisNexis Shepard's citations online.

Case management   Handling the flow of paperwork involved in client cases.

Case Management/Electronic Case Files (CM/ECF)   A comprehensive case management system developed for the federal courts allowing them to receive electronic filings and to maintain case files accessible via the Internet.

Case reporters   Books that contain appellate court decisions. There are official reports and unofficial reporters.

Castle doctrine   The defense that one can use deadly force if necessary to protect one's home and its inhabitants.

Cause of action   A claim that based on the law and the facts is sufficient to support a lawsuit. If the plaintiff does not state a valid cause of action in the complaint, the court will dismiss it.

Cause in fact   See **Actual cause.**

Caveat emptor   Let the buyer beware.

Censure or reprimand   A public or private statement that a lawyer's conduct violated the code of ethics.

Certificated   The status of having received a certificate documenting that the person has successfully completed an educational paralegal program.

Certification   A method of recognizing accomplishment administered by nongovernmental bodies.

Certified   The status of being formally recognized by a governmental or nongovernmental organization for having met special criteria, such as fulfilling educational requirements and passing an exam, established by that organization.

Certified Legal Assistant   A registered trademark of the National Association of Legal Assistants.

Certiorari   See **Writ of certiorari.**

Chain of custody   A record identifying who had control and access to evidentiary materials from the time they were obtained until the time they are introduced into evidence.

Challenge for cause   A method for excusing a prospective juror based on the juror's inability to serve in an unbiased manner.

Charging the jury   After both sides have presented their final arguments, the judge's instructions to the jury on the meaning of the law to be applied to the facts of the case.

Charitable immunity   The prohibition against suing charitable institutions.

Chattel   Personal property.

Check   A specialized form of a draft in which a bank depositor names a specific payee to whom funds are to be paid from the drawer's account.

Checks and balances   Division among the three branches of the federal government so that each one acts as a check on the power of the other two, thereby maintaining a balance of power among the branches.

Child abuse   Intentional harm to a child's physical or mental well-being.

Child neglect   The negligent failure to provide a child with the necessaries of life.

Child support   Money that the noncustodial parent contributes to assist the custodial parent in paying for a child's food, shelter, clothing, medical care, and education.

Circumstantial evidence   Indirect evidence, used to prove facts by implication.

Citation   A stylized form for giving the reader information about a legal authority, generally including the name of the authority, its date, and specifics such as volume and page numbers to help the reader locate it. For court opinions, a citation includes the name of the case, where it can be located, the name of the court that decided it, and the year it was decided. A statutory citation is a formalized method for referring to a statute's chapter (or title) and section numbers. The Bluebook gives precise rules as to how citations are to be written. See also **Bluebook**.

Citator A resource to help ensure the validity of a law.

Cited case The case you are Shepardizing.

Citing case A case listed in Shepard's that cites your case.

Civil action A lawsuit brought to enforce an individual right or gain payment for an individual wrong.

Civil law Law that deals with harm to an individual.

Class action suit A lawsuit brought by a person as a representative for a group of people who have been similarly injured.

Claw-back provision An agreement whereby privileged documents inadvertently produced can be retrieved.

Clear and convincing The standard of proof used in some civil trials. The evidence presented must be greater than a preponderance of the evidence, but less than beyond a reasonable doubt.

Clear title An ownership right that is free from encumbrances or other defects; also known as **marketable title**.

Clearly erroneous The standard used by appellate courts when reviewing a trial court's findings of fact.

Client confidentiality An ethical rule requiring that lawyers and paralegals maintain their clients' secrets.

Client file All of the relevant documents related to a client.

Client trust account A bank account used to hold money belonging to a client or to a third party.

Closed questions Specific questions that usually demand very short or yes/no answers.

Closely held corporation A relatively small business operation in which one person or the members of a family own all the stock.

Closing statement An itemized allocation of all the costs and moneys exchanged among the various parties, including financial institutions and real estate brokers, when a property is sold.

Closing table A table located in digest volumes and pocket parts indicating the last volume and page numbers for the reporters included in that digest.

Code A compilation of federal or state statutes in which the statutes are organized by subject matter rather than by year of enactment.

Code of Federal Regulations (C.F.R.) A compilation of federal administrative regulations arranged by agency.

Codicil A supplement or addition to a will that modifies, explains, or adds to its provisions.

Codification The process of organizing statutes by subject matter.

Codification of the common law The process of legislative enactment of areas of the law previously governed solely by the common law.

Collaborative divorce A non-adversarial process whereby the divorcing couple hires a team of professionals to help them reach a mutually satisfactory agreement.

Collateral heir One who has the same ancestors, but does not descend from the decedent.

Comma splice A type of run-on sentence; two independent clauses joined by a comma.

Commercial impracticability An argument that a contract has become too costly for one of the parties.

Commercial paper A written promise or order to pay a certain sum of money.

Committee hearing Legislative committees often hold public hearings where interested parties can testify about a proposed law. The transcript of the hearing becomes a part of the statute's legislative history.

Committee report When a legislative committee holds public hearings on proposed legislation, the result of those hearings is sometimes published in a committee report, which becomes part of the statute's legislative history.

Common law The body of law that has evolved from judicial decisions in cases that do not involve constitutional, statutory, or administrative regulation interpretation. Law created by the courts.

Common-law marriage A marriage that has not been solemnized but in which the parties have mutually agreed to enter into a relationship in which they accept all the duties and responsibilities that correspond to those of marriage.

Community property state A state that classifies all property acquired by either the husband or the wife during the marriage, with the exception of gifts or inheritance, as marital property to be equally distributed between the spouses at the time of the divorce.

Commutation An executive action that lessens the penalty for a crime without changing the fact of conviction.

Comparative negligence A method for measuring the relative negligence of the plaintiff and the defendant, with a commensurate sharing of the compensation for the injuries.

Compensatory damages Money awarded to a plaintiff in payment for his or her actual losses. Compare **punitive damages**.

Competency Relates to the fitness of a person to perform certain legal actions, such as, meeting the minimum requirements to give testimony in court (must be able to explain to the jury what was seen or heard) or the requirements to serve on a jury (must be able to hear and follow testimony and arguments); the defendant's mental state at the time of the trial (must be able to understand the proceedings and communicate with his or her lawyer), a person's mental state at the time a will is signed (must be of "sound mind," know what property he or she possesses and to whom it should go); or a person's ability to make a binding contract (must be an adult without severe mental impairments).

Complaint The pleading that begins a lawsuit.

Complete defense   A defense that, if proven, relieves the defendant of all criminal responsibility.

Compulsory joinder   When a person must be brought into a lawsuit as either a plaintiff or a defendant.

Concluding paragraph   The final paragraph in a written legal analysis that summarizes the writer's conclusions.

Concurrent conflict of interest   Simultaneously representing adverse clients.

Concurrent jurisdiction   When more than one court has jurisdiction to hear a case.

Concurring opinion   An opinion that agrees with the majority's result, but disagrees with its reasoning.

Conditional fee estate   The current owner of the land retains ownership only as long as certain conditions are met.

Cone of silence   See **ethical screen**.

Confidentiality   The ethical rule prohibiting lawyers and paralegals from disclosing information regarding a client or a client's case.

Conflict of interest   The ethical rule prohibiting lawyers and paralegals from working for opposing sides in a case.

Conflict check   The process of ensuring that there is no conflict of interest between the firm's current or past clients and a potential new client.

Conjunctive adverb   An adverb that joins two clauses. Examples include *also, consequently, furthermore, however, moreover, nevertheless, then*, and *therefore*. These should not be used to join two independent clauses.

Consanguinity   See **Kindred**.

Consent to search   When someone, who has the authority to do so, voluntarily agrees to allow law enforcement to search a dwelling, car, or business.

Consequential damages   Indirect damages that must be foreseeable to be recovered. Also called **Special damages**.

Consideration   Anything of value; it must be present for a valid contract to exist, and each side must give consideration.

Consortium   See **Loss of consortium**.

Conspiracy   An agreement to commit an unlawful act.

Constitutional court   A court established by Article III of the U.S. Constitution.

Constitutional law   The study of the U.S. Constitution, the legal framework it established, and the rights it protects; a body of principles and rules that are either explicitly stated in, or inferred from, the constitutions of the United States and those of the individual states.

Constructive   Not factually true, but accepted by the courts as being legally true.

Constructive delivery   When actual delivery is impossible but the court decides that enough was done to prove intent to relinquish title and control.

Constructive eviction   An act by a landlord that makes the premises unfit or unsuitable for occupancy.

Constructive knowledge   Not actual knowledge but the knowledge that the person should have if reasonable care is taken to be informed.

Content neutrality   The principle that laws may not limit free expression on the basis of whether the speech's content supports or opposes any particular position.

Contextual analysis   A form of statutory analysis in which meaning is inferred from the statement of legislative purpose and other sections of the statute.

Contingency fee   Lawyer compensation that is calculated as a percentage of the settlement or award in the case rather than a flat or an hourly fee.

Contract   A legally enforceable agreement supported by consideration.

Contract reformation   An equitable remedy that allows the courts to "rewrite" contract provisions.

Contributory negligence   Negligence by the plaintiff that contributed to his or her injury. Normally, it is a complete bar to the plaintiff's recovery. See **Comparative negligence**.

Conversion   The taking of someone else's property with the intent of permanently depriving the owner; the civil side of theft.

Coordinating conjunction   A coordinating conjunction can join two independent clauses; examples include *and, but, for, nor, or*, and *yet*.

Copyright   An author or artist's right to control the use of his or her works.

Corporation   A business entity formed by an association of shareholders.

Corpus Juris Secundum (C.J.S.)   West's law encyclopedia; contains cross-references to West digest topics and key numbers.

Correctional system   See **penal system**.

Corroborative evidence   Evidence that supports previous testimony but that comes in a different form.

Count   In a complaint, one cause of action.

Counterclaim   A claim by the defendant against the plaintiff. A compulsory counterclaim relates to the facts alleged in the complaint. A permissive counterclaim can relate to an entirely different factual setting.

Court   A unit of the judicial branch of government that has the authority to decide legal disputes.

Court clerk   A court official responsible for keeping the court files in proper condition and ensuring that the various motions filed by lawyers and the actions taken by judges are properly recorded.

Court commissioner   A title given in some states to a public official with limited judicial powers.

Court of record A court where a permanent record is kept of the testimony, lawyers' remarks, and judges' rulings.

Court reporter A person trained to take a verbatim transcript of a courtroom proceeding or deposition.

Covenant not to compete A promise not to compete within a given geographical area for a specific time period; also known as a **noncompete agreement**.

Cover Finding substitute goods.

Crime An activity that has been prohibited by the legislature as violating a duty owed to society; it is prosecutable by the government, with the possibility of punishment of a fine, imprisonment, or even death.

Criminal complaint A document charging a person with a crime.

Criminal defenses In a criminal case, a fact or legal argument that would relieve the defendant of guilt.

Criminal justice system Used to refer to a combination of legislative, administrative, and judicial agencies that are involved in the development and enforcement of criminal law in the United States.

Criminal law Law that deals with harm to society as a whole.

Criminal procedure The way in which criminal prosecutions are handled; governed by the federal or state rules of criminal procedure.

Cross-claim A claim by one defendant against another defendant or by one plaintiff against another plaintiff.

Cross-examination The questioning of an opposing witness.

Cumulative evidence Evidence that does not add any new information but that confirms facts that already have been established.

Custodial interrogation Occurs when law enforcement authorities question a person who has been deprived of his or her freedom in a significant way.

Custody In criminal law, occurs when the defendant has been deprived of freedom in a significant way. In family law, when couples divorce, the court determines with whom the children will live and how legal decisions, regarding such things as the children's health care and education, will be made.

Damages Monetary compensation, including compensatory, punitive, and nominal damages.

Deadly force A force that would cause serious bodily injury or death.

Decedent A person who died.

Declarant The person who made a statement.

Deductive reasoning A form of logical reasoning based on a major premise, a minor premise, and a conclusion.

Deed A legal document that formally conveys title to property to the new owner. In most sales, a warranty deed is used.

Defamation The publication of false statements that harm a person's reputation.

Defamation per se Remarks considered to be so harmful that they are automatically viewed as defamatory.

Default judgment A judgment entered against a party who fails to complete a required step, such as answering the complaint.

Defendant In a lawsuit, the person who is sued; in a criminal case, the person who is charged with a crime.

Defense A fact or legal argument that would relieve the defendant of liability in a civil case or guilt in a criminal case.

Delegatee A person who owes an obligation to the obligee in a contractual situation.

Delegation The transfer by one of the original parties to the contract of his or her obligations to a third party.

Delegator A person who delegates duties under a contract.

Demand letter A letter from a lawyer demanding that some action be taken, with either an implicit or an explicit threat to take the matter to court if the requested action is not forthcoming.

Dependent clause A clause that contains a subject and a verb but that cannot stand alone, as it does not contain a complete thought. A dependent clause always begins with a subordinating conjunction (e.g., *that, before, after, because*).

Deponent The person who is being asked questions at a deposition.

Deposition The pretrial oral questioning of a witness under oath.

Derogation of the common law A term referring to legislation that changes the common law.

Descendants Lineal heirs who descend from, or issue from, the decedent, such as children and grandchildren; also known as **issue**.

Detrimental reliance See **Promissory estoppel**.

Devise A gift of real estate that is given to someone through a will.

Dictum A statement in a judicial opinion that is not necessary for the decision of the case. Plural is dicta.

Digest A book that contains court opinion headnotes arranged by subject matter.

Direct appellate review Occurs when the courts think a case is so significant that the middle step of going through an intermediate appellate court should be skipped; the case proceeds directly from a trial court to the highest appellate court.

Direct evidence Establishes a direct link to the event that must be proved.

Direct examination The questioning of your own witness.

Directed verdict A verdict ordered by a trial judge if the plaintiff fails to present a prima facie case or if the defendant fails to present a necessary defense.

Disability Under the Americans with Disabilities Act (ADA), a physical or mental impairment that substantially limits a major life activity. An individual with a disability is one who has such an impairment, has a record of such an impairment, or is regarded as having such an impairment.

Disaffirm The ability to take back one's contractual obligations.

Disbarment The revocation of a lawyer's license.

Disclosure The intentional publication of embarrassing private affairs.

Discovery The modern pretrial procedure by which one party gains information from the adverse party.

Disillusionment See **divorce.**

Dismissal with prejudice A court order that ends a lawsuit; the suit cannot be refiled by the same parties.

Dismissal without prejudice A court order that ends a lawsuit; the suit can be refiled by the same parties.

Disparate impact The legal theory applied when the use of a neutral standard has a disproportionate impact on one protected group.

Disparate treatment The legal theory applied when a rejected applicant claims the reason for rejection was based on a discriminatory intent but the employer alleges a nondiscriminatory reason.

Disposition The result reached in a particular case.

Dissenting opinion An opinion that disagrees with the majority's decision and reasoning.

Distinguish To find differences (distinctions) between two situations.

Distinguishable cases Cases that involve dissimilar facts or rules of law.

District attorney A lawyer elected or appointed to prosecute crimes in a particular jurisdiction.

Diversity jurisdiction The power of the federal courts to hear matters of state law if the opposing parties are from different states and the amount in controversy exceeds $75,000.

Diversity of citizenship A situation where the opposing parties are from different states and the amount in controversy exceeds $75,000.

Divided custody A situation in which the court separates the children so that each parent is awarded custody of one or more of the children.

Dividend A distribution of the corporate profit as ordered by the board of directors.

Divorce Also called **disillusionment;** a legal judgment that dissolves a marriage.

Doctrine of equitable distribution A system for distributing property acquired during a marriage on the basis of such factors as the contributions of the spouses, the length of the marriage, the age and health of the spouses, and their ability to make a living.

Doctrine of implied powers Powers not stated in the Constitution, but that are necessary for Congress to carry out other, expressly granted powers.

Doctrine of incorporation In constitutional law, the application of the Fourteenth Amendment's due process protections to incorporate the provisions of the Bill of Rights and make them applicable to the states.

Documentary evidence Consists of records, contracts, leases, wills, and other written instruments, saved as hard copy printouts, computer files on a hard drive or in the cloud, or as a posting on a social network site.

Document harvesting The searching of electronic files for relevant information.

Document preparer An individual who prepares legal documents for people who are attempting to handle their own legal matters **pro se.**

Documents clerk Someone who organizes and files legal documents.

Domestic corporation A corporation doing business in its own state.

Donor A person who creates a trust; also known as a **grantor** or **settlor.**

Double jeopardy A constitutional protection against being tried twice for the same crime.

Draft A three-party instrument in which the **drawer** orders the drawee, usually a bank, to pay money to the **payee.**

Dramshop laws Statutes making bar owners responsible if intoxicated patrons negligently injure third parties.

Drawee On the face of a check or draft, the party that is ordering payment to be made.

Drawer On the face of a check or draft, the party that is ordered to pay.

Due process The principle, guaranteed by the Fifth and Fourteenth Amendments to the U.S. Constitution, that notice and a hearing must be provided before depriving someone of property or liberty.

Durable health care power of attorney A document that gives someone the power to make health care decisions for you if you become incapacitated and cannot make those decisions yourself. Also known as a **health care proxy.**

Durable power of attorney A document that gives someone else power to act for you if you become incapacitated and unable to handle your financial matters on your own. See **Health care proxy.**

Duress In criminal law, a defense requiring proof that force or a threat of force was used to cause a person to commit a criminal act. In contract law, pressure that is so great as to overwhelm the contracting party's ability to make a free choice.

Earnest money The money the buyer turns over to the real estate agent to be applied to the purchase price of property.

Easement A right to use property owned by another for a limited purpose.

Ejusdem generis A canon of construction meaning "of the same class."

Electronically Stored Information (ESI) Information created, disbursed, or stored in an electronic format.

Electronic discovery (e-discovery) The process of gaining information from the adverse party when that information is in electronic form, such as e-mails, voice mails, text messages, photographs, spreadsheets, and documents.

Electronic filing (e-filing) The filing of court documents over the Internet as electronic files.

Electronic signature A means of establishing that a document being sent electronically was properly authorized.

Element A separable part of a statute that must be satisfied for the statute to apply.

Emancipated minor Someone who is still under the legal age of adulthood but who has nevertheless been released from parental authority and given the legal rights of an adult.

Eminent domain The power of government to take private property for public purposes.

Employee A person working for another. Compare **Independent contractor.**

En banc When an appellate court that normally sits in panels sits as a whole.

Enabling act A statute establishing and setting out the powers of an administrative agency.

Enacted law Constitutions, statutes, ordinances, and administrative regulations.

Encumbrance A lien or other type of security interest that signifies that some other party has a legitimate claim to the property.

Entrapment A defense requiring proof that the defendant would not have committed the crime but for trickery or inducement by law enforcement officers.

Equity A principle that allows judges to take action, such as issuing injunctions and ordering specific performance, when otherwise the law would limit their decisions to monetary awards.

Escheat A reversion of property to the state when there are no heirs.

Escrow account A bank account used to hold money belonging to a client or a third party.

Estate In property law, an interest in or title to real property. In probate law, the total property of whatever kind, both real and personal, that a person owns at the time of his or her death.

Ethical screen Also known as an **ethical wall** or **cone of silence** A system developed to shield a lawyer or a paralegal from a case that otherwise would create a conflict of interest.

Ethical wall A system developed to shield a lawyer or a paralegal from a case that otherwise would create a conflict of interest. Also known as an **ethical screen** or **cone of silence.**

Evict To remove a tenant from possession of rental property.

Evidence Information that can be presented in a court of law as proof of some fact. Evidence can consist of witness testimony or documents and exhibits. It is the proof presented at a trial.

Evolutionary approach An approach to constitutional interpretation in which judges seek to determine the underlying purpose that the drafters had in mind at the time they wrote the law and the modern-day option that best advances that purpose.

Exception A lawyer's objection to a trial court's ruling in order to preserve it as grounds for an appeal.

Exclusionary rule A rule that states that evidence obtained in violation of an individual's constitutional rights cannot be used against that individual in a criminal trial.

Exclusive jurisdiction When only one court has the power to hear a case.

Exculpatory clause A provision that purports to waive liability.

Exculpatory evidence Evidence that suggests the defendant's innocence; the opposite of **inculpatory evidence.**

Execute To perform or to sign; in contract law, an executed contract is one that has been completely performed.

Execute a warrant To carry out the provisions of a warrant.

Executive clemency The power of the president or a governor to pardon someone or reduce someone's sentence.

Executive memorandum An official policy directive issued by the president for the federal government, or by the governor of a state, which directs government employees as to how they should implement a law.

Executive order An official policy directive issued by the president for the federal government, or by the governor of a state, which directs government employees as to how they should implement a law. At the federal level, executive orders are published in the *Federal Register.*

Executor/Executrix A person appointed by the testator to carry out the directions and requests in his or her will.

Executory contract A contract that has not been fully performed.

Exemplary damages See **Punitive damages.**

Exhaustion The requirement that appellate courts intervene only after the trial court has had an opportunity to correct its own errors.

Exhaustion of administrative remedies The requirement that relief be sought from an administrative agency before proceeding to court.

Exigent circumstances Generally, an emergency situation that allows a search to proceed without a warrant.

Expert witness A witness who possesses skill and knowledge beyond that of the average person and is allowed to speculate about what caused something or how it happened.

Explanatory parenthetical A parenthetical located at the end of a case citation containing information about the case.

Express contracts Contracts that are formed through words, either oral or written.

Express warranty An express warranty or promise created by an affirmation of fact or a promise made by the seller, a description of the goods sold, or a sample or model provided that forms the basis of the bargain.

Extradition The transportation of an individual from one state to another so that person can be tried on criminal charges.

Fact An actual incident or condition; not a legal consequence.

Fact bound The principle that even a minor change in facts can change the outcome of a case.

False arrest Occurs when a person is arrested (by either a law officer or a citizen) without probable cause and the arrest is not covered by special privilege.

False imprisonment Occurs whenever one person, through force or the threat of force, unlawfully detains another person against his or her will.

False light The intentional false portrayal of someone in a way that would be offensive to a reasonable person.

Fastcase An online legal database containing court decisions and statutes from the entire country, as well as secondary authority; includes a citation checker and AI Sandbox, using artificial intelligence (AI) to analyze data or documents.

Family law The area of the law that covers marriage, divorce, and parent-child relationships.

Federal question A legal issue involving the application of a federal law.

Federal question jurisdiction The power of the federal courts to hear matters of federal law.

Federal Register A daily newspaper in which proposed federal regulations are first printed.

Federal Reporter The West reporter that contains decisions from the U.S. courts of appeals.

Federal Rules of Civil Procedure The rules governing the stages of civil litigation in federal courts.

Federal Sentencing Guidelines Government guidelines that specify an appropriate range of sentences for each class of convicted persons based on factors related to the offense and the offender.

Federal Supplement The West reporter that contains decisions from the U.S. district courts.

Federalism A system of government in which the authority to govern is split between a single, nationwide central government and several regional governments that control specific geographical areas.

Fee simple absolute estate An ownership of land that is free from any conditions or restrictions.

Felony A serious crime, usually carrying a prison sentence of one or more years.

Fiduciary A person who has a legally imposed obligation to act in the best interests of another party.

Fiduciary duty A legally imposed obligation to act in the best interests of the party to whom the duty is owed.

Financing statement A public record of a security interest.

Fine A penalty requiring the payment of money.

Fixed fee A set charge for a specific service, such as drafting a simple will.

Floating lien A security interest in proceeds or after acquired property.

Floor debate Debate that takes place in the legislature before a vote is taken on a proposed statute. It becomes part of the statute's legislative history.

Follow precedent When a court bases its decision on prior similar cases.

Forcible entry and detainer In some states, a summary civil action by a landlord to regain possession of the premises from a tenant who disputes the landlord's right to possession. Also, an action by anyone with the right to possession who has been unlawfully evicted.

Foreclosure The process by which a creditor who holds a mortgage or some other form of a lien on real property can force the sale of that property in order to satisfy the debt to the mortgagee or lien holder.

Foreign corporation A corporation incorporated in one state doing business in another state.

Forensic search In e-discovery, a search that is performed to recover deleted files or older versions of current files to look for any changes.

Forfeiture The loss of money or property as a result of committing a criminal act.

Forgery The alteration or falsification of documents with the intent to defraud.

Formal contract A contract requiring certain formalities, such as a seal, to be valid.

Formal will A will that has been prepared on a word processor or typewriter and that has been properly signed by the testator and the required witnesses.

Fourth branch of government Administrative agencies.

Fraud A false representation of facts or intentional perversion of the truth to induce someone to take some action or give up something of value.

Freehold estate A right of title or ownership to real property that extends for life or some other indeterminate period of time.

Freelance paralegal A paralegal who works as an independent contractor rather than as an employee of a law firm or corporation.

Friend of the court See **Amicus curiae.**

Fruit of the poisonous tree doctrine Evidence that is derived from an illegal search or interrogation is inadmissible.

Full-text database A computerized database that contains the full text of documents, such as court opinions or depositions.

Full-text search A computer search that identifies every place in which the search term appears in the actual text of the document being searched.

Fused sentence A type of run-on sentence; two independent clauses with no separating punctuation.

Garnishment A process through which a court can require an employer to withhold money from an employee's wages and turn this money over to the party to whom a debt is owed.

General damages Damages that you would naturally expect to occur given the type of harm suffered.

General intent An intention to act without regard to the results of the act.

General jurisdiction A court's power to hear any type of case arising within its geographical area.

General partnership A type of partnership in which all partners have the right to manage the business.

Grand jury A group of people, usually 23, whose function is to determine if probable cause exists to believe that a crime has been committed and that the defendant committed it.

Grantor The prior owner.

Guardian A person appointed by the court to manage the affairs or property of a person who is incompetent due to age or some other reason.

Guardian ad litem Someone appointed by the court to speak for the interests of a child.

Guilty Convicted of a crime.

Habitual offender statute A statute that mandates required prison sentences for third-time offenders

Harmless error A trial court error that is not sufficient to warrant reversing the decision.

Hate crime A crime in which the selection of the victim is based on that person's membership in a protected category, such as race, sex, or sexual orientation.

Hate speech Speech directed at a particular group or classification of people that involves expressions of hate or intimidation.

Headnote A summary of one legal point in a court opinion on some databases; written by the editors of the database in question.

Health care proxy A document in which an individual delegates legal authority to make medical or financial decisions for that person if he or she is too incapacitated to make such decisions; also known as a **durable power of attorney.**

Hearing officer Holds administrative hearings, administers oaths, issues subpoenas, oversees depositions, and holds settlement conferences; also known as an **administrative law judge.**

Hearsay Testimony or evidence introduced in court regarding what someone said out of court for the purpose of establishing the truth of what was said.

Heir Someone entitled to inherit property left by the decedent.

History The prior or subsequent history of the case you are Shepardizing; it is always preceded by a one-letter abbreviation.

Holder Someone who receives negotiable paper through proper delivery.

Holder in due course Someone who gives value in good faith (a subjective standard) and without notice that the instrument is overdue or has been dishonored or has any claims against it or defenses to it (an objective standard).

Holding The new legal principle established by a court opinion. In a case brief, the court's answer to the issue presented to it.

Holographic will A will that was handwritten by the testator, without the witness signatures necessary for a formal will; an informal will.

Home page The first page of a website that has multiple links to other places on the website and to other websites.

Homestead exemption A provision in state or local law that provides homeowners with specified types of protection from creditors or special tax deductions.

Homicide The killing of one human being by another.

Hostile witness A witness who shows bias or hostility toward the party that asked him or her to testify; also known as an **adverse witness.**

Hostile work environment Occurs when unwelcome sexual conduct has the purpose or effect of unreasonably interfering with an individual's work performance or creating an intimidating, hostile, or offensive working environment.

Hourly rate A fee based on how many hours lawyers or paralegals spend on the case. Different hourly rates are often charged for different lawyers and paralegals within the firm, based on their seniority and experience.

Id.   A short citation form indicating reference is to the immediately preceding authority.

Immunity   For policy reasons, protection from being sued for negligent acts.

Implied warranty of fitness   An implied promise that the goods being sold will satisfy a special purpose.

Implied warranty of habitability   A requirement that property be fit for the purpose for which it is being rented. Owners are required to repair and maintain the premises at certain minimum levels.

Implied warranty of merchantability   An implied promise that the goods being sold will be usable for the purpose for which they were sold.

Implied-in-fact contract   A contract formed through conduct.

Inchoate crime   An attempted crime.

Incidental beneficiary   Someone who the original contracting parties did not explicitly intend to benefit from the contract.

Inculpatory evidence   Evidence that suggests the defendant's guilt; the opposite of **exculpatory evidence.**

Independent adoption   An adoption that involves a private agreement between the birth parents and the adoptive parents.

Independent clause   A clause that contains a subject and a verb and that can stand alone as a sentence.

Independent contractor   A person who works for another, but who retains the right to control the manner of producing the end result; not an employee.

Independent paralegal   A paralegal working under the supervision of a lawyer in a contractual relationship. Sometimes used to refer to a paralegal providing legal services directly to the public without being under the supervision of a lawyer.

Indictment   A grand jury's written accusation that a given individual has committed a crime. Compare **Presentment.**

Indorsement in blank   When an indorser simply signs his or her name and does not specify to whom the instrument is payable.

Infant   In the law, a name sometimes used to mean any minor child.

Inference   A conclusion reached based on the facts given.

Inferior courts   In the federal system, all courts other than the U.S. Supreme Court.

Informal contract   A contract not requiring any particular formalities to be valid.

Information   A prosecutor's written accusation that a person has committed a crime.

Infra   Below; used to refer to authority cited later in a document. May not be used with citations to cases, statutes, or constitutions.

Initial appearance   The first court hearing for a person charged with committing a crime.

Injunction   A court order requiring a party to perform a specific act or to cease doing a specific act.

Insanity defense   A defense requiring proof that the defendant was not mentally responsible.

Intangible property   Personal property that cannot be touched, such as a stock certificate or a patent.

Intellectual property   Intangible assets that are created by someone's intellectual activity, such as trade secrets, copyrights, patents, and trade or service marks.

Intended beneficiary   A person whom the contractual parties intend to benefit.

Intentional infliction of emotional distress   An intentional tort that occurs through an extreme and outrageous act that causes severe emotional distress.

Intentional tort   A tort committed by one who intends to do the act that creates the harm.

Inter vivos trust   A trust that is created before a person's death.

Interference with a contractual relationship   An intentional tort that occurs if someone induces a party to breach a contract or interferes with the performance of a contract.

International Paralegal Management Association (IPMA)   A national association of paralegal managers.

Internet   A worldwide network of computer networks.

Interrogatories   Written questions sent by one side to the opposing side, answered under oath.

Intestate   The status of a person's estate when that person died without leaving a valid will.

Intimidation   Putting someone in fear, usually of physical harm to themselves or another person they know, to force them to do something or refrain from doing something.

Intoxication defense   A defense requiring proof that the defendant was not able to form the requisite mens rea to commit a crime due to intoxication.

Intrusion   The intentional unjustified encroachment into another person's private activities.

Intrusive phrase   A phrase placed between a sentence's subject and verb.

Invasion of privacy   An intentional tort that covers a variety of situations, including disclosure, intrusion, appropriation, and false light.

Involuntary manslaughter   The unlawful killing of another human being through criminal negligence or recklessness.

IRAC   A method for organizing legal writing; stands for "issue, rule, analysis, and conclusion."

Irresistible impulse test   A test that provides that the defendant is not guilty due to insanity if, at the time of the crime, the defendant could not control his or her actions.

Irrevocable trust   A form of inter vivos trust that the grantor cannot alter.

Issue A circumstance when the law is applied to specific facts and the result is not obvious. In a case brief, the rule of law applied to the case's specific facts. In an IRAC analysis, the statement of the client's problem. In probate law, a lineal heir; see **Decedent**.

Issue of first impression An issue that the court has never faced before.

Jail A place of confinement in a city or county.

Joint and several liability Liability shared collectively and individually.

Joint legal custody Both parents have an equal say in making major decisions, such as those regarding the education of the child.

Joint liability Shared liability, so that if one party is sued, others must be sued also.

Joint tenancy Ownership by two or more persons who have equal rights in the use of that property. When a joint tenant dies, that person's share passes to the other joint tenant(s).

Joint tenancy with right of survivorship Another term for **joint tenancy**.

Judge A court official who presides over courtroom proceedings and decides all legal questions. In a bench trial the judge also decides the facts.

Judgment The decision of the court regarding the claims of each side. It may be based on a jury's verdict.

Judgment notwithstanding the verdict (J.N.O.V.) A judgment that reverses the verdict of the jury when the verdict had no reasonable factual support or was contrary to law.

Judgment proof When the defendant does not have sufficient money or other assets to pay the judgment.

Judicial activism A judicial philosophy that supports an active role for the judiciary in changing the law.

Judicial history See **Procedural facts**.

Judicial notice When a judge formally recognizes something as being a fact without requiring the lawyers to prove it through the introduction of other evidence.

Judicial restraint A judicial philosophy that supports a limited role for the judiciary in changing the law, including deference to the legislative branch.

Judicial review The court's power to review statutes to decide if they conform to the U.S. Constitution.

Jurat A document with content that is sworn to or affirmed to be true by the signer, verbally, before a public official.

Jurisdiction The power of a court to hear particular types of cases or to hear cases within a specific geographic area.

Jurisprudence The study of law and legal philosophy.

Jury trial When a jury decides the facts and determines liability or guilt.

Just compensation The amount of money the government must pay the owner of property it seizes through eminent domain.

Justice of the peace A local public officer with the authority to try minor civil and criminal cases, usually with other limited powers such as to perform marriages.

Juvenile courts Special courts established to deal with juveniles who commit crimes or status offenses, or who are adjudged to be abused or neglected.

Juvenile delinquent A minor, usually under the age of 18, who commits acts that would be considered crimes if committed by adults or who commits status offenses, such as underage drinking or truancy.

Kidnapping An unlawful movement and confinement of the victim.

Kindred Persons related to the decedent by blood; also known as **consanguinity**.

Knowingly Not intending to cause a specific harm, but being aware that such harm would be caused.

Land contract An installment contract for the sale of land.

Landmark decision A court opinion that establishes new law in an important area.

Larceny Another term for **theft**.

Last clear chance The doctrine that states that despite the plaintiff's contributory negligence, the defendant should still be liable if the defendant was the last one in a position to avoid the accident.

Law clerk A law student or a recent law school graduate whose duties usually focus on legal research.

Law office memorandum An unbiased analysis of the client's situation.

Law review A journal generally published by a law school editorial board or by a bar association. The articles usually contain in-depth analyses of current legal topics.

Laws Rules of conduct promulgated and enforced by a government, based on policy decisions that determine legal rights and duties between people or between people and the government.

Lawyer A person who has been officially licensed to practice law in a state or federal jurisdiction. Also referred to as an **attorney**.

Lawyer work product Materials prepared by a lawyer or paralegal in anticipation of litigation.

Lay advocate Generally a nonlawyer who represents persons before administrative agencies that permit this practice.

Lay a foundation The process of providing the qualifications of a witness or properly identifying and authenticating evidence so that it can be introduced.

Lay witness A witness who has not been shown to have any special expertise and is limited to testifying about what was personally observed.

Leading question A question that suggests the answer; generally, leading questions may not be asked during direct examination of a witness.

Lease An agreement in which the property owner gives someone else the right to use that property for a designated period of time.

Leasehold A parcel of real estate held under a lease.

Leasehold estate A right to use real property for a limited period of time.

Legacy See **Bequest.**

Legal aid services See **Legal Services Corporation.**

Legal analysis The process of applying the law to a client's facts; also known as **legal reasoning.**

Legal assistant Synonym for **paralegal;** may also refer to other nonlawyers who assist lawyers.

Legal clinic Usually organized as either a partnership or a professional corporation, law clinics provide low-cost legal services on routine matters by stressing low overhead and high volume.

Legal custody In family law, the designated parent or guardian who has authority to make legal decisions for the child relating to such matters as health care and education.

Legal document preparer (LDP) A nonlawyer, not working under the supervision of a lawyer, who assists with the preparation of legal documents for individuals or companies representing themselves.

Legal fiction An assumption that something that is not real is real—for example, assuming that a corporation is a person for purposes of its being able to sue and be sued.

Legal formalism A legal theory that views the law as a complete and autonomous system of logically consistent principles within which judges find the correct result by simply making logical deductions.

Legal malpractice The failure of a lawyer to act reasonably.

Legal positivism A legal theory whose proponents believe that the validity of a law is determined by the process through which it was made rather than by the degree to which it reflects natural law principles.

Legal realism A legal philosophy whose proponents think that judges decide cases based on factors other than logic and preexisting rules, such as economic and sociological factors.

Legal reasoning The application of legal rules to a client's specific factual situation; also known as **legal analysis.**

Legal research The process of finding relevant legislation, administrative regulations, court opinions, and constitutional provisions.

Legal scrivener The provider of a typing service.

Legal Services Corporation A federally funded program to deliver legal assistance to the indigent.

Legal Services offices Affiliated with the federal government's **Legal Services Corporation,** these offices serve those who would otherwise be unable to afford legal assistance. See also **legal aid services.**

Legal technician A nonlawyer who provides legal services directly to the public without being under the supervision of a lawyer; also known as a **lay advocate.** Absent a statute allowing this activity, it constitutes the unauthorized practice of law.

Legal writing Examples of legal writing include case briefs, law office memoranda, and documents filed with the court.

Legislative courts Courts created under Congress's Article I powers.

Legislative history The background documents created during the process of a bill becoming a statute. These documents can include alternative versions of the legislation, proceedings of committee hearings, committee reports, and transcripts of floor debates.

Legislative history approach A method for interpreting statutes, regulations, and constitutional provisions in which judges attempt to determine what the drafters intended to accomplish by passing the law.

Legislative intent The purpose of the legislature at the time it enacted a statute. In interpreting statutes, the role of the court is to try to discover the intent of the legislature at the time it enacted the statute.

Lessee or tenant The person with right of possession during the term of the lease.

Lesser included offense A crime whose elements are contained within a more serious crime. For instance, theft is a lesser included offense of robbery.

Lessor or landlord The owner of the property being leased.

Lexis An online legal database containing court decisions and statutes from the entire country, as well as secondary authority; such as Am. Jur. 2d and A.L.R.

Liable A finding in a civil suit that a defendant is responsible.

Libel Written defamation.

Liberal construction An approach whereby the courts give a statute a broad interpretation.

Licensed Paralegal Practitioner (LPP) A paralegal in Utah meeting certain educational requirements, who is permitted to advise and assist clients in approved practice areas.

Licensing Governmental permission to engage in a profession.

Life estate An ownership right to real property that lasts only as long as that person, or some other named individual, lives.

Life tenant A person who has ownership under a life estate.

Limited jurisdiction A court's power to hear only specialized cases.

Limited liability company (LLC) A form of business ownership that gives small businesses the advantage of liability limited to the amount of the owner's investment along with single taxation.

Limited liability partnership (LLP) A form of business ownership similar to a general partnership except the partners do not have unlimited personal liability for the wrongful acts of other partners. Unlike a limited liability company, however, the partners remain personally liable for other business debts, such as rent and utilities.

Limited Licensed Legal Technician (LLLT) A nonlawyer in Washington who meets certain educational requirements and is permitted to advise and assist clients in approved practice areas.

Limited partnership A partnership of at least one general partner and one or more limited partners. The limited partners' liability is limited to their investments so long as they do not participate in management decisions.

Lineal heir Someone who is a grandparent, parent, child, grandchild, or great-grandchild of the decedent.

Liquidated damages The result of a provision in a contract that specifies what will happen in case of breach.

Listing agreement A document that spells out the nature of the services a real estate agent will perform with respect to selling real property and how the agent will be compensated for those services.

Litigation A lawsuit; a controversy to be settled in a court.

Litigation hold A requirement that routine alteration or destruction of ESI must stop whenever there is a reasonable belief that litigation may arise.

Living constitution A judicial philosophy that seeks to interpret the Constitution in light of existing societal values; also called "evolutionary" or "living law."

Living trust A form of inter vivos trust that allows a person, while still living, to benefit another.

Living will A document expressing a person's end-of-life health care wishes; also known as a **medical directive**.

Loss of consortium The loss by one spouse of the other spouse's companionship, services, or affection.

Magistrate A title sometimes given to a public official exercising limited judicial power.

Magistrate judge A court official who exercises limited judicial powers such as issuing subpoenas, conducting preliminary hearings, and ruling on procedural motions.

Maintenance See **Alimony**.

Major premise In deductive reasoning, the statement of a broad proposition that forms the starting point; in law, the statement of a legal rule that you can find in a statute or court opinion.

Majority opinion An opinion in which a majority of the court joins.

Maker On the face of a note, the person who signs, promising to pay.

Malice Making a defamatory remark either knowing the material was false or acting with a "reckless disregard" for whether or not it was true.

Malicious prosecution A lawsuit that can be brought against someone who unsuccessfully and maliciously brought an action without probable cause.

Mandatory authority or decisions Court decisions from a higher court in the same jurisdiction involving similar facts and law.

Marital property Property that is subject to court distribution upon termination of the marriage.

Market share theory A legal theory that allows plaintiffs to recover proportionately from a group of manufacturers when the identity of the specific manufacturer responsible for the harm is unknown.

Marketable title See **Clear title**.

Massachusetts Decisions The unofficial reporter published by West covering court decisions from Massachusetts also found in the Northeastern Reporter. The pages containing the court decisions from the other four states reported in the Northeastern Reporter are removed.

Massachusetts Digest A West publication; the digest is a collection of Massachusetts court decision summaries arranged by subject matter.

Massachusetts Digest table of cases An alphabetical listing of court decisions arranged by the plaintiff's last name, giving the citation and relevant topics and key numbers. There is also a defendant-plaintiff table, an alphabetical listing by the defendant's last name.

Massachusetts Practice Series (M.P.S.) A West publication; the Massachusetts equivalent of a legal encyclopedia. Contains cross-references to C.J.S. and Massachusetts Digest topics and key numbers.

Massachusetts Reports The official reporter published by the state of Massachusetts covering Massachusetts Supreme Judicial Court decisions.

Master In law, the name that is sometimes given to an employer.

Material breach A circumstance where there is such a grave failure to fulfill the contractual terms that the other party is relieved of all contractual obligations.

Material fact A fact on which the outcome of the case depends.

Mechanic's lien A claim filed by a contractor or repair person who had done work on a building for which he or she has not been fully paid.

Mediation An ADR mechanism whereby a neutral third party assists the parties in reaching a mutually agreeable, voluntary compromise.

Medical directive See **Living will.**

Meet and confer conference In federal court, a mandated conference at which the parties must develop a discovery plan.

Mens rea Criminal intent.

Merchant's firm offer An offer made by a merchant in a signed writing that assures the buyer that the offer will remain open for a specific period of time. It does not require consideration to be binding.

Metadata Information contained in a document that may include the author of the document, the date it was created, and other data about the document.

Mini-digest A digest located in an advance sheet pamphlet or hardbound volume of court decisions published by West. It contains the headnotes for the cases in that single publication.

Minimum contacts A constitutional fairness requirement that a defendant have at least a certain minimum contact with a state before the state courts can have jurisdiction over the defendant.

Minor A child who is under the age of legal competence.

Minor premise In deductive reasoning, the second proposition, which along with the major premise leads to the conclusion; in law, the minor premise consists of the client's facts.

Miranda **warnings** The requirement that defendants be notified of their rights to remain silent and to have a lawyer present prior to being questioned by the police.

Mirror image rule The requirement that the acceptance exactly mirror the offer or the acceptance becomes a counteroffer.

Misdemeanor A minor crime not amounting to a felony, usually punishable by a fine or a jail sentence of less than a year.

Misfeasance Acting in an improper or a wrongful way.

Mistrial A trial ended by the judge because of a major problem, such as a prejudicial statement by one of the lawyers.

Mitigation of damages The requirement that the non-breaching party take reasonable steps to limit his or her damages.

M'Naghten test A test that provides that the defendant is not guilty due to insanity if, at the time of the crime the defendant suffered from a defect or disease of the mind and could not understand whether the act was right or wrong.

Model Code of Professional Responsibility An older set of standards governing lawyer ethics developed by the American Bar Association (ABA).

Model Penal Code The American Law Institute's proposal for a uniform set of criminal laws; it is not the law unless adopted by a state's legislature.

Model Rules of Professional Conduct A set of ethical rules developed by the American Bar Association (ABA). The Model Rules have been adopted in whole or in part by every state and the District of Columbia.

Motion A request made to the court.

Motion for acquittal A request that the court end the trial by finding for the defendant.

Motion for a continuance A request that the court postpone the proceeding to a later time.

Motion for a directed verdict A request that the court find for the moving party because either the plaintiff failed to present a prima facie case or the defendant failed to present a necessary defense.

Motion for judgment notwithstanding the verdict A request that the court reverse the jury's verdict when the verdict had no reasonable factual support or was contrary to law.

Motion in limine A request that the court order that certain information not be mentioned in the presence of the jury.

Motion for a new trial A request that the court order a rehearing of a lawsuit because irregularities, such as errors of the court or jury misconduct, make it probable that an impartial trial did not occur.

Motion to dismiss In civil litigation, a request that the court dismiss the case based on one of several grounds, including the failure of the plaintiff to state a claim upon which relief can be granted; also known as a **12(b)(6) motion.**

Motion to require a finding of not guilty A defense request that the court find the prosecution failed to meet its burden and that it remove the case from the jury by finding the defendant not guilty.

Motion to suppress A request that the court prohibit the use of certain evidence at the trial.

NALA: The Paralegal Association A national association of paralegals advancing paralegals through certification and professional development.

Narrow holding A statement of the court's decision that contains many of the case's specific facts, thereby limiting its future applicability to a narrow range of cases.

National Federation of Paralegal Associations (NFPA) A national association of paralegal associations advancing the paralegal profession.

National Reporter System West's system for reporting court decisions from every state and the federal courts.

Native format The format used by the program that created the file, such as Microsoft Word or Microsoft Excel.

Natural law A legal philosophy whose proponents think there are ideal laws that can be discovered through careful thought and humanity's innate sense of right and wrong.

Necessaries Normally food, clothing, shelter, and medical treatment.

Necessity A defense requiring proof that the defendant was forced to take an action to avoid a greater harm.

Negligence The failure to act reasonably under the circumstances.

Negligence per se Violation of a statute as proof of negligence.

Negotiable instrument Commercial paper that can be transferred by indorsement or delivery. It must meet the requirements of UCC §3-104 to be negotiable. If it does not, a transferee cannot become a holder, but only gets the rights along with the liabilities of a contract assignee.

New trial A rehearing of a lawsuit granted when irregularities such as errors of the court or jury misconduct make it probable that an impartial trial did not occur.

Next friend A person who represents the interests of someone in court without being that person's legal guardian.

No-fault divorce A form of divorce that allows a couple to end their marital relationship without having to assess blame for the breakup.

No-knock warrant A warrant that allows the police to enter without announcing their presence in advance.

Nolo contendere A defendant's plea meaning that the defendant neither admits nor denies the charges.

Nominal damages A token sum awarded when liability has been found but monetary damages cannot be shown.

Noncompete agreement See **covenant not to compete**.

Nonfeasance Failing to act.

Nonrestrictive phrase A phrase that is not essential to the sense of a sentence; it should be set off with commas.

North Eastern Reporter An unofficial regional reporter published by West covering court decisions from Massachusetts, as well as four other states.

Note A promise to pay money; a two-part instrument in which the maker promises to pay the payee.

Notice Being informed of some act done or about to be done.

Notice pleading A method adopted by the federal rules in which the plaintiff simply informs the defendant of the claim and the general basis for it.

Novation In a contract, when a third party is substituted for one of the original parties.

Nuncupative will An oral will.

Obligee A person owed a contractual benefit.

Obligor A person under a contractual obligation.

Obscenity Sexually explicit material without redeeming artistic, scientific, or political worth.

Offer In contract law, an indication of a firm desire to enter into an agreement that is sufficiently definite that once accepted, a contract is formed.

Official report Governmental publication of court opinions.

On all fours A term used to describe two cases that are almost identical, with similar facts and legal issues.

On point A term used to describe a case that is similar to another case.

Open questions Broad questions that put few limits on the freedom of the respondent.

Option contract A contract in which the buyer gives the seller consideration to keep the offer open for a stated period of time.

Order paper An instrument that is payable to the order of a specific party.

Ordinance A law enacted by a local government; a subcategory of statutory law.

Originalism An approach to constitutional interpretation that narrowly interprets the text of the Constitution in a manner that attempts to be consistent with what most people understood those words to mean at the time that they were written.

Original jurisdiction The authority of a court to hear a case when it is initiated, as opposed to appellate jurisdiction.

Output contract A contract in which one party agrees to deliver its entire output of a particular product to the other party.

Overbreadth A reason for invalidating a statute where it covers both protected and criminal activity.

Overrule A decision is overruled when a court in a later case changes the law so that its prior decision is no longer good law. Compare with **Reverse**.

Overt discrimination When an employer openly refuses to treat all applicants or employees equally.

Paralegal A person who assists a lawyer and, working under the lawyer's supervision, does tasks that, absent the paralegal, the lawyer would do. Paralegals cannot give legal advice or appear in court, nor can they set legal fees.

Parallel citation When reference to two or more reporters is required, each citation is known as a parallel citation. For example, 333 Mass. 99 is the parallel citation for 89 N.E.2d 488; the reverse is also true.

Parallel construction Using the same grammatical structure for clauses or phrases that bear the same relationship to some major idea.

Pardon An executive action that cancels a conviction for a crime and the penalty associated with it.

Parental immunity The prohibition against allowing children to sue their parents.

Parenthetical The parenthetical that occurs at the end of a court citation always contains the year of decision and also the name of the court if that information is not obvious from the name of the reporter.

Parol evidence rule   An evidentiary rule that a written contract cannot be modified or changed by prior verbal agreements.

Parole   Conditional early release from custody.

Partial defense   A defense that reduces a crime to a lesser included offense.

Partnership   A business run by two or more persons as co-owners.

Partnership by estoppel   A partnership created by the words or actions of persons acting as though they were a partnership.

Passive voice   A form of writing where the subject of the sentence is being acted on; opposite of **active voice**.

Patent   A right to exclude others from making, using, or selling one's invention.

Pattern jury instructions   A set of standardized jury instructions.

Penal system   The system of jails, prisons, and other places of confinement, as well as the pardon and parole system. Also known as the **correctional system**.

Peremptory challenge   A method for excusing a prospective juror in which no reason need be given.

Perfected security interest   A creditor's interest in security is perfected if the creditor possesses the security, files a financing statement, or gives money to purchase consumer goods.

Perfection   In secured transactions, a process by which the secured party gives notice of an attached security interest, usually by filing a financing statement, thereby giving the secured party priority to the collateral over the claims of other creditors.

Perfect tender rule   The requirement that the goods delivered exactly meet the contractual specifications.

Periodic tenancy   A tenancy established at a set interval, such as week to week, month to month, or year to year. At the end of each rental period the lease can be terminated with proper notice.

Perjury   Knowingly making a false statement while under oath.

Perpetrator   A person who commits a crime.

Personal defense   In negotiable instrument law, a defense that is good against everyone except a holder in due course. Compare **Real defense**.

Personal jurisdiction   The power of a court to force a person to appear before it.

Personal property   All property that is not **real property**; also referred to as **chattel**.

Personal recognizance bond   A defendant's personal promise to appear in court.

Per stirpes   A method of dividing an intestate estate whereby a person takes the place of the dead ancestor; also known as the **right of representation**.

Persuasive authority or decisions   Court decisions from an equal or a lower court from the same jurisdiction or from a court in a different jurisdiction; also includes secondary authority.

Petitioner or appellant   A person who initiates an appeal.

Physical custody   The child lives with and has day-to-day activities supervised by the designated parent or guardian.

Physical evidence   See **Real evidence**.

Piercing the corporate veil   When a court sets aside the unlimited liability protection normally given to corporate shareholders.

Pinpoint cite   The reference to a particular page within an opinion.

Plain meaning   A method for interpreting enacted law in which the key terms are interpreted in light of their dictionary definitions and use in ordinary conversations.

Plain view doctrine   A policy that allows police to seize contraband or evidence that is openly visible in an area where they are authorized to be.

Plaintiff   A person who initiates a lawsuit.

Plea bargaining   A process whereby the prosecutor and the defendant's lawyer agree for the defendant to plead guilty in exchange for the prosecutor's promise to charge him or her with a lesser offense, drop some additional charges, or request a lesser sentence.

Pleading in the alternative   Including more than one count in a complaint; the counts do not need to be consistent.

Pleadings   The documents that begin a lawsuit; generally, the complaint and the answer.

Pocket part   A pamphlet inserted into the back of a book containing information new since the volume was published.

Popular name table   Located in most codified statutes, this table lists statutes by their popular names along with their citations.

Portable Document Format (PDF)   A format that allows a document to be captured and electronic versions to be sent, viewed, and printed consistently across multiple devices and platforms. Federal courts require all documents to be filed in PDF format.

Postconviction relief   A statutory collateral challenge to a judgment of conviction.

Potential conflict   A situation in which a conflict of interest may arise in the future —for example, representing business partners.

Power of judicial review   A court's power to review statutes to decide if they conform to the federal or state constitution.

Power of sale clause   A clause authorizing a private foreclosure sale that does not require court action.

Practice of law   An activity that requires professional judgment, or the educated ability to relate law to a specific legal problem.

Practitioners' Notes   A section of the Bluebook devoted to citation information for the practicing lawyer.

Precedent   One or more prior court decisions.

Preemption   The power of the federal government to prevent the states from passing conflicting laws, and sometimes even to prohibit states from passing any laws on a particular subject.

Prejudicial error   A trial court error so serious as to require reversal of the trial court's decision.

Preliminary hearing   A hearing in which the prosecutor must present sufficient evidence to convince the judge that there is probable cause to believe the named individual committed the crimes for which the defendant is being charged.

Prenuptial agreement   A document that prospective spouses sign prior to marriage regarding financial and other arrangements should the marriage end; also known as an **antenuptial agreement**.

Preponderance of the evidence   The standard of proof most commonly used in civil trials. The evidence presented must prove that it is more likely than not that the defendant committed the wrong.

Presentment   Acting on its own initiative, a grand jury's charging a person with a crime. Compare **Indictment**.

Pretrial conference   A meeting of the lawyers and the judge to discuss a case prior to the beginning of the trial.

Pretrial motion   A motion brought before the beginning of a trial either to eliminate the necessity for a trial or to limit the information that can be presented at the trial.

Prima facie case   What the prosecutor or the plaintiff must be able to prove in order for the case to go to the jury—that is, the elements of the prosecution's case or the plaintiff's cause of action.

Primary authority   The law itself, such as statutes and court opinions.

Principal   In criminal law, the person who actually commits a criminal act. In agency law, a person who permits or directs another person to act on the principal's behalf.

Prior case history   Information about what happened procedurally to the cited case before it was heard by the cited court. Do not include this information in a citation.

Prisons   Places of confinement for those convicted of the more serious crimes.

Privilege log   A list of factors relevant to determining if evidence in documents and other materials is covered by attorney-client privilege.

Privity of contract   The relationship that exists between the contracting parties.

Pro bono work   Legal representation done without charge.

Probable cause   Not susceptible to a precise definition; a belief based on specific facts that a crime has been or is about to be committed; more than a reasonable suspicion.

Probate   The legal process settling an estate after a person has died.

Probation   An alternative sentence to incarceration that releases the defendant upon agreeing to certain conditions.

Probation officer   A government employee who administers the probation system.

Procedural facts   In a case brief, the facts that relate to what happened procedurally in the lower courts or administrative agencies before the case reached the court issuing the opinion, and how the appellate court disposed of the case. Examples include reversed (rev'd) and affirmed (aff'd).

Procedural law   Law that regulates how the legal system operates.

Process server   A person authorized by law to serve legal papers on defendants.

Product misuse   When the product was not being used for its intended purpose or was being used in a dangerous manner; it is a defense to a products liability claim, so long as the misuse was not foreseeable.

Products liability   The theory holding manufacturers and sellers liable for defective products when the defects make the products unreasonably dangerous.

Professional corporation   A professional entity in which the stockholders share in the organization's profits but have their liability limited to the amount of their investment.

Professional judgment   The educated ability to apply law to specific facts.

Promissory estoppel   Occurs when the courts allow detrimental reliance to substitute for consideration.

Pronoun   A word that substitutes for a noun: examples include *hers, her, his, him, its, them, their,* and *theirs.*

Property   A tangible object or a right or ownership interest.

Property law   Law dealing with ownership and use of property, both real and personal.

Pro se   Representing oneself in a legal matter.

Prosecuting attorney   The lawyer responsible for presenting the state's evidence against the defendant; called "U.S. attorneys" on the federal level and **district attorneys** or **state's attorneys** on the state level.

Prosecutor   A person representing the government who brings criminal charges and presents cases for criminal trial.

Prostitution   Participating in sexual activity for a fee.

Protected categories   Under Title VII, race, color, religion, sex, and national origin.

Protection order A court order issued in domestic violence and abuse cases to keep one spouse away from the other, the children, or the home.

Proving a case within a case The requirement in a legal malpractice case that the plaintiff-client prove that but for the lawyer's negligence, the client would have won.

Proximate cause Once actual cause is found, as a policy matter, the court must also find that the act and the resulting harm were so foreseeably related as to justify a finding of liability.

Public defender A lawyer employed by the state to represent indigent defendants.

Punitive damages Money awarded to a plaintiff in cases of intentional torts in order to punish the defendant and serve as a warning to others.

Purchase money security interest Arises when a seller gives credit to a debtor so that the debtor can purchase an item.

Purposeful Intending to cause a specific harm.

Qualified individual Under the Americans with Disabilities Act (ADA), someone who can perform the essential job functions.

Quasi-contract A scenario in which there is no agreement, but both parties treat it as though one existed. Although no actual contract was formed, the courts will fashion an equitable remedy to avoid unjust enrichment.

Question of fact A question relating to what happened: who, what, when, where, and how. Disputed factual issues are normally for the jury or trial court to decide and cannot be appealed.

Question of law A question relating to the application or interpretation of the law. Disputed legal issues are initially for the trial court to decide but can be appealed.

Question presented In a law office memorandum, the question presented states the legal issue raised by the facts of the problem in as concrete a fashion as possible.

Quid pro quo sexual harassment A situation involving an exchange of sexual favors for employment benefits.

Quiet enjoyment The tenant's right to be free from interference from the landlord with respect to how the property is used.

Quitclaim deed A deed in which the grantor gives up any claims to the property without making any assertions about there being a clear title.

Ratio decidendi The court's reasoning for its decision.

Real defense In negotiable instrument law, a defense inherent in the instrument itself, such as forgery. Compare **Personal defense**.

Real estate See **Real property**.

Real estate closing A meeting at which the buyer and the seller and/or their representatives sign and deliver a variety of legal documents to finalize the sale and transfer of property.

Real evidence Any tangible object, like a bloody glove; also referred to as **physical evidence**.

Real property Land and items growing on or permanently attached to that land; also known as **real estate**.

Reasonable accommodation Under the Americans with Disabilities Act, an accommodation that would not create an undue hardship for the employer.

Reasonable suspicion A suspicion based on specific facts; less than probable cause.

Receiving stolen property Knowingly possessing stolen property.

Recidivist A repeat offender; one who continues to commit more crimes.

Recklessness Disregarding a substantial and unjustifiable risk that harm will result.

Reformation An equitable remedy whereby the court rewrites a contract.

Registered agent The person designated to receive service of legal documents.

Registration The process by which individuals or organizations have their names placed on an official list kept by some private organization or governmental agency.

Regulation A law promulgated by an administrative agency.

Relevancy Determined by whether the evidence leads one to logically conclude that an asserted fact is either more or less probable.

Remand When an appellate court sends a case back to the trial court for a new trial or other action.

Remedial statute A statute enacted to correct a defect in prior law or to provide a remedy where none existed.

Removal The transfer of a case from one state court to another, or from state court to federal court.

Reporters Books that contain court decisions. There are both official and unofficial reporters.

Reprieve An executive action that temporarily postpones the punishment until some future time when another authority can review the sentence.

Reprimand or censure A public or private statement that a lawyer's conduct violated the code of ethics.

Request for admissions A document that lists statements regarding specific items for the other party to admit or deny.

Request for documents A discovery tool whereby one party asks for documents in the other party's possession or control.

Requirements contract A contract in which one party agrees to buy all its requirements for a particular product from the other party.

Res ipsa loquitur "The thing speaks for itself"; the doctrine that suggests negligence can be presumed if an event happens that would not ordinarily happen unless someone was negligent.

Res judicata Occurs when a civil case has a final judgment and is no longer subject to appeal; at that point, the case cannot be relitigated between the original parties.

Rescission The act of canceling the contract and returning the parties to the positions they were in prior to the contract having been formed.

Respondeat superior The tort theory that an employer can be sued for the negligent acts of its employees.

Respondent or appellee The party in a lawsuit against whom an appeal has been filed.

Restatement of the Law of Torts, Second An authoritative secondary source, written by a group of legal scholars, summarizing the existing common law, as well as suggesting what the law should be.

Restatements A series of books—the Restatements of the Law—summarizing the basic principles of the common law, written by the American Law Institute (ALI).

Restitution Repaying the victim for harm caused.

Restrictive covenant A provision in a deed that prohibits specified uses of the property.

Restrictive phrase A phrase that contains essential information; it should not be set off with commas.

Retainer An advance or down payment that is given to engage the services of a lawyer.

Retainer agreement A contract that outlines the lawyer's duties and the client's obligations regarding payment, on either an hourly or a contingency fee basis, as well as the client's responsibility regarding costs and expenses.

Retreat exception The rule that in order to claim self-defense, there must have been no possibility of retreat.

Reversal When an appellate court reverses a lower court decision.

Reverse A decision is reversed when the litigants appeal a lower court decision and the higher court disagrees with the decision of the lower court. Compare with **Overrule**.

Reversible error An error made by the trial judge that is sufficiently serious to warrant reversing the trial court's decision.

Revocable trust A form of inter vivos trust that the grantor can alter.

RICO The federal Racketeer Influenced and Corrupt Organizations Act.

Right of representation See **Per stirpes**.

Road map paragraph An introductory paragraph listing issues to be discussed in the order they are to be discussed.

Robbery Theft through the use of force.

Rule In a case brief, the general legal principle in existence before the case began.

Rule 8 The rule of civil procedure that sets forth the general pleading requirements.

Rule 11 A requirement that lawyers sign a pleading only after conducting a reasonable inquiry into the circumstances supporting it.

Rule 12(b)(6) motion A request that the court find the plaintiff has failed to state a valid claim and dismiss the complaint; also known as a **motion to dismiss**.

Rule 56 motion (summary judgment motion) A request that the court grant judgment in favor of the moving party because there is no genuine issue as to any material fact and the moving party is entitled to judgment as a matter of law. It is similar to a **12(b)(6) motion** except that the court also considers matters outside the pleadings.

Rulemaking hearing An administrative agency hearing that resembles a legislative hearing in which interested parties present evidence and arguments to an administrative agency about what the general law should be.

Rules of criminal procedure Federal and state rules that regulate how criminal proceedings are conducted.

Rules of evidence Federal and state rules that govern the admissibility of evidence in court.

Run-on sentence Two sentences written as one. It can occur either as a comma splice (two independent clauses joined by a comma) or as a fused sentence (two independent clauses with no separating punctuation).

Screen See **Ethical wall**.

Search engine A computer program that allows the user to retrieve web documents that match the key words entered by the searcher.

Search warrant A court's prior permission for the police to search for and seize property.

Secondary authority Information about the law, such as that contained in encyclopedias and law review articles.

Secured transaction An arrangement whereby a creditor asks for and receives a guarantee of repayment from the debtor in the form of collateral.

Security agreement An agreement granting a creditor a security interest in specific property.

Security deposit An amount of money, usually equal to one month's rent, that is collected at the time the lease is signed and then a portion or all of it may be held by the landlord to cover the cost of repairs that may be needed when the tenant moves out.

Security interest A security interest is created when a debtor agrees to put up something as collateral that the creditor can then claim if the debtor fails to pay the debt.

Self-defense The justified use of force to protect oneself or others.

Self-proving clause A notarized affidavit, signed by the attesting witnesses, that may eliminate the need to call witnesses during the probate process to attest to the validity of the will.

Sentence fragment An incomplete sentence.

Sentencing hearing A hearing held after a finding of guilt to determine the appropriate sentence.

Separation of powers The division of governmental power among the legislative, executive, and judicial branches.

Serial comma In a series of three or more items, use a comma after each item until you reach the final conjunction.

Servant In law, an archaic term sometimes used to mean employee.

Service The delivery of a **pleading, subpoena,** or other paper in a lawsuit to another party.

Service mark A mark used to identify a service-oriented business.

Service of process See **Service.**

Session law A statute that is enacted and published for a particular session of the legislature

Settlement The resolution of a dispute between parties independent of the rendering of a final decision by a trial or appellate court.

Settlement agreement A document that contains the arrangements agreed on by the parties to a dispute.

Settlor See **Donor.**

Shareholders The owners of a corporation.

Shepardize Using **Shepard's Citations** to check a court citation to see whether there has been any subsequent history or treatment by other court decisions.

Shepard's Citations A book that contains nothing but citations. It serves three purposes: (1) as a source for parallel citations; (2) as a source for subsequent history for a case or statute; and (3) as a source for treatment by later courts of the case or statute you are Shepardizing.

Short citation form A partial citation that may be used after you have given a complete citation.

Signal A word or a phrase that precedes a citation to indicate the purpose for which the citation is being given.

Simultaneous death clause A clause that states that if a person named as a beneficiary in the will dies within a short period of time after the decedent dies, it will be assumed for purposes of the will that the person in question failed to survive the decedent.

Slander Spoken defamation.

Slip laws A form in which statutes are published; they are printed individually at the time they are first enacted.

Sole custody An individual has both physical and legal custody of the child.

Sole proprietorship A business owned by a single owner.

Solemnized marriage A marriage in which the couple has obtained the proper marriage license from a local government official and has then taken marriage vows before either a recognized member of the clergy or a judge and a designated number of witnesses.

Solicitation Encouraging someone to commit a crime.

Sovereign immunity The prohibition against suing the government without the government's consent.

Special damages Indirect damages that must be foreseeable to be recovered. Also called **consequential damages.**

Specific intent An intention to act and to cause a specific result.

Specific performance When money damages are inadequate, a court may use this equitable remedy and order the breaching party to perform his or her contractual obligations.

Split custody One parent has both physical and legal custody during one part of the year, and the other parent gets both physical and legal custody during the rest of the year.

Spoliation The destruction or alteration of documents relevant to a case.

Spousal immunity The prohibition against one spouse suing the other.

Stalking An intentional or knowing course of conduct that places a person in fear of imminent physical injury or death to that person or that person's family.

Standing The principle that courts cannot decide abstract issues or render advisory opinions; rather, they are limited to deciding cases that involve litigants who are personally affected by the court's decision.

Stand-your-ground laws Statutes that allow citizens to use deadly force without attempting to retreat, even when they are threatened outside their homes.

Stare decisis The doctrine stating that normally once a court has decided one way on a particular issue, it and other courts in the same jurisdiction will decide the same way on that issue in future cases given a similar set of facts unless they can be convinced of the need for change.

State action requirement A requirement that a defendant cannot be charged with a violation of constitutional rights unless the defendant was acting as an agent of a governmental entity

State's attorney A law officer who represents the state in criminal cases. Also known as a **district attorney.**

Statute A law enacted by a state legislature or by Congress.

Statute in derogation of the common law A statute that changes the common law.

Statute of frauds A statutory requirement that in order to be enforceable, certain contracts must be in writing.

Statute of limitations The law that sets the length of time from when something happens to when a lawsuit must be filed before the right to bring it is lost.

Statutes at large or session laws The chronological publication of statutes at the end of a legislative session.

Statutory element A separable part of a statute that must be satisfied for the statute to apply.

Stay the judgment A suspension of the judgment. It is often requested when the trial court judgment is being appealed.

Stipulate To agree.

Stop and frisk The right of the police to detain an individual for a brief period of time and to search the outside of the person's clothing if the police have a reasonable suspicion that the individual has committed or is about to commit a crime.

Strict construction An approach whereby the courts give a statute a narrow interpretation.

Strict liability Liability without having to prove fault.

Strict scrutiny The standard the courts use in equal protection claims involving race-based decisions or "fundamental rights." The government must prove that the challenged action is designed to achieve a compelling government interest and that there is no reasonable alternative method for achieving it.

String citation A series of citations in a row.

Structured database A computerized database that contains key information about the content of documents, such as medical records.

Subject matter jurisdiction The power of a court to hear a particular type of case.

Subordinating conjunction Dependent clauses always begin with subordinating conjunctions; examples include *after, although, as, because, before, even though, if, since, unless, when, where, whereas,* and *while.*

Subpoena A court order requiring a person to appear to testify at a trial or deposition. (Administrative agencies also usually have subpoena powers.)

Subpoena duces tecum A court order that a person who is not a party to litigation appear at a trial or deposition and bring requested documents.

Subsequent case history Information about what happened procedurally to the litigation after the case cited. Include this information in a citation.

Substantial capacity test Part of the Model Penal Code; a test that provides that the defendant is not guilty due to insanity if, at the time of the crime, the defendant lacked either the ability to understand that the act was wrong or the ability to control the behavior.

Substantial performance Although a breach of contract, performance of all the essential terms of the contract will entitle the breaching party to the contractual price minus any damages caused by the breach.

Substantive facts In a case brief, facts that deal with what happened to the parties before the litigation began.

Substantive law Law that creates rights and duties.

Successive conflict of interest Representing someone who is in a position adverse to a prior client.

Summary judgment A judgment based on a finding that there is no genuine issue as to any material fact and that the moving party is entitled to judgment as a matter of law.

Summary judgment motion A request that the court grant judgment in favor of the moving party because there is no genuine issue as to any material fact and the moving party is entitled to judgment as a matter of law. It is similar to a **12(b)(6) motion** except that the court also considers matters outside the pleadings. Also called a **Rule 56 motion.**

Summary jury trial A nonbinding process in which lawyers for both sides present synopses of their cases to a jury, which renders an advisory opinion on the basis of these presentations.

Summons A notice informing the defendant of the lawsuit and requiring the defendant to respond or risk losing the suit.

Superseding cause In negligence, an intervening cause that relieves the defendant of liability.

Support See **Alimony.**

Supra Above; used to refer to authority already cited in the document. May not be used with citations to cases, statutes, or constitutions.

Supremacy Clause A clause in the U.S. Constitution that dictates if there is a conflict between federal law and state law, federal law takes precedence.

Supreme Court Reporter A West publication containing U.S. Supreme Court decisions.

Surrogacy contract A document in which a woman agrees to conceive and give birth to a child, deliver the child to its natural father, and terminate her parental rights so the father's wife can become its adoptive mother.

Suspension A determination that a lawyer may not practice law for a set period of time.

Syllabus A summary of a court opinion that appears at the beginning of the case.

Synthesis The process of integrating a series of cases in such a way that their interrelationship is explained to the reader.

Tabulation A method for writing lists.

Tangible personal property Also known as **chattel**; personal property that can be touched and moved.

Temporary restraining order (TRO) A court order of limited duration designed to maintain the status quo pending further court action at a later date.

Tenancy at sufferance   A situation in which the person in possession of the land has no legal right to be there.

Tenancy at will   An arrangement in which no time period is specified and the lessee can leave or the lessor can reclaim the land at any time.

Tenancy by the entirety   A special type of joint tenancy applicable only to married couples.

Tenancy for a term or estate for years   A right to control real property for a set period of time.

Tenancy in common   Ownership by two or more people. Ownership shares do not have to be equal, but each has an undivided interest in the property. When a tenant in common dies, that person's share passes either by will or by intestate statute.

Testamentary capacity   The mental capacity, also known as *sound mind*, whereby the testator understands the nature of his or her property and the identity of those most closely related to him or her.

Testamentary trust   A trust that is created by a will and does not become effective until after the testator's death.

Testator/Testatrix   The person making a will to direct how his or her assets will be distributed at death.

Testimonial evidence   Consists of the description of events that a witness testifies to under oath in a legal proceeding.

That case   A case that you are citing.

Theft   Also known as **larceny**; the taking of another's property with the intent to permanently deprive the owner.

Third party   Someone who is not a party to the agreement or transaction.

Third-party beneficiary   Although not a party to the contract, someone the contracting parties intended to benefit.

Third-party claim   A claim by a defendant against someone in addition to the persons the plaintiff has already sued.

This case   Your client's case.

Tickler system   A calendaring system that records key dates and important deadlines.

Title insurance   Insurance against any loss due to a defective title.

Title search   An examination of documents recording title to a property to ensure that the owner has clear title to the property.

Tort   Harm to a person or a person's property.

Tort law   Law that deals with harm to a person or a person's property.

Tortfeasor   A person who commits a tort.

Trademark   A name, combination of letters or numbers, or logo that identifies a particular product.

Trade secret   A formula or process that has not been patented and is known by a limited number of individuals working for the company that uses it.

Transferred intent   A legal fiction that if a person directs a tortious action toward A but instead harms B, the intent to act against A is transferred to B.

Transition   In writing, a technique used to help your reader move from one thought to the next and to see the connections between them.

Treason   Attempting to overthrow the government or betraying the government to an enemy of the United States, traditionally defined as a country or organization with which the United States is at war.

Treatise   A book that summarizes, interprets, and evaluates the law.

Treatment   How subsequent cases have affected the case you are Shepardizing. It is sometimes indicated by a one-letter abbreviation before the Shepard's citation.

Trespass   The unauthorized intrusion onto the land of another. Also known as **trespass to land.**

Trespass to personal property   Occurs when someone harms or interferes with the owner's exclusive possession of the property but has no intention of keeping the property.

Trial   The process of deciding a dispute by presenting evidence and witness testimony either to a jury or to a judge.

Trial courts   Courts that determine the facts and apply the law to the facts.

Trust   A legal relationship in which one party holds property for the benefit of another.

Trustee   The person appointed to administer a trust.

12(b)(6) motion   A request that the court find the plaintiff has failed to state a valid claim and dismiss the complaint.

Ultrahazardous activities   Those activities that have an inherent risk of injury and therefore may result in strict liability.

Unauthorized practice of law (UPL)   When nonlawyers do things that only lawyers are allowed to do. In most states, this is a crime.

Unconscionable contract   A contract formed between parties of very unequal bargaining power where the terms are so unfair as to "shock the conscience."

Undue influence   When one party is in a position of trust and misuses that trust to influence the actions of another.

Unenforceable contract   A valid contract that cannot be enforced, for example, because the statute of limitations has passed.

Uniform Commercial Code (UCC)   Originally drafted by the National Conference of Commissioners on Uniform State Law, it governs commercial transactions and has been adopted by all states entirely or in part.

Uniform Partnership Act (UPA) Known as a gap filler, the UPA comes into play only if terms are left out of a partnership agreement.

Unilateral contract A contract where a promise is exchanged for an act.

United States Code (U.S.C.) Federal statutes arranged by subject matter.

United States Code Annotated (U.S.C.A.) Federal statutes arranged by subject matter, published by West.

United States Code Service (U.S.C.S.) Federal statutes arranged by subject matter, published by Lexis Law Publishing.

United States Law Week A publication of U.S. Supreme Court decisions by the Bureau of National Affairs (BNA).

United States Reports The official federal government publication of U.S. Supreme Court decisions.

United States Sentencing Guidelines Government guidelines that specify an appropriate range of sentences for each class of convicted persons based on factors related to the offense and the offender.

United States Supreme Court Reports, Lawyers' Edition A listing of U.S. Supreme Court decisions published by Lexis Law Publishing.

U.S. Constitution Drafted in 1787, it established the structure of the federal government and the relationship between the federal and state governments.

U.S. courts of appeals The intermediate appellate courts in the federal system.

U.S. district courts The general jurisdiction trial courts in the federal system.

U.S. Supreme Court The highest appellate court in the federal system; consists of nine appointed members; established by Article III of the U.S. Constitution.

Unlawful detainer A civil action brought to recover use of property.

Unofficial reporter A private publication of court opinions; examples include the regional reporters, such as N.E.2d, published by West.

Valid In logic, an argument is considered to be valid or sound if the assumptions underlying the argument are true.

Valid contract A contract having all the essential elements needed for a binding agreement.

Venue When the court with the power to hear the case has multiple locations, the proper location for the case to be filed and heard.

Verdict The opinion of a jury on a question of fact.

Verification An affidavit signed by the client indicating that he or she has read the complaint and that its contents are correct.

Vicarious representation The rule whereby all members of a law firm are treated as though they had represented the former client, even if only one lawyer did.

Victim impact statement A written or oral statement made by the victim of the crime (or the family members of a deceased victim) that is presented at the sentencing hearing.

Void A contract that is invalid even if it is not repudiated by either party. In law, if an action is void, it has no legal effect.

Void for vagueness A reason for invalidating a statute when a reasonable person could not determine a statute's meaning.

Void marriage A marriage that is invalid from its inception and that does not require court action for the parties to be free of any marital obligations.

Voidable A valid contract that can be set aside at the option of one of the parties. In law, if an action is voidable, it can be disaffirmed by one of the parties.

Voidable marriage A marriage that was valid when it was entered into and that remains valid until either party obtains a court order dissolving it.

Voir dire An examination of a prospective juror to see if he or she is fit to serve as a juror.

Voluntary manslaughter The unlawful killing of another human being with malice.

Warrant A court's prior permission for the police to search and seize.

Warranty A guarantee, made by the seller or implied by law, regarding the character, quality, or title of the goods being sold.

Warranty deed A deed in which the seller promises clear title to the property.

Web browser A computer program that allows users to access and search the web with a few clicks of a mouse.

West Group A major private publisher of legal materials; its logo is the key symbol.

Westlaw An online legal database containing court decisions and statutes from the entire country, as well as secondary authority; and KeyCite, similar in function to LexisNexis Shepard's online.

Will The document used to express a person's wishes as to how his or her property should be distributed upon death.

Writ A judge's order requiring that something be done.

Writ of certiorari A means of gaining appellate review; in the U.S. Supreme Court the writ is discretionary and will be issued to another court to review a federal question if four of the nine justices vote to hear the case.

Writ of execution A court order authorizing a sheriff to take property in order to enforce a judgment.

Writ of habeas corpus A court order to produce the person detained; designed to give a neutral judge an opportunity to review the charges, to ensure there is a lawful basis for the incarceration.

Table of Cases

*Cases in **bold** have boxed case summaries in the text.*

Index